Real Estate and Property Law for Paralegals

Real Estate and Property Law for Paralegals

Sixth Edition

NEAL R. BEVANS, J.D.

Cover image: tamas/stock.adobe.com

To contact Customer Service, e-mail customer.service@aspenpublishing.com, call 1-800-950-5259, or mail correspondence to:

Aspen Publishing
Attn: Order Department
PO Box 990
Frederick, MD 21705

Printed in the United States of America.

1 2 3 4 5 6 7 8 9 0

ISBN 978-1-5438-2688-3

Library of Congress Cataloging-in-Publication Data application is in process.

About Aspen Publishing

Aspen Publishing is a leading provider of educational content and digital learning solutions to law schools in the U.S. and around the world. Aspen provides best-in-class solutions for legal education through authoritative textbooks, written by renowned authors, and breakthrough products such as Connected eBooks, Connected Quizzing, and PracticePerfect.

The Aspen Casebook Series (famously known among law faculty and students as the "red and black" casebooks) encompasses hundreds of highly regarded textbooks in more than eighty disciplines, from large enrollment courses, such as Torts and Contracts to emerging electives such as Sustainability and the Law of Policing. Study aids such as the *Examples & Explanations* and the *Emanuel Law Outlines* series, both highly popular collections, help law students master complex subject matter.

Major products, programs, and initiatives include:

- **Connected eBooks** are enhanced digital textbooks and study aids that come with a suite of online content and learning tools designed to maximize student success. Designed in collaboration with hundreds of faculty and students, the Connected eBook is a significant leap forward in the legal education learning tools available to students.

- **Connected Quizzing** is an easy-to-use formative assessment tool that tests law students' understanding and provides timely feedback to improve learning outcomes. Delivered through CasebookConnect.com, the learning platform already used by students to access their Aspen casebooks, Connected Quizzing is simple to implement and integrates seamlessly with law school course curricula.

- **PracticePerfect** is a visually engaging, interactive study aid to explain commonly encountered legal doctrines through easy-to-understand animated videos, illustrative examples, and numerous practice questions. Developed by a team of experts, PracticePerfect is the ideal study companion for today's law students.

- The **Aspen Learning Library** enables law schools to provide their students with access to the most popular study aids on the market across all of their courses. Available through an annual subscription, the online library consists of study aids in e-book, audio, and video formats with full text search, note-taking, and highlighting capabilities.

- Aspen's **Digital Bookshelf** is an institutional-level online education bookshelf, consolidating everything students and professors need to ensure success. This program ensures that every student has access to affordable course materials from day one.

- **Leading Edge** is a community centered on thinking differently about legal education and putting those thoughts into actionable strategies. At the core of the program is the Leading Edge Conference, an annual gathering of legal education thought leaders looking to pool ideas and identify promising directions of exploration.

*For my stepchildren, Tamara Tigani and Camilo Lopez-Escobar,
and their mother, my friend and my wife, Nilsa Bevans*

Summary
of Contents

CONTENTS   xi

PREFACE   xxxiii

ACKNOWLEDGMENTS   xxxix

Chapter 1	An Introduction to Real Estate	1
Chapter 2	Estates in Real Property	27
Chapter 3	Property Descriptions and Boundaries	49
Chapter 4	Transferring Title to Real Estate	77
Chapter 5	Rights Associated with Real Estate	109
Chapter 6	Real Estate Contracts	137
Chapter 7	Landlord and Tenant Law	167
Chapter 8	Real Estate Deeds	203
Chapter 9	Mortgages and Financing the Purchase of Real Estate	235
Chapter 10	Public and Private Restrictions on the Use of Land	277
Chapter 11	Real Estate Professions	307
Chapter 12	Title Insurance and Title Examinations	343
Chapter 13	The Closing	379
Chapter 14	Taxation Issues in Real Property	421

APPENDIX: ANSWERS TO REVIEW QUESTIONS AND PRACTICE QUESTIONS
FOR TEST REVIEW   439

GLOSSARY   483

INDEX   489

Contents

PREFACE   xxxiii
ACKNOWLEDGMENTS   xxxix

1 AN INTRODUCTION TO REAL ESTATE 1

Chapter Objectives   *1*
Chapter Outline   *1*

I. INTRODUCTION   **1**

II. REAL PROPERTY VERSUS PERSONAL PROPERTY   **2**

  A. What Makes Real Property So Unique?   3
  B. Physical Characteristics of Land   4
  C. Economic Characteristics of Land   4

III. THE REAL ESTATE MARKET   **7**

IV. CLASSIFYING PROPERTY BY USE   **8**

  A. Unimproved Land   9
  B. Residential Property   9
    1. Single- and Multi-Family Homes   9
    2. Apartments   9
    3. Condominiums and Townhouses   10
      a. Condominiums   10
      b. Townhouses   10
    4. Cooperatives   10
    5. Mobile Homes   11
    6. Manufactured Housing and "Kit" Homes 11
  C. Commercial Property   11
    1. Retail/Wholesale   12
    2. Shopping Centers and Malls   12
  D. Industrial Property   12
    1. Industrial Parks   12
    2. Light Industry/Heavy Industry   12

E. Farm and Rural Property | 13
F. Recreational Property | 13
G. Government-Owned Land | 13

Case Excerpt: Jones v. State Prop. Tax Appeal Bd. | 13

COVID-19 Concern | 20
Chapter Summary | 20
Skills You Need in the Real World | 21
Ethical Issues for the Paralegal: An Introduction | 22
Key Terms and Concepts | 23
End-of-Chapter Exercises | 23
Annotated Document: Real Estate Sales Listing | 25
Practice Questions for Test Review | 25

2   ESTATES IN REAL PROPERTY   27

Chapter Objectives | 27
Chapter Outline | 27

I. INTRODUCTION | **28**

II. REAL PROPERTY ESTATES | **28**

III. FEE SIMPLE ESTATES | **28**

A. Rights of Fee Simple Absolute Owners | 30
B. Conditional Fee Simple Estates | 30
  1. Fee Simple Determinable | 31
  2. Fee Simple on a Condition Subsequent | 31

IV. LIFE ESTATES | **33**

A. Historical Basis of Life Estates | 33
B. Remaindermen | 34
C. Waste | 34
D. Court Doctrines That Affect Life Estates | 34
E. Life Estate *Pur Autre Vie* | 35

V. CONCURRENT OWNERSHIP IN REAL ESTATE | **35**

A. Tenants in Common | 36
B. Joint Tenancy | 36
  1. Right of Survivorship | 36
  2. Specificity Required to Create Joint Tenancy | 37
C. Tenancy by Entirety | 38

D. Tenancy in Partnership   39
E. The Right to Partition   39

Case Excerpt: Vargo v. Adams   40

COVID-19 Concern   42
Chapter Summary   42
Skills You Need in the Real World   43
Ethical Issues for the Paralegal: Drafting Deeds   43
Key Terms and Concepts   44
End-of-Chapter Exercises   44
Annotated Document: Creating a Life Estate   46
Practice Questions for Test Review   46

3 PROPERTY DESCRIPTIONS AND BOUNDARIES 49

Chapter Objectives   49
Chapter Outline   49

I. INTRODUCTION   50

II. THE HISTORY OF PROPERTY BOUNDARIES   50

III. PROPERTY DESCRIPTIONS IN DEEDS   51

A. The Elements of a Valid Property Description   51
B. Legal Requirements for Property Descriptions in Deeds   52
C. Referring to Other Documents to Prove Property Boundaries   52
D. Litigating Property Boundaries   53
E. Ambiguous Property Descriptions   53
    1. Patent Ambiguities   54
    2. Parol Evidence and Property Descriptions   54
    3. Latently Ambiguous Property Descriptions   55

IV. METES AND BOUNDS DESCRIPTIONS   55

A. Drafting Metes and Bounds Descriptions   57
B. Using Technology to Help with Metes and Bounds Drawings   59

V. OTHER METHODS TO DESCRIBE PROPERTY: GOVERNMENT SURVEY SYSTEM   59

A. Tract Indexing   59
B. Plats   60
C. Torrens Registration   60

VI. WATER RIGHTS   **61**

   A. The Right to Use Water   61
      1. Limitations on Right to Use the Water   61
      2. Court Doctrines That Affect Water Rights   61
   B. Natural Forces That Affect Property Boundaries   62
      1. Accretion   62
      2. Erosion   62
      3. Avulsion   62
      4. Reliction   63
   C. Water and Property Boundaries   63
      1. Navigable Waters   63
      2. Non-Navigable Waters   63

*Case Excerpt: In re Foreclosure of Real Prop. Under Deed
of Trust from Vicque*   64

COVID-19 Concern   69
Chapter Summary   69
Skills You Need in the Real World   70
Ethical Issues for the Paralegal: Confidentiality   70
Key Terms and Concepts   71
End-of-Chapter Exercises   71
Annotated Document: Metes and Bounds Description   73
Practice Questions for Test Review   74

4   **TRANSFERRING TITLE TO REAL
ESTATE 77**

Chapter Objectives   77
Chapter Outline   77

I. INTRODUCTION   **78**

II. VOLUNTARY TRANSFERS OF TITLE   **78**

   A. Sale   78
      1. The Differences Between Sale of Personal Property
        and Sale of Real Property   78
      2. The Basic Requirements of Sale of Real Property   80
        a. Mutual Assent   80
        b. Consideration   80
        c. Capacity   81
          i. Infants   81
          ii. Intoxicated Persons   81
          iii. Mentally Incompetent Persons   81
        d. Property Description   82

B. Will (Probate)	84
1. The Minimum Requirements of a Will	84
a. The Will Must Be in Writing	84
b. The Will Must Be Signed by the Testator	84
c. The Will Must Be Witnessed	85
d. The Will Must Clearly Express the Testator's State of Mind	86
e. The Will Must Clearly Devise Property to a Specific Beneficiary	86
2. Wills Versus Sales	86
3. Different Methods Used to Transfer Title Through Wills	87
a. Intestate Succession	87
b. Testate Succession	87
C. Gift	88
D. Dedication	88
E. Homesteading	88
III. INVOLUNTARY TRANSFERS OF TITLE	**88**
A. Foreclosure	89
1. Judicial Foreclosure	89
2. Power of Sale Foreclosure	89
a. The Right to Foreclose	90
b. Default	90
c. Notice to the Borrower	90
d. Steps in Foreclosure	91
e. The Foreclosure Auction	91
f. The Right of Redemption	92
g. Purchasing Property at a Foreclosure Sale	92
h. Terminating the Rights of Other Creditors	93
i. Mortgages and Deeds of Trust	93
B. Eminent Domain (Condemnation)	93
1. The Process of Eminent Domain: Condemnation	94
2. Inverse Condemnation	94
C. Partition	95
D. Escheat	95
E. Civil Judgment	95
F. Adverse Possession	95
1. Why Does the Doctrine of Adverse Possession Exist?	95
2. The Elements of Adverse Possession	96
a. Open, Continuous, Notorious, and Hostile Possession	96
b. Color of Title	97
3. Specified Time Periods for Adverse Possession	97
G. Tax Auctions	98
Case Excerpt: Dip Lending I, LLC v. Cleveland Avenue Properties	*98*
COVID-19 Concern	*101*
Chapter Summary	*101*

Skills You Need in the Real World   102
Ethical Issues for the Paralegal: Fraudulent Transfers   102
Key Terms and Concepts   103
End-of-Chapter Exercises   103
Annotated Document: Notice of Foreclosure   105
Practice Questions for Test Review   106

5   RIGHTS ASSOCIATED WITH REAL ESTATE   109

Chapter Objectives   109
Chapter Outline   109

I. INTRODUCTION   110

II. FIXTURES   110

    A. Determining When Personal Property Becomes a Fixture   111
       1. Intent Test   111
       2. Manner of Attachment Test   112
       3. Use Test   112
       4. Damage Test   112
    B. Trade Fixtures   113

III. EASEMENTS   113

    A. Appurtenant Easements   114
    B. In Gross Easements   115
    C. Easements Run with the Land   116
    D. Creating Easements   116
       1. Agreement   116
       2. Deed Reservation   116
       3. Implication   117
       4. Necessity   117
       5. Prescription   117
       6. Eminent Domain   118
    E. Terminating Easements   118
       1. The Easement Is No Longer Needed   119
       2. The Properties Have Merged   119
       3. The Parties Enter into an Agreement   119
       4. The Easement Is Abandoned   119

IV. LICENSES   120

V. *PROFIT À PRENDRE*   120

VI. LIENS   121

VII. ASSESSMENTS   122

VIII. AIR RIGHTS   122

IX. WATER RIGHTS   124

A. The Right to Draw Water   124
B. Subterranean Water   124
C. Terminology for Water Rights   125

X. MINERAL RIGHTS   125

Case Excerpt: Scott v. Lee & Donna Metcalf Charitable Trust   *126*

COVID-19 Concern   *130*
Chapter Summary   *130*
Skills You Need in the Real World   *131*
Ethical Issues for the Paralegal: Unauthorized Practice of Law   *131*
Key Terms and Concepts   *131*
End-of-Chapter Exercises   *132*
Annotated Document: Lien   *134*
Practice Questions for Test Review   *135*

6   REAL ESTATE CONTRACTS   137

Chapter Objectives   *137*
Chapter Outline   *137*

I. INTRODUCTION   138

II. WHAT IS A CONTRACT?   138

A. Offer   139
  1. Offers Do Not Require Specific Language   140
  2. The Reasonable Person Standard and Offers   140
B. Acceptance   141
  1. The Power of Acceptance   141
  2. Communicating the Acceptance to the Offeror   142
  3. The Mailbox Rule   142
  4. Counteroffers   143
C. Mutual Assent   143
D. Consideration   144
E. Legality   144
F. Capacity   144

III. THE STATUTE OF FRAUDS   145

IV. FORMATION ISSUES IN CONTRACT LAW — 146

   A. Guidelines That Courts Use to Interpret Contracts — 146
   B. Mistake — 147
   C. Fraud — 147

V. REAL ESTATE CONTRACTS — 147

   A. Listing Agreements — 148
      1. Open Listing — 148
      2. Exclusive Listing — 148
      3. Multiple Listing — 148
   B. Offer of Purchase and Contract — 149
      1. Property Description — 151
      2. Purchase of Personal Property — 151
      3. Purchase Price Details — 151
      4. Conditions — 151
      5. Evidence of Title — 151
      6. Property Disclosures — 151
      7. Risk of Loss Provisions — 152
      8. Closing Provisions — 152
      9. Signature Provisions — 152
   C. Options — 152

VI. CONTRACT CLAUSES — 153

   A. Time Is of the Essence — 153
   B. Title — 153
   C. Escrow — 154
   D. Insurance (Risk of Loss) — 154

VII. BREACH OF CONTRACT — 154

   A. Remedies for the Seller — 154
   B. Remedies for the Buyer — 155
   C. Remedies for the Broker — 155

Case Excerpt: Pickett Fence Preview, Inc. v. Zillow, Inc. — 155

COVID-19 Concern — 159
Chapter Summary — 159
Skills You Need in the Real World — 160
Ethical Issues for the Paralegal: Legal Research — 161
Key Terms and Concepts — 161
End-of-Chapter Exercises — 161
Annotated Document: Offer of Purchase for Real Estate — 163
Practice Questions for Test Review — 164

LANDLORD AND TENANT LAW   167

Chapter Objectives   *167*
Chapter Outline   *167*

I. INTRODUCTION   168

II. THE LANDLORD-TENANT RELATIONSHIP   169

    A. Historical Background on Landlord-Tenant Law   169
    B. Modern Changes to the Landlord-Tenant Relationship   170

III. LEASES   171

    A. Fixed-Rent Leases 171
    B. Percentage Leases 171
    C. Net Leases 171
    D. Rent-to-Own Leases 172
    E. Ground Leases 172
    F. Timber Leases 172
    G. Mineral Leases 172
    H. Oil and Gas Leases 173

IV. COMMON LEASE PROVISIONS   173

    A. Rent 173
    B. Late Payments and Fees 174
    C. Pet and Security Deposits 174
    D. Renewal Provisions 174
    E. Persons Permitted on the Leased Premises 174
    F. Acceptance of Leased Premises 175
    G. Modifying or Altering the Premises 175
    H. Subletting 175
    I. Notice 175

V. COMMERCIAL LEASES   176

VI. PUBLIC POLICY CONCERNS IN LEASES   177

    A. Federal Law Requirements 177
    B. Statue of Frauds Considerations 177

IV. RIGHTS AND DUTIES CREATED BY THE
LANDLORD-TENANT RELATIONSHIP   178

    A. Uniform Residential Landlord and Tenant Act 178
    B. Landlords' Duties and Rights 178
        1. Right to Re-Enter Premises 179

2. Duty to Repair   179
3. Duty to Third Parties   181
4. Discriminatory Practices   181
C. Tenants' Duties and Rights   182
1. Right to Use and Enjoyment   182
2. Tenant Duties   182
3. Responsibility for Damages to Leased Premises   183
  a. Ordinary Wear and Tear   183
  b. Safety Deposits   183
  c. Pet Deposits   184
D. Legal Doctrines That Arise in the Landlord-Tenant Relationship   184
1. Warranty of Habitability   184
2. Quiet Enjoyment   184

VIII. REMEDIES FOR BREACH OF DUTY   **184**

A. Tenant Remedies Against Landlord   185
1. Damages That Can Be Awarded to the Tenant   185
  a. Equitable Relief   185
  b. Compensatory Damages   185
  c. Punitive Damages   186
2. Constructive Eviction   186
3. Actions for Wrongful Eviction   187
B. Landlord Remedies Against Tenant: Eviction   187
1. Procedures to Evict   188
2. Self-Help Eviction   188
3. Retaliatory Eviction   189

IX. CLASSIFYING LANDLORD-TENANT RELATIONSHIPS   **189**

A. Tenancy for Years   189
1. Creating a Tenancy for Years   190
2. Terminating a Tenancy for Years   190
B. Tenancy from Year to Year   190
1. Creating a Tenancy from Year to Year   190
2. Terminating a Tenancy from Year to Year   190
C. Tenancy at Will   191
1. Creating a Tenancy at Will   191
2. Terminating a Tenancy at Will   191
D. Tenancy at Sufferance   191
1. Creating a Tenancy at Sufferance   191
2. Terminating a Tenancy at Sufferance   191

Case Excerpt: Alabama Assoc. of Realtors v. U.S. Dept. of Health and Human Services   192

COVID-19 Concern   196
Chapter Summary   196

Skills You Need in the Real World   197
Ethical Issues for the Paralegal: Landlords Who Violate State Law   197
Key Terms and Concepts   197
End-of-Chapter Exercises   198
Annotated Document: Apartment Lease   199
Practice Questions for Test Review   200

8. REAL ESTATE DEEDS 203

Chapter Objectives   203
Chapter Outline   203

I. INTRODUCTION   **204**

II. A BRIEF HISTORY OF DEEDS   **204**

II. ELEMENTS OF DEEDS   **205**

  A. The Deed Must Be in Writing   205
  B. The Deed Must Identify the Grantor and the Grantee   206
  C. The Deed Must Be Signed by the Grantor   207
  D. The Grantor Must Have Legal Capacity   208
  E. The Property Must Be Adequately Described   210
    1. Specific Descriptions   210
    2. Court Interpretations of Ambiguous Property Descriptions   211
  F. The Deed Must Contain Language Indicating an Intention to Convey
    Property Rights   211
  G. The Deed Must Be Delivered by the Grantor and
    Accepted by the Grantee   212
    1. Proving Delivery   213
    2. Delivery in Escrow   214
  H. The Deed Must Be Attested and Acknowledged   214
    1. Attestation   214
    2. Acknowledgment   215
  I. Other Deed Provisions   215
    1. Seals   215
    2. Consideration Recitals   216
    3. Exceptions and Exclusions   216
  J. Nonessential Deed Provisions   216
    1. Witnesses   216
    2. Date   217

IV. TYPES OF DEEDS   **217**

    A. General Warranty Deeds   217
       1. *Seizin*   218
       2. Quiet Enjoyment   218
       3. Against Encumbrances   218
       4. Further Assurance   218
       5. Warranty Forever   218
    B. Special Warranty Deeds   219
    C. Deeds of Trust/Mortgages   220
    D. Quitclaim Deed   221

V. RECORDING STATUTES   **221**

    A. Notice Recording Statutes   221
    B. Race-Notice Recording Statutes   221
    C. Race Recording Statutes   222

Case Excerpt: Corso v. Miser   222

COVID-19 Concern   227
Chapter Summary   227
Skills You Need in the Real World   228
Ethical Issues for the Paralegal: Use of Forms   228
Key Terms and Concepts   229
End-of-Chapter Exercises   229
Annotated Document: General Warranty Deed   231
Practice Questions for Test Review   233

9   MORTGAGES AND FINANCING THE PURCHASE OF REAL ESTATE   235

Chapter Objectives   235
Chapter Outline   235

I. INTRODUCTION   **236**

II. MORTGAGE MARKETS   **237**

    A. Primary Mortgage Market   237
    B. Secondary Mortgage Market   239
       1. Federal Agencies in the Secondary Mortgage Market   240
         a. Fannie Mae   241
         b. Ginnie Mae   241
         c. Freddie Mac   242
         d. HUD   242
         e. The Role of the Federal Reserve Board 242
         f. Troubled Asset Relief Program   242

2. Federal Legislation That Governs Real Estate Financing   242
  a. Dodd-Frank   243
    i. Sweeping Changes in Truth-in-Lending   244
    ii. Potential Problems Under Dodd-Frank   247
    iii. Violations of Dodd-Frank   248
  b. Real Estate Settlement Procedures Act   248

III. THE LEGAL REQUIREMENTS OF A MORTGAGE/DEED OF TRUST   249

A. Mortgages Versus Deeds of Trust   249
B. The Elements of a Mortgage   249
  1. Mortgages Must Be in Writing   250
  2. The Parties Must Be Identified   250
  3. Specific Clauses in Mortgages   251
    a. Property as Collateral   251
    b. Promissory Note   251
    c. Granting Clause   251
    d. Description of the Debt   251
    e. Power of Sale Provision   252
    f. Taxes and Insurance   252
    g. Estoppel Certificate   252
    h. Acceleration Clause   252
    i. Due on Sale Clause   252
    j. Interest Escalation Clause   252
    k. Prepayment Clause   253
    l. Attorney's Fees   253
C. Recording Mortgages   253

IV. TYPES OF MORTGAGES   254

A. Fixed-Rate Mortgages   254
  1. Advantages and Disadvantages of Fixed-Rate Mortgages   254
  2. Amortization   255
B. Adjustable-Rate Mortgages   255
  1. Advantages and Disadvantages of Adjustable-Rate Mortgages   255
  2. Rate Caps   256
C. Other Types of Mortgages   256
  1. Purchase-Money Mortgages   256
  2. Wraparound Mortgages   257
  3. Second Mortgages   257
  4. Equity Lines of Credit   258
  5. Bridge Loans   258

V. QUALIFYING FOR A MORTGAGE   258

A. Underwriting   260

B. Borrower's Credit History   260
   1. Consumer Reporting Agencies   260
   2. The Fair Credit Reporting Act   260
   3. Points   261
C. Appraisal   261
D. The Rise of Internet Lenders   261

VI. DISCHARGING A MORTGAGE   **261**

VII. FORECLOSURE   **262**

A. Judicial Foreclosure   262
B. Power of Sale Foreclosure   262
C. The Foreclosure Auction   262
D. Decreasing Foreclosure Rates   263

Case Excerpt: Mohanna v. Wells Fargo Bank, N.A.   263

COVID-19 Concern   266
Chapter Summary   266
Skills You Need in the Real World   267
Ethical Issues for the Paralegal: Predatory Lending   268
Key Terms and Concepts   268
End-of-Chapter Exercises   268
Annotated Document: Residential Mortgage   270
Practice Questions for Test Review   275

10   PUBLIC AND PRIVATE RESTRICTIONS ON THE USE OF LAND   277

Chapter Objectives   277
Chapter Outline   277

I. INTRODUCTION   **278**

II. PUBLIC RESTRICTIONS ON PRIVATE LAND USE   **278**

A. Zoning   278
   1. Aesthetic Zoning   279
   2. Enforcing Zoning Regulations   279
   3. Zoning Classifications   280
      a. Residential   280
      b. Commercial   281
      c. Industrial   281
   4. Exceptions to Zoning Classifications   281
      a. Nonconforming Use   281
      b. Conditional Use Permit   282
      c. Variance   282

     5. Unconstitutional or Illegal Zoning Regulations   283
       a. Rational Basis Test   283
       b. "Spot" Zoning   283
   B. Building Codes   284
   C. Planning Boards   285
   D. Historic Districts   285
   E. Urban Planning   285
   F. Interstate Land Sales Full Disclosure Act   286
   G. Environmental Issues   286
     1. Clean Water Act   287
     2. The Superfund   287

III. PRIVATE RESTRICTIONS ON PRIVATE LAND USE   287

   A. Restrictive Covenants   287
     1. Creating Covenants   288
     2. Restrictive Covenants "Touch and Concern"   288
     3. Typical Covenants   289
     4. Illegal or Unconstitutional Covenants   289
     5. Enforcing Covenants   290
     6. Terminating Restrictive Covenants   290
       a. Stated Time Period   290
       b. Abandonment   290
       c. Changed Conditions   290
       d. Merger   291
   B. Subdivision Rules and Regulations   291
   C. Nuisance Actions   291
     1. Public Nuisance   291
     2. Private Nuisance   292

Case Excerpt: Moseley v. Arnold   *292*

COVID-19 Concern   *299*
Chapter Summary   *299*
Skills You Need in the Real World   *300*
Ethical Issues for the Paralegal: Discriminatory Restrictive Covenants   *300*
Key Terms and Concepts   *300*
End-of-Chapter Exercises   *301*
Annotated Document: Restrictive Covenants   *302*
Practice Questions for Test Review   *304*

 **REAL ESTATE PROFESSIONS   307**

Chapter Objectives   *307*
Chapter Outline   *307*

I. INTRODUCTION   **308**

II. THE LAW OF AGENCY   **308**

  A. Creating an Agency Relationship   308
  B. Agent's Duty to the Principal   309
    1. Obedience   309
    2. Care   310
    3. Loyalty   310
    4. Accounting   310
  C. Agent's Duty to Third Parties   310
    1. Honesty and Fair Dealing   311
    2. Not to Commit Fraud   311
      a. Material Facts   311
      b. Sales Tactics   312
    3. Avoid Negligent Misrepresentation   312
  D. Principal's Duty to Agent   313
    1. Compensate the Agent   313
    2. Cooperate   313
    3. Not to Unfairly Injure the Agent's Reputation 314
  E. Independent Contractors   314

III. APPLYING AGENCY LAW TO REAL ESTATE AGENTS   **315**

  A. A Real Estate Agent's Duty of Care   315
  B. A Real Estate Agent's Responsibility to Disclose Information 316
  C. Classifications of Real Estate Agents   316
    1. Real Estate Brokers Versus Real Estate Agents 316
    2. Becoming a Real Estate Broker or Agent   317
    3. Regulations That Govern Real Estate Brokers and Agents 318
    4. Services Provided by Real Estate Agents and Brokers 318
      a. Multiple Listing Service   319
      b. Locating and Prequalifying Buyers 320

IV. OTHER REAL ESTATE PROFESSIONS   **321**

  A. Real Estate Investors   321
    1. Advantages of Real Estate Investments   321
      a. Appreciation in Value   322
      b. Impact on Credit Rating   322
      c. Potential Source of Funds   322
      d. Tax Advantages   322
    2. Disadvantages of Real Estate Investments   323
      a. Poor Liquidity   323
      b. Property Taxes   323
      c. Maintenance Costs   323
      d. Financing and Down Payment Costs 323
    3. Real Estate Investment Trusts   323

4. Small Investors and "Do It Yourselfers"	324
B. Loan Officers	324
1. Online Loan Applications	325
2. Internet Mortgage Lenders	325
C. Appraisers	325
1. Process of Appraisal	325
2. The Importance of Real Estate Valuation	326
D. Surveyors	326
E. The Legal Team	328
1. Real Estate Attorneys	328
2. Real Estate Paralegals	328
3. Real Estate Title Searchers	328
4. The Role of Technology in the Real Estate Law Office	329
F. Contractors	329
G. Property Managers	329
H. Inspectors	329
Case Excerpt: Clark v. Taylor Hudson Real Estate	*331*
COVID-19 Concern	*336*
Chapter Summary	*336*
Skills You Need in the Real World	*337*
Ethical Issues for the Paralegal: Real Estate Professionals' Codes of Ethics	*337*
Key Terms and Concepts	*338*
End-of-Chapter Exercises	*338*
Annotated Document: Real Estate Appraisal	*340*
Practice Questions for Test Review	*341*

12 TITLE INSURANCE AND TITLE EXAMINATIONS 343

Chapter Objectives	*343*
Chapter Outline	*343*
I. INTRODUCTION	**344**
II. TITLE INSURANCE	**344**
A. What Title Insurance Does	344
B. Obtaining Title Insurance	345
1. Title Insurance Premium	346
2. Terminating the Policy	346
III. TITLE EXAMINATIONS	**346**
A. What Is a Title Examination?	347
B. Information Needed for a Title Examination	348

  1. Names of the Current Owners   349
     a. Grantor-Grantee Index   349
     b. Tract Index   349
  2. Description of the Property to Be Conveyed   350
  3. Time Period   350
  4. Tax ID Number   350
  5. Deed Book and Page Number   350
  6. Surveys and Plats   351

IV. STEPS IN A TITLE SEARCH   351

  A. Creating a Client File   352
  B. Step 1: Creating the Chain of Title   352
     1. The Tax Office   353
     2. Creating the Links in the Chain of Ownership   353
     3. Technological Innovations in Land Records   354
  C. Step 2: Establishing the Out or Adverse Conveyances   355
     1. Reviewing Title Documents   356
     2. Liens   357
     3. UCC Listings   358
     4. Marriage, Birth, and Death Records   359
     5. Probate Records   359
     6. Judgments   359
  D. Step 3: Compiling the Information   360
     1. Role of Forms   360
     2. Title Abstracts   360
  E. Preliminary and Final Title Certificates   361
     1. Legal Malpractice and Title Examinations   361
     2. Tacking   361
  F. The Paralegal's Role in Title Searches   361

V. COMMON PROBLEMS IN TITLE SEARCHES   363

  A. Subdivided Properties   363
  B. Holes or Breaks in the Chain of Title   364

Case Excerpt: Fid. Nat'l Title Ins. Co. v. Butler   364

COVID 19 Concern   371
Chapter Summary   371
Skills You Need in the Real World   372
Ethical Issues for the Paralegal: Tacking and Other Shortcuts   372
Key Terms and Concepts   373
End-of-Chapter Exercises   373
Annotated Document: Chain of Title   375
Practice Questions for Test Review   377

13 THE CLOSING 379

Chapter Objectives		*379*
Chapter Outline		*379*

I. INTRODUCTION   **380**

II. WHAT IS A CLOSING?   **380**

III. PREPARING TO CONDUCT A CLOSING   **381**

A. Mortgages		381
B. Attorney Representation		382
C. Establishing the Date		382
1. Three-Day Window		382
2. Time Is of the Essence		383
D. Gathering Documents and Information		383
1. Title Search		384
2. Legal Description of the Property		384
3. Loan Payoff Amounts		385
4. Tax Information		385
5. Inspection Reports		386

IV. PEOPLE NORMALLY PRESENT AT THE CLOSING   **387**

A. Settlement Agent		388
1. Attorney		388
2. Paralegal		388
B. Buyer		389
C. Seller		389
D. Real Estate Agent		389

V. THE CLOSING PROCEDURE   **389**

A. Preparing the Loan Package		390
B. Verifying Hazard Insurance		390
C. Exchanging Documents		391
1. General Warranty Deed		391
2. Mortgage		391
a. Promissory Note		391
b. Subordination Agreements		392
3. IRS Forms		392
a. IRS Form 1099		392
b. IRS Form 4506		392
c. W-9 Form		392
4. Lien Waiver Affidavits		392
5. Disclosure Form		393
6. Bill of Sale for Personal Property		393

          7. Compliance Agreement   393
          8. Credit Insurance Documents   393
          9. Loan Application   394
         10. USA Patriot Act Requirements   394
         11. PMI Disclosure   394
         12. Trust Disbursement Records   395
         13. Truth-in-Lending Documentation   396
         14. Termite Inspection Letter   399
         15. Survey   401
      D. Disbursing the Funds   401
          1. Lender's Fees   401
          2. Attorney's Fees   402
          3. Recording Fees   402
          4. Seller's Profit on the Transaction   402
          5. Real Estate Agent's Commission   402
          6. Tax Payments   402
          7. Proration   403
          8. Certified Funds from the Buyer   404

   VI. OTHER CLOSING ISSUES   **404**

      A. "Escrow" Closings   404
          1. Relation Back   405
          2. Modifications to Escrow Closings Under Dodd-Frank   406
      B. Dual Representation   406

   VI. AFTER THE CLOSING   **406**

   Case Excerpt: Johnson v. Alexander   409

   COVID-19 Concern   413
   Chapter Summary   413
   Skills You Need in the Real World   414
   Ethical Issues for the Paralegal: Delegating the Closing to the Paralegal 414
   Key Terms and Concepts   414
   End-of-Chapter Exercises   415
   Annotated Document: Settlement Statement   417
   Practice Questions for Test Review   418

14   TAXATION ISSUES IN REAL PROPERTY   421

   Chapter Objectives   421
   Chapter Outline   421

      I. INTRODUCTION   **421**

II. GOVERNMENTAL POWERS OF TAXATION   422

   A. What Can Be Taxed?   422
   B. Tax Exemptions   423
      1. Homestead Exemption   423
      2. Charitable Exemption   423
      3. Nonprofit Exemption   423
      4. Government Exemption   424

III. HOW TAXES ARE ASSESSED   424

   A. Determining the Property Value   425
      1. Challenging an Assessment   425
      2. Reassessment   426
   B. Calculating the Tax Rate   426

IV. PAYING TAXES   427

   A. Enforcing Tax Regulations   427
   B. Tax Liens   427
      1. Setting Priorities in Tax Liens   428
      2. Foreclosing a Tax Lien   428

V. ASSESSMENTS   429

Case Excerpt: Miller & Rhoads Building, L.L.C. v. City of Richmond   430

COVID-19 Concern   432
Chapter Summary   433
Skills You Need in the Real World   433
Ethical Issues for the Paralegal: Tax Dodges   434
Key Terms and Concepts   434
End-of-Chapter Exercises   434
Annotated Document: County Tax Record   436
Practice Questions for Test Review   437

APPENDIX: Answers to Review Questions and Practice Questions for Test Review   439
GLOSSARY   483
INDEX   489

Preface

INTRODUCTION

The sixth edition is a strong reworking of the previous edition, which was itself a major reworking of the base material. The fifth edition came in on the heels of the Great Recession and the dramatic changes to the real estate world that it ushered in. Dodd-Frank and other changes have now had time to become established procedure for borrowers and lenders. Under other circumstances, this sixth edition might simply be seen as a minor revision.

Then the Great Pandemic hit. COVID-19 and its variants have changed the world. This impact has been felt in every pocket of society, and it has had a dynamic impact on the day-to-day practice of real estate. From "parking lot" closings to Zoom conferences, real estate professionals of every type have had to adjust to new behaviors while waiting for society to return to normal. At the time of this writing, "normal" remains as elusive as ever. The pre-2019 approach to the practice of law may never return. In acknowledging both the large and small changes that the pandemic has brought on the practice of law, this edition has undergone major changes. Predictable, stable, and long-entrenched practices from inspecting a home to conducting a closing have all gone through dramatic changes.

Among the new features of this text is a section directly addressing the impact that COVID-19 has had on real estate law practice. Appropriately named "COVID-19 Concerns," this new element focuses on current and possible changes to real estate practice. In addition, the author has provided another new feature, "Real World Perspectives," which provides the reader with interview excerpts from real estate paralegals, real estate brokers, and others on the practical aspects of real estate law, including the challenges brought on by mask mandates, nationwide moratoriums on evictions, and many other aspects. Case excerpts have also been updated to reflect new developments in many areas of real estate law. The author has updated the materials as much as possible, while continuing to lay a proper foundation in real estate law that covers topics as diverse as the basics of fee simple ownership, landlord-tenant law, restrictive covenants, closing procedures, and taxation, to name just a few.

As in previous editions, the day-to-day practice of law is never far from consideration of the material presented. The text continues to place a strong emphasis on practical applications of real estate law. The author has also extensively updated the graphs, exhibits, and other visual aids. The data show some interesting trends in home ownership, rental rates, and other aspects of real estate law. Ethical issues continue to be a paramount concern. The author emphasizes various ethical issues in every chapter. End-of-Chapter material has also changed, providing sample test questions for the student, including essay, fill in the blank, true/false, and multiple choice questions with the answers provided in the Appendix. There will also be substantial changes to the Instructor's Manual by adding sample syllabi, lesson plans, presentation suggestions, expanded Power Point slides, and suggested video clips available online. All of this is intended to help the instructor with as much ancillary materials as possible.

FEATURES

The book was designed with the reader in mind. The text presents the material in a variety of methods to tap into different learning styles. Many examples of actual documents are provided as figures throughout each chapter. In addition, various features lend a strong visual element to the text. The features found in the text include the following:

Chapter Objectives
Each chapter begins with clearly stated learning objectives to guide readers in their studies.

Real Estate Basics at a Glance
Scattered throughout each chapter are small synopses of issues discussed in the chapter. These synopses are positioned adjacent to the material under discussion, not only as a way of helping the reader synthesize important issues, but also as a visual marker for later study.

Definitions
As each new term is introduced, it is also defined for the student. These on-the-spot definitions provide a handy reference.

Examples
Each chapter contains not only discussions of the theoretical underpinnings of law, but also practical examples to assist the student in building the reasoning skills needed to succeed in the legal field.

Annotated Documents
In addition to the documents provided as figures throughout the text, each chapter contains one relevant annotated document to highlight the practical application of issues discussed in the chapter.

Ethics
Ethics is a vital component of any legal text, so the ethical implications of a real estate practice are emphasized in each chapter. In order to emphasize the important role that ethics plays in law, each chapter contains a separate ethical discussion.

Skills You Need in the Real World
The text places strong emphasis on balancing theoretical discussion with practical examples. This is readily apparent in the "Skills" section found at the

conclusion of each chapter. Here, the author addresses how the student can build an entire skill set, from researching public records to drafting property descriptions.

Case Excerpts
Each chapter contains a case excerpt designed to emphasize some of the points raised in that chapter and to provide material for classroom discussions. These cases have been updated to reflect recent changes in the law since the publication of the first edition.

Case Questions
At the conclusion of each case are questions relevant to that case that spur classroom discussion and ask the student to relate the case to the material brought out in each chapter.

Chapter Summary
Each chapter contains a concise summary of the major issues discussed. This feature helps readers focus on the important points raised in the chapter.

Review Questions
Extensive review questions test the student's comprehension of the issues under discussion. These review questions, coupled with the Discussion Questions, provide rich material for classroom discussions. Answers to these review questions are now provided in the Appendix, allowing students to compare their answers to the ones provided by the author.

Applying What You Have Learned
In this section, the reader is asked to apply the theoretical knowledge from the chapter to practical aspects of real estate law. These applications vary from preparing title examination documents, researching zoning regulations to creating drawings based on real estate property descriptions.

Websites
The Internet is becoming an increasingly vital link for students, and a list of web sites is included at the end of each chapter to assist students in gathering more information about the chapter topics. Web sites in each chapter focus on important real estate concepts or provide direct access to the amazing amount of detail currently provided about real estate topics, including access to public documents.

Key Terms and Concepts
A list of key terms and phrases used in each chapter assists the student in mastering the concepts presented.

Tech Topic
In addition to discussing the ever-expanding role of technology in real estate practice, the author has revised this feature to discuss new technology and the impact that it has had in many different areas of real estate law.

■ **Sample Quizzes in Different Formats**
The text has also been revised to include new sections with sample quizzes in several formats that allow students to check their progress in their comprehension of the materials. Answers to all these questions are provided in the Appendix.

■ **COVID-19 Concerns**
Given the overall impact that the COVID-19 pandemic has had on the world, it is little wonder that it would also have had a continuing impact on real estate law. Each chapter contains a separate section discussing the current and possible impacts of the global pandemic on diverse areas of real estate practice and law.

■ **Non-Gender Specific Language**
In recognition of the changing face of pronoun use and the impact that gender-specific language has on readers, the author has endeavored to avoid the use of gender specific pronouns whenever possible.

PEDAGOGY

The following features are included in the text to take advantage of different student learning styles:

■ Learning objectives stated at the beginning of each chapter
■ Terms and legal vocabulary in bold and defined immediately for the student; also listed in the Glossary for later reference
■ Many different forms of visual aids that illustrate crucial points
■ "Real World Perspectives" to allow the student to hear about various aspects of real estate law in the voices of the people who practice it
■ Lesson plans in the instructor's manual that provide alternative presentations of the material
■ End-of-chapter questions, activities, and assignments to hone the student's understanding
■ End-of-chapter ethical discussion
■ Websites for further research and/or discussion

INSTRUCTOR'S MANUAL

The author has developed an extensive instructor's manual to accompany the text. This instructor's manual provides a wealth of resources for the instructor. The instructor's manual and other ancillary materials are available to download at the companion website to accompany the text, at www.aspenlawschool.com/bevans_realestate3.

■ **Suggested Syllabi**
Suggested syllabi are provided for various versions of an Introduction to Law course, including alternate syllabi for instructors who emphasize theoretical over practical, or practical over theoretical.

Lesson Plans
The author provides several different lesson plans to help instructors who must present introductory courses in 6-, 8-, 10-, 12-, or 16-week formats.

Chapter Lecture Outline and Discussion
Each chapter is outlined for the instructor and annotations are provided throughout the outline to provide additional discussion and classroom material for the instructor.

Additional Web Resources
The instructor's manual also contains additional websites to provide other resources for classroom discussion and assignments.

Additional Assignments
In addition to the chapter review questions and discussion questions, the author also provides more assignments in the instructor's manual.

Answers to Review Questions and Discussion Questions
The end-of-chapter review questions are answered in detail. The author also provides suggested answers for the discussion questions.

Test Bank
The test bank includes a variety of test questions, including:
Essay Questions (five per chapter)
Short Answer (ten per chapter)
Multiple Choice (25 per chapter)
True-False (ten per chapter)

Additional Instructor's Materials
1 Power Point Slides
The author has prepared a PowerPoint® presentation for each chapter of the text.

2 Additional Cases
Additional cases are provided for classroom discussion. These can be used in a variety of ways, including as lecture handouts and additional assignments.

Acknowledgments

The author would like to thank the following for their help in creating this book: Starla Hoke, Debra Holbrook, Betsy Kenny, and Lisa Connery.

An Introduction to Real Estate

Chapter Objectives

- Explain the differences between real and personal property

- Explain the economic characteristics of real property

- Describe the real estate market

- List and explain the various classifications of real property

- Explain the differences between residential, commercial, and industrial property

Chapter Outline

I. Introduction

II. Real Property Versus Personal Property
   A. What Makes Real Property So Unique?
   B. Physical Characteristics of Land
   C. Economic Characteristics of Land

III. The Real Estate Market

IV. Classifying Property By Use
   A. Unimproved Land
   B. Residential Property
   C. Commercial Property
   D. Industrial Property
   E. Farm and Rural Property
   F. Recreational Property
   G. Government-Owned Land

INTRODUCTION

In this chapter we examine the basic concepts of real property. We first examine how real property differs from personal property, and then dig deeper into the issues by showing how the unique qualities of real property are revealed in a wide variety of ways, from how land is classified to how title to real property is conveyed from a seller to a buyer.

REAL PROPERTY VERSUS PERSONAL PROPERTY

All property can be divided into two classifications: real property and personal property. Although the original meanings of these terms had special relevance to how a case was brought — and the court in which the action could be brought — these days the differences have more to do with the way that ownership interests are transferred. In the modern era, real property refers to land and anything permanently attached to land. Personal property refers to all other types of property. As such, real property refers to the land, houses, trees, and any other permanent structures. Personal property refers to non-real estate items, including everything from apples to automobiles.

REAL ESTATE BASICS AT A GLANCE

"Real property" refers to land and anything permanently attached to land.

The reason that the law makes a distinction between these two types of property is that the classification affects many of the rights and legal remedies available to the owners. For one thing, the way that ownership is transferred in real estate is different from the way it is transferred in personal property. We will see time and again that there is a great deal of symbolism in real estate transactions. In Chapter 2, we will see that the modern real estate transaction still holds many of the same features used in the Middle Ages and earlier. This is particularly true when it comes to transferring title to real property.

The transfer of ownership interest in real estate is required to be in writing under the **Statute of Frauds** (explored in greater detail in Chapter 8); however, most transfers of personal property are not required to be in writing. For personal property, possession often equates to ownership. Bills of sale, receipts, and other indicia of title are helpful in proving ownership of personal property, but possession is the best way. In fact, the old common law rule that "possession is nine-tenths of the law" is a maxim that applies to personal property (but not to real property). Real property ownership interests, by contrast, are transferred by deed. The deed is the evidence of ownership, and the delivery and acceptance of the deed are the physical acts that transfer ownership from one person to another.

Statute of Frauds
Originally enacted in England and later adopted in all American states, this statute requires certain types of contracts to be in writing before they can be enforced. Typical contracts covered by the Statute of Frauds include contracts to answer for the debt of another and transactions involving real estate.

REAL ESTATE BASICS AT A GLANCE

Real property ownership interests are transferred in a different way than ownership interests in personal property.

Knowing how to classify property as real or personal also has a practical consideration: In a real estate transaction, there is no need to refer to or list the specific items of real property that are being sold because the sale of real property involves the sale of all items that are permanently attached to the land. The house, trees, soil, and attached garage are never mentioned in the deed. Personal property transactions, on the other hand, must specifically list all items for which the title is changing hands.

In the past, the difference in classification between real and personal property had an effect on probate law. Real property interests were transferred to heirs in different ways than personal property. Although many of those probate rules have changed, there are still important differences that arise in transferring title through an estate proceeding.

Another difference between real property and personal property is taxation. Taxes are assessed differently on personal property and real property. Taxes on personal property are usually imposed based on its sale price, while taxes on real property are based on its assessed value. We explore these and many other differences in later chapters. See Figure 1-1 for a summary of differences between real and personal property.

Personal Property	Real Property	**FIGURE 1-1**
Usually refers to mobile items	Always refers to land	
Often taxed on sale price	Often taxed on assessed value	Differences Between Real Property and Personal Property
Ownership is evidenced by possession	Ownership is evidenced by deed	
Statute of Frauds usually does not apply	Statute of Frauds applies to almost all transactions	

A. WHAT MAKES REAL PROPERTY SO UNIQUE?

Real property is a unique and specialized area of law for several reasons. As we will see throughout this chapter, real property has its own set of rules for selling, buying, mortgaging, and investing. Real property also has unique physical attributes. For one thing, real estate occupies a fixed point on the globe. Rivers may change course, houses may be torn down, but the underlying land remains where it is. Land that is submerged under a lake is still there, albeit inaccessible.

Real property has its own set of laws, statutes, cases, and judicial interpretations that make it an entirely separate branch of law. Many attorneys devote their careers to this one area. It is as specialized as criminal defense, trademark, and labor law. Attorneys and paralegals can spend decades in the practice of real property law and still not learn all its aspects. During the course of this book, we discuss many of the legal implications that arise from real property, from easements to encroachments, from mortgages to metes and bounds descriptions, while learning a great deal about property law in all its rich diversity.

Real property is also unique because of the financial arrangements used to purchase it. Later, we examine the issue of deeds of trust and mortgages and the legal impact of these financing instruments on real estate ownership.

Sidebar

Most states have their own statewide real estate treatises. Usually written by a noted scholar or attorney, a real estate treatise is a great source of information about real property law in a particular state. It provides not only legal background but also practical applications. You should locate and acquire your own copy of the real property treatise for your state.

B. PHYSICAL CHARACTERISTICS OF LAND

Real property has several distinctive characteristics that separate it from personal property (see Figure 1-2). As mentioned above, land occupies a specific point on the globe. Unlike personal property, land is fixed and immovable; it cannot be relocated. For this reason, it is the perfect vehicle for assessing taxes. (In Chapter 14, we explore how real estate taxes are assessed.) Another physical characteristic of real estate is that no two pieces of land are identical. Each one is unique, with its own special characteristics and chain of ownership. Also, because land is located within different jurisdictions, the rules governing real estate transactions vary considerably. Land falls under the law of whatever state it happens to be located in. A single individual can own land in any number of different states, and each parcel falls under different rules and statutes. An owner cannot claim that simply because he is the owner of all the tracts that they should all fall under one set of rules.

FIGURE 1-2	Land is:	
Physical Characteristics of Land	■ Permanently fixed and immovable.	■ Used by local governments for assessing taxes.
	■ Unique; no two pieces of land are exactly the same.	

Personal jurisdiction
A court's power to render decisions based on an individual's personal connections and interactions within the court's geographic boundaries.

In rem jurisdiction
A court's power to render decisions based on the location of the land within the court's geographic boundaries.

This fact controls some of the rules regarding lawsuits involving real estate. In most lawsuits, the court's jurisdiction is based on **personal jurisdiction**, that is, power over the people involved in the suit. However, in some lawsuits, a court acquires jurisdictional power simply because a tract of land lies within its geographic boundaries. There is a specific term for this type of jurisdiction: **in rem jurisdiction**. This is a court's power to enter decisions and rulings simply because the land involved happens to be within the court's geographic limits. We explore many of these jurisdictional questions in Chapter 4.

C. ECONOMIC CHARACTERISTICS OF LAND

In addition to its unique physical characteristics, land also has some interesting economic characteristics. For one thing, land has traditionally been an excellent investment. In the past, a person's wealth was measured by the extent of his real estate holdings. Land ownership continues to be an important source of investment income for many individuals. See Figure 1-3.

Land also offers some economic benefits to persons who are not wealthy. In fact, one of the best economic benefits of land ownership is its tax consequences. In Chapter 4, we explore how a homeowner earns a substantial tax benefit from being able to deduct mortgage interest payments from his yearly income tax return.

Another interesting aspect of real estate is that unlike almost all other purchases, it generally appreciates in value. Because there is a fixed supply of land, and an ever-growing population, the realities of supply and demand put upward pressure on real estate prices. In many areas of the country, the value of a person's home and land increases about 6 percent a year. This makes land an attractive investment even for those of a moderate income. However, like any other item, land can also decrease in value. In recent years, the value of real estate, especially residential real estate, has either failed to rise or has actually dropped. Still, the price fluctuations of land are relatively minor, especially when you compare the long-term prices of real estate to other commodities.

Median Asking Sales Price for Vacant for Sale Units: 1997-2021
(Current Dollars)

Source: U.S. Census Bureau, Current Population Survey/Housing Vacancy Survey November 2, 2021
Recession data: National Bureau of Economic Reseach, <www.nber.org>

FIGURE 1-3

Median Asking Sales Price for Vacant Sale Units: 1997-2021.

In recent years, falling interest rates have also encouraged people to refinance their homes. This has the advantage of allowing an owner to receive some of the **equity** value in a home as cash. Equity is another aspect of the economic characteristics of land ownership. When we say that a person has equity in his or her home, what we are saying is that there is a difference between what the person owes on the home and what the home (and land) are actually worth.

Equity
A homeowner's value in property once the amount owed on the property is subtracted from its current fair market value.

JUAN'S EQUITY

EXAMPLE 1-1

Juan purchased his home 15 years ago and has been making regular monthly mortgage payments on it. His original loan amount was for $150,000. In the past 15 years, he has lowered the balance of the loan to $85,000. However, because Juan's house has steadily been appreciating in value over the years, the house is now worth $220,000. How much equity does Juan have?

Answer: Juan has $135,000 in equity. How do we arrive at this amount? Subtract the amount that Juan owes on the house from the current value ($220,000 – $85,000 = $135,000).

Although this appears to be a simple paper gain, Juan can borrow against his equity. He can apply for a second mortgage and borrow against this "paper value" for real money.

EXAMPLE 1-2

CHANGING THE EQUITY SITUATION

Let's take the same numbers and show how Juan can end up in a situation that is all too common today: with a home value that is "underwater," meaning that his house is worth less than what he owes on it.

Juan's original loan amount, 15 years ago, was $150,000. However, three years ago, he took out a second mortgage on his home for the amount of $40,000. He used the money to fix up the home. Using the same numbers as the first example, Juan has paid down his original loan to $85,000, but because the real estate market has crumbled, Juan's house is worth $100,000. Juan owes $125,000 ($85,000 + $40,000). Juan now owes $25,000 more than the house is actually worth.

Tech Topic
CLOUD-BASED COMPUTING

In an era when the Internet is king and individuals, businesses, and governments alike are moving to online services and storage, it is tempting for law firms to follow suit. Before making the leap, however, it is important to consider both the ethical and the practical implications of a shift to cloud-based computing.

First, what is "cloud-based computing"? In broad terms, it is the use of software and services developed and hosted by third parties and delivered via the Internet rather than stored locally on a single user's computer. This is also known as "Software as a Service" (SaaS). In contrast to the traditional model of a user purchasing a software, installing it on her computer, and storing both it and its products on her local drive, SaaS calls for users to purchase a subscription to a software that they then access online. Rather than on a hard drive, the software and its products are stored in "the cloud," which is a federated group of hardware and software combined together to form an ecosystem through which they deliver users storage, hosting, and software capabilities. It is similar to the idea of a public utility like water or electricity, wherein users share a pool of resources, each drawing on

them when necessary and leaving them free for others to use when not.

While SaaS is undoubtedly an appealing model for legal professionals — given that it usually provides more current software at a lower price, massive amounts of storage without the need to find space locally, and built-in disaster recovery options — there are strong ethical implications inherent in its use. The most obvious issue is, of course, that using the cloud places sensitive and confidential client data outside of the law firm's direct control. As is apparent in the frequent data breaches reported on the news, information stored online is never fully secure, and even the most secure system can be hacked. And while there are segregated cloud environments that cater to the security demands of industries that deal with highly sensitive information (such as government agencies, the health care industry, and education), even those environments are not foolproof.

Different states have different rules and regulations in place regarding attorney use of SaaS. Many of the states that have issued opinions expressly permitting its use have also imposed certain "reasonable care" standards that require users to investigate the security measures in place before using any SaaS. The first step in deciding whether to use cloud-based computing is to find out if the state in which the law firm is located allows attorneys to use SaaS, and then to deal with any restrictions or requirements in place if SaaS is allowed.

It is then up to each attorney or firm to weigh for itself the risks of cloud-based computing versus the gains. Is the increased storage and software power worth a potential breach of privileged data? Is the immediate convenience worth a potential lawsuit down the road? As the use of SaaS continues to expand and more services move to cloud-only options, these are questions more and more of those in the legal profession will find themselves needing to wrestle with.

REAL WORLD PERSPECTIVES: *REAL ESTATE PARALEGAL*

I love it. It's a service profession. I think it's very rewarding. It's all about being a servant. So many agents, they want to shade a deal with their own ideas or comments. It's not about me — it's about the client and moving them forward. It's also about removing yourself personally and not getting in the way. It's important to stay professional. You have to assess the seller's needs and the buyer's needs, regardless of who you represent. Then you try to figure out what the best path is moving forward for both of them. A lot of times an agent will shade a transaction with their own thoughts or ideas.

— D. W., Real Estate Agent

THE REAL ESTATE MARKET

There is a market for land, just as there is a market for commodities or goods. The real estate market has its own rules and regulations. It also has participants, such as brokers, agents, loan correspondents, and attorneys and paralegals, to name just a few. We explore the role played by these participants as we develop the concepts of real estate in later chapters.

We begin our discussion of the real estate market with a straightforward example: Maria and Vern Seller have outgrown their house and want to put it up for sale. They contact Good & Better Real Estate Agency to discuss their options. Alvin Agent tells them that if they sign a listing agreement with the agency, Good & Better will advertise their house for sale, put a sign in their yard, list the home in the Multiple Listing Service, and make every effort to give the house the best chance of being sold.

Maria and Vern decide to list their house with Good & Better. Bill Buyer sees the house listed and decides that he wants to purchase the home. He contacts Good &

Better and gets the price particulars. Then he goes to a bank, meets with a loan officer, and arranges financing to purchase the home. Finally, he buys the home from the Sellers.

Although we have oversimplified the typical real estate transaction in this example, it gives us a starting point to discuss how the real estate market functions.

In any market, there must be buyers and sellers. Maria and Vern are sellers, and Bill is a buyer. Good & Better is acting for Maria and Vern to list the house for sale. In exchange for this service, Good & Better will receive a percentage of the total sale price (called a *commission*). The Sellers could have put their house up for sale on their own. They could have paid for an ad in the local newspaper, put a sign in their yard, and printed brochures to distribute to various places around the city, but they have decided that they would prefer to leave the job of marketing their home to professionals. Later, we will see that listing a home with a real estate agent brings certain advantages that are almost impossible for a single home seller to match.

When Bill Buyer decides to purchase the Sellers' home, he goes to a bank to borrow money. Most people who buy homes must obtain a mortgage because few people have that much ready cash on hand. The real estate market includes banks and other lending institutions. The banks in turn rely on others to review a borrower's application, assess the possible risk of the transaction, and establish the actual value of the home.

Throughout this book, we examine not only the theoretical basis of real property, but also the day-to-day activities of real estate professionals. We will see that, in many ways, the health of the real estate market is an indicator of the strength of the overall economy. The economic downturn that has come to be called "The Great Recession" was based almost exclusively on companies buying and selling mortgages, guaranteeing those transactions with insurance, and then formulating these various loans into packages that could be sold like stocks to individuals, companies, and even foreign countries. In a very real way, when the mortgage market in the United States went wrong, almost the entire economy on Earth went wrong. Then, a few years later, the worldwide COVID pandemic swept the world, dealing another crippling blow. Before we can delve into these topics, we must have a firm understanding of the various ways that real estate is classified.

CLASSIFYING PROPERTY BY USE

One of the oldest and most easily understood methods of classifying property is by the use to which it is put. There are several different categories of property, including unimproved land, residential property, commercial property, industrial property, farm and rural property, recreational property, and government-owned land.

However, before we set out these classifications, we must first examine exactly how the term *land* is defined. For our purposes, we define land as including the grass, soil, trees, and anything else permanently affixed to the ground, including the soil underneath and the structures above. This includes the owner's air rights in the space above the property. With this working definition of land, we can now examine specific subcategories of land.

A. UNIMPROVED LAND

When land contains **improvements**, it means that it contains structures. **Unimproved land** has no buildings or other structures on it, so it is often referred to as *raw land*. Such property can be developed into any number of uses: homes, businesses, farms, or parks. Once land has been improved, it can be reclassified into residential, farm, commercial, industrial, or recreational land. The categories are all based on the way in which the land is used.

Improvements
Buildings, fences, barns, and other structures that add value to raw land.

Unimproved land
Raw land that contains no structures.

"Unimproved land" has no structures placed on it.

REAL ESTATE BASICS AT A GLANCE

B. RESIDENTIAL PROPERTY

Property categorized as residential refers to land that has a structure designed to be used for personal living, such as a home. There are numerous subcategories of residential properties, including single- and multi-family units, apartments, condominiums and townhouses, cooperatives, mobile homes, and manufactured homes.

1. SINGLE- AND MULTI-FAMILY HOMES

The category of single- and multi-family homes includes residential houses, duplexes (two-family units sharing a single roof), triplexes (three-family units sharing a single roof), and four-family homes (four-family units sharing a single roof). When more than four family units share a single roof, the law characterizes that arrangement as an apartment.

2. APARTMENTS

The technical definition of an **apartment** is a type of residential real estate consisting of five or more living units per building; however, we use the term to describe a wide range of landlord-tenant relationships. Even if the technical definition encompasses five or more units under a single roof, most people who rent the living space above their garage to someone would undoubtedly refer to it as an "apartment" as well. The word is open to broad interpretation. In many large urban areas, there may be hundreds of apartments in any given complex. Apartments are popular because the residents have far less responsibility for maintaining the building, they generally have no responsibility for keeping up the grounds, and they do not need to make a large initial investment to move in. On the other hand, while apartment buildings can be a great financial investment for the owners, they provide few, if any, financial advantages for

Apartment
A leased residence containing five or more living units sharing a single roof or foundation.

the residents. Apartment residents, or tenants, pay rent to the apartment owners in exchange for the use of the premises, but they do not gain any ownership interests or equity in the property. We examine landlord-tenant law in greater detail in Chapter 7.

3. CONDOMINIUMS AND TOWNHOUSES

Condominiums and townhouses share many characteristics, but there are important differences that a legal professional should know.

a. Condominiums

Condominium
A form of real property in which the owner has full title to the interior, but not the exterior, of a structure.

A **condominium** resembles an apartment, but it is actually more like a hybrid between a home and an apartment. The tenant in an apartment does not have any ownership interests in the dwelling. He must seek permission from the owner before making changes to the interior and is not allowed to make any changes to the exterior. By contrast, a condominium gives the resident an ownership interest in the interior of the dwelling, but no rights to the exterior. Condominiums are sold, just like homes, but the only thing being sold is what is inside the four walls. No actual land is transferred in the sale of a condominium. The owner of a condominium receives the same favorable tax treatment as a homeowner but does not have the responsibility of exterior upkeep and maintenance. Condominiums are very attractive to people who do not want the burden of home maintenance, yet wish to receive the financial benefits of home ownership.

Condominiums typically have common areas that are owned and maintained by a homeowners' association. These common areas consist of the sidewalks connecting the various units and the amenities, such as swimming pools, tennis courts, gym facilities, and walking trails. A condominium owner usually pays mandatory annual dues to the homeowners' association to defray the cost of maintaining these public areas; homeowners' associations generally contract with maintenance firms to take care of yard work and to maintain the various facilities.

b. Townhouses

Townhouse
A form of real property in which the owner has title to both the interior and exterior of a structure that resembles an apartment instead of a traditional residence.

While condominium owners have legal rights only to the inside of their individual units, **townhouse** residents own the entire unit, both the interior and the exterior. They also own the land that the townhouse is situated on. In many states, there are no specific statutes that govern townhouses. Instead, the same rules and statutes that govern single-family homes control townhouses.

4. COOPERATIVES

Cooperative
A land holding arrangement often organized as a corporation where the owners have shares or ownership rights in the real estate, but do not hold title to the actual land itself.

Cooperatives, unlike condominiums and townhouses, are often large tracts of land or working farms in which several persons have an ownership interest. Both interior and exterior portions of the property — which may include large buildings — are owned jointly by all members of the cooperative.

5. MOBILE HOMES

Mobile homes are usually considered to be personal property, not real property. This classification carries with it some important consequences. The owner of a mobile home does not receive the same kind of favorable tax treatment as does a traditional homeowner. The mobile homeowners cannot, for instance, "write off" their mortgage interest payments for the year on their annual income tax return. Mobile homes can be reclassified as real property, but usually only after removing the wheels of the unit and permanently affixing it to the ground. Because real property houses are by their very nature permanently attached to the land—thus meeting the definition of real property—anything that a mobile homeowner can do to duplicate this process will push the mobile home away from a personal property classification and toward a real property classification. In order for a mobile home to change from a classification of personal property to real property, several actions must take place. Among them are:

Mobile homes
An off-site constructed living structure that can be transported by being hauled to a location, often with the benefit of an understructure that contains wheels and can then be attached to water, electrical, and sewage lines. Considered to be personal property unless and until the understructure is modified in such a way that the unit is permanently mounted to the ground.

- The homeowner establishes the mobile home on the land with an obvious intent to make it permanent.
- The homeowner clearly intends to treat the mobile home as real property.
- The homeowner pays taxes on the mobile home as though it were a house.

When a mobile home is considered personal property, it usually falls under the jurisdiction of the Uniform Commercial Code, not state real property laws. The Uniform Commercial Code governs transactions in personal property and has very specific rules about the transfer of ownership, shipment of goods, and other issues. These rules differ from real property rules in significant ways. Some state decisions actually hold that a mobile home is a form of motor vehicle.

6. MANUFACTURED HOUSING AND "KIT" HOMES

In recent years there has been a huge upswing in the construction of manufactured housing. **Manufactured houses** are homes in which all or some of the fabrication occurs away from the actual home site. In prior decades, manufactured housing fell into the same category as mobile homes. However, because these newer houses are actually permanently affixed to the real estate, and are never intended to be movable, most states have abolished the distinction between manufactured homes and traditional homes that are constructed entirely on the site.

Manufactured houses
An off-site constructed building that is transported to a location where it becomes permanently attached to the ground or to another unit already present; designed to be a permanent structure and once transported is usually reclassified as real property.

C. COMMERCIAL PROPERTY

Commercial property consists of lots and buildings specifically designed for businesses. These properties range from doctors' offices to malls. They all share some common features, however. First, they are not designed as living spaces. People do not reside in commercial properties; they work in them. Second, commercial properties have design features not commonly seen in residential properties: parking lots, elevators, and trade and customer entrances. They must abide by specific federal and state regulations, such as the Americans with Disabilities Act, which dictates design features such as handicapped parking and ramps for wheelchair access.

1. RETAIL/WHOLESALE

Retail real property
Real property containing structures primarily designed to house and display merchandise for sale to the general public.

Retail and wholesale properties are designed for what most of us would term "normal" business purposes. **Retail properties** include stores and shops of an almost infinite variety. Wholesale properties comprise warehouses and supply depots where merchandise is stored. Wholesale establishments are also where business owners go to order the merchandise that they will later sell on a retail basis to members of the public.

2. SHOPPING CENTERS AND MALLS

Malls
A large, often extremely large, structure that houses dozens, sometimes hundreds of individual retail businesses; malls are often designed to include atria and fountains to enhance the consumer's experience while inside.

Malls and shopping centers have become increasingly important to the U.S. economy in the past several decades. Some shopping malls occupy hundreds of square acres and function much like small cities. There are numerous legal issues involved in the selection, construction, and maintenance of such a huge facility. The same concerns are found, to a lesser extent, in shopping centers and other areas specifically devoted to the business of providing merchandise to the public.

D. INDUSTRIAL PROPERTY

Industrial property
Property containing structures primarily designed to manufacture, create, or build items that will then be transported to other locations for further assembly or to be sold to other manufacturers.

Another classification of property is **industrial property**. Industrial property includes factories, research facilities, and other production facilities. Loud noises, noxious fumes, and dangerous manufacturing practices are often associated with these structures. Because of these drawbacks, industrial properties are usually located away from residential areas, where their offensive qualities can be contained, at least to an extent.

1. INDUSTRIAL PARKS

Industrial park
An area set off for buildings where research, education, or experiments are conducted, as well as light industrial processes; industrial parks are often designed to resemble actual parks, with trees, hedges, and even lakes to enhance their appearance.

In recognition of the important role of industry, some towns and cities have created **industrial parks**. These parks are designed to group numerous industrial buildings in a central location, often close to major highways, electrical grids, and other infrastructure that assists the businesses in their operations. They are often landscaped and quite attractive.

2. LIGHT INDUSTRY / HEAVY INDUSTRY

Industrial property can be further broken down into two subcategories: light industry and heavy industry. Light industry includes any manufacturing plant or factory that does not emit excessive odors or machinery noises. Heavy industry, on the other hand, involves noxious odors, heavy traffic in and out of the plant, and/or excessive noise.

Heavy industry is usually located as far from residential properties as possible, not only due to these factors, but also because some factories emit pollution and use dangerous chemicals in their manufacturing processes.

E. FARM AND RURAL PROPERTY

Farm and rural property is a designation for those areas reserved for agriculture. These areas are devoted to the cultivation of crops or livestock. They may also consist of vast tracts of land that are usually not zoned and are often taxed at a low rate.

Farm and rural property
Property primarily designed for growing food, timber, or other products.

F. RECREATIONAL PROPERTY

Recreational property consists of federal-, state-, county-, or city-owned parks. These areas have been set aside specifically for the use of citizens and residents. They are usually located near wooded areas, lakes, or rivers, where people can congregate to enjoy the outdoors.

Recreational property
Property, often set aside by local, state, or federal governments, for the use of the public for trails, camping, and enjoying nature.

G. GOVERNMENT-OWNED LAND

The final classification of real estate is the vast acreage in the United States that is owned by federal or state governments. If you consider the size of military bases, prisons, governmental facilities, state-owned schools, and the numerous other government-owned properties, you will not be surprised to learn the government owns nearly one-third of the land in the continental United States.

Case Excerpt

JONES v. STATE PROP. TAX APPEAL BD.
82 N.E.3d 838 (Ill. 2017)

Opinion

This appeal involves the tax status of a manufactured home installed months before the effective date of a change in the applicable law. Prior to January 1, 2011, mobile homes and manufactured homes were taxed as real property only if they were resting on a permanent foundation. Under current law, all mobile homes and manufactured homes located outside of mobile home parks are taxed as real property. 35 ILCS 515/ 1(a). The law contains a "grandfather clause," which provides that mobile homes and manufactured homes that were taxed as personal property on the effective date of the amendment will continue to be taxed as personal property until they are sold or transferred or moved to a different location outside of a mobile home park. 35 ILCS 200/ 1-130(b). At issue is the applicability of this provision to a manufactured home that was installed before the effective date of the new law but was not assessed or taxed either as real property or as personal property in 2010.

The petitioners, Harlan and Phyllis Jones, installed a manufactured home on their property in May or June of 2010. They did not comply with a requirement that they register the home with the local tax assessor within 30 days. The tax assessor — who ordinarily completes his assessments by July 1 of each year — did not conduct a new assessment of the petitioners' property after the manufactured home was installed, and the property was therefore assessed and taxed as a vacant lot in 2010. The manufactured home was assessed and taxed as real property beginning in 2011. The petitioners challenged this assessment. The Property Tax Appeal Board upheld the assessment, finding decisive the fact that the petitioners failed to register their manufactured home. The circuit court affirmed this decision. The petitioners appeal, arguing that the decision was clearly erroneous. We reverse.

In July 2009, the petitioners purchased a vacant lot in the village of Valier, Franklin County, Illinois. The property was located across the street from Valier city hall. When they purchased the land, the petitioners lived in Mississippi. They intended to install a modular manufactured home on the lot and live in the home. On September 18, 2009, the village of Valier issued a building permit to the petitioners for a 3000 square foot manufactured home.

In March 2010, the petitioners completed vehicle registrations for each of the three modules of the home with the Secretary of State. In April, they filed a vehicle use tax transaction return and paid sales tax for the home.

The petitioners' home was installed on the property during May and June of 2010. As noted previously, they did not file a mobile home registration with the local tax assessor within 30 days of installation as required by statute. Electric service began late in June 2010, and water service began in July. According to Harlan Jones, he and his wife "began moving into" the home in the spring of 2010; however, they did not immediately begin living there full time.

In December 2010, the petitioners received an assessment notice informing them that the property was being assessed and taxed as a vacant lot. In June 2011, township assessor Gerald Owens performed an assessment of the petitioners' property. He believed that the home on the property was a stick-built house and assessed it as real estate.

In November 2011, the petitioners received a notice of "new construction" assessment. They contested this assessment, arguing that their home was a manufactured home, not a stick-built home. On February 27, 2012, the Franklin County Board of Review issued a notice of final decision on assessed value. It affirmed the township assessor's assessment.

On March 20, 2012, the petitioners filed an appeal of that decision with the Illinois Property Tax Appeal Board. They argued, as they do before this court, that because their home was installed before the effective date of the new law, it should be taxed and assessed under the old law.

The matter came for a hearing in January 2014. Harlan Jones testified that he recently retired after working for 23 years as a mobile home salesman in Mississippi. He and his wife, Phyllis, moved from Mississippi to Illinois to be closer to his brother, who had health problems. As a result of his professional experience, Jones was familiar with the proper way to install manufactured and mobile homes. In the spring of 2009, the Joneses bought land in Franklin County. They then purchased the manufactured home at issue from the Mississippi dealership where Jones worked.

Jones testified that the home was a modular home with three components, each of which came with its own title. When the components were transported to Illinois, the Joneses registered them as vehicles with the Secretary of State and paid tax on them. Jones testified that the home was not placed on a permanent foundation. Instead, it rested on blocks and was held in place by "hurricane straps." Once the home was put together on the lot, the Joneses "started moving in." This took place in the spring of 2010. However, they did not stay there full time, in part because their home in Mississippi had not yet been sold. During 2010, Harlan Jones stayed overnight in the manufactured home a few times, the longest being "about two weeks" in August 2010. While he was there, he used the water and electricity in the home and mowed the yard.

Susi Jones, the petitioners' sister-in-law, confirmed Harlan Jones's testimony that he stayed in the home multiple times during 2010. She testified that before he arrived, she would turn up the air conditioner and turn on the water for him.

Township tax assessor Gerald Owens testified that petitioners' property was located across the street from city hall. Owens was familiar with their property because he saw it each time he went to city hall to pick up forms. He testified that in June 2011, he first went to assess the property because it was on what he called a "911 list" of new addresses to assess for 2011. He did not receive a registration of the mobile home or any other type of notification that the home had been placed on the petitioners' property.

Owens testified that he receives the "911 list" each year in January, and he goes out to assess each property on the list between January and July. He explained that he turns in his assessments on July 1, after which time "it's too late to get them in the process." He testified that he assumed the petitioners' home was a stick-built house because that is what it looked like when he first saw it. However, he did not dispute that the home was in fact a manufactured home.

The hearing officer asked Owens what would have happened had he been aware in late June 2010 that the petitioners' home was a manufactured home. Owens indicated that he could have gone to look at the property to verify that information. The hearing officer then asked who would have turned that information in for a privilege tax on the property, to which Owens responded, "Good question." He then stated that he "would have probably conferred with the supervisor of assessments to determine how to get this turned in the right way." Owens acknowledged that other similar homes were taxed as mobile homes in 2010.

The final witness to testify was Cynthia Humm, of the Franklin County supervisor of assessments office. Humm explained that her department's primary argument was "that the mobile home did not follow the statute in not registering within 30 days of placement." She argued that the "grandfather clause" should not apply because the petitioners' mobile home "never paid a privilege tax in order to have that precedent set."

Humm testified that the privilege tax would have been assessed for 2010 if the county supervisor of assessments had received a registration of the home "either from the property owner or the township assessor." The hearing officer asked, "And a homeowner should learn of this registration requirement how?" Humm replied, "Through the news media, and also we sent — and of course, if we didn't know that you had a mobile home, we wouldn't know to send you the registration." At this point, Harlan Jones interjected, "I did have to get a building permit." The building permit was admitted as an exhibit. As stated previously, the permit specified that it was for a manufactured home. Humm testified that the permit would not be accessible to the county supervisor of assessments, but she acknowledged that it would be accessible to the township assessor. She further acknowledged that her office did not place a notice in the newspaper about the registration requirement until December 2010.

The hearing officer asked Humm, "Do you agree that the subject dwelling was installed in 2010?" Humm did not want to stipulate to this fact. She did not dispute that the manufactured home was placed on the property in 2010; however, she testified that there was a factual question as to whether the home was ready for occupancy before 2011. According to Humm, the records her office obtained showed that the water hookup was installed in 2010 but was not turned on until 2011. She explained that in 2012, after the petitioners contested the assessment of their property, her department obtained records from the water department in an effort to determine when the home was ready for occupancy because "this was part of our fact-checking to make sure that we should have put it on real estate and not privilege tax."

The petitioners offered into evidence several exhibits to support Mr. Jones's testimony. Among these exhibits were the building permit issued by the village of Valier for a 3000 square foot manufactured home and billing records showing water and electricity usage during the latter half of 2010.

Also admitted into evidence was a memorandum from the Illinois Department of Revenue explaining the implementation of the new legislation at issue in this appeal. The memorandum contained a frequently asked questions section, which specifically addressed essentially the same situation involved in this appeal — the assessment and taxation of mobile or manufactured homes that were installed "after the assessment cycle was completed" in 2010 and were "not on the tax rolls." The memo stated:

> "The department advises that these homes should be assessed uniformly with other mobile and manufactured homes in the county as provided in the Property Tax Code and Mobile Home Local Services Tax Act in effect for assessment year 2010. If mobile or manufactured homes on private property were assessed as real property, then that same classification should be used. If, however, the mobile or manufactured homes of similar construction were taxed under the Mobile Home Local Services Tax Act, then the home should be taxed under that Act."

On March 21, 2014, the Property Tax Appeal Board issued its final administrative decision. The hearing officer first noted that the following three facts were undisputed: (1) the petitioners' home was a mobile or manufactured home; (2) it was placed on their property in May or June of 2010; and (3) the property was assessed as a vacant lot in 2010. She then noted that neither party presented any evidence on whether the installation requirements of the new legislation were met, but she further noted that the Franklin County Board of Review did not dispute that the home was "installed" in 2010. Turning to the question of when the property was fit for occupancy, the hearing officer specifically found credible the petitioners' evidence that water and electric service and usage began during the summer of 2010.

The hearing officer went on to find that "the most crucial issue" in the case was the fact that the home was never registered as required by section 4 of the Mobile Home Local Services Tax Act (Mobile Home Tax Act). She explained that registration, even before the change in the law, was a "prerequisite to taxation under the Mobile Home Local Services Act." She acknowledged that the petitioners, who never received notice of the registration requirement, "presented a sympathetic argument." However, she concluded that the home was properly taxed as real property.

On April 23, 2014, the petitioners filed a petition in the circuit court seeking review under the Administrative Review Law (735 ILCS 5/3-101 et seq. (West 2012)). On April 14, 2016, the circuit court affirmed the decision of the Property Tax Appeal Board in a docket entry. The court noted that the "home was never taxed under the Mobile Home Tax Act primarily because the petitioners failed to register the property as required, both before and after January 1, 2011." The court concluded that the Property Tax Appeal Board's decision was supported by evidence and was not clearly erroneous. This appeal followed.

One principle of statutory interpretation is the presumption that the legislature intended for statutes relating to the same subject "to be consistent and harmonious." Id. at 60. We must therefore consider all of the provisions of the enactment as a whole, rather than in isolation. Id. Although we presume that the legislature did not intend an absurd, inconvenient, or unjust result (id.), we may not read into the statutes any exceptions, limitations, or conditions that are contrary to the legislature's intent (*JPMorgan Chase Bank, N.A. v. Earth Foods, Inc.*, 238 Ill. 2d 455, 461, 939 N.E.2d 487, 345 Ill. Dec. 644 (2010)). However, if the legislative intent is "otherwise clear," we may read into the statutes language "which has been omitted through legislative oversight." *DeLuna*, 223 Ill. 2d at 60. Finally, although we give substantial deference to an agency's interpretation of a statute it administers, the agency's interpretation is not binding on this court, and we will reject it if we find it to be erroneous. *Denton*, 277 Ill. App. 3d at 774.

This appeal involves Public Act 96-1477 (eff. Jan. 1, 2011), which enacted the Manufactured Home Installation Act (Installation Act) (35 ILCS 517/1 et seq. (West 2010)) and amended portions of the Property Tax Code (35 ILCS 200/1-1 et seq. (West 2008)) and the Mobile Home Tax Act (35 ILCS 515/1 et seq. (West 2008)). Prior to the effective date of the new law, a mobile home was included in the statutory definition of real property only "if the structure was resting in whole on a permanent foundation." 35 ILCS 200/1-130 (West 2008). Similarly, mobile homes resting on permanent foundations were excluded from the Mobile Home Tax Act's definition of a mobile home. Such homes were "assessed and taxed as real property." 35 ILCS 515/1 (West 2008). Mobile homes not resting on permanent foundations were instead subject to a "privilege tax" based on square footage. 35 ILCS 515/3 (West 2008). (We note parenthetically that prior to the enactment, the relevant statutes referred only to "mobile homes," and not to "mobile or manufactured homes." For purposes of the amendments in the new legislation, mobile homes and manufactured homes are synonymous. 35 ILCS 515/1(a) (West 2010).)

Beginning January 1, 2011, the new legislation eliminated the distinction between mobile homes resting on permanent foundations and those not resting on permanent foundations. See Pub. Act 96-1477, §805 (eff. Jan. 1, 2011) (amending 35 ILCS 200/1-130 (West 2008)) (removing this definitional language). Instead, the new law provides that all mobile homes and manufactured homes installed outside of mobile home parks on or after its effective date are to be assessed and taxed as real estate. 35 ILCS 515/1(a) (West 2010) (providing that "mobile homes and manufactured homes outside of mobile home parks must be assessed and taxed as real property"); 35 ILCS 517/10(a) (West 2010) (providing that "a mobile home or manufactured home installed on private property that is not in a mobile home park on or after the effective date of this Act must be classified, assessed, and taxed as real property").

At issue here is a "grandfather clause" for mobile homes that were assessed and taxed as personal property under the Mobile Home Tax Act before the new law went into effect. That provision appears in three different statutes. Section 1-130(b) of the Property Tax Code provides that "mobile homes and manufactured homes that are taxed under the Mobile Home Local Services Tax Act on the effective date of this amendatory Act shall continue to be taxed under the Mobile Home Local Services Tax Act." 35 ILCS 200/1-130(b) (West 2010). The statute further provides that mobile and manufactured homes "that are classified, assessed, and taxed as real property" on the effective date of the new legislation "shall continue to be classified, assessed, and taxed as real property." Id. Section 10(b) of the Installation Act contains identical language. 35 ILCS 517/10(b) (West 2010). Similarly, section 1(b) of the Mobile Home Tax Act provides, "Mobile homes and manufactured homes that are taxed under this Act on the effective date of the amendments must continue to be taxed under this Act," but mobile homes and manufactured homes that are already "classified, assessed, and taxed as real property must continue to be classified, assessed, and taxed as real property." 35 ILCS 515/1(b) (West 2010).

All three statutes address the taxation of mobile homes and manufactured homes that were taxed as real property before the new law went into effect — they continue to be taxed as real property; and all three statutes address the taxation of mobile homes and manufactured homes that were taxed as personal property under the Mobile Home Tax Act prior to the effective date of the new law — they continue to be taxed under that act. The Installation Act addresses the taxation of mobile homes or manufactured homes that are "installed on private property that is not in a mobile home park on or after the effective date of this Act," providing that such homes "must be classified, assessed, and taxed as real property." 35 ILCS 517/10(a) (West 2010). However, none of these provisions explicitly address the assessment or taxation of mobile homes or manufactured homes that were installed prior to the effective date of the new law but were not taxed or assessed under either provision of the old law because they were installed after the local assessor completed assessments for the year.

The petitioners contend that under the "plain and ordinary meaning" of these statutes, all mobile homes and manufactured homes that were in place before the effective date of the new law must continue to be taxed in the same manner they were taxed previously. Both respondents argue that the statutes unambiguously provide that the Mobile Home Tax Act's "privilege tax" is only available to homeowners who have previously paid that tax. We do not find either interpretation persuasive. The problem with the petitioners' argument is that it overlooks the fact that their manufactured home was not taxed either as real property or as a mobile home prior to January 2011. They do not claim their property should continue to be taxed as a vacant lot. The problem with the respondents' argument is that it overlooks statutory language expressly limiting the temporal reach of the new law to mobile homes that are installed "on or after the effective date" of the legislation. 35 ILCS 517/10(a) (West 2010). For the reasons we just discussed, we conclude that the legislation failed to address mobile homes and manufactured homes that, like the petitioners' home, were not installed on or after the effective date of the new legislation and were not assessed and taxed in 2010. We note that a relatively small number of homes are likely to fit into this category. Thus, we presume that this omission was a legislative oversight.

The Franklin County Board of Review argues that any ambiguity created by this omission must be resolved in favor of less preferential tax treatment. See *People ex rel. Kassabaum v. Hopkins*, 106 Ill. 2d 473, 476, 478 N.E.2d 1332, 88 Ill. Dec. 606 (1985) (explaining that statutory provisions granting tax exemptions or "special tax treatments" should be strictly construed). This argument correctly describes an important tool for statutory construction. However, consideration of the interpretation given to this legislative scheme by one of the agencies charged with administering it — the Illinois Department of Revenue — leads us to a different conclusion.

As we discussed previously, guidelines supplied by the Department of Revenue in a memorandum directed local taxing authorities to treat mobile homes that were not on the 2010 tax rolls the same way similar mobile homes that were on the tax rolls were treated. It is worth noting that, prior to the petitioners' challenge in this case, the Franklin County supervisor of assessments appeared to agree with the interpretation of the Department of Revenue. As noted earlier, Cynthia Humm testified that after the petitioners challenged the assessment of their home, her investigation focused on determining whether the home was ready for occupancy before the effective date of the new law. It was because she believed evidence showed that the home was not ready for occupancy until 2011 that Humm refused to stipulate that the home was "installed" in 2010. This inquiry would have been irrelevant if the supervisor of assessments interpreted the law in the manner now urged by the respondents in this appeal. Under that interpretation, the petitioners' home would not be eligible to be taxed under the Mobile Home Tax Act regardless of whether it was ready for occupancy — and, therefore, deemed to be "installed" — before the new law went into effect on January 1, 2011.

The respondents argue, however, that the petitioners' home does not fall within the category of homes addressed by the Department of Revenue's guideline. They contend that this is so because the home was placed on the property sometime in May, which left ample time for the home to be assessed under the Mobile Home Tax Act if only the petitioners had complied with the registration requirement. We note that at oral argument, all parties agreed that the home would not have been assessed and taxed under the Mobile Home Tax Act had the petitioners complied with the registration requirement. This acknowledgement notwithstanding, we are not persuaded by the respondents' contention.

For all of these reasons, we conclude that the decision of the Property Tax Appeal Board was clearly erroneous. We therefore reverse the judgment of the circuit court and set aside the decision of the Property Tax Appeal Board.

Circuit court judgment reversed; Property Tax Appeal Board decision set aside.

QUESTIONS ABOUT THE CASE

1   Prior to the enactment of the new legislation, how were properties containing mobile homes taxed?
2   What argument did the homeowners present to both the trial and appellate courts?
3   The court states that one of the main contentions in this case is the "grandfather clause." What is it and what impact does it have on the court's decision?
4   There is a logical fallacy in the petitioners' argument: What is it?
5   What result did the court reach?

COVID-19 CONCERN

Throughout this text, we will refer to the impact of the ongoing COVID-19 or coronavirus pandemic on real estate law. This feature will address current problems and anticipated issues that may arise over time that are specific to real estate law practice. Although several vaccines are available throughout the world, as of the time of this writing, COVID-19 infections continue to rise, primarily among the unvaccinated. There are also several variants. Eventually, the pandemic will end, but its impact on all areas of society will have lasting consequences. In discussing each chapter's topic, we will also relate it to COVID. What effect will the disease and its aftermath have on the law and procedures followed in real estate practice? We will address these questions in subsequent chapters.

CHAPTER SUMMARY

Property can be divided into two broad categories: real property and personal property. Personal property consists of movable items that are not permanently attached to real estate. Real property, on the other hand, consists of land and anything permanently affixed to land. Real estate has specific and unique characteristics. Among its physical characteristics are that land occupies a fixed point on the globe, no two parcels of real estate are identical, and land is immovable and permanent. Among its economic characteristics are that land generally appreciates in value over time and makes an excellent investment. There is a market for real estate, just as there are markets for other products. The real estate market consists of buyers and sellers, as well as professionals involved in facilitating the sale, funding the sale, and making sure that the legalities of the sale are observed. One way of classifying real estate is by the way that it is used. Unimproved land is vacant land that has no structures placed upon it, while improved land has been developed. Improved land can be further categorized into residential property, which is reserved for living space; commercial property, which is designed for businesses; and industrial property, which is reserved for manufacturing and warehousing products.

SKILLS YOU NEED IN THE REAL WORLD

Each chapter of this text includes a section called "Skills You Need in the Real World." Its purpose is to provide you with practical, hands-on information that you can put to immediate use in real estate practice. We cover topics as varied as reviewing probate records, researching liens, and preparing TRID Closing Disclosures.

In this introductory chapter, one of the most important skills you can acquire as a real estate professional is the ability to quickly and efficiently research real property questions. In the past, paralegals and attorneys relied on printed materials, but modern practice relies a great deal on the Internet. Not only can you find excellent free and paid legal research sites on the Internet, but you can also locate a wealth of real estate information ranging from online real estate transactions to Google Earth and aerial photographs to sites that will give you directions from your current location to the property itself. You should review each of these chapters for the specific websites given, but also develop your own list of helpful websites and keep it handy. More and more public records and other information will be available online so that your problem as a real estate professional will not be whether you can find something, but how to find the most reliable information in a sea of data.

How You Can Do Some Basic Investigative Work

Most real estate professionals are not trained to carry out investigations. Many would be surprised to learn that knowing basic investigative techniques could be a real asset in the marketplace. When a firm needs basic information about a case, the most common method of obtaining it is for the attorney to investigate the basic details and then rely on discovery to ferret out additional details. However, there are times when this process is not efficient. Some cases do not have the financial resources to justify an attorney's time. In such a situation, the other alternative — a private detective — may also be too costly. Not all clients can afford the added expense of a private investigator. However, a real estate professional who knows some basic investigative techniques can learn a great deal about a case, with less of a cost investment, and that professional will become even more indispensable to the firm in the process.

What Facts Do You Need?

Before you can begin to investigate a claim, you must first decide what facts are the most important to discover. For a plaintiff's firm, the most important facts are those that support the cause of action. Without that support, there can be no valid claim.

Using Public Records to Gather Information

Suppose your firm is investigating the defendant (or the person who will be the defendant if the lawsuit is actually filed). What public records can help you learn more information about this person? The best place to start is the local courthouse.

The Courthouse

The local courthouse is a gold mine of information, if you know where to look. Consider the following resources:

- **Clerk's Office:** The local clerk's office maintains records about all civil and criminal cases in the county. Using the computer databases, you can learn whether someone has been sued, divorced, or convicted of a crime.
- **Deed Room or Registrar's Office:** Sometimes called the registrar's office, or the land office, the deed room is where all records of real estate transactions are stored. In this office, you can find out what real estate a defendant owns (useful in evaluating the likelihood of enforcing a judgment against him).
- **Tax Office:** The tax office is required to keep extensive records about real estate and other items. In some tax offices, you can even see a digital photo of the house. In larger counties, such as metropolitan areas, this information is available at public access terminals. A picture of the house and all of the details are just a mouse click away.

Internet

The Internet also offers some valuable research tools. There are numerous sites that allow you to search out a person's address, telephone number, email address, and other information. However, some questionable sites claim to provide you with complete background information on a person for a nominal fee. Unless the site is one that you recognize as a reputable company, you should avoid such sites. A great deal of free information is available about persons, but if you plan on paying for research, the best bet is still a private detective.

Keep these sources in mind if you are ever called upon to do some basic investigative work in a case.

ETHICAL ISSUES FOR THE PARALEGAL

An Introduction

Ethical rules are important for all legal professionals. The state bar maintains strict rules about a wide range of activities associated with real estate practice, especially in the area of trust accounts. Later, we will see that clients routinely deposit large sums of money into attorney trust accounts prior to a real estate closing. This money, including the interest drawn on it, must be monitored with scrupulous care. Real estate ethical standards are strict in regard to attorney-client privilege and self-dealing. Other real estate professionals, including real estate brokers and agents, also have ethical standards. We explore the ethical concerns facing all these professionals in later chapters of this book.

KEY TERMS AND CONCEPTS

Apartment	In rem jurisdiction	Recreational property
Condominium	Industrial property	Retail real property
Cooperative	Malls	Statute of Frauds
Equity	Manufactured houses	Townhouse
Farm and rural property	Mobile homes	Unimproved land
Improvements	Personal jurisdiction	

END-OF-CHAPTER EXERCISES

Review Questions

See Appendix for answers.

1   What is the definition of real property?
2   What is the Statute of Frauds?
3   What are some of the primary differences between real and personal property?
4   What are some of the aspects of real property law that make it unique?
5   List and explain some of the physical characteristics of land.
6   Describe the economic characteristics of real property.
7   What makes real estate such an attractive investment?
8   Explain equity.
9   What is the real estate market?
10 What is unimproved land?
11 List and explain the various classifications of real property.
12 What are the elements that make a residence qualify as an apartment?
13 What is the difference between a condominium and a townhouse?
14 When does a mobile home or manufactured home qualify as real property?
15 What is the difference between residential and commercial property?
16 How much land in the United States is government owned?
17 Why are ethical rules important for real estate practitioners?
18 Explain how cloud computing impacts legal services.

DISCUSSION QUESTIONS

1 Log on to Zillow.com or some other real estate site and identify properties by the
   following categories:
   - Residential
   - Light industrial
   - Farm
   - Heavy industrial
   What features separate these listings? How are they alike? How are they different?

2 We know that real property law has its own rules, regulations, statutes, and history.
   Why has real property law always been dealt with differently than other types of
   property? Explain your answer.

3 Some have said that real estate is the only real source of wealth. Is that statement
   justified? Why or why not?

APPLYING WHAT YOU HAVE LEARNED

1 Go online and find a local house for sale. What can you learn about the home from
   the Internet listing? What is the sale price? How many square feet does the house
   have? Are the sellers offering any incentives to prospective buyers? Does the home
   come with a warranty?

2 Locate websites that explain how and why the real estate market in the United
   States, and in other countries, has suffered so severely in recent years.

WEB SURFING

Real Property Law: Legal Research Institute
http://www.law.cornell.edu/wex/real_property

Nolo's Plain English Dictionary–Real Estate
http://www.nolo.com/dictionary/real-estate-term.html

New York State Bar–Real Property Law
http://www.nysba.org/rpls/

Real Estate Law (HG.org)
http://www.hg.org/realest.html

Real Property vs. Personal Property
https://www.britannica.com/topic/real-property

Tech Topic
ZILLOW

Zillow (http://www.zillow.com) is a real estate website that offers myriad tools for the real estate professional, including a property search function that gives the last date of sale, sale price, and current estimated value (among other information), for any real estate parcel.

ANNOTATED DOCUMENT

Real Estate Sales Listing

Springfield subdivision; three-bedroom, two-bath, garage, finished basement, central air and heat, $225,000 firm. Enjoy spacious living in this contemporary home that has all the amenities. Fireplace, luxurious master bath, and state-of-the-art security system.

The owner's use of the word firm to describe the $225,000 price indicates that the sale price is non-negotiable.

Sales listings put a lot of information into a very small space.

PRACTICE QUESTIONS FOR TEST REVIEW

See Appendix for answers.

Essay Question

List and explain the various classifications of real property.

True–False

1 T F Manufactured houses are never considered to be real property.

2 T F A mobile home may be considered real property, depending on the nature of its attachment to land.

3 T F Shopping centers are examples of residential property.

Fill in the Blank

1   Land containing structures: _____.

2   This term refers to land and anything permanently attached to the land: _____.

3   This term refers to anything that is not land and is not permanently affixed to land: _____.

Multiple Choice

1   All of the following are examples of real property except:

    A   Trees
    B   Houses
    C   Mobile homes
    D   Fences

2   Why does the law make distinctions between real property and personal property?

    A   Because the classification affects the rights and legal remedies available.
    B   Because the classification means that some owners do not have legal rights.
    C   The law does not make a distinction between real and personal property.
    D   All of the above.

3   Modern real estate law still reflects its roots in what era?

    A   The Stone Age
    B   The Middle Ages
    C   The Colonial period
    D   The twentieth century

Estates in Real Property

Chapter Objectives

- Explain the rights created by fee simple absolute estates

- Define the differences between conditional fee estates, such as fee simple determinable and fee simple on a condition subsequent

- Describe how a life estate is created

- Explain the types of estates available to two or more owners of a single parcel of real estate

- Define the rights and obligations of joint owners

Chapter Outline

I. Introduction

II. Real Property Estates

III. Fee Simple Estate
    A. Rights of Fee Simple Absolute Owners
    B. Conditional Fee Simple Estates

IV. Life Estates
    A. Historical Basis of Life Estates
    B. Remaindermen

    C. Waste
    D. Court Doctrines That Affect Life Estates
    E. Life Estate *Pur Autre Vie*

V. Concurrent Ownership in Real Estate
    A. Tenants in Common
    B. Joint Tenancy
    C. Tenancy by Entirety
    D. Tenancy in Partnership
    E. The Right to Partition

INTRODUCTION

In this chapter, we explore the various types of ownership of real property. These property rights, or estates, range from complete ownership in fee simple absolute to estates with fewer rights, such as life estates. We also examine the rights and responsibilities of two or more individuals who own property together.

REAL PROPERTY ESTATES

Estate
A right to use or enjoy real property.

An **estate** is a bundle of rights that accompanies title to property. In discussing land, we define an estate in land as the quality of title that an owner possesses to use and enjoy the property as well as the extent of that ownership. Different estates contain different rights. There are numerous types of estates, from fee simple absolute to life estates to several different forms of concurrent ownership estates. Estates can be either present estates or future estates. A *present estate* confers an immediate benefit on the owner. A *future estate*, on the other hand, will confer a right at some point in the future. For example, a testator can write a will that states that her parcel of real estate will go to a specific heir on the testator's death. The heir does not have an immediate right to it. The heir cannot, for example, mortgage the property, sell it, or take any action on it until the testator dies. The heir only has a potential future interest. In the first part of this chapter, we will focus on present estates, but future estates will figure prominently in our discussion of life estates in the second part of the chapter.

When there is a dispute about the type of estate involved or when the estate was created, courts follow a general rule that what the parties intended is generally controlling. If the parties said that they intended a specific type of estate, such as fee simple, the courts will work to interpret the language so that such an estate is recognized. If there is a dispute about when the estate was created, courts opt for a test that provides that an estate was created as early as possible. These rules give some guidance and a measure of predictability to court actions on estate questions.

FEE SIMPLE ESTATES

Fee simple absolute
The real property estate in which an owner has the most complete set of rights possible, including the right to use, possess, give, sell, mortgage, and lease the property, among other rights.

A person who has **fee simple absolute** ownership in property has the most complete set of rights that it is possible to have in a parcel of real estate. She can give, sell, mortgage, use, and possess the property. Fee simple absolute owners possess all of the following rights:

- The right to make a gift of the property to another
- The right to put the property up for sale

- The right to raise crops on the property and to sell those crops
- The right to use and possess the property
- The right to mortgage the property
- The right to lease the property to others

Fee simple rights are often described as an assorted "bundle" of rights. When a person acquires title in fee simple to a parcel, this bundle of rights is conveyed along with that title. Imagining fee simple rights as a bundle has the added advantage of being able to describe the owner's ability to convey some of the rights to others while retaining other rights herself. The classic example is a landlord-tenant relationship. A landlord conveys some of her fee simple rights to a tenant. The tenant receives the right to use, possess, and enjoy the property, while the landlord retains all the other rights. Because the landlord retains the right to sell and mortgage the property, the tenant cannot do so. On the other hand, the landlord no longer has the right to possess the property and cannot, for instance, move onto the premises after creating a lease arrangement with the tenant. The landlord no longer has that right and will not get it back until the rental agreement terminates. We will explore landlord-tenant relationships in greater detail in Chapter 7.

The word "fee" originated under English law and referred to a grant from the king to an individual landowner. The fee was the emblem of the owner's obligation to provide military or tax support to the monarch. In Chapter 8, when we discuss the details of a typical real estate transaction, we will see that much of the ceremony that accompanied a real estate transaction then still exists in one form or another in modern real estate practice.

Under the modern approach to real estate law, a fee simple absolute estate not only confers specific rights on the owner, but also guarantees that the parcel itself is free from encumbrances. A fee simple title is one that has no liens or other impediments that would prevent the owner from freely transferring it to another. See Figure 2-1 for a historical overview of homeownership rates from 1973 to 2021. The data makes clear that ownership percentages have steadily increased.

FRED. — Homeownership Rate in the United States

Shaded areas indicate U.S. recessions   Source: U.S. Census Bureau   fred.stlouisfed.org

FIGURE 2-1

Homeownership Rate in the United States

Fee simple absolute title is the highest set of rights that a person can possess in real property.

A. RIGHTS OF FEE SIMPLE ABSOLUTE OWNERS

An owner in fee simple absolute has the highest and best form of title in real property, but that does not mean that the owner can do literally anything with the property. All owners have limitations on their rights, whether imposed by law or by practice. Fee simple owners also assume certain obligations when they take title to property. For instance, we will see in Chapter 10 that real estate owners are limited by public laws and private acts. Laws can prevent an owner from carrying out specific actions on her property, such as operating a business in a residential area. Private acts, such as restrictive covenants, can go even further and prevent the homeowner from putting specific structures on the property or even building a home with an unapproved architectural style.

B. CONDITIONAL FEE SIMPLE ESTATES

Although we have said that fee simple absolute ownership is the highest and best form of real estate title, there are legal conditions that may have a significant impact on the owner's use of the property.

When a seller (grantor) places conditions on fee simple ownership, this can be referred to as a *fee simple defeasible* estate. Fee simple defeasible estates fall into one of two categories:

1   Fee simple determinable, or
2   Fee simple subject to a condition subsequent.

When either of these categories exists, an owner who may believe she has taken unconditional title to property actually has a limitation. Because of the legal difficulties that these two conditional fee simple estates have created over the decades, most practitioners no longer use either estate to limit the way that property can be used. These estates are cumbersome and fraught with legal problems; however, they do remain in existence.

Before we discuss the particulars of either of these limiting conditions on a fee simple title, however, we must first address a more fundamental question: Why would anyone impose a condition on fee simple absolute title? The answer is simple: The seller has specific wishes for the property and wants a legal method to enforce these wishes.

BUYING CARLA'S HOUSE

EXAMPLE 2-1

Ramon wants to buy Carla's property, but Carla is reluctant. She has always wanted to deed her property to the state so that it will be used as a park or nature preserve. Ramon suggests deeding it to him and inserting a condition that will satisfy this desire. Carla can deed the property to him as fee simple, but insert a condition stating that the property can only be used as a park or nature preserve. Ramon will have complete ownership in the property, but if he ever violates the condition, either the title will revert to Carla or Carla can sue him for damages.

These days, there are other methods Carla can use to enforce her wishes for the property's use, but in the past Carla did not have such options. The only way for her to be sure about how the property would be used was to create a fee simple with a condition. The main difference between the two types of conditional fee simple estates is what happens when the condition is violated.

1. FEE SIMPLE DETERMINABLE

A *fee simple determinable* estate is created when a person transfers property to another with a stipulation that the property be used in a certain way, as outlined in the example above. Carla conveys her property to Ramon but inserts a stipulation that the property should always be used as a park or nature preserve. If Carla includes language in the deed that automatically conveys title to the property back to her or her heirs should the stipulation be violated, the condition is described as fee simple determinable. Under this classification, when Ramon — or anyone else who later owns the property — violates the condition, the title will automatically revert to the original owner or her heirs. Obviously, this is a drastic measure and one that might cause future buyers to hesitate to buy the property. After all, who wants to spend a great deal of money to buy a parcel of real estate only to learn that title to it might automatically shift to someone else if she violates a condition? The other problem with fee simple determinable estates is that once they are imposed on property, they remain with the title as it passes from owner to owner. Although the original arrangement was between Ramon and Carla, for example, it binds future owners as well.

Because of these problems, modern real estate practitioners do not use fee simple determinable estates. Courts have also been extremely wary of these conditions and have routinely struck down deed clauses where the language creating a fee simple determinable estate was ambiguous or poorly worded. However, fee simple determinable estates are still legal, and a person can create one if she so desires. Modern court decisions require the seller to insert language in the deed that specifically provides that upon the happening of a particular event, title to the property will vest in another. Without that specificity, courts are inclined to ignore the condition and treat the title as a normal fee simple absolute.

2. FEE SIMPLE ON A CONDITION SUBSEQUENT

A *fee simple on a condition* subsequent closely resembles, and is often confused with, fee simple determinable. The distinguishing feature between them is that while the fee simple determinable automatically transfers title when a condition is violated, a fee simple on a condition subsequent only gives the grantor (or grantor's heirs) the right to challenge title. When a deed contains a fee simple on a condition subsequent and a future owner stops using the property in the way prescribed by the original owner, the owner's heirs can file suit to have title awarded to them. They will not, however, automatically receive title to the property.

Both fee simple determinable and fee simple on a condition subsequent estates raise a host of potential problems when they are used. The language used to create them is often strictly interpreted by the courts, rendering them ineffective if they do not follow the exact letter of the law. The other problem with both estates is that they frequently do not achieve their purpose. Because courts scrutinize both so closely, a person who wished to limit the way that land can be used in the future would be better served using some other method, such as restrictive covenants (covered in detail in Chapter 10).

 REAL ESTATE BASICS AT A GLANCE

 Conditional fee simple titles place restrictions on how property can be used; they are generally discouraged under modern real estate practice.

 Tech Topic
ONLINE ACCESS TO REAL ESTATE RECORDS

As recently as a couple of decades ago, the only way to research real estate records was to trudge down to the county courthouse and sift through reels of microfilm indexes. Researching efforts improved vastly when property indexes were computerized, but a trip to the courthouse was still necessary.

Then came the Internet, and most localities were quick to make their records available for purchase online. Armed with only a property owner's name or a parcel number, you can locate real estate records from your home computer, including deeds, mortgages, liens, reconveyances, and releases. In most cases, you will be able to view only the essential elements, such as the name of the property holder and the type of record. To see the details, you will usually have to order the complete document and pay a fee for it. Once you have paid the fee, the documents are either viewable immediately as a PDF file or mailed to you within a few days.

To find property records online, visit your county government's website. Look for a link to recorded deeds, real estate records, or something similar. Chances are you will find a searchable database to help track down what you are seeking.

LIFE ESTATES

In the last section, we saw that fee simple determinable and fee simple on a condition subsequent estates are rarely used. Life estates, however, are extremely common.

A **life estate** is created when an owner leaves her property to another person, but only for as long as the person lives. When the person dies, the title to the property automatically vests in someone else. The typical formula used to create a life estate is as simple as: to A, for her life, then to B.

An owner might include this provision in a deed or a will. As you can see, life estates are relatively easy to create. Unlike fee simple determinable estates, they are not closely scrutinized. The reason that they are not given the same level of review is that they are simple and straightforward devices that provide for an orderly conveyance of property. In the example above, there are very few complications that can arise. Under the life estate, A will receive the property from the owner and hold it for A's life. When A dies, the title to the property automatically vests in B. Of course, there are always complications, but the basic system works very well.

The person who receives the benefit of a life estate is often referred to as a life tenant, or the holder of a life estate. We will use the term **life tenant** to describe this person's estate. A life tenant has almost all of the rights to the property that the original owner enjoyed. A life tenant can possess, use, and grow crops on the real estate. A life tenant can even sell the property, but the person who purchases it has an important limitation: The new purchaser can only possess the property as long as A is alive. When A dies, title to the property will automatically transfer to B. It is unlikely that anyone would be willing to buy the property under this limitation, but it does point out the broad extent of a life tenant's rights to the property. Thus, a life tenant could be described as possessing fee simple absolute rights with a time limit.

A. HISTORICAL BASIS OF LIFE ESTATES

The reason that life estates were created in the first place was to provide a mechanism to allow a surviving spouse to retain rights in the marital property after the death of the other spouse. This was particularly true in the past when wives did not enjoy the same rights as husbands. A surviving husband was free to take any action with the marital property, but a surviving wife faced many legal hurdles. To ensure that wives could retain the marital home after the husband's death, states created the concepts of "dower" and "curtesy."

Under the ancient concepts of **dower and curtesy**, a surviving spouse had a legal right to a priority claim on a fraction of the marital property. This fraction could be from one-third to one-half of the property acquired by the couple during their marriage. The terms actually mean the same thing, but dower refers to the amount that a surviving wife could claim, while curtesy refers to the claim raised by a surviving husband. Under old state laws, the amount that could be claimed varied depending on the sex of the surviving partner; however, those laws have since been ruled unconstitutional because

Life estate
An estate granted to a specific person, allowing that person to use, possess, enjoy, and take profits from the real estate, but only as long as the person lives. On that person's death, title vests in a remainderman.

Life tenant
The person who holds a life estate.

A life estate can have important consequences in taxation. For instance, a life estate created by one spouse for the other can qualify under the federal marital deduction rule, meaning that the surviving spouse may be able to postpone estate taxes until he or she also dies. However, if the life tenant and remainderman agree to sell the property and extinguish the life estate, the tax situation will change dramatically and may be classified as a taxable gift.

Dower and curtesy
A provision of common law that provided that a set portion of the marital property would automatically vest in a surviving spouse. Dower referred to the portion allotted to a surviving wife, while curtesy referred to the portion allotted to a surviving husband.

they are based on sex discrimination. As a result, most states have abolished dower and curtesy and replaced it with **forced share** or **statutory share**. Under either concept, a surviving spouse is automatically granted a life estate in the marital residence and has other rights to checking and deposit accounts, retirement accounts, and other issues that arise under estate proceedings.

Forced share/
Statutory share
The statutory claim that a surviving spouse has in the marital estate.

B. REMAINDERMEN

In the example set out above, A receives a life estate and upon A's death, the title to the property automatically vests in B. In this example, B is the **remainderman**. A remainderman is someone who has future interest, but no present interest, in real estate. (In some states, this future interest is referred to as a reversionary interest.) This division between present interests and future interests is important and merits further discussion. A person with a present interest has the immediate right to the property. This person can make changes to the property, sell it, give it away, and carry out any of the actions that we normally associate with fee simple absolute title. However, a person with a future interest has severe limitations. Her interest in the property will not vest until a future date; in a life estate, the remainderman will not receive the property until the life tenant dies. Until that time, the remainderman has few legal rights and no present rights to use or enjoy the property. The remainderman cannot, for example, enter the premises and make changes to the property. However, because the property will eventually vest in the remainderman, if the remainderman observes that the life tenant is destroying the property, she can bring suit to stop the life tenant. Such an action by the life tenant is referred to as engaging in **waste**.

Remainderman
A person with a future interest in property, but no present rights.

Waste
An action by a life tenant that adversely affects the nature or quality of the remainderman's future interest in real property.

C. WASTE

When we use the term *waste* in the context of a life estate, we are talking about any action taken by the life tenant that adversely affects the quality of the estate that will eventually transfer to the remainderman. In this context, waste takes on a very specific and limited meaning. A remainderman cannot sue for any action that could cause only a diminution in value of her future interest. Instead, the remainderman must allege specific actions taken by the life tenant that could result in a total loss of value. Examples of waste include destruction of fields where crops would be raised, failure to maintain the premises, failure to pay property taxes, and any other action that affects the value of the property. A remainderman can, for instance, bring suit to prevent the seizure of the property for back taxes or to satisfy a civil judgment against the life tenant.

D. COURT DOCTRINES THAT AFFECT LIFE ESTATES

There are several court doctrines that can affect a life estate. One such doctrine is merger. Under the merger doctrine, the same person is designated as the remainderman and the life tenant. When that occurs, there is no longer a life estate. Instead, the title merges in one person and the life estate is eliminated. How would such a situation arise? Consider the following example:

RAUL'S WILL

EXAMPLE 2-2

Raul writes a provision in his will leaving his property to Amy as a life estate, and on Amy's death, to his heirs. When Raul dies, Amy is Raul's only heir. The life estate and the future estate merge, and Amy is the owner in fee simple absolute.

E. LIFE ESTATE *PUR AUTRE VIE*

In addition to the normal configuration of a life estate, in which A receives the property for her life and then it goes to B, there are other options. For instance, there is a provision to allow the life estate to be measured by the life of another. Under a life estate *pur autre vie,* an owner in fee simple conveys a life estate to one person that terminates on the death of another person. The language used to create it is "to A for the life of B." One might wonder why anyone would create such a situation. There are several reasons to create a life estate measured by the life of someone other than the individual who is actually in possession of the premises. The owner might wish to convey the property to an individual, but measure it by the lifespan of a much older person. This would effectively provide the individual with a few years to enjoy the premises before it would transfer to others.

Pur autre vie
(French) "For another's life."

REAL WORLD PERSPECTIVES: *REAL ESTATE PARALEGAL*

Real estate is highly stressful. It's a burnout job, really. There are not a lot of people who stay in the real estate paralegal position for a very long time because you burnout. If you don't work with good people and don't have a lot of good support staff, it can make you lose your mind. It's all the moving parts. You have lenders. You have real estate agents. You have buyers. You have sellers. You have other attorneys' offices, sometimes. It's one of those things that you either love it or you leave it.

— S.C., real estate paralegal

CONCURRENT OWNERSHIP IN REAL ESTATE

Our discussions so far have assumed that there is a single owner of the real property. However, as you know, many parcels of real estate are held in the names of two or more individuals. In this section, we will explore how property rights are apportioned between concurrent owners. Before we can proceed with that discussion, however, we should outline the terminology. When there are multiple owners for a single piece of property, they are referred to as **co-tenants**. There are several different types of co-tenant arrangements, including tenants in common, joint tenancy, and tenants by entirety, to name just a few.

Co-tenants
Two or more persons who have ownership interests in a single property.

A. TENANTS IN COMMON

A tenancy in common is created when real property is conveyed to two or more persons and there is no clear indication about the type of co-tenancy involved. Under a tenancy in common, each co-tenant's share of the real estate transfers to her heirs upon her death. Each co-tenant has equal right to use, possess, and transfer the property, but each may own the property in unequal shares. For instance, one co-tenant might possess 20 percent of the property while the other possesses 80 percent of the property.

Tenancy in common
A type of concurrent ownership in which two or more people own property together without the right of survivorship.

A **tenancy in common** can be created in a variety of ways. An owner might convey title interest to two or more individuals with nothing being said about the nature of the relationship between the co-tenants. In such a situation, most courts would assume that a tenancy in common was intended. A tenancy in common can also be created by gift or by probate proceeding. No matter how the relationship is created, the basic features remain the same as outlined in Figure 2-2.

FIGURE 2-2

Features of Tenancy in Common

- Tenants in common can have separate, unequal interests.
- Each tenant has the right to possess and use the property.
- There is no right of survivorship.
- Each tenant may transfer ownership interest to others.

B. JOINT TENANCY

Joint tenancy
A type of concurrent ownership in which two or more individuals own property together, with equal ownership rights and the right of survivorship.

A **joint tenancy** is a different form of concurrent ownership. While similar to a tenancy in common, joint tenancy has one important difference: Joint tenants enjoy the right of survivorship.

1. RIGHT OF SURVIVORSHIP

Right of survivorship
The right of a co-tenant to take fee simple title to property on the death of the other co-tenant.

The **right of survivorship** provides that in the event that one of the co-tenants dies, her right to the property automatically transfers to the surviving co-tenant. This arrangement effectively precludes the co-tenant's heirs from receiving any of the property interest. Because this arrangement avoids probate proceedings, courts give it close scrutiny and require the parties to specifically state their intention of creating a joint tenancy with the right of survivorship between the co-tenants. Without this clearly stated provision, most courts will interpret language conveying title interest to two or more people as a tenancy in common.

EXAMPLE 2-3

A DEED PROVISION

The following provision appears on the deed: "To Amy and Raul as co-owners." Is it a joint tenancy or a tenancy in common?

Answer: Because this sentence does not contain any specific provision creating a joint tenancy, it must be a tenancy in common.

See Figure 2-3 for a comparison of joint tenancy and tenancy in common.

FIGURE 2-3

Tenancy in Common Compared to Joint Tenancy

Tenants in Common
1. Co-tenants can have unequal interests in the property.
2. Co-tenants do not have right of survivorship.
3. When the arrangement is unclear, tenancy in common is assumed.
4. The interest of the co-tenant is conveyed to her heirs through probate proceeding.

Joint Tenant
1. All co-tenants have equal, undivided interests.
2. Co-tenants have right of survivorship.
3. Joint tenancy must be specifically stated by the parties.
4. Co-tenants' heirs are precluded from receiving an interest in the property; surviving co-tenants automatically receive full title to property.

2. SPECIFICITY REQUIRED TO CREATE JOINT TENANCY

Joint tenancies create the **right of survivorship** among the co-tenants. But what, exactly, is the right of survivorship? Stated simply, it is the right of one co-tenant to assume full ownership of the property on the death of the other co-tenant. However, this simple statement belies a complex area of law. Because the right of survivorship precludes a co-tenant's heirs from receiving property interests through probate proceedings, courts require the degree of specificity in the language creating a joint tenancy to demonstrate that the parties clearly intended to preclude their heirs from receiving any interest in the property. Most states have standing rules declaring that a joint tenancy will never be presumed. (See Figure 2-4 for an overview of multiperson households over time.) This is not to say that the law does not favor the creation of joint tenancies, but it does require the parties to be specific about their intentions. For example, if two or more owners wish to create a joint tenancy, they must employ words such as "to A and B as joint tenants, not as tenants in common, and with the right of survivorship." See Figure 2-5 for a statement of the right of survivorship.

MICHAEL'S DEED

EXAMPLE 2-4

Michael executes a deed containing the following language: "To Conrad and his girl-friend, out of love and respect for all his help, I leave my property on Main Street, Los Angeles, California, to him." Does this create a right of survivorship?

Answer: No. In order to take advantage of the law of joint tenancy, the parties must use the proper terms and make the necessary legal indications before it is created. When courts take a strict view of how and when a joint tenancy is created, this deed will fail the test. It does not use the words "right of survivorship," but more importantly there is no specificity as to who Conrad's "girlfriend" is or, even worse, to which property on Main Street, Los Angeles, Michael is referring. There is no reference to what type of tenancy is created. Therefore, most courts would rule — assuming that the court found the language sufficient to transfer any rights at all — this to be a tenancy in common, not a joint tenancy.

REAL ESTATE BASICS AT A GLANCE

The right of survivorship provides that on the death of the last co-tenant, the remaining owner acquires the property in fee simple absolute.

FIGURE 2-4

Median Household Size

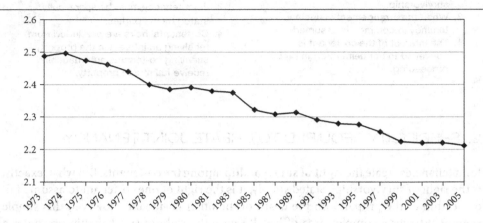

32 Years of Housing Data, Prepared for: U.S. Department of Housing and Urban Development, Office of Policy Development and Research, p. 32.

FIGURE 2-5

Defining the Right of Survivorship

Except as otherwise provided herein, in all estates, real or personal, held in joint tenancy, the part or share of any tenant dying shall not descend or go to the surviving tenant, but shall descend or be vested in the heirs, executors, or administrators, respectively, of the tenant so dying, in the same manner as estates held by tenancy in common. . . . Nothing in this section prevents the creation of a joint tenancy with right of survivorship in real or personal property if the instrument creating the joint tenancy expressly provides for a right of survivorship, and no other document shall be necessary to establish said right of survivorship.

C. TENANCY BY ENTIRETY

Tenancy by entirety
A joint tenancy with the right of survivorship that is only available to lawfully married couples.

Tenancy by entirety is a joint tenancy that is reserved for married couples. Although not all states refer to this arrangement as a tenancy by entirety, all states confer special privileges to married couples that are not enjoyed by domestic partners or live-in lovers. Under this arrangement, when one spouse dies, the other receives full title to the property, pending any other estate proceeding such as forced share or statutory share.

With the decision by the United States Supreme Court in *Obergefell v. Hodges*, 135 S. Ct. 1732 (2015), there is no longer any question about whether tenancy by entirety applies to same-sex couples. The answer is an unequivocal yes. These couples receive the same benefits and protections under state laws of tenancy by entirety as any other legally married couple. There are some states that also preserve these rights for civil unions among same-sex couples.

Tenancy by entirety is a co-tenancy that is reserved for married couples; it creates the right of survivorship.

REAL ESTATE BASICS AT A GLANCE

D. TENANCY IN PARTNERSHIP

Among the other types of concurrent ownership acknowledged under the law is **tenancy in partnership**. A relatively recent phenomenon, tenancy in partnership recognizes a legal relationship between business partners. Under the rules of tenancy in partnership, business partners enjoy the right of survivorship to all business-related property. To qualify for this tenancy, the partners must have a partnership agreement and actually be in business together. Under a tenancy in partnership, no partner can sell, transfer, or mortgage partnership property without the consent of the other partners. The advantage of a tenancy in partnership is that an individual partner's creditors are not permitted to use business property to satisfy a personal debt. Similar to a joint tenancy, the business assets automatically vest in the surviving partners in the event of the death of any partner.

Tenancy in partnership
A type of concurrent ownership among business partners, with the right of survivorship.

E. THE RIGHT TO PARTITION

Regardless of the type of tenancy arrangement, most co-tenants enjoy the right of **partition**. A partition is the division of the property along the ownership lines. In a tenancy in common, for example, where one co-tenant owns 80 percent and the other owns 20 percent, a partition proceeding might divide up the land according to the percentage. However, it isn't always practical or even possible to physically divide up parcels of real estate by the percentage of ownership. Instead, the property will be sold and the proceeds of the sale divided according to the percentage of ownership rights. Obviously, the right to partition is not universal in all concurrent ownership estates. For instance, in a tenancy by entirety, a married couple would not have the right to partition the marital property. Instead, they must first go through a divorce proceeding terminating the marriage. Only then would they have the right to partition marital property. Partitions are most commonly seen in the dissolution of tenancies in common and joint tenancies.

Partition
The right of co-tenants to divide property according to their ownership interests.

Case Excerpt

VARGO v. ADAMS
805 S.E.2d 817 (2017)

BENHAM, Justice.

The parties to this appeal were previously a couple, though unmarried. Appellant Adam Vargo purchased the real property in which the parties formerly resided in his own name as sole owner, and executed a purchase money mortgage on it. Shortly thereafter, Vargo executed a warranty deed conveying the property to himself and appellee Brittany E. Adams as joint tenants with the right of survivorship. The couple broke up and Vargo filed a petition for statutory partition, which was later amended to dismiss that claim and substitute a claim for equitable partition. Vargo testified at the bench trial in this matter that he contributed the down payment to purchase the property and nearly all the mortgage payments made on the loan, and claimed that an inequity exists, requiring equitable partition of the property, due to the disparity of funds he paid toward the purchase of the property compared to that paid by Adams. After conducting a bench trial, the judge found that equitable partition is not an available remedy to parties who hold property as joint tenants with right of survivorship except in actions for divorce. In the order denying Vargo's petition for equitable partition, the trial judge advised Vargo that he may sever the joint tenancy and then seek either a statutory partition under OCGA §44–6–160, or equitable partition if no sufficient remedy at law exists. The order also granted Vargo certain of his claims for conversion of items of personal property retained by Adams, but denied Vargo's claim for attorney fees. Vargo filed this appeal. For the reasons that follow, we affirm.

1. When Vargo dismissed his original claim for statutory partition, he correctly concluded that partition pursuant to OCGA §44–6–160, known as statutory partition, is available only to tenants in common. Because Vargo and Adams are owners of the subject property as joint tenants with the right of survivorship, statutory partition is unavailable to Vargo. See *Wallace v. Wallace*, 260 Ga. 400, 396 S.E.2d 208 (1990). Under the circumstances of this case, equitable partition is also unavailable. OCGA §44–6–140 states as follows: "Equity has jurisdiction in cases of partition whenever the remedy at law is insufficient or peculiar circumstances render the proceeding in equity more suitable and just." Vargo asserts he is entitled to equitable partition under one or both of the requirements described in OCGA §44–6–140 because, since the parties hold the property as joint tenants with the right of survivorship, they lack a remedy at law, and because the accounting issues regarding the parties' respective contributions to the property represent "peculiar circumstances" that render proceedings in equity appropriate. He claims the trial court's conclusion that, because the property is not marital property, he must sever the joint tenancy to create a tenancy in common before seeking equitable partition is unsupported by law or logic. Vargo is mistaken.

The trial court properly applied well-settled property law when it concluded Vargo may seek a partition of the subject property only after the joint tenancy is severed. For example, in *Reed v. McConathy*, Reed was, like Vargo, originally the sole owner of the subject property who later conveyed the property to a person to whom she was not married in a manner that resulted in the two titleholders owning the property as joint tenants with the right of survivorship. Several years later, Reed executed a quit claim deed transferring all her interest in the property to a third party, who then immediately executed a quit claim deed transferring back to Reed all interest the third party held in the property. A number of years afterwards, Reed filed a petition for equitable partition and an accounting. This Court reversed the trial court's order dismissing the petition, finding that because the joint tenancy had been severed, the conclusion that the property could not be equitably partitioned because it was held in a joint tenancy was erroneous. Id. at 473, 788 S.E.2d 769. Pursuant to what is now OCGA §44–6–190 (a) (3), a transfer during the life of one of the joint tenants of all or part of his or her interest in the property serves to sever the joint tenancy. At that point, it becomes property held by tenants in common, which is subject to equitable partition.

The trial court did not err by denying the equitable relief Vargo sought. Further, it offered Vargo a proper solution for severing the joint tenancy with the right of survivorship he created and creating instead a tenancy in common, for which equitable partition may be an available remedy.

2. Vargo sought the equitable partition of real property owned by unmarried parties as joint tenants with the right of survivorship. In her initial response to Vargo's petition, Adams raised the defense that the petition should be dismissed because it failed to state a claim upon which relief can be granted. Vargo was granted a full and fair opportunity to litigate the issue of whether he was entitled to equitable partition pursuant to the circumstances of this case in a two-day bench trial. The trial court noted in its order denying the petition for equitable partition that Vargo had failed to present any authority for equitable partition of property held as joints tenants with the right of survivorship except in actions for divorce. As noted in Division 1, the trial court properly concluded that equitable partition is not available to unmarried parties who own property as joint tenants with the right of survivorship. This distinction between married and unmarried joint tenants is because divorce and the division of marital property have always been regarded as equitable. Generally speaking, marital property is to be equitably divided upon the divorce of married persons, and this includes real property that is marital property whether owned in common by the parties to the marriage or as joint tenants with the right of survivorship.

Adams did not specifically assert this argument as grounds for the dismissal of Vargo's petition. Nevertheless, we reject Vargo's assertion that the trial court's ruling was made "sua sponte" in such a manner that it denied him the fundamental right of due process because it amounted to a dispositive ruling on an issue not raised by the parties, and on which he was not granted the opportunity to be heard. The trial court simply applied the well-settled law of Georgia. In this state, the general rule is that parties who own property as joint tenants with the right of survivorship are not entitled to equitable partitioning, the exception being for married parties who are seeking the equitable division of marital property in a divorce proceeding. That circumstance does not exists in this case, and the trial court properly denied the petition.

Judgment affirmed.

All the Justices concur.

QUESTIONS ABOUT THE CASE

1 What was the ownership arrangement between the two parties?
2 What was the reason that Vargo dismissed his original claim for statutory partition?
3 If statutory partition is unavailable to Vargo, could he then rely on equitable partition?
4 What does the court say must occur before any other action is available to the plaintiff in this case?

COVID-19 CONCERN

We have seen that one of the legal remedies available to joint tenants and tenants in common is to partition the property. A partition can consist of physically sectioning off the property according to the ownership interests of those involved or, when this is impractical, selling the property and dividing the assets based on percentage of ownership. In the era of COVID, would it be a valid claim to assert that the parties must partition the property because one has tested positive or has an active infection while the other does not? The question could extend to those who are vaccinated sharing a household with those who refuse to get the vaccination.

CHAPTER SUMMARY

Ownership in real estate brings with it a wide assortment of rights. When a person owns property in fee simple absolute, she has the highest and best form of real property ownership. Among the rights invested in a fee simple absolute owner are the rights to sell, give away, mortgage, and otherwise encumber the property. Traditionally, there have been two sub-classifications of fee simple absolute title: fee simple determinable and fee simple on a condition subsequent. These two limitations on fee simple absolute title are based on a limitation on how the property can be used. In modern real estate practice, they are rarely seen. A person may also receive a life estate in real property. A person who has a life estate has the authority to use and enjoy the property, but only as long as she is alive. Upon the life tenant's death, the property title transfers automatically to a predetermined person, referred to as a remainderman. A remainderman has a future interest in the property held in a life estate, but has no present interest in it. A remainderman can bring an action for the life tenant's waste or destruction in value of the property but can do very little else until the life estate terminates.

When property is held by two or more people, it is referred to as concurrent ownership. Concurrent ownership comes in a variety of different tenancies. A tenancy in common involves the ownership of the real estate parcel by two or more individuals with unequal shares in the property. Joint tenancy, on the other hand, is a form of concurrent ownership that allows the right of survivorship. When one of the joint tenants dies, the title automatically vests in the surviving tenants, bypassing the estate process. Tenancy by entirety is a concurrent ownership estate reserved for legally married couples. Tenancy in partnership is a legal doctrine that allows business partners to own property together. Partition is the right of co-tenants to bring an action to physically divide property along ownership lines or to sell the property and divide the profit based on percentage of ownership.

SKILLS YOU NEED IN THE REAL WORLD

Identifying Estates

As a real estate professional, it is important for you to be able to identify the different types of real property estates recognized in your state. For instance, does your state recognize fee simple determinable estates? What language is necessary to create such an estate? Similarly, are there limitations on life estates in your jurisdiction? For example, there is an old common law rule — referred to as the rule in Shelley's case — that specifically barred an owner from leaving a life estate to a person who might also be a remainderman. Under that old rule, the property would pass as fee simple title instead of establishing a life estate. Does that rule still apply in your state? In addition to these legal questions, it is also important for you to stay current on real property issues in state and federal appellate decisions that might concern real estate.

ETHICAL ISSUES FOR THE PARALEGAL

Drafting Deeds

Unauthorized practice of law is a crime in all states. Paralegals and legal assistants come close to crossing the line into unauthorized practice of law when they assist others in preparing deeds and other documents related to fee simple absolute and life estates. What might seem like a simple assignment to help another prepare a deed might be construed as practicing law without a license when that deed involves creating a life estate appropriate to the person's probate situation.

KEY TERMS AND CONCEPTS

Co-tenants	Life estate	Statutory share
Dower and curtesy	Life tenant	Tenancy by entirety
Estate	Partition	Tenancy in common
Fee simple absolute	*Pur autre vie*	Tenancy in partnership
Forced share	Remainderman	Waste
Joint tenancy	Right of survivorship	

END-OF-CHAPTER EXERCISES

Review Questions

See Appendix for answers.

1 What is a real property estate?
2 What is the difference between a present estate and a future estate?
3 What are the rights that an owner in fee simple absolute enjoys?
4 What limitations are placed on the rights of a fee simple absolute owner?
5 What is a fee simple determinable estate, and how does it compare to a fee simple absolute estate?
6 What is a fee simple on a condition subsequent estate, and how does it compare to a fee simple determinable and a fee simple absolute estate?
7 Why have fee simple determinable estates fallen into disuse?
8 Draft a deed provision that contains a fee simple determinable clause.
9 What is a life estate?
10 What limitations does a life tenant have on her ability to use the property subject to a life estate?
11 Provide an example of a clause that would create a life estate.
12 What is a remainderman?
13 Explain the concepts of dower and curtesy.
14 What is the historical basis for the creation of life estates?
15 What is waste as that term applies to life estates?
16 What is a life estate *pur autre vie*?
17 Compare and contrast tenancies in common with joint tenancies.
18 What is the right of survivorship?
19 What is a tenancy by entirety?
20 What is a tenancy in partnership?
21 What is partition?

DISCUSSION QUESTIONS

1   If you had to explain the difference between a tenancy by entirety and a joint tenancy to someone who knew nothing about real estate law, what would you say?

2   Are there good reasons for retaining the title of "life estate"? Can you think of better ways to achieve the same end, or is this a concept that should be kept? If so, why?

APPLYING WHAT YOU HAVE LEARNED

1   Should tenancy by entirety be extended to unmarried partners? Suppose that a state allows a classification for "domestic live in lover." Should the tenancy be extended to that category? Why or why not?

2   Draft a clause that would create each of the following estates:
    A   Fee simple on a condition subsequent
    B   Life estate
    C   Joint tenancy
    D   Tenancy in common

WEB SURFING

Life Estate Pur Autre Vie: Legal Information Institute
http://www.law.cornell.edu/wex/life_estate_pur_autre_vie

Findlaw: Joint Tenancy
https://www.findlaw.com/estate/probate/joint-tenancy-with-right-of-survivorship.html

Tenancy in Common
http://realestate.findlaw.com/buying-a-home/difference-between-joint-tenancy-and
-tenancy-in-common.html

Mortgage Professor
https://www.mtgprofessor.com/home.aspx

ANNOTATED DOCUMENT

Creating a Life Estate

Life estates are usually created in a will.

John Doe owns the property.

Mary Doe is the life tenant.

John Jr. and Tammy are the remaindermen.

Last Will and Testament for John Doe

I hereby leave all of my real property to my wife, Mary Doe, for her life and then, on her death, to our children John Jr. and Tammy.

PRACTICE QUESTIONS FOR TEST REVIEW

See Appendix for answers.

Essay

What are the rights and obligations that come with fee simple ownership?

True–False

1 T F Tenancy by entirety is only available to married couples.

2 T F Tenancy in common has the right of survivorship.

3 T F The estate that provides the highest form of ownership rights is fee simple determinable.

Fill in the Blank

1 This is a legal concept that comes into play when one spouse in a legal marriage dies. At that point, the surviving spouse is automatically granted a life estate in the marital residence: _____.

2 A life estate measured by the life of someone other than the life tenant is: _____.

3 A term for when the cotenants decide to divide up their property according to their ownership interests is: _____.

Multiple Choice

1   A right to use or enjoy real property

    A   Fee

    B   Estate

    C   Ordinance

    D   Authority

2   A person with this estate has the most complete set of rights that it is possible to have in a parcel of real estate.

    A   Fee simple

    B   Fee simple determinable

    C   Fee simple with a condition subsequent

    D   None of the above

3   This term originated under English law and referred to a grant from the king to an individual landowner.

    A   Fee

    B   Check

    C   Reversion

    D   Vacancy

Property Descriptions and Boundaries

Chapter Objectives

- Draw a metes and bounds description

- Explain the water rights available to landowners

- Define the role of property descriptions in accurately describing particular real estate tracts

- Demonstrate how ambiguities in property descriptions can lead to issues with the legal validity of a deed

- Describe how property boundaries change when they are bordered by water

Chapter Outline

I. Introduction

II. The History of Property Boundaries

III. Property Descriptions in Deeds
    A. The Elements of a Valid Property Description
    B. Legal Requirements for Property Descriptions in Deeds
    C. Referring to Other Documents to Prove Property Boundaries
    D. Litigating Property Boundaries
    E. Ambiguous Property Descriptions

IV. Metes and Bounds Descriptions
    A. Drafting Metes and Bounds Descriptions
    B. Using Technology to Help with Metes and Bounds Drawings

V. Other Methods to Describe Property: Government Survey System
    A. Tract Indexing
    B. Plats
    C. Torrens Registration

VI. Water Rights
    A. The Right to Use Water
    B. Natural Forces That Affect Property Boundaries
    C. Water and Property Boundaries

INTRODUCTION

In the first chapter, we described real estate as the land and anything permanently attached to it. However, that description does not help when it comes time to properly describe a parcel of real estate that is being sold. Real estate must be accurately described not only to ensure that the correct parcel is changing hands but also because of the peculiar nature of land itself. In this chapter, we will examine how to create accurate property descriptions and then describe how natural processes can affect those boundaries. We will also explore the vitally important issue of water rights.

Before we can discuss how real estate property descriptions are compiled, we must first address a basic question: Why is an accurate property description so important?

When any item is sold, it is important that both parties know exactly what they are buying and that both are able to identify the specific item that is the subject of the sale. With automobiles, this identification might be in the form of the vehicle identification number. For other items, there are serial numbers and other identifying marks. But such forms of identification don't work for land. For one thing, land is fixed; it cannot be transported. For another, one parcel of land looks very much like another. Imagine yourself walking through the woods, breathing in the country air, and generally enjoying the quiet. As you walk, you pay little attention to the fact that you are crossing over the boundaries of various tracts. In fact, without fences or signs to warn you, there is no way for you to determine exactly whose property you are on. Now, consider this same situation from a buyer's perspective. Just as you could not tell where one piece of property began and another ended, the buyer also does not know the exact parameters of his property. With items of personal property, that question is always easy: You own an object. But land is not an object, and the unique nature of real estate raises two interesting and vitally important points:

- What are the boundaries of a property?
- What distinguishes a particular parcel from every other parcel?

Because neither of these questions can be answered from the land itself, buyers and sellers are forced to rely on other sources for answers. This is not a new problem, which explains why surveying and describing tracts of land has an ancient history.

THE HISTORY OF PROPERTY BOUNDARIES

From the moment that societies began dividing up property for use by its members, it became a paramount concern to pinpoint exactly where one person's plot ended and another's began.

Ancient Egyptians used surveying techniques to divide up parcels and as a way to rediscover property boundaries after the yearly floods they suffered. Before the construction of the Aswan Dam in the 1960s, the Nile flooded every year. This flooding submerged the lands along the river and often destroyed fences and other structures used to identify property boundaries. Egyptians used surveying techniques to quickly and efficiently identify property boundaries after the flood waters receded. These surveying techniques were so accurate that they were also employed to build the great Egyptian monuments, such as the Pyramid of Giza and the Luxor Temple.

PROPERTY DESCRIPTIONS IN DEEDS

Because the description of the parcel's boundaries is so important for both buyers and sellers, it has always been necessary to have a system in place to identify land boundaries. However, there are other reasons why adequate property descriptions are important. We have already referred to the Statute of Frauds. That statute requires many aspects of a real estate transaction to be reduced to writing. Therefore, the actual boundaries for each parcel must be written down in order to create a legally valid transaction.

A. THE ELEMENTS OF A VALID PROPERTY DESCRIPTION

There are two critical elements pertaining to a property description:

1 The property description must *sufficiently describe* the property in the deed.
2 The property description can *make reference to other documents* that sufficiently describe the property.

Let's start with one method of property description that we are all familiar with: street address. If we accept that identifying a particular parcel is important, why can't we simply rely on street addresses in all our documents? Although this appears to be a fairly reasonable approach, there are some practical limitations with this method. For one thing, what if there are two streets in the town with the same name? Visitors to Atlanta, Georgia, are often confused by the sheer number of streets with "Peachtree" in the name. If you are selling the lot known as 1001 Peachtree Street, which lot are you selling? A property description must provide a specific method for identifying one tract from all others, and a street address doesn't always meet that standard.

A property description is sufficient in itself when it (1) clearly identifies a unique parcel of real estate and (2) makes specific references to property lines/roadways/other landmarks.

REAL
ESTATE
BASICS AT
A GLANCE

B. LEGAL REQUIREMENTS FOR PROPERTY DESCRIPTIONS IN DEEDS

As we have seen, street address is not sufficient to properly identify a parcel of real estate. Add to this the fact that each state has statutes that mandate particular types of property descriptions, and you begin to see the need for precise property descriptions that not only adequately pinpoint the property in question, but also meet the legal standards. Statutes require a property description that is adequate at the time that the deed is recorded; the property description cannot be added later. The description must stand on its own, giving specific reference points for the boundary lines and making reference to natural or artificial boundaries and landmarks. In states that use a tract indexing method to record deeds (discussed in further detail in a later chapter), the tract must be specific and refer to the correct parcel. In states that follow a metes and bounds system to describe land, the description must show how the parcel is unique compared to all others. The final description must provide enough information that anyone could properly identify the property.

C. REFERRING TO OTHER DOCUMENTS TO PROVE PROPERTY BOUNDARIES

The property description can refer to another document not included in the deed, but that other document must make the property description complete. The category of "other documents" includes plats, surveys, and other information provided in the public records. We will examine the function of plats and surveys later in this chapter. When a property description refers to other documents, those documents become a legally binding aspect of the property description. Both documents are now intertwined, and someone who wished to know the exact boundaries of the property would be forced to refer to both the deed and the other document. Many states have laws that make the document as much a part of the deed as if it were actually written down and included with the deed.

EXAMPLE 3-1

KATIE'S CONVEYANCE
Katie has recently conveyed a one-acre tract to Lisa. In the section of the deed where the property description is provided, Katie has written: "The one-acre lot shown on Plat 45-672, land records of Anywhere County." Is this a sufficient property description?

Answer: Yes. Because Katie has specified a public document that adequately identifies the parcel, the property description is legally valid.

EXAMPLE 3-2

VALID PROPERTY DESCRIPTION
"That one-acre lot that we visited yesterday and that is known as the old Smith place." Is this property description sufficient?

Answer: No. The problem with a description like this is that there are too many unknowns to make this parcel identifiable. The parties may understand what they are talking about, but the law requires more: The property description must be sufficient so that anyone could understand it. This description fails that test.

D. LITIGATING PROPERTY BOUNDARIES

When a question arises about exactly where the property boundaries are, the parties often find themselves in court, presenting their case to a judge and a jury. If there is some confusion about exactly where the boundaries are, how do the parties prove their case?

At a minimum, the parties must prove the following to satisfy the court regarding the boundaries of a particular parcel:

- The description details the boundaries of the parcel,
- The description conforms to the physical features of the parcel,
- The description is accurate, and
- The description refers to natural boundaries and other features that specify a unique parcel of land.

If a party is unable to prove these elements, the court is likely to rule against him. The practical result of a ruling against one party is a ruling in favor of the other. When a property boundary is under dispute, the court will side with one owner or the other.

LISA'S PROPERTY DISPUTE

EXAMPLE 3-3

Lisa owns 1.3 acres. She lives there with her husband and children and has done so for years. The area is rural, and most of the surrounding tracts have never been developed. One day, Lisa gets a letter in the mail from Missy. Missy has purchased the adjoining lot and has noticed that Lisa's fence and shed have been constructed across Missy's property line. Missy demands that Lisa remove both immediately. Lisa reviews her original title documents and finds that her deed makes reference to a large oak tree as forming the corner of her lot with the adjacent lot. It also provides that her property line runs from the old oak tree to a stump that is only a few feet from the road. Walking that straight line clearly places the fence and the shed on her side of the property. Missy has a deed that states that she owns 1.5 acres and describes the boundary line in question as "running along the property adjacent in a north-westerly direction until it reaches Choctaw Road." If this case goes to litigation, who will win?

Answer: Lisa. Why? Her deed provides some information that could give a third party a clear indication of where the property line is. Although referring to an old oak tree isn't the best description, if there is only one oak tree and one stump, it provides a better description than Missy's deed.

E. AMBIGUOUS PROPERTY DESCRIPTIONS

What happens when a property boundary, such as the one in the example above, is ambiguous or open to interpretation? How do the courts resolve ambiguities in property descriptions? There are actually two different classifications of ambiguous property descriptions: patent ambiguities and latent ambiguities. The classification of a particular property description as patently ambiguous or latently ambiguous has enormous consequences when courts address property descriptions.

1. PATENT AMBIGUITIES

Patently ambiguous
A description that is invalid on its face.

A **patently ambiguous** property description is so vague that the property cannot be identified at all. Such a designation has a dramatic effect on the proceedings. Courts will rule that patently ambiguous property descriptions do not convey property, that the deed is invalid, and that the entire transaction is canceled, therefore voiding any sale. The standard that most states use to define a patently ambiguous property description is any description that leaves the land to be conveyed in a state of absolute uncertainty. Patently ambiguous descriptions do not, by their very terms, offer any assistance to help clear up the confusion.

EXAMPLE 3-4	**RICK'S CONVEYANCE**

Rick conveys a half-acre tract to Katie. The property description reads: "All that tract or acreage containing .5 acres and described as 100 feet on each side, forming a perfect square, with one point of the square pointing directly at the winter sun's rising point."

As you can tell from reading this description, any tract that is 100 feet on each side does not equal one half-acre. In fact, a 100-foot-square parcel is considerably less than a half-acre. The other problem with this deed is that the "point" of this square cannot be determined. Where exactly is the winter sun's rising point? The sun rises at different points on the horizon throughout the year. This description fails to provide sufficient explanation of both the size and the orientation of the property.

In the face of a void description, is there some way that the parties can provide additional information? For instance, is it possible to present testimony from the people involved in the transaction to help identify the exact parcel?

2. PAROL EVIDENCE AND PROPERTY DESCRIPTIONS

Parol evidence
Oral testimony offered to explain or interpret the provisions of a written document, such as the property description in a deed.

Parol evidence is oral testimony offered to prove an element in a written document. But is such testimony permissible to help clear up a patently ambiguous property description? No. The rule about parol evidence is simple: Oral testimony cannot rectify a poorly drafted document. The reasons behind the parol evidence rule stretch back for centuries but are based squarely on common sense: A written document must stand on its own. While oral testimony can clear up discrepancies in a document, it cannot prove the document. Why? The temptation would be too great on the parties to spin their testimony to help support their position. Permitting a party to interpret the language in a deed also attacks the fundamental reason to have documents in writing in the first place: to establish the basic terms of the transaction. The parol evidence rule applies not only to deeds, but also to many other written documents.

Under the parol evidence rule, a property description must stand on its own; courts will not consider evidence or testimony that seeks to explain or expand on a patently ambiguous property description.

3. LATENTLY AMBIGUOUS PROPERTY DESCRIPTIONS

What happens when a property description appears to be patently ambiguous, but it refers to another document that exactly pinpoints the property's location? In that situation, the description is classified as **latently ambiguous**. Latently ambiguous property descriptions are insufficient when viewed by themselves but become valid when they refer to some other document through which a more precise identification can be made (see Figure 3-1 for an example). Consider the following description: "I hereby sell to Ben all of my land in Burke County." Such a description would be patently ambiguous. However, if this same wording included a reference to, "as set out in deed book, 432, page 15," this patently ambiguous description becomes a latently ambiguous description. Although the original description does not specify a unique and identifiable property, the reference to the deed book makes it a legally valid description. In order for a latently ambiguous description to be legal, it must refer to some public document or an entry in the public records. Unlike with patently ambiguous descriptions, parol evidence can be used to explain or interpret the provisions in latently ambiguous descriptions.

Latently ambiguous
A description that appears to be invalid but refers to a document through which the property can be adequately described.

Latently ambiguous descriptions appear to be inadequate but refer to other documents that prove the parcel is specific and unique.

The plot to be purchased is + or – 25 acres to be determined by a survey for property behind Mr. Fox's property, to run to the first field by the road. This being the same as the plot shown in tax map 21, Lot 23, in Pearson county.[1]

FIGURE 3-1

Example of a Latently Ambiguous Property Description

IV   METES AND BOUNDS DESCRIPTIONS

The original colonies of the Americas, and the first 13 states of the United States, adopted metes and bounds property descriptions primarily because it was the English system, and the original states adopted English law as the model for the nation. This method of property description continues to be used in those states, and a few others, even though many other states have adopted tract indexing and other methods. Because there is such a diversity of methods used to describe property, we examine metes and bounds descriptions thoroughly in this chapter and then discuss other states' methods in later chapters.

Most of the states along the Eastern Seaboard of the United States use the metes and bounds system to describe land. A metes and bounds description sets out the distance and direction of the property's boundaries. Metes (distance) and bounds (direction) follow the course of the property lines from a point of beginning (P.O.B.) in a clockwise direction, from border to border, until returning to the P.O.B. In many ways, a metes and bounds description is similar to the way treasure maps describe the location of the prize. However, instead of "twelve paces west to an old stump, then twenty paces east to the mouth of a cave" and thus to the buried treasure, a metes and bounds description is actually a step-by-step tour of the entire property line. Along the way, it describes every twist and turn of the property so that there can be no doubt about the exact location of boundary lines. For example:

> Starting from the northwestern-most point of lot 9 Plat Book 28 page 30 thence N. 85 degrees 07' 20" W. 37.40 feet to the point and place of beginning; thence N. 85 degrees 07' 20" W. 102.46 feet; thence N. 11 degrees 18' 10" W. 36.37 feet to a point which is the northeastern-most point of the Smith property; thence S. 70 degrees 38' 18" E. 139.66 feet to the point and place of beginning.

Metes and bounds descriptions are very precise. Distances are given to 1/100 of a foot and directions are given not only in degrees, but also in finer gradations of minutes and seconds. The degrees refer to the hash marks on a typical drawing compass. For instance, "N. 85 degrees 07' 20" W. 37.40 feet," directs the reader directly north, and then seven degrees to the west. The designation 20" W is so tiny that it is almost impossible to see on a typical compass. A surveyor would have instruments delicate enough to discern this gradation, but most real estate practitioners would not. If you were drawing this line, and you designated north as the direction toward the top edge of the page, your line would be at a slight angle toward the upper left corner. We will draw out metes and bounds descriptions in the next section of this chapter.

Metes and bounds descriptions can present problems for legal professionals. For instance, a parcel with an unusual shape could have a description that goes on for dozens of lines. Recopying that description to another document always runs the risk of leaving out a line and thus rendering the entire description invalid. Metes and bounds descriptions must be word perfect from deed to deed.

Another problem for legal professionals involves older metes and bounds descriptions. For one thing, they do not use the same terminology or units of measure. Consider the following example:

> BEING Grant No. 97 by the State to Juan Amigo, dated April 13, 1870, recorded in Book L—2 page 644, Brunswick County Registry, and more particularly described by metes and bounds as follows: BEGINNING at a stake in the southwest corner of the new survey in your old line; running thence South 72 degrees East 150 poles to your corner on the Sea Banks; thence along the sea shore South 18 degrees West 384 poles to a stake at the

end of the bank near a small inlet; thence across the sound South 72 degrees West 115 poles to your old line; thence along said line to the place and point of BEGINNING; containing three hundred acres, more or less.[2]

This description does not describe the directions in finer gradations of degrees; instead, it simply provides "South 72 degrees West." However, that is not the real problem presented by this property description. The real problem is: How long is a "pole"?

In deeds from the 1960s and earlier, units of measure are given in unfamiliar terms, such as "poles," "rods," and "chains." These are all units of distance, in the same way that miles and yards are units of distance. When deciphering these older property descriptions, you must first convert poles and chains into feet and then draw the description based on the conversion. See Figure 3-2 for a conversion chart.

1 chain = 66 feet	1 link = 7.92 inches	**FIGURE 3-2**
1 rod = 16.5 feet	1 acre = 43,560 square feet	
1 pole = 16.5 feet	1 square acre = 208.71 feet on each side	**Conversion Chart for Old Metes and Bounds Descriptors**
1 perch = 16.5 feet	1 mile = 5,280 feet	

A. DRAFTING METES AND BOUNDS DESCRIPTIONS

It is important for any legal professional to know how to draft metes and bounds descriptions, if that is the system used in your state. Being able to draw metes and bounds descriptions helps you visualize the property descriptions in a way that simply reading distances and directions never can. Drawing out the description also allows you to compare your drawing with other, known drawings of the same property, such as plats, tax maps, and other drawings of the parcel. A drawing will help you immediately identify when the property description is in error (or is actually the description for an entirely different parcel).

To draw metes and bounds descriptions, you will need a circular land measure compass or a semi-circular protractor. Land measure compasses can be obtained from many sources; for example, they are given out as a promotional item from title insurance or surveying companies. You will also need a regular straight ruler.

To begin, get a blank piece of paper and then locate a point on the paper to serve as your P.O.B. One way of deciding where your P.O.B. will be is by reading through the entire description and locating the longest boundary line. If the longest described line is on the north-south axis, then your P.O.B. should be toward the bottom of your blank page. If the longest line is on the east-west axis, your P.O.B. should be closer to the left-hand margin of your page. The reason we specify the left-hand margin of the blank page is that metes and bounds descriptions are written in a clockwise fashion, meaning that they usually start on the left-hand side of the page and progress in a clockwise manner from there.

Here is a relatively basic example: From P.O.B., N 30 degrees E, 100 feet, then S 30 degrees E, 100 feet, then S 30 degrees W, 100 feet, then N 30 degrees W, 100 feet to P.O.B.

You can start to draw this description by first locating a spot toward the lower left-hand corner of your blank page. Draw a dot there. Place the center of your compass on this point, with north on the compass pointing directly toward the top of the page. A direction such as "N 30 degrees E," means "North 30 degrees toward the East." Locate north, and then go 30 degrees toward the east. In this situation, you will go right down the curve of your compass or protractor until you locate 30 degrees. Mark that point, and then remove your compass. You should now have two points: your original P.O.B. and the mark indicating North 30 degrees East from that point. You can now draw a line connecting these marks, but before you do, there is one other matter: How long should this line be?

The description states that the line is "N 30 degrees E, 100 feet." Obviously, we must scale down 100 feet to some distance that will fit on a sheet of paper. One way of doing this is to create a scale in which 1 inch equals 100 feet. Most attorneys use a scale closer to 1 inch equals 200 feet to be sure that the drawing actually fits on the page. We will use the 1 inch equals 100 feet scale in this example just to keep things simple. Using that scale, the line connecting the P.O.B. along the N 30 degrees E mark would measure one inch. Place your ruler along the axis of these two lines and measure one inch from the P.O.B. You may find that the line doesn't reach your second mark. No problem. That mark was just there to give you a direction. In fact, as soon as you draw your one-inch

Tech Topic

REAL ESTATE MARKETING TECHNOLOGY

It should be no surprise that technology has made massive inroads into marketing methods for both residential and commercial real estate. In residential real estate alone, the increase in use of mobile devices has produced a concurrent avalanche of marketing tools. Homebuyers have access to websites with profuse details about properties for sale. Smartphone apps can retrieve property information according to GPS coordinates. Furthermore, users can elect to receive alerts about certain types of properties so that when they travel near those properties, an automatic notification is sent to their mobile phone.

Additionally, many realtors are now using Quick Response, or QR, codes (which look like a block of code about an inch square) in their print ads. A prospective buyer uses a smartphone app to take a picture of the QR code, which then reveals details about the property or leads the buyer to the property's website.

Commercial real estate brokers have likewise adopted technology tools in their marketing. In recent years, the industry has embraced online listings that widened their access to prospective investors. Email marketing has allowed commercial real estate firms to market directly to their databases of owners and brokers. Firms have even used social media such as LinkedIn, Facebook, and Twitter to generate leads. Another marketing avenue has been the use of specialized software that provides a targeted approach to generating, tracking, and nurturing leads.

One of the commercial real estate industry's newer approaches is online auctions. Particularly in a down market, these platforms help push through the bottleneck of unsold commercial property by better meeting price expectations and creating a sense of urgency and excitement.

As technology continues to evolve, it is certain that new real estate marketing tools will continue to emerge.

line, you should probably erase that N 30 degrees E mark so that it won't cause any later confusion.

You now have a one-inch line that starts at the bottom left-hand corner of your blank sheet and aims roughly at the upper right corner of the page. Now what? Move your compass to the end of this new line, and dial in your new direction. According to our sample, this new direction is "S 30 degrees E, 100 feet." Following the same process that we outlined above, your line will point in the general direction of the lower right corner of your page and will be 1 inch long. You should end up with a square, with one corner of the square pointing toward the top of your page.

Sometimes a metes and bounds description will give you a direction such as "directly North," or "due North," or simply "N, 100 feet." In this case, the description means directly north, with no angling off to either side.

B. USING TECHNOLOGY TO HELP WITH METES AND BOUNDS DRAWINGS

In the era of the Internet and computer-assisted drawing, it should come as no surprise that many companies have developed software to help title searchers and others to draw metes and bounds descriptions. Programs such as MapDraw (www.informatik.com/mapdraw.html), Version Tracker (www.versiontracker.com/dyn/moreinfo/macosx/22791), and Metes and Bounds Online (www.metesandboundsonline.com/home.html) allow users to plug in the various directions and distances and produce a line drawing that can be compared with the plat for the property. Each of these programs can complete the drawing with an ease that would have astonished a title searcher from even a few years ago.

OTHER METHODS TO DESCRIBE PROPERTY: GOVERNMENT SURVEY SYSTEM

In the Public Land Act of 1785, the federal government created a system for surveying vast tracts of land that it planned to give away to new homesteaders. Most of these tracts were located in the new territories of the Middle and Far West. The original colony states continue to use the old metes and bounds descriptions; however, if you are involved in real property practice in midwestern and western states, you may find that your state uses an entirely different system. These are briefly outlined below, and we will discuss them in greater detail in later chapters.

A. TRACT INDEXING

In Chapter 12, when we discuss the process involved in carrying out a title search, we will see that there are essentially two systems used to record land transactions. One involves a listing of grantors (sellers) and grantees (buyers). The other system is a tract index. We mention tract indexes in this chapter because they are also used to describe property. In states that use the tract-indexing system, the local government will assign a permanent parcel identification number to each parcel of real estate. This number is usually cross-referenced with the county tax or assessor's office. Any action involving the property is then recorded according to this number. In some areas, all transactions involving the property are actually recorded on a series of cards for a particular parcel. Although this system has the benefit of putting all records for a parcel in one place, the system is not used everywhere. In fact, most states continue to use a variation of the grantor-grantee index, along with metes and bounds, plat, or tract references.

B. PLATS

Plats are drawings of property that are prepared by surveyors. A plat can be recorded in the registrar of deeds or land office and often contains all the same information provided in a metes and bounds or government tract survey property description. Most states give plats the status of official, recorded documents, provided that they meet certain requirements. Once recorded, a plat can be one of the documents referred to in a legally valid property description (see Figure 3-3).

FIGURE 3-3

Effect of Reference to Plat in Conveyance, Mortgage, or Other Instrument

When any deed, mortgage, or other instrument conveying an interest in or creating a lien on real property refers to the boundaries, metes, courses, or distances of the real estate delineated or shown on any plat of the property or on any blueprint, tracing, photostatic copy, or other copy of the plat which has been recorded as authorized in Code Section 44-2-26 and when the deed, mortgage, or other instrument states the office, book, and page of recordation of the plat or of the blueprint, tracing, photostatic copy, or other copy of the plat, the reference shall be equivalent to setting forth in the deed, mortgage, or other instrument the boundaries, metes, courses, or distances of the real estate as may be delineated or shown on the plat or on the blueprint, tracing, photostatic copy, or other copy thereof.[3]

C. TORRENS REGISTRATION

Sir Robert Torrens developed a land registration system in the 1850s for use in tracking land sales in Australia. The Torrens method greatly simplified the rules regarding registration of English deeds by gathering together all information about a particular parcel into a single document. The appealing aspect of the Torrens registration scheme is that, when a person wishes to know whether an encumbrance, such as a lien, has been filed against the property, he can simply pull the registration card and read what has been printed there. In many ways, the modern tract-index system used in some states is a direct offshoot of the Torrens system. The Torrens system almost completely eliminates the need for a title search and greatly simplifies other aspects of real property titles.

Torrens registration schemes were adopted by most of the original colony states as a way to deal with some of the problems inherent in metes and bounds descriptions — not the least of which is the confusion that they can cause. Although the Torrens system provided an easy and logical organization scheme for real estate records, it was never popular. Many of the states that enacted it have since repealed it, and even in those states where it is still a legal form of registration, attorneys do not use it. These days, a property that is registered in Torrens is considered to have legal problems, and real estate attorneys will take action to have the property removed from the registry.

When property is recorded under a Torrens system, any encumbrance, lien, or judgment against the property is actually written on the Torrens card corresponding to the unique parcel of land in question.

REAL
ESTATE
BASICS AT
A GLANCE

 **WATER RIGHTS**

The subject of water rights could easily fill an entire volume. Broadly known as **riparian rights**, an owner's right to water is a critical factor in real estate. Without water, land is essentially worthless. Riparian rights can be broken into two broad categories: the right to use water, and the effect that water has on property boundaries. We will address the right to use water first.

Riparian rights
The right to use and draw water for the benefit of real property.

A. THE RIGHT TO USE WATER

What rights do real estate owners have to surface water? The rule in most states is simple: When an owner's land is in contact with water, he has the right to make reasonable use of it.

1. LIMITATIONS ON RIGHT TO USE WATER

Under ordinary circumstances, all owners whose land borders on a body of water, including rivers and streams, have the right to take water from the source. Obviously, this right is limited to the extent that the owner cannot use so much of the water that it prevents others from doing so. Other limitations on owners include the prohibition against altering the course of a river or polluting it to such an extent that the water becomes unusable for other owners whose land also borders the river.

2. COURT DOCTRINES THAT AFFECT WATER RIGHTS

Many states have adopted the "reasonable use" test to determine when an owner's use of water is excessive or injurious to others. Under this rule, the owner may use the water to an extent considered reasonable under the circumstances. The factors that determine reasonableness will vary from case to case. Among the factors that the court will consider are the individual owners' needs for water. Are they drawing water for drinking and bathing, or to run a business? Are they drawing water simply to use it for decorative purposes, such as fountains and displays? The owners who draw water for personal use will have a much stronger case for water access than the second group who simply use the water for display. Whether a particular owner's water use is reasonable is a question to be determined by a jury.

B. NATURAL FORCES THAT AFFECT PROPERTY BOUNDARIES

When one or more boundary lines of a parcel border on water, the question often becomes, where exactly does one draw the property line? Water levels tend to rise and lower not only throughout the course of a year, but sometimes during the course of a single day. Property boundaries can be affected not only by tides, but also by the more gradual natural actions that affect boundary lines. Among these natural forces are:

- Accretion
- Erosion
- Avulsion
- Reliction

1. ACCRETION

Accretion
The natural and gradual deposit of soil against a bank or other barrier.

Accretion is the gradual deposit of soil on an owner's property that expands the total size of the parcel. In this situation, the boundary line shifts to reflect the new expansion of dry land. When accretion occurs by natural forces, it gives the landowner a windfall. Without paying for any additional property, he has gradually acquired more land.

2. EROSION

Erosion
The natural and gradual removal, usually by force of water, of soil from a bank or some other barrier.

Erosion is the opposite of accretion. When the action of water slowly takes away soil from a parcel, the owner's overall lot size gradually decreases. The owner is not permitted to adjust his boundaries to reflect the slow loss of acreage.

3. AVULSION

Avulsion
The sudden separation of land from its main body, usually by action of water.

Avulsion is a lesser-known process wherein dry land is suddenly added or lost by the action of water. Rivers can sometimes shift their courses dramatically, and when this shift results in a sudden change in a property's boundaries, the process is accurately described as avulsion, not accretion or erosion.

4. RELICTION

Reliction is the gradual exposure of dry land by receding waters. Although this process is not common, it can affect a property's boundaries, or even an entire parcel.

C. WATER AND PROPERTY BOUNDARIES

Although government surveys, metes and bounds descriptions, and plat book references are all excellent ways to describe property, there are some situations in which they prove to be inadequate. For instance, none of these written descriptions helps a real estate professional to determine the air rights above the property or the mineral rights under the surface. Property descriptions also run into practical difficulties. When one line of the property is bordered by a river, lake, or stream, where exactly should the property line be located? If the water level varies, as it usually does, doesn't this mean that the property line also varies, sometimes several times a day? Courts follow a two-pronged approach to this issue. The first prong is to determine the classification of the body of water in question. That classification will then determine the rules applicable to boundary lines and watercourses (the second prong). The first question that must be asked when dealing with water is whether the water is navigable.

1. NAVIGABLE WATERS

A "**navigable**" body of water is one that is capable of supporting commercial navigation. This means, in essence, a river, lake, or other body of water that a boat could cross. Here, a "boat" includes pleasure craft. Under the public trust doctrine that is a feature of most states' policies regarding water, when rivers or lakes are navigable and thus capable of use for commercial purposes, these bodies are the property of the state, not individual landowners. The state retains title to these bodies of water as a way of furthering commerce.

When property borders a navigable body of water, the boundary line is the bank, or the mid-distance between low and high water marks (if the property borders the ocean). This arbitrarily chosen midpoint becomes the owner's boundary line, while the water itself is public (or government) property.

Navigable water
Water that can be used for navigation by boats.

2. NON-NAVIGABLE WATERS

When water is classified as **non-navigable**, the rules about boundaries change. When a property is bordered by a non-navigable body of water, such as a stream, the owner's property line runs to the middle of the stream. The opposite owner's boundary line also runs to the middle, effectively dividing the stream in half. If the course of the stream changes, the property boundaries will change with it. Obviously, these rules are not a factor when the stream passes through the middle of a parcel. In that case, the only concern for the property owner is the reasonable use of the water itself.

Non-navigable water
A body of water so shallow or small that it is incapable of supporting navigation.

Case Excerpt

IN RE FORECLOSURE OF REAL PROP. UNDER DEED
OF TRUST FROM VICQUE
2017 N.C. App. 261, 799 S.E.2d 658 (2017)

Opinion

Appeal by respondents from order entered 30 March 2016 by Judge D. Jack Hooks in Onslow County Superior Court. Heard in the Court of Appeals 7 March 2017.

ZACHARY, Judge.

Appellants Vicque and Christalyn Thompson ("the Thompsons") appeal from an order of the trial court that allowed the substitute trustee appointed by appellee USAA Federal Savings Bank ("the Bank") to foreclose on a loan secured by property owned by the Thompsons. On appeal, the Thompsons argue that the trial court erred by failing to vacate an earlier order of the Clerk of Superior Court of Onslow County allowing foreclosure and by entering the order permitting the foreclosure sale to proceed. The Thompsons contend that "the trustee did not hold legal title to the property owned by the Thompsons by virtue of the faulty description in the deed of trust" and that, as a result, the substitute trustee was "not entitled to foreclose under the instrument." For the reasons discussed below, we conclude that the trial court did not err and that its order should be affirmed.

Background

The relevant facts of this case are largely undisputed and may be summarized as follows: On 28 September 2007, the Thompsons acquired property located at 303 Old Pine Court, Richlands, North Carolina ("the property"). In order to purchase the property, the Thompsons borrowed $205,850.00 from the Bank and secured the loan with a Deed of Trust on the property. The Thompsons later defaulted on the loan by failing to make the payment to the Bank that was due on 1 September 2013, or to make any payments thereafter. A letter informing the Thompsons of the default was mailed on 2 February 2014, and a pre-foreclosure notice was mailed to the Thompsons on 2 September 2014. On 23 July 2015, Trustee Services of Carolina, LLC was appointed as substitute trustee for the property. The Bank instructed the substitute trustee to institute foreclosure proceedings.

On 29 July 2015, the substitute trustee filed a notice of a foreclosure hearing to be conducted on 15 September 2015. The foreclosure hearing was continued until 17 November 2015, at which time the Clerk of Superior Court for Onslow County conducted a hearing and entered an order allowing the foreclosure to proceed. The Thompsons appealed the Clerk's order to the Superior Court of Onslow County for a de novo hearing. The trial court conducted a hearing on 15 February 2016. On 8 April 2016, the court entered an order allowing the foreclosure to proceed. The Thompsons entered timely notice of appeal to this Court from the trial court's order.

Right to Foreclose: General Principles

The general principles by which foreclosure must be conducted are well established. "Foreclosure by power-of-sale proceedings conducted pursuant to N.C. Gen. Stat. §45-21.16 are limited in scope. A power-of-sale provision contained in a deed of trust vests the trustee with the 'power to sell the real property mortgaged without any order of court in the event of a default.' " *In re Foreclosure of Collins*, ___ N.C. App. ___, ___, 797 S.E.2d 28, 31, 2017 N.C. App. 51 (2017). N.C. Gen. Stat. §45-21.16(a) (2015) requires that in order to initiate a foreclosure proceeding, the mortgagee or trustee must file a notice of hearing with the clerk of court and serve notice of the hearing upon the appropriate parties. The Thompsons do not dispute that they were properly served with notice of the hearing. Thereafter, a hearing "shall be held before the clerk of court in the county where the land, or any portion thereof, is situated." N.C. Gen. Stat. §45-21.16(d) (2015). At the hearing, the lender "bears the burden of proving that there was a valid debt, default, the right to foreclose under power of sale, and notice." *In re Foreclosure of Brown*, 156 N.C. App. 477, 489, 577 S.E.2d 398, 406 (2003). N.C. Gen. Stat. §45-21.16(d) provides in relevant part that:

> If the clerk finds the existence of (i) valid debt of which the party seeking to foreclose is the holder, (ii) default, (iii) right to foreclose under the instrument, and (iv) notice to those entitled to such under subsection (b), . . . then the clerk shall authorize the mortgagee or trustee to proceed under the instrument, and the mortgagee or trustee can give notice of and conduct a sale pursuant to the provisions of this Article.

Discussion

In this case, the Thompsons' only challenge to the order allowing foreclosure is their contention that the evidence fails to show that the Bank has the right to foreclose on the property. The Thompsons assert that as a result of an error contained in the Deed of Trust's description of the property, the Bank "never received legal title" to the property and therefore has no right to foreclose on the loan secured by the Deed of Trust. Upon careful review of the relevant jurisprudence, in light of the facts of this case, we conclude that the Thompsons' argument lacks merit.

Resolution of this appeal requires an examination of the contents of the General Warranty Deed and the Deed of Trust. Both the General Warranty Deed and the Deed of Trust (1) identify the location of the property as 303 Old Pine Ct., Richlands, N.C., (2) identify the property as being Lot 46 as shown on a plat recorded in Map Book 51, Page 149, Slide 1485 of the Onslow County Registry, and (3) identify the property as having Onslow County Tax Parcel ID Number 46B-153. The Thompsons' appellate argument is based upon a single error in the Deed of Trust, evidenced in the following discrepancy between the documents:

> 1. The General Warranty Deed describes the property as "all of Lot 46 as shown on a plat entitled 'Final Plat Walnut Hills, Section III-C,' prepared by Parker & Associates, Inc., dated August 3, 2006 and recorded in Map Book 51, Page 149, Slide L-1485, Onslow County Registry."

2. The Deed of Trust describes the property as "all of Lot 46, as shown on a plat enti-tled 'Final Plat Walnut Hills, Section II-C' prepared by Parker & Associates, Inc., dated August 3, 2006 and recorded in Map Book 51, Page 149, Slide L-1485, Onslow County Registry."

The sole difference between these documents is that the Deed of Trust describes the property as being located in "Section II-C" of the Walnut Hills subdivision, and the General Warranty Deed identifies the property as being located in "Section III-C" of the Walnut Hills subdivision. The parties agree that the Walnut Hills subdivision did not include a "Section II-C" and that the reference in the Deed of Trust to "Section II-C" was incorrect and referred to a location that does not exist. The Thompsons contend that this error renders the Deed of Trust void as a matter of law. The Bank, however, argues that the Deed of Trust's reference to "Section II-C" is a minor error that cre-ates only a latent ambiguity as to the description of the property, which may be rectified by examination of extrinsic documents referenced in the Deed of Trust. We agree with the Bank's analysis.

Neither the transfer of property from a buyer to a seller, nor the execution of doc-uments securing a loan used to purchase real estate is a modern phenomenon or an unusual occurrence. Property has changed hands throughout North Carolina's history and there have been many occasions in which a party has challenged the validity of a document evidencing a property transaction on the grounds that the document con-tained an error or failed to identify the property with sufficient certainty. Our courts have had numerous opportunities during the last 150 years to consider the effect of an error or misnomer in a deed, promissory note, or other real estate-related document. As a result, the law governing the issue of errors or uncertainty in such documents has been firmly established for more than a century.

N.C. Gen. Stat. §22-2 (2015), known as the statute of frauds, requires that all contracts to convey land "shall be void unless said contract, or some memorandum or note thereof, be put in writing and signed by the party to be charged therewith, or by some other person by him thereto lawfully authorized." The Supreme Court of North Carolina has held that "a valid contract to convey land, therefore, must contain expressly or by necessary implication all the essential features of an agreement to sell, one of which is a description of the land, certain in itself or capable of being rendered certain by reference to an extrinsic source designated therein." *Kidd v. Early*, 289 N.C. 343, 353, 222 S.E.2d 392, 400 (1976). The general rule regarding the validity of the description of property in a deed or related document is as follows:

> The decisions in this State are in very general recognition of the principle that a deed con-veying real estate or a contract concerning it, within the meaning of the statute of frauds, must contain a description of the land, the subject-matter of the contract, "either certain in itself or capable of being reduced to certainty by reference to something extrinsic to which the contract refers."

Patton v. Sluder, 167 N.C. 500, 502, 83 S.E. 818, 819 (1914).

"It is presumed that the grantor in a deed of conveyance intended to convey some-thing, and the deed will be upheld unless the description is so vague or contradictory that it cannot be ascertained what thing in particular is meant." *Duckett v. Lyda*, 223 N.C. 356, 358, 26 S.E.2d 918, 919 (1943). Thus, "while the contract must contain a description of the land to be sold, it is not essential that the description be so minute or particular as to make resort to extrinsic evidence unnecessary. The line of separation is the distinction between a patent and a latent ambiguity." *Gilbert v. Wright*, 195 N.C. 165, 166, 141 S.E. 577, 578 (1928).

Although a description of real property must adequately identify the subject property, the law will support a deed if possible. "When a description leaves the land 'in a state of absolute uncertainty, and refers to nothing extrinsic by which it might be identified with certainty,' it is patently ambiguous and parol evidence is not admissible to aid the description. The deed or contract is void." *Kidd*, 289 N.C. at 353, 222 S.E.2d at 400. "'A description is . . . latently ambiguous if it is insufficient in itself to identify the property but refers to something extrinsic by which identification might possibly be made.' Thus, a description missing or uncertain in one document may be rendered certain by another and together the documents may satisfy the statute of frauds." *River Birch Associates v. City of Raleigh*, 326 N.C. 100, 123, 388 S.E.2d 538, 551 (1990). In sum:

> It is a general rule, that if the description be so vague or contradictory, that it cannot be told what thing in particular is meant; the deed is void. But it is also a general rule, that the deed shall be supported, if possible; and if by any means different descriptions can be reconciled, they shall be, or if they be irreconcilable, yet if one of them sufficiently points out the thing, so as to render it certain that it was the one intended, a false or mistaken reference to another particular shall not overrule that which is already rendered certain.

Proctor v. Pool, 15 N.C., 370, 373 (1833).

We have reviewed our appellate jurisprudence addressing challenges to the validity of the identification of property described in documents such as a deed, deed of trust, or contract for the sale of property, and observe that our Courts have generally affirmed the validity of such documents when it is possible to ascertain the identity of the subject property. For example, in *Carson v. Ray*, 52 N.C. 609, 609 (1860), our Supreme Court upheld as valid a deed in which the grantor agreed to transfer "my house and lot in the town of Jefferson, in Ashe County, North Carolina." The Court noted that "there was no evidence that the grantor owned any other house and lot" in Jefferson, and that the deed presented only a latent ambiguity. Similarly, in *Gilbert v. Wright*, supra, our Supreme Court upheld an order of the lower court ordering specific performance of a contract to sell "the vacant lot" on the grounds that the other documents and the factual circumstances associated with the transaction clearly identified a specific vacant lot.

Where a document that constitutes part of the transfer of property, such as a deed or deed of trust, describes the property in a manner that is uncertain or contains an error, our appellate courts generally have upheld the decision of a trial court to admit extrinsic evidence derived from sources referred to in the challenged document, in order to establish with greater certainty the identity of the subject property. Thus, in *Taylor v. Bailey*, 34 N.C. App. 290, 237 S.E.2d 918 (1977), this Court upheld an order by the trial court granting specific performance of a contract for the sale of property. The contract erroneously described the property as being located in Buncombe County, rather than giving its correct location in Henderson County. We held that this discrepancy created only a latent ambiguity:

> Defendant argues that the description before us for construction is clearly patently ambiguous. We cannot agree. True, there is no metes and bounds description. However, the description gives the acreage and refers to a deed of trust, naming the parties and the date thereof, in which the land is described with particularity. This is adequate to satisfy the "something extrinsic by which identification might possibly be made." Further, the complaint locates the property in Henderson County.

Taylor, 34 N.C. App. at 292, 237 S.E.2d at 919. In *River Birch*, supra, our Supreme Court held that "the trial court incorrectly excluded evidence of the preliminary plat for the purpose of resolving a latent ambiguity in the identity of the common area referred to in the covenants." *River Birch*, 326 N.C. at 126, 388 S.E.2d at 553. And, in *Tomika Invs., Inc. v. Macedonia True Vine Pent. Holiness Ch. of God, Inc.*, 136 N.C. App. 493, 524 S.E.2d 591 (2000), the defendant claimed that the subject deed was void because of the misstatement of the name of one of the parties. This Court held that "there is only a latent ambiguity in the deed" that did not render the deed void. *Tomika*, 136 N.C. App. at 497, 524 S.E.2d at 594.

Applying the principles discussed above to the present case, we conclude that the erroneous reference in the Deed of Trust to "Section II-C" instead of "Section III-C" is merely a scrivener's error and creates only a latent ambiguity in the description of the property. This uncertainty may be remedied by examination of the four corners of the Deed of Trust and documents referenced therein. The Deed of Trust identifies the property as Lot 46 of a subdivision depicted on a plat "prepared by Parker & Associates, Inc., dated August 3, 2006 and recorded in Map Book 51, Page 149, Slide L-1485, Onslow County Registry." This plat correctly identifies Lot 46 as being located in "Section III-C." In addition, the Deed of Trust identifies the property with a street address and tax parcel ID number, both of which correspond to the information in the General Warranty Deed and the plat. Upon examination of the information in the record, in the context of the long-established jurisprudence on this subject, we conclude that the erroneous reference to "Section II-C" in the Deed of Trust did not render the document void and that the trial court did not err by allowing the foreclosure to go forward.

In their arguments seeking a contrary result, the Thompsons do not acknowledge that extrinsic evidence may be utilized to clarify a latent ambiguity and do not discuss the law on this issue or make any attempt to distinguish cases such as those cited above. Instead, the Thompsons cite cases that, although they may involve a deed of trust or the transfer of property, do not address in any respect the principles discussed in this opinion. We conclude that the Thompsons have failed to establish that the trial court erred or that they are entitled to relief on appeal. Accordingly, we conclude that the trial court's order should be

AFFIRMED.

Judges BRYANT and INMAN concur.

QUESTIONS ABOUT THE CASE

1   What is the Thompsons' allegation about whether the trustee held valid legal title to the property and how this impacted the subsequent foreclosure?
2   What provision gives a trustee the power to conduct a foreclosure?
3   What basic steps are required by the trustee in order to carry out a foreclosure on a deed of trust? Were these steps followed in this case?
4   What is the invalid property description referred to by the Thompsons, and does this court believe that this description is sufficient to cancel the foreclosure?

 COVID-19 CONCERN

In order to create a valid legal description, a surveyor is called upon to visit the property. While there, they will measure and find precise directions. This will take place outside of the home. However, several inspections must take place inside the home. With potential COVID exposure in mind, will inspections move towards intermediary steps? We know that drones are in heavy use in almost all industries; why not in real estate inspections, too? Some drones are small enough to easily fly inside a home. Does it make more sense — from considerations of both biological exposure and time required — to use more technology in carrying out inspections of heating and air-conditioning units, roof structures and foundations, and similar systems? One could argue that technology has already crept into these procedures through the use of thermal cameras, "septic cameras," and other technology that allows inspectors to see things that they couldn't unaided.

CHAPTER SUMMARY

One of the most important aspects of real property is the ability to identify a particular parcel that is being transferred. Property descriptions are a way to show how a tract of real property is specific and unique. In this chapter, we have seen that there are several methods used in the United States to describe real property, including the use of metes and bounds descriptions to describe property boundaries. A metes and bounds description is a listing of the distance and direction of each of the boundary lines such that any described parcel may be drawn precisely.

There are many rights that arise directly from ownership of real estate. Among these rights are riparian, or water, rights. Water rights not only include the ability to draw water for use, but they also define how a property's boundaries may change over time by the natural forces that water exerts on the land. Through erosion, accretion, avulsion, or reliction, a landowner's property boundaries may change.

SKILLS YOU NEED IN THE REAL WORLD

Drawing Property Descriptions

In this chapter, we have discussed in detail the various methods used to adequately describe property. We have seen, for instance, that adequate property descriptions are not only a good way of confirming which tract is actually being sold but are also required by state law. This brings us to the issue of learning how to actually prepare written drawings of metes and bounds and other property descriptions. Why would a legal professional need this skill? There will be times, it is true, when you can simply locate a plat or other pre-existing drawing and compare it to the written description for accuracy. However, there are many lots that have never been surveyed and for which there are no maps. In those situations, the only way to be sure that the property boundary makes sense — and that there are no gaps in the description — is to actually draw it out yourself. Once you have acquired the skill, you will find that it comes in handy in many other situations as well. For instance, if you can hand-draw a property description, you can actually make your own drawing and compare it to questionable surveys. Learning how to draw property descriptions is an important skill for any legal professional who specializes in real estate law.

ETHICAL ISSUES FOR THE PARALEGAL

Confidentiality

A thorough understanding of ethical rules is important no matter what area of law you specialize in; however, there is sometimes a temptation to think that real estate practice does not raise many ethical considerations. Nothing could be further from the truth. Attorneys owe their clients confidentiality. That means that a client can expect that private conversations with his or her attorney will not be repeated to others. Confidentiality is one of the core ethical concerns for any legal practitioner, but is confidentiality really all that important in a real estate transaction? Absolutely. Suppose you have a client who is planning to buy several large tracts of land to construct a shopping center. If news of this project leaks out of the law office, the client's plans could be jeopardized. Local owners may unrealistically increase their sale prices, causing the entire project to fail. You should always keep client communications secret.

This means not discussing client business with anyone outside the firm — not other legal professionals, not the friendly people at the land office, not even family members.

Confidentiality is not only required by both paralegal and attorney ethical codes, but a violation of confidential communications might also result in a legal malpractice action against the firm.

KEY TERMS AND CONCEPTS

Accretion	Navigable water	Reliction
Avulsion	Non-navigable water	Riparian rights
Erosion	Parol evidence	
Latently ambiguous	Patently ambiguous	

END-OF-CHAPTER EXERCISES

Review Questions

See Appendix for answers.

1 Why is it important to have an accurate property description for a real estate transaction?
2 Explain the difference between identifying real property and identifying personal property in a sale.
3 Describe the history of surveying real estate property boundaries.
4 What are the two critical elements of a property description?
5 Why is street address not sufficient to describe a parcel of real estate?
6 Explain the legal requirements for property descriptions in a deed.
7 What types of documents can a legal description refer to in creating a valid legal description?
8 What are patently ambiguous property descriptions?
9 What are latently ambiguous property descriptions?
10 What is the parol evidence rule, and how does it apply to patently ambiguous and latently ambiguous property descriptions?
11 What is a metes and bounds description?
12 How long is a "rod"? How long is a "chain"?
13 What equipment do you need to draw a metes and bounds description?
14 What is a tract-indexing system?
15 What is a plat?
16 What is the Torrens registration system?
17 What are riparian rights?
18 Describe the natural forces that can affect property boundaries.
19 Compare and contrast accretion with erosion.
20 Explain the significance of this chapter's case excerpt.

DISCUSSION QUESTIONS

1   Given that metes and bounds descriptions have been around for centuries, is there a better or more preferable way of describing property? If you had the power to change the law, how would you?

2   In the age of GPS, should all other property descriptions be abandoned for GPS grid references? Why or why not?

APPLYING WHAT YOU HAVE LEARNED

1   Based on what you have learned about the various methods used to describe real property, should all states be required to follow the same system? If so, which system would you advocate?

2   For the following exercises, you will need a circular land measure compass and a regular straight ruler. Place the compass center point over the P.O.B., with north always facing the top of the page. Turn the dial to the desired direction, and mark that point with a pencil. Using your straight ruler, measure the corresponding inches from the P.O.B. along the direction indicated. Remember, for purposes of this exercise, our conversion is 1 inch equals 100 ft. Draw the following metes and bounds descriptions:

    a   Beginning at a point on the southwest corner of the lot, then proceeding due North 400 feet to a point, then due East 90 degrees 400 feet to a point, then due South 400 feet to a point, then due West 400 feet to the P.O.B.

    b   Beginning at a point on the southwest corner of the lot, then North 60 degrees East 200 feet to a point, then South 85 degrees East 300 feet to a point, then South 25 degrees East 300 feet to a point, then South 60 degrees West 200 feet to a point, then North 50 degrees West 550 feet to the P.O.B.

    c   Beginning at a point on the north side of the property, South 52 degrees East 250 feet to a point, then South 30 degrees West 250 feet, then South 68 degrees West 300 feet to a point, then North 90 degrees 40 feet to a point, then North 65 degrees East 200 feet to a point, then North 9 degrees West 150 feet to a point, then North 52 degrees West 100 feet to a point, then North 41 degrees East 200 feet to the P.O.B.

WEB SURFING

Patently Ambiguous Descriptions: U.S. Supreme Court Case
http://www.law.cornell.edu/supremecourt/text/355/554

Metes and Bounds Descriptions Video: Youtube.com
http://www.youtube.com/watch?v=kjCdSUOPWs4

California Division of Water Rights
http://www.swrcb.ca.gov/waterrights

Tech Topic
SOFTWARE THAT DRAWS METES AND BOUNDS DESCRIPTIONS FOR YOU

For some time, there have been programs that can translate the words of a metes and bounds description and translate them into a drawing. If you have tried making a hand-drawing of a metes and bounds description using only a compass, a ruler, and a pencil, then you know how difficult creating such drawings can be. But there are now robust software packages out there that can do the heaving lifting for you.

For example, there is the aptly named "metes and bounds" that not only can create a basic drawing of a metes and bounds description, it can also calculate square feet and square acres. It will accept measurements in feet, or the older versions of rods, and even meters. A quick Internet search will also reveal several other quality software programs that are capable of doing the same thing.

ANNOTATED DOCUMENT

Metes and Bounds Description

This deed, made this the 21st day of June, 1991, by and between Elizabeth Wilson, widow, the grantor, and Gary Brown, the grantee, of 1001 Maple Street, Anywhere.

That the grantor, for valuable consideration paid by the grantee, the receipt of which is hereby acknowledged, has and by these presents does grant, bargain, sell, and convey on to the grantee in fee simple, all that certain lot or parcel of land situated in Anywhere Township, State of Placid, and more particularly described as follows:

"Adjoining the lands of Eric Siegel, Ernest Bovine, and Edward White, and beginning at an iron stake in the West side of a Street, said stake being located 249.91 feet South 1° five minutes West from the iron stake at the Ernest Bovine corner in the edge of said street and running North 76° 32 minutes West for 595.11 feet along the line on the Ernest Bovine property to an iron stake in Eric Siegel's line; thence South 8° 42 minutes West for 150 feet along the Eric Siegel line to an iron stake; thence South 77° 15 minutes East for 361 feet to a post; thence South 80° East for 252.5 feet to a stake in the edge of said street; thence North 1° five minutes East for 130 feet to the beginning, and containing 1.96 acres, more or less."

Metes and bounds descriptions always provide a point of beginning ("249.91 feet South 1° five minutes West").

Property boundaries are described by distance and direction ("running North"; "minutes West").

Metes and bounds descriptions usually provide total acreage ("1.96 acres").

PRACTICE QUESTIONS FOR TEST REVIEW

See Appendix for answers.

Essay

List and describe the natural forces that affect property boundaries.

True–False

1   T   F   Describing property boundaries is a relatively recent phenomenon.

2   T   F   A patently ambiguous property description is not valid.

3   T   F   Plats and deeds are the same thing.

Fill in the Blank

1   A court will rule that this type of property description is so vague that a deed containing it cannot be legally valid: _____.

2   In limited circumstance, courts may allow oral testimony to assist in proving a deed. This oral testimony is called:_____.

3   In the original North American colonies and then, later, in the early United States, this method was used almost exclusively to describe the boundaries of real estate:_____.

Multiple Choice

1   The society that first institutionalized the use of property descriptions to track property boundaries.

    A   The Ancient Romans
    B   The Etruscans
    C   The Cappadocians
    D   The Ancient Egyptians

2   Which of the following is not an element of a legally valid property description?

    A   It must sufficiently describe the property in the deed.
    B   It must make reference to other documents that sufficiently describe the property.
    C   It must refer to the owners' mental capacity.
    D   All of the above are elements of a legally valid deed.

3   At what point in time is a property description evaluated for legal validity?

    A   When it is written.
    B   When it is recorded.
    C   When the property is assessed for taxes.
    D   When the property is sold to the government.

ENDNOTES

[1] Adapted from *Wolfe v. Villines*, 610 S.E.2d 754 (N.C. Ct. App. 2005).
[2] *Resort Development Co. v. Phillips*, 278 N.C. 69, 178 S.E.2d 813 (1971).
[3] S.C. Code Ann. §30-5-10.

Transferring Title to Real Estate

Chapter Objectives

▪ Distinguish between voluntary transfers and involuntary transfers of title in real estate

▪ Explain the basic requirements of a will

▪ Compare and contrast dedication and homesteading as a means to transfer real estate title

▪ Explain foreclosure

▪ List and explain the elements of adverse possession

Chapter Outline

I. Introduction

II. Voluntary Transfers of Title
   A. Sale
   B. Will (Probate)
   C. Gift
   D. Dedication
   E. Homesteading

III. Involuntary Transfers of Title
   A. Foreclosure
   B. Eminent Domain (Condemnation)
   C. Partition
   D. Escheat
   E. Civil Judgment
   F. Adverse Possession
   G. Tax Auctions

INTRODUCTION

In this chapter, we will examine the various ways that title to property can be transferred, both voluntarily and involuntarily. Under the category of voluntary transfers, there are sales, wills, gifts, and other means. Involuntary transfers include foreclosure of property rights by a mortgage lender, seizure of property by governmental action through eminent domain, partition of the property, and loss of property rights through adverse possession.

VOLUNTARY TRANSFERS OF TITLE

In this section, we will examine the various ways that a property owner can use to voluntarily transfer property rights to others. The methods are listed from the most frequently to the least frequently used. Sale of property is by far the most common way of voluntarily transferring title.

A. SALE

When a property owner has title to the property, she is entitled to sell that title to anyone else. In its most basic state, the sale of real property is similar to the sale of personal property. The current owner surrenders title in exchange for something of value, usually money. The purchaser acquires title in exchange for surrendering the purchase price to the previous owner. It is tempting, then, to think that the sale of real property resembles the sale of personal property in other ways, but that approach would be incorrect. There are important and fundamental differences between real and personal property, as becomes evident when we consider how title to each is transferred.

REAL
ESTATE
BASICS AT
A GLANCE

Sale is the most common form of voluntary title transfer in real estate.

1. THE DIFFERENCES BETWEEN SALE OF PERSONAL PROPERTY AND SALE OF REAL PROPERTY

In personal property, one of the best indicators of ownership is possession. The old rule, which we have all heard in one context or another, that "possession is nine-tenths of the law," applies only to personal property, not real property. This rule, an old common law principle, guided courts in determining the ownership of diverse types of personal property, especially property that could not readily be identified. However, ownership of real property has always been characterized differently. The reason for the different approach to ownership — and the transfer of ownership rights — in real property probably stems from several critical factors. For one thing, land has often been a source of wealth. It certainly was the basis of the early English system of patronage between king and subjects. But the significance of land title has survived the societies that created it. Land continues to be an important source of revenue and obligation in modern society. For most people, purchase of the family home is still their largest financial undertaking (though recent data from the U.S. Census Bureau shows a downward trend in homeownership in recent years, as seen in Figure 4-1).

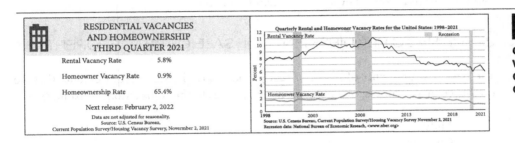

FIGURE 4-1

Quarterly Residential Vacancies and Home Ownership, Third Quarter 2021

Historically, the procedures involved in transferring title to land also followed different, more rigid controls than those used to transfer title to personal property. Although this is not a history lesson on the development of real property issues, it is interesting to note that there is an entire body of both English and American law concerning the procedures used to transfer real estate title, including "*seizin*," "fee," and other terms that we will return to in Chapter 8 when we address the concept of real estate deeds.

The issue of the many important differences between real property and personal property transactions comes up again and again in issues as diverse as the creation of real estate deeds (Chapter 8), financing real estate purchases (Chapter 9), and the public and private limitations on the way that real property can be used (Chapter 10). Having said this, however, it is interesting to note that the preliminary requirements for the sale of real property are as straightforward as those for the sale of personal property.

The original American colonies were all conveyed by the government of England to one or more individuals. The usual form of this conveyance was by royal charter. These charters gave the residents specific rights to use and to convey the property to others, subject to certain conditions, such as regular tax payments to the king. Then the Declaration of Independence and the subsequent Revolutionary War severed all ties between the colonies and England. This raised an interesting question: If the original authority to hold land in the colonies arose from the king's permission, what was the source of authority after the American Revolution? The colonies generally adopted an approach that simply substituted the state for the king and made property ownership subject to the power of the new American state governments. For states that came into existence after the Revolution, a different system of property authority developed. In many areas, it was the federal government — not individual state governments — that

had original ownership of the land. This ownership may have derived from purchase from foreign governments, negotiation with Indian tribes, or simple assertion of a claim to vast tracts of land.

A question often arises when discussing the sales of real estate: Why should we be concerned about the original source of title for a particular parcel? The original source of title is important because of an ancient principle in real estate law. A person can only receive the quality of title that the previous owner possessed. In other areas of law, a purchaser may actually improve the quality of their title when the purchaser can show that the property was acquired under certain circumstances. However, that is not the case with real property. The quality of title of the new owner derives from the previous owner, and so on, until the original grant of title. If that title had defects, those defects haunt the transactions of every subsequent purchaser.

2. THE BASIC REQUIREMENTS OF SALE OF REAL PROPERTY

The basic requirements of a sale of real property are the same requirements that we might see in any contractual obligation. The parties to the transactions must have:

- Mutual assent
- Consideration
- Capacity
- Property description

REAL
ESTATE
BASICS AT
A GLANCE

A sale is a contract between buyers and sellers and must therefore meet all legal requirements of a contract.

---

a. Mutual Assent

Mutual assent is a contract law element that requires that both parties to the contract know and understand the material features of the contract. For instance, both the buyer and the seller must be in agreement about the property that is the subject of the transaction. Each must understand that they are undertaking a legal obligation.

b. Consideration

Consideration is a requirement for most types of contracts, including the sale of real property. Consideration is often referred to as "bargained-for exchange." This is a legal requirement that both parties to the transaction have a stake in the outcome. Seller A is surrendering something of value in exchange for receiving something else of value. In a typical real estate transaction, Seller A is surrendering title to the property in exchange for money. Buyer B is surrendering money in exchange for title to the property. This exchange would seem to be a given in any contract, so why do all jurisdictions require consideration as an element? Consideration has more to do with enforcing the contract than proving that one existed. If one party to the contract neither gives up nor receives anything of value, how can she truly be said to be bound? Exchange is the core issue in any contract, and if one party does not give or receive, how would the contract be enforced? What recourse would the court have in ordering the party to conform to the details of the agreement if the party has no obligations? We will return to the topic of consideration in several other contexts throughout this book, both in drafting real estate contracts (Chapter 6) and the importance of consideration in deeds (Chapter 8).

c. Capacity

Another requirement of any contractual agreement is that all parties to the transaction have legal capacity to enter into a transaction. **Capacity** refers to the party's ability to know and understand the consequences of entering into a legal contract. Persons who lack capacity cannot become parties to a binding contract. Examples of persons who lack capacity include:

Capacity
The ability to know and understand the consequences of entering a legally binding agreement.

- Infants
- Intoxicated persons
- Mentally incompetent persons

i. Infants
At law, an infant is anyone under the age of 18. Contracts cannot be enforced against children. When a party to a contract is revealed to be underage, the court is authorized to void the contract and return the parties to the positions they were in before the contract was created.

ii. Intoxicated Persons
If a person can show that she was under the influence of alcohol or some other drug at the time that a contract was created, the court is authorized to void the contract in much the same way that the court can when a party is underage. Here, **intoxication** refers to a state in which a person is so under the influence that she could not understand the consequences of the obligation. Intoxication does not simply mean that a person had had something to drink. Instead, a person must be intoxicated to the point that she could not form the mental state necessary to enter into a contract.

Intoxication
A state in which a person suffers from the effects of alcohol or other drug to the point that he or she is unable to comprehend the legal obligations of entering into a legally binding agreement.

iii. Mentally Incompetent Persons
A person who suffers from a mental or physical condition that makes it impossible for her to understand the legal obligations imposed by a contract cannot be a party to a contract. In some cases, a court may have declared that a specific person was mentally incompetent and appointed a guardian to handle all of this person's affairs. In other situations, the person may be deemed mentally incompetent after the contract has been created. In such a case, a court would be authorized to void the contract and refuse to enforce it against the mentally incompetent person.

d. Property Description

The previous three requirements of a binding real estate contract have all focused on the capacity of the parties, something required in all contract proceedings. However, this last element is unique to real property: adequate property description. As we saw in the previous chapter, adequate property description is something more than a mere street address. Whether a particular state uses metes and bounds descriptions, plats, tracts, or surveys, it is absolutely essential that the contract set out a specific, unique, and identifiable parcel of real estate as the subject of the real estate contract.

EXAMPLE 4-1	Cory writes out the following document and hands it to Raul:

"I hereby sell to you that parcel of land known as my house, Anytown, USA. The price for this sale is your continued friendship.
"Signed: Cory, age 12
"Signed: Raul, age 12"

Is this a valid real estate transaction?

Answer: No. We can attack this transaction on several grounds. First, there is no consideration for the sale. "Continued friendship" sounds very nice, but most courts would not recognize it as a legal finding of consideration. Even if the court were tempted to rule that consideration exists, there is another problem: The property description is hopelessly vague. Added to that, there is the issue of infancy. Both the "buyer" and the "seller" are under the legal age to carry out such a transaction. What changes to the details would result in a valid transaction?

Tech Topic
ADOBE ACROBAT AND PDF FILE

Although many people use Adobe Acrobat to transfer documents in portable document format (PDF), law firms have not been as active in this area as many other professions. Many law firms continue to complete document-preparation tasks using programs like Microsoft Word and do not use PDFs as often as one might think.

For example, it is quite common for state-approved sales contracts to be made available in both Word and PDF. PDFs can be created through either saving a word processing file as a PDF or scanning a physical document to a digital PDF. In either case, the result is a universally readable PDF document. It is only in the last few years that attorneys have been taking advantage of this file format to decrease their paper load and streamline many of the document-related tasks that are so time-consuming to complete by hand.

Bates numbering (also called "Bates labeling," "Bates coding," "Bates stamping," and "Bates branding"), for example, has long been used to assign a unique numerical or alphanumerical identifier to each page of a legal document. Traditionally, this was accomplished by means of a physical stamp applied to each page; more recently, preprinted Bates labels were stuck by hand onto the pages of a document. Adobe Acrobat, however, allows the process to be completed electronically, with a few clicks of the mouse applying Bates numbering to all desired pages of a document, or even a group of documents. For additional security in more sensitive documents, there are safeguards that can be applied to a document in Adobe Acrobat to ensure that no changes are made to the Bates numbering once it has been applied.

What about occasions when information in a document needs to be redacted? It is no longer necessary to attack each page with a black pen; instead, Adobe Acrobat allows its users to use the Redact tool to hide any information that must remain private. This process can usually be accomplished fairly quickly even in long documents through searching the document for key words and phrases (although it should be noted that the Find Text tool does not work in secured or encrypted PDFs). The user also has the option of leaving the redacted area blank or covering it with a colored (usually black) box.

There may also be situations in which a PDF needs to be edited. Adobe Acrobat features an Optical Character Recognition (OCR) tool that allows most PDFs to have their text edited without the need for a word processing program — though it should be noted that the effectiveness of the OCR tool depends heavily upon the clarity of the PDF's text and functions best when the PDF was created via a word processing program rather than a scanner. In an ideal situation, the OCR tool scans the document and converts the image of the text into actual editable text, which prevents the need to return to the original file and start from scratch when just a few words here or there need to be changed.

Adobe Acrobat has many more uses for attorneys and law firms, and it is rapidly becoming a popular software among the legal community.

REAL WORLD PERSPECTIVES: *REAL ESTATE PARALEGAL*

The most important attribute for a paralegal who works in real estate is attention to detail. That is critical. You have to have it set up like a checklist so that you can monitor every step of process and make sure that everything is done correctly. You have to have all the pieces of the puzzle, and that's frustrating. Because it's not always possible to bring all the pieces together in the way that you want at the time that you want. Sometimes the lender is slow getting you what you need. Sometimes the seller is slow on signing and returning the paperwork. At any given time, I might be working on 5, 10, or even 15 different closings, all of them at different stages. Closing dates become more of a suggestion than a hard and fast deadline. Closings are constantly being rescheduled.

— S.C., real estate paralegal

B. WILL (PROBATE)

Determining whether a transaction is by sale or by will is important because the two transactions have such different elements. Sales, as we have seen, are primarily based on contract law. Transfer by will, on the other hand, must meet all the minimum requirements of any testamentary document. We will discuss those minimum requirements in the next few sections, but we must first address a more fundamental question: What is the difference between a sale and a disposition through a will? The question seems so basic as to require little thought to answer it: A sale is a voluntary transaction between living parties; a will is a document that disposes of property after the owner's death. However, in the practical world of real estate transactions, it isn't always so easy to distinguish one from the other.

REAL ESTATE BASICS AT A GLANCE

The ability to leave property to one's heirs is considered an important right for all citizens.

1. THE MINIMUM REQUIREMENTS OF A WILL

Before any property can be passed through a will, the document itself must meet some basic requirements. For instance, it must:

- Be in writing
- Be signed by the testator
- Be witnessed
- Be signed by the testator
- Clearly express the testator's state of mind
- Clearly devise property to a specific beneficiary

a. The Will Must Be in Writing

Wills must be in writing. This has been a requirement of both English and American law for centuries. The Statute of Frauds specifically states the requirement for written wills and provides that an unwritten will cannot be enforced. However, the statute is not specific about what constitutes a "writing," and this has spawned thousands of cases addressing exactly what is—and what is not—a written document. This is a discussion that could easily take up a chapter in itself. We will sidestep the issue here by simply stating that a will must be in writing and that "a writing" refers to ink on paper, either typed or handwritten.

b. The Will Must Be Signed by the Testator

The testator's signature on a will has been a staple of American law for centuries. The original English Statute of Frauds required wills to be in writing, and that statute was

Sidebar

Traditionally, sales were classified as inter vivos (Latin for "between the living") as a way of distinguishing these transactions from testamentary transactions, which only take effect after the property owner dies.

adopted by the American colonies and later by all states in the Union. The signature requirement remains the law of the land today. However, there are some interesting features under the law about what actually constitutes a signature. For instance, many states still allow a person to sign a will with a mark, such as a fingerprint, instead of a handwritten signature. Many states also have provisions that allow another person to sign for the testator, such as when the testator is too ill to sign for himself. In those situations, the person must be acting under the direction of the testator and the signing must be done in the testator's presence. [2]

Although we have said that wills must be in writing, there is a narrow exception that allows oral wills to be probated. A **nuncupative will** is an oral declaration by a testator, usually made shortly before death, before witnesses, about the disposition of her property. Such wills were drastically limited under the Statute of Frauds and usually have strict requirements, such as that three witnesses hear the testator's oral declaration and that the declaration be made when the testator knows death is imminent. Some states also impose a third requirement: that the statement be made inside the testator's home.[3] As a result of these strict requirements, nuncupative wills are rarely presented for probate.

Nuncupative will
An oral will, usually only permitted when the testator is in the last stages of life and is unable to draft a written will.

c. The Will Must Be Witnessed

When the testator creates a will, all states require that her signature and acknowledgment of the will be witnessed, although there is a split about whether the witnesses must actually see the testator sign the document or even whether they need to know that the document they are witnessing is actually a will. The function of witnesses is obvious: They can testify about the testator's state of mind at the precise moment that the testator signed the will. If the testator was not mentally competent, witnesses could testify to this fact. In some states, the testator must specifically announce that the document is her "last will and testament." This is referred to as **publication** of the will.

In some situations, the witness requirement for a will can be waived. One such instance is a **holographic will**. A holographic will is one that the testator writes out in her own handwriting and signs. Such a will can be considered valid, even if it is not witnessed.

Publication
The announcement by a testator to witnesses that she has created a will and wishes to have it witnessed.

Holographic will
A will written entirely in the testator's handwriting.

There are many different types of wills and their legal requirements differ greatly from those required in a contract for sale of real property.

REAL ESTATE BASICS AT A GLANCE

ANTHONY'S CANCER

EXAMPLE 4-2

Anthony has been diagnosed with inoperable cancer and has only a few months to live. He makes an audio recording at home one night, when he is all alone, that states his clear intention to leave all his property, both real and personal, to his brother Michael. On the tape, he acknowledges that he is making the transaction because he knows that he is dying. He seals the tape in an envelope that bears the typed message: "Open in the event of my death."

Is this a valid will?

Answer: If the minimum requirements of a will are that it be the stated intention of the decedent, witnessed by others, this audio tape does not meet that standard. Anthony's statement made in the presence of others shortly before his death would qualify as a nuncupative will, but that is not the case here. Anthony's recording was not made in front of others, and it was not made shortly before his death. The writing on the outside of the envelope also does not help the situation. Those words were typed, and there is no signature. The audio tape is not a will.

d. The Will Must Clearly Express the Testator's State of Mind

In addition to being written, signed, and witnessed, a will must also express the testator's mental status. If a person is suffering from some form of mental or physical impairment that renders her incapable of understanding the significance of creating a will, the resulting document is void. Courts will not enforce a will drafted by a person who is mentally incompetent — or drafted by someone else under the testator's direction. This is one reason for the famous phrase found in wills, "I, _____, being of sound mind . . . ." Although this statement is not dispositive of the issue of mental competence, it does point out the significance of the testator's state of mind when the will is executed.

e. The Will Must Clearly Devise Property to a Specific Beneficiary

Devise
To transfer property in a will.

Beneficiary
A person named in a will that the testator intends to receive an interest in property.

Devisee
Another term for beneficiary.

Wills often **devise** (award) property. When a will devises property to a specific person, the person who receives the property is the **beneficiary** or **devisee**. Although there are many technical rules surrounding who may receive property (and in what amount) under a will, the general rules are simple: The beneficiary must be someone who is clearly identifiable and who can be located. There is no requirement that the testator actually identify the beneficiary by name, although that is obviously the best practice. A testator could, for instance, leave property to "my sister's children." Under this clause, any children of the testator's sister alive at the time that the testator dies would be entitled to receive a portion of the estate. However, problems occur in devising the property if it turns out that the testator has more than one sister or if her sister has no children. This is one reason why it is so important to draft a will carefully. Attention to detail in specifying beneficiaries can forestall many problems later on.

2. WILLS VERSUS SALES

Although the differences between wills and sales seem obvious, it is important to summarize those differences. The most common differences focus on the nature of the rights conferred on others. Deeds transfer immediate present interests; wills transfer future interests. A present interest is a party's right to enter the land immediately and begin using the land. Wills, by their very nature, cannot transfer present interests. Instead, they transfer future interests. In a will, the beneficiary has a future right to property that will only become a present interest when a specific condition occurs, namely the death of the owner.[4]

Consider the situation in Example 4-3.

FRANCESCA'S DEED

Francesca owns a house that sits on three acres. She agrees to sell her property to her son, Darrell, for $10,000. She writes out a deed with the following provisions: "To my son, Darrell. To take effect on my death."

Is this a sale or transfer through testate proceeding?

Answer: If this is a sale, what present right has Darrell received? He does not have the immediate right to take possession of the property. In fact, his right is not triggered until his mother's death. However, if this is a will, it fails to meet the basic legal requirements for such a document.

When faced with the difficulties inherent in such transactions, courts have come up with some basic guidelines. For instance, when there is any ambiguity about what kind of transaction is involved, the courts will opt for an interpretation that the document is a deed instead of a will. The simple reason for this guideline is that it is easier to meet the minimum requirements of a deed than of a will. The other reason for this interpretation is that most such cases arise with documents that the parties themselves consider to be deeds, not wills.[5]

3. DIFFERENT METHODS USED TO TRANSFER TITLE THROUGH WILLS

Testators may transfer rights to property in many ways. Because this book does not address the complexity of probate issues, we focus on only two of the most common methods: intestate transfer and testate transfer.

a. Intestate Succession

In situations in which the owner of property dies without a will, they are said to have died **intestate**. Persons who die intestate do not leave any instructions about how their property should be divided among their heirs. In this situation, the probate court will appoint an administrator, who disperses the property based on intestacy statutes. These statutes provide that the decedent's closest heirs, such as their spouse and children, should receive the estate. In situations in which the decedent has no close relatives, the statutes also dictate the share that the decedent's heirs should receive after the estate is settled.

Intestate
The term for a person who dies without a will.

A person who dies with a will is said to have died testate; a person who dies without a will is said to have died intestate.

REAL ESTATE BASICS AT A GLANCE

---

b. Testate Succession

When a person dies after having created a will, and that will is judged to be legally sufficient, they are said to have died **testate**. In such a situation, courts will work to carry out the testator's intentions in regard to the transfer of her property.

Testate
The term for a person who drafts a valid will before dying.

C. GIFT

A property owner is always free to give property away, assuming that there is no outstanding mortgage or other indebtedness on the property. If there is such an indebtedness, a court may void the transaction, especially if it appears that the transaction was specifically designed to avoid claims raised by creditors. In situations in which a valid gift of real property has occurred, the recipient may also have tax issues to consider. The value of the property may be considered as a gain for purposes of calculating yearly income tax.

D. DEDICATION

Dedication
A grant of private land to the government.

When land is transferred by **dedication**, it means that the owner has given the land over to the government for a specific use. One of the most common uses of dedicated land is for public parks, playgrounds, or recreation areas.[6] Dedication is a term that is reserved for a donation of land to the government, not transfers made to religious groups or charities. In those situations, the transfer is normally seen as a gift. Dedication is a process used to provide land for public use, not for private individuals, societies, or institutions.

E. HOMESTEADING

In some areas of the country where there is an abundance of land but relatively few people, some states still use a system of awarding land rights to homesteaders. Under this system, which became popular in the late 1800s and early 1900s, a family could claim up to 160 acres of land by simply taking possession of it, residing there, and working the land as a farm. Most states have done away with this system, but it still exists in the less populous states. A homesteader must claim her 160 acres from government-owned land. Homesteading is not a means for one person to usurp property rights held by another.

INVOLUNTARY TRANSFERS OF TITLE

So far, our discussion has focused on voluntary transfers of title interests in real property. However, there are many transactions in which a person's rights to property may be taken away involuntarily. These methods include:

- Foreclosure
- Eminent domain (condemnation)
- Partition
- Escheat
- Civil judgment
- Adverse possession
- Tax auctions

A. FORECLOSURE

Although we will discuss financing real estate purchases in Chapter 9, it is important to note the process of **foreclosure** here. When a person buys real estate and finances that purchase, the lender will insist on a provision in the loan agreement that allows the lender to auction off the property in the event that the borrower fails to make regular payments on the loan. Foreclosure is an action brought by a lending institution or some other party who has received property interest as part of the financial arrangements to purchase real property. Foreclosure is usually the last resort of a lender who is no longer receiving monthly mortgage payments. Part of the paperwork involved in obtaining a mortgage involves transferring a right from the owner to a lending institution to foreclose as a means of protecting its interest in the property.

Foreclosure
The right of a lender (mortgagee) to initiate an action to auction off property for outstanding indebtedness in a mortgage or deed of trust.

Foreclosure is a legal remedy available to lenders to enforce the obligations in a mortgage.

REAL
ESTATE
BASICS AT
A GLANCE

The legal theories underlying foreclosure vary from state to state. In some states, for example, when a borrower defaults on the loan, legal title to the property passes to the lender. In other states, the foreclosure action is similar to a lien on the property that can only be foreclosed after judicial action. In still other states, where deeds of trust are common, the financial arrangement is more like a trust whereby a trustee has the right to foreclose on behalf of the lender.

There are generally two types of foreclosure proceedings used in the United States: judicial foreclosure and power of sale foreclosure.[7]

1. JUDICIAL FORECLOSURE

Judicial foreclosure is similar to any other legal action. In a judicial foreclosure, a party requests that a court enter an order divesting the borrower's rights to the property. Because many states have ruled that a judicial foreclosure that fails to abide by each statutory requirement is a void action, most lenders opt for power of sale foreclosure.

Judicial foreclosure
Foreclosure based on state statutes.

2. POWER OF SALE FORECLOSURE

Under **power of sale foreclosure**, a lender inserts a contract provision in the mortgage agreement that allows the lender to institute foreclosure actions when the borrower defaults on the loan. This procedure has the benefit of less judicial involvement and gives the lender more latitude in deciding when to bring the foreclosure action. In the next sections, we will examine the steps involved in bringing a power of sale foreclosure. The first step is to determine whether the lender has the right to foreclose.

Power of sale foreclosure
Foreclosure brought pursuant to a mortgage agreement.

a. The Right to Foreclose

The right to foreclose only becomes available when a borrower fails to meet one of the stipulations in the mortgage agreement. The most common stipulations in mortgage financing are that the borrower:

- Make regular monthly payments on the loan
- Insure the property
- Pay real estate taxes on the property
- Maintain the premises

Failure to meet one of these conditions is referred to as default, and it triggers the foreclosure procedure.

b. Default

Default
Violation of a contractual duty.

When a borrower fails to live up to the agreements in the mortgage, such as failing to make regular monthly payments on the loan, the borrower is considered to be in **default** on the loan. Default has a specific, legal connotation. When a borrower defaults, the lender has the right to initiate foreclosure action. In many ways, a borrower's default on a mortgage is similar to a party's failure to fulfill a contract provision. The lender has the right to cancel the mortgage in the same way that a contract party may sue to terminate a contract.

Mortgage agreements contain specific provisions detailing what actions constitute a default. The most common reason for a foreclosure is the failure to make payments on the loan. Banks often will attempt to work out some type of arrangement short of foreclosure. Foreclosure can be a costly proposition, and most lenders opt for it only as a last resort. As we will see in Chapter 9, a foreclosure is often seen as an error on the lender's part. Proper background checks and underwriting should have revealed the possibility that the borrower would go into foreclosure.

Although failure to make payments on the loan is the most common type of default, there are other situations that technically might qualify as a default. In the previous section, for example, we listed four general promises or stipulations that a borrower makes to the lender in the mortgage agreement.

A violation of any of these stipulations could result in a foreclosure action. For instance, if the borrower failed to obtain insurance on the property or failed to pay real estate taxes, the lender could initiate foreclosure proceedings. However, in the hard-headed world of residential mortgage lending, there are other, less drastic methods of dealing with these problems. The lender might take out an insurance policy on the residence and then bill the borrower for the premiums. The lender might also pay real estate taxes to keep the property from being auctioned off for back taxes, and then pass these charges on to the borrower.

c. Notice to the Borrower

Once the lender has decided that foreclosure is the only option, the first step in bringing the action is to notify the borrowers that they are in default and that a foreclosure action is about to commence. The purpose of notifying the borrower is to satisfy the elements of the mortgage that require the lender to accelerate the loan provisions. On default, the lender has the right to notify the borrower that the entire balance of the loan is now due. This is part of the acceleration clause found in most mortgages. Of course, if a borrower is having trouble making monthly mortgage payments, it is highly unlikely that she would be able to pay the entire loan balance. The notice to the borrower usually contains a specific date by which the borrower must pay the entire loan balance or foreclosure actions will begin.

d. Steps in Foreclosure

In states where a foreclosure action must be brought as a form of civil action, the lender must present the case to a judge. In order to bring a foreclosure action, the lender must prove the following elements:

- That the property owner owes a debt to the lender
- That the property owner has failed to make payments on that debt
- That the lender has the right to foreclose on the property

Once the lender has proven these three elements, the lender is entitled to a judicial order forcing foreclosure of the property. Although borrowers are usually permitted to attend this judicial hearing, there is very little room for the borrower to argue against foreclosure. When the judge makes a finding that the borrower is in default, the judge has no option except to order foreclosure of the property pursuant to the mortgage agreement.

The power of sale provision is authorized by statute and must be strictly complied with. These requirements vary from state to state but all have some of the same basic requirements, including:

- Providing notice provisions to the borrower
- Acceleration of the balance of the loan
- Posting the power of sale provision in the paper for a specific period of time
- Conducting an auction at the time and place stated in the posting

The first step in bringing a foreclosure action is for the lender to post the power of sale provision. This notice, a sample of which appears at the end of the chapter, is usually posted at the local courthouse and in the legal section of the local newspaper. Most states have provisions that require that the power of sale provision be published at least four weeks in a row before the foreclosure auction can be held.

e. The Foreclosure Auction

Once the preliminary steps in a foreclosure action have been completed, including publishing of the power of sale provision, the lender is authorized to auction off the property for the balance due on the loan. The actual auction process varies considerably from state to state. In some states, for example, foreclosure auctions can only be held on a specific day of the month, such as the first Tuesday. In other states, foreclosure auctions can occur on any regular business day. Because auctions have been subject to fraud in the past, many states limit their foreclosure auction procedures to specific times during regular business hours at specific locations. Common limitations on foreclosure actions include provisions that the lender must place the property for auction at the time stated in the advertised notice and at the location given in that notice. In many states, foreclosure auctions do not occur at the property location; they are held at the local courthouse.

f. The Right of Redemption

Because a typical foreclosure action is a form of contract proceedings, many states recognize that the borrower has a right of redemption. The right of redemption is the power of the borrower to purchase the property at the foreclosure auction or to pay off the loan balance prior to the auction to prevent foreclosure in the first place. In some states, the borrower's right to redeem the property is conclusively terminated when the property is sold to another at the foreclosure auction. Other states allow a redemption period that follows the sale. This redemption period, which can be as long as 10 business days, allows the borrower the right to redeem the property from the auction purchaser.

Courts have not always recognized the right of a borrower to redeem the property. Historically, default on a mortgage loan was enough to authorize foreclosure and immediate seizure of the property. Another way of defining foreclosure is to say that the foreclosure action terminates the borrower's right to redeem the property.[8]

g. Purchasing Property at a Foreclosure Sale

The process of purchasing property at a foreclosure sale is another area that varies considerably from state to state. However, there are some common elements found in all foreclosure auctions. The procedure involved in beginning the auction is usually straightforward: The lender or lender's representative reads the power of sale provision aloud and then opens bidding on the property. The lender has a standing bid for the balance owed on the mortgage. If no one appears to bid for the property at the foreclosure sale, the lender automatically becomes the winning bidder and receives title to the property. Lenders do not wish for this to happen. Taking over title to a property means that the lender now has the responsibility to maintain the premises, to pay taxes on it, and also to arrange for its sale. In many respects, it is easier for the lender when someone appears at the auction and bids on the property.

When a person bids on property at a foreclosure sale, their bid must be higher than the standing bid that the lender has on the property. Suppose that a particular property has an $80,000 mortgage outstanding and is now up for auction. The property, however, is actually worth $90,000. If a person bids at the foreclosure auction in excess of the lender's outstanding claim on the property, they are entitled to receive full title to the property, regardless of the fact that they did not pay the full market price of the property. The possibility of acquiring property at less than market rate is one of the most attractive features of a foreclosure auction. Unlike other types of auctions, such as law-enforcement asset seizures, there is no requirement that the bidder pay fair market value on the property. Obviously, the higher the value of the property and the lower the amount of the outstanding mortgage, the greater the chance that there will be competitors in the bid process.

Some states allow a successful bidder several days to come up with the full amount of the bid. In those states, the successful bidder usually must post a percentage of the total bid price, which the bidder will forfeit if they fail to come up with the full bid amount. Other states allow bidders to present letters of credit from banks or other lending institutions that specify that the bidder's credit is good up to a specific amount.

h. Terminating the Rights of Other Creditors

When property is foreclosed, all junior lienholders' claims on the property are extinguished. A junior lienholder is someone who has a claim against the property that was filed at some point in time after the mortgage was created. If there is a lien or claim against the property that was filed before the mortgage, which is unlikely, that right would not be terminated by a foreclosure action. However, as we will see in Chapter 9, most banks insist that their first mortgage have priority over all other types of claims; therefore, if the lender brings a foreclosure action, all other claims against the property are extinguished. This means that the successful bidder at a foreclosure auction can usually take possession of the property without having to pay other claims. However, this general rule is subject to some specific exceptions. For instance, tax liens and other government assessments automatically take priority over all other claims, including first mortgages.

i. Mortgages and Deeds of Trust

So far, our discussion about foreclosure has made certain assumptions. One of these assumptions is that mortgages, which are the most popular form of financing of real estate in the United States, and deeds of trust, which are an older form of mortgage financing, proceed along the same lines in a foreclosure action. This is not true; a deed of trust is similar to a mortgage only in superficial ways. In a typical foreclosure action, a mortgage lender proceeds against the borrower in a way that closely resembles a typical lawsuit. Deeds of trust follow a different procedure. When a person obtains a deed of trust, a three-way arrangement is created. The borrower transfers the right of foreclosure to a trustee, who acts as a middleman between the lender and the borrower. If the borrower defaults on the loan, the bank notifies the trustee to bring foreclosure proceedings. Because the borrower has already transferred certain rights to the trustee, foreclosing on a deed of trust is a much simpler process than foreclosing on a mortgage. The trustee must notify the borrower that they are in default, and then the trustee is allowed to post a power of sale provision in a local newspaper and begin foreclosure proceedings. Deed of trust foreclosures involve much less judicial interaction and therefore can proceed much more quickly than mortgage foreclosures. We will discuss deeds of trust in greater detail in Chapter 9.

B. EMINENT DOMAIN (CONDEMNATION)

Although foreclosure is the most common way to involuntarily transfer title to real estate, it is not the only method. Another common process is eminent domain. Federal and state governments have the right to seize property, even property held by private individuals, for public use. The power of eminent domain is considered to be one of the inherent powers of government. Without it, governments could not build roads, set aside state parks, or create the infrastructure that we all rely upon.

REAL
ESTATE
BASICS AT
A GLANCE

Eminent domain is the power of the government to seize property for governmental purposes.

1. THE PROCESS OF EMINENT DOMAIN: CONDEMNATION

Eminent domain refers to the power of the government to seize property; condemnation is the method to carry it out. When the federal or state government decides that a certain parcel of land should be seized, it condemns the property for public use. The landowner cannot challenge the government's right to seize property. As long as the property is used for governmental purposes, a condemnation action will proceed. The only issue in a condemnation action is the amount of the landowner's compensation. The U.S. Constitution provides that landowners must be compensated for any land seized by the government. The amount of compensation is fair market value for the parcel that has been condemned. Fair market value refers to the value of the property that a willing buyer would pay to acquire the land.

The determination of fair market value for the seized property often results in a battle of experts, one set hired by the government and the other hired by the landowner. The government's experts may testify that the fair market value of a particular piece of property is $10,000, while a landowner's expert may testify that the actual fair market value of the property is $20,000. The ultimate determination of the amount falls to a judge or jury.

2. INVERSE CONDEMNATION

Occasionally, landowners will complain that government action has resulted in a diminution in value of their property. A landowner might claim, for example, that the installation of a sewage treatment plant next to their property has essentially rendered their property valueless. In such a situation, the landowner might bring an inverse condemnation action, alleging that although the government did not directly condemn their property and seize it, government action has resulted in an indirect seizure of the property because the landowner is now unable to sell it to anyone else. When a landowner brings an inverse condemnation action, a judge must determine whether the government's actions have actually resulted in a diminution or total destruction of the landowner's rights and enjoyment in the property.

C. PARTITION

When two or more individuals own property together, each owner has the right to bring a partition action against the other owners. A partition action does exactly what its name suggests: It divides the property by the percentage of ownership in each individual owner. We discussed partition in Chapter 2.

D. ESCHEAT

When a property owner dies and leaves no heirs, title to the property transfers to the state or local government. The process of transferring title under these circumstances is referred to as **escheat**. Before the government can claim ownership in the property, it must demonstrate reasonable efforts to locate anyone who would qualify as the decedent's heir. Receiving property through escheat often causes government officials many problems. For instance, there is the issue of upkeep and maintenance. Most governments would prefer not to receive property this way and work diligently to locate individuals who qualify as heirs of the decedent so that they may receive the property instead. Escheat is governed by state statute and must be strictly complied with before title passes to the government.

Escheat
Transfer of title to property to local government when a person dies without heirs.

E. CIVIL JUDGMENT

A person may also lose title to property through the enforcement of a civil judgment. When a person is sued and loses that suit, the winning party has the right to seek payment of the judgment. The winning party may petition the court for an order allowing that party to seize personal assets or real estate owned by the losing party in a civil suit. If the judge authorizes such an action, the losing party's real property may be auctioned off to satisfy the monetary judgment.

F. ADVERSE POSSESSION

One of the more unusual ways for a person to involuntarily lose title to property is the process known as **adverse possession**. Under the doctrine of adverse possession, when a person can show that they have claimed the property owned by another and held that property openly and notoriously, under color of title and for a specific period of time, that person may petition the court to be awarded fee simple absolute title in the property.

Adverse possession
An action that can be brought by a person who possesses land owned by another, holds that land openly and against the claims of others, and continues in possession for a minimum period of time, such as seven years.

1. WHY DOES THE DOCTRINE OF ADVERSE POSSESSION EXIST?

Why would courts and legislatures create a rule such as adverse possession? There is a simple and practical reason: Because land has been, and continues to be, an important source of wealth, any action that tends to cloud title on real property, or result in a vacuum in ownership rights, is actively discouraged. The law frowns upon freezing title in land in such a way that no one can make use of it. Adverse possession is one way of keeping land usable.

REAL ESTATE BASICS AT A GLANCE

Adverse possession is a legal theory that allows a person to claim lands owned by another after a period of time.

Doctrine of laches
The legal principle that states that a person who fails to assert a legal right loses it.

Some commentators have said that the statutes authorizing adverse possession arise out of a societal need for the settlement of title issues.

Another theory underlying adverse possession is one found in all areas of law. In civil law, there is something known as the **doctrine of laches**. Under the doctrine of laches, when an individual has the right to challenge an action and fails to do so, they eventually lose that right. In criminal law, when a prosecutor fails to charge an individual with a crime within a specified time period, the statute of limitations bars that prosecution forever. One could easily argue that all branches of law are built on the premise that, when an individual has a right and fails to exercise it, the right will be lost. Our legal system is based on the belief that it is always better to know when a particular action is barred forever. Such knowledge helps individuals by allowing them to go on with their lives. It also prevents courts from litigating cases that are decades old, when witness memories, physical evidence, and other relevant information have faded away.

Adverse possession, then, is built on two premises: (1) Real estate is a vital part of our economy and parcels should remain in the stream of commerce, and (2) Parties who have rights and fail to exercise them will often lose them forever.

2. THE ELEMENTS OF ADVERSE POSSESSION

Before a person can be awarded title to property through adverse possession, they must satisfy each and every element of the doctrine. Those elements include:

- Open continuous, notorious, and hostile possession,
- Under color of title, and
- For a specified period of time.

When a party proves all the elements of adverse possession, the court is authorized to award that party full title in fee simple, based on the finding that the original owner neglected the property and failed to assert their rights.[9]

a. Open, Continuous, Notorious, and Hostile Possession

One of the key elements of adverse possession is the requirement that the party actually possess the property. It is not enough for a person to claim title to the land. They must physically move on to the property and demonstrate possession for all to see.[10] In addition to openly possessing the property, the claimant must assert their claim so that it is hostile to the original owner's. This means that the claimant must act as though the property is theirs, and prevent others from entering the property, using the property, or taking possession of it. This "hostile" use is the manifestation of the claimant's intent to bring an adverse possession claim at some point in the future.

If the claimant fails to maintain possession in an open, notorious, and hostile fashion, the claimant cannot show the central element of an adverse possession claim: actual possession. Without proof of possession, the claimant will fail.

EXAMPLE 4-4

PERRY'S DEED

Perry records a deed granting him property that he technically has no right to use. After recording the deed, he does not move on to the property, but he does pay real estate taxes on the land for 21 years. Will Perry be awarded the property through adverse possession?

Answer: No. In order to prove a claim of adverse possession, all the elements must be met, especially the first: possession. Merely paying taxes on another's property does not meet all the elements of adverse possession, and Perry will not be awarded title to the disputed property.[11]

b. Color of Title

Most states require not only that a claimant possess the property but also that the claimant originally enter onto the property under "color of title." This phrase means that the claimant's original claim is based, at least in some way, on a legal, viable claim to the property. The claim may not be perfect, but it should at least create an arguable right to the property. Examples of color of title are tax deeds. In this case, a person attends a tax auction, bids on the property, and receives a deed from a local official. This deed may not grant fee simple title, but it is at least color of title that should satisfy the courts. Color of title is required in many states to prevent persons who have no rights or claims to a property from simply trespassing and then claiming ownership. Color of title also helps establish the time period in which the claimant took open and hostile possession of the property. Without some independent evidence of when the claimant took possession, they might be tempted to exaggerate the amount of time that they have been in possession in order to hurry the process along.

3. SPECIFIED TIME PERIODS FOR ADVERSE POSSESSION

All states have specific time periods that must elapse before a claimant can be awarded title through adverse possession. In some states, especially when a person claims color of title through a tax deed, that time may be as short as 5 years,[12] while in others, it could be as long as 20 years.[13]

The claimant must also possess the property continuously during the statutory period. Intermittent possession will not satisfy this element of adverse possession. Instead, the claimant must show that during the mandatory period (which can be as long as 21 years in some states), they had continuous possession of the property and did not permit others to take possession of it.

In some situations, a previous possessor's use of the property can be tacked onto a new possessor's use. Tacking is the process of adding time periods together to reach the statutory minimum time period, and it can be used in adverse possession. Tacking is a principle we return to in later chapters when we discuss issues such as encroachment and other time-sensitive concerns in real property.

G. TAX AUCTIONS

All states have provisions in their laws that allow governments to enforce the payment of property taxes through the use of tax auctions. Without such power, landowners might be inclined to ignore tax bills. The assessment and collection of real estate taxes is one of the primary sources of revenue for local governments. Most state statutes that authorize an auction of property for unpaid taxes are similar to the California statute shown in Figure 4-2. Several states permit a successful bidder at a tax auction the right to claim the property under fee simple title, while others require that the successful bidder file a separate action and request that a court award fee simple title.

FIGURE 4-2

Seizure of Property for Unpaid Taxes

Whenever any supplier is delinquent in the payment of the tax, the Controller or his or her authorized representative may forthwith collect the tax due in the following manner: The Controller shall seize any property, real or personal, of the supplier, and thereafter sell the property, or a sufficient part of it, at public auction to pay the tax due together with any penalties, interest and any costs incurred on account of the seizure and sale. Cal. Com. Code §§7891-7895.

Case Excerpt

DIP LENDING I, LLC v. CLEVELAND AVENUE PROPERTIES
812 S.E.2d 533 (2018)

BETHEL, Judge.

These appeals arise from the trial court's partial grant and denial of cross motions for summary judgment in a wrongful foreclosure action between Cleveland Avenue Properties, LLC (hereinafter "Cleveland") and Dip Lending I, LLC (hereinafter "Dip Lending"). In Case No. A17A1410, Dip Lending contends the trial court erred by finding that Dip Lending (1) failed to comply with the statutory notice provisions of OCGA §44–14–162.2, and (2) breached its duty to provide Cleveland notice of the foreclosure sale. Dip Lending further contends the trial court erred when applying the standard for the defense of equitable estoppel. In Case No. A17A1411, Cleveland argues the trial court erred by finding Cleveland was not entitled to the equitable remedy of setting aside the foreclosure sale of its two properties because it had not tendered the amounts due on the note. For the reasons explained, we affirm.

So viewed, the evidence shows that in 2010, ATA Properties, Inc. (hereinafter "ATA"), deeded two properties ("Properties") located in East Point, Georgia to Cleveland. At the time of the transfer, the Properties were subject to a lien held by

Rockbridge Commercial Bank which was under the control of its receiver, the Federal Deposit Insurance Corporation ("FDIC"). In 2015, the FDIC assigned its interest in the Properties to Dip Lending. Dip Lending sold the Properties through a non-judicial foreclosure sale.

Cleveland filed an action for wrongful foreclosure alleging that Dip Lending failed to send it notice of the foreclosure and that Cleveland was entitled to have the fore-closure sale of the Properties set aside. Dip Lending answered and denied Cleveland's claim that it was never notified that the Properties were being foreclosed. Both parties moved for summary judgment. The trial court partially granted Cleveland's motion for summary judgment on the elements of legal duty and breach of legal duty on its claim for wrongful foreclosure based on its conclusion that Dip Lending failed to provide Cleveland notice pursuant to OCGA §44–14–162.2. The trial court partially granted Dip Lending's motion for summary judgment on Cleveland's request for the equita-ble remedy of setting aside the foreclosure sale because Cleveland failed to tender the amounts due. These appeals followed.

Dip Lending argues the trial court erred in finding that it failed to comply with the notice provisions of OCGA §44–14–162.2 because the foreclosure sale notices were sent to the appropriate address and otherwise substantially complied with the statute's requirements. In support of its argument, Dip Lending contends that Cleveland had actual notice of the foreclosure sale and filed a subsequent petition to enjoin the sale because notice was provided. We disagree.

OCGA §44–14–162.2 (a) provides in part that

Notice of the initiation of [foreclosure] proceedings . . . shall be given to the debtor . . . shall be in writing, shall include the name, address, and telephone number of the individual or entity who shall have full authority to negotiate, amend, and modify all terms of the mort-gage with the debtor, and shall be sent by registered or certified mail or statutory overnight delivery, return receipt requested, to the property address or to such other address as the debtor may designate by written notice to the secured creditor.

OCGA §44–14–162.1 defines the term "debtor" to mean the "grantor of the . . . lien contract." In the event the encumbered property has been transferred by the original debtor, the same statute provides that the "debtor" is "the current owner of the property encumbered by the debt."

The record reflects that as of April 1, 2015, the registered address for Cleveland was 963 Cleveland Avenue, and the registered address for ATA was 1827 Warren Way. It is undisputed that Dip Lending sent notices of the initiation of foreclosure proceed-ings for the Properties to ATA, Cleveland's predecessor in interest, and ATA's registered agent, Tony White, at the 963 Cleveland Avenue address. When the notices were sent, Dip Lending knew Cleveland was the owner of record for the Properties, but it did not list Cleveland as a recipient on the notices as required by the statute. However, Dip Lending argues that the notice statute only required that the notices be sent to the proper address. Dip Lending's argument is without merit.

OCGA §44–14–162.2 not only requires that foreclosure notices be sent to the proper address, but also requires that notices be sent to the "current owner of the prop-erty encumbered by the debt." Nowhere does the plain language of the statute specify or even suggest that the foreclosure notice can be sent to anyone other than the debtor.

Contrary to Dip Lending's argument, addressing the notices to a third-party located at the proper address is not sufficient to satisfy the statutory notice requirement.

We are also unpersuaded by Dip Lending's argument that because Cleveland had actual knowledge of the initiation of foreclosure proceedings, as evidenced by their petition to enjoin the foreclosure sale, the trial court erred in finding Cleveland lacked the required statutory notice. OCGA §44 14 162.2 requires a showing that the initiator of the foreclosure proceedings complied with statutory and contractual notice requirements. The record reflects that

Dip Lending did not send the foreclosure sale notices to Cleveland as required by statute. It is of no consequence that Cleveland was made aware of the foreclosure via ATA or Tony White. As we have ruled in regard to other notice requirements in the context of a foreclosure, actual knowledge does not relieve a party of its statutory duty to provide notice.

Neither the plain language of the statute nor our prior holdings permit us to do what Dip Lending suggests. "Where the plain language of the statute is clear and susceptible to only one reasonable construction, we must construe the statute according to its terms." *Ray v. Atkins*, 205 Ga. App. 85, 89 (2), 421 S.E.2d 317 (1992) "OCGA §44–14–162.2, being in derogation of common law, must be strictly construed according to its terms." *Id*. Thus, the trial court did not err in finding Dip Lending failed to comply with the notice provisions of OCGA §44–14–162.2

Lastly, we see no merit in Cleveland's argument that it was entitled to the equitable remedy of setting aside the foreclosure. It has long been established that "[h]e who would have equity must do equity, and . . . under the application of this maxim, before the complainant would be entitled to equitable relief, he or she must do equity and tender the amount due under the security deed and note." *Stewart v. Suntrust Mortg., Inc.*, 331 Ga. App. 635, 640 (6), 770 S.E.2d 892 (2015).

The record reflects that the Properties were encumbered by a lien which was later assigned to Dip Lending. Despite Cleveland's assertions that there is a dispute as to the amounts still owed, the record shows that no payments have been made on the debt since December 2009 and Cleveland has not tendered any amounts owed since that time. Because setting aside a foreclosure sale requires that Cleveland first tender to Dip Lending the amount of principal and interest due, we find no error in the trial court's denial of its motion for summary judgment to set aside the foreclosure. See *Hill v. Filsoof*, 274 Ga. App. 474, 475 (1), 618 S.E.2d 12 (2005).

Judgment affirmed.

McFADDEN, P.J., and BRANCH, J., concur.

QUESTIONS ABOUT THE CASE

1   Cleveland filed an action for wrongful foreclosure on what basis?
2   Dip Lending argued that it substantially complied with the foreclosure statute. What actions did it take?
3   Did the trial court find that substantial compliance was enough to sustain an action for foreclosure?
4   Dip Lending counters that even if the notice went to the wrong party, Cleveland was aware of the foreclosure proceeding and therefore the basic requirements of the statute were met. Did the appellate court agree?

COVID-19 CONCERN

This chapter discusses the ramifications of a person's failure to pay their mortgage or tax payments. The result may be an auction. At present, there are few rules to allow such auctions to be held virtually. Should this be changed, given restrictions such as those imposed by COVID-19 precautions? If school classes and company meetings can be held virtually, why not a real estate auction? In the era of fast moving COVID variants, wouldn't it make more sense to allow a virtual auction? This would also open up the auction to people who do not live in the immediate area. In a sense, anyone on the planet could "attend" the auction. Is that a good thing? Don't we want the auctioneers to bring in as much money as possible? Would this open up the auction process to companies with representatives prepared to outbid anyone else, especially local townspeople, bidding on the property? Is COVID simply pushing this technology along faster than might have happened in the ordinary course of business?

CHAPTER SUMMARY

In this chapter, we explored both the voluntary and the involuntary transfers of title to real property. Voluntary real property transactions involve sales, gifts, and transfer through probate proceedings. Sale of real property is the most common way that title is transferred. A sale must meet certain minimum requirements, including contractual elements such as capacity and mutual assent. When property is transferred through a probate proceeding, it can be done in one of two ways. When a person dies with a will, they are said to have died testate, and courts will attempt to carry out the decedent's wishes. When a person dies without a will, referred to as dying intestate, the court must determine what the decedent's intentions likely were. Courts are guided by intestate succession statutes that dictate which of the heirs should be given priority in receiving title to property.

Involuntary transfers of title to property can also occur through a borrower's failure to make mortgage payments. Lenders are authorized to institute foreclosure actions in such situations and auction off the real estate for the amount of the outstanding mortgage. Governments may bring condemnation proceedings through their power of eminent domain, which allows them to seize real property from private individuals. When governments seize property, they must compensate the owners by paying fair market value for the property. Co-owners may bring partition actions to divide the ownership of the property. Property may also be lost through escheat, whereby a person dies without heirs and the government takes title to the property. Real estate may also be auctioned off to satisfy civil judgments or back taxes. Finally, title to property may be lost through the process of adverse possession, whereby a person claims property owned by another, takes possession of the property for a specified time, and holds it openly and adversely to other claims. Eventually, the claimant may bring a legal action to have the title awarded to them.

SKILLS YOU NEED IN THE REAL WORLD

Reviewing Probate Records

During the course of your work as a real estate professional, it is vitally important for you to know and understand the types of records that are stored at the local courthouse. Although most of your work may center on the land office or deed room, it also is important for you to be able to locate probate records.

When a person dies with a will, the will is probated and made a matter of public record. There is often a special index listing all people who have received real property through the provisions of a will or by intestate proceeding. When you are trying to locate these records, be aware that they are not always kept in or near the deed room. In some states, there is a separate probate court that maintains all records of probate proceedings. In other states, probate records are stored in the clerk of court's office. Wherever they are kept, you should be able to locate them in order to determine if real property has been transferred through a probate proceeding.

ETHICAL ISSUES FOR THE PARALEGAL

Fradulent Transfers

There are times when clients approach legal professionals with requests to carry out questionable transfers. Individuals who are facing divorce actions or tax audits often wish to transfer title to property to close friends or family members with the understanding that, when the legal difficulties are over, they will receive title back. Such transfers are fraudulent, and legal professionals should not become involved in them. Signs that a transfer is designed to defraud creditors include:

- The sale price is well below market value;
- The client wishes to disguise features of the sale or wishes to wait before recording the deed;
- The client asks for advice on ways to shield the transaction from the public records; and
- The property is given as a gift under circumstances that are unusual.

KEY TERMS AND CONCEPTS

Adverse possession	Devisee	Intoxication
Beneficiary	Doctrine of laches	Judicial foreclosure
Capacity	Escheat	Nuncupative will
Dedication	Foreclosure	Power of sale foreclosure
Default	Holographic will	Publication
Devise	Intestate	Testate

END-OF-CHAPTER EXERCISES

Review Questions

See Appendix for answers.

1 What are some examples of voluntary transfer of real estate title?
2 Why is the question of origin of title so important?
3 What are the minimum requirements of a legal sale?
4 What basic elements must a will have before it is considered legally valid?
5 What are the differences between a will and a sale?
6 What is dedication as that term applies to real estate?
7 How can a person acquire title to real estate through homesteading?
8 When and under what circumstances does foreclosure occur?
9 Explain the basic steps involved in a foreclosure proceeding.
10 What is the right of redemption as that term applies to foreclosures?
11 What is eminent domain?
12 What is condemnation, and how does it apply to eminent domain?
13 Explain partition.
14 Describe escheat.
15 How may a person lose title to property through the enforcement of a civil judgment?
16 What is adverse possession? List and explain the basic elements of adverse possession.
17 What is color of title as that term applies to adverse possession?
18 What effect does a tax auction have on the original property owner's rights?
19 Why is it important to be able to locate probate records?
20 Explain the information that can be found in a notice of foreclosure.

DISCUSSION QUESTIONS

1   Is the doctrine of adverse possession a good thing or a bad thing for society? Explain your answer.

2   Should the requirements for transfer of title by sale and transfer of title by will be the same? Why or why not?

APPLYING WHAT YOU HAVE LEARNED

1   Go through real estate brochures to locate houses that are for sale. What inducements do the sellers offer to potential buyers to encourage them to purchase a home?

2   Visit your local courthouse and review a will that has been probated. Probated wills are part of the public record and are freely accessible. Locate an estate in which real estate was conveyed to beneficiaries. How many beneficiaries received a share of the property? What findings did the court make in order to determine that the will was valid?

WEB SURFING

Mutual Assent: Legal Research Institute
http://www.law.cornell.edu/wex/mutual_assent

Consideration: Duhaime.org
http://www.duhaime.org/LegalDictionary/C/Consideration.aspx

Requirements of a Will: 'Lectric Law Library
http://www.lectlaw.com/filesh/qfl06.htm

Intestate Succession: Findlaw.com
http://estate.findlaw.com/estate-planning/estate-planning-overview/estate-planning-overview-intestate.html

Tech Topic
MLS FORECLOSURE SEARCH

The Multiple Listing Service (ML) website includes a foreclosure search tool (http://www.mls.com/ ForeclosureListings) that allows you to search for foreclosures by city, county, state, or ZIP code, with the option to further narrow your search by property type. The search results display in both a map and a list; the list includes information about each property, such as status, square footage, bedrooms/bathrooms, and price.

ANNOTATED DOCUMENT

Notice of Foreclosure

NOTICE OF FORECLOSURE UNDER POWER OF SALE

NOTICE IS HEREBY PUBLISHED of the following default on conditions of the following described mortgage, to wit:

DATE OF MORTGAGE: August 22, 2022

MORTGAGOR(S): Dail J. Doe and John M. Doe, Wife and Husband.

MORTGAGEE: Borrowers' Mortgage, Inc.

DATE AND PLACE OF RECORDING: Recorded August 22, 2022, Town of Anywhere, State of Placid, Document No. 000123445.

COUNTY IN WHICH PROPERTY IS LOCATED: Barnes County

ORIGINAL PRINCIPAL AMOUNT OF MORTGAGE: $153,000.00

AMOUNT DUE AND CLAIMED TO BE DUE AS OF DATE OF NOTICE, INCLUDING TAXES, IF ANY, PAID BY MORTGAGEE: $143,234.56

That prior to the commencement of this mortgage foreclosure proceeding Mortgagee/Assignee of Mortgagee complied with all notice requirements as required by statute; That no action or proceeding has been instituted at law or otherwise to recover the debt secured by said mortgage, or any part thereof;

PURSUANT to the power of sale contained in said mortgage, the above-described property will be sold by the Sheriff of said county as follows:

DATE AND TIME OF SALE: January 11, 2023, at 10:00 A.M.

PLACE OF SALE: Barnes County Courthouse, PL, to pay the debt then secured by said Mortgage, and taxes, if any, on said premises, and the costs and disbursements, including attorneys' fees allowed by law subject to redemption within six (6) months from the date of said sale by the mortgagor(s), their personal representatives, or assigns.

REDEMPTION: Pursuant to the laws of the state of Placid, the mortgagee has the right to redeem the property within ten (10) business days of the auction and sale by posting the AMOUNT DUE with the Clerk of Superior Court of Barnes County, State of Placid.

Notice Date: November 4, 2022
CLARENCE D. ARROW
BAUGH & ARROW, PLLC
Attorney for Mortgagee

> The Notice of Foreclosure is a notice of default.

> The names of the borrowers are Dail J. Doe and John M. Doe ("mortgagors").

PRACTICE QUESTIONS FOR TEST REVIEW

See Appendix for answers.

Essay Question

What are the basic requirements of a will?

True–False

1 T F Sales are the most common way to transfer title to real property.

2 T F Historically, the procedures involved in transferring title to real property were more relaxed than those used to transfer title to personal property.

3 T F Real estate contracts do not require mutual assent.

Fill in the Blank

1 This statute has been in existence for hundreds of years, both in the U.S. and in England. It demands that a will must be in writing to be valid:_____.

2 The legal requirement for a testator to announce to witnesses that he or she has created a will and wishes to have it witnessed: _____.

3 When a person decides to leave his or her property to the government following death: _____.

Multiple Choice

1 The contract law element that requires that both parties to the contract know and understand the material features of the contract.

    A Mutual convenience
    B Mutual assent
    C Mutual adverse
    D Mutual commitment

2 The legal requirement that both parties to the transaction have a stake in the outcome.

    A Capacity
    B Mutual Commitment
    C Intelligence
    D Consideration

3 A contract party's ability to know and understand the consequences of entering into a legal contract.

A Capacity

B Consideration

C Mutual assent

D Assertion

ENDNOTES

[1] *Johnson v. M'Intosh*, 21 U.S. (8 Wheat.) 543, 5 L. Ed. 681 (1823).

[2] *In Re Will of Cox*, 139 Me. 261, 29 A.2d 281 (1942).

[3] *Christianson v. Rumsey*, 91 Idaho 684, 429 P.2d 416 (1967).

[4] *Hall v. Hall*, 214 Ky. 596, 283 S.W. 957 (KY, 1926).

[5] *Nelson v. Parker*, 687 N.E.2d 187 (Ind. Ct. App. 1996); *Quickel v. Quickel*, 261 N.C. 696, 136 S.E.2d 52 (1964).

[6] *Biglin v. Town of West Orange*, 46 N.J. 367, 217 A.2d 135 (1966).

[7] *National Tailoring Co. v. Scott*, 65 Wyo. 64, 196 P.2d 387 (1948).

[8] Coote on Mortgages 1026 (9th ed. 2004).

[9] *Republic Nat'l Bank of Dallas v. Stetson*, 390 S.W.2d 257 (Tex. 1965).

[10] *Bailey v. Shanks*, 199 Neb. 29, 255 N.W.2d 866 (1977).

[11] *Perry v. Alford*, 225 N.C. 146, 32 S.E.2d 665 (1945).

[12] O.C.G.A. §23-3-62.

[13] N.C. Gen. Stat. §41-40.

ENDNOTES

Rights Associated
with Real Estate

Chapter Objectives

▨ Explain how courts determine what qualifies as a fixture

▨ Describe how easements are created

▨ Define the air and mineral rights that real property owners possess

▨ Explain the purpose of liens

▨ Describe the importance of water rights

Chapter Outline

I. Introduction

II. Fixtures
   A. Determining When Personal Property Becomes a Fixture
   B. Trade Fixtures

III. Easements
   A. Appurtenant Easements
   B. In Gross Easements
   C. Easements Run with the Land
   D. Creating Easements
   E. Terminating Easements

IV. Licenses

V. *Profit à Prendre*

VI. Liens

VII. Assessments

VIII. Air Rights

IX. Water Rights
   A. The Right to Draw Water
   B. Subterranean Water
   C. Terminology for Water Rights

X. Mineral Rights

INTRODUCTION

In this chapter, we will explore the many different rights associated with real property ownership. From fixtures to licenses, we will see that ownership of real property carries with it numerous rights and obligations. We will begin our discussion by examining the legal consequences of attaching personal property to real property — the subject of fixtures.

FIXTURES

Our discussion of the rights associated with real property ownership begins with the interplay between real and personal property. We have seen that personal property consists of items as disparate as apples and airplanes, but what happens when personal property becomes permanently affixed to real property? What effect does this union have on personal property? Does it retain its separate identity? This is more than a theoretical question; there are practical concerns here as well. For example, when title to real property is exchanged, there is no need to list all the individual components that make up the real estate parcel. As we will see in our discussion of deeds (Chapter 8), the only item described in a real estate transaction is the property because everything permanently attached to the property is transferred with the deed. This explains why structures such as houses are never listed on a real property deed. Because they are permanently attached to the land, they are transferred along with the underlying ground.

REAL
ESTATE
BASICS AT
A GLANCE

A fixture is personal property that has become permanently attached to real property.

Fixture
Personal property that has become permanently attached to real property.

The same thing happens when personal property becomes permanently attached to real estate. The term for these items is "fixtures." A **fixture** is an item that was formerly classified as personal property but has become real property by virtue of being attached to the real estate. When this attachment (sometimes called *annexation*) occurs, the personal property is reclassified as real property and will continue to be considered real property.

| EXAMPLE 5-1 | **THE MISSING CHANDELIER** |

Tonya has placed her house for sale, and a young couple has agreed to buy it. On the day of the sale, just before Tonya leaves the house forever, she unbolts a crystal chandelier from the ceiling of the dining room and loads it into her car. When the new owners arrive at the house, they immediately notice that the chandelier is gone. They want to sue Tonya. How is the judge likely to rule?

Answer: The judge will rule that the chandelier, once an item of personal property, has now become a fixture and must remain with the house when it is sold. Unlike other items of personal property, such as furniture, books, and table lamps, the chandelier is permanently attached to the real property and must remain with the house when it is sold. The judge will order Tonya to return the chandelier.

Fixtures belong to the persons who own the real estate.

REAL
ESTATE
BASICS AT
A GLANCE

A. DETERMINING WHEN PERSONAL PROPERTY BECOMES A FIXTURE

Because the determination of when personal property becomes a fixture is so important and can have such dire effects, courts have created several tests to help determine when something has crossed the boundary between personal property and real property. Although different states have different standards and tests for determining what constitutes a fixture, there are some general guidelines. For instance, courts could use any or all of the following tests:

- Intent,
- Manner of attachment,
- Use, or
- Damage resulting from removal.

1. INTENT TEST

Courts always look to the intent of the party who placed the item to see whether the personal property was placed there with the idea that it would become part of the real property. In the previous example involving Tonya and the chandelier, one could certainly argue that, by bolting the chandelier to the dining room ceiling, Tonya had clearly intended that it should remain there permanently. Contrast this with a table lamp, the placement of which is clearly designed to be temporary. Under the intent test, the chandelier would qualify as a fixture.

Although the courts have ruled that the parties' intentions are controlling when it comes to the issue of determining a fixture, there are times when it is difficult, if not impossible, to determine the parties' intentions. The original parties may no longer be available, or they may have made conflicting statements about their intentions. In those situations, the courts would opt for the manner of attachment test.

2. MANNER OF ATTACHMENT TEST

Another method used to determine whether an item qualifies as a fixture is the manner of attachment test. Under this test, the more permanent an attachment, the more likely the item would be classified as a fixture.

EXAMPLE 5-2

THE MISSING PAINTING

Once the new owners have moved into Tonya's old house, they also notice that, in addition to the missing chandelier, a painting that they liked very much has also been removed. Tonya took the painting down on the same day that she removed the chandelier. The new owners are now requesting that in addition to returning the chandelier, Tonya also return the painting. Does the painting qualify as a fixture?

Answer: Here is an example in which the intent test might not provide an answer to this question, but the manner of attachment test does. Under the manner of attachment test, a painting that hangs on the wall by a nail and wire is obviously not intended to remain there permanently. Under the manner of attachment test, the painting would not qualify as a fixture, and therefore the new owners cannot compel Tonya to return it.

3. USE TEST

In situations in which intent and manner of attachment do not help to resolve the question of whether an item is a fixture, the use test provides another mechanism. Under the use test, personal property is considered to be a fixture when the item is essential to the use of the real property.

EXAMPLE 5-3

THE HEAT PUMP

Carlos has come to our firm with the following problem: He is being transferred out of state and must put his house up for sale. He has also recently installed a heat pump. Carlos wants to know if the heat pump must remain when he sells the house or if he can take it with him. Put another way: Is a heat pump a fixture?

Answer: Under the intent and manner of attachment tests to determine fixture status, there is no equivocation on the question. However, is a heat pump necessary to the use of the real property? The new owners will need to heat and cool their home, so it is obvious that the heating mechanism is necessary for the use of the property. The heat pump is a fixture.[1]

4. DAMAGE TEST

The final test used to determine whether a specific item qualifies as a fixture is to determine how much damage it would cause to remove it. Under this test, if removal of an item would cause extensive damage to the site, courts are more likely to rule that the item is a fixture. Examples of items that would fit into this category would be built-in wall units or furniture constructed on site that would require opening up an exterior wall for removal. Under the damage test, such items would be classified as fixtures.

If an item satisfies any of the court-created tests, it is classified as a fixture and must remain with the land when the property is sold.

REAL
ESTATE
BASICS AT
A GLANCE

B. TRADE FIXTURES

The rules about fixtures change when an item is classified as a **trade fixture**. A trade fixture is equipment that is necessary to run a commercial enterprise. Even though this equipment may be permanently attached to the real estate, such as heavy machinery that is bolted to the floor, the person who owns the equipment is allowed to remove it when he sells or otherwise leaves the real property. The rules about trade fixtures are different because trade fixtures are necessary to run a business, and it would not make much sense, financial or otherwise, to require someone who had invested thousands of dollars in equipment to leave it behind when the real property was sold. As far as the law is concerned, trade fixtures always remain personal property and can be removed.[2]

Trade fixture
A fixture that is necessary to the operation of a business.

So far, our discussion has centered on the rights that owners have to use items on or remove items from real property. In the next section, we will discuss rights that others have to use a portion of another's property.

A trade fixture may be removed when the business vacates the premises, even though it may have been permanently attached to the real estate.

REAL
ESTATE
BASICS AT
A GLANCE

 **EASEMENTS**

An **easement** is a right held by someone other than the real property owner. When someone has an easement, it means that he has the right to use part of another parcel of land, even though he has no ownership interests in it. Easements are very common. If you consider the layout of a typical neighborhood, you will discover easements existing on almost every parcel.

Easement
The right of a person other than the landowner to use a portion of the owner's land: for example, a driveway or a right of way.

| EXAMPLE 5-4 | **DRIVEWAY TROUBLE** |

Juan has recently purchased a new home in a nice subdivision. One day as he is out walking the boundary lines of his property, he realizes that his next-door neighbor's driveway actually cuts across his boundary line. Juan has come to our firm to find out if there is anything that he can do to have the driveway moved.

Our firm investigates the situation and learns that there is an easement on record, granting the next-door neighbor the use of that portion of Juan's property. Barring an agreement by the neighbor to surrender the easement, there is nothing that Juan can do to stop his next-door neighbor from using the driveway, even though it crosses over onto Juan's property.

REAL
ESTATE
BASICS AT
A GLANCE

Easements give non-owners the right to use a small portion of the owner's property.

Easements give a non-owner the right to use the owner's property. The reason that easements exist is to provide the maximum possible access from one parcel to another. Allowing a person to cross over another person's property to get access to the public streets is seen as a small price to pay to ensure that all property has access.

Easements are broken down into two categories: appurtenant easements and in gross easements. Driveways are examples of appurtenant easements.

A. APPURTENANT EASEMENTS

Appurtenant easement
An easement created for an adjoining, dominant estate.

An **appurtenant easement** is the right of an adjoining landowner to use a portion of another parcel for his own benefit. Appurtenant easements always involve two tracts of land and two different owners. One is classified as the *dominant estate* and the other, the *servient estate* (see Figure 5-1). In the example above, we see that the servient estate is the one that has the driveway placed across it for the benefit of the other, dominant, estate. Fortunately, many courts are moving away from this terminology and are focusing more on the parcels that receive the benefit of the easement and the other that must bear the burden of the easement.

REAL
ESTATE
BASICS AT
A GLANCE

Appurtenant easements involve two tracts of land.

FIGURE 5-1

A dominant estate is the land for which the easement is used. When A passes over a portion of B's property to access his property, the driveway benefits A's property. A's property is the dominant estate.	A servient estate is the land on which the easement is found. When A passes over a portion of B's property, he is using the servient parcel.

Terminology Used in Easements

B. IN GROSS EASEMENTS

An **in gross easement** is the right of another to enter onto a specific parcel. There is only one parcel involved in an in gross easement. An example of an in gross easement is the right given to local utilities to enter onto the property to service telephone poles or underground lines. A person or company that has an in gross easement is not required to seek permission to enter onto the premises.

In gross easement
An easement that allows someone to enter onto the land; there are no dominant or servient estates with in gross easements.

In gross easements involve only one tract of land.

REAL ESTATE BASICS AT A GLANCE

Tech Topic
CELLPHONE TOWER EASEMENTS

Now that more than 80 percent of the world's population owns a cellphone, the placement of cellphone towers has added a new wrinkle to the world of real estate. Cellphone towers are an essential factor in wireless communication, and they have to be erected somewhere. Wireless carriers spend a great deal of money designing systems around specific radio frequency engineering standards, and they often target specific geographic locations.

Many jurisdictions have zoning ordinances that either allow or prohibit cellphone towers. If a property is an industrial parcel surrounded by residential property, the likelihood that a wireless carrier could use it is high. On the other hand, if a residential property is surrounded by industrial property, the likelihood decreases. Thus, wireless carriers not only have to find a desirable property, they also have to make sure zoning ordinances allow for a tower to be built in that location.

Once a wireless carrier identifies a suitable location, it then must negotiate a lease with the property's owner. In exchange for monetary consideration, either in the form of a monthly lease payment or a lump sum payment, the carrier gains an exclusive easement over the property. The easement includes the transmission and reception of all wireless communication signals and the construction and operation of towers, antennas, and related facilities.

C. EASEMENTS RUN WITH THE LAND

Run with the land
A right that transfers with the title to the property.

When an owner grants an easement to another, this right is said to **run with the land**. Put another way, this right, once granted, automatically transfers when the property is transferred. New owners are not required to renegotiate terms. The easement remains, and if a new owner interferes with the other's use of the easement, the new owner can be sued and enjoined from taking any action to prevent access.

D. CREATING EASEMENTS

Now that we have seen how important easements are, we can examine how they are created. Easements can be created in any number of ways, but the most common methods are:

- Agreement,
- Deed reservation,
- Implication,
- Necessity,
- Prescription, and
- Eminent domain.

1. AGREEMENT

The easiest and most direct way to create an easement is by the agreement of the parties. For instance, a property owner might sell a portion of a much larger tract and then enter into an agreement with the new owner that the new owner will have an easement over a portion of the larger tract. This easement could be recorded and made part of the public record, but it might just as easily remain an informal agreement between the parties that eventually ripens into an important legal right for future owners. In order for such an easement to be a legally effective agreement, however, the Statute of Frauds dictates that it must be in writing.

When the parties enter into an agreement establishing an easement, they should not only put the agreement in writing, they should also specify the exact location of the easement so that there will not be a question for future owners.

2. DEED RESERVATION

Another method used to create an easement is by simply reserving one in the deed between seller and buyer. The seller can insert a provision in the deed specifying that an easement is created on the recently sold property. This is commonly referred to as *deed reservation* and is just as binding as an agreement between the parties.

3. IMPLICATION

Another method to create an easement is to assume that the parties intended to create one in their transaction but failed to list it in the deed. Here, courts will rule that the parties must have intended to create an easement but simply forgot to do so. To rule otherwise might create a situation in which a person who buys property cannot access it. After all, when a person crosses another person's property without permission, he is committing trespass. Rather than rule that every time a person who is trying to gain access to his own property is committing a fresh trespass, the courts will rule that the original parties obviously intended to create an easement and neglected to list it in the deed or other documents.

4. NECESSITY

In addition to the voluntary actions of the parties, courts can also take an active role in determining easements. Creating an easement by necessity is based on the commonsense notion that no one would purchase property to which he could not gain access. When a dispute arises about access and the existence of an easement, courts often find that an easement existed simply because one is required to give an owner access to his land. This does not mean that the landowner gets to pick the best or most advantageous easement. It simply means that every landowner is entitled to physical access to property — not necessarily convenient access. When courts create easements by necessity, they try to place the easement so that it gives an owner access to public roadways, but they are not required to create an easement that is aesthetically pleasing or even the shortest and most convenient route to those public roads.

GETTING AN EASEMENT

EXAMPLE 5-5

Earl purchased a lot last month, and when he tried to drive onto his property, the adjoining landowner, Carl, refused to let Earl cross his property to gain access. There are no easements recorded for the property, and Carl has consistently refused to agree to an easement. Earl brings suit, asking the local court to create an easement by necessity. The judge rules in Earl's favor, but creates a winding, circuitous route across the back edge of Carl's property. Earl wants an easement that is shorter and more direct. Will he get it?

Answer: No. Earl is entitled to access his property, and the court can create an easement across Carl's property to give Earl that access, but the court does not have to place the easement where Earl wants it. Access is access.

5. PRESCRIPTION

When a party acquires an easement by prescription, he is using a method similar to adverse possession, discussed in the previous chapter. As we saw with adverse possession, all states have rules that permit a person who exercises open, notorious, and hostile possession against an original owner to eventually receive full title to the lot. A similar theory will result in the creation of an easement.

In easement by prescription, an adjoining landowner simply begins using a portion of another person's property as a driveway. After a period of time, which varies from state to state, the use will ripen into an easement. The theory underlying easement by prescription is that when the property owner has the right to stop another from using a portion of his property for access and fails to do so, he eventually waives the right to bring any action opposing the use. To satisfy the elements of an easement by prescription, the original use must be without permission. Additionally, the party seeking to have an easement declared must also establish the following elements:

- That the easement was established adversely to the rights of the landowner,
- That the use has been open and notorious and obvious to all, and
- That the use has been uninterrupted and continuous for a period of time (as long as 21 years in some states).[3]

6. EMINENT DOMAIN

The final method used to create easements is by the power of the government to seize property. We saw in the last chapter that all governments — local, state, and federal — have the power of eminent domain: the power to seize a private individual's property to use for a government-related project. Of course, the owner must be reimbursed for the value of his property. Eminent domain actions can also apply to easements. Governments can just as easily seize a portion of a lot to use for a new roadway or to widen an existing roadway.

If you think that the rules are stacked in favor of creating an easement on properties, you are correct. Courts in all states have ruled that it is important for individuals, and society as a whole, that real property be freely exchanged. Anything that would make certain parcels off limits for real estate transactions, such as prohibiting a person from accessing his own property, is considered an undesirable result. As a consequence, many of the real estate rules that we address throughout this book have, as their underlying principle, the idea that real estate should be made as freely transferable as possible and that anything that prevents that freedom of transfer should be eliminated.

If the rules about easements seem to make the creation of easements simpler, the opposite can be said about terminating them.

E. TERMINATING EASEMENTS

When one owner decides that he does not want his next-door neighbor to continue to use a driveway across his property, is there an action that he can take to terminate the easement? Can an owner place a fence or some other obstruction across the easement and declare the easement terminated? The answer is no. One party cannot, unilaterally, cancel an easement. In fact, there are only a few ways that an easement can be extinguished. They include the following:

- The easement is no longer needed,
- The properties have merged,
- The parties enter into an agreement, and
- The easement is abandoned.

1. THE EASEMENT IS NO LONGER NEEDED

One way of terminating an easement is to eliminate the need for it. Suppose that Jorge has an easement that gives him access to a public highway. The county builds a new road that runs along a different side of Jorge's property and closes the other highway. Jorge no longer needs an easement to the first highway, because it no longer exists, and he has ready access to the new highway. In this situation, the court would rule that the easement has been extinguished through loss of purpose.

2. THE PROPERTIES HAVE MERGED

The basic premise behind an appurtenant easement is that there are two tracts, one of which has an easement across it to allow access to another. However, suppose that the same owner buys both parcels. In that situation, the easement would disappear. Both parcels have merged, and there is no longer a need for an easement. On a more fundamental level, there is no longer a dominant and a servient estate, only a single parcel. A person cannot grant an easement to himself, so the easement terminates through **merger**.

Merger
The combination of two formerly separate tracts into a single unit.

3. THE PARTIES ENTER INTO AN AGREEMENT

The individual parties are always free to enter into an agreement extinguishing the easement. In such a situation, the person who has the easement can simply release his rights to the easement, surrendering those rights to the original landowner. In this situation, the agreement rescinds the easement, and the other landowner would no longer be required to allow access across his property. Just as with creating an easement, the Statute of Frauds requires a release of an easement to be in writing.

4. THE EASEMENT IS ABANDONED

Abandoning an easement is the opposite of creating one by prescription. In **abandonment**, the party who has the easement stops using it, or the other landowner blocks off the easement and the easement-holder fails to object. Just as with easements by prescription, when a party has a right and fails to use it, that right will be lost. In this case, the easement-holder will eventually lose his right to the easement by failing to object to the other landowner's actions.

Abandonment
Giving up or surrendering all legal rights.

LICENSES

License
Permission to do a
specific act.

A **license** is a right granted to a specific individual to come onto someone else's property for a specific purpose. An example of a license is allowing certain people onto the property to hunt or fish. Both private and governmental owners are permitted to license the use of their property. It is very common for governmental agencies to license the use of public lands for logging or hunting and to require payment from individuals who seek these licenses. A license is different from an easement in that the party who comes onto the land with a license does so for a specific purpose. Licenses do not run with the land as easements do. Instead, a license is more like a contract between the landowner and the person who wishes to enter the property.

REAL ESTATE BASICS AT A GLANCE

A license gives a specific person the right to enter onto the land to do a specific action.

PROFIT À PRENDRE

Profit à prendre
(French) The right of a person
to enter onto land owned by
another and remove an item
or items previously agreed
upon, for example, crops.

Real property owners have the right to transfer a portion of their rights to others. We have seen this with easements and licenses; however, the owner can transfer other rights as well. For instance, an owner can grant *profit à prendre* to another person. *Profit à prendre*, or profits, involves taking products generated on the parcel. Examples include harvesting crops from the land, removing timber, or mining the soil. In this situation, a person or company who had been granted a profit could enter the land, remove the specified items, and then resell them. Obviously, the landowner and the person taking the products have negotiated this right.

EXAMPLE 5-6

GROWING CROPS

Juan owns 16 acres of mountain land that is not suitable for growing crops and is too far away from town to develop as home sites. However, the land is perfect for growing Christmas trees. Juan plants hundreds of trees and then negotiates a contract with Trees 'R Us, granting the company the right to enter onto the land and harvest the trees every year before the Christmas season. Juan has created a *profit à prendre* arrangement with Trees 'R Us.

How do profits compare with easements? When a person or company has a profit, they can enter onto the land and remove items. Easement holders are allowed to pass over the land but are certainly not permitted to remove items. Profit holders are also different from license holders, because persons with licenses enter the property for a specific activity, such as hunting or fishing, not harvesting the products of the land itself.

Examples of *profit à prendre* include allowing someone to come onto the land to:

- Graze cattle,[4]
- Remove sand from a beach,
- Harvest timber, and
- Harvest crops.

The right to profits from the land means that someone other than the owner has the right to enter onto the land and remove items, such as crops, minerals, trees, and so on.

REAL
ESTATE
BASICS AT
A GLANCE

LIENS

So far, our discussion about the rights associated with real property ownership has focused on the privileges that ownership brings. However, there is a downside to real property ownership. For instance, creditors are permitted to file actions against the property to force a landowner to pay a debt. This action usually comes in the form of a **lien**.

A lien is an action filed by a creditor that prevents the sale of the property until the debt is satisfied. This is a very powerful tool to put in the hands of a creditor, so courts and statutes have given it only to specific types of creditors. There are two classes of creditors who can file a lien against property:

1 Materialmen, and
2 Mechanics.

These terms are somewhat archaic, but there are important differences between materialmen and mechanics. When a person is classified as a **materialman**, it means that he has provided supplies to a landowner. These supplies might be building materials, livestock feed, or even fuel. A **mechanic**, on the other hand, is a person who provides a service to the landowner. The service might be helping to harvest crops, building a barn, or providing any other service to the landowner. In either situation, the creditor has the right to file a lien against the property when he is not paid.

Although the terms "materialman" and "mechanic" continue to be used, most states have stopped making a distinction between them. Because they both have the right to file a lien, it no longer matters if they provided a service or supplies.

We began this section by saying that a lien acts to prevent the sale of real property, but the issue is actually more complicated than that. In most situations, a lien may

Lien
A monetary claim against property brought by a creditor that may ripen into a judgment.

Materialman
A creditor who has provided supplies for the benefit of a real property owner.

Mechanic
A creditor who has provided a service for the benefit of a real property owner.

prevent the sale outright, but in other situations, the lien may simply attach to the real property title, eventually ripening into a judgment that a court will insist must be paid. Whether a lien immediately prevents the sale of property or will eventually become a judgment against the property depends on applicable state law. However, most banks and lending institutions will not allow a prospective buyer to borrow funds to purchase a home that has a lien placed against it. In practical terms, then, the type of lien is unimportant. Because a lender won't provide funds to purchase a property that has a lien against it, the practical result is that all liens prevent the sale of the property. Before the title can change hands, the lien must be cleared up, at least to the lender's satisfaction. We will see, in later chapters, the effect that lending institutions have had on the field of real property law, often indirectly exerting power to correct issues such as liens and other encumbrances against real property.

When a general contractor builds a home, for example, he will often obtain a lien waiver from subcontractors in exchange for their payment. This waiver prevents the subcontractors from filing a lien against the property to satisfy an outstanding bill owed by the general contractor. When a creditor files a lien and the homeowner pays the bill, the homeowner should insist on a signed lien waiver from the creditor. See Figure 5-2 for an example of California's lien waiver form.

ASSESSMENTS

Assessment
A payment made above and beyond normal taxes owed for real property.

No discussion of the rights and obligations of landowners would be complete without mentioning assessments. An **assessment** is a bill by a governmental agency for improvement in or near the property. An example of assessments would be putting in sidewalks in subdivisions and then billing the residents for the costs associated with creating the sidewalks. Assessments can come in a wide variety of forms, but most of them focus on improvements created by the government that directly benefit specific parcels of land.

AIR RIGHTS

Before the invention of the airplane, the issue of air rights did not rank very high on the roster of real property issues. Legal commentators simply assumed that a landowner's rights to the air above his property extended as far into the sky as he wished. The old common law maxim stated air rights very succinctly: "The rights of the owner extend all the way to heaven and all the way to hell."[5]

However, the issue changed dramatically when air travel became a new means of transportation. Suddenly, those clearly defined rights were causing legal problems. After all, when a plane crosses over the boundaries of someone's property, even at 20,000 feet, this is technically a trespass. Even a short plane ride would result in hundreds, if not thousands, of trespass cases. On a more practical level, courts began

CONDITIONAL WAIVER AND RELEASE ON PROGRESS PAYMENT

FIGURE 5-2

NOTICE: THIS DOCUMENT WAIVES THE CLAIMANT'S LIEN, STOP PAYMENT NOTICE, AND PAYMENT BOND RIGHTS EFFECTIVE ON RECEIPT OF PAYMENT. A PERSON SHOULD NOT RELY ON THIS DOCUMENT UNLESS SATISFIED THAT THE CLAIMANT HAS RECEIVED PAYMENT.

California Conditional Waiver and Release upon Progress Payment Form

Identifying Information

Name of Claimant:

Name of Customer:

Job Location:

Owner:

Through Date:

Conditional Waiver and Release

This document waives and releases lien, stop payment notice, and payment bond rights the claimant has for labor and service provided, and equipment and material delivered, to the customer on this job through the Through Date of this document. Rights based upon labor or service provided, or equipment or material delivered, pursuant to a written change order that has been fully executed by the parties prior to the date that this document is signed by the claimant, are waived and released by this document, unless listed as an Exception below. This document is effective only on the claimant's receipt of payment from the financial institution on which the following check is drawn:

Maker of Check:

Amount of Check: $

Check Payable to:

Exceptions

This document does not affect any of the following:
(1) Retentions.
(2) Extras for which the claimant has not received payment.
(3) The following progress payments for which the claimant has previously given a conditional waiver and release but has not received payment:
     Date(s) of waiver and release:_____
     Amount(s) of unpaid progress payment(s): $_____
(4) Contract rights, including (A) a right based on rescission, abandonment, or breach of contract, and (B) the right to recover compensation for work not compensated by the payment.

Signature

Claimant's Signature:

Claimant's Title:

Date of Signature:

7/1/12

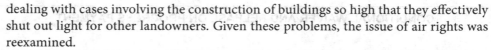

dealing with cases involving the construction of buildings so high that they effectively shut out light for other landowners. Given these problems, the issue of air rights was reexamined.

The current state of the law is that a landowner possesses rights in the air above his property to a reasonable height. Determining this reasonable distance depends on several factors. For instance, a farmer might go as high as 100 feet to construct a windmill to draw water or to generate power, while the owners of a high-rise building would need a much greater height to complete the building. One landowner's use of air space also depends on the effect that this use will have on adjoining landowners. The greater the impact on the neighbors, the more likely the court will rule that the use is unreasonable and must be discontinued.

WATER RIGHTS

The right to use water is one of the most important rights a landowner has. In cities, where water systems are connected to city water lines, homeowners may give little thought to water. But in the countryside, where homeowners draw their water from pumps and wells, the absence of water can mean the difference between a thriving community and a desert. There are entire books written exclusively about this important right. Although our discussion of water rights is not that detailed, it is important for anyone learning about real property law to understand the unique features of water rights.

A. THE RIGHT TO DRAW WATER

The right to draw water is considered one of the most essential and necessary rights that a real property owner possesses. Many states, especially those in the western United States, have crafted statutes specifying exactly how water can be used.

When property borders a river, stream, or lake, the property owner has the right to some of that water for his own use. In most states, the owner is restricted to "reasonable" use of water. Although the definition of reasonable varies from state to state, most courts define reasonable as use that is commensurate with need and that does not deprive other owners of water for their own purposes.[6]

B. SUBTERRANEAN WATER

If a property owner has rights to surface waters, what about underground waters? Most people who depend on water get it, in one form or another, from underground sources. However, the issues here can become very complicated. When we are discussing surface waters, the owner's right to the water derives from the simple fact that the property borders on the water. However, can the same be said of subterranean water? For instance, what is the source of a landowner's rights to this water? By its very nature, the water source cannot be seen, and the actual location of the water may be difficult, if not impossible, to establish. There is no way to establish that the property borders on a large underground lake. What, then, gives a property owner the right to use this water?

Most legal authorities point to the deed and the owner's title to the property as the source for the owner's additional right to draw water. This right to draw and use water applies not only to surface waters but also to subterranean waters. Under this theory, the right to draw water is identical to the rights that property owners have to harvest crops grown on the property, to mine for minerals, or to use the air space above the property. However, that analogy does not hold up under close scrutiny. For one thing, all of those other features are stationary and held within the boundaries of the property. Water, on the other hand, is free-flowing, moving from place to place.

C. TERMINOLOGY FOR WATER RIGHTS

There is some important terminology related to both surface and underground waters. For instance, water that soaks through the soil and pools at some point below the surface is referred to as "percolating" water. On the other hand, water that flows in an underground river is commonly referred to as a "watercourse." These terms are important not only because they distinguish between different types of water, but also because the rights associated with them vary according to their classification. An underground river, for instance, is usually controlled by the same statute that controls aboveground streams. However, percolating water is treated differently.[7]

MINERAL RIGHTS

The final category of rights associated with real property is mineral rights. One of the rights that comes with property ownership is the ability to take useful items from the soil. Property owners can mine for gold, silver, or other useful materials, assuming that such activities do not violate zoning or other ordinances. In many cases, however, previous owners may have already transferred mineral rights to another party. In the late 1800s and early 1900s, for example, it was not uncommon for mining companies to purchase mineral rights to huge swaths of countryside. Because those rights have already been conveyed away, current owners no longer possess them and therefore have no right to sink mines in their own properties.

Case Excerpt

SCOTT v. LEE & DONNA METCALF CHARITABLE TRUST
381 Mont. 64, 358 P.3d 879 (2015)

Opinion

Justice MICHAEL E. WHEAT delivered the Opinion of the Court.

Terrance Scott and Laurie Scott (the Scotts) appeal from the order of the Montana First Judicial District Court, Lewis and Clark County, resolving cross-motions for summary judgment in favor of the Lee and Donna Metcalf Charitable Trust (the Trust). We affirm.

Issues

We review the following issues:

1. Did the District Court err by deciding that the Metcalf Restrictions were enforceable against the Scotts by the Trust?

Factual and Procedural Background

On January 3, 1996, Donna Metcalf (Metcalf) transferred a 40-acre parcel of land located near Lake Helena to Richard Thieltges (Thieltges) by warranty deed. The deed stated that:

> Metcalf, for and in consideration of the sum of One Dollar and other valuable consideration . . . to her in hand paid by Thieltges, . . . does by these presents grant, bargain, sell, convey, warrant and confirm unto Thieltges and to his heirs and assigns forever, the hereinafter-described real estate. . . .
>
> Metcalf does hereby impose and charge all of the above-described property with certain exceptions, with the covenants, restrictions, conditions and charges as follows:
>
> 1. Thieltges shall not engage in any activity nor shall he permit another to use the property in any way so as to reduce the quality of the stream running through the property below the water quality as it exists on the date of this conveyance, nor shall Thieltges utilize the riparian area surrounding the stream in any way such that the quality of the said riparian area shall be reduced below that existing at the time of this conveyance.
>
> 2. The above-described parcel has several improvements, including a log dwelling house situated thereon. No more than one single-family residence, in addition to the existing log dwelling structure, shall be placed upon this parcel, and the said parcel may not be subdivided beyond its existing forty acres.
>
> These restrictions and covenants are to run with the land and shall be binding upon Thieltges, his successors, heirs or assigns. Enforcement shall be by proceedings at law or in equity against any person or persons violating or attempting to violate any covenants, either to restrain violations or to recover damages.

The "covenants, restrictions, conditions and charges" imposed in paragraphs 1 and 2 will hereinafter be referred to as the Metcalf Restrictions. Thieltges recorded the deed with the Lewis and Clark County Clerk and Recorder on January 10, 1996.

On September 1, 2000, Thieltges transferred the full 40-acre parcel to the Scotts by warranty deed. The deed incorporated by reference a title insurance report, which specifically mentioned the Metcalf Restrictions. In light of this and based on their communications with Thieltges, the Scotts admit that they had actual knowledge of the Metcalf Restrictions at the time of the transfer.

On July 12, 2013, the Scotts filed a complaint in the District Court seeking permission to subdivide their 40-acre parcel. The Scotts asked the District Court to invalidate the Metcalf Restrictions and allow them to subdivide the property. In the complaint, they named the Trust and Lewis and Clark County as defendants. Lewis and Clark County disclaimed an interest in the suit, and it has not participated in the case since. The Trust answered the Scotts' complaint and then filed a counterclaim asking the Court to enforce the Metcalf Restrictions.

Soon thereafter, both parties filed motions for summary judgment. They agreed there were no factual issues to be resolved, and that the case could be decided based on construction of the Metcalf Restrictions. The District Court granted summary judgment in favor of the Trust on November 12, 2014. It decided that the Metcalf Restrictions were covenants of which the Scotts had actual notice. It also decided that Metcalf and Thieltges intended the Metcalf Restrictions to run with the land. For these reasons, it concluded that the Metcalf Restrictions were enforceable against the Scotts and any other of Thieltges's successors with actual notice of them. It refused to invalidate the restrictions. The Scotts appeal.

Discussion

1. Did the District Court err by deciding that the Metcalf Restrictions were enforceable against the Scotts by the Trust?

The Trust argues that the Metcalf Restrictions are real covenants enforceable against Thieltges and his successors in interest, the Scotts. The Scotts, on the other hand, argue that the Metcalf Restrictions are an easement in gross that is unenforceable against them by the Trust. For this reason, they argue that the District Court erred when it granted summary judgment in favor of the Trust. We do not wholly agree with either party. We hold that the Metcalf Restrictions are enforceable against the Scotts by the Trust as an easement in gross.

An easement in gross is a nonpossessory interest in land that benefits the holder of the easement personally. *Bos Terra, LP v. Beers*, 380 Mont. 109, 354 P.3d 572 (2015). It is distinguishable from an easement appurtenant, which benefits a particular parcel of land. Both easements in gross and easements appurtenant burden a parcel of land, which is termed the servient estate. Easements appurtenant also benefit an associated parcel of land, which is termed the dominant estate. No such dominant estate exists for easements in gross.

We agree with the Scotts that when Metcalf and Thieltges made the Metcalf Restrictions they created easements in gross. We have held that a servitude or restriction is properly classified as an easement in gross if it falls within the scope of §70-17-102, MCA, and if there is no dominant estate that the servitude or restriction benefits.

The parties in this case agree that the Metcalf Restrictions were made for conservation purposes. Additionally, the Scotts have repeatedly argued that the benefit of the easement is not attached to any dominant estate. The Trust has not disagreed nor has it provided evidence indicating that such a dominant estate exists. Moreover, we cannot identify any estate benefited by the Metcalf Restrictions from the terms of the Restrictions or from any other part of the record. As such, there is no genuine issue that there is no dominant estate benefitted by the Metcalf Restrictions. Thus, the Metcalf

Restrictions created an easement in gross since they comply with §70-17-102(7), MCA, and they do not benefit any dominant estate.

We disagree with the Scotts' conclusion that this characterization of the Metcalf Restrictions — characterization of them as easements in gross — compels the conclusion that the Metcalf Restrictions are unenforceable against them. For an easement to be enforceable against parties that were not the original parties to the easement, the burden of the easement must pass to the original easement grantor's successors in interest and the benefit of the easement must pass to the original easement grantee's successors in interest. Since both pass in this case and since the Scotts base their arguments concerning enforceability only on whether the benefit and burden passed, we conclude that the easement was enforceable by the Trust against the Scotts.

The burden of the easement passed to the Scotts. According to §70-20-308, MCA, an easement remains attached to a servient estate despite transfer of that estate. Here, the 40-acre parcel became the servient estate of the easement when Thieltges and Metcalf created the Metcalf Restrictions and Thieltges thereby granted an easement to Metcalf. By §70-20-308, MCA, Thieltges's subsequent transfer of the parcel to the Scotts did not extinguish the easement.

We have suggested that an easement may not survive certain transfers where the original parties to the easement have no intent for the easement to pass to successors or where a successor to the servient estate succeeds to the estate without notice of the easement. Neither requirement provides grounds for the Scotts to avoid the burden of the easement in this case. Metcalf and Thieltges intended the Metcalf Restrictions to pass with the servient estate. In their deed, they specifically stated that "these restrictions and covenants are to run with the land and shall be binding upon Thieltges, his successors, heirs or assigns." Also, the Scotts took the property with both record and actual notice of the Metcalf Restrictions. They admitted in their briefs to this Court and to the District Court that they had actual knowledge of the Metcalf Restrictions. Indeed, the restrictions were acknowledged in the deed they took from Thieltges. The Metcalf Restrictions also had been recorded with Lewis and Clark County at the time Metcalf transferred the property to Thieltges. The Scotts also, therefore, had record notice of the easement. For the foregoing reasons, the burden of the easement passed with the servient estate when it was transferred to the Scotts.

The benefit of the easement also passed when it was transferred from Metcalf to the Trust. Both parties assume that the Trust is Metcalf's successor in interest, presumably as the devisee of her estate. The Scotts contend that the easement, as an easement in gross, was extinguished upon Metcalf's death and that it was not devisable, descendible, or otherwise transferrable to the Trust. We disagree.

We have held that "whether or not . . . an easement may be alienated and apportioned depends upon the manner and the terms of the creation of the easement." *Lindley*, 198 Mont. at 199, 645 P.2d at 431. In *Lindley*, we decided that an easement in gross survived transfer of the benefit of the easement from the original grantee of the easement to his successor in interest. We held that the easement in gross was enforceable against the grantor's successor in interest by the grantee's successor in interest. We reasoned that there was "no language in the warranty deed limiting the grantee's right to freely alienate and apportion the easement." *Lindley*, 198 Mont. at 199, 645 P.2d at 431.

Similarly, in this case, neither the deed from Metcalf to Thieltges nor the deed from Thieltges to Scott contains any language limiting Metcalf's right to freely transfer the easement. As in *Lindley*, we hold that the easement in gross comprising the Metcalf Restrictions was freely transferrable. It was, therefore devisable to the Trust. The easement in gross was not rendered unenforceable by its transfer or by Metcalf's death.

We also recognize that our holding—allowing Metcalf to transfer the benefit of her easement in gross absent language in the deed limiting her right to do so—is at odds with the laws of many other jurisdictions. Most jurisdictions in the United States strictly limit the transfer of easements in gross. However, our law governing easements has not always tracked the rule followed by the majority of states, and we do not feel compelled to follow the majority rule here. Moreover, our conclusion is not wholly inconsistent with the jurisprudence of the rest of the country. For example, the Restatement (Third) of Property states that benefits of servitudes in gross are transferrable and devolve either as property of their owners or as contractual obligations of their obligor. Restatement (Third) of Property: Servitudes §5.8 (citing cases from Colorado, Florida, Georgia, Illinois, and Wisconsin, in addition to this Court's decision in *Lindley*). We do not adopt the Restatement, but we note that we have quoted it approvingly in the past and we cite it here as authority that our holding in this case is not wholly unique.

For the foregoing reasons, we conclude the Metcalf Restrictions created an easement in gross, and that the benefit of the easement passed to the Trust and that the burden of the easement passed to the Scotts. Because we find the parties' arguments to the contrary unpersuasive, we conclude that the Metcalf Restrictions are enforceable against the Scotts by the Trust as an easement in gross.

Conclusion

The District Court did not err by granting summary judgment in favor of the Trust. When Metcalf and Thieltges created the Metcalf Restrictions, Thieltges granted an easement in gross to Metcalf. It was immaterial to the creation of the easement that the easement might have been enforced via a Title 76, Chapter 6, MCA, conservation easement. The terms of the easement did not prevent its transfer and the easement was not extinguished when Metcalf died or when Metcalf transferred the easement to the Trust. It also was not extinguished when Thieltges transferred the servient estate to the Scotts. For these reasons, the District Court correctly concluded that the Metcalf Restrictions could be enforced by the Trust against the Scotts. We affirm its decision to grant summary judgment in favor of the Trust.

/S/ Michael E Wheat

QUESTIONS ABOUT THE CASE

1 How did the restrictive covenants become an issue in this case?
2 Did the court rule that the restrictive covenants were enforceable, or did the court reach a different classification for the actions by the original owners?
3 The Scotts argue that if the restrictions are considered to be an easement in gross instead of a restrictive covenant, then the conditions no longer apply to them. How does the court deal with that argument?

COVID-19 CONCERN

With politics coloring nearly every aspect of U.S. life, it is not outside the realm of possibility that a seller would refuse to sell their property to a person who is or isn't vaccinated against the COVID-19 virus or its variants. In the past, sellers have refused to sell to people of color or to people of a specific religion or national origin. Although it is almost certain that refusal to sell on the basis of a personal medical diagnosis will be ruled unconstitutional, at present there are no rulings. Is it possible that the unvaccinated (or vaccinated) will become a "sub-class" of people who are denied basic rights, such as the right to purchase or acquire other rights in real estate?

CHAPTER SUMMARY

Fixtures are items of personal property that have become permanently attached to real property. At the moment of attachment, personal property is reclassified as real property. This reclassification has both philosophical and practical consequences. When something becomes permanently attached to real property, it remains with the property when the parcel is sold and there is no requirement to list it separately on the deed.

Easements are the rights of non-owners to use a portion of a real estate parcel. Easements come in two forms: appurtenant easements and in gross easements. An appurtenant easement gives a non-owner the right to use a portion of the owner's property. The most common example of an appurtenant easement is a driveway. An adjoining landowner has the right to use a portion of property that does not belong to him in order to access his own parcel. An in gross easement gives a non-owner the right to enter on the owner's property, usually for the purpose of maintaining utilities.

There are many other rights and obligations associated with real property ownership. Real property owners can be charged for governmental improvements on or near the property. Real property owners can give licenses to others to use their property for specific purposes, such as hunting and fishing. Owners also have specific rights arising from ownership of a real property parcel. For instance, owners have air rights, which give them the right to use the air above their property to a reasonable distance. Owners also have rights in the soil, referred to as mineral rights. These rights give the owner the ability to mine the soil for metals and other useful materials. Finally, an owner can transfer certain rights to others while retaining full ownership. An owner might, for example, transfer the right to harvest crops or the right to mine for minerals to another person.

SKILLS YOU NEED IN THE REAL WORLD

Researching Liens and Other Assessments

We have seen that liens and other types of assessments against property can result in any of a number of potential problems for homeowners. Many of these problems do not surface until the homeowner has put the house up for sale. Then there is little time to correct some of these legal problems. To check the status of real estate for any liens or assessments, you must learn your state's system for recording these items. In some states, for example, liens are filed in the clerk of court's office. They are sometimes cross-referenced with the deed office or land office, but that isn't always the case. You can learn how to search for liens and other assessments by visiting the local government agencies that track them. Learn what office inside the local courthouse or land office is responsible for tracking liens and practice locating liens before you actually need this skill. The time that you spend in this preparation is a wise investment toward building a skill set that will help you throughout your career.

ETHICAL ISSUES FOR THE PARALEGAL

Unauthorized Practice of Law

Paralegals should always be keenly aware of the dangers posed by answering questions and offering advice to others about legal matters. All states have some variation of the following law: "It shall be unlawful for any person except members of the State Bar who are admitted and licensed to practice in this state, to appear as attorney or counselor at law in any action or proceeding before any judicial body, except in his own behalf as a party thereto; or, by word, sign, letter or advertisement, to hold himself, or themselves, as competent or qualified to give legal advice or counsel, or to prepare legal documents."[8]

As you can see, a paralegal might be guilty of the crime of unauthorized practice of law for giving legal advice or carrying out other actions normally reserved for attorneys. The safest course to take to avoid an allegation of unauthorized practice of law is to review your own state's statutes and also make sure that you identify yourself as a paralegal. Many non-lawyers preface their remarks with the statement, "I cannot give you legal advice," or, "You understand that I cannot act as a lawyer, since I'm not a member of the bar." Such statements, and strict compliance with state law, will help you avoid an allegation of unauthorized practice of law.

KEY TERMS AND CONCEPTS

Abandonment	Assessment	Fixture
Appurtenant easement	Easement	In gross easement

License	Mechanic	Run with the land
Lien	Merger	Trade fixture
Materialman	*Profit à prendre*	

END-OF-CHAPTER EXERCISES

Review Questions

See Appendix for answers.

1   What is a fixture?
2   What are some of the tests that courts have used to determine when something qualifies as a fixture?
3   What is the difference between a fixture and a trade fixture?
4   What is an easement?
5   What are the two different types of easements?
6   List and explain the ways that easements can be created.
7   List and explain the ways that easements can be terminated.
8   What are assessments?
9   How are licenses and easements different?
10   Explain "profits" from the land.
11   Compare and contrast profits, licenses, and easements.
12   What is the difference between materialmen's liens and mechanics' liens?
13   What are air rights?
14   How would a real property owner's air rights in the eighteenth century compare to those same rights today?
15   How did the development of air travel affect property owners' air rights?
16   Why are water rights important?
17   What rights does an owner of real property have to subterranean water?
18   What are "percolating waters"?
19   Explain mineral rights.
20   Explain the decision in this chapter's case excerpt.

DISCUSSION QUESTIONS

1   Should all adjoining landowners always be granted an easement or are there situations where courts should rule that an easement should not be allowed?

2   Air rights for property underwent a dramatic change when airplane travel became common. There is now a possibility that certain companies may begin delivering items by drone. Does this create a new problem for property owners? Why or why not?

APPLYING WHAT YOU HAVE LEARNED

1   Do statutes and court rules favor the creation of easements? Explain your answer.

2   Why is water such an important component of property rights? Explain your answer.

3   Visit your local real estate or land office and locate a copy of an easement, lien, or assessment that has been filed against a particular title. What are the details provided on this filing?

WEB SURFING

Fixtures: Upcounsel
https://www.upcounsel.com/legal-def-fixtures

Trade Fixtures: Duhaime.org
https://www.duhaime.org/Legal-Dictionary/Term/TradeFixtures

Easements by Implication: Pennsylvania Legislator's Municipal Deskbook (at pg. 127)
http://www.lgc.state.pa.us/download.cfm?file=/Reports/deskbook20/Deskbook%206th%20Edition%202020.pdf

Mineral Rights: Michigan Department of Environmental Quality
http://www.michigan.gov/documents/deq/ogs-oilandgas-mineral-rights_257977_7.pdf

Tech Topic
TAX LIEN SEARCH

The Foreclosures and Tax Lien Sale Records Resources website (http://publicrecords.onlinesearches.com/Foreclosures-and-Tax-Lien-Sales.htm) offers links to the online foreclosure and lien search functions of nearly all counties in the United States. While there are advertisements for paid searches on the website, the links themselves go to the free search resources available on each county's website, giving you a central location from which to search for tax liens filed against property anywhere in the country.

ANNOTATED DOCUMENT

Lien

Form 9

Notice of Other Lien Filling

Name and Telephone Number of Contact at Filer (optional)

Return copy to: (Name and Mailing Address)

John Doe
123 Maple Drive
Anywhere, PL 00030

Creditor filing lien

☑ Notice of filing of lien.

Check one ☐ Notice of full release or discharge of lien.

☐ Notice of change of lien

1. Debtor Name: Insert only one debtor in 1a. or 1b.

	For Secretary of State Use Only
MARY ROE, INC.	*ROE* *MARY* *R.*
1a. Entity's Name	1b. Individual's Last Name: First: Middle: Suffix:
1001 BURKE DR.	*ANYWHERE* *PL* *CA.* *00030*
1c. Mailing Address	City State Country Postal Code

Landowner who owes debt

2. Additional Debtor Name: Insert only one debtor in 2a. or 2b.

N/A	
2a. Entity's Name	2b. Individual's Last Name: First: Middle: Suffix:
2c. Mailing Address	City State Country Postal Code

3. Lienor's Name: Insert only one lienor name in 3a. or 3b.

SAME AS ABOVE	
3a. Entity's Name	3b. Individual's Last Name: First: Middle: Suffix:
3c. Mailing Address	City State Country Postal Code

4. Type of lien/statutory authority

☐ Federal tax lien ☐ State Tax lien ☐ Town tax lien on manufactured housing ☐ Aircraft registration lien

☐ Child support lien ☐ Housing Finance Authority lien ☐ Hazardous Waste lien ☐ Employment Security lien

☐ Writ of attachment ☐ Road Toll lien ☑ Creditors bill lien ☐ State Food Security Act lien

5. Complete if filing is a release, discharge or change.

Filing Location of initial lien: *N/A*

Filing Date of initial lien: _____

File Number: assigned to initial lien: _____   other lien form 9, version 1.1

PRACTICE QUESTIONS FOR TEST REVIEW

See Appendix for answers.

Essay Question

Describe how easements are created.

True–False

1　T　F　A kitchen cabinet is an example of a fixture.

2　T　F　Intent is not a feature that helps determine whether an item is a fixture.

3　T　F　When it will cause a great deal of damage to remove an item, it is more likely to be ruled a fixture.

Fill in the Blank

1　This court-created test states that an item formerly classified as personal property can be considered to be a fixture when the item is essential for the day-to-day use of the real property:_____.

2　A fixture, often machinery or equipment, that is essential to running a business: _____.

3　When a person or company is granted the right to use part of another's property for access to equipment or as a driveway: _____.

Multiple Choice

1　An item that was formerly classified as personal property but has become real property by virtue of becoming attached to it.

　　A　Requisite
　　B　Improvement
　　C　*Seizin*
　　D　Fixture

2　All of the following elements help determine whether an item is a fixture, except:

　　A　Intent of the party who installed it
　　B　Manner of attachment
　　C　Use
　　D　All of the above will make an item qualify as a fixture

3　The process of attaching a fixture to real property.

　　A　Attestation
　　B　Acknowledgement
　　C　Annexation
　　D　Acquisition

ENDNOTES

[1] *Household Finance Corp. v. BancOhio*, 62 Ohio App. 3d 691, 577 N.E.2d 405 (1989).

[2] *Colonial Pipeline Co. v. State Dep't of Assessments & Taxation*, 371 Md. 16, 32 (2002).

[3] *Mitchell v. Golden*, 107 N.C. App. 413, 420 S.E.2d 482 (1992).

[4] *Burlingame v. Marjerrison*, 204 Mont. 464, 665 P.2d 1136 (1983).

[5] *Jones v. Loan Association*, 252 N.C. 626, 637, 114 S.E.2d 638, 646 (1960).

[6] *Pine Knoll Association, Inc. v. Cardon*, 126 N.C. App. 155, 484 S.E.2d 446 (1997).

[7] *Bull v. Siegrist*, 169 Or. 180, 126 P.2d 832 (1942).

[8] N.C. Gen. Stat. §84-4.

Real Estate Contracts

- Define the basic components of any legally binding contract

- Explain the minimum requirements of a valid offer

- Define when and under what circumstances a valid acceptance is made

- Explain the importance of the Statute of Frauds to real estate transactions

- List and describe the various types of clauses that are routinely inserted into real estate contracts

I. Introduction

II. What is a Contract?
   A. Offer
   B. Acceptance
   C. Mutual Assent
   D. Consideration
   E. Legality
   F. Capacity

III. The Statute of Frauds

IV. Formation Issues in Contract Law
   A. Guidelines That Courts Use to Interpret Contracts
   B. Mistake
   C. Fraud

V. Real Estate Contracts
   A. Listing Agreements
   B. Offer of Purchase and Contract
   C. Options

VI. Contract Clauses
   A. Time Is of the Essence
   B. Title
   C. Escrow
   D. Insurance (Risk of Loss)

VII. Breach of Contract
   A. Remedies for the Seller
   B. Remedies for the Buyer
   C. Remedies for the Broker

INTRODUCTION

In this chapter, we will explore the topic of contract law as it applies to real property transactions. There has always been a close relationship between real estate law and contract law. The two topics are closely interwoven, and it is difficult, if not impossible, to understand one without understanding the other. Real estate practice is rife with examples of contracts, from the lease between a landlord and a tenant, to the offer of purchase between a prospective buyer and seller, to the real estate agent's commission with the seller. Contracts appear at nearly every phase of a real estate transaction. (See Figure 6-1 for statistics on home ownership in metropolitan areas.)

We will explore the relationship between contract and real property law by first addressing the basic components of a contract. We then proceed to specific examples of contracts in real estate practice and the common provisions found in real estate contracts.

But first we must answer the question: What is a contract?

FIGURE 6-1

Quarterly Home Ownership 1998-2021

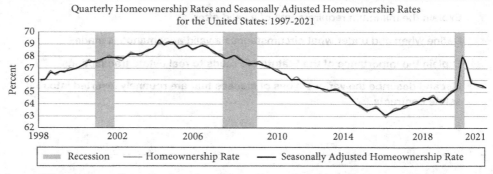

Sourcce: U.S. Census Bureau, Current Population Survey/Housing Vacancy Survery, November 2, 2021, Recession data: National Bureau of Economic Research, <www.nber.org>

WHAT IS A CONTRACT?

Contract
A legally recognized agreement that gives both parties the right to enforce the obligation through legal means.

A **contract** is an agreement between two or more parties in which those parties agree to exchange something of value. The value may be in the form of a service for which a person will be paid, or it could be the exchange of title for a particular item, such as a car or a house. The important point to make about contracts is that, when one is created, it gives both parties certain rights. Among these rights is the option of using the court system to enforce the contract provisions in the event that one party fails to live up to her agreements.

We will concentrate on real estate contracts in this chapter, but the introductory material here applies to all types of contracts. When a contract is created, it gives the parties specific rights and obligations. If a party breaches the terms of the contract, the other party has the right to sue for damages or seek equitable relief.

No matter what the subject of the contract, all contracts have some basic elements. There must be:

- An offer,
- An acceptance of that offer,
- Mutual assent,
- Consideration,
- Legality, and
- Capacity.

A. OFFER

An offer is one party's indication of her willingness to enter into a contract. Offers are specific; they invite another person to enter into a legally binding agreement. The details that must be present in an offer include the following:

- Who will be bound by the contract?
- What (services, property, title) will be exchanged?
- What are the terms?
- What is the manner of performance?

If an offer sets out these terms, it will be valid, even if it is vague on some points. For instance, there is no requirement that the offer anticipate all possible issues, or even that it define specific items such as manner and time of payment. If the questions in Figure 6-2 can be answered, the offer will be considered legally valid. Beyond that, an offer can be silent on other issues.

A valid offer must provide answers for the following questions:
- Who can accept?
- What is being offered?
- What will be exchanged?
- What are the terms?
- How can a party indicate acceptance of the offer?

FIGURE 6-2

Terms of a Valid Offer

SIMON'S "FOR SALE" SIGN

EXAMPLE 6-1

Simon puts a "For Sale" sign on his front yard. Is Simon's sign a valid, legal offer?

Answer: No. Simon's "For Sale" sign cannot be considered an offer because it lacks sufficient information. It does not, for example, specify who can accept, what the sale price is, what the terms are, or what exactly Simon is offering for sale. After all, based on the sign's location, he might just as easily be selling the sod in his front yard. Barring any further developments, courts will not consider Simon's sign to be a valid offer.

1. OFFERS DO NOT REQUIRE SPECIFIC LANGUAGE

If Simon's sign is not an offer, does it have any legal significance? Many legal commentators would refer to Simon's sign as an "invitation for offers." Simon is effectively stating to the world his intention of receiving an offer on his home.

There is no requirement for offers to contain legal-sounding phrases, such as "party of the first part" or other "legalese." A valid offer can be couched in everyday language, and the words used will be given their ordinary meaning. Another test that we can apply to an offer is even more basic: Does the offer create something that another person could accept?

Tech Topic
COMMUNICATING OFFERS VIA E-MAIL, TEXT, OR TWITTER

State law varies on the enforceability of unsigned or oral contracts, although most states affirm that if an oral contract is partially performed, the contract is then binding. However, real estate law generally states that an offer on a property must be signed by the buyer, show an acceptance by the seller, and have a written contract by both parties. But with the proliferation of communication by way of email, text message, and Twitter, could electronic offers be enforceable?

In general, the answer is no. The key element of a legitimate offer is the signature. A signed offer can certainly be scanned and faxed or attached to an email, but a simple electronic communication absent the signature will not suffice. Electronic and digitally encrypted signatures are becoming more commonplace and might possibly be an acceptable alternative to a live signature one day. But the underlying technology required to create such signatures would be cumbersome in the fast-paced exchange of offers and counteroffers.

There are provisions that allow for electronic signatures and, where those laws have been enacted, such an offer might be considered legally valid. The best practice is to refer to your state's laws about electronic or digital signatures.

2. THE REASONABLE PERSON STANDARD AND OFFERS

An offer is judged by the reasonable person standard. Under this standard, a particular statement will be construed to be an offer when a reasonable person would have interpreted it that way. Under the reasonable person test, the subjective intent of the parties is not the central issue. Instead, the courts will look to the surrounding circumstances and ask the question, "Under these facts, would a reasonable person have believed that an offer had been made?"

Jan is jogging through her neighborhood when a man accosts her. The man is obviously intoxicated. He points at the house on the corner and says to Jan, "You're going to buy that house for $100,000, or you'll regret it." When Jan later refuses to purchase, the man sues. What is the result?

Answer: There is no contract. Leaving aside the issue of the man's obvious intoxication, which would affect his capacity, there is the issue of the reasonable-person standard. No one would interpret the man's actions as an offer. Besides that, Jan has not indicated an acceptance.

B. ACCEPTANCE

When a valid offer has been made, the party to whom the offer was made — referred to as the "offeree" — has one of several possible options. The offeree can simply ignore the offer, and her failure to act will be construed as a rejection of the offer. The offeree can actively reject the offer by stating that she has no intention of accepting it. The offeree can accept the offer. Finally, the offeree can make a counteroffer. We examine each of these possible scenarios.

An offer indicates a person's willingness to enter into a contract; it is also specific about what is being offered and how a person can accept.

1. THE POWER OF ACCEPTANCE

When a person rejects an offer, there is no possibility of contract because a rejected offer cancels the basic prerequisite of a contract: The offeree no longer has any power to accept it. In fact, courts often term this phase of the negotiations as *placing the power of acceptance in another person*. If a person has the **power of acceptance**, it means that she can accept an offer and create a contract. Rejecting an offer cancels the power of acceptance. It is as if the offer has died and cannot be revived. Once it has been rejected, the only way to resurrect a contract is by making a new offer. The original party might restate the offer, at which point the offeree could accept.

Power of acceptance
The legally recognized capacity of a party to accept an offer and create a binding, enforceable contract.

SIMON'S "FOR SALE" SIGN, PART 2   EXAMPLE 6-3

Simon puts up a sign in his front yard that reads, "For sale: 3br/2bath/living room/fireplace/full basement, 2200 sq. ft., $120,000, o.b.o."

Sara sees this sign and correctly interprets it to mean: for sale, house with three bedrooms, two bathrooms, living room, fireplace, full basement, 2,200 square feet at $120,000, or best offer.

Sara goes to Simon's door and says, "Okay."

Has a contract been formed?

Answer: It certainly appears that Simon's sign meets many of the requirements of an offer. It has specific details about what is being offered and for how much. But what about the issue of who can accept? Under Simon's terms, is there anything to indicate that Sara can accept? Put another way, has Simon's sign given anyone who comes by his house the power of acceptance?

Since the answer is no, the sign is not an offer. Just as we saw in an earlier example, Simon's sign is still an invitation to others to make an offer — and to incorporate some of the terms that Simon has laid out.

REAL ESTATE BASICS AT A GLANCE

A contract is the product of a valid offer that has been accepted by another.

EXAMPLE 6-4

FOLLOWING UP ON THE "FOR SALE" SIGN

Maria has seen Simon's sign and drafts an offer to him containing the following provisions:

- ◻ Offer: $115,000, cash at closing
- ◻ Fee simple absolute title
- ◻ Contingent on financing from a lender at 5 percent interest for 30 years
- ◻ Contingent on the home passing an inspection
- ◻ Offer is revoked if not accepted within 10 days

Is this a statement that a reasonable person would consider to be a valid offer?

Answer: It is specific about terms and to whom the offer is being made. It is also specific about how and when the offer will expire. If Simon were to accept this offer, a binding contract would result. Simon has the power of acceptance, and therefore this is a legally valid offer.

2. COMMUNICATING THE ACCEPTANCE TO THE OFFEROR

When an offer is accepted, the acceptance must be communicated to the offeror. If the offeree fails to communicate her intention to accept, there is no binding agreement. Unless the offer specifically limits the method used to communicate the acceptance, it can be sent through any means; an oral offer can be accepted by written correspondence, and vice versa (however, when an acceptance is made through the mail, special rules apply).[1] Later, however, we will see that the Statute of Frauds, which requires certain contracts to be in writing, usually dictates that offers and acceptances involving real property must be made in writing.

3. THE MAILBOX RULE

The so-called "mailbox rule" states that an acceptance is legally effective at the moment when it is deposited in the U.S. postal system. All states have some version of the mailbox rule.[2] The reason for the rule is simple: Without it, any offer accepted by mail would not be effective until received. We all know that it takes a posted letter from one to three days to reach its intended destination. In the fast-paced world of negotiations, 72 hours is a lifetime. Without a rule that states that an acceptance is effective the moment that it is posted, accepting contracts by letter would be nearly impossible.

Under the mailbox rule, an acceptance is legally effective when it is posted.

REAL
ESTATE
BASICS AT
A GLANCE

4. COUNTEROFFERS

A counteroffer technically rejects the original offer and replaces it with a new offer. Although most people don't phrase it this way, a counteroffer actually states the following: "I hereby reject your original offer and instead substitute my own offer for it."

THE COUNTEROFFER   `EXAMPLE 6-5`

Simon likes Maria's offer, except for the term regarding price. He decides to raise it to $118,000. What is the significance of his change in the price?

    Answer: This is a counteroffer.

    Who has the power of acceptance now?

    Answer: Maria does. She can accept the counteroffer and create a contract; if she rejects it, there will be no contract.

People make counteroffers in negotiations all the time without being aware of the legal consequences. Let's see if we can diagram what has happened in the example above.

Maria made the original offer. At that point, Simon had the power of acceptance. Had he accepted, a binding contract would have been created. However, Simon made a counteroffer, which flipped the transaction. At this point, Maria has the power of acceptance. When she accepts Simon's counteroffer, Simon and Maria become parties to a valid contract.

So far, our discussion about contracts has focused on the offer and acceptance. But there are other equally important components of a contract, including mutual assent, capacity, and legality.

C. MUTUAL ASSENT

Mutual assent is the consequence of a valid offer and acceptance. Otherwise known as a "meeting of the minds," mutual assent is the requirement that all parties know and understand the basic features of the contract. Both parties should be in agreement about what is being sold and for how much. When the parties have a basic misunderstanding about these core issues, the contract may be invalidated on the basis of a mistake. (We will discuss mistake later in this chapter.)

Mutual assent
"Meeting of the minds"; the requirement that the parties to the contract have the same understanding about the contract.

D. CONSIDERATION

Consideration
The contractual requirement that both parties incur some form of legal detriment in exchange for receiving something of value; consideration ensures that both parties are bound to the contract.

Another requirement for a valid contract is **consideration**. Consideration is the requirement that both parties give up something of value in exchange for receiving something else of value. Essentially, consideration is an element of contracts that ensures that both parties are bound to the contract's terms. A contract that binds only one person is no contract at all. Consideration is sometimes referred to as "bargained-for exchange." Both parties to a contract must negotiate away a right, service, or object in order to receive some other right, service, or object. In a common example, when homeowners sell their property to others, they are giving up title to the land in exchange for something of value, that is, money. The buyers, on the other hand, are giving up cash in exchange for the title. Consideration is usually not a question in most contracts, where the terms make clear that value is being exchanged. This is especially true in real estate transactions.

REAL ESTATE BASICS AT A GLANCE

Consideration ensures that both parties to a contract are giving up something of value in exchange for something else of value; it is also called "bargained-for exchange."

E. LEGALITY

Legality
The requirement that a contract must have a legal subject or action as its topic.

Legality is one of the most understated of contractual requirements. It almost goes without saying that before a contract can be enforced, it must contemplate a legal action. Contracts to carry out crimes are not contracts at all; at least, they are not contracts that can be enforced. Without the provision of enforcement, one could easily argue that the agreement does not qualify as a valid contract.

Although it would appear that legality would not be a question in a typical real estate transaction, there are times when legality becomes an issue. For instance, if a lender is charging a mortgage rate higher than that permitted by law, the courts could void the mortgage agreement.

F. CAPACITY

Capacity
The requirement that all parties to agreements know and understand the consequences of entering a legally binding contract.

While legality may not be a common concern in contracts, a party's **capacity** frequently is. The requirement of capacity goes directly to each party's state of mind at the time that the contract was created. A person is considered to be incompetent to enter into a contract when she lacks the ability to understand the nature and consequences of the agreement. Certain classes of persons are presumed to lack capacity, and any contract entered into by them will be considered void. See Figure 6-3 for a list of classes of persons who lack capacity.

FIGURE 6-3

Persons Who Lack
Capacity

Persons who lack capacity include:
- Minors (under the age of 18)
- Persons declared to be mentally incompetent
- Persons who have had their civil rights suspended (prisoners)
- Intoxicated persons

In some circumstances, the court may rule that a contract with a person who lacks capacity is voidable, that is, capable of being cancelled by either of the parties at their option. Examples of voidable contracts include those made with minors or persons who are intoxicated. When the legal impediment disappears, the parties can affirm the contract and create a perfectly legal agreement.

THE STATUTE OF FRAUDS

The Statute of Frauds was developed in England in the 1600s. Originally given the more descriptive name of "The Statute to Prevent Frauds," the statute was an early legislative attempt to protect consumers by requiring certain types of contracts to be in writing before they could be enforced through the court system. Examples of contracts that fall under the jurisdiction of the Statute of Frauds include:

- Wills,
- Contracts to answer for the debt of another,
- Contracts in anticipation of marriage (prenuptial/antenuptial agreements),
- Contracts for the sale of land,
- Contracts that cannot be performed within one year of the date of their creation,
- Contracts for the sale of goods exceeding $500 in value, and
- Contracts for the sale of securities (stocks, bonds).

Although these classes of contracts are important for different legal areas, for the purposes of real property, only two are important: contracts for the sale of land and contracts that cannot be performed within one year of their creation. We will address the first of these classifications in this chapter and the second when we discuss landlord-tenant law in Chapter 7. Most states have a version of the Statute of Frauds that is similar to the one provided in Figure 6-4.

FIGURE 6-4

Statute of Frauds

All contracts to sell or convey any lands, tenements, or hereditaments, or any interest in or concerning them, and all leases and contracts for leasing land for the purpose of digging for gold or other minerals, or for mining generally, of whatever duration; and all other leases and contracts for leasing lands exceeding in duration three years from the making thereof, shall be void unless said contract, or some memorandum or note thereof, be put in writing and signed by the party to be charged therewith, or by some other person by him thereto lawfully authorized.[3]

The Statute of Frauds applies not only to contracts for the sale of real property, but also to any transaction involving a property right, from mineral leases to option contracts.

The practical effect of the Statute of Frauds is to require that all contracts involving the transfer of real property interests be in writing. If they are not, they are unenforceable. Anyone who brings suit over an oral purchase contract for a real estate parcel, for instance, will have the case dismissed before it reaches a discussion of its merits.

The question of what constitutes a "writing" often comes up in the context of discussing the Statute of Frauds. There is no requirement, for instance, that specific types of forms, or even particular formulations of words, must be used before a contract satisfies the statute. In fact, the statute is vague about what constitutes a written contract. In most contexts, even the most cursory of documents will satisfy the Statute of Frauds writing requirement.

REAL ESTATE BASICS AT A GLANCE

The Statute of Frauds has been enacted in one form or another across the United States. It requires that specific types of contracts must be in writing before they will be legally enforceable.

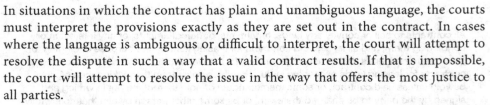

FORMATION ISSUES IN CONTRACT LAW

Contract disputes are some of the most common types of lawsuits in the United States. Because of this, courts frequently must interpret contracts and rule on the legality of particular provisions. This puts the courts in an unusual situation: They must decipher the intent of parties who are now hotly contesting those specific issues. Fortunately, over the years, courts have developed general guidelines to assist them in interpreting ambiguous or confusing contract provisions.

A. GUIDELINES THAT COURTS USE TO INTERPRET CONTRACTS

In situations in which the contract has plain and unambiguous language, the courts must interpret the provisions exactly as they are set out in the contract. In cases where the language is ambiguous or difficult to interpret, the court will attempt to resolve the dispute in such a way that a valid contract results. If that is impossible, the court will attempt to resolve the issue in the way that offers the most justice to all parties.

In some situations, the court may find that no contract was ever formed. Such a conclusion would be justified when the parties can prove mistake.

B. OFFER OF PURCHASE AND CONTRACT

An offer of purchase and contract is a written document that presents the details of the buyer's offer to the seller to purchase real estate. This contract reflects the negotiations between the buyer and seller and the final terms of their agreement (see Figure 6-5 for an example). Among the specifics set out in an offer of purchase and contract are:

- A description of the real estate involved;
- A provision for the purchase of any personal property located on the premises;
- Purchase price details, including earnest money deposit;
- Conditions, including the buyer's financing condition and loan commitment letter;
- Evidence of title;
- Property disclosures;
- Risk of loss provisions;
- Closing provisions; and
- Signature provisions.

FIGURE 6-5

Sample Offer of Purchase and Contract

THIS OFFER OF PURCHASE AND CONTRACT OF SALE, dated _____ the day of _____ 20 ___ between _____ and _____ (collectively referred to herein as the "Seller") whose address is _____ and _____ and (collectively referred to herein as the "Buyer") whose address is _____.

1 The Property. The Seller agrees to sell to the Buyer, and the Buyer agrees to purchase from the Seller, the fee simple real property located in _____, real property, whose legal description is as follows:

_____

Included in the property hereby sold are all permanently attached fixtures, and the following items, if any, now on the property: kitchen stove and oven, refrigerator, alarm systems, water filters, carpet, fireplace screens, draperies, shades, screens, storm doors and windows, venetian blinds, curtain rods, awnings, shrubbery, light fixtures, television aerial, dishwasher, garbage disposal, clothes washer, clothes dryer, window air conditioning units, and _____.

_____

2 Purchase Price. The purchase price for the property is _____ Dollars ($), of which the Buyer has paid _____ Dollars ($) as Earnest Money. The balance of the purchase price shall be paid by the Buyer to the Seller in cash at settlement.

3 Time and Place of Settlement. Unless the parties agree otherwise, settlement shall take place at A.M./P.M., at _____.

4 Financing Contingency. The Buyer's obligation to purchase the property is contingent upon the Buyer obtaining, from a lending institution, a commitment for a mortgage loan, secured by the property, in the principal amount of not less than_____ Dollars ($), at an interest rate not to exceed _____ percent (_____ %) per annum, repayable in equal monthly installments of principal and interest over a period of not less than thirty (30) years, and requiring the payment of _____of points/fees of not more than _____

FIGURE 6-5

(continued)

(_____ %) percent of the total loan amount. The Buyer shall apply for and receive a commitment of financing from a suitable lending institution within (ten) 10 days of the date of this contract.

5 Termite Infestation or Damage. The Buyer shall have the right to have the dwelling on the property inspected by a licensed pest control operator within ten (10) days of the date of this contract. The fees for this inspection will be borne exclusively by the Buyer. If the inspecting company should report an infestation by termites or other wood-boring insects, the Buyer shall notify the Seller of this fact, in writing, including a written report prepared by the inspecting company. The Seller shall have _____ days to correct, repair, or take other suitable action to repair the damage and shall certify this action to the Buyer, in writing.

6 Home Inspection. The Buyer shall have the right at the Buyer's expense to have the dwelling on the property inspected by a home inspection service or engineer within ten (10) days of the date of this contract. This inspection will involve a visual inspection of the mechanical, electrical, plumbing, and structural elements of the premises. Neither the Buyer nor the inspector shall damage the property during the inspection process. The Buyer shall provide the Seller with a copy of the inspector's written report, within a reasonable period of time after the inspection. The failure of the Seller to provide the Buyer or the Buyer's inspector access to said premises will be deemed a violation of this contract and in that event, the Seller shall return the Buyer's earnest money deposit.

7 Evidence of Title. At the closing or settlement of this contract, upon the Buyer's complete payment of all outstanding purchase monies, the Seller shall provide the Buyer evidence of title through a general warranty deed, in fee simple absolute, detailing the Seller's title to the property, free and clear from any encumbrances.

The Seller will convey title to the Buyer at the closing. The Seller is responsible for paying any transfer taxes, conveyance fees, or other sales taxes based on this transaction.

8 Risk of Loss. The property shall be held at the risk of the Seller until the settlement occurs. Upon receipt of all closing documents, risk of loss shall vest in the Buyer.

9 Default by the Buyer. In the event of the Buyer's default under this contract, the Seller shall have the right to retain all deposits and earnest money paid by the Buyer as liquidated damages under this contract. The Seller reserves the right to seek additional damages and equitable remedies against the Buyer for a willful breach of this contract.

10 Real Estate Commission. The Seller agrees, at the time and place of closing, to pay a commission of 6 percent to the real estate brokers who have produced a buyer who is ready, willing, and able to conclude the transaction.

11 Entire Agreement. This contract contains the entire agreement of the parties. This contract will not be modified by any parol evidence or other communications not contained herein.

12 Contract Addendum. Time is of the essence in this contract. The closing date for this transaction is the 15th day of May 2021.

The laws of the State of Placid shall govern this contract.

WITNESS the hands and seals of the parties.

Seller _____   Buyer _____

Date _____   Date _____

1. PROPERTY DESCRIPTION

The property in question should be adequately described. An adequate description must be something beyond the street address. Most states have forms that have been preapproved by the state bar or state real estate commission that provide blanks not only for the street address of the property but also for its city and town location and its legal description.

2. PURCHASE OF PERSONAL PROPERTY

The buyer and seller may, in addition to purchasing real property, also negotiate the purchase of certain items of personal property located on the premises. Because personal property is a separate and distinct class from real property, any personal property items that are purchased along with the real estate must be listed separately.

3. PURCHASE PRICE DETAILS

The offer of purchase and contract will not only include the purchase price but will also make provision for an earnest money deposit. **Earnest money** is the money put down by the buyer early in the negotiation process as proof of good faith of the buyer's intention to enter into a contract. This money must be accounted for later on in the sale process.

Earnest money
The money deposited by a potential buyer to show good faith and a willingness to enter into a contract for the purchase of the real estate.

4. CONDITIONS

The buyer will usually make her offer contingent upon certain events, particularly financing. The buyer's offer usually contains a condition revoking the offer in the event that the buyer is unable to obtain suitable financing. Other conditions may include the buyer's express condition of sale of her current home prior to concluding the purchase of the new home.

5. EVIDENCE OF TITLE

The evidence of title provision in the offer to purchase and contract is the seller's promise to use her best efforts, including hiring attorneys and conducting title searches on the property, to ensure that the buyer receives marketable title to the property in question.

6. PROPERTY DISCLOSURES

Most states require that the buyer receive a copy of the real property disclosures prior to the signing of the offer to purchase and contract. This provision also allows the buyer to conduct a property inspection within a specific time period after signing the contract.

7. RISK OF LOSS PROVISIONS

The offer of purchase and contract provides that the risk of loss — specifically whose insurance company will pay for any damages to the property — rests squarely on the seller prior to closing. After the closing, however, the risk of loss shifts to the new owner and her insurance company.

8. CLOSING PROVISIONS

The offer of purchase and contract will also contain provisions concerning the actual closing. In some cases, the buyer may elect to include a "time is of the essence" contract clause provision. This is a clause that requires the closing to occur at a specific date; otherwise, the contract will be considered null and void. We will discuss this and other common contract provisions later in this chapter.

9. SIGNATURE PROVISIONS

In Chapter 8, we will see that for a deed to be legally effective, the grantor must sign it. The grantor, or seller, is the only person required to sign a deed, but that is not the case with an offer of purchase and contract. This contract has signature provisions for all parties concerned and must be signed by both buyer and seller. Without the signatures, the contract is legally insufficient and cannot be enforced.

REAL WORLD PERSPECTIVES: *REAL ESTATE BROKER*

The trend that I see locally isn't so much about the length of time it takes for closings, but who is present. When I was paralegal working for real estate attorney, it was common to have all parties present. The trend now is that we separate parties, which is better. The longer the transaction takes, the more volatile the issues can become. People get tired, the transaction gets tired. There's a psychology that runs the transaction. At the beginning, everyone is excited. "Oh, we've got an offer." And then you start doing the hard stuff, like the due diligence. You might have appraisal issues. Inspection issues. Then you basically renegotiate the terms of the entire offer, sometimes.

— D. W., real estate broker

Option
A contract between a seller and buyer, whereby the seller agrees not to sell the property to another person for a stated period of time.

C. OPTIONS

An **option** is a contract between a seller and a prospective buyer, whereby the seller agrees that he will not sell the property to some other person, but only for a stated period of time. A prospective buyer might seek an option on the property instead of simply buying the property when she is attempting to negotiate contracts with other vendors and is not sure about the ultimate prospects of success. Negotiating an option with a potential seller involves only a small fraction of the money that it would take to actually purchase the property. In this case, the terms of the contract are simply that the seller will not sell or that, if she does decide to sell, she will offer the property to the option-holder first. If the option-holder does not close the transaction within the prescribed period or the time expires, the contract is canceled and the seller is free to sell the property to anyone else she chooses.

 ## CONTRACT CLAUSES

As you can see from Figure 6-5, there are numerous clauses and provisions contained in an offer to purchase and contract. We will now examine the more important ones and discuss their significance to the transaction. Important provisions include the following:

- Time is of the essence,
- Title,
- Escrow, and
- Insurance (risk of loss).

A. TIME IS OF THE ESSENCE

When a contract contains a "time is of the essence" provision, it means that the closing must occur on the date specified or the contract will be void. This provision is often included in time-sensitive transactions, when a closing must occur at a certain date in order to free up funds for another transaction. For instance, if A is buying a new home, A needs the funds from the sale of her previous home in order to complete the transaction. Therefore, the closing on the sale of A's home must occur prior to the purchase of her new home. In such a situation, a "time is of the essence" provision puts all parties on alert that the contract has strict time limitations. These provisions have a way of galvanizing the people involved in the transaction to ensure that the closing occurs on or before the date listed in the contract.

B. TITLE

A title clause in a contract (numbered paragraph 7 in Figure 6-5) is a provision that spells out exactly what type of title the buyer is expecting to receive at the closing. For instance, in Figure 6-5, the buyer is expecting to receive the highest and best type of title: fee simple absolute. We discuss the ramifications of the various types of titles in Chapter 8.

C. ESCROW

When a contract contains a provision for escrow, it means that the parties have agreed to take advantage of an unusual feature of real estate law in order to conclude the closing. As we will see in Chapter 13, an escrow closing allows the parties to sign the documentation for a closing at different times and still complete the closing as though all parties were actually present. To take advantage of this provision, the parties must first agree to it in the offer of purchase and contract.

D. INSURANCE (RISK OF LOSS)

An insurance, or risk of loss, provision in an offer of purchase and contract simply details which party bears the risk of loss during the transaction, and when the risk of loss for any damage or destruction of the premises transfers from the buyer to the seller. In Figure 6-5, this provision is found in numbered paragraph 8. The provision provides, in part, "The property shall be held at the risk of the Seller until the settlement occurs." This clause places the burden of property loss or destruction on the seller until the settlement, or closing, occurs. When the closing is complete, the risk of loss then shifts to the buyer, who is now the new owner. The risk of loss provision is important because it dictates which party's insurance company will be liable for damage to the property and when this liability is triggered.

BREACH OF CONTRACT

Equitable remedies
The power of a trial court to order a party to undertake specific actions, or to refrain from taking specific actions, such as injunctions and specific performance.

Specific performance
A court's order compelling a party to abide by the terms of a contract to which that party was previously in agreement.

When one party refuses to live up to her obligations under the contract, the other party is relieved of any further obligation in the contract and may sue for breach of contract. Breach of contract gives the non-breaching party the right to sue for damages or **equitable remedies**. A court can exercise its equity power to order an injunction, **specific performance**, or other action that is separate and distinct from the court's power to award monetary damages.

Contract law provides several different remedies and damages for the non-breaching party. The remedy sought often depends on which party is seeking the damages; sellers might seek a different remedy for a breach than buyers would.

A. REMEDIES FOR THE SELLER

When the buyer breaches the contract, the seller might retain the earnest money deposit, which was originally offered to evidence the buyer's good faith and on the condition that it would be forfeited on the buyer's failure to conclude the contract. However, the seller might well seek other remedies. For instance, the seller might decide to sue for monetary damages. Suppose that the seller sold the house to another buyer later on, but at a lower price. The seller would be authorized to sue the breaching buyer for the difference between the original contract price and the reduced price she later obtained.

B. REMEDIES FOR THE BUYER

Although a buyer might also be authorized to sue for monetary damages from a breaching seller, the buyer's main concern is probably concluding the contract. In this situation, the buyer might sue under the equitable remedy of specific performance. Under this doctrine, a court would be authorized to force the seller to comply with the terms of the original contract and sell the house to the buyer.

C. REMEDIES FOR THE BROKER

When a seller refuses to go through with a sale and the broker has completed all of her contractual duties, the broker has a cause of action against the seller for the real estate commission. This commission becomes due when the broker produces a buyer who is ready, willing, and able to conclude the transaction and the sale fails to occur because of the seller's actions. In this situation, the broker would be entitled to the commission even though the sale did not occur.

Case Excerpt

PICKETT FENCE PREVIEW, INC. v. ZILLOW, INC.
No. 2:21-cv-00012, U.S.D.C. D. Vermont

CHRISTINA REISS, United States District Court Judge

Picket Fence Preview, Inc. brings this action against Defendant Zillow, Inc., alleging violations of the Vermont Consumer Protection Act (the "VCPA"), 9 V.S.A. §2453(a) (Count I); the Lanham Act, 15 U.S.C §1125 (Count II); and state law unfair competition (Count III); arising out of Defendant's policy of providing free online listings for homes that are for-sale-by-owner ("FSBO"). Plaintiff is seeking compensatory and exemplary damages as well as injunctive relief.

Pending before the court is Defendant's motion to dismiss Plaintiff's Complaint on the grounds that Plaintiff lacks standing to bring suit on behalf of third parties and otherwise fails to state a claim for which relief can be granted. On March 25, 2021, Plaintiff opposed the motion and on April 8, 2021, Defendant replied.

I. Allegations in the Complaint.

Plaintiff is a FSBO For Sale By Owner publication business which began in 1993 and was one of the first publications to provide a marketplace where private homeowners could pay to advertise their property directly to potential buyers, bypassing the use of real estate agents or brokers. "A major incentive for homeowners to advertise with Plaintiff is reaching potential buyers directly through Plaintiff's publications and avoiding a 6-8% real estate commission" that is typically paid to real estate agents and brokers.

Defendant was incorporated in 2004 and launched its website in 2006, which provides an online portal for the general public to advertise real property and realtor services. Plaintiff alleges that Defendant's business depends on its ability to attract advertisers and partners to its online portal, including by "creating an advertising network and providing leads to its Premier Agents."

Defendant permits FSBO sellers to list their real property on its website at no cost, however, Plaintiff alleges that when an FSBO seller lists real property on Defendant's website, the web-page that a potential buyer sees contains "a big bar below that says 'Contact Agent' prominently displayed." If a potential buyer clicks on the "Contact Agent" button, they are routed to a "Premier Agent." Each website listing and each page allegedly contains a link that informs "Premier Agents" how to pay to get their name on the listing or to be the only contact for a listing.

To find the seller's contact information on Defendant's website, a potential buyer must click on a tab labeled "Get More Information" which lists the contact information for "Premier Agents" first "and the owner is listed at the bottom of the list." Id. In the "Get More Information" section of Defendant's FSBO listings, a potential buyer can enter their contact information to express an interest in a property, however "even if one checks the owner box the response goes to Defendant who connects the buyer with an agent." Plaintiff alleges that, on some listings, "the only way to find the owner's phone number is to scroll through all of the information, including past a page allowing for contact with an agent as well as a section showing nearby properties and similar homes."

Defendant's FSBO listings, when viewed on mobile devices such as cell phones and tablets, allegedly often do not have any owner contact information immediately visible, unless the owner includes such information in the description of the real property or the potential buyer scrolls through the entire listing to find the owner's phone number at its end. When viewing an FSBO listing on a cell phone, a "Call Agent" or "Message Agent" button is prominently displayed at the bottom of the screen.

Plaintiff contends that Defendant has "engaged in illegal and unfair methods of competition as well as fraud and deceit by setting up a bait and switch scheme for its 'free' listings for For-Sale-By-Owners and then making it difficult, or impossible, for prospective buyers to contact those sellers directly." It asserts that FSBO sellers "may lose potential sales" from these listings "because Premier Agents may redirect potential purchasers to other properties if the FSBO seller is not willing to share a commission with the Premier Agent" or if another property would provide the Premier Agent with "a better commission." Plaintiff further asserts that Defendant's "pricing scheme is predatory" because while Defendant "claims that it is offering a service for free, in reality it is charging the Premier Agents so they can advertise on the website of those free ads and receive hijacked inquiries from deceived buyers."

Because Defendant's FSBO listings allegedly make it "difficult, and in many cases impossible" for potential buyers to contact the FSBO seller directly and instead direct them to Premier Agents, FSBO sellers "end up having to pay a commission" on the sale of their property. Plaintiff maintains that this practice effectively "hides the fee from the For-Sale-By-Owners and deceives them into believing by listing their property on Defendant's site they would avoid commissions." FSBO sellers thus allegedly "end up paying a significantly higher cost to sell their property than if they had listed it with a traditional For-Sale-By-Owner publication, like Plaintiffs," that charges a listing fee. Plaintiff contends that Defendant "deceives and defrauds the seller who posted the free For-Sale-By-Owner ad as it steals this ad making it neither For-Sale-By-Owner nor free."

Prior to Defendant's offering free FSBO listings on its website, Plaintiff "was enjoying dynamic and consistent growth" and beginning to "expand and franchise its business model." Because the cost of adding pages to its publication and adding listed properties to its website was relatively low, its profits increased as it gained more customers. Between 1994 and 2006, Plaintiffs revenue grew at a compounded annual rate of 16% per year. Its lost profits in 2017 are estimated at $3,400,000 and, at a projected 16% growth rate, from 2018 to 2030, Plaintiff contends it would have earned over $128,467,758.50 in profits but for Defendant's FSBO services. It alleges it will lose $142,000,000 in profits by 2030 and will have additional losses associated with potential expansion to other markets and franchising fees that it claims are "in the hundreds of millions of dollars."

Plaintiff asserts that there were numerous other FSBO publications across the country but that it is now one of the last remaining publications of its type due to Defendant's FSBO services.

II. Conclusions of Law and Analysis.
Whether Plaintiff Plausibly Pleads a Lanham Act Claim.

Pursuant to 15 U.S.C. §1125(a):

> (1) Any person who, on or in connection with any goods or services, or any container for goods, uses in commerce any word, term, name, symbol, or device, or any combination thereof, or any false designation of origin, false or misleading description of fact, or false or misleading representation of fact, which —
>
>   (A) is likely to cause confusion, or to cause mistake, or to deceive as to the affiliation, connection, or association of such person with another person, or as to the origin, sponsorship, or approval of his or her goods, services, or commercial activities by another person, or
>
>   (B) in commercial advertising or promotion, misrepresents the nature, characteristic, qualities, or geographic origin of his or her or another person's goods, services, or commercial activities,
>
> Shall be liable in a civil action by any person who believes that he or she is or is likely to be damaged by such act.

15 U.S.C. §1125(a)(1).

Defendant contends that Plaintiffs Lanham Act claim must fail because Plaintiff does not have standing to bring a claim based on Defendant's services and because Plaintiff fails to allege that Defendant made any false statement. "A statutory cause of action extends only to plaintiffs whose interests 'fall within the zone of interests protected by the law invoked.'" *Lexmark Inf I, Inc. v. Static Control Components, Inc.*, 572 U.S. 118, 129 (2014). "To come within the zone of interests in a suit for false advertising under §1125(a), a plaintiff must allege an injury to a commercial interest in reputation or sales." Such an injury must "flow directly from the deception wrought by the defendant's advertising, which "occurs when deception of consumers causes them to withhold trade from the plaintiff." The relevant question is "whether the harm alleged is proximately tied to the defendant's conduct."

Plaintiff has alleged that it has suffered economic injury as a result of Defendant's allegedly deceptive FSBO services which has caused consumers to "opt for the free listing of their properties on Defendant's site instead of using Plaintiff, a For-Sale-By-Owner paid advertising publication. . . . Since the Lanham Act authorizes suit only for commercial injuries, the intervening step of consumer deception is not fatal to the showing of proximate causation required by the statute." *Lexmark*, 572 U.S. at 133. At the pleading stage, Plaintiff has adequately alleged standing under Lexmark to bring a false advertising claim under the Lanham Act.

"To prevail on a Lanham Act false advertising claim, a plaintiff must establish that the challenged message is (1) either literally or impliedly false, (2) material, (3) placed in interstate commerce, and (4) the cause of actual or likely injury to the plaintiff." *Church & Dwight Co. v. SPD Swiss Precision Diagnostics*, 843 F.3d 48, 65 (2d Cir. 2016). "To establish literal falsity, a plaintiff must show that the advertisement either makes an express statement that is false or a statement that is 'false by necessary implication,' meaning that the advertisement's 'words or images, considered in context, necessarily and unambiguously imply a false message.'" *Church & Dwight Co.*, 843 F.3d at 65.

Defendant's promise of a "free" FSBO listing is not literally false because, as Plaintiff admits, Defendant does not charge sellers to post FSBO listings on its website. Plaintiff nonetheless maintains that this statement was impliedly false because Defendant did not "disclose that interested shoppers would be directed to Premier Agents." To be impliedly false the statement must be "likely to mislead or confuse consumers." *Apotex*, 823 F.3d at 63. "Such an implicit falsity claim requires a comparison of the impression left by the statement, rather than the statement itself, with the truth." Id.

Plaintiff fails to point to any representation by Defendant that any sales will be "commission free" or any promise that a real estate agent will not be involved in a subsequent sale. Defendant's only promise to FSBO sellers is that it will list their real property at no cost to them. An FSBO seller remains free to refuse to deal with a real estate agent and free to refuse to pay a real estate agent's commission even if it uses Defendant's website. Defendant's listing focuses only on a preliminary step in a real estate transaction with no promise as to what happens thereafter. Stated differently, a customer who is promised a free listing is not promised a commission free sale either directly or by implication.

Because Plaintiff has failed to allege that Defendant's message was "either literally or impliedly false," Church & Dwight Co., 843 F.3d at 65, within the meaning of 15 U.S.C. §1125(a)(1), Defendant's motion to dismiss Plaintiffs false advertising claim under the Lanham Act (Count II) is GRANTED.

Conclusion

Defendant's motion to dismiss (Doc. 15) is GRANTED. Plaintiffs Complaint (Doc. 12) is DISMISSED. Plaintiff is GRANTED leave to file an Amended Complaint within twenty (20) days of the date of this Opinion and Order consistent with the Federal Rules of Civil Procedure and this court's Local Rules.

SO ORDERED.

QUESTIONS ABOUT THE CASE

1 What is the plaintiff's business? What is the defendant?
2 What are the plaintiff's allegations against the defendant?
3 What is necessary for the plaintiff to prove in order to bring an action under the Lanham Act?
4 What does the court say about the plaintiff's claim?

COVID-19 CONCERN

Although virtual meetings, such as Zoom, have been seen as an acceptable alternative to in-person meetings, there are times when the virtual world does not deliver the same qualities as live interactions. There is a feeling of disconnect in a virtual meeting that can have consequences for the negotiation process. In the world of residential real estate, it is unlikely that the sellers will meet the persons making the offer at any time during the negotiations. However, that is not true of the real estate agents. They may be used to communicating face-to-face and getting those subtle body language clues that we all rely on, whether we realize it or not. If the COVID virus continues to be a part of everyday existence, then this may affect all types of negotiating.

CHAPTER SUMMARY

A contract is a legally binding agreement between two or more parties that is a result of negotiations between those parties and consists of an offer, which is one party's stated intention to enter into a binding contract, and the acceptance by the other party of all the terms stated in that offer. When an offer has been accepted, a contract is created. In addition to a valid offer and acceptance, there are some additional contract law requirements. For instance, both parties to the contract must have legal capacity. Legal capacity refers to a party's competence to know and understand the consequences of entering into a contractual obligation. Consideration is another contractual element that requires a bargained-for exchange between the parties. This is a contract requirement that necessitates that both parties surrender something of value in exchange for something else of value before an enforceable contract will be found under the law.

Contract law is of vital importance in real estate transactions because so many real estate conveyances involve contract principles. In this chapter, we explored offers of purchase, which consist of the binding contract between the seller and buyer, as well as many other types of contracts. We also explored various contract clauses, including the "time is of the essence" clause. This contract clause requires that the closing must occur at a specific date; otherwise the contract will be null and void.

SKILLS YOU NEED IN THE REAL WORLD

Deciphering Real Estate Contracts

One skill that you will need to master is the ability to decipher the various types of contracts that are the meat of real estate practice. Whether they are listing agreements, brokerage agreements, offers of purchase, or any of the other contracts that are involved in real estate transactions, you should learn how to take such contracts apart.

Real estate contracts often appear very intimidating when you first read them. Usually they are very long and have small print and confusing terms. Here are some guidelines to help you decipher real estate contracts.

Start with Who

The first and most important aspect of any contract is the identity of the parties: Who is actually bound by this contract? Identifying the parties goes a long way toward discovering the intent of the contract and pinpointing the issues. For instance, if the contract is a listing agreement, then the parties are the seller and the real estate agent. Chances are that the issues between these two parties will revolve around attempts to sell the house and whether the real estate agent earned her commission. Simply identifying the parties helps you understand the potential issues that arise in the contract.

What Is Involved?

What rights, duties, or obligations are put forth in the contract? Put another way, who has the obligation to act, and what are they obligated to do? When you pinpoint these parts of the contract, you begin building a solid understanding of what the contract is about.

What Are the Penalties?

Contracts often list the potential penalties for nonperformance. Does the contract detail what rights a party has when the other party defaults? Has one party contractually agreed to a limitation of possible penalties? Is there a provision calling for the use of a particular state's law to determine breach of contract duty? If you can detail these basic elements of a contract, you will have gone a long way toward understanding even the most complex real estate contract.

ETHICAL ISSUES FOR THE PARALEGAL

Legal Research

It might seem odd to refer to ethical requirements in performing legal research, but it is one of the most overlooked and potentially dangerous areas for any legal professional. Performing adequate legal research is an ethical requirement for attorneys. As a result, it behooves paralegals to understand the importance of legal research as well. Staying current and up to date on legal issues is one of the most basic parts of the service that legal professionals provide to clients. It also prevents embarrassing situations, such as relying on statutes that have been ruled unconstitutional or cases that have been reversed by higher courts. In addition to general embarrassment, shoddy legal research can also leave attorneys open to claims of legal malpractice.

KEY TERMS AND CONCEPTS

Capacity	Legality	Option
Consideration	Listing agreement	Power of acceptance
Contract	Mistake	Specific performance
Equitable remedies	Mutual assent	

END-OF-CHAPTER EXERCISES

Review Questions

See Appendix for answers.

1   What are the elements of a legally enforceable offer?
2   How does real property law define the "power of acceptance"?
3   What is mutual assent?
4   What is consideration, and why is it a necessary component for a contract?
5   Explain how a contract may be unenforceable when it does not have a legal subject.
6   What is legal capacity to contract? Provide some examples of individuals who lack such capacity.
7   What is the Statute of Frauds, and why is it important in real estate contracts?
8   How is contractual mistake defined in real property?
9   What are the basic elements of an offer of purchase and contract?

10   List and explain at least three important provisions of an offer to purchase and contract.

11   Why does the law require that both the seller and the buyer sign the offer to purchase and contract?

12   What is an option?

13   How is an offer to purchase and contract different from an option?

14   Explain the significance of a "time is of the essence" contract clause.

15   What are some of the penalties that a seller can seek against a buyer for the buyer's wrongful refusal to perform under the offer to purchase and contract?

16   What are some of the buyer's remedies against a seller who wrongfully refuses to perform under a contract of sale?

17   What types of damages is a seller entitled to against a buyer who refuses to fulfill the obligations of an offer to purchase and contract?

18   Explain why it is so important to understand contract clauses.

19   Describe how you would begin to draft an offer of purchase and contract.

20   What is specific performance?

DISCUSSION QUESTIONS

1   Can a person accept an offer to purchase real estate without saying a word?

2   Would it be possible for a person to use Twitter, Facebook, or some other new communication program to create a legally valid contract? Why or why not?

APPLYING WHAT YOU HAVE LEARNED

1   The Statute of Frauds was created in a time when most people could not read and write. Requiring a contract to be put in writing necessitated the help of someone who could read and write. Is the Statute of Frauds still relevant when the vast majority of people in this country are literate?

2   Using Figure 6-5, create a new contract of sale based on the following facts:
   ■   Date of contract: January 11, 2022 Sal Seller and Bill Buyer. Sal's address is 10 Sol Street. Bill's address is 12 Third Avenue. The property address is 21 Robin Lane, Morgan, State of Placid.
   ■   Included in the sale are some built-in tool storage cabinets in the basement.
   ■   The purchase price is $121,000. Bill put down $1,000 earnest money. No additional money will be paid prior to closing. The closing is to take place on May 11, 2022, at 3 P.M. in the offices of Al Attorney, 100 Shyster Boulevard, Burnett City, State of Placid.
   ■   Bill's offer is based on being able to obtain financing at 9 percent or lower, in the amount of $115,000, for a 30-year loan. He doesn't want to pay more than two points.

- Sal wants Bill to apply for financing as soon as possible, at least within 10 days of the contract being signed. Bill wants a termite inspection within 10 days of signing the contract.
- If termites are found, Sal wants at least 30 days to fix whatever is wrong.
- Bill wants to inspect the home within 10 days of signing the contract.
- The real estate agent's name is Ron Realtor.

WEB SURFING

National Association of Realtors
https://www.nar.realtor

Women's Council of Realtors
http://www.wcr.org

Real Estate Contract Law: Legal Information Institute
http://www.law.cornell.edu/topics/real_estate.html

Tech Topic
MULTIPLE LISTING SERVICE

The Multiple Listing Service (MLS) Website (http://mls.com) allows you to search for real estate listings and homes for sale across the United States, in addition to many other useful real estate tools.

ANNOTATED DOCUMENT

Offer of Purchase for Real Estate

This offer, dated the 23rd day of May, 2021, between Marvin Meaty and Melba Meaty, hereafter known as "Seller," and Beula Buyer, hereafter known as "Buyer," sets out the details of an offer to purchase real estate located at 123 Maple Drive, Anywhere, Placid, 00030.

1. The Seller agrees to sell to the Buyer, and the Buyer agrees to purchase from the Seller, the real property located at 123

Offers always identify the parties (Marvin and Melba Meaty ("Seller") and Beula Buyer ("Buyer")).

Offers provide the street address of the property ("123 Maple Drive, Anywhere, Placid, 00030"), but that is not enough.

The property description refers to tax maps and plats.

Maple Drive, Anywhere, Placid, 00030, more fully described as Burke County Tax Map 12400564, as shown in Plat Book 41-1546.

2. Seller agrees to provide Buyer title in fee simple absolute, free of any encumbrances and in marketable condition.

The buyer obviously wishes to receive the best type of title: fee simple ("Seller agrees to provide Buyer title in fee simple absolute").

PRACTICE QUESTIONS FOR TEST REVIEW

See Appendix for answers.

Essay Question

What are the basic elements of a legally binding contract?

True–False

1   **T   F**   Oral contracts are not enforceable.

2   **T   F**   Contracts create rights in both parties.

3   **T   F**   When a valid contract exists and one-party breaches, the other party has the right to sue.

Fill in the Blank

1   When one party indicates a willingness to be bound by a contract, this person makes a(n):_____.

2   Courts try to be objective when evaluating the terms of a contract. What standard do they use?: _____.

3   The effect that making a counter-offer has on the original offer: _____.

Multiple Choice

1   A legally recognized agreement gives both parties the right to enforce the obligation to legal means.

   A   Document
   B   Public record
   C   Contract
   D   None of the above

2   What remedy does a party have when the other party to a contract breaches?

    A   The party has no remedy.
    B   The party must appeal to the state Supreme Court.
    C   Party may bring a civil action.
    D   None of the above.

3   All contracts have the same basic elements. Which of the following is not an element of a contract?

    A   An offer
    B   An acceptance
    C   Regulatory intent
    D   Capacity

ENDNOTES

[1] *Dudley A. Tyng & Co. v. Converse*, 180 Mich. 195, 146 N.W. 629 (1914).
[2] *Woody v. State, ex rel. Dep't of Corrections*, 83 P.2d 257 (Okla. 1992).
[3] N.C. Gen. Stat. §22-2, Contract for sale of land; leases.
[4] *Yeazell v. Copins*, 98 Ariz. 109, 402 P.2d 541 (1965).
[5] *Lancaster v. Lancaster*, 138 N.C. App. 459, 530 S.E.2d 82 (2000).

Landlord and Tenant Law

- Explain the origin of the obligations between landlords and their tenants

- Define the basic features of leasehold estates

- Describe the impact of contract and property law on leasehold estates

- Explore how the law of landlord and tenant relations has changed over time

- Explain how various tenancies are created, administered, and terminated

I. Introduction

II. The Landlord-Tenant Relationship
   A. Historical Background on Landlord-Tenant Law
   B. Modern Changes to the Landlord-Tenant Relationship

III. Leases
   A. Fixed Rent Leases
   B. Percentage Leases
   C. Net Leases
   D. Rent-to-Own Leases
   E. Ground Leases
   F. Timber Leases
   G. Mineral Leases
   H. Oil and Gas Leases

IV. Common Lease Provisions
   A. Rent
   B. Late Payments and Fees
   C. Pet and Security Deposits
   D. Renewal Provisions
   E. Persons Permitted on the Leased Premises
   F. Acceptance of Leased Premises
   G. Modifying or Altering the Premises
   H. Subletting
   I. Notice

V. Commercial Leases

VI. Public Policy Concerns in Leases
   A. Federal Law Requirements
   B. Statute of Frauds Considerations

VII. **Rights and Duties Created by the Landlord-Tenant Relationship**
   A. Uniform Residential Landlord and Tenant Act
   B. Landlord's Duties and Rights
   C. Tenant's Duties and Rights
   D. Legal Doctrines That Arise in the Landlord-Tenant Relationship

VIII. **Remedies for Breach Of Duty**
   A. Tenant Remedies Against Landlord

   B. Landlord Remedies Against Tenant: Eviction

IX. **Classifying Landlord-Tenant Relationships**
   A. Tenancy for Years
   B. Tenancy from Year to Year
   C. Tenancy at Will
   D. Tenancy at Sufferance

INTRODUCTION

This chapter is devoted to a discussion of the relationship between landlords and tenants. We have already seen that ownership in fee simple brings with it a host of rights. Many of those rights can be transferred piecemeal. In a life estate, for example, a fee simple owner may transfer most of the rights inherent in real property ownership, but for a limited period. We will face a similar situation when discussing **leasehold estates**.

A leasehold estate is one that gives the possessor many of the obvious rights associated with real property but only conveys those rights for a short period. When the lease term is over, the rights revert to the fee simple owner. The parties to a leasehold arrangement are the landlord and the tenant. The **landlord** is usually the owner in fee simple, who conveys some of his or her interests in a property to the **tenant**. When these rights are conveyed, it means that the landlord no longer possesses:

Leasehold estate
The body of rights conveyed to a tenant from a landlord.

Landlord
The owner of the premises; the landlord retains all the rights normally associated with ownership except use, possession, and enjoyment.

Tenant
The possessor of certain rights transferred away from the landlord; these rights include use, possession, and enjoyment.

■ The right to use the property,
■ The right to occupy the property, and
■ The right to possess the property.

Just as important as the rights that are conveyed to tenants are the rights that are not conveyed. For instance, a tenant does not have the right to sell the property; that right remains vested in the landlord. Similarly, the tenant has no right to mortgage the property and also bears no responsibility for paying real estate taxes. The tenant's rights are usually limited to the use and possession of the property.

In this chapter, we will examine how the landlord-tenant relationship is created, the rights and obligations that this relationship establishes, and how the relationship is terminated.

THE LANDLORD-TENANT RELATIONSHIP

A leasehold arrangement can be created in a number of ways. (See Figure 7-1 for a summary of median rents over a twenty year period.) Once created, the relationship carries with it certain obligations for both parties. However, the historical basis of the relationship was not always so mutually dependent.

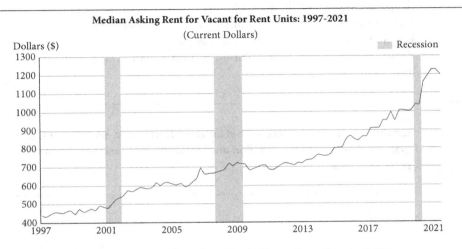

Median Asking Rent for Vacant for Rent Units: 1997-2021
(Current Dollars)

Source: U.S. Census Bureau, Current Population Survey/Housing Vacancy Survey November 2, 2021
Recession data: National Bureau of Economic Reseach, www.nber.org.

FIGURE 7-1

Median Asking Rent 1997–2021

A. HISTORICAL BACKGROUND ON LANDLORD-TENANT LAW

The history of landlord-tenant law stretches back thousands of years. Some of the most prominent members of ancient Roman aristocracy were landlords. Unfortunately, that history is fraught with examples of the one-sided nature of the relationship. Under English and early American common law, landlords had few obligations and were able to evict tenants for any of a number of reasons. Eviction could be a violent process, with landlords engaging in "self-help" eviction, which consisted of physically dragging tenants out of the premises and throwing their belongings onto the street. Until the twentieth century, landlords had few obligations to their tenants beyond providing a dwelling. It was not until the 1900s that American law began changing its view of the landlord-tenant relationship. States gradually began changing their laws by imposing more requirements on landlords, such as maintaining structures, with the recognition that legal doctrines such as the warranty of habitability applied to landlords.

B. MODERN CHANGES TO THE LANDLORD-TENANT RELATIONSHIP

Every state has now modified, to a greater or lesser extent, its landlord-tenant law. Some of these changes have been brought about by judicial decisions that placed greater responsibilities on landlords while others were required by changes in the statutes governing landlord-tenant relationships.

Under the modern definition of landlord-tenant relationships, landlords have specific duties to their tenants. Among these duties are:

- Keeping the premises in good repair,
- Maintaining the premises in a fit and habitable condition,
- Keeping all common areas in a safe state, and
- Ensuring that the electrical, plumbing, heating, and ventilating systems are all in working order.

REAL ESTATE BASICS AT A GLANCE

Landlord-tenant law refers to that large body of cases, statutes, rules, and regulations that govern the creation and termination of residential and commercial property leases.

Tech Topic
USING WI-FI TO LURE TENANTS

In a down rental market, landlords go to extremes to entice renters, including the promise of free wireless Internet service. On the surface it is a tempting perk, but it comes with some underlying dangers.

Many Wi-Fi users are not aware that, when they connect to Wi-Fi through hot spots (such as those at a coffeehouse, a hotel, or even a place of business), their online activity can be monitored and intercepted — including account numbers and passwords. A landlord who provides free Wi-Fi to tenants becomes the de facto Internet service provider. If the landlord is technologically savvy, he can monitor the traffic on the network he is providing — and so can the neighbors.

There are steps that tenants can take to protect their data while at the same time enjoying the benefit of free Wi-Fi. One is to be sure to use only secure, encrypted connections while making online transactions. Websites whose URL begins with HTTPS (instead of HTTP) are secured, and although the landlord might be able to see the site that is being visited, he cannot see any of the data sent to it or displayed on it.

Another solution is to use a Virtual Private Network (VPN) service. A VPN ensures protected access to the Internet. Originally designed for people who travel frequently or those who often work away from the office, a VPN provides an extra layer of protection from prying eyes.

LEASES

Leases raise a host of issues because of their dual nature. A **lease** is the embodiment of the contractual agreement between landlords and tenants and therefore must contain all the basic contractual elements. However, a lease is not *only* a contractual agreement and therefore must also contain some additional elements that arise because the agreement involves a real estate transaction. We will discuss all these elements later in this chapter. But first we must address the various lease categories, including:

- Fixed-rent leases,
- Percentage leases,
- Net leases,
- Rent-to-own leases,
- Ground leases,
- Timber leases,
- Mineral leases, and
- Oil and gas leases.

Lease
The contractual arrangement between a landlord and tenant.

A. FIXED-RENT LEASES

A fixed-rent lease assesses a flat fee that must be paid periodically. The most common example of a fixed-rent lease is a residential lease. In this arrangement, the tenant agrees to pay a specific amount in rent every month. The amount of the rent does not vary from month to month, and the tenant is not responsible for paying out additional sums for expenses.

B. PERCENTAGE LEASES

Unlike fixed-rent leases, percentage lease rents change over time. Because they are based in whole or in part on the tenant's income, the amount of the rent may vary from month to month. Percentage leases are used in commercial settings, where the tenant is a business. The landlord receives a report of the tenant's total income for the month and assesses a percentage of the proceeds as the monthly rent. Percentage leases come in many different forms and may be based on gross or net sales, or even a combination of percentage of income plus a flat fee.

C. NET LEASES

Net leases make the tenant responsible not only for paying rent but also for paying all costs associated with the premises, including electricity, water, sewage, and any other expenses.

D. RENT-TO-OWN LEASES

Rent-to-own leases are often popular when the economy is in a downturn. Under the most common provisions of a rent-to-own lease, the landlord applies some portion of each month's rent toward a down payment on the purchase of the home. These leases are sometimes referred to as a lease with option to purchase, but whatever the terminology, the basic arrangement is the same: The tenant gets credit for some portion of the rent paid over a period of time and has the right to apply that amount toward the purchase of the premises.

| EXAMPLE 7-1 | **TONY'S RENT TO OWN** |

Tony has been renting a house for over five years now. The original arrangement between Tony and his landlord was simple: 10 percent of Tony's monthly rent would be applied toward a down payment on the purchase of the house. When the amount reached $10,000, Tony would then have the option of purchasing the home. However, the amount was nonrefundable because it was part of Tony's rent. The agreement also provided that no modifications to the original agreement were permissible. Tony has found an apartment he likes better than the house and wants to sue the landlord for the amount that has been slowly building up as credit toward his down payment. That amount is $2,800. Will Tony win his suit?

Answer: No. Because the agreement provided that the down payment would be based on a percentage of his rent (as opposed to an additional amount paid every month), Tony is not entitled to a return of any of the money he has paid.[1]

E. GROUND LEASES

Ground leases are arrangements between landlords and tenants wherein the tenant rents vacant land, often for the purpose of farming or for constructing a building on the lot.

F. TIMBER LEASES

A timber lease allows the tenant to enter onto the landlord's land for the purpose of harvesting trees. The landlord will be paid for the timber that is removed, and the tenant, usually a mill or paper company, often has the additional duty of replanting new trees after removing the old ones.

G. MINERAL LEASES

Mineral leases give the tenant the right to enter onto the property, test for the presence of various ores, sink mines, and carry out other actions to extract minerals and other materials from the soil. Most states have provisions that require mineral leases to be in writing before they are considered legally enforceable. Mineral leases often raise interesting legal questions. For instance, a mining company might possess a license, but not a lease.

When discussing leases, especially mineral or gas leases, there is often an important point about terminology. In some cases, for example, a company might have the right to enter onto a person's property for the purpose of harvesting soil or crops, but have no right to actually possess the property or to make other use of it. The company that holds a **license**, for example, has the right to specific products of the land, but no rights in the real estate. Only leases convey real property interests. Licenses solely convey personal property rights.

License
The right to the products of the land, but not the land itself; a licensee might have the right to enter the premises to harvest, but no right to any other use of the property.

A license grants the owner the right to enter onto the land for a specific purpose. A leaseholder, on the other hand, has all the rights normally associated with possession.

REAL ESTATE BASICS AT A GLANCE

Licenses fall into the category of "*profits à prendre*," or the right to take soil, minerals, stones, or other materials from the property, but no right to any other use of the property. (See Chapter 5 for additional discussion of *profits à prendre*.)

H. OIL AND GAS LEASES

Just as the names suggest, oil and gas leases give the tenant the right to explore for oil and natural gas and to remove those products from the property. This category of leases can become quite complicated, given the speculative nature of drilling for oil, and these leases often involve additional clauses and provisions that provide for new arrangements between the parties if oil or gas is discovered on the property.

IV COMMON LEASE PROVISIONS

Although there is a wide variety of leases available, some common clauses and provisions are often found in any actual written lease, regardless of type. We will examine the contract clauses of a typical residential lease in order to better understand lease provisions. (For a complete residential lease form, see the Appendix.)

A. RENT

One of the most obvious, and most important, provisions of any lease is the issue of rent. Landlords go into the business of renting property for the income that it will generate. Without rent, there is no revenue. All leases have provisions that specify not only the amount of the rent but also when it should be paid. Most leases also have provisions detailing the consequences of late rental payments.

B. LATE PAYMENTS AND FEES

Many states have provisions that limit how much residential landlords can charge delinquent renters. For instance, a lease may contain a provision that specifies a late fee of $15 or $20 in addition to the outstanding rent. Other states limit late charges to a percentage of the total rent. For instance, state law may allow a late fee of up to 5 percent of the total monthly rent.

C. PET AND SECURITY DEPOSITS

In addition to rent, a lease may contain provisions for a wide variety of other matters. Landlords are permitted to charge deposits to renters with pets, as well as security deposits. The reasoning behind such deposits is that they may help to pay for any damages to the premises caused by the renter or the renter's pet. However, as we will see later in this chapter, landlords are not permitted to assess tenants for charges for ordinary wear and tear. See Figure 7-2 for an example of the limitations on security deposits.

FIGURE 7-2

Statutory Limitations on Security Deposits

(a) Upon termination of the tenancy, property or money held by the landlord as security must be returned less amounts withheld by the landlord for accrued rent and damages which the landlord has suffered by reason of the tenant's noncompliance. Any deduction from the security/rental deposit must be itemized by the landlord in a written notice to the tenant together with the amount due, if any, within thirty days after termination of the tenancy and delivery of possession and demand by the tenant, whichever is later.[2]

D. RENEWAL PROVISIONS

It is common for leases to contain clauses specifying how, or even if, the lease can be renewed. For instance, a lease might provide that the leasehold arrangement automatically renews every year unless the tenant indicates a desire to terminate the relationship. On the other hand, a lease might provide that the lease is terminable at the will of either party after giving specified notice.

E. PERSONS PERMITTED ON THE LEASED PREMISES

Landlords are allowed to restrict the number of persons permitted to be on the leased premises. The lease might contain a provision specifying exactly who is permitted to reside at the rental unit. This provision not only protects the landlord from the additional damage that other individuals might do to the premises but may also be required by fire codes or other statutes designed to limit the number of individuals residing at one location.

F. ACCEPTANCE OF LEASED PREMISES

Residential leases often contain a provision whereby the tenant explicitly accepts the premises as they appear. This provision demonstrates that, at a specific point in time, the tenant was aware of the conditions of the rental unit and found them acceptable.

G. MODIFYING OR ALTERING THE PREMISES

Another provision that is very common in residential leases is a clause that specifically prohibits the tenant from making alterations or modifications to the structure. This does not prevent the tenant from decorating or hanging pictures on the walls. Instead, this provision prevents the tenant from tearing down walls or making other substantial changes to the floors, walls, or ceilings.

H. SUBLETTING

The general rule is that a tenant is free to **sublet** the rented premises to another tenant unless the lease provides otherwise. There are many reasons why a tenant would wish to sublet a unit. The tenant may suddenly need to relocate to another town, and renting the unit to someone else may be a more cost-effective remedy than paying the balance on the lease. There are also rental units in areas where rent is strictly controlled by the local government. In places such as New York City, a person might be very happy to sublet a unit where rent control keeps the rent at or below a specific amount.

    The reasons why a person might want to sublet are the same reasons why a landlord would be eager to deny such access. With a new tenant, one free from a pre-existing lease, the landlord is free to charge a higher rent or impose other favorable conditions. Many residential leases outside of rent-controlled areas contain provisions that specifically bar the current tenant from subletting to others. Another variation on the theme prevents subletting unless it is with the landlord's prior approval.

Sublet
One tenant rents the leased premises to another tenant.

I. NOTICE

Notice provisions in leases cover a wide assortment of activities. Leases may contain notice provisions that specify when a tenant must notify the landlord if the tenant intends to move out at the end of the lease term. Other notice provisions might include changes to the list of persons permitted on the premises. Notice provision requirements imposed in the lease may also pertain to the landlord. For instance, the landlord might be required to give so many days' notice to a tenant before he seeks to evict that tenant for nonpayment of rent.

    Although we will discuss eviction in much greater detail later in this chapter, we must note here that many residential leases have clauses that detail how and when the **eviction** process may begin. The most common reason to evict a tenant is for nonpayment of rent, but leases also usually contain provisions that allow landlords to initiate

Eviction
The legal process of removing a tenant from the leased premises.

eviction procedures when the tenant is unruly, causing public nuisance, or violating the law.

EXAMPLE 7-2

THE STAGE

Alton has just started college and has moved into his first apartment. He likes the place very much, but it is missing something that Alton considers very important: Because he wants to be an actor, he wants a stage in his living room. He buys lumber, screws supports into the floor and walls, and creates a stage that is three feet high and runs the length of the back wall in his living room. He lives in the apartment for four years, and upon graduation, he notifies the landlord that he will be dismantling the stage and taking it with him. The landlord tells Alton that the stage must remain. Alton wants to sue for the right to remove the stage. Will he win?

Answer: No. Because of the way that the stage was constructed, it is a fixture and will remain with the property (at the option of the landlord).

COMMERCIAL LEASES

So far, our discussion has focused on residential leases. Commercial leases involve very different issues. Commercial leases are generally for retail, wholesale, or warehouse businesses, so many of the issues we have discussed, such as pet deposits and persons permitted on the premises, do not apply. However, other concerns will be reflected in a commercial lease. It is not unusual, for instance, for a commercial landlord to require accounting statements, business plans, or other documentation before entering into a lease with a business.

Commercial leases often contain provisions allowing the landlord to forcibly enter the premises and seize inventory or other items to secure rent. The landlord also has the right to bar access to the premises of a tenant who has defaulted on the rental agreement. Obviously, such tactics could not be used with residential leases. The rules are different in commercial leases, and that is even more evident when we consider fixtures.

Rules about fixtures change when the lease involves commercial property. Trade fixtures are items of personal property that qualify as fixtures but are used for the tenant's business. Because of their commercial use, the rules about these fixtures are different. When tenants give up their commercial leasehold, they are permitted to remove these fixtures, even when they are fully attached to the real property and even when it must cause some damage to do so.

EXAMPLE 7-3

THE BAGEL STORE

Haley runs a bagel store downtown. Her lease has expired, and she is going to move her business to another location. She needs to take her big dough mixer with her. It stands 6 feet tall, weighs 400 pounds, and is bolted to the floor. The landlord is refusing to allow her to remove it, saying that she would leave two bolt holes in the floor and would have to take off one of the doors in order to get it out. Will Haley be permitted to remove the mixer?

Answer: Yes. Because the mixer qualifies as a trade fixture, Haley will be allowed to remove it, even though it is bolted to the floor and she will have to take off a door to get it out.

PUBLIC POLICY CONCERNS IN LEASES

As we will see later in this chapter, there are both state and federal laws that govern the creation of leases. One of the most important is the Uniform Residential Landlord and Tenant Act (URLTA). All states, whether they have adopted URLTA or not, have provisions in their laws that prevent landlords from requiring tenants to negotiate away legal rights as a condition of obtaining the premises. Such a lease provision would be considered a violation of public policy or unconscionable and would not be enforced. Figure 7-3 provides an example of state law on this issue.

---

(2) if any provision of a rental agreement was unconscionable when made, the court may enforce the remainder of the agreement without the unconscionable provision or limit the application of any unconscionable provision to avoid an unconscionable result; or
(3) if a settlement in which a party waives or agrees to forego a claim or right under this chapter or under a rental agreement was unconscionable when made, the court may refuse to enforce the settlement, enforce the remainder of the settlement without the unconscionable provision, or limit the application of any unconscionable provision to avoid an unconscionable result.[3]

FIGURE 7-3

Violation of Public Policy in Leases

A. FEDERAL LAW REQUIREMENTS

In addition to some of the state-based legislation that governs rental properties, there are also some federal laws that regulate residential real estate. The Federal Residential Lead-Based Hazard Reduction Act of 1992[4] requires landlords who own and lease houses built prior to 1978 to make certain disclosures to potential tenants. These disclosures require the landlord to give the tenant a lead hazard information pamphlet, to disclose the existence of lead-based paint known to be on the premises, and to give the tenant ten days to conduct his own risk assessment or to inspect the premises for lead-based paint.

B. STATUTE OF FRAUDS CONSIDERATIONS

Each state has its own version of the Statute of Frauds. The statute, originally created in England in the 1600s and imported to the American colonies, requires certain types of contracts to be in writing before they are enforceable. Examples of contracts that fall under the modern Statute of Frauds include prenuptial agreements, contracts to answer for the debts of another, and any agreement that cannot be performed within a year. This category of agreements that cannot be performed within a year creates Statute of Frauds concerns in leases. When a rental agreement is for a period longer than 12 months, the Statute of Frauds requires it to be in writing. Without a writing, neither the landlord nor the tenant can enforce the provisions of the lease.

VII   RIGHTS AND DUTIES CREATED BY THE LANDLORD-TENANT RELATIONSHIP

The landlord-tenant relationship confers specific rights and duties on both the landlord and the tenant. In this section, we will examine those rights and duties.

A. UNIFORM RESIDENTIAL LANDLORD AND TENANT ACT

URLTA provides a basic framework for the many issues that arise in landlord-tenant relationships, from creating the lease to establishing the reasons and procedures to evict a tenant (see Figure 7-4).

FIGURE 7-4 **URLTA: Purpose**	(b) Underlying purposes and policies of this chapter are: (1) to simplify, clarify, modernize, and revise the law governing rental of dwelling units and the rights and obligations of landlords and tenants; (2) to encourage landlords and tenants to maintain and improve the quality of housing.[5]

URLTA provides many other rules, including guidelines for written leases. If the lease is never signed or properly delivered, URLTA creates a landlord-tenant relationship as soon as the tenant accepts the leased premises (see Figure 7-5).

FIGURE 7-5 **URLTA Provisions Concerning Unsigned Leases**	Effect of unsigned or undelivered rental agreement. (a) If the landlord does not sign and deliver a written rental agreement which has been signed and delivered to the landlord by the tenant, acceptance of rent without reservation by the landlord gives the rental agreement the same effect as if it had been signed and delivered by the landlord.[6]

B. LANDLORDS' DUTIES AND RIGHTS

Although landlords had very few duties under the common law of old, modern statutes have substantially changed the landlord's role in the landlord-tenant relationship. The idea that landlords have few, if any, obligations to their tenants has slowly given way to new statutory obligations and civil liability. These days, landlords have numerous legal requirements and obligations that they owe to their tenants.

1. RIGHT TO RE-ENTER PREMISES

Because the landlord surrenders possession of the premises to the tenant as part of the lease arrangement, the landlord has no right to re-enter the premises as he wishes. Although the law does permit a landlord to re-enter the premises to make reasonable repairs and inspections (see Figure 7-6) and to demand payment for rent, the landlord has no additional rights to use and possess the premises; the tenant has the absolute right to the use and enjoyment of the property. Of course, the landlord has the right to re-enter the premises when the tenant vacates, even if the tenant leaves before the lease term expires.

When a tenant breaks a lease, the landlord has three possibilities: ■ Refuse to retake possession and continue to collect the rent.	■ Give notice to tenant, retake possession, and rent the premises to another tenant. ■ Re-enter the premises, take possession, and cancel the lease.[7]

FIGURE 7-6

Excerpt from the Uniform Residential Landlord and Tenant Act

THE CREEPY LANDLORD

EXAMPLE 7-4

Meredith has recently rented an apartment from a landlord named Andy. Meredith is concerned because lately she has found Andy in her bedroom when she comes home from work. She isn't sure about her rights and needs advice about how to proceed. Andy has told her that because he is the landlord, he can come and go as he pleases. What can she do?

Answer: Meredith would be within her rights to bring a civil action against Andy for trespass or invasion of privacy. Although Andy has the right to re-enter the premises for the limited purpose of making reasonable repairs, the key word here is "reasonable." Andy does not have the right to visit Meredith's apartment whenever he wishes, and he certainly has no right to be in Meredith's bedroom without some express purpose.

2. DUTY TO REPAIR

Although the common law of old imposed no duty on landlords to make repairs, that obligation has changed over time.[8] Under the modern view of landlord-tenant relationships, the landlord has the obligation to keep the premises in good condition (see Figures 7-7 and 7-8). This imposes on the landlord the duty to make repairs to ensure the tenant's safety. Failure to do so is considered a breach of the lease and is also a violation of other statutory obligations now imposed on landlords. However, before a landlord becomes liable to make repairs, the tenant must report the condition, especially if it is not immediately apparent to the landlord.

FIGURE 7-7 **Landlord's Obligations to the Tenant**	▪ Ensure that the premises are safe and habitable. ▪ Comply with building and housing codes.	▪ Make all repairs required to keep the premises safe. ▪ Remove garbage and trash from common areas.

FIGURE 7-8 **Landlord's Obligation to Maintain Premises**	(1) The landlord at all times during the tenancy shall: (a) Comply with the requirements of applicable building, housing, and health codes; or (b) Where there are no applicable building, housing, or health codes, maintain the roofs, windows, screens, doors, floors, steps, porches, exterior walls, foundations, and all other structural components in good repair and capable of resisting normal forces and loads and the plumbing in reasonable working condition. However, the landlord shall not be required to maintain a mobile home or other structure owned by the tenant.[9]

EXAMPLE 7-5	## THE LOOSE STEPS

Griffin has rented an upstairs apartment, and in the last few weeks he has noticed that when he comes downstairs to go to his car, the two top steps seem a little loose. Two weeks ago, he called the landlord and reported the loose steps. Last night, as he was leaving for work, one of the steps snapped under his weight and he was injured. He wants to sue the landlord. Does he have a case?

Answer: Yes. Because he gave notice to the landlord of the defective steps, and because the landlord failed to take any action to repair them, Griffin has a solid case against the landlord.

Some state statutes, such as Rhode Island's Landlord-Tenant Act, permit the landlord to shift some repair duties to the tenant. Routine repairs can fall to the tenant, but anything requiring the premises to meet state or building codes remains the responsibility of the landlord.[10] Landlords are not permitted to negotiate away their obligations in a lease, even in exchange for lower-than-average rent. Landlords continue to bear the burden of making major repairs and cannot pass this burden on to tenants.[11] When the landlord fails to meet this responsibility, the tenant is permitted to sue for damages, including the cost incurred by the tenant to make the repair.[12] See Figure 7-9 for a list of the repair duties imposed upon the landlord by URLTA.

FIGURE 7-9 **Duty to Make Repairs Under URLTA**	▪ Comply with all applicable building, safety, and housing codes. ▪ Make all necessary repairs to keep the premises in a fit and habitable condition. ▪ Keep all common areas clean, safe, and free of garbage.	▪ Maintain and keep in good working order all appliances provided with the leased premises. ▪ Provide running water and hot water. ▪ Provide heat.[13]

3. DUTY TO THIRD PARTIES

In addition to the duties that landlords owe their tenants, they also have some duties to third parties. For instance, all states require landlords to keep both residential and commercial rental units free from dangerous conditions. Landlords have a duty to warn tenants about unsafe conditions. Some states go further and impose duties on the landlord to actively protect tenant guests and customers.

4. DISCRIMINATORY PRACTICES

Landlords are barred from engaging in specific types of discriminatory practices. The federal Fair Housing Act and Fair Housing Amendments Act[14] prohibit landlords from engaging in practices such as refusing to rent to individuals on the basis of:

- Race,
- Religion,
- National origin,
- Sex,
- Marital status, and
- Mental or physical disability.

Some states extend this list to include the categories of age or sexual orientation. (See Figure 7-10 for a statement of the property rights of citizens.) In addition to these overt tactics, the Fair Housing Act also prohibits more subtle forms of discrimination, such as failing to accommodate individuals with disabilities, establishing different terms and conditions for different tenants, and using inconsistent policies for some tenants on issues such as pets and late payments.

However, these statutes do permit certain types of discrimination. For instance, a landlord can refuse to rent to a person or business that does not meet specific financial criteria or that has negative references from previous landlords. As long as these rules apply to all renters, the landlord is permitted to refuse to rent to individuals or businesses that do not meet the established criteria.

Sidebar

Renters who are the victims of discrimination can contact the Department of Housing and Urban Development to file a complaint. They may also bring actions under state law.

All citizens of the United States shall have the same right, in every State and Territory, as is enjoyed by white citizens thereof to inherit, purchase, lease, sell, hold, and convey real and personal property.[15]

FIGURE 7-10

Property Rights of Citizens

REAL WORLD PERSPECTIVE: *LANDLORD*

It's not like what you see on those late night informercials. I had this kind of silly idea that I'd buy a place, rent it out, and sit back and cash those rent checks. I was pretty naïve. I had to learn the hard way that you need to check your tenants' backgrounds before you lease. There is a ton of stuff in the public record that can warn you about problematic tenants. I had to learn to document everything, even the people who didn't get the apartment. I had to take notes on when, where, how much I spent on making repairs. I got this program that let me download my texts because I had to show them in court to a small claims judge. I guess it's like a lot of things: the reality is a lot different than what you think. It's a lot more work. I have six units now and they keep me pretty busy. And I've got a full-time job. So, I work on the weekends, making repairs that I can do or supervising guys to do the plumbing or HVAC. It was already a tough job, then the whole Covid thing comes along and boom! You can't evict people who don't pay. But I still got to make my mortgage payments. We were pretty lucky. Out of the six, we only had one tenant who just wouldn't pay. We worked out new payment schedules for the others, lowering the rent so we could at least have some money coming in and so they wouldn't worry about eviction if they lift the ban.

— E. V., landlord

C. TENANTS' DUTIES AND RIGHTS

The landlord-tenant relationship confers specific rights and duties on the tenant. For instance, not only does the tenant have the absolute right to use, possess, and enjoy the leased premises, tenants also have the duty to pay the rent.

1. RIGHT TO USE AND ENJOYMENT

The tenant has the right to use and enjoy the premises. *Use and enjoyment* includes many of the rights normally associated with fee simple title, including full access to all amenities and the right to redecorate the interior, hang pictures, lay carpets, and bring in furniture. The tenant is free to decorate in a variety of ways, as long as she does not make any structural changes or cause damage to the building. In essence, the landlord has divested those rights and has only a reversionary interest in the premises. When the lease terminates, the property rights automatically revert to the landlord.

2. TENANT DUTIES

The landlord-tenant relationship creates duties not only for landlords, but also for tenants. The most obvious tenant obligation is to pay rent, but there are several other important responsibilities that the tenant assumes when entering into a lease (see Figure 7-11).

FIGURE 7-11

**Duties Tenants Owe to
Their Landlords**

- They must pay rent.
- They must keep the premises clean.
- They must dispose of garbage.
- They must keep plumbing fixtures clean.
- They are prohibited from destroying, altering, or defacing the leased premises.
- They are obligated to pay for any damages above normal wear and tear.

Landlords and tenants can enter into agreements to restrict the nature of the relationship, as long as this agreement does not violate state statutes or public policy. For instance, a lease can contain a provision that the premises will be used for limited purposes. Commercial leases often have clauses that limit the manner of use. Such a lease might contain a provision that limits use to a retail business and prohibits it for use as a residence.

3. RESPONSIBILITY FOR DAMAGES TO LEASED PREMISES

Although the tenant duties outlined in Figure 7-11 are self-explanatory, one category merits further discussion: When a tenant causes damage to the property, he is responsible for paying for the repairs. The question always becomes: What is the extent of the tenant's responsibility for damages? What constitutes "damage" in this context? In this context, damage refers to any destruction or defacing of property that is beyond ordinary wear and tear.

The tenant is responsible for keeping the premises clean; the landlord is responsible for all major repairs and upkeep.

REAL
ESTATE
BASICS AT
A GLANCE

a. Ordinary Wear and Tear

Although the tenant is responsible for any damages to the premises that qualify as structural, the landlord cannot insist that the tenant pay for **ordinary wear and tear**. "Wear and tear" is a phrase that covers all the normal dents and scrapes that occur through daily use. Examples of ordinary wear and tear include:

Ordinary wear and tear
The normal dents and scrapes that occur through daily use.

- Light scratches on walls and doors,
- Wear on carpeting and floors,
- Accumulated dirt and grime, and
- Nail holes in walls.

b. Safety Deposits

As we have already seen, landlords are authorized to assess safety deposits as part of the rental process. These deposits can help defer the costs of repairing any damages that the tenant does to the leased premises. Safety deposits are usually a percentage of one month's rent and can be returned to the tenant if there is no major damage at the end of the lease term.

c. Pet Deposits

As with safety deposits, landlords can also require a pet deposit to defer the costs for stains or torn carpeting that are often associated with pet ownership.

D. LEGAL DOCTRINES THAT ARISE IN THE LANDLORD-TENANT RELATIONSHIP

Throughout this chapter, we have alluded to the obligations now placed on landlords that were not a feature of the historical landlord-tenant relationship. There are several legal doctrines that apply in this context, including the warranty of habitability and quiet enjoyment.

1. WARRANTY OF HABITABILITY

Warranty of habitability
A legal doctrine that imposes on landlords the implied duty to provide leased premises that are fit for human habitation.

Historically, tenants had no legal right to habitable premises. Under this rule, the landlord could provide a dwelling in nearly any condition. However, all jurisdictions have modified this original rule, and most have adopted the warranty of habitability. The **warranty of habitability** is a legal doctrine that requires the landlord to provide a living environment that meets basic standards of cleanliness, safety, and livability. It also imposes a duty on the landlord to maintain the premises in this condition. In many ways, this doctrine is similar to the warranties that courts have implied in other commercial settings. When consumers buy products, courts will often imply warranties covering the fitness of the product for its advertised purpose. Similarly, the landlord provides habitable and safe premises in exchange for the rent paid by the tenant. In this relationship, the obligation of one is premised on the action of the other. The warranty of habitability applies to residential properties only, not commercial leases.

2. QUIET ENJOYMENT

Quiet enjoyment
The right of a tenant to use the leased premises unmolested.

The tenant has the right of **quiet enjoyment** in the leased premises. This means that the tenant has the absolute legal right to live in or use the premises free from interference by others. The tenant has the right to order other individuals off the property and to institute trespass actions for people who refuse to leave. Rented apartments and houses can be the subject of burglary actions under the theory that although someone else actually owns the property, the tenant is the person in possession and has the right to quiet enjoyment.

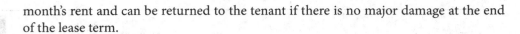

REMEDIES FOR BREACH OF DUTY

Because the landlord-tenant relationship creates mutual obligations, both parties have actions against the other when those obligations are breached.

A. TENANT REMEDIES AGAINST LANDLORD

When a tenant believes that a landlord has infringed on his rights, he is free to bring suit. The civil action could be based on contract principles. Under this theory, the tenant alleges that the lease was a contract entered into between the two parties and that the landlord has breached this contract by interfering with the tenant's quiet enjoyment or violating the warranty of habitability. But tenants also can bring suits under an entirely different legal theory; for example, they can sue under tort law.

When a tenant sues under tort law, he alleges that the landlord had a duty to him and failed to meet that duty. He might allege, for instance, that because the landlord had a duty to keep the premises safe, when the landlord failed to repair a hole in the sidewalk, the landlord was responsible for the tenant's injuries when the tenant fell into the hole. The issue of tort law involves a set of concerns that could easily justify its own textbook.

1. DAMAGES THAT CAN BE AWARDED TO THE TENANT

If the tenant can prove a case against the landlord, she, like any successful plaintiff, is entitled to damages. There are many different types of damages, including:

- Equitable relief,
- Compensatory damages, and
- Punitive damages.

a. Equitable Relief

A tenant can ask a court to exercise its powers of equity in dealing with the issues pending in a landlord-tenant suit. Equity powers refer to a court's authority to order individuals to carry out specific actions, or in some cases, to stop carrying out actions. The most common type of equitable relief is an injunction. An injunction is a court order demanding that an individual cease carrying out specific actions. In a landlord-tenant case, for example, a court could use its equity powers to order a landlord to stop discriminating against renters, to reinstate a dispossessed tenant, or even to make specific repairs.

b. Compensatory Damages

In addition to ordering specific forms of equitable relief, a court can also award monetary damages. If a tenant proves financial losses directly tied to the landlord's actions, the court may order the landlord to reimburse the tenant for those losses. Of course, the opposite situation also holds true. A tenant who wrongfully terminates a lease may be ordered to pay damages to a landlord.

In such cases, the question often becomes: How does the court determine the actual amount of damages? Usually, the court calculates damages by using the difference between the rent the landlord could have received and the rent the landlord actually received.

| EXAMPLE 7-6 | **TONYA'S ABANDONED APARTMENT** |

Tonya Tenant abandoned her leased property six months prior to the lease termination. Her monthly rent was $600. The premises were vacant for two months before the landlord rented it to another tenant; however, the landlord had to reduce the rent by $100 per month to attract a new tenant. The landlord requests damages in the amount of $3,600, which is what he would have received if Tonya had remained on the premises for the remainder of her lease. When the landlord sues Tonya, what are his damages?

Answer: Although the landlord would have received $3,600 if Tonya had remained on the premises, he did find a new tenant who leased the property for the remaining four months of Tonya's lease. The court determines that the landlord is entitled to $1,600 in damages. How did it arrive at this figure?

The court calculated that the total damages that the landlord would have been entitled to receive were $3,600. However, the landlord mitigated his damages by renting the unit to another tenant. This tenant paid $500 per month, meaning that the landlord lost $100 per month for four months, or $400. The premises were also vacant for two months, for a total of $1,200. Adding these two amounts together, the court awards $1,600 in damages.

REAL
ESTATE
BASICS AT
A GLANCE

Fair rental value is often determined by the amount of the rent paid by the new tenant.

A court can also calculate compensatory damages for the tenant by calculating the fair market rental of a unit. In cases where the premises have become unfit for habitation, the court will calculate the difference between the rental value of the premises as they should have been and compare that with the rental value of the premises as they are. The difference is the amount of damages that a court can award to a tenant. The tenant is also entitled to compensation for out-of-pocket expenses directly related to the landlord's failure to maintain the premises.

c. Punitive Damages

In some cases, a tenant may be entitled to an award of punitive damages. Punitive damages are designed to do exactly what the name suggests: They punish the landlord by assessing monetary damages against him that are in excess of the tenant's out-of-pocket and other expenses.

2. CONSTRUCTIVE EVICTION

Constructive eviction
A legal doctrine that holds that leased premises that are unfit for human habitation effectively prevent the tenant from continuing to live there.

One ground that a tenant can allege in a suit against the landlord is **constructive eviction**. An action for constructive eviction states that the landlord allowed conditions at the rental to deteriorate to such an extent that it was no longer fit for human habitation. Under common law, a tenant could sue a landlord for wrongful eviction only when the landlord used physical force to evict the tenant. However, all jurisdictions now recognize the theory of constructive eviction.

Under constructive eviction, the tenant must show that the landlord, or someone working for the landlord, created conditions that effectively made the premises uninhabitable. Some of the elements that the tenant must show are that the conditions interfered with her quiet enjoyment of the premises, that she had to abandon the premises, and that she left under protest. If the tenant continues to live in the rental unit, she cannot allege constructive eviction. Some authorities hold that the landlord's acts must amount to something "grave and permanent" and must clearly indicate the landlord's intention to deprive the tenant of the enjoyment of the leased premises.

LARRY'S LOCK OUT

EXAMPLE 7-7

Larry Landlord has decided that he wants to get out of the landlord business. He has only one remaining tenant, Teresa. He can't find a legal reason to evict her. One day, when Teresa is at work, he boards up all her windows and padlocks her door. Does Teresa have an action for constructive eviction?

Answer: Yes. Many states recognize a cause of action for constructive eviction when the landlord blocks access to the premises. Teresa will most likely win her suit.

KEISHA'S DOG

EXAMPLE 7-8

Keisha owns a dog and rents an apartment. One day, the landlord stops by, and when he sees Keisha's dog, he revs his car engine and threatens to run the dog over. Does Keisha have grounds for constructive eviction?

Answer: No. An action for constructive eviction alleges that the landlord has taken some action to make the premises unfit. Threatening the tenant's dog does not qualify.[16]

3. ACTIONS FOR WRONGFUL EVICTION

Because eviction is now governed by state statute, landlords who violate the law in evicting tenants are subject to several different sanctions. For instance, the court may allow the tenant to recover possession of the leased premises and is also authorized to assess the landlord for monetary damages. If the tenant brings an action for wrongful eviction and proves the case, he would be entitled to:

- Recover possession of the leased premises,
- Terminate the lease, or
- Recover monetary damages against the landlord for various costs he incurred.

B. LANDLORD REMEDIES AGAINST TENANT: EVICTION

So far, our discussion has focused on the remedies that the tenant has against the landlord. Landlords also have several possible actions against a tenant who defaults on a lease. The most obvious of these is eviction.

Eviction is the most common, and perhaps most effective, form of sanction that a landlord can bring against a tenant. A landlord is permitted to bring an eviction against a tenant for any of number of reasons, but the most common is for failure to pay rent. Under modern eviction statutes (see Figure 7-12), a landlord must bring a civil action and request a judicial ruling that the tenant is in violation of the lease and can be evicted from the premises.

FIGURE 7-12 **Notice Required in an Eviction Procedure (Ohio)**	A party desiring to commence an action under this chapter shall notify the adverse party to leave the premises, for the possession of which the action is about to be brought, three or more days before beginning the action, by certified mail, return receipt requested, or by handing a written copy of the notice to the defendant in person, or by leaving it at his usual place of abode or at the premises from which the defendant is sought to be evicted. Every notice given under this section by a landlord to recover residential premises shall contain the following language printed or written in a conspicuous manner: "You are being asked to leave the premises. If you do not leave, an eviction action may be initiated against you. If you are in doubt regarding your legal rights and obligations as a tenant, it is recommended that you seek legal assistance."[17]

1. PROCEDURES TO EVICT

An eviction action often falls under the jurisdiction of small claims court or another specifically designated court. To bring an eviction action, the landlord must prove several elements, including that she notified the tenant that he was in default, usually by certified mail or by personal service. Once proper notice is given, the landlord may bring an action in the appropriate court, stating that the tenant failed to pay the rent and that proper notice was given, and requesting that the court order the tenant to vacate the premises. The landlord may also request payment for outstanding rent.

2. SELF-HELP EVICTION

Although the common law once allowed landlords to forcibly evict residential tenants, this remedy is no longer available. Such actions are fraught with potential dangers, including the possibility of violence from angry tenants. In almost all jurisdictions in the United States, **self-help eviction** is not an option, at least in residential leasing. Instead, landlords must follow state statutes that create specific steps that must be followed to evict a tenant who has not paid his rent.

Self-help eviction
The landlord acts without legal process to evict a tenant and instead relies on physical force; no longer permitted in most states, at least for residential leases.

When landlords violate the rules against self-help eviction, they can be civilly liable to the tenant. The tenant is permitted to sue the landlord, including for claims such as intentional infliction of emotional distress.[18] The landlord may also be required to pay for any damage to the tenant's possessions and the costs associated with the tenant's relocation. The court may also reinstate the tenant on the leased premises and invoke the provisions of the previous lease. In some circumstances, the tenant may be entitled to punitive damages, especially when the landlord has acted without legal authority. Commercial tenants may be entitled to damages that include lost future income.

3. RETALIATORY EVICTION

Landlords are not permitted to use the eviction process as a way to get rid of tenants who complain about conditions on the premises or tenants who report the landlord's deficiencies to local government officials. Tenants are allowed to raise the defense of retaliatory eviction when the landlord terminates their lease in response to their complaints. Under URLTA, a landlord is prevented from evicting a tenant when:

- The tenant has complained to a governmental agency with jurisdiction over housing and building codes,
- The tenant has complained to the landlord about the failure to maintain to the premises, or
- The tenant has organized or joined a tenants' union.

Allowing a landlord to evict tenants when they complain about the landlord's actions is a violation of public policy.[19] The courts are allowed to presume that the landlord has committed retaliatory eviction when the tenant does any of the above activities and is then evicted. However, courts are not allowed to reach this conclusion when the tenant bases a complaint on any of the actions set out above after he is evicted. If the tenant proves a claim for retaliatory eviction, a court is permitted to reinstate the lease and is also permitted to assess other damages against the landlord. Courts are allowed to apply the statutes prohibiting retaliatory eviction in a liberal way.[20]

 **CLASSIFYING LANDLORD-TENANT RELATIONSHIPS**

Landlord-tenant relationships come in several different forms, including:

- Tenancy for years,
- Tenancy from year to year,
- Tenancy at will, and
- Tenancy at sufferance.

Each of these tenancies has unique features, including when and how they are created, the duties imposed on the parties, and the ways that each is terminated.

A. TENANCY FOR YEARS

A tenancy for years is any lease arrangement that will terminate on a specific date. Many of these tenancies run for set periods, such as one month or one year. Because of the confusion inherent in calling something a "tenancy for years" that could actually expire in less than a year, many legal commentators have suggested that a more appropriate name for this tenancy would be an "estate for a stated period."

1. CREATING A TENANCY FOR YEARS

Tenancies for years are created by the express terms of the lease. The parties specify when the lease begins and when it ends.

2. TERMINATING A TENANCY FOR YEARS

A tenancy for years expires by its own terms. The parties are not required to give notice to one another of their intention to terminate the lease. Instead, if they wish to continue the arrangement, they must express their intention to renew the lease prior to the termination point, or the lease will automatically expire.

B. TENANCY FROM YEAR TO YEAR

The deceptively named tenancy from year to year is a lease arrangement that usually does not run for a year. Instead, it runs for a series of specific intervals. The most common example is a month-to-month lease. There is also a push to change the name for this tenancy to an "estate from period to period." By whatever name, this tenancy automatically renews at the end of the agreed-upon term unless the parties agree to terminate it.

1. CREATING A TENANCY FROM YEAR TO YEAR

Tenancies from year to year are often created when a tenant has a tenancy for years arrangement and then remains on the premises past the expiration date of that original lease. Most states have provisions that convert an expired tenancy for years into a tenancy from year to year. The significance of this reclassification is found in the method used to terminate the arrangement.

2. TERMINATING A TENANCY FROM YEAR TO YEAR

Tenancies from year to year do not terminate automatically; instead, the parties must give notice to cancel the lease. The question in such cases often concerns the amount of notice required. By its very nature, there are few details provided in a tenancy from year to year, so the courts cannot refer to a lease for guidance about notice. What courts have done instead is to fashion a notice period based on the lease period. If the tenancy runs for a year, the parties must give at least one month's notice to terminate. If the lease runs from month to month, they must give at least seven days' notice. Without proper notice, the tenancy will automatically renew.

REAL
ESTATE
BASICS AT
A GLANCE

The notice required to cancel different types of tenancies depends on their legal status. For instance, in a tenancy from year to year, notice to cancel must be received at least one month prior to the stated term of the lease for the notice to be legally effective.

C. TENANCY AT WILL

Tenancies at will have no set terms. This is a lease arrangement wherein the landlord and the tenant have an informal agreement to lease the premises "for as long as the tenant desires," or under some similar formula. The lack of specificity about the arrangement means that the tenancy can be created at any time. See Figure 7-13 for URLTA's rules governing tenancy at will.

(d) Unless the rental agreement fixes a definite term, the tenancy is week to week in case of a roomer who pays weekly rent and in all other cases month to month.[21]	**FIGURE 7-13** **URLTA: Rental Payment Determines Tenancy**

1. CREATING A TENANCY AT WILL

The parties create a tenancy at will when they fail to specify the lease terms in regard to length, notice, renewal, or any other material terms usually found in a landlord-tenant relationship.

2. TERMINATING A TENANCY AT WILL

Either the landlord or the tenant can terminate a tenancy at will at any time. The only requirement is that one give "reasonable notice" to the other of the intention to terminate. What constitutes reasonable notice is determined on a case-by-case basis. The requirement for reasonable notice is to give the tenant enough time to remove personal items from the leased premises.

D. TENANCY AT SUFFERANCE

A tenancy at sufferance is not really a tenancy at all. In the three previous examples, there was an agreement between the landlord and the tenant; however, in tenancy at sufferance, there is no agreement. Instead, the tenant remains on the premises without permission. This situation often arises when a tenant remains on the premises after a lease has expired and refuses to leave after being given notice to do so. A tenancy at sufferance relationship often arises while an eviction action is pending.

1. CREATING A TENANCY AT SUFFERANCE

The parties do not create a tenancy at sufferance. Instead, this tenancy comes into existence when the tenant is on the leased premises without permission.

2. TERMINATING A TENANCY AT SUFFERANCE

Because this tenancy is not a voluntary arrangement, there is no notice required to terminate it. Instead, the court may authorize the ejection of a tenant at sufferance when the court rules in the landlord's favor in an eviction action.

Case Excerpt

ALABAMA ASSOC. OF REALTORS v. U.S. DEPT. OF HEALTH AND HUMAN SERVICES
No. 20-cv-3377 (2021)

As part of the Coronavirus Aid, Relief, and Economic Security Act (CARES Act), Pub. L. No. 116-136, 134 Stat. 281 (2020), Congress enacted a 120-day eviction moratorium that applied to rental properties receiving federal assistance, *id.* §4024(b). After that moratorium expired, the U.S. Department of Health and Human Services (HHS), through the Centers for Disease Control and Prevention (CDC), issued an order implementing a broader eviction moratorium that applied to all rental properties nationwide, 85 Fed. Reg. 55, 292 (Sept. 4, 2020), which prompted this suit. Since then, Congress has granted a 30-day extension of the CDC Order, and the CDC has extended the order twice itself. The current order is set to expire on June 30, 2021.

In this action, the plaintiffs raise a number of statutory and constitutional challenges to the CDC Order. Before the Court is the plaintiffs' Motion for Expedited Summary Judgment, as well as the Department's Motion for Summary Judgment, and Partial Motion to Dismiss. For the reasons that follow, the Court will grant the plaintiffs' motion and deny the Department's motions.

I. Background

On March 13, 2020, then-President Trump declared COVID-19 a national emergency. Two weeks later, he signed the CARES Act into law. The CARES Act included a 120-day eviction moratorium with respect to rental properties that participated in federal assistance programs or were subject to federally-backed loans. In addition, some-but not all-states adopted their own temporary eviction moratoria. The CARES Act's federal eviction moratorium expired in July 2020.

On August 8, 2020, then-President Trump issued an executive order directing the Secretary of HHS ("the Secretary") and the Director of the CDC to "consider whether any measures temporarily halting residential evictions of any tenants for failure to pay rent are reasonably necessary to prevent the further spread of COVID-19 from one State or possession into any other State or possession."

Weeks later, on September 4, 2020, the CDC issued the "Temporary Halt in Residential Evictions To Prevent the Further Spread of COVID-19" ("CDC Order"), pursuant to §361 of the Public Health Service Act, 42 U.S.C. §264(a), and 42 C.F.R. §70.2. 85 Fed. Reg. 55, 292 (Sept. 4, 2020). In this order, the CDC determined that a temporary halt on residential evictions was "a reasonably necessary measure . . . to prevent the further spread of COVID-19." 85 Fed. Reg. at 55, 296. As the CDC explained, the eviction moratorium facilitates self-isolation for individuals infected with COVID-19 or who are at a higher-risk of severe illness from COVID-19 given their underlying medical conditions. *Id.* at 55, 294. It also enhances state and local officials' ability to implement stay-at-home orders and other social distancing measures, reduces the need for congregate housing, and helps prevent homelessness. *Id.* at 55, 294.

The CDC Order declared that "a landlord, owner of a residential property, or other person with a legal right to pursue eviction or possessory action shall not evict any covered person." *Id.* at 55, 296. To qualify for protection under the moratorium, a tenant must submit a declaration to their landlord affirming that they: (1) have "used best efforts to obtain all available government assistance for rent or housing"; (2) expect to earn less than $99,000 in annual income in 2020, were not required to report any income in 2019 to the Internal Revenue Service, or received a stimulus check under the CARES Act; (3) are "unable to pay the full rent or make a full housing payment due to substantial loss of household income, loss of compensable hours of work or wages, a lay-off, or extraordinary out-of-pocket medical expenses"; (4) are "using best efforts to make timely partial payments"; (5) would likely become homeless or be forced to move into a shared residence if evicted; (6) understand that rent obligations still apply; and (7) understand that the moratorium is scheduled to end on December 31, 2020. *Id.* at 55, 297.

Unlike the CARES Act's moratorium, which only applied to certain federally backed rental properties, the CDC Order applied to all residential properties nationwide. *Id.* at 55, 293. In addition, the CDC Order includes criminal penalties. Individuals who violate its provisions are subject to a fine of up to $250,000, one year in jail, or both, and organizations are subject to a fine of up to $500,000. *Id.* at 55, 296.

A. Procedural History

The plaintiffs — Danny Fordham, Robert Gilstrap, the corporate entities they use to manage rental properties (Fordham & Associates, LLC, H.E. Cauthen Land and Development, LLC, and Title One Management, LLC), and two trade associations (the Alabama and Georgia Associations of Realtors) — filed this action on November 20, 2020. They challenge the lawfulness of the eviction moratorium on a number of statutory and constitutional grounds. The plaintiffs allege that the eviction moratorium exceeds the CDC's statutory authority, violates the notice-and-comment requirement, and is arbitrary and capricious, all in violation of the Administrative Procedure Act (APA).

B. Relevant Decisions

This Court is not the first to address a challenge to the national eviction moratorium set forth in the CDC Order. In the last several months, at least six courts have considered various statutory and constitutional challenges to the CDC Order. Most recently, the Sixth Circuit denied a motion to stay a district court decision that held that the order exceeded the CDC's authority under 42 U.S.C.

The Agency's Statutory Authority

Section 361 of the Public Health Service Act empowers the Secretary to "make and enforce such regulations as in his judgment are necessary to prevent the introduction, transmission, or spread of communicable diseases" either internationally or between states.1 42 U.S.C. §264(a). "For purposes of carrying out and enforcing such regulations," the Secretary is authorized to "provide for such inspection, fumigation, disinfection, sanitation, pest extermination, destruction of animals or articles found to be so infected or contaminated as to be sources of dangerous infection to human beings, and other measures, as in his judgment may be necessary." *Id.* The Secretary is also authorized to, within certain limits, make and enforce regulations to apprehend, examine, and, if necessary, detain individuals "believed to be infected with a communicable disease" or who are "coming into a State or possession" from a foreign country. *Id.* §264(b)-(d).

By regulation, the Secretary delegated this authority to the Director of the CDC. 42 C.F.R. §70.2. Pursuant to this regulation, when the Director of the CDC determines that the measures taken by health authorities of any state or local jurisdiction are insufficient to prevent the spread of communicable disease, "he/she may take such measures to prevent such spread of the diseases as he/she deems reasonably necessary, including inspection, fumigation, disinfection, sanitation, pest extermination, and destruction of animals or articles believed to be sources of infection." *Id.*

The CDC, with the approval of the Secretary, is authorized to make and enforce such regulations as in his judgment are necessary to prevent the introduction, transmission, or spread of communicable diseases from foreign countries into the States or possessions, or from one State or possession into any other State or possession. For purposes of carrying out and enforcing such regulations, the Secretary may provide for such inspection, fumigation, disinfection, sanitation, pest extermination, destruction of animals or articles found to be so infected or contaminated as to be sources of dangerous infection to human beings, and other measures, as in his judgment may be necessary. 42 U.S.C. §264(a).

Other subsections of the Act authorize, in certain circumstances, the quarantine of individuals in order to prevent the interstate or international spread of disease. See *id.* §264(b)-(d). Though the Public Health Service Act grants the Secretary broad authority to make and enforce regulations necessary to prevent the spread of disease, his authority is not limitless.

Section 264(a) provides the Secretary with general rulemaking authority to "make and enforce such regulations," *id.* §264(a) (emphasis added), that "in his judgment are necessary" to combat the international or interstate spread of communicable disease, *id.* But this broad grant of rulemaking authority in the first sentence of §264(a) is tethered to-and narrowed by-the second sentence. It states: "For purposes of carrying out and enforcing such regulations," *id.*, the Secretary "may provide for such inspection, fumigation, disinfection, sanitation, pest extermination and destruction of animals or articles found to be so infected or contaminated as to be sources of dangerous infection to human beings." *Id.*

These enumerated measures are not exhaustive. The Secretary may provide for "other measures, as in his judgment may be necessary." *Id.* But any such "other measures" are "controlled and defined by reference to the enumerated categories before it." *Id.* at 522 (applying the ejusdem generis canon to interpret the residual catchall phrase in §264(a)). These "other measures" must therefore be similar in nature to those listed in §264(a). *Id.* And consequently, like the enumerated measures, these "other measures" are limited in two significant respects: first, they must be directed toward "animals or articles," 42 U.S.C. §264(a), and second, those "animals or articles" must be "found to be so infected or contaminated as to be sources of dangerous infection to human beings," *id.*; see Skyworks, 2021 WL 911720. In other words, any regulations enacted pursuant to §264(a) must be directed toward "specific targets 'found' to be sources of infection." *Id.*

The national eviction moratorium satisfies none of these textual limitations. Plainly, imposing a moratorium on evictions is different in nature than "inspecting, fumigating, disinfecting, sanitizing, . . . exterminating or destroying," 42 U.S.C. §264(a), a potential source of infection. Moreover, interpreting the term "articles" to include evictions would stretch the term beyond its plain meaning. See Webster's New International Dictionary 156 (2d ed. 1945). And even if the meaning of the term "articles" could be stretched that far, the statute instructs that they must be "found to be so infected or contaminated as to be sources of dangerous infection to human beings." 42 U.S.C. §264(a). The Secretary has made no such findings here. The fact that individuals with COVID-19 can be asymptomatic and that the disease is difficult to detect, Mot. Hr'g Tr. at 27, Dkt. 65, does not broaden the Secretary's authority beyond what the plain text of §264(a) permits.

Accepting the Department's expansive interpretation of the Act would mean that Congress delegated to the Secretary the authority to resolve not only this important question, but endless others that are also subject to "earnest and profound debate across the country." *Gonzales*, 546 U.S. at 267. Under its reading, so long as the Secretary can make a determination that a given measure is "necessary" to combat the interstate or international spread of disease, there is no limit to the reach of his authority.

"Congress could not have intended to delegate" such extraordinary power "to an agency in so cryptic a fashion." *Brown & Williamson Tobacco Corp.*, 529 U.S. at 159. To be sure, COVID-19 is a novel disease that poses unique and substantial public health challenges, see Def.'s Cross-Mot. at 14, but the Court is "confident that the enacting Congress did not intend to grow such a large elephant in such a small mousehole." *Loving*, 742 F.3d at 1021.

It is also telling that the CDC has never used §264(a) in this manner. As the Department confirms, §264(a) "has never been used to implement a temporary eviction moratorium," and "has rarely been utilized . . . for disease-control purposes." See Defs.' Cross-Mot. at 13-15, 23. "When an agency claims to discover in a long-extant statute an unheralded power to regulate a significant portion of the American economy," the Court must "greet its announcement with a measure of skepticism." Util. Air Regul. Grp., 573 U.S. at 324.

In sum, the Public Health Service Act authorizes the Department to combat the spread of disease through a range of measures, but these measures plainly do not encompass the nationwide eviction moratorium set forth in the CDC Order. Thus, the Department has exceeded the authority provided in §361 of the Public Health Service Act, 42 U.S.C. §264(a).

Conclusion

For the foregoing reasons, the plaintiffs' motion for expedited summary judgment is granted and the Department's motion for summary judgment and partial motion to dismiss are denied. A separate order consistent with this decision accompanies this memorandum opinion.

QUESTIONS ABOUT THE CASE

1 What provisions from the CARES act applied to evictions?
2 How did the CDC become involved in a moratorium on evictions?
3 How could the CARES Act apply to landlords?
4 Did the CDC order implement a broader moratorium on evictions? If so, how?
5 What were the plaintiffs' allegations against the CDC?
6 How did the court rule on the CDC order?

COVID-19 CONCERN

Just as the reaction to the COVID-19 pandemic resulted in a nationwide moratorium on evictions, at least until it was challenged in court, COVID is going to change many other aspects of renting. Renters may demand that new HVAC systems be put into place that screen for airborne infectants. Landlords may be hesitant or outright refuse to rent to an infected person. Others may require proof of vaccination before they consider renters' applications.

CHAPTER SUMMARY

The topic of landlord-tenant law has many legal implications. The basics of the arrangement are established when a landlord conveys some of his rights to the tenant. These rights include the right to occupy, use, and enjoy the property. The landlord retains all other rights. The lease sets out the terms of the rental agreements. During the time that a tenant is in possession of the property, referred to as a tenancy, the tenant has both rights and obligations that arise from the relationship. Similarly, the landlord owes duties to the tenant. There are four different classifications of tenancy relationships. A tenancy for years has a specific termination date, after which the landlord-tenant relationship automatically terminates. A tenancy from year to year runs for a specific period of time. A tenancy at will is created when the parties do not specify the terms of the lease arrangement. A tenancy at sufferance arises when the tenant wrongfully remains on the premises after the lease has expired.

SKILLS YOU NEED IN THE REAL WORLD

Researching Landlord-Tenant Law

Because the area of landlord-tenant law is rich with case law decisions and statutes, be aware that this area of law changes constantly. Most states have statutes that specifically govern residential leases, and it is not uncommon for these laws to change every few years. Similarly, there is a large body of case law that constantly refines and expands on this topic, not only from state appellate courts but also from federal courts. After all, there are always disgruntled tenants suing landlords and exasperated landlords seeking to evict nonpaying tenants. You should also be aware that the standards in these cases have slowly changed over time. Fifty years ago, there were virtually no court decisions dictating that landlords must provide air conditioning or even hot water to their tenants as a basic requirement for habitation. As society's standards have slowly risen, so have the courts' expectations of landlords.

ETHICAL ISSUES FOR THE PARALEGAL

Landlords Who Violate State Law

The legal professional should always be on the lookout for recent cases that illustrate a landlord's responsibility to tenants. As this chapter's case excerpt clearly shows, landlords have numerous obligations to tenants and the failure to meet those obligations can have severe monetary consequences. As case law develops on this point, it behooves legal professionals to keep track of recent decisions by the state appellate courts that modify those obligations or expand on them. Landlord clients should be informed of recent changes in the law in order to keep them on the right side of the law.

KEY TERMS AND CONCEPTS

Constructive eviction	Leasehold estate	Sublet
Eviction	Ordinary wear and tear	Tenant
Landlord	Quiet enjoyment	Warranty of habitability
Lease	Self-help eviction	

END-OF-CHAPTER EXERCISES

Review Questions

See Appendix for answers.

1   What rights does a landlord transfer to a tenant in a typical lease arrangement?
2   List the landlord's duties to the tenant.
3   Explain the difference between a fixed-rent lease and a percentage lease.
4   What is a ground lease?
5   What is a mineral lease?
6   What are the rules that govern pet and security deposits?
7   What is subletting?
8   Give an example of an action that would be permissible under a commercial lease but not a residential lease.
9   How does the Statute of Frauds affect leases?
10 What is the Uniform Residential Landlord and Tenant Act?
11 Name at least three different statutes that are important in residential leasing, and explain why they are important.
12 What discriminatory practices are prohibited under federal and state law?
13 What is "ordinary wear and tear"? Briefly describe the two legal doctrines that have evolved in modern landlord-tenant law.
14 What is "self-help" eviction?
15 What are the characteristics of a tenancy for years?
16 What are the characteristics of a tenancy from year to year?
17 How is a tenancy at will created?
18 What is a tenancy at sufferance?
19 Create a table showing the different ways that the four tenancies discussed in this chapter can be terminated.
20 Summarize the chapter's case excerpt.

DISCUSSION QUESTIONS

1   Are all of these different tenancies really necessary? Is there a way to structure a residential agreement between landlords and tenants that simplifies the process?

2   Is it too easy to evict someone or too difficult? Justify your answer.

APPLYING WHAT YOU HAVE LEARNED

1   Has the law of constructive eviction unfairly shifted the legal burden in the landlord-tenant relationship to the landlord? Is constructive eviction too vague? Does it allow tenants to escape their obligations under the lease?

2 Using the form available at the product page that accompanies this text at www .aspenpublishing.com, create a residential lease for Tonya Tenant and her cat, Missy. They will live in Apartment 301 of Kensington Arms Apartments. The lease will begin on January 1 of next year and run through December 31. The rent is $750 per month. The landlord will charge 5 percent of the first month's rent as a damage deposit and another 5 percent as a pet deposit.

WEB SURFING

Georgia Superior Court Cooperative Authority
http://www.gsccca.org/search

National Apartment Association
www.naahq.org

Search: "just cause eviction"

Tech Topic
LEASE CALCULATOR

This free online lease calculator (http://www .calculator.net/lease-calculator.html) allows you to calculate either the monthly payment or the interest rate for a lease. The website also includes links to many other types of real estate calculators, such as a mortgage calculator, a mortgage payoff calculator, and a refinance calculator.

ANNOTATED DOCUMENT

Apartment Lease

IN CONSIDERATION of the rent to be paid. Calvin Cash as landlord (the "Landlord") does hereby lease and rent to Sid Savage as tenant (the "Tenant") and the Tenant does hereby lease and rent from the Landlord the apartment unit known as Apartment Number 24, Building C, of the apartment complex known as Qualls Roost located at 324 Queen Street, Apt C24, Morganton, North Carolina 28655

The lease identifies the landlord (Calvin Cash) and the tenant (Sid Savage).

The lease provides the address of the rental unit.

(the "apartment") in accordance with the following terms and conditions.

1. Term: The terms of this lease shall be for 12 months commencing October 10, 2021, and expiring October 9, 2022 (the "Initial Term"). Either Landlord or Tenant may terminate the tenancy at the expiration of the Initial Term by giving written notice to the other at least thirty (30) days prior to the expiration date of the Initial Term.

The term of the lease is clearly identified.

The date of termination of the lease is clearly identified.

PRACTICE QUESTIONS FOR TEST REVIEW

See Appendix for answers.

Essay Question

What rights does a landlord convey to the tenant in a typical landlord-tenant relationship?

True–False

1 T F Landlords do not surrender any rights to tenants in a typical landlord-tenant relationship.

2 T F Landlords usually own the leased premises in fee simple.

3 T F Tenants usually have no responsibility to pay real property taxes.

Fill in the Blank

1 A lease grants this person or persons the right to use and possess the property. This person or persons are called: _____.

2 When the tenant violates the term of the lease, the landlord is permitted to bring this action: _____.

3 Under this arrangement, tenants transfer their rights to another for the balance of the lease term:_____.

Multiple Choice

1 The body of rights conveyed to the tenant from the landlord.

   A   Franchise
   B   Freehold estate
   C   Leasehold estate
   D   None of the above

2 Which of the following rights is conveyed by the landlord to the tenant in a typical landlord-tenant relationship?

A The right to use the property.
B The right to occupy property.
C The right to possess property.
D All of the above.

3 The owner of the leased premises.

A Landlord
B Tenant
C Grantor
D Grantee

ENDNOTES

[1] *Corbray v. Stevenson*, 98 Wash. 2d 410, 656 P.2d 473 (1982).

[2] S.C. Code Ann. §27-40-410.

[3] S.C. Code Ann. §27-40-230.

[4] 42 U.S.C. §4851.

[5] S.C. Code Ann. §27-40-20.

[6] S.C. Code Ann. §27-40-320.

[7] *Wilfred Laboratories, Inc. v. Fifty-Second Street Hotel Associates*, 133 App. Div. 2d 320, 519 N.Y.S.2d 220 (1987).

[8] *Conley v. Emerald Isle Realty, Inc.*, 350 N.C. 293, 513 S.E.2d 556 (1999).

[9] Fla. Stat. Ann. (West's) §83.51.

[10] R.I. Gen. Laws (1956) §34-18-22(c); *State Water Resources Bd. v. Howard*, 729 A.2d 712 (R.I. 1999).

[11] URLTA §1.404.

[12] 40 A.L.R.3d 1369.

[13] URLTA §2.104.

[14] 42 U.S.C. §§3601-3619, 3631.

[15] 42 U.S.C. §1982 Ch. 21.

[16] *Honce v. Vigil*, 1 F.3d 1085 (10th Cir. 1993).

[17] Ohio Rev. Code Ann. §1923.04.

[18] *Williams v. Guzzardi*, 875 F.2d 46 (3d Cir. 1989).

[19] *Morford v. Lensey Corp.*, 110 Ill. App. 3d 792, 66 Ill. Dec. 372, 442 N.E.2d 933 (1982).

[20] *Kriz v. Taylor*, 92 Cal. App. 3d 302, 154 Cal. Rptr. 824 (1979).

[21] S.C. Code Ann. §27-40-310.

Real Estate Deeds

8

- Explain how deeds symbolize the real estate transaction

- Describe the various types of deeds

- Define the minimum legal requirements for a deed

- Explain the function of deed clauses

- Describe the warranties made by specific types of deeds

I. Introduction

II. A Brief History of Deeds

III. Elements of Deeds
   A. The Deed Must Be in Writing
   B. The Deed Must Identify the Grantor and the Grantee
   C. The Deed Must Be Signed by the Grantor
   D. The Grantor Must Have Legal Capacity
   E. The Property Must Be Adequately Described
   F. The Deed Must Contain Language Indicating an Intention to Convey Property Rights
   G. The Deed Must Be Delivered by the Grantor and Accepted by the Grantee

H. The Deed Must Be Attested and Acknowledged
   I. Other Deed Provisions
   J. Nonessential Deed Provisions

IV. Types of Deeds
   A. General Warranty Deeds
   B. Special Warranty Deeds
   C. Deeds of Trust/Mortgages
   D. Quitclaim Deed

V. Recording Statutes
   A. Notice Recording Statutes
   B. Race-Notice Recording Statutes
   C. Race Recording Statutes

INTRODUCTION

Deed
The written instrument that conveys real property interests.

In this chapter, we examine the many aspects of deeds. A **deed** is an unusual document in that it embodies both contract and real property law. On one hand, a deed is a contract, setting out basic rights and obligations between parties. On the other hand, it is the written expression of the transfer of legal rights in real property from one party to another. Deeds have a unique and interesting history that continues to have significance in daily real estate practice.

A BRIEF HISTORY OF DEEDS

In ancient times, a real estate transaction was a symbolic ceremony in which a grantor transferred property and title to a grantee. We saw in Chapter 1 that there are important differences between real property and personal property. This distinction becomes readily apparent when we examine the laws surrounding transfer of title between these two different types of property. In personal property, title changes hands when the actual item is transferred from one owner to another. Let's consider how someone would sell something like a book or an antique desk: After the buyer and seller negotiate a price agreeable to both, the seller accepts money from the buyer and the buyer takes physical possession of the item. Here, physical possession is the best indicator of ownership. Although the sale may be accompanied by a bill of sale or some other written expression of the transfer of ownership, possession is the best way to establish the buyer's rights. This approach works well for most types of personal property, but it presents practical difficulties when dealing with real property.

First of all, land is immobile and therefore cannot be transferred in the same way that personal property can be. An owner cannot always be in physical possession of land in the same way that she could be of a personal item such as a book. Owners routinely leave their real property to conduct other business and to go to work. Because owners cannot always be in physical possession of their land, there has to be some other way to prove ownership. There are other practical problems presented by real property ownership: If you cannot simply take the land with you, how do you prove that you own it? How, for instance, do you pass this title on to others? How do your heirs prove that you held interest in the land? The deed was created as a way of solving many of these problems.

REAL ESTATE BASICS AT A GLANCE

Deeds must meet the requirements of both contract law and real property law.

ELEMENTS OF DEEDS

Real estate deeds are unique because they serve two different functions at the same time: (1) They embody the contractual agreement between the parties, and (2) they serve to declare that real property interests have transferred from one party to another. As a result, they must have the required elements of a contract as well as statutory requirements. The end result is a document that is a hybrid: It is both a contract and a declaration.

Before we can go any further into our discussion of deeds, it is important to clarify some of the terminology. Deeds do not list "buyers" and "sellers." Instead, they refer to "grantors" and "grantees." A **grantor** is a person who transfers a property interest, and a **grantee** is a person who receives a property interest. Grantors and sellers are often, but not always, synonymous. The reason for this distinction is that a person could transfer some, but not all, rights in real estate to another without actually selling the property.

Grantor
One who conveys a real property interest.

Grantee
One who receives a real property interest.

LINDA'S LIFE ESTATE

EXAMPLE 8-1

Uncle Joe has always had a soft spot in his heart for his niece, Linda. One day, he decides to give Linda a life estate in a house that sits on several acres just outside of town. When it comes time to write up the deed, who is listed as grantor and who is listed as grantee?

Answer: Uncle Joe is conveying his interests, so he is listed as grantor; Linda is receiving rights, so she is listed as grantee.

All states have minimum requirements that deeds must satisfy before they are considered to have any legal significance. These minimum requirements include the following:

- The deed must be in writing,
- The deed must identify the grantor and the grantee,
- The deed must be signed by the grantor,
- The grantor must have legal capacity,
- The property conveyed must be adequately described,
- The deed must contain language clearly showing the intent to convey property rights,
- The deed must be delivered by the grantor and accepted by the grantee, and
- The deed must be attested and acknowledged.

Sidebar

In the past, when real estate transactions took on a more literal meaning, property owners would actually transfer some physical representation of the land to the new buyer. The handover of this "fee" would symbolize the transfer of property rights from the seller to the buyer. Deeds now take the place of that physical transfer. This accounts for many of the features found in deeds that seem odd or out of place.

A. THE DEED MUST BE IN WRITING

One of the most obvious requirements for any deed is the requirement that it be in writing. Oral deeds are unenforceable. The reason that a deed must be in writing is that it falls into that small category of contracts governed by the Statute of Frauds.

The Statute of Frauds was originally created in England as a way to prevent fraud. In those days very few people could read, and requiring that important contracts be in writing was a safeguard against unscrupulous practices. The Statute of Frauds was enacted in all states and continues to exist, in one form or another, across the United States. The statute covers several different categories of writings, including promises to answer for the debts of another person, prenuptial agreements, contracts involving the purchase of goods worth more than $500, and the transfer of real estate interests. See Figure 8-1 for a typical Statute of Frauds.

Although state statutes require deeds to be in writing, there has never been a requirement that particular deed forms must be used. The parties are free to create their own, handwritten deeds. However, in the age of the Internet and the availability of forms that have passed muster with state bar associations, it makes a great deal of sense to use pre-prepared forms.

FIGURE 8-1	A conveyance of an estate of inheritance, a freehold, or an estate for more than one year, in land and tenements, must be in writing and must be subscribed and delivered by the conveyor or by the conveyor's agent authorized in writing.[1]
Statute of Frauds (Texas)	

REAL ESTATE BASICS AT A GLANCE

The Statute of Frauds requires that all deeds must be in writing.

B. THE DEED MUST IDENTIFY THE GRANTOR AND THE GRANTEE

In addition to being in writing, deeds must also identify the grantor and the grantee. Here we encounter some unusual provisions of deed law. The grantor must always be identified by name, but there is authority for transferring property to an unnamed grantee. Although the grantee can be unnamed, she must be identifiable. In a situation in which a grantor deeds property to an unnamed individual, the description of that individual must be specific and unique enough to identify a specific grantee.

EXAMPLE 8-2	**ECCENTRIC UNCLE HARRY**

Uncle Harry has always been a little bit eccentric. Last week, he wrote up and signed a deed for 100 acres of prime farmland. In the grantee line, he wrote, "That redheaded girl who walks by my house every day at 3 o'clock." Uncle Harry's family members have decided to challenge this deed on the grounds that he is obviously mentally unstable. Is this description of the grantee sufficient to meet the legal requirements for a deed?

Answer: It depends. If there is only one redheaded girl who walks by Uncle Harry's house every day at 3 o'clock (presumably after school lets out), then the transaction may be valid. However, if there is more than one redheaded girl, or even girls whose hair may be various shades of red to auburn, the transaction will be void for vagueness.

Although there is flexibility in the method used to identify the grantee, the same does not hold true for the grantor. The grantor must be clearly identified by name (see Figure 8-2). There is some flexibility when it comes to the grantor's full, legal name and the way that the grantor signs her name. For example, a deed showing the grantor as "William A. Cortez" and signed "Bill Cortez" would be acceptable in any court. "Bill" is a common nickname for "William," and barring any other complications, such as there being more than one William Cortez in the family, the deed would be sufficient to pass title. The grantor's signature indicates his intention to pass title to the grantee. Interestingly enough, there is usually no requirement for the grantee to sign a deed. The grantee takes ownership by accepting the deed when it is offered.

WILSON COUNTY

THIS DEED, made this 30th day of August, 2019, by and between JOHN M. BARNES and wife, AMY C. BARNES, GRANTORS, and AMY C. BARNES, GRANTEE, 3400 Teal Drive, Wilson,

FIGURE 8-2

Grantor's Name Excerpt from a General Warranty Deed

Another common problem that directly relates to the names of grantors and grantees is the problem of misnomer. This occurs when the grantor incorrectly identifies the grantee in the deed. When presented with this problem, courts will attempt to resolve the question by trying to identify the person to whom that the grantor actually intended to pass title interest. When that is impossible, the deed will be ruled a nullity and no title interest will pass. Misnomer applies not only to incorrectly named individuals, but also to incorrectly named corporations.

THE CONTRADICTING DEED

EXAMPLE 8-3

Our firm is looking into a deed that contains a contradiction. In the main part of the deed, the grantor is identified as Samuel S. Johnson, conveying ten acres to Thomas S. Johnson. However, in the body of the deed, there is a reference to ten acres owned in fee simple by "Samuel S. Jones." Samuel S. Johnson signs the deed, and that signature is notarized. Is this a valid deed?

Answer: Because the deed refers to the grantor by his correct name at every other point in the transaction except one, and because the grantor signed and notarized his signature as Samuel S. Johnson, the deed is acceptable.[2]

C. THE DEED MUST BE SIGNED BY THE GRANTOR

In addition to correctly identifying the grantor and the grantee, the deed must also bear the grantor's signature. The signing of the deed indicates the grantor's desire to transfer the interest to the property and that this transfer is done willingly. Many states require the grantor's signature before the deed is considered legally effective.[3] There is, however, no requirement that the grantee must sign the deed. Later we will see that the important action from the grantee's viewpoint is not signing the deed but accepting it.

The grantor's signature on the deed indicates her knowing and voluntary transfer of property interests to the grantee.

Why should there be a rule that requires only the grantor to sign the deed? At this point in the transaction, the courts focus on the grantor. After all, it is the grantor who is transferring real property interests. To show a valid transaction, the parties must show that the grantor had the mental ability to transfer real property interests; that she did so voluntarily; and that she was not subject to any force, threat, or intimidation. Many of the requirements to finalize a deed, such as acknowledgment and notarization, help establish these elements. See Figure 8-3 for some examples of deed signature provisions.

D. THE GRANTOR MUST HAVE LEGAL CAPACITY

At the time of the signing, delivery, and acceptance of the deed, the grantor must have the mental capacity to carry out the transaction. A grantor who lacks the capacity to enter into a contract is similarly barred from divesting real property rights through a deed. To ensure that the transaction is legally effective, the parties must be able to demonstrate that, at the time of the transaction, the grantor was free of any mental disease or defect that affected her ability to know and understand the consequences of the transaction.

Because there is a close affinity between contract law and real property law on the question of capacity, it is helpful to point out certain conditions that give rise to a presumption that a person lacks capacity. For instance, a person lacks capacity when she:

- Is under the legal age of majority (18 years old, in most states),
- Is under the influence of alcohol or some other drug, or
- Has been declared mentally incompetent.

If it can be proven that at the time of transaction the grantor lacked legal capacity, the court is empowered to negate the entire transaction and return the property interests to the grantor. The court may also appoint a guardian to oversee the grantor's business affairs in order to avoid similar situations in the future.

BOOK 1785 PAGE 113

FIGURE 8-3

**Signature Provision
from a Deed**

THIS INSTRUMENT PREPARED BY JULIE T. WILLIAMS, ATTORNEY
NO TITLE SEARCH PERFORMED - NO OPINION ON TITLE RENDERED

2193

NORTH CAROLINA

WILSON COUNTY

THIS DEED, made this 30th day of August, 2019, by and between JOHN M. BARNES and wife, AMY C. BARNES, GRANTORS, and AMY C. BARNES, GRANTEE, 3400 Teal Drive, Wilson, NC 27893.

W I T N E S S E T H :

That said GRANTORS, in consideration of Ten Dollars ($10.00) and other good and valuable considerations in hand paid, the receipt of which is hereby acknowledged, have bargained and sold and by this deed do hereby bargain, sell and convey unto said GRANTEE, her heirs and assigns, in fee simple, that certain lot or parcel of land lying and being situate in the City of Wilson, Wilson County, North Carolina, and more particularly described as follows:

BEING all of Lot 70 as shown on that map of section One, Millbrook Subdivision as recorded in Plat Book 14, page 260, Wilson County Registry. For reference, see deed recorded in Book 1492, page 169, Wilson County Registry. And being the identical property conveyed in deed dated February 28, 1996 from Charles M. Carter and wife, Margaret S. Carter, recorded in Book 1580, Page 633, Wilson County Registry.

TO HAVE AND TO HOLD the above described lot or parcel of land with all privileges and appurtenances thereunto belonging or in anywise appertaining unto them, the said GRANTEE, her heirs and assigns in fee simple forever.

Pursuant to N.C.G.S. Section 39-13.3(c) and any other applicable statutes, the tenancy by the entirety ownership formerly held by GRANTORS is hereby dissolved and ownership is now solely held by the GRANTEE.

AND the said GRANTORS do hereby covenant that they are seized of said premises in fee and have the right to convey the same in fee simple; that the same is free and clear of all encumbrances, and that they hereby warrant and will forever defend the title to the same against the lawful claims of all persons whomsoever.

IN TESTIMONY WHEREOF, the GRANTORS have hereunto set their hands and seals the day and year first above written.

_____ (SEAL)
JOHN M. BARNES

_____ (SEAL)
AMY C. BARNES

WILSON COUNTY NC   10/31/2020
$14.00
STATE OF NORTH CAROLINA
Real Estate Excise Tax

Mail: Grantee

FIGURE 8.3
(continued)

TO HAVE AND TO HOLD said lands and premises unto the parties of the second part, their heirs and assigns, in fee simple, together with all privileges and appurtenances thereunto belonging.

And the parties of the first part covenant with the parties of the second part that they are seized in fee simple of the land above described and have good right and title to convey the same; that the same is free and clear of all liens and encumbrances, except 2017 ad valorem taxes, and that they will forever warrant and defend the title to the same against all lawful claims and demands of all persons whomsoever.

IN WITNESS WHEREOF, the parties of the first part have hereunto set their hands and affixed their seals, this the day and year first above written.

Bobby Gene Weathington (SEAL)
BOBBY GENE WEATHINGTON

Janice Carol Weathington (SEAL)
JANICE CAROL WEATHINGTON

E. THE PROPERTY MUST BE ADEQUATELY DESCRIBED

The deed between the grantor and the grantee must contain a description of the property conveyed. This description must be sufficient to show how this particular parcel is separate and unique from all other parcels. As a result of this requirement, street address or mailing address is not sufficient to adequately describe property in a deed, unless the town is laid out in a municipal grid or the deed refers to some other government-imposed survey system.

1. SPECIFIC DESCRIPTIONS

Most states require specific descriptions, such as metes and bounds, tract index, or reference to a government survey. Without this type of specific description, the deed may fail because it is impossible to identify with precision the parcel of land to be transferred between the parties. Incorrect property descriptions are one of the most common problems in modern real estate practice. See Figure 8-4 for a list of methods used to describe real estate to overcome these problems.

- Metes and bounds description
- Tract index
- Government survey
- Subdivision and lot number

THE DEED FROM UNCLE THEO

Uncle Theo writes out the following deed: "I hereby leave all of my property to my nephew, Theo, Jr." Is this a sufficient description of the land involved?

Answer: Although the description fails to give specifics, if Uncle Theo owns only one tract of land, this description may just be enough to effectively pass title to his nephew.[5]

2. COURT INTERPRETATIONS OF AMBIGUOUS PROPERTY DESCRIPTIONS

In cases in which the description in a deed is ambiguous or unclear, a court may be called upon to interpret the language in the deed. Generally, courts try to give effect to the parties' intentions and will attempt to discern the actual location referred to in the deed. When the language is not helpful, the courts may fall back on other evidence, such as the public record, recorded plats, natural landmarks referred to in the deed, surveys of other adjoining properties, total acreage, and distance and directions given in the deed that indicate which parcel is being sold. Only when these methods fail will the court void the deed for vagueness (see Figure 8-5).

No deed or other writing purporting to convey land or an interest in land shall be declared void for vagueness in the description of the thing intended to be granted by reason of the use of the word "adjoining" instead of the words "bounded by," or for the reason that the boundaries given do not go entirely around the land described: Provided, it can be made to appear to the satisfaction of the jury that the grantor owned at the time of the execution of such deed or paper-writing no other land which at all corresponded to the description contained in such deed or paper-writing.[6]

F. THE DEED MUST CONTAIN LANGUAGE INDICATING AN INTENTION TO CONVEY PROPERTY RIGHTS

It is not enough for the parties simply to indicate that they wish to transfer interests in real estate. The deed must also contain unambiguous language clearly showing the intent of the grantor to transfer all of her interest to the grantee. The two most important deed clauses that convey this intention are the **habendum clause** and the **granting clause**.

The purpose of these two clauses is to show the grantor's present intent to transfer her property interests to the grantee. The habendum clause describes the nature of the title that is being transferred. In most situations, the habendum clause would include

Habendum clause
A deed clause that conveys specified rights to the grantee.

Granting clause
A deed clause that demonstrates the grantor's willingness to engage in the transaction.

provisions showing that the grantee is receiving fee simple absolute title (see Figure 8-6 for an example). The granting clause, on the other hand, is the clause that declares the grantor's intention to actually transfer the land to the grantee. Some courts have held that without both clauses, there can be no legal transfer.

REAL ESTATE BASICS AT A GLANCE

Habendum clauses discuss the quality or type of title interests conveyed to the grantee; granting clauses show the grantor's intent to transfer.

This is not to say that the law requires a specific formula of words to create a legally valid deed. Both the habendum and the granting clauses will be interpreted from the language used by the parties. If, for instance, a grantor uses the word "grant" or "convey," these words will be considered sufficient to satisfy the granting clause. Similarly, if the grantor mentions the quality of the title passed to the grantee, this will often satisfy the requirements of the habendum clause. Courts generally are liberal in their interpretations of the language used in deeds. The language used can be as simple as, "I do hereby grant and convey to you fee simple title to this land."

FIGURE 8-6

Habendum Clause

TO HAVE AND TO HOLD the aforesaid tract or parcel of land, and all of the privileges and appurtenances thereto belonging, to the said party of the second part, its successors and assigns in fee simple absolute.[7]

G. THE DEED MUST BE DELIVERED BY THE GRANTOR AND ACCEPTED BY THE GRANTEE

The requirement of delivery and acceptance of a deed goes back to the ancient history of real estate transactions. So far, our discussion about deeds has focused on their qualities as a contract between the grantor and the grantee. However, when it comes to the issues of delivery and acceptance, we diverge from contract law into other aspects of real estate law. The deed transfer now takes the place of the transfer of a piece of earth as a symbol of the land itself. When the grantor signs the deed and delivers the deed to the grantee, this physical act symbolizes the transfer of the grantor's interest in the property. In order for the transaction to be complete, the grantee must accept the deed offered by the grantor. When this delivery and acceptance is complete, title to the land has changed hands.[8] If anything occurs that interrupts the process of delivery and acceptance, the real estate transaction is not complete. If, for some reason, the grantor signs the deed but fails to deliver it, there is no completed transaction. If the grantor signs and delivers the deed but the grantee refuses to accept it, we reach the same result.

GERALD'S DEED

EXAMPLE 8-5

Gerald Grantor has signed a deed and is about to deliver it to Al Grantee. However, before he can hand the deed over, Gerald suffers a heart attack and dies. Al takes the deed out of his hands and declares the transaction complete. Has there been a valid transaction?

Answer: No. Real estate law requires not only that the grantor sign a deed but also that he voluntarily deliver it to the grantee. Although it seems clear from the surrounding circumstances that Gerald intended to deliver the deed, the fact that he never did so means that there can be no valid transaction. Title has not changed hands in this scenario.

To have a valid transaction, the deed must be both delivered and accepted.

REAL
ESTATE
BASICS AT
A GLANCE

---

1. PROVING DELIVERY

In some cases, it may be necessary for the parties to prove that a valid delivery and acceptance actually occurred. The elements that the parties must prove are the following:

1 The grantor intended that the deed transfer real property to the grantee.
2 The grantor's action placed the deed beyond her possession and control.
3 The grantee accepted the deed.[9]

Just as important as the grantor's delivery is the grantee's acceptance of the deed. When the grantee accepts the deed, she is bound by the terms contained in it. As we have already seen, there is no requirement that the grantee must sign the deed. When the deed is recorded, courts will usually presume that a valid delivery and acceptance occurred.

Tech Topic

ELECTRONIC RECORDING

The act of recording means to physically enter into the public record executed real estate records, including deeds, mortgages, easements, and other instruments that affect title. The purpose of recording is to detail the various interests that people have in a particular property. Recording establishes a priority, in other words, who holds the dominant legal interest in a property.

Until recent years, the executed documents involved in a real estate transaction would be transported to the recording entity either by mail or in person. Nowadays, e-recording is supplanting the traditional method.

The difference between traditional recording and e-recording is that the documents are delivered to the recording office via the Internet, usually through a third-party document service. The benefit of e-recording is that the recording entity can process the information more quickly and speed the return of an image of the recorded documents.

In general, this is how e-recording works:

1　After closing, the lender or the title company scans the executed and notarized documents into a PDF file.

2　The PDF file is uploaded to the third party's website.

3　The documents are submitted (along with appropriate indexing information) to the appropriate county.

4　The county records the documents and returns an electronically stamped copy—sometimes within a couple of hours. (When recording is done using the traditional method, the wait for returned documents can take weeks.)

Not all lenders and title companies have fully embraced e-recording, but it is only a matter of time before it completely replaces traditional methods.

2. DELIVERY IN ESCROW

An escrow closing allows the grantor to deliver the deed prior to the actual date of closing and relieves the grantor of the responsibility of being present at the actual closing. We will discuss escrow closings in greater detail in Chapter 13.

H. THE DEED MUST BE ATTESTED AND ACKNOWLEDGED

In order for a deed to be valid, it must be both attested and acknowledged. These are somewhat archaic terms that refer to signatures and witness provisions.

1. ATTESTATION

Attestation
Signing a document.

A deed must be attested. **Attestation** is another word for signature. Although these days most people sign a deed by writing their name, attestation originated in previous times when most people were illiterate and therefore were allowed to sign with a thumbprint or mark as a way to attest the deed. See Figure 8-7 for a sample attestation clause.

FIGURE 8-7

Attestation Clause from a Deed

IN WITNESS WHEREOF, the grantor has executed this deed on the date set forth above.

Mark Goodson

2. ACKNOWLEDGMENT

When grantors acknowledge a deed, they are presenting proof that they are who they claim to be. The best way to accomplish **acknowledgment** for a deed is to appear before a notary public and sign the deed in the notary's presence. Notaries are supposed to ask for identification and then witness signatures on deeds. Although there are other provisions that satisfy the acknowledgment requirement, such as appearing before the clerk of court or in some cases before a judge, notarizing a signature is the most common way to prove acknowledgment. These days, acknowledgments are usually not an official deed requirement under state law. See Figure 8-8 for a sample acknowledgment provision.

Acknowledgment
Proof that the person who signed a document is who she claims to be.

STATE OF GEORGIA)
)ss:
COUNTY OF COBB   )

The foregoing instrument was acknowledged before me this 30th day of October, 2001 by the persons to me known as the person(s) described in and who executed the foregoing instrument and Acknowledged before me that (s)he executed the same.

Witness my hand and official seal

April Barnard
NOTARY PUBLIC

FIGURE 8-8

Acknowledgment Provision from a Deed

I. OTHER DEED PROVISIONS

So far, we have outlined the minimum legal requirements for a deed. However, state law may also impose other provisions. For instance, state law might also require that deeds contain:

- Seals,
- Consideration recitals, and
- Exceptions and exclusions.

1. SEALS

The use of seals in important documents goes back centuries. In many states, seals were required on all deeds before they could be filed. Placing a seal on a document had a very particular legal significance. For instance, a document under seal did not have to be supported by consideration and was protected by other presumptions under the law. However, seals have steadily lost importance over the years. In fact, most states no longer require a seal on a deed, or they make a provision that the person's signature will substitute for the seal requirement.

2. CONSIDERATION RECITALS

Consideration is a requirement for contracts. In the context of a commercial transaction, consideration establishes that both parties have surrendered something of value in exchange for something else of value. Because deeds resemble contracts, many states have provisions in their deeds for a recital of the consideration between the grantor and the grantee. Rather than requiring a specific monetary sum as consideration in the deed, most states simply fall back on a requirement that the deed is given for "valuable consideration" or "good consideration." The issue of consideration usually only rears its head in situations in which a grantor has made a gift of a parcel of real estate. Because this gift may have important tax consequences, courts often look very closely at the consideration involved in a real estate gift transaction.

3. EXCEPTIONS AND EXCLUSIONS

The deed may also contain exceptions and exclusions. These are statements inserted by the grantor that seek to limit the grantor's promises or warranties made to the grantee. A grantor might, for example, include an exception in a deed stating that the property is free and clear of all encumbrances with the exception of an existing easement. These exceptions and exclusions serve two purposes: (1) They put the grantee on notice of specific situations, and (2) they insulate the grantor from claims that she failed to provide full disclosure about the nature of the title. See Figure 8-9 for a sample exception and exclusion.

FIGURE 8-9

Sample Exception and Exclusion from a Deed

The property hereinabove described was acquired by Grantor by instrument recorded in the Stanly County Public Registry in Deed Book 360, at Page 482.

A map showing the above described property is recorded in Plat Book N/A page .
TO HAVE AND TO HOLD the aforesaid lot or parcel of land and all privileges and appurtenances thereto belonging to the Grantee in fee simple.

And the Grantor covenants with the Grantee, that Grantor is seized of the premises in fee simple, has the right to convey the same in fee simple, that title is marketable and free and clear of all encumbrances, and that Grantor will warrant and defend t e title against the lawful claims of all persons whomsoever except for the exceptions hereinafter stated.
Title to .he property hereinabove described is subject to the following exceptions:

(1) Easements, conditions and restrictions of record in the chain of title;
(2) 1989 ad valorem taxes, which have been assumed by the Grantees.

J. NONESSENTIAL DEED PROVISIONS

Although dates are not required on deeds, the presence of a date on a deed creates a rebuttable presumption that the deed was delivered.

Deeds often contain additional information and entries that are not strictly required by state law. Among these nonessential deed provisions are witness signatures and dates.

1. WITNESSES

In most situations, there is no requirement for a deed to be witnessed by someone other than the person who acknowledged the grantor's signature. In contrast to wills, which require more than one witness, the person who witnesses the grantor's signature is sufficient.

2. DATE

There is also no requirement that the deed contain a date. Obviously, a date is helpful in fixing time periods and determining exactly when certain actions occurred, but the only date that is absolutely essential is the date that the deed was recorded. Other date provisions are generally irrelevant.

REAL WORLD PERSPECTIVES: *REAL ESTATE PARALEGAL*

We call it a 'dry closing' when we get all the signatures but we haven't recorded the deed yet. That can be a scary time. Say that the closing doesn't finish up until after 5 P.M. You have to wait until the courthouse opens the next day. Suppose something occurs at the property in the meantime? The insurance companies can have quite a battle over who has to pay for damages. Buyers want to get moved in, but the sellers say not until the deeds are recorded. I think it's a bad idea for the buyers to move in before anything is recorded. Besides the legal issues involved, when you move in you have moved in everything that you own. If the house burns down, no matter whose insurance is going to cover the loss, you still lost everything that you own.

—S. C., real estate paralegal

 **TYPES OF DEEDS**

There are numerous types of deeds, and they all serve different functions. Among the most important are:

- General warranty deeds,
- Special warranty deeds,
- Deeds of trust/mortgages, and
- Quitclaim deeds.

A. GENERAL WARRANTY DEEDS

When a grantor wishes to convey fee simple absolute rights to the grantee, the deed that does so is a general warranty deed. This deed contains a series of promises or warranties that make specific assertions. Among the warranties made in a general warranty deed are:

- *Seizin*,
- Quiet enjoyment,

- Against encumbrances,
- Further assurance, and
- Warranty forever.

1. *SEIZIN*

Seizin
(French) Possession of real property.

When a general warranty deed provides a covenant of *seizin*, it simply means that the grantor is in full possession of the property and has the right to convey it to another. *Seizin* usually refers to ownership.[10]

2. QUIET ENJOYMENT

The covenant or promise of quiet enjoyment is the grantor's assurance that the grantee can take possession of the premises secure in the knowledge that no other person can claim an ownership interest in the property. The covenant of quiet enjoyment ensures that the new owner has full right to possess the property.

3. AGAINST ENCUMBRANCES

The warranty against encumbrances is the grantor's promise that there are no outstanding encumbrances on the property that will affect the title. Examples of encumbrances include liens, assessments, foreclosure actions, judgments, or any other legal action that could interfere with the grantee's possession of the land.

4. FURTHER ASSURANCE

The grantor's warranty of further assurance is the grantor's promise that, should any claims arise against the property, the grantor will provide evidence that the title passed to the grantee was free and clear.

5. WARRANTY FOREVER

Finally, the covenant of warranty forever is simply the grantor's guarantee that she will continue to support the grantee's claims at any point in the future, should it become necessary.

REAL ESTATE BASICS AT A GLANCE

General warranty deeds make the most promises or warranties to the grantee.

B. SPECIAL WARRANTY DEEDS

Special warranty deeds resemble general warranty deeds, but while general warranty deeds provide several different promises, a special warranty deed usually only makes a single promise. This single promise is often as simple as stating that the grantor has taken no action during the time that the property was in the grantor's possession that will affect the grantee's rights. See Figure 8-10 for an example of a special warranty deed.

SPECIAL WARRANTY DEED

FIGURE 8-10

Special Warranty Deed

THIS INDENTURE, made the 21st day of May, 2004, between Marge Simpson and Homer Simpson of the County of Springfield, State of Placid, hereinafter called "Grantor," and Ester Jenkins, whose address is 20 Robinwood Ave, Asheville, North Carolina, of the County of Buncombe, hereinafter called "Grantee" (the terms "Grantor" and "Grantee" designate both the singular and plural, as the context demands).

WITNESSETH that: Grantor, for and in consideration of Ten Dollars ($10.00) and other good and valuable considerations to said Grantor in hand paid by said Grantee, the receipt which is hereby acknowledged, has granted, bargained and sold and by these presents does grant, bargain and sell unto the said Grantee, and Grantee's heirs and assigns forever, land situate, lying and being in Springfield County, Placid and more particularly described as follows:

Tract 10-1254 in Springfield County Tract Index

TO HAVE AND TO HOLD the said tract or parcel of land, with all and singular the rights, members and appurtenances thereof, to the same being, belonging, or in anywise appertaining, to the only proper use, benefit and behalf of the said Grantee forever in FEE SIMPLE.

This conveyance and the warranties are limited to the issues of a mortgage found at DB 101/123 and by this special warranty, grantor hereby releases any claims under that document.

AND THE SAID Grantor will only warrant and forever defend the right and title to the above described property unto the said Grantee against the claims of those persons claiming by, through or under Grantor, but not otherwise.

IN WITNESS WHEREOF, the Grantor has signed, sealed and delivered this Deed, the day and year above written.

WITNESSES:
Grantor(s)

_____

_____

STATE OF PLACID
COUNTY OF SPRINGFIELD

THE FOREGOING INSTRUMENT was acknowledged before me this _(17)_ day of 22nd day of May, 2004, by Troy McClure.

_____
Notary Public
My Commission Expires: _____

C. DEEDS OF TRUST/MORTGAGES

A deed of trust is the deed that specifies the lender's rights to the property in the event that the buyer defaults on her mortgage. Also referred to as a mortgage, this document sets out the rights of the lender, creates a promissory note between the buyer and the lender, and gives the lender the right to foreclose on the property in the event of the buyer's default. We will discuss deeds of trust and mortgages in greater detail in Chapter 9.

 REAL ESTATE BASICS AT A GLANCE

Mortgages and deeds of trust set out the rights of the lender.

FIGURE 8-11

Quitclaim Deed

2003-120226-0
Recording Dist: 301 - Anchorage
11/17/2003 8:39 AM Pages: 1 of 1
ALASKA

Filed for Record at Request of:
First American Title of Alaska

AFTER RECORDING MAIL TO:

Name   John H.B. Smith
Address   3670 Richard Evelyn Byrd Street
City, State Zip Anchorage, AK 99517

Escrow Number: 0310041 **12.5**

Statutory Warranty Deed

THE GRANTOR   The Petersen Group, Inc., an Alaska corporation

whose mailing address is: 3820 Lake Otis Parkway #204, Anchorage, AK 99508

for and in consideration of   TEN DOLLARS AND OTHER GOOD AND VALUABLE CONSIDERATION

in hand paid, conveys and warrants to   John H.B. Smith and Barbara A. Smith, husband and wife

the following described real estate, situated in the Recording District of   Anchorage
State of Alaska:

Lot 7, Block 1, BROADMOOR ESTATES WEST ADDN. NO. 1, according to the official plat thereof, filed under Plat Number 73-63, Records of the ANCHORAGE Recording District, THIRD Judicial District, State of ALASKA.

SUBJECT TO reservations, exceptions, easements, covenants, conditions and restrictions of record, if any.

Dated this   14th   day of November , 2003

The Petersen Group, Inc.

BY:
Robert C. Petersen, President

D. QUITCLAIM DEED

A quitclaim deed does exactly what its name suggests: It surrenders any rights that the grantor may have in the property. Quitclaim deeds do not make any representations about the nature or quality of the rights that the grantor has; they simply surrender them to the grantee. See Figure 8-11 for an example of a quitclaim deed and Figure 8-12 for a checklist of things to consider when examining any deed.

FIGURE 8-12

Deed Checklist

- What type of deed is it?
- Who are the parties to the transaction?
- What is the complete, legal name of the grantor?
- Is the grantee clearly identifiable?
- Does the deed contain habendum and granting clauses?
- Is the deed signed by the grantor(s)?
- If the deed is a warranty deed, does it contain the appropriate covenants (*seizin*, quiet enjoyment, against encumbrances, further assurance, and warranty forever)?
- Has the deed been notarized?
- Has the deed been acknowledged?
- Does the deed contain the appropriate words of conveyance?
- Is this a standard deed form, such as one approved by the state bar, or did the parties develop it?

V. RECORDING STATUTES

Recording statutes were an invention of early American law. England, the source of most of our laws, had no recording statutes that set priorities. There, the rule was simple: Whoever filed first had priority over anyone else. However, various states in the United States have created several different models for recording title to land and the consequences of that recording. There are three general approaches:

1. Notice,
2. Race-notice, and
3. Race.

A. NOTICE RECORDING STATUTES

Under a pure notice system, a party who has given notice of a claim, but who has not yet filed it, will receive priority over others who have filed.

B. RACE-NOTICE RECORDING STATUTES

Race-notice statutes, on the other hand, allow the first person to record a claim that does not have notice of pending claims to receive the highest priority.

C. RACE RECORDING STATUTES

Pure race statutes allow a party to have a superior claim if she is the first to record, whether or not the party has notice of any other outstanding, but unfiled, claims. Only three states follow a pure race system for recording claims.

Case Excerpt

CORSO v. MISER
2020 Ohio 5293 (Ohio App. 2020)

Opinion and Judgment Entry

Defendant-Appellant/Cross-Appellee George W. Miser appeals the decision of Jefferson County Common Pleas Court granting summary judgment and quieting title to the oil and gas for Plaintiffs-Appellees/Cross-Appellants Rebecca M. Corso and Paula D. Modransky. Appellees/Cross-Appellants appeal the trial court's decision denying their request for attorney fees. These issues are raised in this appeal. First, does the language of the 1949 deed reserve the oil and gas to George T. Miser and Isabelle Miser, Appellant/Cross-Appellee's predecessor in interest. Second, if the language is ambiguous, does the parol evidence indicate that the language was meant to reserve the oil and gas interest.

For the reasons explained below, the language of the 1949 deed is ambiguous and susceptible to different interpretations. However, there is no parol evidence indicating whether or not there was an intent by George T. Miser and Isabelle Miser, Appellant's predecessor in interest, to reserve the oil and gas. Thus, the language is construed against the grantor.

Statement of the Case

This case involves the ownership of oil and gas underlying approximately 140 acres of real estate in Springfield Township, Jefferson County, Ohio. George M. and Mary Miser were the owners of the real estate and subsurface. In 1906 they conveyed the coal, except the number 8 seam, to Henry Wick. In 1943 George M. and Mary conveyed a portion of their estate to George T. and Isabelle Miser. George T. and Isabelle Miser are Appellant/Cross-Appellee's parents. One exception in this deed stated:

> EXCEPTING that part of the coal underlying said premises heretofore sold and conveyed to Henry Wick, a reference to this deed of conveyance heretofore on record in the Recorder's Office of Jefferson County, Ohio, will more fully show, and being the same premises as is described in Mortgage Record 79, Page 22 of said county.

1943 Deed.

In 1964, George T. and Isabelle Miser leased the oil and gas rights to Humble Oil & Refining Company. The oil and gas estate leased was identified as, "That certain mineral reservation by lessor appearing in deed dated September 30, 1949, recorded in

Book 257, Page 152." This lease is dated March 26, 1964. This lease was signed by the Misers, notarized, and recorded.

In 2011, Appellees/Cross-Appellants entered into a lease with Chesapeake Exploration LLC for the oil and gas rights underlying the land at issue in this case. In 2014, Chesapeake Exploration LLC entered into a lease with Appellant/Cross-Appellee for the oil and gas rights underlying the land at issue in this case. Chesapeake is withholding royalties from both Appellant/Cross-Appellee and Appellees/Cross-Appellants due to the parties' competing claims to ownership over the oil and gas interest.

In 2018, Appellees/Cross-Appellants filed an action to quiet title or in the alternative for declaratory judgment based on the Marketable Title Act against Appellant/Cross-Appellee. Appellees/Cross-Appellants asked for an order granting them all rights, title, and interest to the oil and gas underlying the real estate.

Appellant/Cross-Appellee answered and asked for the court to dismiss the claims with prejudice, award him attorney fees and courts costs, and any other equitable relief the court deemed appropriate. 8/22/18 Answer.

The parties filed their competing summary judgment motions and argued that the plain language was in their respective favors. Appellant/Cross-Appellee asserted the plain language of the deed meant that the oil and gas interest was reserved. Response to Summary Judgment Motion; Appellees/Cross-Appellees asserted the language on its face indicated the oil and gas interest was not reserved and accordingly was transferred to their predecessors in interest and therefore inherited by them.

The trial court denied the motions explaining:

> While the Court does have some extrinsic evidence such as the newly-entered oil and gas lease and the statements of both sides claiming that they always thought they owned the oil and gas rights the Court is not convinced that it has access to all of the extrinsic evidence that would be out there or would be available after discovery. For these reasons the Court cannot grant a Summary Judgment to either party. 11/30/18 J.E.

A hearing on the summary judgment motions was held on June 17, 2019. Thereafter, the trial court granted summary judgment for Appellees/Cross-Appellants. It held that the word "minerals" standing alone and without qualifying words would have created an effective reservation. However, the word "minerals" was followed by qualifying language and that qualifying language was ambiguous. Therefore, the court looked to parol evidence and stated there was no parol evidence indicating the Misers intended to reserve the oil and gas. Therefore, the limiting language was construed against the drafters, i.e., the grantors Misers, and it was found that the oil and gas interest passed to the Wylies and then to the Appellees/Cross-Appellants.

First Assignment of Error

"The trial court erred when it granted summary judgment to Appellees because the plain language of the reserving deed excluded the minerals from the conveyance."

Both parties assert the language of the deed is plain and clear. Appellees/Cross-Appellants contend the plain language indicates the oil and gas was not reserved. Appellant/Cross-Appellee contends the plain language of the deed indicates the oil and gas was reserved.

The issue before us requires a review of the deed as a matter of law. Written instruments "are to be interpreted so as to carry out the intent of the parties, as that intent is evidenced by the contractual language." *Skivolocki v. East Ohio Gas Co.*, 38 Ohio St.2d 244, 313 N.E.2d 374 (1974). "The principles of deed construction dictate that a court presumes that a deed expresses the intentions of the grantor and grantee at the time of execution. . . . A court cannot interpret the parties' intent in a manner contrary to the clear, unambiguous language of the deed." *American Energy Corp. v. Datkuliak*, 174 Ohio App.3d 398, 2007-Ohio-7199, 882 N.E.2d 463. When determining the grantor's intent, a court must analyze the language used in the deed, "the question being not what the parties meant to say, but the meaning of what they did say, as courts cannot put words into an instrument which the parties themselves failed to do." *Id.*

However, when the plain language of the written instruments is ambiguous, then a court can look to parol evidence to resolve the ambiguity and ascertain the parties' intent. Terms in a contract are ambiguous if their meanings cannot be determined from reading the entire contract, or if they are reasonably susceptible to multiple interpretations. Parol evidence is used only to interpret the terms, and not to contradict the terms. *Id.* "The decision as to whether a contract is ambiguous and thus requires extrinsic evidence to ascertain its meaning is one of law."

If parol evidence fails to clarify the meaning of the contract, then the contract is strictly construed against the drafter. *Envision Waste Services, LLC v. Cty. Of Medina*, 2017-Ohio-351, 83 N.E.3d 270, ¶ 15 (9th Dist.).

The language at issue in this case is the reservation from the 1949 deed. It states:

> Excepting and reserving from the above described Real Estate, all coal and minerals underlying the same with the right to mine and remove the same as shown in the deed to Henry Wick, wherein said coal was conveyed, reference to which is hereby made for a more complete statement thereof. 1949 Deed.

The trial court determined that the language of the 1949 Deed was ambiguous or susceptible to different meanings:

> While it is true that the word "minerals" standing alone without qualification or limited words would have created an effective reservation, that word does not stand alone in this Case. Clearly, the words "As shown in Deed to Henry Wick, wherein said coal was conveyed . . ." defines, qualifies or limits something. The question is what is defined, qualified or limited by those words. Those limiting words could define, qualify or limit the "right to mine and remove" immediately preceding the limiting words. Or, the limiting words could limit "and minerals underlying the same with the right to mine and remove same." Or it could limit the entire exception/reservation. There is no way to know for sure, but there is a clue.
>
> While we cannot know with absolute certainty from the words alone, we can say with absolute certainty that the words are ambiguous.

In reviewing deed language, we agree with the trial court's well thought out analysis and conclusion that the deed is ambiguous and susceptible to more than one reasonable interpretation.

Given the grammatical construction of the reservation in the 1949 Deed, the reference to the 1906 Wick Deed could be interpreted to be qualifying language. The reservation/exception may have just been notice of the prior conveyance and not a separate reservation of oil and gas. There is not a separate sentence that the grantor was reserving and excepting the minerals for himself. And then, a separate sentence giving notice of the prior coal conveyance.

Another possible interpretation is that this one sentence reservation was a reservation of minerals to the grantor and a notice provision of the prior coal conveyance to Wick.

Appellant/Cross-Appellee asserts George T. and Isabelle Miser could have repeated the reservation language from the 1943 deed in the 1949 deed. However, they did not and omitted the limiting language "heretofore sold and conveyed" and added mineral language which Appellant/Cross-Appellee contends thereby plainly indicates they were reserving the minerals.

We agree that is one possible interpretation of the language used. However, we disagree that when reading the 1943 deed in conjunction with the 1949 deed the language is plain that Appellant/Cross-Appellee was reserving the subsurface that was not previously conveyed. It is true the same language from the 1943 deed could have been used in the 1949 deed to show that everything was being conveyed except the coal that was previously conveyed to Henry Wick. It is also true that they changed the language.

In conclusion, we agree with the trial court's analysis that the words used are susceptible to multiple interpretations. We find no merit with this assignment of error and hold that the reservation language is ambiguous.

Second Assignment of Error

"The trial court erred when it granted summary judgment to Appellees because Appellant produced parol evidence indicating that oil and gas production was prevalent in the area of the reservation at the time of the reservation."

As we have found that the deed is ambiguous, we must address this assignment of error. As stated above, if the language is deemed ambiguous, we can look to parol evidence to determine the intent of the parties to the deed. In looking at parol evidence, the trial court explained:

> We also know that ambiguous words are resolved against the scrivener, which in this case is the Grantor or maker of the Deed. Because those words were chosen and used by George T. Miser and Isabelle Miser in their 1949 Deed to John P. Wiley we must resolve the ambiguity against George T. Miser and Isabelle Miser and in favor of John P. Wiley after applying whatever parole evidence might be out there to resolve the ambiguity.
>
> Defendant points out no parole evidence tending to indicate that the Misers intended to reserve Oil and Gas. Defendant's sole argument seems to focus on the word "minerals" carefully avoiding the words that follow. None of the language or parole evidence is conclusive to the intended meaning of the 1949 Exception/Reservation but it all leans toward Plaintiffs.

"Leans toward" is not normally sufficient for a Summary Judgment but here it is. That is because Plaintiff need not prove its interpretation to be correct. It need only prove that the Exception/Reservation fails to "clearly" appear in the Deed to prevent Grantor's entire Estate from passing to Grantee pursuant to Section 8510-1, General Code which was effective in all of 1949. While it is clear that the Henry Wick coal was reserved nothing beyond that is clear hence, Grantor's entire Estate (except for the Henry Wick coal) passed in 1949 to John, Mary and Dula Wylie and then on to Plaintiff. 7/16/19 J.E.

As aforementioned, parol evidence is used to interpret the terms, not to contradict them. If parol evidence fails to clarify the meaning of the contract, then the contract is strictly construed against the drafter, which in the case of an exception or reservation it is construed in favor of the grantee.

Appellant/Cross-Appellee points to the language of the 1949 Deed versus the 1943 Deed. As stated above, while the language of the deeds are different, the differences do not clarify the ambiguity. In fact, it could be suggested that the differences make it murkier. As the trial court noted the drafted language is sloppy.

Appellant/Cross-Appellee also asserts that in our case law the word "minerals" includes oil and gas and helps to resolve the ambiguity. As stated under the first assignment of error the use of the word "minerals" in 1949 in our area would include oil and gas. The problem here is that the language used in the 1949 deed modified the word "minerals." Thus, the issue is what the language used to modify the word "minerals" means. As stated above the word "minerals" could have been used to indicate that any minerals conveyed to Henry Wick were being excepted/reserved. Since none were conveyed to him none were excepted/reserved. Thus, the use of the word "minerals" does not help resolve the ambiguity in this instance.

Appellant/Cross-Appellee also points to the historic well information provided by the Ohio Department of Natural Resources. While it is clear there were oil and gas wells drilled at the time of the 1949 Deed, that does not necessarily indicate it was the intention of the Misers to reserve those minerals for themselves. Mere production of oil and gas in the vicinity does not show an intention to reserve/except the oil and gas to the grantor.

Consequently, there is no parol evidence indicating the intent of the parties. Therefore, pursuant to rules of construction, we construe the reservation against the drafter/grantor of the exception and conclude that the oil and gas was not reserved by the Misers and therefore it was conveyed to the Wylies and passed to Appellees/Cross-Appellants. The trial court's grant of summary judgment for Appellees/Cross-Appellants is affirmed.

Conclusion

For the reasons expressed above, all assignments of error raised in the appeal and cross-appeal lack merit. The trial court's decision is affirmed in all respects.

QUESTIONS ABOUT THE CASE

1 Why is the language in the deed ambiguous?
2 When a court is presented with a clearly ambiguous deed, what procedures do they follow?
3 What are the "principles of deed construction"?
4 In the absence of parol evidence, what must a court do to interpret a deed with ambiguous language?
5 How did the court rule? Did the deed reserve mineral and oil rights or not?

 COVID-19 CONCERN

One change that the COVID-19 pandemic has facilitated is a move toward more virtual encounters between people involved in a real estate transaction. One area that was ripe for technological improvement was the topic of notarization. By its very nature, notarization requires that the notary meet with a person intending to sign a document, review that person's ID, and then stamp or print a seal stating that the person who signed the document had been correctly identified. All of these steps involve both parties being in close proximity to one another.

E-notary laws seek to change that, however. Some states, like Georgia, have already implemented a virtual notary scheme in which a notary can be at a different location than the person signing a document (such as a deed). For some, this attacks the very notion of what a notary is. For others, it is a concession not only to technology but also to the realities of social distancing in the face of a deadly disease.

CHAPTER SUMMARY

Deeds have basic, legal requirements. For instance, they must be in writing in order to satisfy the Statute of Frauds. They must also be signed by the grantor and have clearly identifiable parties. Deeds must also contain an adequate property description, often in the form of a metes and bounds description or reference to a government survey.

There are several different types of deeds. General warranty deeds contain numerous warranties from the grantor to the grantee, such as the assurance that the grantor is in legal possession of the property (*seizin*) and that there are no encumbrances against the title. A quitclaim deed, on the other hand, is a deed by the grantor to the grantee wherein the grantor surrenders any rights that she may have to the real estate, with no promises or warranties of any kind.

SKILLS YOU NEED IN THE REAL WORLD

Locating Deeds in the Public Records

One of the most fundamental skills that you need in real estate practice is the ability to locate specific deeds quickly. No matter how deeds are organized in your state, whether on a tract index or by grantors' names, you should take the time to master locating deeds. The first step is to visit your local courthouse to see where the deeds are stored. In some states, there is a separate office referred to as the registrar of deeds office, while in other states it is referred to as the land office or the deed room. Whatever the name, the function remains the same: This office is primarily responsible for housing all real estate records. When people come in to transfer title to real estate, they do so in this office. You should learn how the deeds are indexed. In some rural areas, deed information is still maintained by handwritten entries in a deed index. In those offices, researching deeds can be a time-consuming process. Fortunately, most deed rooms are now computerized and have as much as the last ten years of real estate transactions available in a computer database. Computer databases allow you to cross-reference grantor's or grantee's names in order to locate deeds.

In addition to the deed room, you should also visit the local tax office. The tax office is responsible for keeping track of real property tax payments, and it usually has up-to-date records about not only a particular parcel but also the most current deed references where this parcel was bought or sold. Investing a few hours now learning your local system will pay big dividends in the future.

ETHICAL ISSUES FOR THE PARALEGAL

Use of Forms

With the subject of deeds, there is always a question about the use of preprinted forms. There are some companies that sell preprinted deed forms that they claim are perfectly valid in all areas of the country. However, before using such a form, you should review it carefully to make sure that it conforms to your state's rules about deeds. A deed form that is sufficient for California may not be sufficient in New York. This can raise an ethical problem because attorneys who rely on faulty preprinted forms can open themselves up to a legal malpractice claim. Some states have preprinted forms that have been approved by the state bar. You can generally rely on those forms without any further research, but you should still be on guard whenever you use any preprinted forms. The Internet has only made this problem worse. You can find a wealth of "legal forms," including deed forms, on the Web. A form downloaded from the Internet is not guaranteed to meet your state's legal requirements.

KEY TERMS AND CONCEPTS

Acknowledgment   Grantee   Habendum clause
Attestation   Granting clause   *Seizin*
Deed   Grantor

END-OF-CHAPTER EXERCISES

Review Questions

See Appendix for answers.

1   List and explain at least five minimum requirements that any deed should have.
2   Who is required to sign a deed, and why?
3   Is the grantee required to sign the deed? Explain your answer.
4   What constitutes a valid legal description of the property conveyed in a deed?
5   What is a habendum clause, and what purpose does it serve?
6   What is the difference between a habendum clause and a granting clause?
7   Provide an example of "words of conveyance" that should be found in a deed.
8   What is the significance of delivery and acceptance of a deed?
9   Compare and contrast attestation and acknowledgment.
10 What is a seal?
11 Is consideration required in a deed? Explain your answer.
12 What is the covenant of *seizin*?
13 What is the covenant against encumbrances?
14 What is the covenant of warranty forever?
15 What is the difference between a special warranty deed and a general warranty deed?
16 What are deeds of trust?
17 What function does a quitclaim deed serve?
18 Under what circumstances would a quitclaim deed be used?
19 Why would a buyer prefer a general warranty deed to a quitclaim deed?
20 Describe the three statutory approaches to recording title.

DISCUSSION QUESTIONS

1   If you had to explain the differences between a general warranty deed and a quitclaim deed to someone who knew nothing about real estate law, what would you say?

2   Has the language in deeds become hopelessly out of date? Should it be updated? Why or why not?

APPLYING WHAT YOU HAVE LEARNED

Locate a deed from your state and then answer the following questions:

■   What language does the deed have concerning consideration?
■   Does the deed contain a covenant of *seizin*?
■   Does the deed make reference to "quiet enjoyment"?
■   What language in the deed qualifies as a "granting" clause?

WEB SURFING

General Warranty Deed: Ohio
http://codes.ohio.gov/orc/5302.05

Deeds of Trust: Legal Information Institute
http://www.law.cornell.edu/wex/deed_of_trust

Tech Topic
DEED SEARCH

The Land Records and Deeds Resources website (http://publicrecords.onlinesearches.com/Land-Records-and-Deeds.htm) offers links to the online land records and deeds search functions of nearly all counties in the United States. While there are advertisements for paid searches on the website, the links themselves go to the free search resources available on each county's website, giving you a central location from which to search for property deeds anywhere in the country.

ANNOTATED DOCUMENT

General Warranty Deed

<u>WARRANTY DEED</u>

KNOW ALL MEN BY THESE PRESENTS, that CAROLYN DRAPER MCCALL, ◄——— Identifies grantor and grantee
an unmarried woman, hereinafter called the "Grantor", for and in consideration of the sum of TEN AND NO/100THS ($10.00) DOLLARS in cash and other good and valuable consideration, in hand paid to the Grantor by BILLY L. JOHNSTON, JR. and DIANE B. JOHNSTON, hereinafter called the "Grantee", the receipt and sufficiency of which is hereby acknowledged, subject to all matters and things hereinafter set forth, has this day bargained and sold and by these presents does hereby GRANT, BARGAIN, SELL AND CONVEY unto the said Grantees, for and during their joint lives, and upon the death of either of them, then to the survivor of them, in fee simple, together with every contingent remainder and right of reversion, all that real property situated in the County of Baldwin, State of Alabama, described as follows, to wit:

Lot 32, First Addition to Cooper's Landing Subdivision, ◄——— Describes property
according to the map or plat thereof recorded in Map Book 4, page 95 in the records in the Office of the Judge of Probate of Baldwin County, Alabama.

LESS AND EXCEPT such as oil, gas, and other mineral interests and all rights and privileges in connection therewith as may have been reserved or conveyed by prior owners, if any.

THIS CONVEYANCE IS MADE SUBJECT TO THE FOLLOWING:

1.   Oil, gas and mineral lease, and all rights in connection therewith, by Vanway v. McRaven to Shell Oil Company, dated January 7, 2011 and recorded in Real Property Book 86, page 276.

2.   Rights of other parties, the United States of America or State of Alabama in and to the shore, littoral or riparian rights to the property described above lying and adjacent to unnamed canal.

TOGETHER WITH ALL AND SINGULAR, the rights, members, privileges and appurtenances thereunto belonging, or in anywise appertaining.

TO HAVE AND TO HOLD the said above described property unto ◄——— Habendum clause
the said Grante es during the term of their joint lives, and upon the death of either of them, then to the survivor of them, in fee simple, and to the heirs and assigns of such survivor, forever, together with every contingent remainder and right of reversion.

And except as to taxes hereafter falling due which are ◄——— Exceptions
assumed by the Grantees, and except as to the above mentioned encumbrances, the Grantor does, for herself and her heirs and assigns, hereby covenant with the Grantees that she is seized of an indefeasible estate in fee simple in said property, is in peaceable possession thereof, that said property is free and clear of all encumbrances, and that she does hereby WARRANT AND WILL FOREVER DEFEND the title to said property and the peaceable possession thereof, unto the Grantees, and to the survivor of

them, and to the heirs and assigns of such survivor, against the
lawful claims of all persons whomsoever.

Carolyn Draper McCall
CAROLYN DRAPER MCCALL

STATE OF <u>Alabama</u>

COUNTY OF <u>Baldwin</u>

    I, <u>Cleveland L. Landreth</u>, the undersigned authority, a
Notary Public in and for said County in said State, hereby
certify that CAROLYN DRAPER MCCALL, whose name is signed to the
foregoing conveyance and who is known to me, acknowledged before
me on this day, that being informed of the contents of said
conveyance, she has executed the same voluntarily on the day the
same bears date.

    Given under my hand and seal this the <u>10th</u> day of <u>April,</u>
<u>2022.</u>

Notary Public Provision

Cleveland L. Landreth
Notary Public

My Commission Expires:

<u>April, 14, 2025</u>

This Instrument Prepared by:

G. DAVID CHAPMAN III, P.C.
Attorney at Law
Post Office Box 1508
Gulf Shores, Alabama 36547
Fiule 95.2373

Grantor's Address:

P.O. Box 207
Bon Secour, AL 36511

Grantees' Address:

375 Rock Products Road
Heber Sp[rings, AR 72543

PRACTICE QUESTIONS FOR TEST REVIEW

See Appendix for answers.

Essay Question

What are the minimum legal requirements of the deed conveying ownership interests from one person to another?

True–False

1 T   F   Deeds embody both contract and real property law in a single document.

2 T   F   Deeds have symbolic significance stretching back hundreds of years.

3 T   F   Only certain types of deeds are required to be in writing.

Fill in the Blank

1   In both contracts and deeds, the parties must meet the legal standard of knowingly and voluntarily entering a legally-binding arrangement: _____.

2   This deed clause conveys specified rights to the grantee, commonly called the right "to have and to hold": _____.

3   This document has aspects of a contract and of a public declaration and is filed in the public records to show change of ownership: _____.

Multiple Choice

1   The document that sets out both the contractual obligation between buyer and seller and serves as the written expression of the transfer of legal rights in real property.

    A   Option.
    B   Attestation.
    C   Deed.
    D   Lien.

2   The name for the person who transfers property to another.

    A   Bailiff.
    B   Auctioneer.
    C   Grantor.
    D   grantee.

3   The name for the person who receives real estate interests.

    A   Bailiff.
    B   Auctioneer.
    C   Grantor.
    D   Grantee.

ENDNOTES

[1] Tex. Code Ann. Prop. §5.021.
[2] *Jenkins v. Jenkins*, 148 Pa. 216, 23 A. 985 (1892).
[3] *Matter of Mills*, 68 N.C. App. 694, 315 S.E.2d 716 (1984).
[4] *Campbell v. Everhart*, 139 N.C. 503, 52 S.E. 201 (1905).
[5] *Snyder v. Bridewell*, 267 S.W. 561 (Ark. 1924).
[6] N.C. Gen. Stat. §39-2.
[7] Excerpted from an actual deed.
[8] *Klouda v. Pechousek*, 414 Ill. 75, 110 N.E.2d 258 (1953).
[9] *Jones v. Saunders*, 254 N.C. 644, 119 S.E.2d 789 (1961).
[10] *Scott v. Fairlie*, 81 Fla. 438, 446, 89 So. 128 (1921).

Mortgages and Financing the Purchase of Real Estate

Chapter Objectives

- Describe the important role played by mortgage lenders in the real estate market

- Define the purpose of the secondary mortgage market

- List and explain the function of corporations such as Fannie Mae, Ginnie Mae, and Freddie Mac

- Explain the common clauses and provisions found in mortgages and deeds of trust

- Describe the various types of mortgages available to fund the purchase of real property

Chapter Outline

I. Introduction

II. Mortgage Markets
   A. Primary Mortgage Market
   B. Secondary Mortgage Market

III. The Legal Requirements of a Mortgage/Deed of Trust
   A. Mortgages vs. Deeds of Trust
   B. The Elements of a Mortgage
   C. Recording Mortgages

IV. Types of Mortgages
   A. Fixed-Rate Mortgages
   B. Adjustable-Rate Mortgages
   C. Other Types of Mortgages

V. Qualifying for a Mortgage
   A. Underwriting
   B. Borrower's Credit History
   C. Appraisal
   D. The Rise of Internet Lenders

VI. **Discharging a Mortgage**

VII. **Foreclosure**

    A. Judicial Foreclosure

B. **Power of Sale Foreclosure**

C. **The Foreclosure Auction**

D. **Decreasing Foreclosure Rates**

INTRODUCTION

Mortgage
A contractual agreement in which a borrower transfers specific real property rights to a lender in exchange for the lender's pledge of funds to purchase the real estate.

Purchasing a home is the single largest investment that most people will ever make. Because few people are able to purchase a home for cash, financing the purchase is the only way to own a home. The method used to finance the purchase of real estate is a **mortgage** (also called a deed of trust). Whatever the name, the arrangement is essentially the same: The borrower transfers some rights to the lender in exchange for the money to purchase the property. The borrower not only transfers important rights, such as the right to foreclose, but also makes additional promises, such as to make monthly mortgage payments, pay real estate taxes, and maintain appropriate insurance on the premises. In this chapter, we examine the ways that mortgages are created, the rights and duties imposed by the arrangement, the different types of mortgages available, and the consequences when a borrower defaults on a mortgage.

In some ways, financing the purchase of real estate resembles financing the purchase of any expensive item. When individuals purchase a new car, for instance, the purchaser borrows money from a lender to provide the funds. There is a temptation to assume that real estate financing is similar to other types of financing. Real estate financing is quite different. When a person finances a car purchase, for example, the lender retains title to the automobile until the last payment is made. When a person buys a home, however, he will receive the title at the closing. The lender does not own the property. Instead, the lender receives a specific set of rights and holds those rights until the mortgage is paid off or the house is sold to someone else. Mortgage financing can be a complex issue. We begin by exploring the business of mortgages and then proceed to the features of mortgages.

In some states, a mortgage resembles a lien. If the borrower fails to make payments on the loan, the lien gives the lender the right to bring a foreclosure action to pay off the outstanding indebtedness. Mortgage lending is regulated on both the state and federal level. Many states regulate not only how mortgages can be made, but also their basic contents. Consider Figure 9-1.

FIGURE 9-1	A mortgage in substance following the form set forth in this section, when duly executed in accordance with Chapter 5301 of the Revised Code, has the force and effect of a mortgage to the use of the mortgagee and the mortgagee's heirs, assigns, and successors, with mortgage covenants and upon the statutory condition, as defined in sections 5302.13 and 5302.14 of the Revised Code, to secure the payment of the money or the performance of any obligation specified in the mortgage. The parties may insert in the mortgage any other lawful agreement or condition.

Mortgage Statute (Ohio)[1]

FIGURE 9.1

(continued)

MORTGAGE

_____, _____ (marital status), of _____ (current mailing address), for ___
_____ Dollars paid, grant(s), with mortgage covenants, to _____, of
_____ (current mailing address), the following real property:
(Description of land or interest in land and encumbrances, reservations, and exceptions,
if any.)
(A reference to the last recorded instrument through which the mortgagor claims title. The
omission of the reference shall not affect the validity of the mortgage.)
This mortgage is given, upon the statutory condition, to secure the payment of
_____ Dollars with interest as provided in a note of the same date.
"Statutory condition" is defined in section 5302.14 of the Revised Code and provides
generally that, if the mortgagor pays the principal and interest secured by this mortgage,
performs the other obligations secured by this mortgage and the conditions of any prior
mortgage, pays all the taxes and assessments, maintains insurance against fire and other
hazards, and does not commit or suffer waste, then this mortgage shall be void.
_____, wife (husband) of the mortgagor, releases to the mortgagee all rights of dower
in the described real property.
Executed this day of _____.
(Signature of Mortgagor)

MORTGAGE MARKETS

When we discuss mortgage markets, we are referring to lending institutions, banks, savings and loan associations, and a myriad of other organizations that make some or all of their income from lending money to others. The mortgage market has two levels: (1) The primary mortgage market, consisting of lenders and borrowers, and (2) a secondary mortgage market, consisting of governmental agencies and others who are in the business of purchasing mortgages from lenders.

A. PRIMARY MORTGAGE MARKET

When we think of the process of acquiring a mortgage to buy a house, we are focused exclusively on the primary mortgage market. Banks and other lending institutions are in the business of loaning money; they earn interest on the money that they loan out to others. Essentially, a mortgage is a simple proposition: The lender gives the borrower money that the borrower can then use to purchase something. In exchange for the money, the borrower gives the lender certain rights and pledges the item as collateral for the loan. When the loan arrangement concerns personal property, these rights include the power to repossess the collateral if the borrower defaults. When the loan concerns real property, the lender does not have the right to repossess but does have an equally powerful tool: the right to foreclose.

Loaning money to individuals is both risky and lucrative. If the individual makes regular monthly payments, the interest that the bank earns can be used to finance other ventures. On the other hand, if the individual defaults on the loan, the bank may be forced to go through a long and costly process of foreclosing on property that may not be worth the amount owed on the loan. As a result, all lenders screen potential borrowers and attempt to reduce the risk of loan defaults.

In an oversimplified version, a bank earns profits by taking in deposits from investors. Suppose, for example, that First Bank pays a rate of 1 percent on all deposit accounts. It then takes the money from those accounts and lends it out to borrowers at 5 percent. The difference between what the bank pays out and what it earns is the bank's profit.

If we examine the basic financial model in the previous paragraph, we will see an obvious flaw in the system: If First Bank takes in deposits and then lends those funds out to borrowers, it will soon run out of funds. After all, it only has so much money on hand from savings accounts, and when those funds are exhausted, the bank is unable to lend any additional money. This leads us to the world of the secondary mortgage market.

REAL ESTATE BASICS AT A GLANCE

The primary mortgage market is where lenders and borrowers arrange financing for home purchases.

Tech Topic
SPEECH-RECOGNITION SOFTWARE

Law firms can save a great deal of time and effort by employing speech-recognition software. Not only is it valuable for dictation transcription, it is also an excellent tool for document creation, computer commands, and workflow streamlining. By far the most popular speech-recognition software among the legal community is Nuance's Dragon, which has software specifically geared for those in the legal profession.

Dragon Legal Group is Nuance's product for its customers in the legal community. The software is designed with a specialized legal vocabulary to increase its accuracy, and it gives users the ability to create commands that will automatically insert

predetermined clauses into documents. Attorneys have the flexibility to both dictate and format contracts, briefs, and legal citations. In essence, Dragon makes it possible to do anything done with a keyboard and mouse with the voice instead.

While such software is quite powerful and has the potential to greatly reduce a firm's transcription workload, there are a few things to keep in mind when preparing to install and use Dragon (or any speech-recognition software). The first is that the efficacy of the program depends heavily upon the quality of the microphone used for dictation. A mic that garbles speech will not produce nearly as good of a document as one that records speech clearly, so it is important to do research and find a high-quality microphone that is compatible with both the computer and the software being used.

The second consideration is the quality of the speech itself. While speech-recognition software is becoming increasingly advanced, it still does not hold the same comprehension power as human ears. Slurred or mumbled words might be understood by another person but likely will not be transcribed properly by software. It is also important to speak loud enough (though not yell) for the microphone to pick up every word. Speech-recognition software tends to work best when the user speaks in longer sentences, as those give the program more context and enable it to better guess the words being said, so try to avoid short sentences or phrases as much as possible.

And finally, it is important to learn the software's commands before starting to use it. Different programs — and sometimes even different versions of the same program — have different commands to indicate formatting, and most of them also include various modes (normal, dictation, command, spell, and so on) to better accommodate the needs of the users. The software will be much more effective and the final product will contain far fewer errors if the user is familiar with all the commands and modes prior to beginning dictation and can transition smoothly from one to the next.

Speech-recognition software is gaining in popularity among those in the legal profession, and it is almost certain that it will continue to do so as the technology continues to improve. It is not unreasonable to believe that the future will see all legal transcription being completed and most legal documents being prepared by speech-recognition software.

B. SECONDARY MORTGAGE MARKET

In 1929, the United States, like many other countries, experienced a financial catastrophe. Although there were many causes for the Great Depression, one of the most important involved the simple paradigm of home mortgages. As the previous section suggested, when a bank loans all its funds, it can neither make new mortgage arrangements nor pay passbook accounts if there should be a sudden run on the bank. In 1929, with the economy going downhill very quickly, many banks found themselves faced with hundreds of customers demanding the balance of their accounts, sometimes all on the same day. When the banks couldn't pay out that money, primarily because it had been loaned to others, they failed. Individuals lost their life savings, and a financial downturn became a full-blown panic as passbook savers across the country rushed to their banks to redeem their savings before that money disappeared as well. This run on banks had a series of consequences: banks failed, businesses closed, individuals were unable to make their mortgage payments, and banks foreclosed on them. The United States teetered on the brink of total financial collapse.

The road out of the Great Depression was long and bumpy. President Franklin D. Roosevelt proposed a series of reforms to avoid a similar catastrophe in the future. One of the most far-reaching, at least in terms of real estate, was the creation of governmental agencies that would purchase mortgages from banks.

The idea of a secondary mortgage market was elegantly simple: The federal government would purchase mortgages from banks, giving them additional funds that they could use to repay passbook accounts or loan to other borrowers. Each mortgage arranged by the bank would be bought up by a governmental agency, creating a cycle whereby banks would never have all their money tied up in outstanding loans. The federal government also shored up confidence in passbook accounts by creating the Federal Deposit Insurance Corporation, which guaranteed payment on accounts in member banks. See Figure 9-2 for a summary of some benefits of the second mortgage market.

EXAMPLE 9-1	**$1 MILLION TO LEND**

ABC Bank has a pool of $1 million in funds available to disburse to mortgage borrowers. If it makes ten mortgages, each at $100,000, ABC Bank will have used all its available funds. Without some arrangement to obtain new funding, ABC Bank cannot support any new mortgages. The secondary mortgage market provides that new funding.

REAL ESTATE BASICS AT A GLANCE

The secondary mortgage market consists of federal agencies that purchase mortgages from primary lenders.

FIGURE 9-2	The benefits provided by the secondary mortgage market are that it:

The Importance of the Secondary Mortgage Market

The benefits provided by the secondary mortgage market are that it:
- Makes capital available to lending institutions,
- Permits lenders to originate more loans,
- Keeps capital flowing, and
- Stabilizes the U.S. economy.

1. FEDERAL AGENCIES IN THE SECONDARY MORTGAGE MARKET

In 1934, the Great Depression still had a stranglehold on the U.S. economy, but there were some bright spots. For instance, Congress had passed the National Housing Act that authorized the creation of governmental agencies whose sole purpose was to improve the mortgage market. The first of these agencies was the Federal National Mortgage Association, FNMA, created in 1938. Quickly nicknamed "Fannie Mae," this agency began buying up mortgages. The procedure was simple: Banks would approach Fannie Mae and offer to sell it mortgages that the bank had recently negotiated. Fannie Mae would purchase these mortgages and administer them for the life of the loan.

In a somewhat simplified version, suppose that First Bank has negotiated a mortgage for $50,000, at 4 percent, for 30 years. If the bank were to hold that loan for the full 30 years, it would receive something on the order of $120,000, between interest payments and repayment of the original $50,000. However, the bank would have to wait the full 30 years to receive that amount. On the other hand, if First Bank sold the mortgage to Fannie Mae for $80,000, it would have the immediate benefit of extra cash that it could loan out to others. Fannie Mae would then receive the mortgage payments and would be responsible for the mortgage from that point on. The borrower might not even be aware of the fact, or care, that Fannie Mae now owned the mortgage. In fact, the bank might continue to receive the monthly mortgage payments, charge a minimal fee to Fannie Mae for the administrative costs, and then forward the mortgage payment.

a. Fannie Mae

Fannie Mae had an enormous impact on the mortgage market. Because banks were anxious to sell mortgages to Fannie Mae, they followed its policies in regard to risk analysis, forms, and procedures. This created, over time, a uniform system across the United States. Almost incidentally, Fannie Mae also began to earn huge profits. After all, the agency had purchased mortgages at a discount, and as mortgage payments poured in from across the country, Fannie Mae found itself in the enviable position of having too much money. The more mortgages it purchased, the more money it made. However, these profits generated new problems: The government is not supposed to be a for-profit business. In 1968, Congress severed all ties with Fannie Mae and authorized it to become a private, for-profit business. Fannie Mae's success spawned new governmental agencies, including the Government National Mortgage Association (Ginnie Mae) and the Federal Home Loan Mortgage Corporation (Freddie Mac).

In September 2008, both Fannie Mae and Freddie Mac were taken over by the federal government and placed into conservatorship. During this period, the day-to-day business of both companies was regulated by government officials.

Fannie Mae is the largest member of the secondary mortgage market. Recent downturns in the real estate market have called many of its decisions into question.

REAL
ESTATE
BASICS AT
A GLANCE

---

b. Ginnie Mae

Like Fannie Mae, Ginnie Mae is a government agency that plays a substantial role in mortgages. It guarantees timely payment of principal and interest on mortgages backed by the Federal Housing Administration or the Department of Veterans' Affairs. Ginnie Mae operates under the authority of the Department of Housing and Urban Development (HUD). Besides administering Ginnie Mae and similar secondary mortgage agencies, HUD also plays a huge role in the housing market through its rules and regulations and its closing settlement form, which we examine in detail in Chapter 13.

Fannie Mae has provided financing for the purchase of over 63 million homes since 1938.

c. Freddie Mac

Freddie Mac was created in 1970 to provide another vehicle for the purchase of mortgages. A government-sponsored corporation, it is publicly owned and traded. It was designed to purchase single- and multi-family mortgages in order to encourage that market. Freddie Mac reviews and approves individual loans and continues to play an active role in the secondary mortgage market.

d. HUD

Originally authorized by the 1937 U.S. Housing Act, the Department of Housing and Urban Development was raised to a cabinet-level department in 1965. HUD plays an important role in many different phases of real estate financing. For instance, it regulates Fannie Mae and Ginnie Mae and insures mortgage loans to help people buy or refinance their current homes. It also provides borrowers with a list of approved lenders who often help individuals purchase a home with little or no money down.

e. The Role of the Federal Reserve Board

Along with governmental agencies such as Freddie Mac and private corporations such as Fannie Mae, there is another federal agency that plays an important role in the home mortgage market: the Federal Reserve System. Usually referred to as the Federal Reserve, it is the nation's central bank. Created in 1913, the role of the Federal Reserve has changed over time. Originally intended to create a stable foundation for the U.S. financial system, the "Fed" now sets the country's monetary policy, regulates the banking industry, and sets short-term interest rates. This last responsibility puts the Fed in an extremely important position as far as home mortgage interest rates are concerned. When the Fed raises short-term interest rates, most lending institutions follow suit. The practical result is that a borrower will pay more money in interest over the life of a loan because the Fed adjusted its rate upward. Of course, the opposite is also true. In recent years, the Fed has been credited with softening the economic recession by moving its interest rates to historic lows.

f. Troubled Asset Relief Program

Signed into law by President Bush in 2008, the Troubled Asset Relief Program (TARP) was designed to assist financial institutions in liquidating real estate assets that had lost their value and had begun to drag on the rest of the economy. Under TARP, the U.S. government pledged $700 billion to various lenders to assist them in jump-starting the lending process. Although much of the money lent to financial institutions has been paid back, many Americans see TARP as a failure.

2. FEDERAL LEGISLATION THAT GOVERNS REAL ESTATE FINANCING

In 2010, in response to the past several years of recession, which has since become known as the "Great Recession," Congress passed and President Obama signed the Dodd-Frank Act, also known as the Mortgage Reform and Anti-Predatory Lending Act. For the sake of clarity, we will refer to this act as "Dodd-Frank."

Some of the biggest changes brought about by Dodd-Frank were the changes to the Truth in Lending Act and the Real Estate Settlement Practices Act. We will address the issues tied to Dodd-Frank and closings in Chapter 13, but will focus on changes surrounding mortgage practice in this chapter.

See Figure 9-3 for a summary of federal real estate legislation.

FIGURE 9-3

Summary of Important Federal Legislation Related to Housing and Real Estate Financing

- Federal Home Loan Bank System (1932)
  This legislation created 12 regional banks and also authorized the creation of the Federal Home Loan Bank Board that provided short-term credit to lending institutions.
- Home Owners' Loan Corporation (1933)
  During the Great Depression, it provided refinancing for mortgages across the country.
- Housing Act of 1934
  This act brought the Federal Housing Administration (FHA) into existence. The FHA insured private mortgage loans and helped encourage lending institutions to provide more long-term mortgages to borrowers.
- Housing Act of 1937
  This act authorized the financing of low-rent housing.
- Federal National Mortgage Association (FNMA, or "Fannie Mae") (1938)
  Fannie Mae is a governmental agency created to provide a secondary market for mortgages.
- Servicemen's Readjustment Act of 1944 (the GI "Bill of Rights")
  The GI Bill of Rights created the VA mortgage loan program for veterans.
- Housing and Urban Development Act of 1968
  This act created the Government National Mortgage Association (GNMA, or "Ginnie Mae"), which took over the duties of the recently privatized Fannie Mae.
- The Dodd-Frank Wall Street Reform and Consumer Protection Act of 2010

---

a. Dodd-Frank

The original Truth in Lending Act (15 U.S.C.A. §1601) was enacted in 1968 and required that borrowers be given specific types of information so that they can make informed choices about their borrowing options. The Truth in Lending Act was designed to protect consumers by requiring lenders to give specific types of disclosures about the key terms of all types of lending agreements, including mortgages, and to disclose specific facts to borrowers, including the total cost of the credit arrangement and the annual percentage rate. The disclosures are supposed to be made in plain English that a layperson can understand and use as a means to compare one lender's terms to another's.[2]

One of the primary functions of Dodd-Frank was to force lenders to push consumers toward loans that the consumer could afford to repay or to deny loans to consumers who could not conceivably repay them. The changes in the Truth in Lending Act (TILA) have been extensive. Lenders must make a good-faith determination of a consumer's ability to repay a loan; verify the information provided by the consumer; and also provide substantial information to the consumer about the costs associated with not only obtaining the loan, but also the amount that the consumer will repay over the life of the loan.

Other limitations imposed by Dodd-Frank include the elimination of most forms of balloon payment mortgages, a limit on debt acceleration, and in particular, a strong focus on the various fees that consumers are expected to pay before and during the mortgage loan process. Dodd-Frank also imposes new restrictions on how appraisals are conducted.

i. Sweeping Changes in Truth-in-Lending

Since the passage of the Truth in Lending Act and the Real Estate Settlement Procedures Act in 1974, the disclosures made by lenders to borrowers have remained more or less fixed. Perhaps the biggest changes brought about by Dodd-Frank concern disclosures that must be made to consumers. TILA documents have been modified to make them simpler and easier to understand. The same has occurred with settlement documents. As we will see in Chapter 13, the old HUD-1 Settlement Statement has been replaced by a multi-page document that attempts to explain the various expenditures and disbursements in plain English.

Because Dodd-Frank combined elements of both the Truth in Lending Act and the Real Estate Settlement Procedures Act, real estate professionals refer to the new law by the short form, "TRID." Under TRID, dramatic changes have been made to the traditional Good Faith Estimate, the TILA disclosures, and the rules that govern client protection, particularly any sensitive information that might be used to defraud clients, such as Social Security numbers, date of birth, and other sensitive information that is now classified as Non-Public Information (NPI). TRID has made dramatic changes in the way that all phases of a real estate transaction transpire, from applying for financing through to closing and even record keeping that must occur after the closing has been consummated.

TRID now requires that these documents must be provided to the consumer at least three business days before the closing is completed (or "consummated"). In the past, Good Faith Estimates were required to be given to the consumer before the scheduled closing, as were the TILA disclosures, but whether this actually happened was an open question. The old legislation certainly did not provide a three-day window between receiving the disclosures and completing (or consummating) the closing. Under the old system, there were borrowers who can attest to the fact that the old GFE and TILA forms were not provided until the day of the closing and sometimes only within a few hours of the scheduled closing.

The Loan Estimate. The new approach consolidates four existing disclosure forms down to two. They are called the Loan Estimate and Closing Disclosure, both of which must be supplied to the borrower three business days before the scheduled closing. See Figure 9-4. It applies to almost all mortgages and deeds of trust where the collateral is real property. The new forms purport to simplify terms and make it easier for consumers to locate important information. Among those important items of information are:

- Interest rate,
- Monthly payment, and
- Closing costs.

FICUS BANK

4321 Random Boulevard · Somecity, ST 12340

Save this Loan Estimate to compare with your Closing Disclosure.

Loan Estimate

DATE ISSUED	2/15/2013	LOAN TERM	30 years
APPLICANTS	Michael Jones and Mary Stone	PURPOSE	Purchase
	123 Anywhere Street	PRODUCT	Fixed Rate
	Anytown, ST 12345	LOAN TYPE	☒ Conventional ☐FHA ☐VA ☐_____
PROPERTY	456 Somewhere Avenue	LOAN ID #	123456789
	Anytown, ST 12345	RATE LOCK	☐ NO ☒ YES, until 4/16/2013 at 5:00 p.m. EDT
SALE PRICE	$180,000		

*Before closing, your interest rate, points, and lender credits can change unless you lock the interest rate. All other estimated closing costs expire on **3/4/2013** at 5:00 p.m. EDT*

Loan Terms

		Can this amount increase after closing?
Loan Amount	$162,000	**NO**
Interest Rate	3.875%	**NO**
Monthly Principal & Interest *See Projected Payments below for your Estimated Total Monthly Payment*	$761.78	**NO**
		Does the loan have these features?
Prepayment Penalty		**YES** • As high as $3,240 if you pay off the loan during the first 2 years
Balloon Payment		**NO**

Projected Payments

Payment Calculation	Years 1-7	Years 8-30
Principal & Interest	$761.78	$761.78
Mortgage Insurance	+ 82	+ —
Estimated Escrow *Amount can increase over time*	+ 206	+ 206
Estimated Total Monthly Payment	**$1,050**	**$968**

		This estimate includes	In escrow?
Estimated Taxes, Insurance & Assessments *Amount can increase over time*	$206 a month	☒ Property Taxes	YES
		☒ Homeowner's Insurance	YES
		☐ Other:	
		See Section G on page 2 for escrowed property costs. You must pay for other property costs separately.	

Costs at Closing

Estimated Closing Costs	$8,054	Includes $5,672 in Loan Costs + $2,382 in Other Costs – $0 in Lender Credits. *See page 2 for details.*
Estimated Cash to Close	$16,054	Includes Closing Costs. *See Calculating Cash to Close on page 2 for details.*

Visit **www.consumerfinance.gov/mortgage-estimate** for general information and tools.

REAL ESTATE BASICS AT A GLANCE

The new Dodd-Frank real estate rules do not apply to home equity loans, reverse mortgages, or mortgages for mobile homes.

The new rules also apply to loan types not previously covered by TILA requirements, including:

- Construction loans,
- Loans secured by vacant land, and
- Trusts established for estate planning.

The new rules are provided by the Consumer Financial Protection Bureau, an independent agency of the U.S. government, and are available online and in print. However, the printed version runs to 91 pages, so instead of reproducing the entire handout here, we will examine parts of it that have a direct bearing to financing and mortgages. For instance, on page 22 of the "TILA-RESPA Integrated Disclosure Rule" (a copy of which is provided in the online resources, available at the product page that accompanies this text), the agency discusses the requirements of the new Loan Estimate disclosure form.

The requirements of the Loan Estimate disclosure form include the following:

- It must provide information about credit costs,
- It must provide information about transaction terms,
- It must provide all information in writing, and
- It must conform to U.S.C.A. §1026.37.

The Loan Estimate must be delivered to the consumer three business days before the closing and it must contain precise and accurate information about:

- Projected payments, and
- Costs at closing.

The second page of the Loan Estimate requires that creditors must provide closing cost information including the Good Faith Estimate (GFE) and a section called "Calculating Cash to Close" and additional information including:

- Adjustable Payment Table for adjustable rate mortgages, and
- Adjustable Interest Rate also for adjustable rate mortgages.

Under the new rules, "loan costs" include any payments by the borrower made to the creditor or third party to originate the loan. "Other costs" include taxes and recording fees. When state law requires additional disclosures, they must be added to the new forms. The Loan Estimate must also contain contact information, comparison tables for various payment options, and a signature provision.

Under the rules, the various new disclosure requirements are triggered when the consumer completes an application for a loan. The Dodd-Frank bill is even specific about what is and what is not considered to be an application. For example, to be considered an application, Dodd-Frank requires six items:

1 Consumer's name
2 Consumer's income
3 Social Security number (for purposes of ordering a credit report)
4 Property address
5 Estimate of the value of the property
6 Mortgage amount sought

There are provisions that allow creditors to request additional information, but these six items must be provided. Lenders are not allowed to get around the six pieces of information by requiring something else and therefore not providing a Loan Estimate. Dodd-Frank also requires that consumers receive a special information booklet about borrowing, including home equity lines of credit.

Can a Consumer Waive the Three-Day Requirement? There are provisions that allow the consumer/borrower to waive the three-day requirement, but only when there is a bona fide financial emergency. The consumer must give a written statement to the creditor explaining the financial emergency, specifically stating that he or she is waiving the three-day requirement. The letter must be signed by the consumer. A bona fide financial emergency is limited to situations where the consumer is facing foreclosure or some other equally disastrous financial issue. It is not a financial emergency that the consumer is behind on paying his or her bills or that the consumer has no money in savings. In this case, emergency means some pending legal action that could affect the consumer's legal rights.

Fees Under Dodd-Frank. In the past, lenders have charged borrowers a wide variety of fees, some of which could be negotiated, some which could not. Under the new legislation, no fees can be imposed on the borrower until the borrower has received the Loan Estimate and he or she has indicated that they wish to proceed with the loan process. In addition, Dodd-Frank also limits imposing fees on:

Lenders are still authorized to charge reasonable credit report fees under Dodd-Frank.

- Applications,
- Appraisals, and
- Underwriting.

ii. Potential Problems Under Dodd-Frank

The most problematic aspect of the new rules and regulations under Dodd-Frank is not that all this information must be provided to consumers. In one form or another all of this information has been provided to borrowers before — although the new rules expand greatly on the basic information that must be provided to consumers. The issue is the timing. The new rules require that this information be delivered to the consumer three business days before the scheduled closing. If it is sent by mail, then it must be deposited into the U.S. mail no later than seven business days before the closing. The only exception to the minimum requirements is when the consumer has what the law considers to be a financial emergency, such as pending foreclosure.

Real estate professionals must comply with these new rules concerning disclosures, but in the past, the typical approach has been to get this information to the consumer as soon as possible, but with some information, especially related to last-minute adjustments to closing numbers, only received on the day of the closing, sometimes within minutes of the closing. The new rules mandate three business days, and that could mean a radical restructuring of how lenders process their loans as well as how closings are handled in the future.

iii. Violations of Dodd-Frank

If the ultimate charges paid are greater than those provided in the Loan Estimate, then the creditor is considered not to have acted in good faith. It is good faith if the final charges are less than the estimate. Obviously, creditors will overestimate loan closing charges to avoid this particular part of the law. We will discuss the implications of the new rules on real estate closings in Chapter 13.

REAL WORLD PERSPECTIVES: *REAL ESTATE PARALEGAL*

There is so much wire transfer fraud in real estate financing, that it is horrifying. That's one reason why we use the encrypted email. All of our emails have a disclaimer at the bottom that says if you received wiring instructions from our firm, you must call to confirm. It just explains that fraud is happening everywhere.

— S. C., real estate paralegal

REAL
ESTATE
BASICS AT
A GLANCE

Federal Truth in Lending laws require that consumers and borrowers receive specific information about mortgages and other loans.

---

b. Real Estate Settlement Procedures Act

Although we discuss the Real Estate Settlement Procedures Act (RESPA) in greater detail in Chapter 13, it is important to point out that RESPA plays an important role when it comes to mortgage financing. Like other aspects of real estate financing, RESPA has been substantially altered by the Dodd-Frank Act. We discuss those changes in depth in Chapter 12.

THE LEGAL REQUIREMENTS OF
A MORTGAGE/DEED OF TRUST

Mortgages all share some common features: Regardless of the terms, a borrower (the mortgagor) transfers rights to the lender (the mortgagee) in exchange for money. In this example, there are two parties: the borrower and the bank. However, there is another type of financial arrangement that is popular in many states that involves three parties: the deed of trust.

A. MORTGAGES VERSUS DEEDS OF TRUST

In most situations there is no practical difference between a mortgage and a deed of trust. They are both financial arrangements used to finance the purchase of real estate. However, there are a few important differences to note.

Unlike mortgages, which usually only have two parties, the lender and the borrower, a **deed of trust** has three parties: the lender, the borrower, and the trustee. In this arrangement, the trustee acts as an intermediary between the borrower and the lender. When the deed of trust is created, the borrower transfers rights to the trustee, who holds them for the lender, unlike a mortgage relationship, in which the borrower transfers these rights directly to the lender. In the event of a default by the borrower, the trustee acts on behalf of the lender to institute foreclosure.

Deed of trust
A type of real estate financing in which a lender and a borrower authorize a third party, the trustee, to act on their behalf in the event of a loan default.

The deed of trust arrangement is only followed in a few states, but it does offer significant advantages over mortgages, at least from the bank's perspective. The advantage of a deed of trust arrangement is that the process of foreclosure is more streamlined and requires less contact with the legal system than does the foreclosure of a mortgage. As we will see later in this chapter, foreclosing a mortgage can be a time- and money-consuming enterprise. Instead of the several months of civil actions a bank must endure before foreclosing on a mortgage, however, a trustee can begin a foreclosure action as soon as the bank determines that the borrower is in default. The only requirement is a notice of sale and a brief hearing before the local clerk of court.

Deeds of trust are popular in such states as Virginia and North Carolina.

Deeds of trust and mortgages closely resemble each other.

REAL
ESTATE
BASICS AT
A GLANCE

B. THE ELEMENTS OF A MORTGAGE

Although there are important differences between mortgages and deeds of trust when it comes to foreclosure, they share many of the same elements when it comes to other aspects. In this next section, we do not make any distinction between mortgages and deeds of trusts when discussing their components. For the sake of clarity, we will use the term "mortgage" here to describe both.

Whether a financing arrangement is deemed a deed of trust or a mortgage, some basic elements apply to each. These elements include:

1 The mortgage must be in writing.
2 The parties must be properly identified by name.
3 The mortgage must contain specific clauses, such as:
    ▪ Property as collateral,
    ▪ Promissory note,
    ▪ Granting clause,
    ▪ Description of the debt,
    ▪ Power of sale provision,
    ▪ Provisions for taxes and insurance,
    ▪ Estoppel certificate,
    ▪ Acceleration clause,
    ▪ Due on sale clause,
    ▪ Interest escalation clause,
    ▪ Prepayment clause, and
    ▪ Attorney's fees.

1. MORTGAGES MUST BE IN WRITING

In our discussion of deeds in the last chapter, we pointed out that each state has a version of the Statute of Frauds. This statute requires that certain types of contracts must be in writing before a court will enforce them (see Figure 9-5 for an example). As we saw in that chapter, any contract that conveys a real estate interest must be in writing. Because mortgages involve the transfer of real estate rights between the borrower and the lender, the mortgage must be in writing to be enforceable.

Mortgages are often filed with general warranty deeds. The general warranty deed conveys fee simple title to the buyer, and the contemporaneous filing of the mortgage assures that no other claim will have priority over the mortgage holder. We discuss the issue of priority in greater detail later in this chapter.

FIGURE 9-5

Florida Statute Requiring Mortgages to Be in Writing

A debtor may not maintain an action on a credit agreement unless the agreement is in writing, expresses consideration, sets forth the relevant terms and conditions, and is signed by the creditor and the debtor.[3]

2. THE PARTIES MUST BE IDENTIFIED

Just as we saw in our discussion of deeds, the parties to a mortgage must be identified. The borrower's name must be listed in order to bind him to the agreement, and the lender's name must appear in order to substantiate its claim on the collateral.

3. SPECIFIC CLAUSES IN MORTGAGES

In addition to the general requirements of writing and identified parties, mortgages have several other clauses that are required in order to make the document binding on all parties. The first of these requirements is that the property must be listed as collateral for the loan.

a. Property as Collateral

Collateral is the security for a loan. When a borrower defaults on a loan, the lender is authorized to seize the collateral in lieu of further payments. Although lenders can routinely repossess personal property posted as collateral for a loan, the situation is more complicated when real property is the loan collateral. In that situation, the lender must institute foreclosure proceedings.

Collateral
Any type of asset that is used to secure a loan.

b. Promissory Note

A **promissory note** is a borrower's agreement to repay a specific amount of money. Promissory notes are seen in a wide variety of loan agreements, and they all have the same elements:

Promissory note
A written document that binds the borrower to pay a specific amount at a specific time.

- The borrower agrees to repay a specific sum.
- The note sets out the terms of the indebtedness.
- The note bears the borrower's signature.

Mortgages should contain specific details about the amount that has been borrowed, including the interest rate, the total amount to be repaid (including interest payments), and the total term of the mortgage.

All mortgages must contain a promissory note, or a promise to pay back a specific amount, before they will be considered legally sufficient.

REAL
ESTATE
BASICS AT
A GLANCE

---

c. Granting Clause

We have already encountered granting clauses in our discussion on deeds. There we saw that a granting clause indicates the parties' intentions to transfer rights. The granting clause in a mortgage serves a similar purpose. Here, it substantiates the borrower's intention of transferring the right to foreclose to the lender in exchange for the money provided for the purchase of the real estate.

d. Description of the Debt

The law is flexible about how the debt is described. The parties are free to negotiate their own terms, and courts will not interfere with their negotiations unless they are clearly insufficient. Although the debt terms can be described somewhat loosely, there must be sufficient specificity to identify the amount borrowed, the collateral for the loan, and the terms of repayment.

e. Power of Sale Provision

The power of sale provision authorizes the lender to begin foreclosure proceedings in the event of loan default. The lender can auction off the property for the total debt owed by the borrower. If this provision is missing, the lender has no right to institute a foreclosure action.

f. Taxes and Insurance

The lender may also require as a condition of the mortgage that the borrower pay all taxes and assessments made on the property. Because property can be auctioned off by the local government for failure to pay real estate taxes, lenders require the borrower to keep all tax payments current. The mortgage also provides the lender with the authority to pay the taxes for the borrower in order to stave off further action and to assess these fees back against the borrower.

In addition to taxes, the borrower must also maintain hazard insurance on the premises. The insurance will pay the balance of the loan in the event that the house is destroyed.

g. Estoppel Certificate

Estoppel certificate
The borrower's acknowledgment of the total amount borrowed in the mortgage.

An **estoppel certificate** is the borrower's certification of the amount that has been borrowed from the lender. This acts as a bar to any claim that the borrower was not aware of the total amount of the loan and also provides additional information about the loan terms.

h. Acceleration Clause

An acceleration clause allows the lender to request payment in full for the entire balance of the loan in the event of the borrower's default. This demand is usually the first step in bringing a foreclosure action. By requesting the entire amount due, the lender is establishing the exact figure owed on the loan. Of course, if the borrower is unable to make regular monthly payments on the loan and has defaulted on the mortgage, it is highly unlikely that he will be able to pay the entire balance.

i. Due on Sale Clause

A due on sale clause requires payment of the entire loan balance in the event that title to the property shifts to another individual. This provision bars a borrower from transferring title to the premises as a way of avoiding responsibility for the debt, or more likely, to have someone else take over payments on a mortgage. The due on sale provision requires the payment of the entire loan balance before title can change hands.

j. Interest Escalation Clause

The interest escalation clause allows the lender to increase the amount of interest charges on the loan when it goes into default. The provisions allowing interest escalation must appear in the mortgage and cannot violate other state or federal laws concerning maximum permissible annual percentage rates.

k. Prepayment Clause

The prepayment clause specifies how payments on the loan will be assessed. For instance, if the borrower overpays on his monthly mortgage payment, the prepayment clause may dictate that the overage must be applied to the principal, instead of future interest payments. There are also important federal laws that bear on the issue of prepayment, which we discuss in greater detail in Chapter 13.

l. Attorney's Fees

The attorney's fees provision authorizes the lender to seek reimbursement from the borrower for any legal actions required to foreclose on the loan. These fees can include billing for the attorney's time to institute the foreclosure action and to bring it to a successful conclusion.

C. RECORDING MORTGAGES

In the previous chapter we discussed the role of recording statutes regarding deeds. The same recording statutes also govern mortgages. The general rule, "first in time — first in line," applies in almost all scenarios. Under this rule, the first mortgage recorded receives the highest level of priority. This means that, in the event of a foreclosure or other judgment, this mortgage will be paid before any others.

Priority is an important issue when dealing with mortgages for a very practical reason: If there is more than one claim on real estate, the claim-holder who has the highest priority will be paid first. Only after this claim is paid in full will other claims be paid. Because of this rule, lenders are always eager to file their mortgages contemporaneously with the general warranty deed in the transaction. This gives the lender the highest priority against any other claims that might be brought on the property.

There are times when the parties can alter the rules about priority. Suppose, for example, that the parties are in agreement that a mortgage that is subordinate to another mortgage can simply change places. This would give the formerly subordinate mortgage a higher priority. Why would the parties agree to such an action?

OWNER FINANCING

Maria has advertised her house for sale. Her asking price is $125,000. In her advertisement, she includes the following language: "Owner financing possible." Kendra sees the ad and contacts Maria. Maria presents the following terms: She will "take back" $10,000 as an owner-financed mortgage as long as Kendra can get the balance of the mortgage from another lender. The advantage of this arrangement is that when Kendra approaches a local bank to seek a mortgage, she will only be requesting to borrow $115,000 on a house that is worth $125,000. This should help Kendra qualify for a mortgage more easily. However, the lender has some concerns, not the least of which is the priority of the mortgages. Because Maria is providing a purchase-money mortgage in the amount of $10,000, her mortgage will take priority over the lender's loan, even though the bank is providing most of the purchase price. The lender insists on a subordination agreement before it will provide the purchase price to Kendra. Maria agrees to subordinate her mortgage to the lender's mortgage, and the sale goes through.

TYPES OF MORTGAGES

There are many different types of mortgages, with new variations created almost daily. However, we can organize the vast field of mortgages into two basic categories: fixed-rate and adjustable-rate.

A. FIXED-RATE MORTGAGES

Fixed-rate mortgages are the more traditional type of mortgage. In a fixed-rate mortgage, all terms remain the same throughout the loan repayment period. The term of the loan is usually 30 years, and the monthly payment and interest rate remain constant over the entire life of the loan. Fixed-rate mortgages are attractive to many borrowers because they are predictable. The borrower will always know exactly what his monthly payment will be and can refer to an amortization schedule to see how each monthly payment is apportioned between interest payments and principal reduction.

1. ADVANTAGES AND DISADVANTAGES OF FIXED-RATE MORTGAGES

However, along with the advantages (listed in Figure 9-6), there are also some disadvantages to fixed-rate mortgages. Their biggest disadvantage is that if the borrower gets his mortgage when interest rates are high, those rates will remain with the loan, even when interest rates fall for new loans.

Banks and other lenders usually offer incentives for first-time buyers, such as fixed-rate mortgages with financing up to 95 percent of the purchase price. This means that the buyers will only have to come up with 5 percent of the purchase price from their own funds.

FIGURE 9-6

Benefits of Fixed-Rate Mortgages

- They are inflation-proof: Monthly payments remain the same for the life of the loan, regardless of what happens to interest rates.
- They help with long-term planning: Borrowers can predict exactly what their payments will be and how long it will take to pay off the mortgage.
- They are low risk: The chances of the lender going into bankruptcy are virtually zero, because most lenders are backed by agencies such as the FDIC, Fannie Mae, or Ginnie Mae.

2. AMORTIZATION

The month-by-month allocation of a mortgage payment to the interest charges and outstanding principal is called an amortization schedule. **Amortization** refers to the process of balancing out payments on the loan principal with payments on the interest. Amortization can be arranged in any number of ways. For instance, the lender might simply apply 50 percent of each payment to the principal and 50 percent to the interest charge. However, most lenders use a different approach. Instead of balancing each payment over the life of the loan, banks vary the percentage of payment, weighing early payments toward interest and later payments toward principal. Banks realize that most people sell their homes in seven years or less, and skewing the payments in this way maximizes the bank's profits. See Figure 9-7 for some examples of fixed-rate mortgage interest rates.

Amortization
The gradual paying down and elimination of a debt through an application of payments toward both principal and interest.

When economic times are good and interest rates are low, fixed-rate mortgages are the most popular choice for borrowers.

REAL ESTATE BASICS AT A GLANCE

FIGURE 9-7

Examples of Fixed-Rate Mortgages

With a maximum borrow amount of $349,999:
- Conventional 30-years fixed has a rate of 5.875%.
- Conventional 20-years fixed has a rate of 5.75%.
- Conventional 15-years fixed has a rate of 5.625%.
- Conventional 10-years fixed has a rate of 5.625%.

B. ADJUSTABLE-RATE MORTGAGES

Unlike fixed-rate mortgages, adjustable-rate mortgages have one or more terms that fluctuate over time. The most common example of an adjustable-rate mortgage is one in which the interest rate fluctuates according to a predetermined formula. An adjustable-rate mortgage might be based on any index, but many are based on the national prime lending rate. As this lending rate rises or lowers, so too does the interest rate assessed on the borrower's mortgage.

1. ADVANTAGES AND DISADVANTAGES OF ADJUSTABLE-RATE MORTGAGES

Adjustable-rate mortgages are extremely attractive when the economy is uncertain and the possibility of rapid interest rate changes makes the logic of obtaining a fixed-rate mortgage questionable.

Adjustable-rate mortgages often have interest rates that are lower than the rates available for fixed-rate mortgages.

Adjustable-rate mortgages are also good alternatives for individuals whose income may vary over time. If the borrower believes that he will be making more money in the next few years, an adjustable-rate mortgage might make a great deal of sense. After all, if the borrower's salary increases, he can afford higher monthly mortgage payments should the adjustable rate climb.

There are a wide variety of formats for adjustable-rate mortgages. They usually come in variations such as 3/27, 5/25, and others. The first number before the slash refers to the number of years that the rate may adjust before being locked in. Most adjustable-rate mortgages have provisions that allow for adjustable rates for only a percentage of the total life of the loan. When that point is reached, the adjustable-rate mortgage converts into a fixed-rate mortgage.

The feature that makes an adjustable-rate mortgage so attractive can also be a substantial downside. If the index on which the adjustable-rate mortgage is based increases over time, this means that the interest rate charged to the borrower also increases. This will result in either a higher mortgage payment per month, or if the payment is fixed, less money going toward paying off the principal and more going toward paying the interest charges. One way of avoiding dramatic shifts in interest rates over time is through the use of rate caps.

2. RATE CAPS

All adjustable-rate mortgages have rate caps. Sometimes known as "ceilings" or "floors," these are limitations on the degree of change that an adjustable-rate mortgage can undergo in a particular time frame. For instance, an adjustable-rate mortgage might come with a 1 percent cap. This means that during a specified period, the most that the interest rate could change either upward or downward is 1 percent. Many adjustable-rate mortgages also have lifetime caps that limit the total amount that the interest rate can change during the course of the loan. Rate caps help provide some measure of predictability to mortgages that are, by their very nature, variable.

C. OTHER TYPES OF MORTGAGES

In addition to fixed-rate mortgages and adjustable-rate mortgages, there are numerous other types of real estate financing available. They include:

- Purchase-money mortgages,
- Wraparound mortgages,
- Second mortgages,
- Equity lines of credit, and
- Bridge loans.

1. PURCHASE-MONEY MORTGAGES

Purchase-money mortgages are commonly seen in "owner financing." When a seller advertises his house for sale and includes a provision that allows for owner financing, it means that the owner is offering to finance part of the sale. The buyer could then obtain another mortgage for the remaining balance of the sale price. Owners typically offer some percentage of the total sale price under owner financing terms, meaning that the buyer would make two mortgage payments: one to the seller and another to the bank. Here, a purchase-money mortgage literally allows the purchase of the property through an owner-financed mortgage.

Purchase-money mortgages can also come in other forms, such as installment contracts. In this arrangement, the seller retains title to the property until the borrower makes the final payment. When that final payment is made, the seller transfers the title to the borrower.

2. WRAPAROUND MORTGAGES

A wraparound mortgage consists of two mortgages. Suppose that the seller has a mortgage that is a non-qualifying assumable loan with a favorable interest rate. The buyer would like to take over that loan, but the amount owed does not reflect the actual sale price. In this situation, the buyer would obtain another mortgage that would encompass the terms of the first and make up the difference between the original mortgage and the new sale price. The buyer would then make one mortgage payment, and this payment would be divided between the two mortgages.

NON-QUALIFYING ASSUMABLE LOAN   `EXAMPLE 9-3`

Sue purchased her home 15 years ago. She has a 30-year non-qualifying assumable loan at a 1 percent interest rate. Paula wants to buy Sue's home and likes the fact that she can take over the payments on Sue's mortgage. However, Sue currently owes $15,000 on that loan, and the sale price of the home is $50,000. Paula can take over the payments on the first loan, but she will still need to come up with an additional $35,000 to meet Sue's price for the property. Paula goes to a bank and obtains a loan for $35,000, creating a wraparound mortgage that allows her to keep the original loan and make payments on both.

These days, the chances of coming across a non-qualifying assumable loan are very slim. Banks and other lenders have slowly weeded out these loans to avoid the precise circumstance set out in the example above.

3. SECOND MORTGAGES

A second mortgage isn't really a mortgage in the conventional sense. So far, our discussion of mortgages has focused on the initial financing necessary to purchase property. A second mortgage, however, allows the current owner the chance to borrow against the equity that he has built up over time. Suppose that the homeowner has been making regular monthly payments on the property for 10 or more years. The homeowner's payments have been steadily reducing the outstanding principal on the loan — but the situation has not remained static. In those 10 years, the house may have appreciated in value considerably. In fact, most homes appreciate about 6 percent in value each year. The difference between the value of the home and the amount owed on it is equity.

An owner can borrow against that equity, taking out money to use for additional improvements on the property, college tuition, or any other purpose. The advantage of taking out a second mortgage on a home is that this second mortgage usually enjoys the same advantages as the first mortgage: The homeowner can deduct the amount of interest payments from his personal income tax return. However, the disadvantages apply with the same force: A lender is permitted to foreclose on a second mortgage just as easily as it can foreclose on a first mortgage.

4. EQUITY LINES OF CREDIT

An equity line of credit is a variation on a second mortgage. In this scenario, the owner negotiates a new loan using the accumulated equity in his home as collateral. However, instead of taking out a specific amount, the owner negotiates a possible maximum and then has the option of withdrawing that amount in smaller increments. An equity line of credit can function like a second bank account, acting as a financial reserve that the owner can tap into whenever he has monetary needs. Like any other form of mortgage, an equity line of credit can result in foreclosure if the borrower defaults on the loan.

5. BRIDGE LOANS

Bridge loan
A loan arrangement where a short-term loan is offered by a lender that anticipates a future event, such as selling one home and waiting to purchase another or buying vacant land and then completing a home on the site.

There are times when both borrowers and lenders have short-term objectives in financing. A borrower may want sufficient money to buy and build on unimproved property, but no long-term plans. In this situation, the borrowers might apply for a **bridge loan**. A bridge loan gives the borrower enough money to purchase the property and build on it and then to either convert to a different loan or to sell the property to another. Bridge loans often have short life spans, some as short as 12 to 24 months. The interest rate is higher, but the borrower is willing to put up with that because the project is short term, and when it is complete the borrower will either sell the property or arrange for different financing with better interest rates and repayment provisions.

QUALIFYING FOR A MORTGAGE

When a borrower approaches a bank to obtain financing, there are several important steps that occur. The borrower will fill out an application (see Figure 9-8 for an example), and part of that application will provide personal information about the borrower that the bank can use to evaluate the risks of lending money to him. The process of evaluating risk is referred to as underwriting. This is an area where Dodd-Frank has made substantial inroads. Under the Act, banks have been forced to tighten their criteria for granting loans to consumers. For example, a lender must be able to certify that a potential borrower is capable of repaying the loan.

FIGURE 9-8

Uniform Residential Loan Application: Fannie Mae (First Page Only)

To be completed by the Lender:
Lender Loan No./Universal Loan Identifier _____ Agency Case No. _____

Uniform Residential Loan Application

Verify and complete the information on this application.
information as directed by your Lender.

Section 1: Borrower Information. This section asks about your personal information and your income from employment and other sources, such as retirement, that you want considered to qualify for this loan.

1a. Personal Information

Name *(First, Middle, Last, Suffix)* _____

Alternate Names – *List any names by which you are known or any names under which credit was previously received (First, Middle, Last, Suffix)*

Social Security Number ____ – ____ – _____
(or Individual Taxpayer Identification Number)

Date of Birth   **Citizenship**
(mm/dd/yyyy)   ○ U.S. Citizen
____ / ____ / _____   ○ Permanent Resident Alien
                                ○ Non-Permanent Resident Alien

Type of Credit
○ I am applying for **individual credit.**
○ I am applying for **joint credit.** Total Number of Borrowers: _
  Each Borrower intends to apply for joint credit. **Your initials:** _____

List Name(s) of Other Borrower(s) Applying for this Loan
(First, Middle, Last, Suffix) Use a separator between names

Marital Status   **Dependents** *(not listed by another Borrower)*
○ Married   Number __
○ Separated   Ages _____
○ Unmarried
  (Single, Divorced, Widowed, Civil Union, Domestic Partnership, Registered Reciprocal Beneficiary Relationship)

Contact Information
Home Phone (____) ____ – _____
Cell Phone (____) ____ – _____
Work Phone (____) ____ – _____   Ext. _____
Email _____

Current Address
Street _____ Unit # _____
City _____ State _____ ZIP _____ Country _____
How Long at Current Address? ___ Years ___ Months **Housing** ○ No primary housing expense ○ Own ○ Rent ($ _____ /month)

If at Current Address for LESS than 2 years, list Former Address ☐ *Does not apply*
Street _____ Unit # _____
City _____ State _____ ZIP _____ Country _____
How Long at Former Address? ___ Years ___ Months **Housing** ○ No primary housing expense ○ Own ○ Rent ($ _____ /month)

Mailing Address – *if different from Current Address* ☐ *Does not apply*
Street _____ Unit # _____
City _____ State _____ ZIP _____ Country _____

1b. Current Employment/Self-Employment and Income   ☐ *Does not apply*

Employer or Business Name _____ Phone (____) ____ – _____
Street _____ Unit # _____
City _____ State _____ ZIP _____ Country _____

Position or Title _____
Start Date ____ / ____ / _____ *(mm/dd/yyyy)*
How long in this line of work? ___ Years ___ Months

☐ **Check if you are the Business Owner or Self-Employed**
○ I have an ownership share of less than 25%.
○ I have an ownership share of 25% or more.

Check if this statement applies:
☐ I am employed by a family member, property seller, real estate agent, or other party to the transaction.

Monthly Income (or Loss)
$ _____

Gross Monthly Income
Base	$ _____	/month
Overtime	$ _____	/month
Bonus	$ _____	/month
Commission	$ _____	/month
Military Entitlements	$ _____	/month
Other	$ _____	/month
TOTAL	$ _____	/month

Uniform Residential Loan Application
Freddie Mac Form 65 • Fannie Mae Form 1003
Effective 1/2021

(The entire form is available in the online resources, available at the product page that accompanies this text.)

A. UNDERWRITING

Before any lending institution loans money to a borrower, it must evaluate the risk of the investment. Underwriters are professionals who review a borrower's history, credit rating, current income, and other factors to determine how much of a risk a particular borrower is. If the risk is acceptable, the underwriters approve the loan. If the borrower has a bad credit history or other negative factors, the underwriters will not approve the loan.

Underwriting is all about assessing potential risks to the lender. In order to fully evaluate the potential risk of a mortgage loan, the lender must know a great deal about both the borrower and the property. Evaluating the borrower centers on reviewing the borrower's credit history. Evaluating the property involves appraisals and inspections.

B. BORROWER'S CREDIT HISTORY

One of the most important elements in underwriting is evaluating the potential risk of foreclosure if the lender enters into a mortgage arrangement with the borrower. One way of evaluating that risk is to review the borrower's credit history. Credit histories are maintained by consumer reporting agencies, such as credit bureaus.

1. CONSUMER REPORTING AGENCIES

Consumer reporting agencies (CRA) are in the business of compiling information about anyone who might apply for any type of credit. Whenever a person applies for a credit card, a personal loan, or even insurance, a file is created in a CRA database. These companies are in the business of selling this information to merchants so that they can make informed decisions about the people to whom they should extend credit. Consumer reporting agencies fall under the jurisdiction of the Fair Credit Reporting Act.

2. THE FAIR CREDIT REPORTING ACT

The Fair Credit Reporting Act (FCRA) was designed to improve the accuracy and privacy of credit reports. It imposes specific responsibilities on consumer credit reporting agencies such as Equifax and Experian. The act gives consumers the right to know exactly what is in their credit reports. Credit reporting agencies collect enormous amounts of information, including the consumer's name, birth date, Social Security number, places of employment, payment histories, addresses where the consumer has lived in recent years, and a great deal of additional information besides. Credit reports may also contain information from the public record, such as tax liens, judgments, bankruptcies, and foreclosures.

Lenders use information provided by credit bureaus to assess a potential borrower before entering into a loan agreement with him. The credit report plays a

significant role in this process. However, it is not the only element that lenders use in order to assess the potential risk of an investment. Lenders also insist on appraisals.

3. POINTS

Points are fees that mortgage lenders assess against borrowers as part of the loan application process. A point equals 1 percent of the loan balance. Suppose that a borrower has obtained a loan for $100,000 and must pay two points as part of the application fee. The borrower would be obligated to pay a fee of $2,000 in addition to any other fees associated with applying for and obtaining the mortgage. Points are assessed in a wide variety of ways and are often negotiable. Some lenders assess points to justify a lower interest rate on the loan. There are plenty of mortgages where no points are assessed at all, but the interest rate is usually higher. If the borrower has a questionable credit history, he may be required to pay higher points on a mortgage.

C. APPRAISAL

In addition to risk assessment of the individual, the lender will also want an independent analysis of the value of the real estate. This is where an appraiser enters the picture. An appraiser is in the business of providing estimates of the value of homes and real estate. Appraisers inspect the premises, compare it to others with similar features, and reach a consensus about the value of the property under consideration. Some lenders will not loan money unless the appraiser can establish conclusively that the home is worth the amount requested by the borrower. We discuss the role of appraisers in greater detail in Chapter 11.

D. THE RISE OF INTERNET LENDERS

In the era before the Internet, the idea that a lender in one part of the country would finance a home purchase in another part was virtually unheard of. However, the Internet has provided new resources for borrowers. These days, a borrower has the option of going not only to local lenders, but also to online lenders to arrange for mortgages, equity lines of credit, and second mortgages. However, no matter what lender a borrower seeks out, the lender must comply with the provisions of Dodd-Frank.

 ## DISCHARGING A MORTGAGE

The term "discharge" means to satisfy a contractual obligation. A borrower can discharge a mortgage in one of two ways: (1) He can make all monthly payments until the loan amount is paid off, or (2) he can sell the house and pay off the outstanding balance. The second situation is far more common than the first. When we discuss the closing process, we will see how the outstanding mortgage is discharged as part of the real estate settlement.

FORECLOSURE

Although we discussed foreclosure in Chapter 4, it is important to point out some important features of foreclosure as it applies to mortgages and deeds of trust. The process of foreclosure varies from state to state, but there are some general guidelines that are followed in all states. For instance, a foreclosure is authorized when the borrower defaults on the loan. The most common reason to default is failing to make regular monthly payments (see Figure 9-9). When a borrower becomes 90 or 120 days late on a mortgage, the lender is authorized to institute foreclosure proceedings. As we saw earlier in this chapter, the mortgage itself provides the framework for the foreclosure process. There are two general types of foreclosure actions: judicial foreclosure and power of sale foreclosure.

FIGURE 9-9

Most Common Reasons for a Default on a Mortgage

- Failure to make monthly payments,
- Failure to pay property taxes, or
- Failure to obtain hazard insurance.

A. JUDICIAL FORECLOSURE

A judicial foreclosure is the process used in the majority of states. The lender institutes a civil action, after giving notice to the borrower of his default and after demanding the balance of the loan be paid by a specific date. The lender essentially brings a civil complaint against the borrower and requests a judge to rule that the borrower is in default and that the lender has the authority to auction off the property for the outstanding balance on the loan.

B. POWER OF SALE FORECLOSURE

Power of sale foreclosures are seen in states that follow the deed of trust model for financing real estate. The deed of trust contains a provision that allows the trustee to institute foreclosure proceedings and initiate an auction once apprised of the borrower's default by the lender. Power of sale foreclosures have several distinct advantages over judicial foreclosures. For one thing, these types of foreclosures do not require a judicial proceeding. In order to conduct a foreclosure under power of sale, the trustee must give notice of default to the borrower, advertise the auction for a specified number of weeks in the local paper, and then conduct the auction on the courthouse steps. Many would argue that the reason for the continued viability of deeds of trust is that they offer lenders expedited foreclosures.

C. THE FORECLOSURE AUCTION

Foreclosure sales must be held in the county where the property is located. When the day for the auction arrives, the bank's representative will read out the foreclosure notice. These auctions often occur at the entrance to the courthouse, although there are provisions that allow them to be held at the property as well. Many individuals attend foreclosure auctions in hopes of purchasing a property well below fair market value; however, the chances that a prime piece of real estate will sell for pennies on the dollar is more urban myth than reality. Usually there are plenty of bidders on choice real estate, and they will bid up the price until someone prevails.

Once the auction is completed, the lender will take its outstanding debt from the sale price. If the auction resulted in more money than the lender was owed, the balance will go to the former owner. If the auction failed to bring in enough money to satisfy the mortgage, the lender may institute a deficiency action against the former owner for the balance. The chances of succeeding on such an action are usually slim.

D. DECREASING FORECLOSURE RATES

In 2007 and 2008, many lenders began noting an increase in foreclosure rates. However, the market has bounced back in recent years, with foreclosure rates flattening out from sharp upward trends. These days, foreclosure rates have dropped back to their more or less traditional small percentage of overall loans.

Many point to questionable lending practices by marginal lenders as a cause of the Great Recession. Conventional wisdom points to lowered underwriting standards by greedy companies eager to cash in on the booming real estate market. These companies offered attractive terms with uglier terms buried in fine print. Some companies have come under government scrutiny for a wide range of questionable — if not illegal — practices, such as disguising interest rates, balloon payments, and excessive fees. These practices were among the many reasons why Dodd-Frank was enacted in 2010 in hopes of avoiding a similar real estate disaster in the future.

Case Excerpt

MOHANNA v. WELLS FARGO BANK, N.A.
No. 21-cv-03797-DMR (D.C.N.D., 2021)

DONNA M. RYU, United States Magistrate Judge

Plaintiff Keyhan Mohanna, representing himself, filed this case on May 20, 2021. Docket No. 1 ("Compl."). He brings claims for wrongful foreclosure and violation of California Commercial Code §3302 et seq. against Defendant Wells Fargo Bank, N.A. ("Wells Fargo"). Jurisdiction is based on diversity. Wells Fargo moves to dismiss the complaint. Mohanna opposes. The court held a hearing on August 26, 2021. Mohanna did not appear at the hearing.

For the reasons stated below, the motion is granted.

I. Background

The following facts are alleged in the complaint. On December 21, 2006, Mohanna took out a loan from World Savings Bank, FSB ("WSB"). The loan was secured by a deed of trust recorded against real property located at 1405 Greenwich Street, Unit #1, San Francisco, CA 94109. WSB later became Wachovia Mortgage, FSB, which was in turn acquired by Wells Fargo. However, Mohanna alleges that when Wells Fargo "acquired the remaining assets of Wachovia, it did not include Plaintiff's debt obligation." This is because Wachovia allegedly transferred the debt to a mortgage pass-through certificate prior to Wells Fargo acquiring Wachovia.

Mohanna fell behind in payments on the loan due to the financial crash in 2007 and 2008. On February 12, 2010, Wells Fargo recorded a Notice of Default on the loan. Wells Fargo proceeded with a non-judicial foreclosure against the subject property on July 25, 2014. Mohanna asserts that Wells Fargo had no legal right to enforce the deed of trust because it never acquired his loan from Wachovia. He alleges that Wells Fargo negligently and/or fraudulently filed false records in order to complete the foreclosure on the property, even though it knew it was not entitled to enforce the deed of trust. Mohanna also alleges that, despite exercising reasonable diligence, he could not have discovered Wells Fargo's unlawful conduct.

Mohanna brings claims for wrongful foreclosure and violation of California Commercial Code §3302 et seq.

Discussion

Wells Fargo moves to dismiss Mohanna's claims for wrongful foreclosure and violation of California Commercial Code §3302. For the reasons explained below, the court finds that Mohanna's claims for wrongful foreclosure and section 3302 are untimely. It is therefore unnecessary to reach Wells Fargo's remaining arguments.

A. Wrongful Foreclosure

Under California law, a plaintiff bringing a claim for wrongful foreclosure must establish that "(1) the trustee or mortgagee caused an illegal, fraudulent, or willfully oppressive sale of real property pursuant to a power of sale in a mortgage or deed of trust; (2) the party attacking the sale . . . was prejudiced or harmed; and (3) in cases where the trustor or mortgagor challenges the sale, the trustor or mortgagor tendered the amount of the secured indebtedness or was excused from tendering." *Sciarratta v. U.S. Bank Nat'l Assn.*, 247 Cal. App. 4th 552, 561-62 (2016). The statute of limitations for wrongful foreclosure based on alleged fraudulent conduct is three years. Cal. Civ. Proc. Code §338(d). A claim brought under section 338(d) "is not deemed to have accrued until the discovery, by the aggrieved party, of the facts constituting the fraud or mistake." *Id.* The tolling of a claim based on a party's lack of knowledge of the factual basis for his claims is known as the "discovery rule." *Fox v. Ethicon Endo-Surgery, Inc.*, 35 Cal. 4th 797, 807 (2005). "A plaintiff discovers, or has reason to discover, a cause of action based on a particular act of wrongdoing by a particular defendant, only when he at least suspects, or has reason to suspect, that act of wrongdoing by that defendant." *Id.* at 812, n. 6.

In this case, it is undisputed that Wells Fargo's alleged wrongful conduct took place more than three years prior to the filing of this complaint. Specifically, Wells Fargo completed a non-judicial foreclosure on the subject property on July 25, 2014, but Mohanna did not file this case until nearly seven years later on May 20, 2021. Thus, the only remaining question is whether Mohanna has adequately pleaded that the discovery rule should apply to toll his wrongful foreclosure claim. The court concludes that he has not. The complaint generically alleges that tolling should apply in this case because

Mohanna "could not have discovered, and did not discover, and was prevented from discovering, the wrongdoing complained of herein." These allegations are entirely conclusory. Mohanna's opposition merely repeats the conclusory statements in his complaint. Mohanna also does not allege when he discovered the factual basis for his claims or explain whether that discovery happened within three years of filing this case.

Moreover, the record establishes that Mohanna cannot amend his complaint to cure this defect. Mohanna brought a similar action against Wells Fargo in the key period during which he purportedly was unable to discover the facts constituting the alleged fraud by Wells Fargo. On December 10, 2014, Mohanna filed a case against Wells Fargo in the San Francisco Superior Court. Def. RJN, Ex. K. He alleged, among other things, that Wells Fargo wrongfully foreclosed on the subject property. *Id.* at 3, 16. That wrongful foreclosure claim, like the one Mohanna brings here, was also premised on the theory that WSB and its successors and/or assigns transferred the deed of trust for the subject property to a securitized trust before Wells Fargo acquired WSB, and that as a result, Wells Fargo did not hold a valid deed of trust and was not entitled to enforce the security interest on the property. *Id.* at 8, 15-17. Mohanna also alleged that Wells Fargo "acted with malice, oppression and fraud" in conducting a foreclosure sale to which it was not entitled. *Id.* "While the court cannot accept the veracity of the representations" Mohanna made in the 2014 state court case, "it may properly take judicial notice of the existence of those documents and of the representations having been made therein." *NuCal Foods, Inc. v. Quality Egg LLC*, 887 F. Supp. 2d 977, 984 (E.D. Cal. 2012). Mohanna's allegations in the 2014 case are substantially similar to his factual claims in this case, which definitively undermines his contention that he did not discover the factual basis for his wrongful foreclosure claims within the three-year statute of limitations.

Mohanna also brings a claim under California Commercial Code §3302. This statute "allows the authenticity of an instrument to be questioned if the instrument bears evidence of forgery, alteration, or is otherwise irregular or incomplete." *Martineau v. Fed. Home Loan Mortg., Inc.*, 2012 WL 2529416 (C.D. Cal. July 2, 2012). In this claim, Mohanna appears to assert that Wells Fargo is not a "holder in due course" of the deed of trust as defined under section 3302 and therefore was not entitled to foreclose on Mohanna's property.

Assuming without deciding that a private right of action exists under section 3302, the claim is untimely. Mohanna's section 3302 claim is essentially a predicate to his wrongful foreclosure claim, which the court found to be time-barred. In other words, even if Wells Fargo was not entitled to enforce the deed of trust because it was not a "holder in due course," Mohanna still cannot challenge the foreclosure because the statute of limitations on that claim has passed. This is sufficient to dismiss the section 3302 claim with prejudice.

Accordingly, to the extent it exists, Mohanna's claim for violation of section 3302 fails because it is untimely. Because Mohanna cannot allege additional facts to cure this defect, it is dismissed with prejudice.

IV. Conclusion

For the reasons stated above, Wells Fargo's motion to dismiss is granted and the case is dismissed with prejudice. The Clerk shall enter judgment for Wells Fargo and against Mohanna and close this case.

IT IS SO ORDERED.

QUESTIONS ABOUT THE CASE

1   What is Mohanna's contention in this suit?
2   What must a plaintiff show under California law to establish a case of wrongful foreclosure?
3   Does the court address the wrongful foreclosure or provide a hint about how it would rule if the case had reached the merits on wrongful foreclosure?
4   In the end, why did the court dismiss Mohanna's action?

COVID-19 CONCERN

In many ways, real estate transactions follow patterns set down decades before. One such ritual that is quickly being abandoned is the face-to-face meeting with the loan officer. In the past, potential borrowers would set an appointment at a local bank, meet with a loan officer, and present their documentation for review. Before the pandemic, there were already loan companies and banks that allowed people to apply entirely online. This trend is accelerating under COVID-19. The reality of those old meetings is that the loan officer rarely made the loan decision anyway. The documentation was presented to a board and approved later. These days, the loan documentation is sifted by algorithms, and a determination is made based solely on the numbers — at least at many lending companies. It is almost certain that the human touch — the face-to-face meeting with the loan officer — is going to die a quick death in the face of the COVID-19 pandemic.

CHAPTER SUMMARY

Real estate purchases are financed through the use of mortgages and deeds of trust. Although the issues involved in real estate financing can be complex, the basic arrangement is relatively simple: A borrower applies to a lender for funds that the borrower will use to purchase the real estate. In exchange for these funds, the lender requires that the borrower transfer certain real estate rights to the lender. Among these rights is the right to foreclose on the property if the borrower defaults on the mortgage.

There are two mortgage markets, the primary and secondary. The primary mortgage market consists of lenders who are in the business of loaning funds to individuals to purchase real estate. These lenders can be institutions as varied as banks, savings and loan associations, credit unions, and insurance companies. The secondary mortgage market consists of both governmental and private corporations that are in the business of purchasing mortgages from lenders. The agencies purchase mortgages at a discount from lenders, freeing up funds that the lenders can then use for other mortgages. The secondary mortgage market is a vital component of the American economy and ensures the continued vitality of the American mortgage market.

Whether a particular state follows a mortgage or deed of trust arrangement in real estate financing, the legal elements used to create these documents are generally the same. Mortgages must be in writing, and they must contain specific clauses, including the granting clause, promissory note clause, and power of sale provision. The lender's right to foreclose on the loan is also a common provision found in both mortgages and deeds of trust.

There are numerous types of mortgages, all of which have radically different features. The two broadest categories of mortgages include fixed-rate mortgages and adjustable-rate mortgages. In a fixed-rate mortgage, all of the terms—including interest rate, monthly payment, and borrowed amount—remain the same for the life of the loan. In an adjustable-rate mortgage, on the other hand, one or more of the terms fluctuates. It is very common for adjustable-rate mortgages to have fluctuating interest rates that are indexed to some other figure, such as the national prime lending rate or other national index.

SKILLS YOU NEED IN THE REAL WORLD

Deciphering Mortgages

One the most important skills you can develop in a real estate practice is the ability to locate and decipher mortgage agreements. Because mortgages are recorded, they are a matter of public record. They may be cross-referenced by the borrower's name or by the particular tract index, but whatever method is used in your area, you should spend some time learning how to quickly and efficiently locate them. Once located, you should review the entire mortgage, clause by clause, and decipher the important features of that mortgage, including:

- Default provisions,
- Type of foreclosure authorized,
- Interest and other acceleration clauses, and
- Redemption rights.

This list is not meant to be exhaustive. Most of the features are self-explanatory, except the last one. "Redemption rights" refer to the borrower's ability to redeem or pay off the loan balance at or before the foreclosure auction. Sometimes these redemption rights also give the borrower the right to challenge the foreclosure auction or even to bid at the auction. You should be familiar with all the terms of mortgages in your state and keep a folder of some of the more unusual mortgages that you come in contact with. This will be time well spent and will help you master mortgage law in your state.

ETHICAL ISSUES FOR THE PARALEGAL

Predatory Lending

With the tremendous expansion in the availability of capital funding for all levels of income, there have also been some problems. Unfortunately, some unscrupulous lenders are taking advantage of individuals by engaging in practices that fall under the heading of "predatory lending." These practices continue to exist even in the face of Dodd-Frank and new legislation designed to protect borrowers from such practices. All legal professionals should be aware of predatory lending practices, which can include any of the following:

- Excessive fees to process loan paperwork,
- Excessive interest rates,
- Single-premium credit insurance,
- Loans made to individuals without inquiring into their ability to repay the loan,
- Loan "flipping," or refinancing the same loan several times within a short period of time, or
- Prepayment penalties.[4]

(Dodd-Frank pays particular attention to the issue of prepayment penalties and although they are extremely restricted, this does not stop unethical lenders from attempting to slip them by unwary borrowers.)

Predatory lenders often strip away the one remaining asset that low- and middle-income individuals still have: the equity in their homes. After assessing excessive interest rates, hidden fees, and other penalties, the predatory lender then institutes a foreclosure action against the individual. Legal professionals should work hard to make sure that predatory lenders are reported to the appropriate state and federal agencies and should not work with such lenders not only because of the ethical concerns, but also because predatory lenders are often prosecuted.

KEY TERMS AND CONCEPTS

Amortization	Deed of trust	Mortgage
Collateral	Estoppel certificate	Promissory note

END-OF-CHAPTER EXERCISES

Review Questions

See Appendix for answers

1   How is the secondary mortgage market different from the primary mortgage market?
2   What is Fannie Mae?

3   Explain the significance of the secondary mortgage market.

4   How has Dodd-Frank changed the way that mortgages are granted?

5   What is the difference between a mortgage and a deed of trust?

6   What is a granting clause in a mortgage?

7   What were the reasons for the creation of the Dodd-Frank Act?

8   What is a power of sale provision?

9   What is an estoppel certificate?

10   What are the rules of priority when it comes to mortgages?

11   What is a subordination agreement?

12   What is the difference between a fixed-rate mortgage and an adjustable-rate mortgage?

13   How does Dodd-Frank affect Truth-in-Lending laws?

14   What is a wraparound mortgage?

15   What is mortgage underwriting?

16   What qualifies as a default under a mortgage?

17   What are some of the common reasons for a borrower to default on a mortgage?

18   Explain the difference between judicial and power of sale foreclosure.

19   What is predatory lending?

APPLYING WHAT YOU HAVE LEARNED

1   Does your state allow mortgages, deeds of trust, or both types of real estate financing? What are the advantages of one over the other?

2   Go to your local courthouse, locate a mortgage or deed of trust, and answer the following questions:
-    What is the borrower's full name?
-    What is the lender's name?
-    What is the total amount financed?
-    When is the final payment due?

WEB SURFING

Freddie Mac
http://www.freddiemac.com/index.html

Fannie Mae
http://www.fanniemae.com

The Dodd-Frank Act
http://www.cftc.gov/LawRegulation/DoddFrankAct/index.htm

Experian
http://www.experian.com

Tech Topic
MORTGAGE CALCULATOR

This free online mortgage calculator (http://www .mortgagecalculator.org) asks you to input various mortgage parameters and then generates a great deal of mortgage repayment information in the form of charts, graphs, and numerical figures. The calculator even offers comparisons of different payment schedules, a useful tool in determining how to save money on mortgage repayment.

ANNOTATED DOCUMENT

Residential Mortgage

MORTGAGE

THIS INDENTURE, this the 22nd day of May, 2021, between Homer and Marge Simpson, hereinafter referred to as "Mortgagor," and First National Bank, hereinafter referred to as "Mortgagee," recognizing that for the purpose of this document singular and plural references shall constitute references to the above-named parties and that any gender references also be applied to the individual parties.

WITNESSETH

"NOTE"

WHEREAS, Mortgagor is justly indebted to Mortgagee in the sum of one hundred and forty-nine thousand DOLLARS ($149,000) in U.S. currency and mortgage has and by these presents does agree to repay the same, with interest, according to the terms of said indenture, and by the terms of a note hereinafter referred to as the "Note," given by the Mortgagor to Mortgagee, bearing the date set out below.

DESCRIPTION OF THE PROPERTY SUBJECT TO THE NOTE:

In consideration of the sum set out above in the note provision and the premises that secure such note, Mortgagor has granted, bargained, sold, and conveyed, and by these presents does grant, bargain, sell, and convey, unto Mortgagee a parcel of real estate situated in Springfield County, State of Placid, more particularly described in Exhibit "A" attached hereto and by this reference made a part hereof;

TOGETHER with all buildings, structures, fixtures, and other improvements now or which will hereafter be located on, above, or below the surface of the property described in Exhibit "A," or any part and parcel thereof; and,

TOGETHER with all and singular tenements, hereditaments, easements, riparian and littoral rights, and appurtenances thereunto belonging or in anywise appertaining, whether now owned or hereafter acquired by Mortgagor, and including all rights of ingress and egress to and from adjoining property (whether such rights

The first paragraph identifies the parties to the mortgage.

The second paragraph identifies the amount borrowed for the purchase of the home.

The property is fully described in a separate and attached document (as mentioned in the third paragraph).

currently lender's exist or subsequently arise) together with the reversion or reversions, remainder and remainders, rents, issues, and profits thereof; and also all the rights, titles, interests, claims, and demands whatsoever of Mortgagor of, in, and to the same and of, in, and to every part and parcel thereof; and,

> The parties describe the nature of the lender's interest in the property in the fifth paragraph.

TOGETHER with all the common elements appurtenant to any parcel, unit, or unit which is all or part of the Premises; and,

ALL the foregoing encumbered by this Mortgage being hereinafter referred to as "Premises";

TO HAVE AND TO HOLD the Premises hereby granted to the use, benefit, and behalf of the Mortgagee, forever.

EQUITY OF REDEMPTION

This agreement is subject to the following conditions: If Mortgagor shall promptly pay or cause to be paid to Mortgagee, at its address listed in the Note, or at such other place which may hereafter be designated by Mortgagee, its or their successors or assigns, with interest, the principal sum of one hundred and forty nine thousand DOLLARS ($149,000) with final maturity, if not sooner paid, as stated in said Note unless amended or extended according terms of the Note executed by Mortgagor and payable to the order of Mortgagee, then these presents shall cease and be void, otherwise these presents shall remain in full force and effect. Said right is granted to Mortgagor as set out in state statute PL 3-25-14 and in accordance therewith.

> The Equity of Redemption provision gives the borrower the right to pay off the loan balance before the property goes to foreclosure.

I. COVENANTS OF MORTGAGOR

Mortgagor covenants and agrees with Mortgagee as follows:

1-1. Secured Indebtedness.

This Mortgage is given as security for the Note and also as security for any and all other sums, indebtedness, obligations, and liabilities of any and every kind arising, under the Note or this Mortgage, as amended or modified or supplemented from time to time, and any all renewals, modifications, or extensions of any or all of the foregoing (all of which are collectively referred to herein as the "Secured Indebtedness"), the entire Secured Indebtedness being equally secured with and having the same priority as any amounts owed at the date hereof.

> The Secured Indebtedness paragraph details the actual obligation to repay the amount borrowed.

1-2. Performance of Conditions Set out in Note, Mortgage.

Mortgagor shall perform, observe, and comply with all provisions hereof and of the Note and shall promptly pay, in lawful U.S. currency, to Mortgagee the Secured Indebtedness with interest thereon as provided in the Note, this Mortgage, and all other documents constituting the Secured Indebtedness.

1-3. Payments Other Than Principal and Interest.

Mortgagor shall pay, when due and payable, (1) all taxes, assessments, general or special, and other charges levied on, or insurance and assessed, placed, or made against the property taxes Premises, this instrument or the Secured during the period Indebtedness or any interest of the Mortgagee of the mortgage, in the Premises or the obligations secured hereby; (2) premiums on policies of fire and other hazard insurance covering the

> The borrower also agrees to pay the insurance and property taxes during the period of the mortgage in the Payments Other Than Principal and Interest paragraph.

Premises, as required herein; (3) ground rents or other lease rentals; and (4) other sums related to the Premises or the indebtedness secured hereby, if any, payable by Mortgagor.

1-4. Hazard and Property Insurance.

Mortgagor shall, at its sole cost and expense, keep the Premises insured against all hazards as is customary and reasonable for residential properties of similar type and nature located in Springfield County, State of Placid.

1-5. Care and Maintenance of Pledged Property.

Mortgagor shall maintain the Premises in good condition and repair and shall not commit or suffer any material waste to the Premises.

1-6. Prior or Pre-Existing Mortgages.

With regard to prior or pre-existing mortgages, lines of credit, second mortgages, or other indentures for which premises are pledged as security, Mortgagor hereby agrees to: (i) Pay promptly, when due, all installments of principal and interest and all other sums and charges made payable by the Prior Mortgage; (ii) Promptly perform and observe all of the terms, covenants, and conditions required to be performed and observed by Mortgagor under the Prior Mortgage, within the period provided in said Prior Mortgage; (iii) Promptly notify Mortgagee of any default, or notice claiming any event of default by Mortgagor in the performance or observance of any term, covenant, or condition to be performed or observed by Mortgagor under any such Prior Mortgage; (iv) Mortgagor will not request nor will it accept any voluntary future advances under the Prior Mortgage without Mortgagee's prior written consent, which consent shall not be unreasonably withheld.

II. DEFAULT

2-1. Definition of Default.

A default is triggered by any of the conditions detailed in the Definition of Default paragraph and is the first step in putting the property up for auction through foreclosure.

The occurrence of any one of the following events which shall not be cured within ten (10) days after written notice of the occurrence of the event, if the default is monetary, or which shall not be cured within ten (10) days after written notice from Mortgagee, if the default is non-monetary, shall constitute a "Default": (a) Mortgagor fails to pay the Secured Indebtedness, or any part thereof, or the taxes, insurance, and other charges, as herein before provided, when and as the same shall become due and payable; (b) Any material warranty of Mortgagor herein contained, or contained in the Note, proves untrue or misleading in any material respect; (c) Mortgagor materially fails to keep, observe, perform, carry out, and execute the covenants, agreements, obligations, and conditions set out in this Mortgage, or in the Note; (d) Foreclosure proceedings (whether judicial or otherwise) are instituted on any mortgage or any lien of any kind secured by any portion of the Premises and affecting the priority of this Mortgage.

2-2. Options of Mortgagee in the Event of Default.

Upon the occurrence of any default, as that term is described in paragraph 2-1, the Mortgagee may immediately do any one or more of the following: (a) Declare the total Secured Indebtedness, including without limitation all payments for taxes, assessments, insurance premiums, liens, costs, expenses, and attorney's fees herein specified, without notice to Mortgagor (such notice being hereby expressly waived by Mortgagor), to be due and collectible at once, by foreclosure or otherwise; (b) In the event that Mortgagee elects to accelerate the maturity of the Secured Indebtedness and declares the Secured Indebtedness to be due and payable in full at once as provided for in Paragraph 1.02(a) hereinabove, or as may be provided for in the Note, or any other provision or term of this Mortgage, then Mortgagee shall have the right to pursue all of Mortgagee's rights and remedies for the collection of such Secured Indebtedness, whether such rights and remedies are granted by this Mortgage, any other agreement, law, equity, or otherwise, to include, without limitation, the institution of foreclosure proceedings against the Premises under the terms of this Mortgage and any applicable state or federal law.

III. MISCELLANEOUS PROVISIONS

3-1. Prior Liens.

Mortgagor shall keep the Premises free from all prior liens (except for those consented to by Mortgagee).

3-2. Notice, Demand, and Request.

Every provision for notice and demand or request shall be deemed fulfilled by written notice and demand or request delivered in accordance with the provisions of the Note relating to notice.

3-3. Construction of Terms and Phrases.

The words "Mortgagor" and "Mortgagee" whenever used herein shall include all individuals, corporations (and if a corporation, its officers, employees, or agents), trusts, and any and all other persons or entities, and the respective heirs, executors, administrators, legal representatives, successors, and assigns of the parties hereto, and all those holding under either of them. The pronouns used herein shall include, when appropriate, either gender and both singular and plural. The word "Note" shall also include one or more notes and the grammatical construction of sentences shall conform thereto.

3-4. Severability.

In the event that any provision of this Mortgage or any other Loan Document or the application thereof shall, for any reason and to any extent, be deemed invalid or unenforceable by a court of law, neither the remainder of the instrument in which such provision is contained, nor the application of the provision to other persons, entities, or circumstances, nor any other instrument referred to hereinabove shall be affected thereby, but instead shall be enforced to the maximum extent permitted by law. Clauses shall be construed in order to give effect to the clauses as individually set out.

> A Severability clause is found in many contracts; it allows courts to construe the clauses independently and will not result in a void contract if one clause is illegal.

3-5. Applicable Law.

The terms and provisions of this Mortgage are to be governed by the laws of the State of Placid. No payment of interest or in the nature of interest for any debt secured in part by this Mortgage shall exceed the maximum amount permitted by law. Any payment in excess of the maximum amount shall be applied or disbursed as provided in the Note in regard to such amounts that are paid by the Mortgagor or received by the Mortgagee.

3-6. Descriptive Headings.

The descriptive headings used herein are for convenience of reference only, and they are not intended to have any effect whatsoever in determining the rights or obligations of the Mortgagor or Mortgagee, and they shall not be used in the interpretation or construction hereof.

3-7. Attorney's Fees.

As used in this Mortgage, attorney's fees shall include, but not be limited to, fees incurred in all matters of collection and enforcement, construction, and interpretation, before, during, and after suit, trial, proceedings, and appeals. Attorney's fees shall also include hourly charges for paralegals, law clerks, and other staff members operating under the supervision of an attorney.

3-8. Exculpation and Release.

Notwithstanding anything contained herein to the contrary, the Note which this Mortgage secures is a non-recourse Note and such Note shall be enforced against Mortgagor only to the extent of Mortgagor's interest in the Premises as described herein and to the extent of Mortgagor's interest in any personal property as may be described herein.

IN WITNESS WHEREOF, the Mortgagor has caused this instrument to be duly executed as of the 22nd day of May, 2021.

Witnessed by:

_____

_____

STATE OF PLACID

COUNTY OF SPRINGFIELD

THE FOREGOING INSTRUMENT was acknowledged before me this day of 22nd day of May, 2021, by Troy McClure.

Notary Public

_____

My Commission Expires: _____

PRACTICE QUESTIONS FOR TEST REVIEW

See Appendix for answers.

Essay Question

What are the basic elements of the mortgage?

True–False

1   T   F   The secondary mortgage market is where borrowers go to obtain second mortgages on their loans.

2   T   F   Fannie Mae is an organization that purchases mortgages from lenders.

3   T   F   Federal Truth in Lending laws do not apply to mortgages.

Fill In the Blank

1   The primary purpose of this "market" is to purchase mortgages from lenders and free up capital so that lenders can lend to other borrowers: _____.

2   The year that Fannie Mae became a private corporation: _____.

3   The name of the U.S. national bank, created in 1913: _____.

Multiple Choice

1   The most common method used to finance the purchase of real estate.

    A   Mortgage
    B   UCC financing statement
    C   Bond
    D   Surety

2   In typical mortgage financing, who holds the title to the real estate during the mortgage period?

    A   The borrower
    B   The lender
    C   The trustee
    D   All of the above

3   Lending institutions that routinely accept mortgages from borrowers in order to finance the purchase of real estate are said to be in what market?

    A   The primary market
    B   The secondary market
    C   The tertiary market
    D   None of the above

ENDNOTES

[1] Ohio Rev. Code Ann. §5302.12.

[2] 15 U.S.C.A. §1631(a).

[3] Fla. Stat. Ann. (West's) §687.0304.

[4] Government Accounting Office, http://www.gao.gov/new.items/d04280.pdf.

Public and Private Restrictions on the Use of Land

Chapter Objectives

- Describe the nature and purpose of zoning regulations
- Explain the importance of urban planning
- Define important state and federal laws that affect the rights of private landowners
- Explain the importance of restrictive covenants
- Describe the area of nuisance law

Chapter Outline

I. Introduction

II. Public Restrictions on Private Land Use
   A. Zoning
   B. Building Codes
   C. Planning Boards
   D. Historic Districts
   E. Urban Planning
   F. Interstate Land Sales Full Disclosure Act
   G. Environmental Issues

III. Private Restrictions on Private Land Use
   A. Restrictive Covenants
   B. Subdivision Rules and Regulations
   C. Nuisance Actions

INTRODUCTION

In this chapter, we will examine the many ways that a landowner's use of her land can be restricted. Public laws, such as zoning, and federal environmental laws can have a huge impact on what a private landowner is permitted to do with her property. In addition to these legislative restrictions, there are also private restrictions, usually in the form of restrictive covenants. We will begin our discussion with an exploration of the legislative, or public, restrictions on land use.

PUBLIC RESTRICTIONS ON PRIVATE LAND USE

Your home may be your castle, but that does not mean that you are free to carry out any activity you wish there. In fact, local, state, and federal governments have the right to impose any number of restrictions on the way that private individuals use their property. We will examine these public restrictions by starting with local ordinances, such as zoning regulations, and then proceed through state and federal legislation that also limits how a private landowner may use her land.

A. ZONING

Zoning
The division of land in a local area into separate districts that are regulated by their use and development.

Local governments have the right to impose **zoning** rules and regulations as part of the police power vested in the government through state and federal constitutions. Zoning regulations restrict the way that both private and business landowners may use their property. Of course, not all property in the United States falls under zoning ordinances. In fact, there are vast tracts of land in the country that are not regulated by any type of zoning. Generally speaking, zoning ordinances are enacted by municipalities and towns that have reached a certain level of development. Farming communities and vast tracts of unimproved land generally do not have local zoning boards to contend with. When a city or town does have a zoning board, zoning regulations are designed to serve four primary purposes:

1 Promote health and morals,
2 Reduce traffic congestion and improve traffic flow,
3 Emphasize safety from fire and other potential hazards, and
4 Provide adequate heat, light, and airflow for residents.

Local governments frequently use zoning regulations as a means to control development and to make effective use of available space. Zoning is often seen as a planning tool for local governments. Through zoning ordinances, municipal governments can concentrate industry and commercial development in particular parts of town while designating other parts for residential use only. This has the benefit of keeping residential areas as far away as possible from industrial and commercial enterprises.

The authority to issue zoning ordinances arises under a city or town's police powers.

A zoning ordinance is usually enacted as some form of protective legislation; a zoning regulation might attempt to protect general health and safety or help ensure property values. For instance, a zoning ordinance will specify that structures must have a minimum setback distance from the road or that only specific types of materials may be used for buildings. The most common example of a zoning ordinance is a limitation on the use of the property, such as designating one area for residential use only, while other areas are zoned for commercial use only. Zoning regulations also carry with them enforcement provisions that allow the zoning board to issue citations against landowners who do not conform to the ordinance. The citation can result in prosecution if the landowner fails to abide by the zoning regulations.

Although zoning is an interference with a private individual's use of property, courts have ruled that it is a constitutional interference and that most zoning ordinances are perfectly legal.[1] However, there are certain zoning regulations that have been ruled unconstitutional. A zoning ordinance that prohibited individuals from certain ethnic groups or races from owning property, for example, would obviously be a violation of the Constitution.

It is important to draw a distinction between zoning and other types of municipal ordinances. For instance, building codes, which limit the manner in which buildings can be erected or rehabilitated, are not a form of zoning. Building codes focus on safety and health issues and therefore have greater latitude than zoning ordinances, which are usually more general in nature.

1. AESTHETIC ZONING

Some cities and towns enact **aesthetic zoning** ordinances to maintain a general overall appearance for their structures. These ordinances may require all architecture to meet specified standards. For example, Asheville, North Carolina, has set aside an area referred to as "Biltmore Village," where all commercial structures must have mission-style architectural features.

Aesthetic zoning
The requirement that all commercial and residential structures in a specified area have the same general appearance.

The most common function of aesthetic zoning ordinances is to control physical aspects of buildings. For instance, an ordinance might require a minimum setback that a building must have from the road. Any structure that is closer to the road than this minimum distance would be in violation of zoning ordinances and would be cited.

2. ENFORCING ZONING REGULATIONS

The city of Helen, Georgia, has a set of zoning ordinances that requires all commercial structures to maintain a Bavarian theme.

Courts consistently require zoning regulations to be limited in their focus to specific areas, such as safety, health, and general welfare. When a zoning ordinance goes beyond one of these issues, courts may strike down the regulation as excessive or overbroad.[2] The general limitation on any zoning ordinance or regulation is that it must serve a justifiable governmental purpose. Examples of permissible governmental purposes include controlling traffic, noise, or pollution. If a city can show that a zoning ordinance meets a justifiable goal, courts will usually uphold the ordinance as constitutional.

3. ZONING CLASSIFICATIONS

Zoning regulations divide land up into three broad categories: residential, commercial, and industrial. In each of these areas, use is limited to the specific classification. By limiting use in particular areas, zoning boards hope to control development and provide greater health and safety for residents. When an area is zoned for commercial use, for example, it means that private owners in that area may only operate businesses in that location; they cannot build a home there. Although there are three broad zoning categories, most cities have numerous additional zoning classifications and subclassifications that can complicate the issue.

a. Residential

Residential classifications can include a number of different types of dwellings, such as detached homes, single-family residences, townhouses, apartments, and group living structures (such as assisted-living facilities), as well as public accommodations from college dormitories to fire departments. Zoning ordinances establish minimum square footage for each of these dwelling types, including a general percentage of how much floor space can be devoted to a particular use. See Figure 10-1 for a sample residential ordinance.

FIGURE 10-1	§17-2-0500
City of Chicago Zoning Ordinance for Townhouses	Townhouse Developments

§17-2-0500

Townhouse Developments

17-2-0500-A Purpose. The purpose of these standards is to establish setback, building spacing, landscaping and design standards that are tailored to townhouse developments. Such standards are intended to ensure that townhouse developments are compatible with the traditional character of Chicago's neighborhoods.

17-2-0500-B Applicability. The townhouse development standards of this section apply in all districts in which townhouses are allowed.

17-2-0500-C Number of Buildings on Zoning Lot. Multiple townhouse buildings are expressly allowed on a single zoning lot in those townhouse developments that comply with the townhouse development standards of this section (Sec. 17-2-0500" destination-id="JD_17-2-0500">17-2-0500), provided that each building contains no more than 9 townhouse units.

17-2-0500-D Lot Frontage. The minimum lot frontage for a townhouse development is 35 feet.

(See Sec. 17-17-0303 for rules governing the measurement of lot frontage.)

17-2-0500-E Building Setbacks for Front and Rear Walls.

1. Front and Rear Walls Defined. Front walls and rear walls are those walls that are generally perpendicular to party walls. These walls are typically the primary sources of light and air for a townhouse unit.

2. Front or Rear Walls Facing a Public Street.

b. Commercial

Commercial designations cover a number of different types of business establishments. Here, the focus of the zoning ordinances is on total square footage, fire and safety issues, and minimum setbacks. Business and commercial district zoning may include requirements pertaining to the materials used in constructing the buildings as well as the placement of firewalls and the width of walls adjoining other businesses.

c. Industrial

Industrial classifications can include light, medium, and heavy industry, with appropriate regulation governing the placement of the structures in relation to residential areas as well as limitations on the types of chemical and manufacturing processes that are allowed on site.

Although there are three general categories of zoning regulations, many local governments create numerous other subcategories.

REAL ESTATE BASICS AT A GLANCE

---

4. EXCEPTIONS TO ZONING CLASSIFICATIONS

Although zoning boards have the power to enforce their rules and regulations by issuing citations, there are often structures within zoned areas that do not conform to the existing ordinances. They may not conform because the structure existed prior to the enactment of the zoning regulation, or the zoning board may have made an exception that allowed a structure to be built that does not conform to the zoning regulations. There are three different exceptions that permit structures to continue to be used even when they do not conform to zoning rules and regulations:

- Nonconforming use,
- Conditional use permit, and
- Variance.

a. Nonconforming Use

The exception of **nonconforming use** (see Figure 10-2) is reserved for a structure that predates the enactment of a zoning regulation. A new zoning ordinance cannot force the closure of a pre-existing business or force an individual out of her home. When the structure is already in existence at the time the zoning ordinance is created, it is allowed to stand even though its use may violate the new rule or the general classification for the area.

Nonconforming use
A structure that violates a zoning classification because it predates the enactment of the rule.

Las Vegas, Nevada, Ordinance Code Definition of Nonconforming Use

19.16.030 REGULATIONS

A. Nonconforming Use of a Conforming Building

1. **Expansion or Redevelopment of Use.** A nonconforming use of a conforming building shall not be continued following redevelopment of the property nor extended or expanded into any other portion of the conforming building; provided, however, that an existing use which was made nonconforming by one or more of the following may be continued following redevelopment or expanded in accordance with Subsection (2) of this Section (A):

   a. The adoption of a Special Use Permit requirement for that type of use;

   b. The adoption of a 400-foot or 1500-foot separation requirement between that type of use and a protected use;

   c. The adoption of a 1500-foot separation requirement between two uses of that type;

   d. The establishment of a protected use that, by virtue of a 400-foot or 1500-foot separation requirement, would otherwise prohibit the existing use from expanding or from continuing following redevelopment; or

   e. The adoption of a different method of measuring distance for purposes of a separation requirement.

b. Conditional Use Permit

Conditional use permit
An exception to a zoning classification granted by a zoning board, usually to benefit area residents.

There are times when a city wishes to encourage business development for commercial services within a residential area. In such a situation, the board might issue a **conditional use permit** that allows a business entity to operate in an area that has been reserved for residential use. Conditional use permits allow the property to be used in a way that is not in strict compliance with the zoning classification, but that does provide an essential service. Examples of conditional use permits would include authorizing a grocery store or gas station to operate in a residential area for the convenience of local residents. There are strict limitations on the issuance of conditional use permits, however. The zoning board cannot act in an unreasonable or capricious way. For instance, the zoning board cannot limit conditional use permits to members of a zoning board member's family or to a specific company.

c. Variance

Variance
An exception to a zoning classification granted by a zoning board.

In addition to conditional use permits, boards are also authorized to make exceptions to zoning classifications. An exception is referred to as a **variance**. A landowner might, for example, request a variance to operate her home-based business in an area reserved for residential use only. In this situation, the landowner would have to apply to the zoning board for a variance that would allow her to conduct a commercial enterprise in a residential area. Zoning boards issue variances to allow a degree of flexibility in zoning regulations, recognizing that it is extremely difficult to limit use entirely. Individuals and companies request variances all the time, and this is often the main item of business at zoning board meetings.

5. UNCONSTITUTIONAL OR ILLEGAL ZONING REGULATIONS

Interestingly enough, there is no prohibition against enacting zoning rules and regulations that discriminate on neutral grounds. Zoning ordinances are, by their very nature, prohibitions on the ways that landowners can use their land and thus could be construed as discriminatory in any form. However, as long as zoning rules and regulations apply equally to everyone in the same territory, and are not based on unconstitutional practices, they will be upheld by the courts. What is illegal is enacting them on the basis of discrimination. At times in the past, zoning rules and regulations have been used to discriminate against some members of society. For example, in the early twentieth century, there were zoning ordinances that prohibited African Americans from living in predominantly white neighborhoods. Eventually, those zoning ordinances were struck down as unconstitutional.

a. Rational Basis Test

Zoning boards must always justify their zoning ordinances by the "rational basis" test. Under this test, courts require zoning boards to demonstrate that there is a connection between the zoning ordinance and the ultimate goal of that ordinance. If the ultimate goal is to promote safety, health, or any other justifiable end, there is a strong likelihood that the zoning ordinance will be upheld as constitutional. However, there are certain classifications that are considered suspect. For instance, any zoning ordinance based on race, religion, or ethnic origin would automatically fall into a suspect classification and would most likely be ruled unconstitutional.[3] Zoning boards must demonstrate that they balance the interests of individual homeowners against the needs of society.

LIMITING BILLBOARDS

EXAMPLE 10-1

The town of Springfield has recently enacted a new zoning ordinance that limits billboards and landscaping along a newly constructed street. This zoning ordinance does not apply to other streets in the town. Landowners on the newly constructed street have filed suit alleging that this new zoning ordinance violates the Constitution. The zoning board counters that the new regulation is designed to ease traffic flow, promote traffic safety, and also meet aesthetic requirements. Based on what you have learned so far about zoning rules and regulations, who will win this lawsuit?

Answer: The town should win. Because the town can satisfy the rational basis test by showing that the new regulation is based on legitimate concerns of traffic safety and aesthetics, the court will most likely rule in favor of the town.[4]

b. "Spot" Zoning

Spot zoning is a practice used by zoning boards to single out a particular parcel for special treatment. Courts generally take a dim view of spot zoning because it places greater emphasis on individual parcels than the general community. An example of spot zoning would be the zoning board changing the zoning for a particular property

Spot zoning
A practice that is often ruled unconstitutional, in which a particular parcel is singled out for special treatment that does not further any of the stated goals of zoning regulations.

but not the rest of the area. Spot zoning was often used as a way of forcing out criminal and other undesirable activity in neighborhoods. Many states consider spot zoning to be illegal, no matter how good the intentions. Courts have created the following criteria to identify instances of illegal spot zoning:

- The zoning ordinance is aimed at a single parcel or a limited area.
- The ordinance is inconsistent with surrounding zoning classifications.
- The ordinance was not created to benefit the community as a whole or to further public health, safety, or other permissible reasons and is arbitrary or capricious.[5]

Tech Topic
VIRTUAL PLANNING

Along with population increases comes the need for expanded development, both residential and commercial. Residents not only like to know about plans for development, but they also prize having input to help shape the future of their community.

Historically, this has meant a long process of public meetings designed to allow residents the opportunity to learn about prospective development projects and deliver their support or opposition in person. Typically, most of those in attendance represented organized groups on both sides, and the measure of legitimate support or opposition by the public in general was hard to come by.

Although the length of the process has not changed much, the method of gathering public opinion has. Nowadays, residents are often invited to express their opinions on planned projects by visiting websites designed expressly for that purpose. Carefully created surveys collect and sort data, producing an overview of how the public is reacting to a proposed project. Even though the results might not qualify as statistically valid because of the voluntary nature of the process, they are every bit as reliable as opinions gathered from a public meeting. Furthermore, it affords those unable to attend a public meeting the chance to weigh in, thereby increasing the number of people involved in the process.

It is doubtful that virtual planning meetings will completely supplant public meetings anytime soon, but they have provided a welcome adjunct to the process.

B. BUILDING CODES

Building codes are different from zoning ordinances. Building codes are local or state rules and regulations that place specific restrictions on the way that buildings can be constructed, that heating and air-conditioning systems can be installed, and that plumbing and electrical work can be completed. Building codes are designed to protect the health, safety, and general welfare of the community. Because these codes are focused solely on safety and health issues, courts generally enforce them, even when building contractors and others claim the regulations are onerous.

C. PLANNING BOARDS

In addition to zoning boards, many communities also have planning boards. These boards are responsible for managing the development of the local community. They engage in long-term studies and work closely with the zoning board to effectuate an overall plan to benefit the local citizens; reduce congestion, noise, and air pollution; and also maintain real estate values.

D. HISTORIC DISTRICTS

Many communities have areas of historical significance. When a particular area is designated as a historic district, it receives special protection on both the local and the state level (see Figure 10-3). This protection can come in the form of special tax incentives for individuals who own designated historic sites as well as limitations on the repair and refurbishment of those structures.

FIGURE 10-3

Authorization of Historic Districts

Legislative findings. The historical heritage of our State is one of our most valued and important assets. The conservation and preservation of historic districts and landmarks stabilize and increase property values in their areas and strengthen the overall economy of the State. This Part authorizes cities and counties of the State within their respective zoning jurisdictions and by means of listing, regulation, and acquisition: (1) To safeguard the heritage of the city or county by preserving any district or landmark therein that embodies important elements of its culture, history, architectural history, or prehistory; and (2) To promote the use and conservation of such district or landmark for the education, pleasure, and enrichment of the residents of the city or county and the State as a whole.

Character of historic district defined. Historic districts established pursuant to this Part shall consist of areas which are deemed to be of special significance in terms of their history, prehistory, architecture, and/or culture, and to possess integrity of design, setting, materials, feeling, and association.

Designation of historic districts. Any municipal governing board may, as part of a zoning or other ordinance enacted or amended pursuant to this Article, designate and from time to time amend one or more historic districts within the area subject to the ordinance.[6]

E. URBAN PLANNING

Entire texts are written on the topic of urban planning; we will only touch on the highlights in this chapter. At its simplest, urban planning consists of any short- or long-term planning that seeks to conserve the value of a community or to enhance its living standards over time. However, that simple explanation belies some very complicated issues. Whether addressing water use, urban landscaping, traffic flow patterns, census data, birth rates, or any of a number of other issues, urban planners attempt to control growth or at least to give it an appropriate outlet. Without such planning, the local community would soon suffer an overload of people, traffic, and pollution, as well as depleted resources.

Urban planners must take into account not only the current state of the community but also the likely complexion of the area in 10, 20, or even 50 years. Along with the issues surrounding population growth, there are also issues of resource allotment, tax incentives to bring in more businesses, and the most appropriate method to use local government budgets to anticipate future problems. These days, urban planners must also take into account technological aspects that did not figure into local government plans even 10 years ago. For instance, what is the distribution of broadband Internet access and cellphone towers? Without such access, a community would be hard-pressed to attract new businesses to the area.

F. INTERSTATE LAND SALES FULL DISCLOSURE ACT

So far, our discussion concerning public restrictions on land has been limited to topics such as zoning or urban planning. Both of these are local government concerns, often handled at town council or other meetings. However, there are several important pieces of federal legislation that can play an important role in the way that landowners can use their property. One such federal act is the Interstate Land Sales Full Disclosure Act.[7] Passed in 1968 after a notorious series of frauds committed by individuals with access to prior knowledge of the planned route of the new U.S. interstate system, this legislation requires land promoters to make specific disclosures about land on or near the interstate highway system. For instance, any promoter who plans to sell 25 or more lots must disclose:

- The identity of the owners of the land that is being subdivided and offered for sale;
- A description of the physical properties of the land (farm land, swamp land, partially covered by timber, etc.);
- A description of the access and availability of utilities for the new lots; and
- A statement about the condition or existence of access roads to the new lots.

The Act also requires promoters to register their land sales with appropriate government agencies, to provide buyers with disclosures at least 48 hours prior to purchase, and to allow buyers a seven-day period to change their minds about the sale. The Act establishes stringent guidelines about fraud and misrepresentation and authorizes federal prosecutions for land promoters who violate the Act's provisions.

G. ENVIRONMENTAL ISSUES

Besides the Interstate Land Sales Full Disclosure Act, there are other important federal laws that can have an impact on a landowner's use of her property.

1. CLEAN WATER ACT

A common example is the Clean Water Act. This act provides strict guidelines for the use of wetlands and imposes limitations on the way that areas that qualify as wetlands can be used. Under the Clean Water Act, a wetland is described as "those areas that are inundated or saturated by surface or ground water at a frequency and duration sufficient to support, and that under normal circumstances do support, a prevalence of vegetation typically adapted for life in saturated soil conditions. Wetlands generally include swamps, marshes, bogs, and similar areas." On the basis of that definition, many areas fall under the jurisdiction of the Clean Water Act.

The Environmental Protection Agency is the branch of the federal government that is responsible for enforcing various environmental rules and regulations, including the Clean Water Act.

2. THE SUPERFUND

The Comprehensive Environmental Response, Compensation, and Liability Act (CERCLA), which is commonly known as the EPA Superfund, became law in 1980. The Act created a tax that is imposed on chemical and petroleum industries to help defer the costs associated with cleaning up hazardous chemical spills. Among other things, CERCLA has:

- Created rules that prohibit the development of certain sites that were formerly hazardous waste sites,
- Created a fund to assist in the cleanup of those sites, and
- Imposed liability on companies and individuals who created the hazardous sites in the first place.

PRIVATE RESTRICTIONS ON PRIVATE LAND USE

So far, our discussion has centered on governmental restrictions on the ability of private landowners to use their land. In the following sections, we examine private actions that individuals can bring against one another to control the way that land is used. The most common form of private restriction on land use is the restrictive covenant. In many ways, restrictive covenants resemble zoning regulations, except that they are imposed and enforced by private individuals.

A. RESTRICTIVE COVENANTS

Like zoning regulations, **restrictive covenants** control issues such as minimum setbacks from roadways, appearance, architecture, minimum lot sizes, and a host of other

Restrictive covenant
A condition or restriction on the way that land may be used that is imposed by private individuals.

issues. However, the important difference between restrictive covenants and zoning regulations is that restrictive covenants are imposed by private individuals on other private individuals.

Restrictive covenants are imposed through deeds or other public record documents. They are said to "run with the land," which means that once a restrictive covenant is imposed on a parcel of land, it remains with that parcel no matter how many times ownership of the land changes hands. Restrictive covenants imposed on present owners will be binding on future owners.

Developers often use restrictive covenants as a way to control use in planned communities, such as subdivisions or other commercial developments. Landowners often create restrictive covenants when there are no zoning rules or regulations imposed by the local government. Courts recognize the right of landowners to create restrictive covenants of property as long as they fall within certain guidelines. For instance, restrictive covenants cannot be used to discriminate against potential owners any more than zoning rules or regulations can.[8]

REAL
ESTATE
BASICS AT
A GLANCE

Restrictive covenants are used by private individuals to control how property can be used, even to the extent of what structures can be placed on the land, how far the house can be set back from the road, and the minimum and maximum square footage of residences.

---

1. CREATING COVENANTS

A restrictive covenant is, in essence, a contract.[9] A seller can create a series of covenants and record them, or put them in a deed, and the new owner takes the property subject to those limitations. The new owner does not have the option of ignoring those conditions. The most common ways to create restrictive covenants are:

- Including them in a deed from the grantor to the grantee,
- Recording them in the public records, and
- Recording a plat that contains them.

Just as we have seen in other contexts dealing with real property, restrictive covenants must be in writing to satisfy the Statute of Frauds. If they are not in writing, they cannot be enforced.

2. RESTRICTIVE COVENANTS "TOUCH AND CONCERN"

When valid restrictive covenants are created, they impose conditions on the way that the property can be used — that is, they "touch and concern" the land. This colorful phrase means that the conditions placed on the new owner must concern the real estate, not the parties. A restrictive covenant cannot, for example, forbid the new owner from practicing a particular religion or from espousing particular politics. Instead, the conditions must apply to the parcel itself.

3. TYPICAL COVENANTS

Restrictive covenants can come in an enormous variety, but there are some basic principles that they all must follow. As we have already seen, each covenant must touch and concern the land. Because of this rule, the most common restrictive covenants:

- Establish minimum lot sizes;
- Limit use of the property, such as to residential use only;
- Limit the number of outbuildings on the parcel;
- Restrict the types of animals that can live on the premises, such as forbidding farm animals; or
- Require that all buildings conform to a general architectural theme.

4. ILLEGAL OR UNCONSTITUTIONAL COVENANTS

We have seen that restrictive covenants must touch and concern the real property and cannot be used as a vehicle to carry out discriminatory policies. Under this rule, restrictive covenants cannot be used to prevent people of a certain race, religion, or national origin from owning property in specific neighborhoods. Restrictive covenants were once used in this way but were eventually abolished by the U.S. Supreme Court. In *Shelley v. Kraemer*,[10] the Court ruled that restrictive covenants were being used as a method to keep African Americans out of white neighborhoods. In that case, white neighbors had banded together and recorded the following restrictive covenant:

> The said property is hereby restricted to the use and occupancy for the term of Fifty (50) years from this date, so that it shall be a condition all the time and whether recited and referred to as (sic) not in subsequent conveyances and shall attach to the land, as a condition precedent to the sale of the same, that hereafter no part of said property or any portion thereof shall be, for said term of Fifty-years, occupied by any person not of the Caucasian race, it being intended hereby to restrict the use of said property for said period of time against the occupancy as owners or tenants of any portion of said property for resident or other purpose by people of the Negro or Mongolian Race.[11]

The Supreme Court ruled that such a condition was unconstitutional and a denial of equal protection under state and federal laws. The restrictive covenant was struck down.

For a restrictive covenant to have legal impact, the restrictions must focus on how the property is used, not the religious, racial, or ethnic origin of the people owning the land.

REAL ESTATE BASICS AT A GLANCE

---

5. ENFORCING COVENANTS

Enforcing restrictive covenants is a relatively straightforward affair. Unlike zoning regulations, which allow the local government to cite the offending homeowner, restrictive covenants must be enforced through civil lawsuits by adjoining landowners. These landowners, who must be bound by the same restrictive covenants, are permitted to sue the offending landowner to enforce the restrictive covenants that they agreed to when they purchased the property.

6. TERMINATING RESTRICTIVE COVENANTS

Restrictive covenants can be terminated in several ways. The most common ways for restrictive covenants to terminate are:

- When the restrictive covenants have a stated time period,
- When the restrictive covenants have been abandoned,
- When the neighborhood has undergone substantially changed conditions, or
- When the properties affected have merged.

a. Stated Time Period

It is not uncommon for restrictive covenants to have a predetermined time period. For instance, the owners might state that the conditions will only apply for 20 years. There is, however, no requirement that restrictive covenants give a specific time period. When they fail to do so, they are considered binding in perpetuity.

b. Abandonment

Restrictive covenants terminate when they have been abandoned by the people they were designed to protect. Abandonment can occur in a number of ways. Suppose, for example, that the local owners have been disregarding the restrictive covenants for years. When it has become obvious that the restrictive covenants no longer have any legal significance, courts will not enforce them. In one case, a court stated, "Restrictive covenants will not be enforced merely to harass and annoy some particular person, when it is clear to the court that the objective for which the restrictive covenants were originally entered into have already failed."[12]

c. Changed Conditions

Restrictive covenants may also be extinguished when the current conditions on the real property no longer have any relation to the original conditions. Suppose, for example, that, when the restrictive covenants were enacted, the entire area consisted of farmland and groves. However, what was once farmland now consists of retail establishments and apartment buildings. In this case, subsequent owners have abandoned the original intent of the restrictive covenants. The standard that courts use to determine if there has been a sufficient change of conditions to terminate restrictive covenants is that there is a fundamental change in the use of the property to such an extent that the original purpose of the restrictive covenants no longer applies.[13]

d. Merger

Merger is a doctrine we have encountered in several situations already. For instance, we saw in life estates that, when a person is both the remainderman and a life tenant, the estate merges into one complete unit owned by the single individual. The idea behind merger in the context of restrictive covenants is relatively simple: When a single individual owns all affected parcels, there are no longer any outside interests involved, and the individual is free to dispose of the restrictive covenants. In this case, merger would apply only if a single individual owned every parcel affected by the restrictive covenants. If this individual owned all but even one parcel, merger would not apply and restrictive covenants would not be terminated.

B. SUBDIVISION RULES AND REGULATIONS

Many cities and towns across the country have been vested with the power to adopt subdivision regulations for neighborhoods in their areas. Towns can adopt ordinances that require a real estate developer to create a plat designating the streets, easements, rights of way, and boundary lines for all tracts contained in a particular subdivision, as well as any other limitations that are reasonable for safety or health reasons.

C. NUISANCE ACTIONS

Nuisance actions are a type of civil lawsuit that gives one landowner the right to sue another. A landowner might sue her neighbor when the neighbor is engaging in activities that make it difficult or impossible for other neighbors to enjoy their property. A civil nuisance action would be authorized, for instance, when the neighbor is engaged in some chemical or manufacturing process that involves loud noises or odors that interfere with the enjoyment of the property. Nuisance actions are commonly seen in situations in which fumes, liquids, or other substances are leaking from one person's property to another's.

Nuisance
A cause of action that is authorized when the defendant's behavior results in a loss of enjoyment or value in the plaintiff's property.

1. PUBLIC NUISANCE

There are actually two different types of nuisance actions: public and private. A public nuisance is some condition that affects the rights of citizens in general. This condition could be a health risk or a general annoyance. When a condition is classified as a public nuisance, local government officials are authorized to bring an action for the good of the community. New federal statutes have made the use of nuisance actions even more valuable to those claiming that large corporations are polluting groundwater or dumping hazardous waste. Working through the Environmental Protection Agency, many agencies use federal statutes to force companies to pay for the complete cost of cleaning up a site that has been designated hazardous.

Private individuals are usually prevented from bringing a claim under public nuisance laws; such actions are generally reserved for the government. Placing such limitations on public nuisance lawsuits is a direct reflection of the fact that there are many things in life that we must all put up with, and allowing a private person to bring a public nuisance suit for these things would grind the legal system to a halt. However, those limitations disappear when the allegation is a private nuisance.

2. PRIVATE NUISANCE

Private nuisance actions have fewer limitations than public nuisance actions. Neighbors are free to sue other neighbors for actions that affect the quality, use, and enjoyment of their property.

EXAMPLE 10-2

TOO MANY RABBITS?

Juan lives on a typical suburban street. His next-door neighbor Chip has recently acquired 100 rabbits and keeps them in cages in his backyard. That number of rabbits produces a strong odor, and Juan wants to know if he can bring a civil nuisance action against Chip to force Chip to get rid of the rabbits. Will his suit be successful?

Answer: Most likely. If Juan can establish that the odor from the rabbits is affecting his ability to use and enjoy his property, he may be able to prove his suit and have a judge order Chip to get rid of the rabbits.

REAL ESTATE BASICS AT A GLANCE

The elements of a private nuisance action are that the defendant maintains a condition that substantially interferes with the plaintiff's right to use and enjoy his property.

Case Excerpt

MOSELEY v. ARNOLD
486 S.W.3d 656, 2016 Tex. App. LEXIS 1627

Opinion

For at least the last twenty-four years, the five-acre tract at the southeast corner of Interstate Highway 20 and Texas Highway 43 in Harrison County, on which was once located a business known as Moseley's Truck Stop, has been unimproved property. But, back in 1985, when the five-acre tract and its personal property had been sold as a package by Douglas B. Moseley for a price of almost $1 million, it had hosted the truck stop. As part of the sale, the five acres was benefitted by a restrictive covenant on the 6.379 acres located at the northeast corner of the same intersection and owned by Moseley (the Retained Tract). That covenant provided that the Retained Tract "may not be developed and used as a truck stop and fuel stop." Now, three decades after the sale, a dispute has arisen between Moseley and the current owner of the five acres, Sherrie Arnold, concerning the restrictive covenant's enforceability against the Retained Tract.

The trial court granted Arnold summary judgment that the restrictive covenant was enforceable against the Retained Tract. Moseley's appeal argues that Arnold lacked standing to enforce the covenant and that fact issues on the presence of changed conditions make Arnold's summary judgment improper. We reverse the summary judgment and remand this matter to the trial court because, while (1) Arnold has standing to enforce the restrictive covenant, (2) fact issues regarding changed conditions preclude summary judgment.

Generally, a restrictive covenant may be enforced only by the parties to the restrictive covenant agreement and those parties in privity with them. "Privity of estate exists when there is a mutual or successive relationship to the same rights of property." *MPH Prod. Co.*, 2012 Tex. App. LEXIS 3989, 2012 WL 1813467. Further, "any person entitled to benefit under the terms of a restrictive covenant may enforce it." *Girsh v. St. John*, 218 S.W.3d 921, 923 (Tex. App. — Beaumont 2007, no pet.). The summary judgment evidence establishes that Arnold is the successor of the Gormans' interest in the five acres. The resolution of this issue, then, requires us to construe the intent of the parties, as expressed in the restrictive covenant agreement, to determine whether Arnold, as the successor of the Gormans' interest in the five-acre tract, is an intended beneficiary who is entitled to benefit under the terms of the restrictive covenant agreement.

We construe restrictive covenants using the general rules of contract construction. "Whether restrictive covenants are ambiguous is a question of law. Courts must examine the covenants as a whole in light of the circumstances present when the parties entered the agreement." Restrictive covenants "are 'unambiguous as a matter of law if they can be given a definite or certain legal meaning.'" If we find there is no ambiguity, we "must determine the intent from the language used in the document." *Silver Spur Addition Homeowners v. Clarksville Seniors Apartments*, 848 S.W.2d 772, 774 (Tex. App. — Texarkana 1993, writ denied). Our primary purpose "is to ascertain and give effect to the true intention of the parties as expressed in the instruments." However, if a restrictive covenant is "susceptible to more than one reasonable interpretation, it is ambiguous." *Pilarcik*, 966 S.W.2d at 478. If the restrictive covenant is susceptible to two or more reasonable interpretations, then it "creates a fact issue as to the parties' intent." *TX Far W., Ltd. v. Tex. Invs. Mgmt., Inc.*, 127 S.W.3d 295, 302 (Tex. App. — Austin 2004, no pet.) (citing *Columbia Gas Transmission Corp.*, 940 S.W.2d at 589). "In construing the intent, a court is not to concern itself with the merits of restrictions because the parties to the restrictions had a right to adopt any type of restrictions they chose." *Id.*

The operative clause of the restrictive covenant agreement contains three clauses relevant to determining the parties' intent regarding its intended beneficiaries. First, it states that the purpose of the restrictive covenant is to benefit the Gormans, their successors and assigns. Second, it provides that the restrictive covenant is given "to protect the value and desirability of" the five-acre tract being purchased by the Gormans. Finally, the operative clause expresses the parties' intent that the restrictive covenant run with the land and binds all parties owning any interest in the Retained Tract. Moseley's construction requires us to consider the first clause only and renders the remaining clauses meaningless. However, when an agreement is unambiguous, "the instrument alone will be deemed to express the intention of the parties, for objective intent controls, not subjective intent. Generally the parties to an instrument intend every clause to have some effect and in some measure to evidence their agreement." *City of Pinehurst v. Spooner Addition Water Co.*, 432 S.W.2d 515, 518 (Tex. 1968) (citations omitted). Therefore, we examine the agreement in its entirety and consider every clause. When the clauses are read together, it is clear that the restrictive covenant is meant to benefit the five-acre tract the Gormans were purchasing, and that the Gormans and their successors and assigns are meant to be beneficiaries only to the extent of their ownership interest in the five-acre tract. Since the summary judgment evidence establishes that Arnold owns the five-acre tract and is a successor to the Gormans' interest in the five-acre tract, she is a beneficiary under the plain terms of the restrictive covenant agreement and may enforce the restrictions. See *Girsh*, 218 S.W.3d at 923. Therefore, Arnold has standing to enforce the restrictive covenant.

Fact Issues Regarding Changed Conditions Preclude Summary Judgment

Since Arnold established that she has standing to enforce the restrictive covenant and Moseley conceded that it ran with the land, the trial court's granting of Arnold's motion for partial summary judgment would be proper unless Moseley produced sufficient evidence to raise a fact issue on each element of his defense of changed conditions. Texas courts have long recognized that "a court may refuse to enforce a restrictive covenant if there has been such a change of conditions that it is no longer possible to secure in a substantial degree the benefits sought to be realized through the covenant." *TX Far W., Ltd.*, 127 S.W.3d at 306-07. In other words, "where the reason for enforcing a restrictive covenant has ceased, equity will no longer enforce the covenant." *La Rocca v. Howard-Reed Oil Co.*, 277 S.W.2d 769, 772 (Tex. Civ. App. — Beaumont 1955, no writ). Further, when the conditions have sufficiently changed, it may bring about a termination of the restrictive covenant. Generally, determining whether conditions have changed to the degree that justifies the non-enforcement, or termination, of a restrictive covenant is a fact question.

Moseley contends that the trial court erred in granting partial summary judgment because genuine issues of material fact exist regarding his claim of changed conditions. Moseley argued at trial and argues in this Court that the restrictive covenant was granted within the context of the purchase and sale of the truck stop as a going concern. Within this context, the original purpose of the restrictive covenant, he argues, was to protect the value of the truck stop. In support of this argument, he points to the contract of sale, that evidences the sale of the truck stop, and to his affidavit in which he avers that the Gormans' and his original intention was that the restrictive covenant protect the value of the truck stop. Since this was the original purpose of the restrictive covenant, he argues, the destruction and non-rebuilding of another truck stop constitutes changed circumstances that frustrates the purpose of the covenant. He points to the evidence that the truck stop burned down, then all the remaining remnants of the buildings and the underground fuel tanks were removed over twenty-four years ago. Since that time, the five-acre tract has been sold several times, and none of the owners have sought to rebuild a truck stop on the property or operated any business on the five-acre tract that the covenant was intended to protect. Therefore, he argues, the restrictive covenant no longer secures the benefits to the five-acre tract as originally intended.

Arnold admits that the Gormans purchased the five-acre tract with an existing and operational truck stop and that one of the negotiated terms of the contract of sale was for a restrictive covenant to be placed on the Retained Tract. Nevertheless, she argues that Moseley has failed to raise any issues of material fact, and alternatively, that there is no evidence, that shows changed conditions that would justify the non-enforcement of the restrictive covenant. She argues that none of the facts on which Moseley relies prevent her from securing the benefits of the restrictive covenant such that it defeats the purpose of the restrictions. Although she does not contest the underlying facts relied on by Moseley, she argues that none of the actions or inactions of the various owners of the five-acre tract prevents it from being used as a truck stop. Further, she argues that she derives a substantial benefit from the fact that she has no competition from the property across the street because of the restrictive covenant. Finally, she argues that the fact that she was able to prevent Moseley from selling the Retained Tract for use as a truck stop establishes the benefit of the restriction to the five-acre tract. Although her argument regarding the purpose of the restrictive covenant is not well-developed, her response assumes that the purpose of the restrictive covenant was to protect the value of the five-acre tract, as long as it is capable of supporting a truck stop.

Arnold relies heavily on Texas cases involving residential subdivisions having a general plan that applies a residential-only restriction to all lots in the subdivision. In those cases, the courts stressed that the changed conditions must have occurred in the restricted area (i.e., the residential subdivision) or the surrounding area, and balanced the equities favoring the particular owner seeking to avoid the restrictive covenant against the equities favoring all of the other owners in the subdivision who purchased their lots in reliance on the residential restrictions. The courts are understandably cautious in granting non-enforcement of the residential-only restriction, since not enforcing the residential restriction as to some lots may adversely affect the value of all the remaining residential lots in the subdivision, and "the entire purpose and intention originally expressed to create a restricted residential subdivision could be thwarted." *Scaling*, 167 S.W.2d at 281. Nevertheless, even in those cases, when the conditions in the restricted area or the surrounding area have changed to such a degree that it defeats the purposes of the restrictive covenant, the restriction may be terminated.

In *Overton*, Ragland owned two lots bordering Broadway Street in Lubbock. *Ragland v. Overton*, 44 S.W.2d 768, 768-69. The deed to Ragland's predecessor in interest in 1908 contained a restriction limiting the lots use to residential purposes. *Id.* Before 1925, the neighborhood consisted of residences and farmland, and Broadway was used only for residential traffic. *Overton*, 54 S.W.2d at 242. However, in 1925, Texas Technological College was established on the west end of Broadway and College Avenue, which bordered the college and intersected Broadway. *Id.* By the time of trial, the traffic along Broadway was fifty times what it had been before the establishment of the college and was then used primarily for commercial and other non-residential purposes. In addition, numerous businesses had been erected on College and Broadway, such that Ragland's two lots were now located near the center of the business district. *Id.* Testimony established that the lots had a value of $3,000.00 for residential purposes and $15,000.00 for business purposes. *Id.* After a jury found that the changes rendered the lots unfit for residential purposes, Overton appealed, arguing that since testimony showed the lots still had a value of $3,000.00 as residential property, the evidence was insufficient to show that the lots were unfit for residential property. *Id.* at 241-42. In upholding the jury's verdict, the Amarillo Court of Appeals noted that "changed conditions in a neighborhood brought about by agencies outside of the parties themselves will terminate a building restriction limiting or restricting property in use for residential purposes only." *Id.* at 243. Thus, even though the lots had some value as residential lots, the restrictive covenant's purpose of maintaining the residential nature of the neighborhood had been essentially destroyed by the intervening events.

The gravamen of these changed-conditions cases is that, if the purpose of the restrictive covenant can no longer be realized in a substantial manner, the courts will terminate, or refuse to enforce, the restrictions. If the purpose of the restrictive covenant can no longer be realized at all, then, ipso facto, it is no longer possible to secure in a substantial degree the benefits sought to be realized through the covenant. Therefore, determining what the parties intended to be the purpose of the restrictive covenant is essential.

A Fact Issue Regarding the Purpose of the Restrictive Covenant Precludes Summary Judgment

"A written contract must be construed to give effect to the parties' intent expressed in the text as understood in light of the facts and circumstances surrounding the contract's execution, subject to the parol evidence rule." *Houston Exploration Co. v. Wellington Underwriting Agencies, Ltd.*, 352 S.W.3d 462, 469 (Tex. 2011). Further, the parol evidence rule "does not prohibit consideration of surrounding circumstances that inform, rather than vary from or contradict, the contract text." *Id.* "Those circumstances include . . . 'the commercial or other setting in which the contract was negotiated and other objectively determinable factors that give a context to the transaction between the parties.'"

In this case, the operative clause of the restrictive covenant agreement provides that the Retained Tract "may not be developed and used as a truck stop and fuel stop to protect the value and desirability of the 5 acre tract or parcel of land purchased by the Gormans." Although this phrase expresses the parties' intent to benefit the five-acre tract, it does not, by itself, give us insight into the nature of the five-acre tract that makes it valuable and desirable. Without knowing the nature of the five-acre tract that the parties are trying to protect, we cannot know the purpose of the restrictive covenant. For instance, if the five-acre tract was to be the site of a residential subdivision, the purpose of the restrictive covenant forbidding the development of a fuel or truck stop on the Retained Tract would clearly be to preserve the value and desirability of the five-acre tract as residential property. In our case, the parties agree that the Gormans purchased the five-acre tract with an existing and operational truck stop and that one of the negotiated terms of the transaction was for a restrictive covenant to be placed on the Retained Tract. Knowing these circumstances informs us of the nature of the five-acre tract when purchased — commercial property containing an operational truck stop — and that the restrictive covenant was negotiated to protect the value and desirability of the property, at least as commercial property capable of supporting a truck stop, as Arnold argues, or perhaps, as Moseley argues, only so long as it is supporting an operational truck stop. Both of these are reasonable interpretations of the purpose of the restrictive covenant, based on the language in the operative clause and informed by the surrounding circumstances. Thus, the language of the operative clause is ambiguous.

When the operative clause is ambiguous, we may "look at recitals to ascertain the intent of the parties in executing the contract." *Universal Health Servs., Inc. v. Thompson*, 63 S.W.3d 537, 543 (Tex. App. — Austin 2001). As we have seen above, the recital paragraphs refer to the contract of sale in which Moseley agreed to sell the five-acre tract to the Gormans and recites that the parties desire to fulfill the terms and provisions of the contract of sale. See infra note 1. Since the recital paragraphs direct us to the contract of sale, we may also consider this prior agreement to determine if it will aid in establishing what the parties intended. See Restatement (Second) of Contracts §214 (1981) ("Agreements . . . prior to or contemporaneous with the adoption of a writing are admissible in evidence to establish . . . (c) the meaning of the writing, whether or not integrated."). As we have seen, the contract of sale shows that the sale of the five-acre tract included the sale of the then-existing and operating truck stop. See infra note 1. Included in the contract of sale was Moseley's agreement to restrict the Retained Tract "to preclude its development and use as a truck stop." Absent from the contract of sale, however, is any language that clearly states that the purpose of Moseley's agreement to restrict the Retained Tract is to protect the value of the five-acre tract only so long as there is an operational truck stop. Therefore, while the contract of sale may provide some evidence in support of Moseley's interpretation, we cannot say that it provides definitive evidence as to the purpose of the restrictive covenant intended by the original parties.

Thus, after considering the language of the restrictive covenant, the surrounding circumstances, and the contract for sale, the different interpretations of the parties as to the purpose of the restrictive covenant remain reasonable. If a restrictive covenant is "susceptible to more than one reasonable interpretation, it is ambiguous." *Pilarcik*, 966 S.W.2 at 478. This, then creates a fact issue as to the purpose of the restrictive covenant intended by the original parties. See *TX Far W., Ltd.*, 127 S.W.3d at 302. Therefore, we hold that, because the ambiguous language of the restrictive covenant cannot establish the purpose of the restrictive covenant intended by the original parties, a fact issue remains that precludes summary judgment.

Fact Issues Regarding Changed Conditions Preclude Summary Judgment

Under either interpretation of the purpose of the restrictive covenant asserted by the parties, the summary judgment evidence, when viewed in the light most favorable to Moseley, shows there remains a fact question regarding whether there has been such a change in conditions that it is no longer possible to secure in a substantial degree the benefits sought to be realized through the covenant. The contract of sale shows that the purchase of the five-acre tract included the sale of the truck stop as a going concern, that it had a sales price of $971,500.00, and that Moseley promised to place the restrictive covenant on the Retained Tract as part of the terms of the sale. Moseley also submitted summary judgment evidence that the truck stop had burned down and that all of its buildings and underground fuel tanks had been removed, over twenty-four years ago. He also brought forth evidence that the five-acre tract had been sold at least four times since the destruction and removal of the truck stop and that none of subsequent owners had rebuilt a truck stop on the property. Although there was no evidence of the purchase price paid for the five-acre tract by any purchaser after the truck stop was destroyed, Moseley testified by affidavit that the five-acre tract is currently valued at $49,500.00 by the Harrison County Appraisal District. In contrast, Moseley was recently offered $850,000.00 for the Retained Tract in contemplation that it would be used for the development of a truck stop.

Arnold sought to counter this evidence in her affidavit in support of her motion for partial summary judgment by attesting, "The Restrictive Covenant makes my five (5) acre tract or parcel of land more valuable as a result of having no competition for a truck and fuel stop directly across Interstate 20." Of course, this is her opinion and falls short of conclusive proof of that fact. Viewing the evidence in the light most favorable to Moseley, the absence of a functioning truck stop on the five acres for over twenty-four years, and the valuation of the five acres at $49,500.00 by the appraisal district, would seem to belie this opinion, especially since Moseley was offered $850,000.00 for the Retained Tract. Even assuming, arguendo, that Arnold is correct that the purpose of the restrictive covenant was to protect the value and desirability of the five-acre tract as commercial property capable of supporting a truck stop, the non-development of the tract for over twenty-four years and the stark difference in the values of the tracts is some evidence that there has been such a change of conditions that it is no longer possible to secure in a substantial degree the benefits sought to be realized through the covenant.

Since issues of fact remain regarding (1) the purpose of the restrictive covenant intended by the original parties, and (2) whether there has been such a change of conditions that it is no longer possible to secure in a substantial degree the benefits sought to be realized through the covenant, we find that the trial court erred in granting partial summary judgment, and final judgment, in favor of Arnold.

We reverse the judgment of the trial court and remand this case to the trial court for further proceedings consistent with this opinion.

Josh R. Morriss III
Chief Justice

QUESTIONS ABOUT THE CASE

1 Explain the restrictive covenant that is the basis of the dispute between the parties in this case.
2 According to the court, there is an essential element that must be present in order to create a binding restrictive covenant between the parties. What is that element, and was it met in this case?
3 The court states that Moseley's argument requires consideration of only one element of contract interpretation. What is that element, and how does it impact the remaining elements?
4 Have the conditions of the property changed so much that the restrictive covenant should no longer be applied? Why or why not?

COVID-19 CONCERN

As this chapter has demonstrated, both public and private restrictions on real estate have been used in discriminatory ways in the past. Restrictive covenants, now ruled unconstitutional, once forbid sale of real estate parcels to Black persons. Is it possible that a similar discrimination may now develop against those suffering with the long-term effects of COVID-19 infection? Some may feel that the "long haul" COVID sufferers offer a risk of disease that they find unacceptable. Might sellers feel that eliminating them from the pool of potential buyers is a safe, if inadvisable, step?

CHAPTER SUMMARY

In this chapter, we have seen that there are numerous restrictions on a private individual's ability to use her land. Zoning is one of the most common types of local governmental control on private property use. Zoning rules and regulations must have a rational basis and must attempt to enforce safety, health, or other concerns. Zoning rules and regulations can be enforced through citations. There are three broad categories of zoning: residential, commercial, and industrial. When a structure predates the enactment of a zoning regulation and thus violates it, it is referred to as a nonconforming use. If a landowner wishes to use property in a way that is inconsistent with existing zoning rules and regulations, she can apply for a zoning variance. Zoning boards occasionally grant exceptions, called conditional use permits, to encourage businesses to go into residential areas. Zoning cannot be used to discriminate against individuals. An example of a potentially discriminatory zoning practice is spot zoning. In addition to zoning rules and regulations, individuals are also bound by state and federal laws that can severely limit how an individual uses her property.

Restrictive covenants are a way of regulating use by private individuals. Restrictive covenants are created by previous owners and act as conditions that limit use for future owners. The typical provisions of restrictive covenants include minimum lot sizes, minimum square footage in houses, and aesthetic issues. Restrictive covenants can be terminated by their own terms, if they are abandoned, if a court rules that conditions have changed to such an extent that they are no longer applicable, or if merger has occurred. In addition to restrictive covenants, private individuals can also bring nuisance actions against neighbors who are engaging in practices that limit a person's use and enjoyment of her property.

SKILLS YOU NEED IN THE REAL WORLD

Locating Restrictive Covenants

The process of locating restrictive covenants isn't always as easy and straightforward as you might think. In some cases, restrictive covenants are filed with the general warranty deeds. In other situations, however, they are filed as a separate document and the deeds are cross-referenced to the filing. In still other situations, the restrictive covenants may be contained on a plat or some other document. In any event, you should develop your skills in locating restrictive covenants. Talk to courthouse personnel; they are a gold mine of information and can often recall details about certain areas that aren't clearly reflected in the public records. They can also save you a lot of time by directing you to the correct filing. Once you have located a copy of the restrictive covenants for a particular neighborhood, make a copy of all clauses and review them. Also note any property to which these restrictive covenants apply. If a question comes up about the application, constitutionality, or validity of the covenants, others will certainly want to see a hard copy of them.

ETHICAL ISSUES FOR THE PARALEGAL

Discriminatory Restrictive Covenants

Legal professionals should always be on guard against unscrupulous or unconstitutional practices. In the area of restrictive covenants, with its long history of discriminatory practices, it is always a good idea to review proposed restrictive covenants for any clause that could be used to discriminate against a particular group. Unlike the early twentieth century, when covenants contained clauses that were clearly discriminatory, modern covenants may be more subtle. For instance, a discriminatory covenant might require a "sponsor" before a person will be allowed to live in a specific neighborhood. Other covenants might contain provisions establishing minimum income limits for ownership or control who can be a member of the neighborhood association. Any such provision should be viewed with skepticism, and when doubt exists, the provision should be thoroughly researched to make sure that it is not an unconstitutional infringement on a buyer's right to live in a certain place.

KEY TERMS AND CONCEPTS

Aesthetic zoning	Nuisance	Variance
Conditional use permit	Restrictive covenant	Zoning
Nonconforming use	Spot zoning	

END-OF-CHAPTER EXERCISES

Review Questions

See Appendix for answers.

1   What is zoning?
2   What is aesthetic zoning?
3   How are zoning regulations enforced?
4   What are the three broad categories of zoning regulations?
5   What is nonconforming use?
6   What is a conditional use permit?
7   What is a variance?
8   What are some examples of unconstitutional zoning regulations?
9   What is the "rational basis test" as it applies to zoning?
10 What is spot zoning?
11 How do building codes compare with zoning rules and regulations?
12 What is a historic district?
13 What is the Interstate Land Sales Full Disclosure Act?
14 What is the role of environmental issues in restricting a private landowner's use of
    property?
15 Explain restrictive covenants.
16 What are some of the methods used to create restrictive covenants?
17 How can restrictive covenants be terminated?
18 Provide examples of some of the typical provisions found in restrictive covenants.
19 What does it mean when we say that restrictive covenants must "touch and
    concern" the land?
20 What are some examples of unconstitutional restrictive covenants?

DISCUSSION QUESTIONS

1   Is it possible that there are too many zoning rules and regulations? In a country that
    prides itself on freedom of expression, can you make a case for the use of zoning to
    stifle creativity?

2   Turning that last question on its head, what are some non-economic arguments to
    expand zoning rules and regulations that are not currently zoned?

APPLYING WHAT YOU HAVE LEARNED

1   Having zoning regulations that regulate health and safety seems like a good idea,
    but what about aesthetic zoning? Why should a local government be able to dictate

to a private landowner or businessperson how a particular structure should look? Is there a good reason for such zoning regulations? Explain your answer.

2   At your local deed office or land registry office, locate a copy of restrictive covenants. What types of limitations are contained in these restrictive covenants?

WEB SURFING

City of Chicago, IL, Zoning
http://www.cityofchicago.org/city/en/depts/dcd/provdrs/admin.html

Planning and Zoning — City of Miami
www.miamigov.com/planning

Official Zoning Map — City of San Diego, CA
https://www.sandiego.gov/development-services/zoning

Tech Topic
FIELD GUIDE TO ZONING LAWS AND ORDINANCES

The National Association of Realtors' Field Guide to Zoning Laws and Ordinances (http://www.realtor.org/field-guides/field-guide-to-zoning-laws-ordinances) includes a great deal of useful information about what zoning restrictions are and how to handle them. The resources include links to sites that allow you to search for zoning restrictions and municipal codes in counties across the country.

ANNOTATED DOCUMENT

Restrictive Covenants

Item 1 sets the time limit for the covenants.

1. These covenants are to run with the land and shall be binding on all parties and all persons claiming under then until January 1, 2023, at which time said covenants shall be automatically extended for successive periods of ten (10) years, unless by vote of those persons then owning a majority of said lots it is agreed to change said covenants in whole or in part.

2. If the parties hereto, or any of them or their heirs, or successors or assigns, shall violate or attempt to violate any of the covenants herein, it shall be lawful for any other person or persons owning

any real property situated in said subdivision as shown on said plat to prosecute any proceedings at law or in equity against the person or persons violating or attempting to violate any such covenant and either to prevent him or them from so doing, or to recover damages or other dues for such violation.

Item 2 permits civil action to enforce the covenants.

3. Invalidation of any one of these covenants by judgment or court order shall in no way affect any of the other provisions, which shall remain in full force and effect.

4. All numbered lots in said subdivision as shown on said plat shall be known and described as residential lots, and no part of said lots shall be used for any type of business or stores. No structure shall be erected, altered, placed, or permitted to remain on any lot other than one detached single-family dwelling, except storage buildings which are of the same construction as the residence located on said lot.

Item 4 restricts the lot use to residential only.

5. None of said numbered lots as shown on said recorded plat shall be re-subdivided so as to create an additional building lot. Where a residence has been erected on a plot consisting of two or more lots, none of said lots shall thereafter be sold separately if such sales would result in a violation of Paragraph 8 below.

6. No trailer, basement, garage, or other outbuildings erected on these residential lots shall be, at any time, used as a residence temporarily or permanently, nor shall any residence be moved onto a building plot in the subdivision. No mobile homes, either temporary or permanent, shall be allowed on any lot in this subdivision.

Item 6 prohibits the use of mobile homes.

7. No single-family residence having less than 1,200 square feet of heated floor space exclusive of garage, carport, basement, or other auxiliary structure shall be erected on the lot. Any residence having living quarters on more than one floor must contain at least 1,000 square feet of heated floor space on the principal floor and a total of not less than 1,600 square feet of heated floor space exclusive of garage, carport, basement, or other auxiliary structure.

8. All dwellings constructed shall have a setback of a minimum of 40 feet from the front property line and 12 feet from either side property line. On corner lots, all dwellings constructed shall have a set-back line of a minimum of 20 feet from the side street.

9. No signs of any kind shall be displayed to the public view on any lot, except one sign of not more than 5 ft. advertising property for sale or rent, or signs used by a builder to advertise the property during the construction and sales term.

10. No lots shall be used or maintained as a dumping ground for rubbish, trash, garbage, or other waste. All trash and garbage must be kept in a sanitary container. All trash containers shall be maintained in a location that is not visible from the street.

11. Grass and weeds are to be kept down on all vacant lots to prevent an unsightly and unsanitary condition. This is an obligation of the owner and is to be done at his or her expense.

12. All homes constructed in this subdivision shall be principally of brick, stone, or wood siding of 4 inches or larger. No concrete or cinder blocks shall appear.

> Item 12 limits the type of material that can be used in building a home.

13. The grantors reserve an easement of 10 feet along the rear property line, and 5 feet along the side property line, of each and every lot for present or future utility needs, such as telephone, electricity, water, sewer, gas lines, and drainage from streets and slopes. Any easements which have heretofore been granted by the grantors are also reserved. The easement area of each road and all improvements on it shall be maintained continuously by the owner of the road except for improvements for which a public authority or utility company is responsible.

14. No animals, livestock, or poultry shall be raised or kept on any lot, except that dogs, cats, or other household pets may be kept, provided that they are not kept, bred, or maintained for any commercial purposes.

PRACTICE QUESTIONS FOR TEST REVIEW

See Appendix for answers.

Essay Question

Explain restrictive covenants.

True–False

1   T   F   Private individuals are usually prevented from bringing a claim under public nuisance.

2   T   F   Many towns have the power to create ordinances that restrict the way that private subdivisions can be developed.

3   T   F   A restrictive covenant may be extinguished when the situation under which it was created has changed substantially.

Fill in the Blank

1   Single family residences fall into this category: _____.

2   This exception to zoning regulations is created when local government wishes to encourage business development: _____.

3   There are two different types of nuisance actions public and _____.

Multiple Choice

1   Governmental regulations that restrict the way both private and business landowners may use their property.

    A   Statutes
    B   Zoning
    C   Codes
    D   All of the above

2   All of the following are reasons for zoning regulations except:

    A   Promote health and morals.
    B   Reduce traffic congestion.
    C   Emphasize safety fire and other hazards.
    D   All of the above.

3   Zoning ordinances that require all properties to maintain the same general overall appearance.

    A   Maintenance zoning
    B   Appearance zoning
    C   Aesthetic zoning
    D   Hazard zoning

ENDNOTES

[1] *King v. Caddo Parish Com'n*, 719 So. 2d 410 (La., 1998).

[2] N.C. Gen. Stat. §153A-341.

[3] *Corn v. City of Lauderdale Lakes*, 997 F.2d 1369 (11th Cir. 1993).

[4] *Craft v. City of Fort Smith*, 335 Ark. 417, 984 S.W.2d 22 (1998).

[5] *Griswold v. City of Homer*, 925 P.2d 1015 (Alaska 1996).

[6] N.C. Gen. Stat. §160A-400.1.

[7] 15 U.S.C. §1701.

[8] *Sheets v. Dillon*, 221 N.C. 426, 431, 20 S.E.2d 344, 347 (1942).

[9] *Beall v. Hardie*, 177 Kan. 353, 279 P.2d 276 (1955).

[10] 334 U.S. 1, 68 S. Ct. 836, 92 L. Ed. 1161 (1948).

[11] *Shelley v. Kraemer*, 334 U.S. 1, 68 S.Ct. 836, 92 L. Ed. 1161 (1948).

[12] *Logan v. Sprinkle*, 256 N.C. 41, 123 S.E.2d 209 (1961).

[13] *Nature Conservancy v. Congel*, 296 A.D.2d 840, 744 N.Y.S.2d 281 (N.Y. App. Div., 2002).

[14] *Meredith v. Washoe County. Sch. Dist.*, 84 Nev. 15, 19, 435 P.2d 750 (1968).

Real Estate Professions

- Identify the various real estate professions

- Define the role played by real estate brokers in the sale of property

- Explain the importance of agency law for real estate brokers

- Describe the function of real estate inspectors and surveyors

- Identify the important duties of the legal professionals in a real estate practice

I. Introduction

II. The Law of Agency
  A. Creating an Agency Relationship
  B. Agent's Duty to the Principal
  C. Agent's Duty to Third Parties
  D. Principal's Duty to Agent
  E. Independent Contractors

III. Applying Agency Law to Real Estate Agents
  A. A Real Estate Agent's Duty of Care
  B. A Real Estate Agent's Responsibility to Disclose Information
  C. Classifications of Real Estate Agents

IV. Other Real Estate Professions
  A. Real Estate Investors
  B. Loan Officers
  C. Appraisers
  D. Surveyors
  E. The Legal Team
  F. Contractors
  G. Property Managers
  H. Inspectors

INTRODUCTION

There is a dizzying array of professions tied directly or indirectly to real estate. In this chapter, we will examine not only the rules and regulations associated with real estate brokers but also the role of appraisers, surveyors, loan officers, and the legal professionals who specialize in real estate law, especially paralegals.

The most well-known example of professionals who work in real estate every day is real estate brokers. These professionals are regulated by state law, have their own code of ethics, and are bound by the law of agency. But there are many others who are closely involved in real estate law. For instance, there are loan officers at lending institutions whose job it is to evaluate prospective borrowers. There are also appraisers, surveyors, investors, and many others. We will begin our examination of real estate professions by exploring an area of law that is closely intertwined with many of those professions: the law of agency.

THE LAW OF AGENCY

Agency
A business relationship between a principal (who is the source of the authority for the transaction) and the agent (who has the power to carry it out).

Principal
The person for whom an agent works.

Agents have existed in one form or another for centuries. Essentially, an **agency** relationship is created when a person is unable or unwilling to conduct business on his own behalf and instead retains another person to act for him. The person who hires an agent is referred to as the **principal**. The principal works out an arrangement with an agent, giving this agent the power to conduct certain transactions and the authority to see those transactions through to completion. The law of agency is very fluid and allows for a multitude of different relationships.

Once an agency arrangement is created, the agent has the power to legally bind the principal to contracts and other relationships. The agent can negotiate on behalf of the principal and, depending on the nature of the agreement between the agent and the principal, carry out an entire series of business transactions without the principal's direct involvement. Because this arrangement can bind the principal to serious legal obligations, most agency relationships are carefully crafted and written out. The agency agreement usually states the exact parameters of the agent's responsibility and authorization. One of the best examples of an agency relationship in real estate practice is the listing agreement between a home-seller and a real estate broker, discussed in Chapter 6.

A. CREATING AN AGENCY RELATIONSHIP

Although agency relationships can be created in a wide variety of ways, the most common way is by express agreement between the principal and the agent. In this agreement, which is often written out, the principal provides the exact parameters of the agent's authority, including details about particular transactions. The agent, for his part, will also want details about compensation and authority spelled out clearly to avoid any misunderstandings and potential legal liability. Putting an agency relationship into writing makes a great deal of sense, but there are numerous situations in which the principal-agency relationship rests completely on a verbal agreement.

An agency relationship can be created in a number of ways.

REAL
ESTATE
BASICS AT
A GLANCE

B. AGENT'S DUTY TO THE PRINCIPAL

As soon as the principal-agency relationship is created, certain duties are imposed on both parties. Agents are fiduciaries to principals. A **fiduciary** is someone who owes legal and ethical duties to another. The fiduciary relationship has been recognized under American and English law for centuries. Because an agent is a principal's fiduciary, the law imposes several key duties on the agent, including:

Fiduciary
A person who holds a special position of trust and confidence in relation to another.

- Obedience,
- Care,
- Loyalty, and
- Accounting.

1. OBEDIENCE

An agent's first—and some would argue most important—duty is to obey the principal's instructions. The entire reason for a principal-agency relationship is so that the principal can have some transaction carried out. Obviously, the principal must have faith that the agent will follow the instructions given. The law reinforces this duty by making obedience to the principal's instructions one of the core responsibilities of an agent. Disobedience of a principal's instructions is a primary ground for a successful lawsuit by the principal against the agent.

There is a certain amount of flexibility under agency law when it comes to the principal's instructions. A principal might, for example, spell out the exact parameters and directions that the agent must follow. However, there are numerous situations in which the principal is either unable or unwilling to dictate all of the agent's actions. In fact, in situations in which the agent has special training and education, the principal would not want to control the agent's actions because the principal might make an elementary error. Beyond that, the principal uses an agent in order to take advantage of the agent's training and experience.

2. CARE

In addition to obedience, the agent must also demonstrate diligence and due care in performing his duties. If the agent fails to live up to this standard, the principal would be authorized to bring a civil action against the agent. The standard of care that an agent must follow is not determined on a case-by-case basis. Instead, the agent's actions are compared with the actions that other reasonable and prudent agents in the same situation would have taken. If the agent fails to live up to the duty of care created by other agents, he is liable to the principal.

3. LOYALTY

The duty of loyalty is considered one of the most important duties that an agent owes to a principal. This duty requires the agent to act in the best interests of the principal and to avoid situations in which there is a conflict of interest between the agent's desires and the principal's needs. If such a conflict arises, the agent must at least inform the principal of the potential conflict of interest and may also be required to withdraw from representing the principal in any way. The duty of loyalty requires the agent to place the business interests of the principal ahead of other considerations.

The duty of loyalty also imposes on an agent the requirement to avoid self-dealing. This term refers to the agent's unethical use of confidential information related to the principal to help enrich the agent at the principal's expense.

EXAMPLE 11-1

MARIO'S AGENT

Sally is Mario's agent. While working for Mario, she learns that he intends to purchase hundreds of acres of farmland in order to build an amusement park. Mario has understandably kept his plans secret to avoid a run-up in price on local farmland. Sally negotiates with local farmers to purchase the property herself, and then approaches Mario with an offer to buy the land at a substantially increased price. Can Mario bring suit against Sally alleging that she has violated her duty of loyalty? If so, who will win this suit?

Answer: Mario can bring suit against Sally and will likely win. Because Sally was Mario's agent, she cannot use information gathered from that relationship to personally enrich herself, especially at her principal's expense.

4. ACCOUNTING

Our discussion of the duties that an agent owes the principal would not be complete without including some of the more practical aspects of the relationship. An agent must make a full accounting of all financial arrangements and distributions that have arisen in the principal-agency relationship.

C. AGENT'S DUTY TO THIRD PARTIES

We have seen that agents have specific duties that they owe to their principals. However, questions often arise about an agent's duty to individuals who are outside the principal-agency relationship. Agents are not fiduciaries to third parties, so they obviously do not owe the same duties to them that they owe to their principals. So what duties does an agent owe to third parties? Under a principal-agency relationship, agents have the following duties to third parties:

- Honesty and fair dealing,
- Not to commit fraud, and
- To avoid negligent misrepresentation.

1. HONESTY AND FAIR DEALING

Although agents do not have fiduciary duties to third parties, they do have general duties. Perhaps the most important of these is the duty of honesty and fair dealing. Agents must avoid using deceptive trade practices, fraud, or any other illegal practices. As we will see later in this chapter, this duty requires that real estate agents make certain disclosures to potential buyers. It also imposes upon them the obligation to make sure that buyers understand that real estate agents work for and are paid by sellers.

2. NOT TO COMMIT FRAUD

The word **fraud** is used in everyday conversation and can have a wide variety of meanings. However, in the legal context, fraud has a very specific meaning (see Figure 11-1). Fraud is deliberate concealment or deceit that causes injury to a third party or gives the agent an unconscionable advantage in a business transaction. If an agent conceals or actively deceives someone about a material fact, this constitutes fraud.

Fraud
An intentional deception that causes injury to another person.

- An agent made a representation of a material fact or concealed a fact.
- The representation was false.
- The agent knew that the representation was false.
- The agent made the representation with the intent that a third party would rely on the representation.
- The third party's reliance on the representation was reasonable under the circumstances.
- The other party suffered injury from his reliance on the representation.

FIGURE 11-1

Legal Elements of Fraud

a. Material Facts

Fraud can be both a criminal and a civil action. As you can see in Figure 11-1, there are several elements involved in proving a fraud action. These elements do not change in any significant way from civil cases to criminal cases. Both require the intentional misrepresentation of a **material fact**. A material fact is a critical negotiating point or understanding that, if changed, would likely alter the outcome of a business transaction. For instance, a person who claims that he has title to an object and proposes to sell that object to another person when in fact he does not have title is affecting the outcome of a transaction. His ownership is a material fact, and the defrauded party would be entitled to bring either a civil or a criminal action against him.

Material fact
An important or central fact in contract or business negotiations that if fully revealed would change the outcome of the transaction.

b. Sales Tactics

There is an important limitation on the law of representations and material facts: The law makes exceptions for statements that are normally associated with salesmanship. When a salesperson makes a claim such as, "this is the prettiest property I have ever seen in my entire life," such a comment is not intended to be taken literally. Put another way, the salesperson's opinion about the beauty of the property is not a material fact. The buyer would have a difficult time proving that the salesperson had seen prettier tracts at other times. As a result, many of the comments and statements that all consumers hear from salespersons are usually not taken literally unless they are presented as facts.

| EXAMPLE 11-2 | **ARNOLD'S STATEMENTS** |

Arnold is an agent representing Alberta. Alberta wishes to sell her home. One day, while Arnold is showing the house to prospective buyers, he makes the following statements:

"This house has some of the finest craftsmanship you'll ever hope to see."

"Look at those windows — they are double paned and the best that money can buy."

"Take a look at those floors. They are so clean you could eat off them."

If any of these comments proved to be inaccurate, which one could be the basis of a fraud allegation?

Answer: Only the second. The first and third comments are opinions and are not actionable as fraud. However, if it turns out that the windows are not double paned or are not the best that money can buy, the buyers would have an action against Arnold for fraudulent statement.

---

3. AVOID NEGLIGENT MISREPRESENTATION

Negligent misrepresentation
Liability for a statement that proved to be untrue when the person making the statement had no reasonable belief in its accuracy.

In addition to avoiding fraud, agents must also be aware that they face potential liability for **negligent misrepresentation**. There is a fine line between fraud and negligent misrepresentation. Both involve the communication of facts that are not correct, but there is an important difference: Fraud is considered an intentional action, while negligent misrepresentation is considered unintentional. As a result, fraud is always punished more severely than negligent misrepresentation. When we say that an agent has the duty to avoid negligent misrepresentation, what we are actually saying is that an agent must be aware of the truth about statements that he makes before he makes them. If an agent is not sure about the veracity of the statement and makes it anyway, and the statement proves to be untrue, the agent would be liable under the theory of negligent misrepresentation (see Figure 11-2). This is true even if the agent believes that the statement is true but has made no effort to verify it. An action for negligent misrepresentation can also be brought when an agent makes a statement with reckless disregard for its truth. Under any of these circumstances, an agent can be liable to a third party and may end up paying substantial monetary damages to the people who rely on the statement.

FIGURE 11-2

Elements of Negligent Misrepresentation

▦ A false statement made by an agent,	▦ But that the agent had not verified, or made with reckless disregard as to its truth, and
▦ That the agent believed was true,	▦ That resulted in a financial loss to a third party relying on the statement.

Fraud is an intentional action; negligent misrepresentation is an unintentional action.

REAL
ESTATE
BASICS AT
A GLANCE

D. PRINCIPAL'S DUTY TO AGENT

Now that we have discussed the duties that agents owe to principals and third parties, we can focus on the duties that principals owe to agents. Given the nature and quantity of duties that agents owe to their principals, it may be surprising to learn that principals have very few legal obligations to their agents. Generally speaking, principals have only three duties to their agents:

- ▦ To compensate the agent,
- ▦ To cooperate, and
- ▦ Not to unfairly injure the agent's reputation.

1. COMPENSATE THE AGENT

It should come as no surprise that the primary duty the principal owes to an agent is to compensate the agent for his actions on behalf of the principal. The agent's compensation can come in a wide variety of forms. An agent might be paid a flat fee for a service or receive an hourly rate. As we will see later in this chapter, real estate agents are often paid on a commission basis. A commission is a percentage of the sale price. If the principal refuses to pay an agent's commission, then the agent is entitled to sue the principal for the outstanding amount plus any additional charges that the agent has incurred in attempting to receive payment. Principals are often responsible for paying not only for an agent's services but also for any expenses incurred by the agent during his representation.

2. COOPERATE

In addition to paying the agent, the principal also has the duty to cooperate with the agent. Although this would seem to be a duty that should go without saying, there are situations in which a principal might choose not to cooperate with an agent in order to avoid paying the agent's fee. In such a situation, the agent could bring a civil action against the principal alleging a failure of the principal to abide by the duty to cooperate.

THE DEPRESSED MARKET

Arnold has been representing Alberta in her attempt to sell her house. Unfortunately, the market is depressed in her area and there have been few offers on her house. There is less than two weeks to go on the contract that Arnold signed with Alberta to represent her. When those two weeks are up, Alberta is free to hire another agent or to sell the house herself. A potential buyer, Calvin, approaches Alberta with the following proposition: If Alberta will stop cooperating with Arnold and wait for the two-week period to pass, she can avoid paying Arnold's commission when she sells the house to Calvin. Alberta refuses to show the house anymore and cuts off all contact with Arnold. Later, Arnold learns that Calvin had approached Alberta prior to the expiration of his listing agreement with her. Arnold sues for his commission. Will he get it?

Answer: Yes. Because Alberta violated her duty of cooperation with Arnold and engaged in an agreement with Calvin to cheat Arnold out of his commission, Arnold will receive his commission, despite the fact that the sale occurred after Arnold's contract of representation terminated.

The duty to cooperate means not only that the principal must pay the agent's commission, but also that the principal should not terminate the agency relationship for an unjust or capricious reason. The principal is required to act reasonably to assist the agent in carrying out his duties and not to impose unreasonable demands on the agent.

3. NOT TO UNFAIRLY INJURE THE AGENT'S REPUTATION

In addition to the principal's other duties to compensate and cooperate, the principal is also under the obligation to refrain from unfairly injuring the agent's reputation. In many ways, this obligation resembles a defamation suit, in which a person is sued for making false statements about another. Here, however, the suit would be specific to the principal-agency relationship and would depend on the nature of the statements made by the principal. The principal is permitted to use the same defense that defendants use in defamation cases: that the statement was true.

E. INDEPENDENT CONTRACTORS

In our discussion of agency relationships, it is important to point out other relationships that do not follow the agency pattern. When a person is classified as an independent contractor, he is not an agent. Independent contractors are specialists. They make their own decisions about how the job will be completed, and other than cursory instructions from the employer, they do not take direction about how they should complete their jobs. They are truly independent, and with this independence comes the freedom from being classified as an agent, with the attendant legal and ethical duties that arise from that classification. There are times when the line between being an agent, being an independent contractor, or having some other business relationship is unclear.

Independent contractors do not qualify as agents and do not have the same level of responsibility or duties as agents.

APPLYING AGENCY LAW TO REAL ESTATE AGENTS

So far, our discussion about agency law has been very general. It is time for us to apply the general law of agency to the specialized world of real estate professionals.

The most common example of an agency relationship in real estate is the real estate agent. A real estate agent is, in every legal sense of the word, an agent. The real estate agent has a principal, has both ethical and legal duties to that principal, and receives his compensation from the principal. In a typical real estate agency relationship, a person who is legally authorized to act as a real estate agent enters into an agreement with a person who wishes to sell a home. In this scenario, the seller is the principal. The seller negotiates specific details of the agent's representation, including how long the relationship will last, what the agent is authorized to tell others about the home, when and how the agent will show the house to prospective buyers, and the amount of the agent's compensation. In most real estate transactions, a real estate agent works on a straight commission basis: The agent's compensation is a percentage of the final sale price.

Real estate agents owe the same duties to their principals as any other agent. However, because they are licensed by the state, real estate agents often owe additional duties to their principals. These differences also extend to the standard of care that is imposed on real estate agents.

A. A REAL ESTATE AGENT'S DUTY OF CARE

Real estate agents actually have a more rigorous standard of care than that seen with other agency relationships. State laws impose on them the duty to use skill, care, and diligence in the performance of their duties. They must demonstrate the same level of skill and care as other real estate agents. It isn't enough for a real estate agent to meet a general standard of skill and care; when it comes time for a court to weigh the real estate agent's actions, he will be compared to the standards of other real estate agents and held to those same high standards, regardless of the fact that he may be a novice in the profession. When it comes to diligence, courts are even more specific. To demonstrate diligence, a real estate agent must show that he acted with reasonable diligence in obtaining the most advantageous result for the principal. That translates into two factors: That the agent obtained (1) the best possible price and (2) the best possible terms for the principal. Failure to do either may make the agent liable to the principal.

B. A REAL ESTATE AGENT'S RESPONSIBILITY TO DISCLOSE INFORMATION

It should come as no surprise that the primary duty the principal owes to an agent is to compensate the agent for his actions on behalf of the principal. The agent's compensation can come in a wide variety of forms. An agent might be paid a flat fee for a service or receive an hourly rate. As we will see later in this chapter, real estate agents are often paid on a commission basis. A commission is a percentage of the sale price. If the principal refuses to pay an agent's commission, then the agent is entitled to sue the principal for the outstanding amount plus any additional charges that the agent has incurred in attempting to receive payment. Principals are often responsible for paying not only for an agent's services but also for any expenses incurred by the agent during his representation.

Real estate agents not only have a legal obligation to disclose certain information, they also have an ethical obligation to preserve confidential information. Because the real estate agent represents the seller, the agent is not permitted to disclose to the buyer the seller's absolute lowest sale price or any other confidential information that the seller has relayed to the agent.

C. CLASSIFICATIONS OF REAL ESTATE AGENTS

So far, our discussion about the duties of real estate agents has presumed that there is only one classification: agent. However, there are actually two classifications of real estate professionals: real estate brokers and real estate agents.

1. REAL ESTATE BROKERS VERSUS REAL ESTATE AGENTS

A real estate broker carries out the full range of activities normally associated with real estate transactions. A real estate broker is someone who is licensed by the state and is authorized to earn a commission. A real estate agent, on the other hand, is usually a person who works under the authority of a real estate broker. The agent assists the broker and in exchange earns part of the commission. It is important to remember that the terminology used here can vary considerably from state to state. For instance, some states may recognize the two classifications as "brokers" and "salespersons," while another state might refer to these individuals by other titles. In some instances, states have eliminated entire categories, such as real estate agents, and now refer to all members of the profession as brokers. For the sake of clarity, we will refer to these two categories as real estate brokers and real estate agents.

Both the broker and the agent often work for a company that has other staff, including other brokers and agents, salespersons, secretaries, and office managers. Whether a real estate professional works for a firm or is self-employed, his responsibilities to the seller remain the same.

Although working as a real estate broker or agent offers a certain measure of freedom, there are downsides. For one thing, brokers and agents often work evenings and weekends and may also be on call to their clients at other times. Novice agents also face stiff competition from older, more established real estate professionals who have better connections in the community.

Notice that we have not used the term "Realtor." This term is a trademarked symbol owned by the National Association of Realtors (NAR) and can only be used by members of that organization. The NAR has been in existence since 1913, and the vast majority of real estate brokers and agents in the United States are members.

2. BECOMING A REAL ESTATE BROKER OR AGENT

Every state requires real estate brokers and agents to be licensed. There are some minimum requirements that all applicants must meet. They include:

- Must be a high school graduate,
- Must be at least 18 years of age, and
- Must pass a written examination.[1]

In addition to these minimum requirements, most states also require:

- Proof of good moral character, and
- Successful completion of real estate education requirements.

Most states require that candidates complete a minimum number of hours of classroom instruction. For instance, some states require a minimum of 60 hours of classroom instruction before an applicant is allowed to take the written examination.[2] Once a real estate broker or agent obtains a license, he must also complete continuing education credits to maintain standing with the state. See Figure 11-3 for sample real estate broker wages.

		FIGURE 11-3
2020 Median Pay	$51,220 per year $24.63 per hour	**2021 Quick Facts: Real Estate Brokers and Sales Agents (Bureau of Labor Statistics)[3]**
Typical Entry-Level Education	High school diploma or equivalent	
Work Experience in a Related Occupation	See: https://www.bls.gov/ooh/sales/ real-estate-brokers-and-sales-agents .htm#tab-4	
On-the-Job Training		
Number of Jobs, 2020	518,800	
Job Outlook, 2020–30	4% (slower than average)	
Employment Change, 2020–30	21,800	

REAL ESTATE
BASICS AT
A GLANCE

Real estate brokers and sales agents help clients buy, sell, and rent properties. Although brokers and agents do similar work, brokers are licensed to manage their own real estate businesses. Sales agents must work with a real estate broker.

3. REGULATIONS THAT GOVERN REAL ESTATE BROKERS AND AGENTS

Because states require real estate brokers and agents to be licensed, all states have some form of real estate commission that is responsible not only for admitting new members, but also for sanctioning brokers and agents who violate state regulations. State real estate boards are authorized to take disciplinary action against brokers and agents who violate rules and regulations. Among the more common actions that can result in sanctions are:

- Negligent misrepresentation,
- Fraud,
- Making false promises designed to influence or persuade a person,
- Dual agency without full disclosure,
- Failing to account for client funds, and
- Absconding or embezzling settlement funds.

If the state agency that governs real estate brokers and agents finds that a member has committed these or any other infractions, it is entitled to bring disciplinary action. A real estate broker or agent may have his license permanently suspended for serious infractions or temporarily suspended for a less serious violation. For a summary of other possible sanctions against real estate professionals, see Figure 11-4.

FIGURE 11-4

Summary of Possible Sanctions Against Real Estate Professionals

- Temporary or permanent suspension of license,
- Civil liability to the client or third party, and/or
- Criminal liability.

4. SERVICES PROVIDED BY REAL ESTATE AGENTS AND BROKERS

Buyers and sellers turn to real estate agents because of their training, education, and experience with the real estate market. A real estate broker can be an invaluable asset to a seller by providing several services that are unavailable anywhere else. Brokers meet with prospective buyers and ask them questions in order to determine the best possible match between what the buyer can afford and the properties currently available. The broker will then turn to the "hot sheet" or, more likely, a computer database to investigate the properties currently listed for sale to meet the buyer's specifications.

In addition to locating buyers, real estate brokers may also be responsible for arranging title searches and meeting with prospective sellers to sign listing agreements. Brokers often have a network of loan officers and mortgage brokers who can help the borrower begin the process of qualifying for a loan. Depending on the state, the broker may be the person responsible for coordinating the entire transaction, from the initial meeting of the buyer and seller to the closing or settlement. In other states, real estate attorneys handle those details.

Although brokers work for sellers, they may spend days or even weeks with a particular buyer. This sometimes creates a false impression for the buyer. The buyer may believe that the real estate broker has his best interests in mind, forgetting the basic agency relationship that exists between the real estate broker and the owner of the property that is eventually sold.

a. Multiple Listing Service

The Multiple Listing Service (MLS) is a feature provided by real estate agents and brokers. Essentially, the MLS is a database listing all available properties. The MLS both advertises these properties and offers to split commissions with other brokers and agents in the area. Listings in the MLS contain extensive descriptions along with exterior photographs and other information, such as lot size, internal and external features of the residence, and information about total square footage, bathrooms, bedrooms, and many other aspects of the property. By offering to split the commission with other real estate agents, the MLS essentially puts all real estate agents in the community to work for the house-seller. Although the MLS was once only a printed document, these days brokers and agents can access property listings online. In the days before the widespread ability to access the Internet, the most recent postings in the MLS were referred to as the "hot sheet." The hot sheet would be printed once a week and distributed to local real estate agents. These days, a hot sheet is usually found online, not in hard copy. Because the MLS is only available to real estate brokers and agents, it continues to be an extremely valuable resource.

A multiple listing service is both an advertisement of available properties and an offer to other brokers to share in a commission.

REAL
ESTATE
BASICS AT
A GLANCE

Tech Topic
ELECTRONIC BILLING

Traditionally, attorneys and their support staff have relied on spreadsheets to keep track of their time for billing purposes and then have needed to transfer those hours to template-style invoices in a word processing program for submission to clients. While this system works, it has several downsides, among them much room for error, the need to shift focus frequently in order to record time spent on various activities, and the time-consuming process of actually filling in invoices.

Fortunately, modern technology offers several software options that automate the time-tracking and billing processes. Generally, these programs run in the background and capture all of a computer's activity, tracking when a user switches from one project to another via a variety of methods, including timers, screenshots, assignment of certain windows to certain projects, and usage of a calendar for appointments. The program then produces an invoice based on this tracked time, using its preprogrammed legal codes to assign the appropriate billing code to each activity. This invoice can be sent electronically to the client, eliminating part of the heavy paper load carried by most law firms. In many cases, the software allows clients to pay invoices online

as well, shortening the time it takes for firms to receive payment.

Timeslips is perhaps the longest-used and most popular of the software options. The fact that it includes myriad predefined reports and supports industry-standard billing codes makes it appealing to those already using it, but it is limited by the fact that it is both desktop-based and Windows-only compatible. It is also one of the pricier time-tracking/billing software options, so firms new to electronic billing will likely favor a different program.

The cloud-based Timesolv and Bill4Time are more tech-friendly options designed just for the legal community. They both allow users to track time across multiple devices simultaneously and include some additional useful budgeting and reporting features. Timesolv has a mobile app for both iOS and Android, and it integrates seamlessly with QuickBooks for accounting purposes. Bill4Time includes a payment portal that allows clients to pay invoices through PayPal, LawPay, and Stripe.

Unsurprisingly, more and more attorneys are choosing to use such time-tracking and billing software in their practices, streamlining the billing process for law firms and clients alike.

b. Locating and Prequalifying Buyers

The primary purpose for the existence of a real estate broker or agent is to bring buyers and sellers together. To that end, real estate brokers not only enter into listing agreements with sellers to advertise and promote the sale of property, but also to actively seek potential buyers. It is not unusual for brokers and agents to prequalify buyers by meeting with them in person, asking them general questions about their financial condition, and putting them in contact with local lenders. Obviously, it is in the broker's best interest to ensure that a buyer can produce the funds necessary to complete the transaction. The broker's ultimate responsibility is to produce a buyer who is ready, willing, and able to complete the transaction. The phrase "ready, willing, and able" has particular legal significance. If a broker or agent produces such a buyer and the seller reneges on the transaction, the real estate agent is still entitled to his commission, even if the transaction never occurs.[4]

REAL WORLD PERSPECTIVES: *REAL ESTATE BROKER*

Up until a few years ago, a real estate agent would do a lot more dual representation. However, it's only about 5 percent of what I do now. With the weight of the listings online with Zillow or others, it will say that this property is listed with a specific agent. It automatically puts in the buyers' mind that the person listed must represent sellers, therefore they think they need a different agent to represent their interests.

— D. W., real estate broker

 **OTHER REAL ESTATE PROFESSIONS**

In this section, we will examine many other types of real estate professions, including:

- Real estate investors,
- Loan officers,
- Appraisers,
- Surveyors,
- The legal team,
- Contractors,
- Property managers, and
- Inspectors.

A. REAL ESTATE INVESTORS

At one time or another, we have all heard the general statement that real estate makes a good investment. There are many appealing aspects to real estate as part of a financial portfolio, but there are also considerable risks that can prove to be disasters for the uninformed investor.

1. ADVANTAGES OF REAL ESTATE INVESTMENTS

In general, real estate is a wise investment. Houses and land generally appreciate in value over time and offer other advantages. The advantages of real estate include that it:

- Generally appreciates in value,
- Improves a homeowner's credit rating,

Provides a ready source of funds for equity loans, and
Offers tax advantages.

a. Appreciation in Value

Real estate makes a good investment because it generally appreciates in value. When something appreciates, it gains in value over time without substantial reinvestment on the part of the owner. There are several reasons why land appreciates in value. For one thing, a growing population demands more housing. As the population becomes more affluent, individual buyers seek bigger and more expensive properties. Although the population steadily increases, the supply of land is fixed and the laws of supply and demand dictate that prices rise in this situation. However, the fact that land generally appreciates in value does not mean that all parcels will be worth more next year than they are worth this year. Periodically, land sales have dipped dramatically and prices have fallen, causing great economic hardship for individual homeowners.

b. Impact on Credit Rating

Homeownership is a great way of improving an individual's credit standing. Regular payments on a monthly mortgage contribute to a positive credit history for an individual, allowing him to borrow additional funds for other purchases.

c. Potential Source of Funds

As a homeowner slowly builds equity in land, the equity provides a ready source of cash if the homeowner chooses to borrow against it. As we have already seen in previous chapters, equity is the difference between the value of the property and the amount that is owed on it. If a person has $20,000 of equity in his home, lenders will use this equity as collateral for a new loan. A homeowner can take advantage of this equity in order to make improvements on a home, take an expensive vacation, or fund a child's college education.

d. Tax Advantages

One of the best advantages that comes from homeownership is the tax advantage it gives individual taxpayers. The Internal Revenue Service allows homeowners to deduct interest charges on monthly mortgage payments from their annual income tax returns. This gives mortgage loans an advantage not seen with other types of lending. The ability to write off mortgage interest is a powerful incentive to purchase a home to help reduce an individual's personal income tax liability in any given year. Recent changes in the tax code may have a substantial impact on this provision, however. For example, taxpayers may no longer write off all of their interest. They may only do so for any home where the mortgage is $750,000 or less. In the past, city, county, and state property taxes were also deductible on annual income tax returns. That has now been limited to $10,000 for individuals. Writing off mortgage interest on home equity loans, which was formerly limited to loans of $100,000 or less, has now been completely eliminated.

2. DISADVANTAGES OF REAL ESTATE INVESTMENTS

Although there are numerous advantages to investing in real estate, there are also some important disadvantages, including:

- Poor liquidity,
- Property taxes,
- Maintenance costs, and
- Financing and down payment costs.

a. Poor Liquidity

One of the biggest disadvantages to homeownership is the lack of liquidity in the investment. **Liquidity** refers to the ease with which an investor can convert funds for use in other investments. Because the sale of a home can take weeks or months, it is not easy for a homeowner to take profits out of a real estate investment. If an individual needs cash quickly, tying up money in a real estate investment is a bad choice.

Liquidity
The ease to which an investment can be converted into ready cash.

b. Property Taxes

An individual homeowner is responsible for paying property taxes. These taxes are assessed on an annual basis and can run to thousands of dollars per year. If a homeowner is unable to pay these taxes, the local government is authorized to foreclose on the property to satisfy the tax bill.

c. Maintenance Costs

Unlike rental situations, a homeowner is responsible for all maintenance costs to keep the premises in good repair. Depending on the quality of the home, maintenance costs can easily take more out of a homeowner's budget than property taxes and mortgage payments combined. Some homes are in such poor shape that they require tremendous capital investment. The homeowner is responsible for all these maintenance costs, and if the homeowner is unable to meet upkeep costs, the house will slowly deteriorate, losing value over time.

d. Financing and Down Payment Costs

Last, but certainly not least, there are many costs associated with purchasing a house. A potential homeowner may have to come up with as much as 10 percent of the total purchase price as a down payment before a lender will even consider providing a mortgage. In addition to down payment costs, banks also assess other fees as part of the lending process. Many of these fees can cause substantial financial hardship for individuals with limited financial resources.

3. REAL ESTATE INVESTMENT TRUSTS

A real estate investment trust (REIT) is a security that trades like a stock on any of the major national stock exchanges. In many ways, it resembles a mutual fund. The trust devotes itself to the business of purchasing, managing, and selling tracts of real estate for profit. Investors buy shares in the trust, and this money is then used to purchase real property around the nation. Profits from real estate investment are then passed back to the investors based on the number of shares that they have purchased in the trust. REITs can be an attractive alternative for individuals who wish to take advantage of the generally positive investment potential for real estate while avoiding many of the disadvantages. REITs usually receive special tax considerations, while also providing the investor with the kind of high liquidity that is not normally found in individual real estate ownership. Individual investors can buy and sell their shares on an open market in the same way that other investors buy and sell stocks and bonds. There are numerous types of REITs, including some that specialize in mortgages, commercial property, and apartment complexes, among many others.

REAL ESTATE BASICS AT A GLANCE

REITs offer many of the advantages of real estate investing while avoiding some of the common disadvantages.

4. SMALL INVESTORS AND "DO-IT-YOURSELFERS"

There are some individuals who specialize in buying and selling individual parcels of real estate. Some of them purchase distressed real estate with the idea of making improvements to it and then selling it for a profit. Others acquire properties to hold as rental units. This can be an attractive investment alternative for individuals who know a lot about construction and can do much of the work themselves. For individuals who lack those skills, many of the profits that could come from the sale of a "fixer-upper" are lost in labor costs to pay others to improve the property. As we will see in Chapter 14, there are important tax considerations that go into any decision to buy, fix up, and resell real estate. State and federal capital gains taxes can eat into any potential profit.

EXAMPLE 11-4

HE BUYS UGLY HOUSES

Juan posts signs around town reading, "I buy ugly houses." He wants to buy houses that may not be considered as desirable as others. Why would Juan do such a thing?

Answer: If Juan chooses correctly, it can be a lucrative business. Even with the costs associated with fixing up the homes, and factoring in capital gains taxes, Juan may still make $10,000 to $20,000 per home. It only takes several homes per year to earn him a substantial salary.

B. LOAN OFFICERS

Although the classification of real estate investors covers several important areas, these are not the only individuals who earn their income directly or indirectly from the real estate profession. Loan officers are another important category. They play a critical role in the sale and purchase of real estate for the simple reason that most people do not have thousands of dollars of ready cash on hand to purchase real estate. Buyers must go to a local banker or other lending institution and borrow funds for the purchase. The problem with a term such as "loan officer" is that it is very broad. In any typical residential mortgage situation, there are literally dozens of individuals who are involved in various phases of the transaction. Lenders have individuals who act as customer service representatives who meet with potential borrowers, underwriters to evaluate the risk of extending credit to the buyer, and committees that are responsible for reviewing loan applications and making decisions about mortgages. All these individuals earn their living either directly or indirectly from real estate.

1. ONLINE LOAN APPLICATIONS

Many lenders have moved to an Internet-based loan application process. Even traditional banks have websites on which prospective borrowers may complete an application and submit it to the loan department, all without ever having to step inside the bank itself.

2. INTERNET MORTGAGE LENDERS

Traditional lenders are also getting stiff competition from lenders that are entirely Web-based. In previous years, borrowers would go to lenders in the community in order to finance the purchase of a home. These days, a borrower can just as easily obtain a mortgage from an Internet-based mortgage lender with offices on the other side of the country.

C. APPRAISERS

The topic of appraisal is complicated enough to fill a book by itself. Although new regulations under Dodd-Frank have restricted some aspects of how an appraisal can be carried out, the traditional approach is still used. Appraisers are professionals who evaluate properties and assess the fair market value of real estate. Like real estate brokers, appraisers are state certified and licensed. Banks and lenders often require an appraisal before loaning money in a particular transaction. After all, the lender is providing funds based on the value of the property and it would be foolish to do so without determining that the property is worth the amount loaned.

1. PROCESS OF APPRAISAL

Appraisers usually visit the seller's house and inspect it. They list the various features and also evaluate the neighborhood. They use several different methods to determine a final value for the real estate. Among the techniques used by appraisers is a comparison of the property for sale with other, similar parcels. They will seek out information about recent sale prices of similarly situated properties. They may also use other techniques, such as:

- Reviewing tax records,
- Examining deeds and recent sales,
- Measuring property boundaries, and
- Reviewing MLS listings.

The appraiser may also visit several different local government offices, including the following:

- Registrar of deeds office (land office or registry office),
- Property tax office,
- Zoning board, and
- Permits and applications department, among many others.

Once the appraiser puts together his report, he forwards it to the lender. Many lenders require that the appraisal amount meet or exceed the amount of the mortgage before authorizing a release of funds in the closing.

2. THE IMPORTANCE OF REAL ESTATE VALUATION

Even before an appraiser enters the picture, the seller and listing agent will attempt to come up with a reasonable sale price for the home. Putting a price on real estate is important for many reasons. For instance, real property taxes are based on property value. Without an appraisal, how do real estate agents value property? Generally, they prepare a comparative market analysis (CMA).

When a real estate broker or agent prepares a CMA, it is not the same thing as an appraisal. CMAs are meant to be more general than the specific report provided by an appraiser. They are prepared for real estate clients to provide guidance in setting the sale price. A CMA is a summary of recent sales of similar properties, based on the sale price of homes with similar features, amenities, and locations as the house currently up for sale. The CMA uses this as a means to provide a general framework to set a price for the current home. In some states, brokers can charge a fee for the CMA, while in others the report is prepared as part of the duties that the broker carries out for the seller.

D. SURVEYORS

Surveyors physically check the accuracy of property boundary lines. Surveying requires careful attention to detail. A surveyor must go to the property and measure off distances and directions with carefully calibrated equipment. When he has completed the physical measurements, he prepares a drawing showing the property boundaries. See Figure 11-5 for a sample survey. In creating a survey, a professional surveyor will not simply visit the site. He will also review the public records, tax records, and other surveys or plats prepared in the past. From these, surveyors use their equipment to

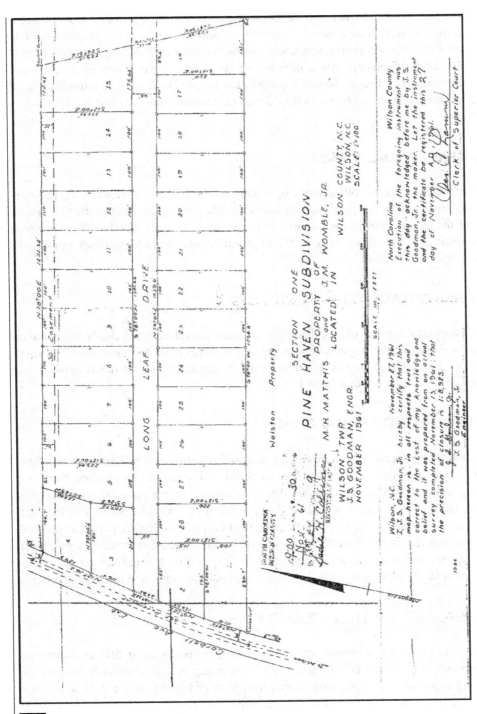

Survey of Pine
Haven Subdivision

measure the precise distance and direction at each point of the property where there is a turn. In most situations, a survey simply shows the boundaries of the property with no reference to the physical structures, such as the house or outbuildings. However, there are also "as-built" surveys. An as-built survey is a map of the property boundaries and the physical structures on the site, especially the house. These surveys often include all improvements, such as fences, outbuildings, extensions, add-ons, and installed water features.

E. THE LEGAL TEAM

Lawyers and paralegals often play a significant role in real estate transactions. In some states, lawyers draft the deeds of conveyance while paralegals conduct the title search under the supervision of the lawyers. In other states, brokers or others may perform these tasks, but there is no denying the importance that sound legal advice can have in a real estate transaction.

1. REAL ESTATE ATTORNEYS

Real estate attorneys are often called upon to draft general warranty deeds and to advise lenders about the legal aspects of mortgages or deeds of trust. In many states, attorneys also conduct closings or real estate settlements during which all funds between the buyer and the seller are distributed.

2. REAL ESTATE PARALEGALS

Real estate paralegals play an absolutely essential role in real estate transactions. They carry out many of the daily activities associated with a real estate practice, from preparing deeds to confirming closing dates. Paralegals, in some states, also conduct title examinations to determine the marketability of title for a particular parcel. In addition to these activities, paralegals also coordinate many of the events that are part of a real estate transaction. They work closely with real estate brokers, agents, loan officers, title insurance agents, and many others. In the next few chapters, we will outline the role played by paralegals in areas such as title insurance, title examinations, and the closing process.

3. REAL ESTATE TITLE SEARCHERS

Some real estate professionals earn their living by performing title examinations. Commonly referred to as "title searchers," this group includes not only lawyers and paralegals but also other individuals who have learned how to carry out these activities and market them to law firms and title insurance companies. In other states, individuals might work to prepare abstracts of title documents. The methods used to compensate these individuals vary. In some cases, they are paid by the job, while in others they are paid by the hour. We will discuss the role of title searchers and abstractors in greater detail in the next chapter.

4. THE ROLE OF TECHNOLOGY IN THE REAL ESTATE LAW OFFICE

Although the practice of law has lagged behind other professions in terms of technological innovation, modern real estate practice now employs a broad range of technology. Any legal professional considering a career in real estate law must have a solid foundation in using computer systems, scanners, flash drives, and the Internet. There are also several different types of legal software now available that are used to do everything from keeping track of client appointments to preparing a HUD settlement statement.

F. CONTRACTORS

In addition to loan officers, real estate investors, and legal professionals, general contractors also play an essential role in real estate. A general contractor is a person who may be licensed by the state to construct residential or commercial structures. Some states do not require licensure of contractors, while others do. Most states require that an individual post a bond or complete a written examination to become a general contractor. Most states also require general contractors to have at least a minimum level of financial resources before they can engage in business. General contractors often hire subcontractors to perform specialized tasks. While a general contractor may coordinate the entire building process, a subcontractor may only complete a small portion of it. As we will see in the chapter on real estate closings, most lenders require a general contractor to submit proof that all subcontractors have been paid before the closing can be completed.

G. PROPERTY MANAGERS

Property managers supervise rental properties for owners. The actual owner may be unable or unwilling to manage the property and therefore will bring in a professional to do it. A property manager may be paid a flat fee or a percentage of the total rents paid during a particular month.

H. INSPECTORS

Our final category of real estate professionals is building inspectors. An inspection is often a condition in the offer of purchase and contract between the buyer and the seller. The buyer will insist that a certified or licensed inspector's report state that there are no major flaws or structural defects in the home. Lenders often insist on an inspection as well.

Real estate inspectors examine properties in painstaking detail to come up with an accurate overview of the condition of the premises. Thorough real estate inspections ensure that buyers will not discover any major problems with the home after taking possession of it. Inspections also protect the interests of the mortgage lender. A real estate inspection resembles an appraisal, but there are important differences.

The purpose of an appraisal is to determine the value of the property. An inspection, on the other hand, is designed to discover any major or minor flaws with the premises.

It is important to make a distinction here between private inspectors and government inspectors. Private inspectors are in the business of inspecting residential properties and issuing reports to buyers and sellers as part of the real estate transaction. However, there is an entirely separate class of inspectors who work for local governmental agencies and are responsible for inspecting new construction to make sure that it complies with building codes. We have discussed the role of governmental inspectors in previous chapters. They are usually not involved in a typical real estate transaction in which there is a pre-existing structure on the property.

Real estate inspectors produce a final report listing all of the important house systems and any major or minor problems with those systems. For an example of a real estate inspector's checklist, see Figure 11-6. Unlike the example provided here, the final report will often run to dozens of pages and provide detailed information on every aspect of the house. For an overview of the type of pay that building and construction inspectors earn, see Figure 11-7.

FIGURE 11-6		Condition				
Typical Inspection		Good	Fair	Poor	Bad	Comments
Checklist	Exterior					
	Windows					
	Siding type: Vinyl Composite Wood siding Other					
	Doors					
	Chimneys					
	Roof ventilation					
	Interior					
	Overall appearance					
	Ceiling					
	Walls					
	Systems: Heating/Air conditioning Electrical (Amp service) Water Sewage					

Quick Facts: Construction and Building Inspectors	
2020 Median Pay	$62,860 per year $30.22 per hour
Typical Entry-Level Education	High school diploma or equivalent
Work Experience in a Related Occupation	5 years or more
On-the-Job Training	Moderate-term on-the-job training
Number of Jobs, 2016	129,300
Job Outlook, 2016–26	–3% (Decline)
Employment Change, 2016–26	–3,800

Source: Bureau of Labor Statistics, downloaded January 31, 2022.
https://www.bls.gov/ooh/construction-and-extraction/construction-and-building-inspectors.htm

FIGURE 11-7

Inspector Pay[5]

Construction and building inspectors ensure that construction meets local and national building codes and ordinances, zoning regulations, and contract specifications.

WHAT CONSTRUCTION AND BUILDING INSPECTORS DO

Case Excerpt

CLARK v. TAYLOR HUDSON REAL ESTATE
SC 1583/2019 (Decided on June 7, 2021)

RICHARD J. GUERTIN, J.

This is a Small Claims action by Nicole Clark ("Plaintiff") against Victoria Yankovoy d/b/a Taylor Hudson Real Estate ("Defendant"). The Plaintiff, in her Application to File Small Claims, alleged the Defendant failed to refund the real estate fee after the prospective landlord rejected the lease agreement for the Plaintiff to rent the property at 38 Wickham Avenue, Goshen, New York ("the Wickham Property"). As a result, the Plaintiff is seeking $1,800.00 in damages from the Defendant. The Defendant filed a counterclaim against the Plaintiff and alleged the Plaintiff owes the Defendant $1,900.00 for the real estate rental fee/commission owed for property the Plaintiff leased and occupied located at 15 Phillips Place, Goshen, New York ("the Phillips Property").

On April 2, 2021, the parties appeared in court for trial; the Plaintiff and the Defendant each appeared pro se. The Court conducted the trial and reserved decision after the trial. At the trial, the Plaintiff and the Defendant both testified under oath as did the Plaintiff's witness, Roman Zawojski ("Zawojski"). The Plaintiff and the Defendant also submitted documentary evidence for the Court's consideration.

Findings of Fact

The credible evidence at the trial showed the following:

The Plaintiff and the Defendant, a licensed real estate broker, on October 9, 2019, entered into a "Rental Fee/Commission Agreement" by which the Plaintiff agreed to pay the Defendant "the commission/real estate rental fee amount equal to one (1) month's rent for the Defendant's services for showing me/us and or referring me/us to any rental property which results in me/us leasing the property/signing a lease agreement and or occupying the rental property." (Defendant's Exhibit E, in evidence). The Defendant worked with the Plaintiff in gathering the necessary information and submitting a rental application for the Wickham Property to the owners of that property, as detailed in various text messages exchanged between the parties and contained in Plaintiff's Exhibit 3, in evidence (including a text from the Plaintiff to the Defendant on October 9th stating "I love the house — I think it's perfect for me!" and another on October 10th stating "Thank you so much again for all your help!"). On October 11, 2019 the Plaintiff signed the lease for the Wickham Property (Plaintiff's Exhibit 2, in evidence; according to the lease, the term was one year commencing November 1, 2019, and the monthly rent was $1,800.00 per month). The Defendant transmitted the lease to the owners of the Wickham Property for their signature, and the Plaintiff deposited money into the owners' account at Chase Bank for the security deposit and pet fee (Plaintiff's Exhibits 3 and 5, both in evidence). The Plaintiff, also on October 11th, paid the Defendant the $1,800.00 commission due to the Defendant pursuant to the parties' agreement, as shown in the receipt given by the Defendant to the Plaintiff (Plaintiff's Exhibit 1, in evidence).

On October 16, 2019, the Defendant sent a text to the Plaintiff indicating the Defendant reminded the owners of the Wickham Property to "scan and email the signed and dated lease to the Defendant" (Exhibit 3). The Plaintiff sent a text to the Defendant on October 19th, inquiring about the lease (Exhibit 3). On October 26, 2019, the Defendant reported to the Plaintiff that the father-in-law of one of the owners called the Defendant and "said the executed lease will be back to us Monday or Tuesday. Thanks for your patience. I don't understand why it took 2 weeks to get the lease back," to which the Plaintiff responded "thank you so much for being so on top of this for me" (Plaintiff's Exhibit 3). On October 27, 2019, the Defendant reported to the Plaintiff that the Defendant "just picked up a hard copy of your fully executed lease . . . finally!" (Plaintiff's Exhibit 3).

The Plaintiff was supposed to move into the Wickham Property on November 1, 2019. That never happened. The Plaintiff and Ursula Rozov, a purported owner of the Wickham Property, exchanged a number of emails on October 29, 2019 and November 1, 2019 (Plaintiff's Exhibit 4, in evidence; Defendant's Exhibit D, in evidence). In those emails, Ursula Rozov alleged that the Defendant altered the signed lease causing the lease to be null and void. Ms. Rozov also alleged the Plaintiff's rental application was not accurate. The Plaintiff disputed those claims; she stated her rental application was accurate and provided details, and she also stated her copy of the lease had no alterations. She also stated she "did not hire Victoria as an agent," despite the fact the

Plaintiff signed the agreement with the Defendant as described in Defendant's Exhibit E. The Plaintiff, on November 1, 2019, indicated by email to Ursula Rozov that she had the executed lease in her possession and was ready to move in, but Ms. Rozov replied by email that same day that she was refunding the Plaintiff's deposit and reiterated the "lease is not valid as it was altered with white out by your broker after we executed" (Plaintiff's Exhibit 4).

The Rozovs refunded the Plaintiff's rent and fee deposit via Zelle on November 23, 2019 and December 18, 2019 in the total amount of $2,065.00 (Plaintiff's Exhibit E, in evidence).

The Plaintiff, in her testimony, claimed that after the owners of the Wickham Property declared the signed lease "null and void," she thought it was best not to work any further with the owners of the Wickham Property or the Defendant. The Plaintiff did not tell the Defendant she wasn't going to work with her any further, and the Plaintiff testified she contacted Ms. Clark directly around October 31, 2019, after receiving text messages from the Defendant regarding the Phillips Property. The Plaintiff also testified that after the Wickham Property fell through, she and her boyfriend (Zawojski) decided to rent a property together (she was going to rent the Wickham Property on her own).

The Plaintiff claimed that Zawojski started looking at other properties to rent before the Wickham Property fell through and that he mentioned the Phillips Property to her around mid-October 2019. She admitted on cross-examination, however, that Zawojski saw the listing for the Phillips Property some time after it was listed on October 24, 2019 (Defendant's Exhibit A). Zawojski himself testified he believed he found information about the Phillips Property around the same day the Plaintiff was supposed to get the key to move into the Wickham Property; she originally was supposed to move in on November 1st.

On November 11th, the Plaintiff sent the following text to the Defendant: "Hi Victoria. I hope you're doing well. I am moving forward with renting another property. Please send me the $1800 realtor fee back as I did not rent the Wickham Avenue property through you or any other property. Thank you."

Discussion

"A real estate broker is entitled to recover a commission upon establishing that it (1) is duly licensed, (2) had a contract, express or implied, with the party to be charged with paying the commission, and (3) was the procuring cause of the transaction." (*Gluck & Company Realtors, LLC v Burger King Corporation*, 164 AD3d 562, 562-563 2d Dept 2018.)

The court in Gluck & Company Realtors identified two other circumstances in which a broker could claim entitlement to a commission. The first could occur if other parties to a transaction exhibited bad faith. As the court stated, "even if the plaintiff were not the procuring cause of the transaction, it would still be entitled to recover a commission, as the evidence established that the property owner terminated the plaintiff's activities in bad faith and as a mere last-minute device to escape the payment of the commission" (*Gluck & Company Realtors* at 563). The second circumstance would occur to avoid unjust enrichment of a party. According to the court, even if there were no contract between a broker and another party, the broker "would be entitled to recover for its services in quantum meruit in order to avoid the unjust enrichment of the property owner. The plaintiff established that it performed services in good faith, that the property owner accepted the services, that it expected to be compensated therefor, and the reasonable value of the services" (*Id.*).

There is no question that the Defendant expended a significant amount of time and resources to assist the Plaintiff in entering into a rental agreement for the Wickham Property. In fact, the Court finds the Defendant was the procuring cause for that agreement, and the Defendant's efforts on the Plaintiff's behalf resulted in a signed lease agreement for the Wickham Property (although one of the listed landlords did not sign it). Although the rental fell through, the credible evidence before the Court indicates neither the Plaintiff nor the Defendant was at fault. If anything, the owner of the Wickham Property may have been at fault in not going forward with the agreement on October 29 and November 1, 2019.

Once the owners of the Wickham Property refused to go forward with the rental agreement, the Defendant used her best efforts to secure another rental for the Plaintiff. The Defendant brought the Phillips Property to the Plaintiff's attention and made arrangements for the listing broker to show the Phillips Property to the Plaintiff. The Defendant also exchanged text messages with the Plaintiff about the Phillips Property as well as the listing broker to pave the way for the Plaintiff to rent the Phillips Property. While there is no indication the Defendant was directly engaged in negotiations between the Plaintiff and the owner of the Phillips Property, the Defendant appears at least to have created an "amicable atmosphere" (*Gluck & Company Realtors* at 563) for the negotiations to take place and the rental agreement to occur. The Plaintiff testified she signed a lease for the Phillips Property on November 13, 2019 but did not offer that lease into evidence. The Plaintiff also admitted she did not tell the Defendant she wasn't going to work with her any further, and the Plaintiff admitted she contacted Ms. Clark directly around October 31, 2019, after receiving text messages from the Defendant regarding the Phillips Property.

Based on the language of the Plaintiff's agreement with the Defendant (Defendant's Exhibit E, in evidence), the Defendant seeks a commission for both the Wickham Property and the Phillips Property. The parties' agreement states that a commission in the amount of one month's rent was due from the Plaintiff "for showing me/us and or referring me/us to any rental property which results in me/us leasing the property/signing a lease agreement and or occupying the rental property." While the agreement in Exhibit E has no ending date and potentially could continue ad infinitum, the credible evidence shows the Defendant's activities on behalf of the Plaintiff occurred over approximately a one-month period. There can be no dispute the Defendant's efforts resulted in the Plaintiff "signing a lease agreement" for the Wickham Property, and the credible evidence also shows the Defendant referred the Plaintiff to the Phillips Property and made other arrangements on the Plaintiff's behalf which ultimately resulted in her signing a lease agreement and occupying the Phillips Property.

While the Defendant could argue she is entitled to a commission for both the Wickham Property and the Phillips Property, under all the circumstances of this case and the open-ended language of the agreement between the Plaintiff and the Defendant, the Court determines it would be unjust for the Defendant to recover two commissions from the Plaintiff. Ultimately, the Defendant's job under Exhibit E was to help the Plaintiff procure a rental property which the Plaintiff could occupy. When the Wickham Property fell through, the Defendant immediately went to work to find another property for the Plaintiff, and the Defendant found the Phillips Property for the Plaintiff. The Plaintiff, within approximately two weeks of the Defendant bringing that property to the Plaintiff's attention, signed a lease for the Phillips Property and now occupies it. The Defendant did the job required under Exhibit E and found a place the Plaintiff could actually occupy.

The Court, in this small claims action, must "do substantial justice between the parties" (Uniform City Court Act §1804). Based on the facts, evidence, and discussion above, and under the terms of the parties' agreement in Exhibit E, it is the Court's determination that "substantial justice between the parties" requires the Court to find that the Defendant is entitled to recover a commission equal to one month's rent. The rental for the Wickham Property was to be $1,800.00 per month; the rental for the Phillips Property when the Plaintiff started occupancy was $1,900.00 per month (Defendant's Exhibit A and Exhibit B, both in evidence). The Court determines that substantial justice would be served by awarding the Defendant one month's commission in the total amount of $1,900.00.

Because the Plaintiff previously paid the Defendant the sum of $1,800.00, which the Defendant has retained, the Defendant is entitled to recover a net amount of $100.00 from the Plaintiff.

Decision

After hearing the testimony at the trial, giving appropriate weight to the testimony of the Plaintiff, the Plaintiff's witness, and the Defendant, and reviewing all documentary evidence produced by the parties at the trial, it is

ORDERED, that Plaintiff's claim is denied and dismissed, and it is further

ORDERED, that the Defendant's counterclaim is granted in the amount of $1,900.00, and it is further

The foregoing constitutes the Decision and Order of this Court.

Dated: June 7, 2021

QUESTIONS ABOUT THE CASE

1 What are the three circumstances where real estate agents are due their commission?
2 The rental agreement in this case never went through. Are there situations, other than those outlined in question one, where real estate agents may still be due their commission?
3 Why did the court rule that the real estate agent was due one commission, but not both?

COVID-19 CONCERN

Real estate agents owe many duties to their principals. Listing agents must reveal specific problems with a house, such as an active mold or rodent infestation. Loan companies often demand certifications from others that there are no termite colonies in the wooden parts of the home. Will real estate agents be required to reveal that the previous owner had a COVID-19 infection or that the previous owner was not vaccinated?

CHAPTER SUMMARY

An agency relationship is created between an agent and a principal. An agent has strict duties that he must comply with while representing the principal. Among these duties are the duties of obedience, loyalty, and accounting. The most common example of an agency relationship in real estate law is the real estate broker-seller relationship. In this relationship, a real estate broker represents the interests of a home-seller. When the agent locates a buyer who is ready, willing, and able to purchase the home, the agent is entitled to a commission, which is based on a percentage of total sale price.

There are several other important professions closely related to real estate practice. Investing in real estate can be a lucrative business on both a large and small level. Real estate investment trusts (REITs) are publicly traded securities that pool funds in order to manage and sell large parcels of real estate. Individual investors can also purchase real estate in order to fix it up and resell it or to manage it as rental property. Other professions closely tied to real estate practice include loan officers, appraisers, and surveyors. Loan officers evaluate potential borrowers and handle paperwork associated with a mortgage. Appraisers are professionals whose duty is to determine the value of real estate. Surveyors are responsible for determining the exact physical boundaries of a particular parcel of real estate. Real estate inspectors are responsible for examining structures on the premises and making a complete and detailed report to the buyer and the lender to assure both that the property has no major flaws.

SKILLS YOU NEED IN THE REAL WORLD

Understanding Commissions

If the calculations in real estate commissions make it appear that real estate agents are earning a lot of money for relatively little effort, take a closer look not only at the numerous duties that the agents carry out, but also at the reality of how commissions are paid.

A real estate agent who produces a buyer who is ready, willing, and able to purchase the property has earned a commission. The commission is usually 6 percent of the sale price. However, we know that one of the main advantages of using a real estate broker is his access to the MLS. This service essentially advertises homes for sale with the promise of splitting the commission with an agent who can produce a buyer. The chances of the listing agent also being the person who produces the buyer are very slim. Instead, most transactions involve at least two brokers: the listing agent and the procuring agent. If we assume that the final sales price for a home is $100,000, the commission is $6,000. This amount is split between the two agents, resulting in a net of $3,000 apiece. However, the calculations are not over.

Because most agents work for companies, they have arrangements to split their earned commission with the company in exchange for providing office space, secretarial services, and other amenities. This can mean that the agent ends up splitting 50 percent of his earned commission with the company for whom he works. That means that of the $3,000 that the agent earned, he may only end up pocketing $1,500. (Even this math is a little misleading, given the fact that agents may also have to pay other expenses, and they will certainly have to pay both state and federal income tax.) If you understand how real estate commissions are actually doled out, you will have a better understanding of the system — and possibly more empathy for real estate agents.

ETHICAL ISSUES FOR THE PARALEGAL

Real Estate Professionals' Codes Of Ethics

The National Association of Realtors has its own code of ethics. As a legal professional, it is not enough for you to be aware of your own ethical code; you must also understand the ethical codes imposed on other professionals. For instance, you should review the National Association of Realtors' ethical code, which can be found online. Individual states also have their own ethical rules and standards of practice that you should review to make sure that you do not inadvertently violate a real estate agent's ethical codes.

KEY TERMS AND CONCEPTS

Agency	Liquidity	Negligent
Fiduciary	Material fact	misrepresentation
Fraud		Principal

END-OF-CHAPTER EXERCISES

Review Questions

See Appendix for answers.

1   What is an agent?
2   Are agency relationships required to be in writing? Why or why not?
3   List and explain the four duties that an agent owes to a principal.
4   What is a fiduciary?
5   What is "self-dealing"?
6   List and explain the three duties that agents owe to third parties.
7   What is fraud in the legal context?
8   What duties does a principal owe to an agent?
9   What is the difference between an agent and an independent contractor?
10 In a typical real estate transaction, who is the principal, who is the agent, and who is the third party?
11 What is the difference between a real estate broker and a real estate agent?
12 What is the Multiple Listing Service?
13 What are some of the advantages of real estate as an investment?
14 What are some of the disadvantages of real estate as an investment?
15 What are Real Estate Investment Trusts?
16 Explain the role of a real estate appraiser.
17 What is a comparative market analysis?
18 What are some of the duties carried out by real estate paralegals?
19 Explain the role of a real estate inspector.
20 Explain the commission system for paying real estate agents.

DISCUSSION QUESTIONS

1   Of the professions described in this chapter, do any appeal to you? If so, why?

2   What are the strengths and weaknesses of working as a real estate broker?

APPLYING WHAT YOU HAVE LEARNED

1 Given the fact that most real estate agents work for sellers, should there be a larger class of buyer's agents? What advantages and disadvantages do buyer's agents bring to a real estate transaction?

2 Contact a local real estate agent and interview him. What got him interested in real estate as a profession? What are the advantages and disadvantages of a career as a real estate agent? What is the biggest misconception about real estate agents? Would this person recommend it as a profession? Why or why not?

WEB SURFING

National Association of Real Estate Investment Trusts
http://www.nareit.com

National Association of Realtors
https://www.nar.realtor

California Real Estate Inspection Association
http://www.creia.org

Ohio, Division of Real Estate and Professional Licensing
https://com.ohio.gov/wps/portal/gov/com/divisions-and-programs/real-estate-and-professional-licensing/real-estate-and-professional-licensing

Texas Real Estate Commission
https://www.trec.texas.gov

Tech Topic
REAL ESTATE COMMISSION CALCULATORS

Mortgage Calculator's real estate commission calculator (http://www.mortgagecalculator.biz/c/commissions.php). You can also do a general

Internet search for mortgage calculators and commission calculators.

ANNOTATED DOCUMENT

Real Estate Appraisal

Uniform Residential Appraisal Report   File

The purpose of this summary appraisal report is to provide the lender/client with an accurate, and adequately supported, opinion of the market value of the subject property.

| Property Address | 21 MAPLE DRIVE | City ANYTOWN | State PL | Zip Code 00300 |

Borrower BILL BORROWER   Owner of Public Record SAME   County BARNES

Legal Description SEE ATTACHED

Assessor's Parcel # BA-11350   Tax Year 2005   R.E. Taxes $ 2012

Neighborhood Name SIMPSON ESTATES   Map Reference   Census Tract

Occupant ☑Owner ☐Tenant ☐Vacant   Special Assessments $ 0   ☐PUD   HOA $ ☐per year ☐per month

Property Rights Appraised ☑Fee Simple ☐Leasehold ☐Other (describe)

Assignment Type ☑Purchase Transaction ☐Refinance Transaction ☐Other (describe)

Lender/Client FIRST NATIONAL BANK   Address 123 ELM STREET

Is the subject property currently offered for sale or has it been offered for sale in the twelve months prior to the effective date of this appraisal? ☐Yes ☑No

Report data source(s) used, offering price(s), and date(s). N/A

I ☐did ☑did not analyze the contract for sale for the subject purchase transaction. Explain the results of the analysis of the contract for sale or why the analysis was not performed.

Contract Price $ N/A   Date of Contract   Is the property seller the owner of public record? ☐Yes ☐No   Data Source(s)

Is there any financial assistance (loan charges, sale concessions, gift or downpayment assistance, etc.) to be paid by any party on behalf of the borrower? ☐Yes ☐No

If Yes, report the total dollar amount and describe the items to be paid.

Note: Race and the racial composition of the neighborhood are not appraisal factors.

Neighborhood Characteristics	One-Unit Housing Trends	One-Unit Housing	Present Land Use %
Location ☐Urban ☑Suburban ☐Rural	Property Values ☑Increasing ☐Stable ☐Declining	PRICE $(000) / AGE	One-Unit 100 %
Built-Up ☑Over 75% ☐25-75% ☐Under 25%	Demand/Supply ☐Shortage ☑In Balance ☐Over Supply	100 Low / 25 yrs	2-4 Unit 0 %
Growth ☐Rapid ☑Stable ☐Slow	Marketing Time ☐Under 3 mths ☑3-6 mths ☐Over 6 mths	High	Multi-Family 0 %
Neighborhood Boundaries .25 - .5 ACRE LOTS		Pred.	Commercial 0 %
			Other 0 %

Neighborhood Description GENERALLY, 2-3 BEDROOM HOMES OLDER NEIGHBORHOOD, GOOD CONDITION, NEIGHBORS KEEP GOOD YARDS

Market Conditions (including support for the above conclusions) FAVORABLE, SEE ATTACHED REPORT SUMMARY ⟵ Neighborhood description

| Dimensions 52 X 35 | Area 1900 | Shape L SHAPE | View 1980 |

Specific Zoning Classification R-1   Zoning Description RESIDENTIAL ONLY

Zoning Compliance ☑Legal ☐Legal Nonconforming (Grandfathered Use) ☐No Zoning ☐Illegal (describe)

Is the highest and best use of the subject property as improved (or as proposed per plans and specifications) the present use? ☑Yes ☐No If No, describe

Utilities	Public	Other (describe)		Public	Other (describe)	Off-site Improvements—Type	Public	Private
Electricity	☑		Water	☑		Street	☑	
Gas	☑		Sanitary Sewer	☑		Alley	☐	

FEMA Special Flood Hazard Area ☐Yes ☑No   FEMA Flood Zone   FEMA Map # N/A   FEMA Map Date N/A

Are the utilities and off-site improvements typical for the market area? ☑Yes ☐No If No, describe

Are there any adverse site conditions or external factors (easements, encroachments, environmental conditions, land uses, etc.)? ☐Yes ☐No If Yes, describe

ELECTRICAL EASEMENT (FRONT YARD), NO OTHER EASEMENTS ⟵ Adverse site conditions or external factors

General Description	Foundation	Exterior Description materials/condition	Interior materials/condition
Units ☑One ☐One with Accessory Unit	☐Concrete Slab ☐Crawl Space	Foundation Walls C-BLOCK	Floors HARDWOOD
# of Stories	☐Full Basement ☐Partial Basement	Exterior Walls SIDING (W)	Walls DRY WALL
Type ☐Det. ☑Att. ☐S-Det/End Unit	Basement Area 700 sq. ft.	Roof Surface ASPHALT SH.	Trim/Finish PAINT
☐Existing ☐Proposed ☐Under Const.	Basement Finish BLOCK 10 %	Gutters & Downspouts GOOD COND.	Bath Floor TILE
Design (Style) RANCH	☐Outside Entry/Exit ☐Sump Pump	Window Type DOUBLE PANE	Bath Wainscot NONE
Year Built 1980	Evidence of ☐Infestation NONE	Storm Sash/Insulated ✓	Car Storage ☐None
Effective Age (Yrs) 25	☐Dampness ☐Settlement	Screens ✓	☑Driveway # of Cars 2
Attic ☐None	Heating ☑FWA ☐HWBB ☐Radiant	Amenities ☐Woodstove(s) #	Driveway Surface ASPHALT
☑Drop Stair ☐Stairs	☐Other Fuel	☑Fireplace(s) # ☑Fence	☑Garage # of Cars 1
☐Floor ☐Scuttle	Cooling ☑Central Air Conditioning	☑Patio/Deck 3 ☑Porch	☐Carport # of Cars
☐Finished ☐Heated	☐Individual ☐Other	☐Pool	☐Att. ☐Det. ☐Built-in

Appliances ☑Refrigerator ☑Range/Oven ☑Dishwasher ☐Disposal ☑Microwave ☐Washer/Dryer ☐Other (describe)

Finished area above grade contains: 6 Rooms 3 Bedrooms 2 Bath(s) 1800 Square Feet of Gross Living Area Above Grade

Additional features (special energy efficient items, etc.)

Describe the condition of the property (including needed repairs, deterioration, renovations, remodeling, etc.) WATER DAMAGE ON N. SIDE PORCH NEAR DOWNSPOUT ⟵

                                                                    ⟵ Condition of property

Are there any physical deficiencies or adverse conditions that affect the livability, soundness, or structural integrity of the property? ☐Yes ☑No If Yes, describe

Does the property generally conform to the neighborhood (functional utility, style, condition, use, construction, etc.)? ☑Yes ☐No If No, describe

PRACTICE QUESTIONS FOR TEST REVIEW

See Appendix for answers.

Essay Question

Explain the law of agency.

True–False

1 T F Agents can bind principals to legally enforceable agreements.

2 T F Agents can carry out an entire series of business transactions without the principal's direct involvement.

3 T F Most agency relationships are oral agreements.

Fill In the Blank

1 This person who holds a special position of trust and confidence to another and must act in the best interests of that other person: _____.

2 Under this duty, an agent must demonstrate diligence in performing his or her duties: _____.

3 This intentional deception causes injury to another person: _____.

Multiple Choice

1 A relationship that is created when a person is unable or unwilling to conduct business on her behalf and instead retains another person to act for her.

   A Representation
   B Agency
   C Subordination
   D Putative

2 The person for whom an agent works.

   A Employer
   B Subordinate
   C Master
   D Principal

3 Which of the following is a duty owed by an agent to a principal?

   A Obedience
   B Care
   C Loyalty
   D All of the above

ENDNOTES

[1] Bureau of Labor Statistics, U.S. Department of Labor, Occupational Outlook Handbook, Real Estate Brokers and Sales Agents, at https://www.bls.gov/ooh/sales/real-estate-brokers-and-sales-agents.htm (visited January 17, 2022).

[2] Bureau of Labor Statistics, U.S. Department of Labor, Occupational Outlook Handbook, Real Estate Brokers and Sales Agents, at https://www.bls.gov/ooh/sales/real-estate-brokers-and-sales-agents.htm (visited January 17, 2022).

[3] Bureau of Labor Statistics, U.S. Department of Labor, Occupational Outlook Handbook, Real Estate Brokers and Sales Agents, at https://www.bls.gov/ooh/sales/real-estate-brokers-and-sales-agents.htm (visited January 17, 2022).

[4] *Bigman Assoc. v. Fox*, 133 A.D.2d 93, 518 N.Y.S.2d 630 (1987).

[5] Bureau of Labor Statistics, U.S. Department of Labor, Occupational Outlook Handbook, Real Estate Brokers and Sales Agents, https://www.bls.gov/ooh/construction-and-extraction/construction-and-building-inspectors.htm (visited January 31, 2022).

Title Insurance and Title Examinations

- Explain the importance of title insurance
- List and explain the basic steps involved in carrying out a title examination
- Describe why a title examination is necessary
- Describe the impact of legal malpractice claims on title searches
- Explain the extent of information that can be located through public records

I. Introduction

II. Title Insurance
   A. What Title Insurance Does
   B. Obtaining Title Insurance

III. Title Examinations
   A. What Is a Title Examination?
   B. Information Needed for a Title Examination

IV. Steps in a Title Search
   A. Creating a Client File
   B. Step 1: Creating the Chain of Title
   C. Step 2: Establishing the Out or Adverse Conveyances
   D. Step 3: Compiling the Information
   E. Preliminary and Final Title Certificates
   F. The Paralegal's Role in Title Searches

V. Common Problems in Title Searches
   A. Sub-divided Properties
   B. Holes or Breaks in the Chain of Title

INTRODUCTION

In this chapter, we explore the importance of title insurance and explain the basic steps involved in a title examination. The manner and method used to carry out a title examination vary considerably from state to state. As a result, we examine the basic reasons why such a search is necessary and then discuss how these examinations are carried out in different states. We also examine the important role played by attorneys and paralegals, in both states that require attorney-certified title searches and states where attorney involvement is not required. Throughout this chapter, we also demonstrate the vitally important role played by real estate paralegals across the country. However, before we explore the issue of title examinations, let's begin with the role of title insurance in modern real estate practice.

TITLE INSURANCE

Title insurance
An insurance policy that protects against legal claims on title to real property.

Title insurance is an insurance policy similar to automobile or life insurance. Title insurance, however, focuses on a very narrow issue: the marketability of the title to property. A title insurance policy is designed to pay for any costs associated with claims raised against a title after the transaction has been completed. It is title insurance that accounts for the need for a title examination.

A. WHAT TITLE INSURANCE DOES

Title insurance is a simple concept with profound implications for real estate law. What a title insurance company agrees to do in its policy is to pay the legal costs associated with defending any claim against the property by someone who purports to have a title interest.

LONG-LOST SON'S CLAIM

Uncle Harry decided to put his house and surrounding property up for sale last year. Demetria liked the house and put in a bid on the property. They haggled over the price and eventually settled on a figure that both found acceptable. Demetria went to a local bank to arrange financing, and the bank insisted that Demetria obtain a title insurance policy, which she did. After the transaction was complete, Uncle Harry's long-lost son, Micah, arrived in town and claimed that he had a half interest in the property. He brought suit against Demetria. Fortunately, she had her title insurance policy and the insurance company hired a local attorney to represent her. The case went to trial, and the jury eventually found in Demetria's favor. Had Demetria been forced to pay her own legal fees, she would never have been able to hire an attorney; hence the need for title insurance.

Title insurance protects not only the buyer, but also the lender. If a claim suddenly arises that affects the buyer's interest in the land, the lender's claim is also in jeopardy. This is the reason why many lenders require title insurance.

A title insurance policy protects against any claim that says someone else has title rights to the buyer's property.

REAL
ESTATE
BASICS AT
A GLANCE

B. OBTAINING TITLE INSURANCE

Obtaining title insurance resembles the process of obtaining any other type of insurance. Just as an applicant might be required to submit to a medical examination before a health insurer issues a **policy**, a title insurer must have some indication about the current state of the title before it will issue a policy. In some states, title insurance companies rely on attorneys to give legal opinions about the title before they will issue a **binder**. In other states, this duty may fall to the title insurance company itself, or to some other legal professional.

Policy
The contract of insurance between the insurance company and the insured.

Binder
A preliminary agreement to issue an insurance policy.

Title insurance works just like any other insurance; a policyholder pays a premium and receives a policy that binds the insurance company to take certain actions on the policyholder's behalf.

REAL
ESTATE
BASICS AT
A GLANCE

A title insurer will want to know the answers to questions like:

- Who has an interest in the property?
- Have all of these interests been properly conveyed to the buyer?
- Are there any outstanding issues in the public records that could affect title to the property, such as outstanding or unpaid taxes, liens or assessments, judgments, federal tax liens, or complications from divorce or probate?

This list provides only a general outline of the types of problems that could have an impact on the title. As a result, the title insurance company will require a title examination to determine whether any of these problems exist. If they do, the insurer will probably demand that those potential legal issues be cleared up.

Once the title insurance company is satisfied about the legal status of the property, it will issue a policy. An insurance policy is a contract between the insurance company and the insured. The policy sets out the duties and limitations for both parties. The title insurance company, for instance, declares that it will defend a suit brought about the property for a title defect. The insured, for her part, pays a premium in exchange for this service. The American Land Title Association creates general forms that are followed in most states. The insurance policy sets out what property is covered and any exceptions to coverage. For an example of a title insurance policy, see the online resources, available at the product page that accompanies this text.

There are two general types of title insurance: owners' policies and lenders' policies. Owners' policies are designed to protect the owner from any legal claim made against the property, while a lender's policy protects the lender's interest.

Exceptions to what is covered under a title insurance policy include matters of record or other legal claims for which the title insurance company will not provide coverage. Examples of exceptions could be claims by a spouse during a divorce proceeding or foreclosure provisions in a mortgage. Any exceptions must be prominently noted on the policy.

1. TITLE INSURANCE PREMIUM

Premium
The periodic payment to keep an insurance policy in effect.

Unlike other forms of insurance, title insurance has only a one-time **premium**. This premium is paid as part of the closing or settlement on the property, and no additional premiums are ever paid. The amount of the policy is often a percentage of the total sale price, such as one-half of 1 percent.

EXAMPLE 12-2

VONDRA'S PREMIUM

Vondra wants to obtain a title insurance policy to cover the purchase of her new home. The sale price is $125,000. How much is Vondra's title insurance premium?
   Answer: Multiply $125,000 by .5%. The answer is $625.

2. TERMINATING THE POLICY

Title insurance remains in effect as long as the owner who purchased the property continues to hold title. However, it automatically terminates when the owner sells the property or has title taken away, such as through a foreclosure process. Policies are not transferable from one owner to another; a new owner must obtain a new insurance policy.

TITLE EXAMINATIONS

Title examination
The process of reviewing public records to determine whether there are any outstanding claims that will affect the marketability of title to real property.

Although not all states use the **title examination** process to determine the marketability of titles, nor even use the term "title examination," all states have some process for recording claims against property in the public records. Whether this recordation process involves a grantor-grantee index or a tract system, there are many types of claims that can adversely affect title to property. This is one of the main reasons to conduct a title examination.

REAL WORLD PERSPECTIVES: *REAL ESTATE PARALEGAL*

We do all of the preliminary work after we get the contract. We do a preliminary title search. Then we see if a title insurance policy has ever been issued. We have a pre-prepared form that we send to the seller's agent, requesting basic information about their sellers. A lot of times, when we are working for the buyers, we don't have a lot of information about the sellers. When you work with real estate agents, it's nice. They tend to be very organized and they know the information that the law firm needs. If there is a mortgage on the property, then we need all of that information. We have to have a signed authorization to get the payoff on the current mortgage.

— S. C., real estate paralegal

A. WHAT IS A TITLE EXAMINATION?

Title examinations are necessary in order to determine the legal status of a parcel of real estate. As we have seen throughout this book, there are many actions that a real estate owner can take that will have a significant impact on future owners. A title examination (or *title search*) is the method used to discover any claims on the current owner or the property that could have an adverse effect on the transaction. The primary purpose of a title examination is to discover any legal problems and to solve them before the closing, but there are some parcels that have so many attendant legal problems that they are virtually impossible to sell. The reason for this is that it would take so much time, money, and effort to clean up the title that a prospective buyer would just as soon buy another parcel that does not have such problems.

In some states, the final product of a title examination is an attorney's legal opinion about the current state of the property. When an attorney issues an opinion stating that the title is free and clear of all encumbrances, this is an assurance that the buyer can take the property without fear of losing it to some adverse claim. It also gives the title insurance company justification in issuing a policy. In states that do not use the attorney-certification process, a title examination is still conducted. However, instead of an attorney, a professional title searcher will review the public records and make a report to the prospective buyer and the title insurance company.

Title searches are necessary in order to ensure that title to property is free and clear of all liens, judgments, assessments, and other actions that could cloud a title.

REAL
ESTATE
BASICS AT
A GLANCE

B. INFORMATION NEEDED FOR A TITLE EXAMINATION

The title search usually begins when a law office or professional title examiner is contacted by a real estate broker, lender, or buyer and asked to review the title for the land in question. In almost all situations, the buyer will ultimately pay for the title examination, either directly or indirectly.

To begin a title search, the examiner must know the real property's street address, parcel number, tax map ID number, or some other information that helps to identify the parcel. Once the examiner has this information, she can review the real estate records for any filing that might affect legal title to the property. (See Figure 12-1 for a sample title search form.) At its simplest, title examination involves a review of the public records. To do as complete a job as possible, a title examiner should have the following information:

- The names of the current property owners;
- A legal description of the real property that is the subject of the transaction;
- The real property's street address;
- The real property's parcel number, tax ID number, or other identifying information;
- The time period that the title search must cover; and
- The real property's deed book and page number, if available.

REAL ESTATE BASICS AT A GLANCE

A title examiner can begin a search with very little information, perhaps only the sellers' names and the property's street address, but having more information is always helpful.

FIGURE 12-1

Title Search Form

Title Examination Worksheet

Examination prepared for: _____

Date of title examination: _____

Type of loan: _____

CHAIN OF TITLE

1.

Book: _____ page: _____

Grantors: _____

Grantees: _____

Type of transaction: _____

Date of transaction: _____

Date recorded: _____ time of recording: _____

Acreage: _____

Brief description: _____

_____

FIGURE 12-1

(continued)

2.

Book: _____ page: _____

Grantors: _____

Grantees: _____

Type of transaction: _____

Date of transaction: _____

Date recorded: _____ time of recording: _____

Acreage: _____

Brief description: _____

UNCANCELLED DEEDS OF TRUST/MORTGAGES

Book: _____ page: _____

Date of transaction: _____

Date recorded: _____ time of recording: _____

Lender: _____

Amount: $ _____

Book: _____ page: _____

Date of transaction: _____

Date recorded: _____ time of recording: _____

Lender: _____

Amount: $ _____

1. NAMES OF THE CURRENT OWNERS

It is essential to get the current owners' names to begin a title search. The current owners are the ones who will be transferring title to the buyer. Getting the owners' names not only ensures that the title searcher is researching the correct parcel but also guards against early misunderstandings, such as when the people involved own more than one parcel of real estate. In states where the parcel is cross-referenced by address or ID number, having the owners' names also serves as a means to double-check that the title examiner received the right information in the first place.

a. Grantor-Grantee Index

In many states, properties are listed by owners' and buyers' names only, under a system known as the **grantor-grantee index**. In those states, the only way to research the title is to work through the names of the previous owners to see if any action taken by or against them could have a possible impact on the legal status of the property.

Grantor-grantee index
A listing of all property by the names of individuals who buy and sell it.

b. Tract Index

In other states, property is indexed by parcel number. In those states, any judgments or other actions that could affect the property are listed on a card or in a database entry. Not all the necessary information can be found on a property card, however, so it is always helpful to have additional information about the parties involved in the transaction because the title search process involves researching other public records. Examples of helpful information about the parties include:

- What are the ages of all parties? (Is everyone involved a legal adult?)
- Have any of the parties been declared mentally incompetent?
- Are any of the parties married? If so, what are the complete legal names of their spouses? Have the spouses also signed all deeds and other documents?
- When did the grantor/current owner acquire the property, and from whom? (It helps to double-check information.)

2. DESCRIPTION OF THE PROPERTY TO BE CONVEYED

It is vitally important to a legal professional to properly identify the property in question before beginning the search. Sometimes street addresses are incorrect and the parties' descriptions may not have sufficient detail to correctly identify the property in question. It is extremely easy to confuse different real estate tracts, especially when the only information available is a poorly drafted description. Pinpointing the actual tract involved in the transaction is an absolute necessity to a successful title search.

3. TIME PERIOD

When a title searcher reviews the public records concerning property and owners, the normal search period is at least 40 years. The reason for conducting such a lengthy search through the records is to ensure that a title searcher locates any document that could potentially have a legal impact on the property today. Although many practitioners search back 50 years or more, most states have provisions that invalidate judgments that are older than three or four decades.

Some title searchers not only search the period that each owner possessed the property but also extend the search period up to two years beyond that time. This acts as a safety precaution to catch any probate matters that might not have arisen during the actual term of ownership.

4. TAX ID NUMBER

The local tax office assigns tax ID numbers or other identifiers to every parcel of real estate in the county. This tax ID number can be extremely helpful to a title searcher, not only in helping to identify the property, but also in taking advantage of the enormous amount of information available in the tax office. We discuss the role of the tax office, and the information that it collects, in the final chapter of this book.

5. DEED BOOK AND PAGE NUMBER

One of the best starting places for a title examiner is the last deed that conveyed an interest in the property. This information, coupled with the tract index or grantor-grantee index, will provide a wealth of information. Unfortunately, most clients do not realize the significance of the previous deeds and usually fail to provide one to the title examiner. Deed book volume and page numbers are always helpful in beginning a title examination. The format for a deed book reference varies from state to state, but most states follow a formula such as "DB 909, Page 102." The first number in this citation gives the title examiner the volume number of the book in which a copy of the deed can be found. The second number is the page of that volume that corresponds to the deed. These days, the growing use of digital technology has made substantial inroads into storing deeds and other information, but most title examiners find that the ancient system of categorization is still used, despite the fact that deeds may not even be stored in actual books anymore.

A copy of the deed for prior transactions is a gold mine of information. As we saw in Chapter 8, a general warranty deed not only identifies the parties but also describes the property, lists its geographic features, and even explains unusual aspects of the deed's history. In addition to all of this information, a previous title examiner may have included helpful information to explain some unusual aspect of the legal title, thus helping clear up a potential problem.

6. SURVEYS AND PLATS

In addition to the basic information outlined above, it is also helpful to have a copy of the most recent plat or survey of the property. Human beings have a strong bias toward visual information, and a well-drawn plat can clear up many issues that written deed provisions only obscure. If the title examiner can also obtain a copy of the most recent title insurance policy, that is always a huge help. That policy will list any features that the parties considered to be important enough to explain and may save hours of work sorting through the public records to explain a feature that a previous title examiner cleared up in the notes or exclusions accompanying a title insurance policy.

Many title insurance companies offer this information to a title examiner with directions to simply "bring the title current." This phrase means that a title insurance company only wishes a title examiner to research the public records from the time that the last title insurance policy was issued through to the present. The theory is that the previous title examination would have discovered any legal problems and the only real concern is what has happened since. There are many who dispute this approach, pointing out that something that was missed in the first title search will not be discovered in the second if the examiner is not permitted to prepare a complete title search.

IV   STEPS IN A TITLE SEARCH

Title examination can be a very rewarding and interesting profession. It can also be tedious and dull. A title examiner must employ many different legal skills, from interpreting probate and divorce records to chasing down civil judgments and criminal convictions. Another attractive feature of working as a real estate title examiner is the assurance of having work, because lenders and title insurance companies need title searches. The level of pay, however, varies considerably, not only from state to state, but also from city to city.

There are different ways of conducting a title search. The reason for these variations has a lot to do with the way that real estate records are stored. In some states, searching a title is a relatively straightforward matter: All information relevant to a particular tract is recorded on a card that corresponds to the property. However, in other states, information must be gleaned from a wide variety of sources. Because this second process is more involved than the first, in the next sections we outline how it is done. Even if this method is not the procedure used in your state, you may find some helpful suggestions about information stored in the public records that can prove to be extremely valuable.

A. CREATING A CLIENT FILE

No matter what system a state uses to store land records, there is a practical step that all title examiners follow: creating a client file. A client file contains the following information:

- The client's name,
- The date that the title examination is due,
- The street address/plat number/ID number of the property,
- The method of payment for the search,
- Notes from previous title insurance policies or old title examinations, and
- Unusual or noteworthy information about the particular tract.

Some or all of this information will be stored in a physical file or in a file on the company computer. Title examiners should remember that some or all of this information may be confidential and should not be shared with others.

B. STEP 1: CREATING THE CHAIN OF TITLE

Chain of title
A complete listing of all owners of a particular parcel of real estate for a specified time period.

Once the client file has been created, and the necessary basic information has been gathered, the title searcher is ready to begin the actual title search. In states that do not follow the tract information system, which records all important information for a parcel in one place, the title examiner must create a chain of ownership, also known as a **chain of title**, listing every owner for the property going back a specific period of time. Most title examiners search back at least 30, if not 40, years. Although you might think that the land office or deed room is the best place to start, actually one of the best sources of information is the local tax office.

REAL ESTATE BASICS AT A GLANCE

The chain of title establishes each owner and the time period that each possessed the property going back for 30, 40, or even 50 years.

1. THE TAX OFFICE

The local tax office contains a wealth of information about real estate in the area, including owners' names, total acreage, parcel ID numbers, tax maps, tax ID numbers, and deed references. In some states, this information is still stored on a paper "tax card," but in most it is available in a computer database that provides not only all the information set out above but also basic floor plans, square footage, and even digital photos of the property in question. Some states even provide this information on the Internet. The tax office is also a great resource because it keeps complete records of all real property located in the city or county and has its own set of tax maps. These maps can be cross-referenced with plats or surveys of the property to help clear up confusing issues or even to help identify the exact parcel in question. In some states, the tax office is also cross-referenced with the land office or deed office and provides information such as deed book references and other information that can be a big time-saver later on.

Another reason to begin a title examination with tax records is that the title examiner must check on the status of the property taxes. If the current owner is in default on her taxes, this may stop the entire transaction. If the property were facing tax foreclosure, no buyer would invest the time and energy to purchase the property when it might be auctioned off within days. The title examiner must also know the amount of taxes paid so that the amount can be prorated between the buyer and seller during the closing. We discuss prorations in greater detail in the next chapter.

2. CREATING THE LINKS IN THE CHAIN OF OWNERSHIP

In states that follow a grantor-grantee index model, the title examiner's first step is to search the grantee index and look up the name of the current owner of the property. The grantee index lists all conveyances through which a party received an interest in real estate. Because the current owner received her title from the previous owner of a particular parcel, that person's name will be listed in the index. The entry in the grantee index will give a deed book and page number reference. Using that reference, the title searcher can find the deed. This deed will provide the name of the previous owner, and the title searcher will repeat the process, looking up the previous owner's name in the grantee index to see from whom she purchased the property and so on, going back through the records until the title searcher has covered the specified time period. See Figure 12-2 for a sample chain of title form.

The purpose of creating a chain of title is to learn both the names of each owner and the dates of ownership. A title searcher should make sure to note the exact date that each owner acquired the property and the exact date that each sold the property. These dates are important because they not only determine the time periods during which each owner held the property, but they also form the basis for the next phase of the search: checking the "outs" or adverse entries for each owner.

FIGURE 12-2		
Chain of Title Form	Current Owner(s):	Bryan and Beth Gartman
	Grantor Name(s):	Rod and Lisa Burnett
	Grantee Name(s):	Bryan and Beth Gartman
	Date of Transaction:	November 4, 2023
	Date Recorded:	November 18, 2023
	Deed Book Reference:	4678/pp. 10–06
	Brief description of the property:	.25 acres, Burke Estates Subdivision

Prior Transaction:

Grantor Name(s):		Leslie and George McKesson
Grantee Name(s):		Rod and Lisa Burnett
Date of Transaction:		April 26, 1996
Date Recorded:		April 26, 1996
Deed Book Reference:		4563/pp. 9–12
Brief description of the property:		.25 acres, Burke Estates Subdivision

Prior Transaction:

Grantor Name(s):		Tara Bevans
Grantee Name(s):		Leslie and George McKesson
Date of Transaction:		May 2, 1985
Date Recorded:		May 4, 1985
Deed Book Reference:		3476/p. 122
Brief description of the property:		.25 acres, Burke Estates Subdivision

Prior Transaction:

Grantor Name(s):		Marvin and Paula Barnes
Grantee Name(s):		Tara Bevans
Date of Transaction:		October 13, 1981
Date Recorded:		October 13, 1981
Deed Book Reference:		2163/p. 208
Brief description of the property:		.25 acres, Burke Estates Subdivision

3. TECHNOLOGICAL INNOVATIONS IN LAND RECORDS

Before the widespread use of computers in land record offices, information about parcels was manually recorded, sometimes handwritten. That added an extra level of complexity to title searches: A title examiner had to know not only how to find information, but also how to decipher it. Modern innovations such as computer databases have taken away that tedious aspect of title examinations. Nowadays, a title examiner can simply type in a person's name or a tract reference and pull up all the information needed to complete the search. However, although the computer solved many old problems, it also created some new ones. For example, if a person's name or reference number has been incorrectly entered into the database, finding it again may prove to be a challenge. Title examiners should keep in mind common misspellings of names and also remember that numbers can easily be transposed. See Figure 12-3 for a list of common problems in title searches.

FIGURE 12-3

■ The previous owner's name has changed (through marriage, name change).
■ The parties' names have been incorrectly entered into the database.
■ The party used a common nickname to sign a document ("Jack" for John, for example).

Common Problems in Title Examinations

Tech Topic
ONLINE TITLE SEARCHES

Much of the business of real estate has been automated, thanks to technology advances that allow for the marketing and sale of properties largely online. Virtually everything related to real estate can be accomplished online, with one notable exception: title searches.

Researching the history and provenance of a piece of property could easily be accomplished online. All the relevant information has long been computerized in searchable databases, and one could theoretically perform an accurate title search with little more than a laptop and a Wi-Fi connection.

So why has this not become standard practice? The answer is complicated. On the one hand, title companies have enormous political power and have a vested interest in maintaining the status quo. Another factor is the technology itself. In those deed offices that have scanned their deeds, many picked an arbitrary date to start the process and have scanned every deed that came in after

that point. Other deed offices not only began scanning all new documents filed with them, but also went back an arbitrary number of years as well. As a result, there is no uniformity in the online sites. A modern title searcher who needs to locate a deed that is more than 30 years old may find herself forced to visit the courthouse or deed room because the required deed has not been scanned and is not available online.

Eventually, as time passes and all new documents are scanned, the history of deed transactions will go sufficiently into the past to make it possible to complete a majority of title searches online. Suppose, for example, that a deed room chose to scan every document from 1980 onward. By 2020, that would encompass 40 years and would be more than sufficient for most title searches. But not all deed rooms chose that date and some began the process much later. As a result, visiting the deed office is going to be a reality for most title examiners for years to come.

C. STEP 2: ESTABLISHING THE OUT OR ADVERSE CONVEYANCES

When the chain of ownership has been established, the next step in the title search is to review the adverse conveyances, sometimes referred to as the "out" conveyances. This is a search of the records to see what actions the individual owners took during the time that they owned the property and also to determine if any of these actions have had an effect on the property. Previous owners can perform any of a number of actions that can have repercussions extending into the future. An owner might have granted an easement to a neighbor, or she might have failed to pay real estate taxes. All of these are good reasons to check the public records.

In states with grantor-grantee indexes, there are two primary sources for information to complete the adverse conveyance worksheet. The first is the grantor index itself. This is the index in which any out conveyance is recorded, even if the conveyance was not done voluntarily. Foreclosures will be listed here, with the previous owner's name as grantor. If a lien has been recorded, it will be indexed under the name of the owner at the time that the lien was given. Because all these actions must be recorded in order to be effective, the title searcher can feel confident that the grantor index will show entries for such actions.

The other place to look for adverse conveyances in states that follow the grantor-grantee model is the clerk's office. We address the clerk's office in detail in the section dealing with judgments.

In states that follow a property card or tract index system, actions that affect legal title to the property will be listed in the entry for that property. This makes checking out conveyances an easy and straightforward activity.

When a title examiner finds any adverse listing, the best practice is to look up the actual document and to review its provisions to make sure that it has no legal impact on the property.

1. REVIEWING TITLE DOCUMENTS

Each document that contains an owner's name should be reviewed to ensure that the listing does not involve the property for which the title examiner is searching or, if it does, that it causes no legal problems for the current title. Any questionable document should be copied and discussed with the title insurance company or real estate attorney to determine its legal significance.

Among the title documents that title examiners routinely encounter are:

- Mortgages or deeds of trust,
- Assignments,
- Easements for utility companies,
- Rights of way,
- Restrictive covenants,
- Leases,
- Water rights declarations, and
- Subordination agreements.

One of the most important items to track down in checking the adverse conveyances are the financing documents. As we saw in Chapter 9, there are two preferred methods used to finance the purchase of real estate: mortgages and deeds of trust. Mortgages are the most common method, but it is always important to understand the function of deeds of trust. A title searcher must be able not only to locate a copy of a mortgage but also to show that each previous mortgage was paid in full or satisfied. In some cases, the mortgage or deed of trust may actually be stamped with the word "Satisfied." In other situations, a separate document will be filed indicating that the mortgage was paid in full. In every situation, the title searcher must show that the financial document for prior transactions was canceled or satisfied. Without such proof, there may be an outstanding and unsatisfied mortgage on the property. In such a situation, a new buyer might be purchasing more than she bargained for.

Outstanding or unpaid mortgages are a problem for the transaction; many lenders will not approve disbursement of funds until these questions are cleared up.

REAL
ESTATE
BASICS AT
A GLANCE

---

2. LIENS

Another important item in the adverse conveyances part of a title search is the presence of liens on the property. When we discussed the legal importance of liens in Chapter 5, we saw that a lien is a mechanism that allows creditors to place encumbrances on titles that must be satisfied before title to the property can be transferred. A proper title examination must always seek to uncover any and all liens and ensure that the parties satisfy these liens before the transaction can resume.

Any liens located in checking the out conveyances should be noted prominently on the title search forms. See Figure 12-4 for an example of an adverse conveyances worksheet.

Out Conveyances		**FIGURE 12-4**
		Adverse Conveyances Worksheet
Current Owner:		
John Farthing		
Period checked: 10-10-23 to present		
a. Out conveyances:	None	
b. Lawsuits:	None	
c. Taxes paid:	Yes; 2023 — $546.43; taxes are current	
d. UCC listings:	Yes; for J. Farthing, 2005 Ford Fiesta; dollar amount not listed	

FIGURE 12-4		
(continued)	Previous Owner:	
	Katie Burnett	
	Period checked: 6-17-04 through 10-10-23	
	a. Out conveyances:	None
	b. Lawsuits:	None
	c. Taxes paid:	No past-due notices
	d. UCC listings:	N/A, beyond 5-year limit
	Previous Owner:	
	Michele Saw	
	Period checked: 2-2-90 through 6-17-04	
	a. Out conveyances:	None
	b. Lawsuits:	Yes; 4-17-01, Equity One $3,062.89
		2-02-01, Weary Regional Medical Center $1,188.25
		Judgment outstanding and unpaid
	c. Taxes paid:	N/A
	d. UCC listings:	N/A, beyond 5-year limit

3. UCC LISTINGS

The Uniform Commercial Code listings are required whenever a borrower pledges personal property as collateral for a loan. The most common example is a car loan. When a person finances an automobile purchase, she executes a document that lists the automobile as collateral for the loan. Under this arrangement, if the borrower defaults on the loan, the lender is authorized to repossess the collateral. The document that records a creditor's interest in personal property is a UCC filing. Why would it be necessary to check UCC filings when conducting a title examination? There are times when a UCC filing is recorded on a fixture. As we saw in Chapter 5, a fixture is an item of personal property that becomes permanently attached to real property and reclassified from personal property to real property. The practical effect of this is that a UCC filing for personal property suddenly has implications for real estate.

EXAMPLE 12-3	**DECKS 'R US**
	Shana has been working construction for years, and last year she formed her own company, called "Decks 'R Us." Shana finances the construction of a deck in the same way that the purchase of a car or a boat is financed. In order to properly record her interest in the decks that she builds for her customers, Shana files UCC statements for all the

decks that she builds on the installment plan. Do these UCC filings have a potential impact on the real estate?

Answer: Yes. Because a deck is, by its very nature, permanently attached to real property, Shana's UCC filing might ripen into a lien or other encumbrance that could have a substantial impact on the property. As a result, the title examiner should note any UCC filing from Decks 'R Us.

4. MARRIAGE, BIRTH, AND DEATH RECORDS

Marriage, birth, and death records can provide vital information for a title examiner. Marriage records can show that a previous owner was married and can clear up an issue of whether the spouse should have signed the deed conveying it to the next owner in the chain. Birth and death records can establish family relationships and can clear up who has title to lands that have been transferred from family member to family member over the years. They can also indicate when a person is a "junior" or a "senior." Men have a tendency to drop the "junior" designation after their names upon the deaths of their fathers. This can cause a great deal of confusion in the records that can be cleared up by reference to birth certificates.

5. PROBATE RECORDS

Probate records are essential when dealing with any real estate that has passed by testate or intestate proceedings. As we saw in Chapter 4, when a person dies with a will, she is said to have died *testate*. In such a case, the courts will attempt to give effect to the provisions of the person's will, passing title to real estate to whoever is designated. Once probated, a will becomes a matter of public record. The will can explain how and when a person obtained title to property. When a person dies without a will, she has died *intestate*. In that situation, a probate court will appoint an administrator who will distribute the decedent's property according to state law. Records of real estate transferred pursuant to intestate proceedings will also be a matter of public record.

6. JUDGMENTS

Establishing out conveyances involves not only the deed room but also other government records. A title searcher will spend a great deal of time in the clerk of court's office in order to make sure that there are no liens, judgments, delinquencies, assessments, foreclosures, or pending civil actions or judgments that have been assessed against the owners or the property. The clerk's office is the office responsible for maintaining records for all civil and criminal actions in the county. Almost all the records in the clerk's office are open to the public. Juvenile and adoption records are usually sealed, but other proceedings, from divorce to criminal actions, are all open to the public for review.

A title examiner may also need to visit the federal courthouse to look up information on bankruptcies or federal tax liens. Any of these actions could have a potential impact on the property. These days, most of this information is available on terminals inside the clerk's office and, in many cases, through databases provided on the Internet.

Title examinations involve sifting through many different types of public records.

D. STEP 3: COMPILING THE INFORMATION

The final step of a title examination is to compile all the information into a final report. The information must be complete and provide answers to the obvious questions: Are there taxes outstanding for the year, and if so, in what amount? Are there any outstanding or unsatisfied mortgages? In many ways, a title examiner must have a practical, no-nonsense attitude about the search. If there are any problems with the title, these must be addressed and cleared up or the sale will not be completed. Many title examiners take the attitude that, in the absence of proof that a problem has been resolved, one should assume that it has not.

1. ROLE OF FORMS

There are numerous forms provided in this chapter and in the online resources, available at the product page that accompanies this text, concerning title examination. However, the job is not about forms; it is about details. No matter how good the form is, the title examination will be a failure if the title examiner does not to pay close attention to details.

Law firms that specialize in closings and title examinations often use their own forms to check the accuracy of a title search.

2. TITLE ABSTRACTS

Title abstract
Forms that summarize important information about title to a particular piece of real estate.

The forms provided in this book are merely a guide to help someone who is conducting a title search double-check certain information. Many title insurance companies and title attorneys require a title examiner to use particular forms, called **title abstract** forms. These forms summarize the important features of a parcel and encapsulate all the important information in such a way that it is readily available.

E. PRELIMINARY AND FINAL TITLE CERTIFICATES

In states that require attorneys to certify the marketability of title, the end result of a title search is a final title certificate (see Figure 12-5). The preliminary title certificate is issued prior to the closing and details any potential problems with the title and what actions the legal team will take to clear up those problems. The final title certificate details the exact legal nature of the title and offers the attorney's legal opinion that the title is free and clear of any encumbrance that would affect the transaction. A title search must be exacting because an attorney who offers an opinion about the legal status of a real estate title is putting her reputation on the line. More important, an inaccurate title opinion can result in a claim of legal malpractice.

1. LEGAL MALPRACTICE AND TITLE EXAMINATIONS

When an attorney offers a final opinion on the nature of a real property title, the attorney is certifying that there are no legal impediments to the sale. If the attorney's opinion is wrong because the legal team has missed an important entry or failed to notice an outstanding legal claim against the property, the borrower, lender, and title insurance company all may have causes of action against the attorney for legal malpractice. In previous decades, legal malpractice was a very rare action. These days, it is quite common. Title insurance companies no longer hesitate to sue attorneys for malpractice when the attorney certifies a title and then the insurance company must pay out a large settlement in an action that was clearly a matter of public record.

2. TACKING

There are also some practices engaged in by legal professionals that may put the attorney in danger of a legal malpractice action, including "tacking." **Tacking** refers to the process of relying on a previous title search and simply conducting a review of the public records since the last title search was conducted. We discussed this practice earlier in our discussion of title insurance. Tacking is permissible when the title insurance company is aware of the process and even suggests it. However, tacking can be an ethical violation if an attorney or title examiner submits a full title search without explaining that all she really did was to review the last few years' public records. The appeal of tacking is obvious: It saves time. Tacking presents legal and ethical problems, however, when the client is not aware that it is being done.

Tacking
The process of merely updating a previous title search.

F. THE PARALEGAL'S ROLE IN TITLE SEARCHES

In states where attorneys certify real estate titles, it often falls to paralegals to actually conduct the work involved. Paralegals or legal assistants review the public records and title documents and even prepare the preliminary and final title opinions (but do not sign them). The process of using paralegals to carry out all phases of an attorney's

---

FIGURE 12-5

**Final Title
Opinion Letter**

FINAL OPINION ON TITLE FOR

AMERICAN TITLE INSURANCE COMPANY

The undersigned has examined the record title on the Barnes County records (and

municipal tax and assessment records if within a municipality) for the period shown below relative

to title to the real property described below, and gives the following opinion of status:

Owner(s): **Rod S. Burnett and wife, Lisa M. Burnett**
Interest or estate: **Marketable Fee Simple**
Property Description: (or attach copy of legal description)

**Being all of Lot 7 of Mimosa Hills, Section I as shown on a plat recorded in Plat Book 10,
Page 11A of the Barnes County Registry.**

Subject to the un-initialed **STANDARD EXCEPTIONS** on reverse side hereof.
Also subject to the following **SPECIAL INFORMATION AND EXCEPTIONS:**
Taxes:

1.	Ad valorem taxes are paid through and including those for the year:	**2021**.
2.	Taxes now due and payable:	**2022 taxes for $854.02**.
3.	Taxes, a lien, deferred or otherwise, but not yet due and payable:	**2022 & subsequent years**
4.	Special levies or assessments now due or payable in future installments:	**0.00**.
5.	Estate or inheritance taxes:	**0.00**.

Restrictive Covenants? No (Attach Copy).
1.Book, Page.
2.Burnett's survey and/or public record indicate a violation?
3.Contain reversionary or forfeiture clause?
4.Building Setback Line(s)
5 Easements/Other Matters: **None recorded**

Survey and Inspection Report Attached? NO

Recorded Plat? Yes
1.Plat Book 10, Page 11A.
2.Building Setback Line(s): **25 feet from side street**
3.Violated? **Unknown**
4.Easements/Other Matters: _____.

Access to Public Right of Way? Yes
Direct (If private easement, attach copy).
If over a private easement, has a search been made of adjoining property on which easement

crosses? N/A

Property Occupied By: Owners

Updating from Previous Title Insurance Policy? Yes (Attach Copy). If "Yes", has a search of

the public records been accomplished for such period of time within which judgments, liens or other

matters could affect the property, regarding the owner(s) of the property on and after the date of

said policy? **Yes**

Title Ins. Co. Policy #12X456

Other Easements, Liens, Deeds of Trust, Objections or Defects:

**Deed of Trust from John S. Burnett and wife, Jane A. Burnett for Clarence D. Arrow, Trustee
for First National Bank, dated May 15, 2022 at 2:00 p.m. in Book 1101, page 45, in the Office
of the Register of Deeds for Barnes County, North Carolina, and securing the amount of
$135,000.00 (To Be Paid and Cancelled).**

This opinion of title is for the parties to whom it is furnished, is not transferable, and may not be

used by any other person or entity without the prior written consent of the undersigned.

certification short of actually signing the certification letter raises a host of ethical issues. In states where attorneys do not certify titles, paralegals may still work as title examiners. There, the potential ethical dilemmas between attorneys and paralegals, at least on this topic, disappear.

With all of the advances in computers, software, and digital storage, it should come as no surprise that advanced technology has begun to come to the rescue of the title searcher. At the beginning of the millennium, a title searcher would carry out his or her duties in much the same way that a title searcher in the 1970s would have. But there have been recent and, some would argue, long overdue changes in title search work. For instance, many of the preliminary steps of a title search can be carried out online without even visiting the courthouse in person.

It is fairly common practice for a title searcher to access recent deed room or land office records through local county websites. These websites offer a huge time-saving feature for title searchers: Instead of having to wait until the title searcher can physically visit the courthouse, he or she can access these public documents through the Internet, any day of the week and at any time of day. Tax offices are also now routinely providing high-quality data for title searchers that may obviate the need to visit the tax office entirely.

But recent innovations in title search work go beyond limited online access to deeds, mortgages, and tax records. Other innovations are more sweeping. Consider the program Eflite, for example. Created by Investor's Title (https://eflite.invtitle.com/Login.aspx), this program has quietly revolutionized the historical approach to title searching. This program allows title searchers to complete online forms and then store them on servers for later retrieval by attorneys. The long-anticipated paperless title search might actually become a reality. Using this program, a title searcher can effectively work from his or her home, submit materials to the attorney online, and then move on to the next assignment. The attorney can review the entire search, including documents, online and when satisfied, generate preliminary and final title opinions that can then be automatically forwarded to the title insurance company for review. Eflite even interfaces with SoftPro® to generate many of the typical forms used in closings.

V. COMMON PROBLEMS IN TITLE SEARCHES

In this last section of the chapter, we will explore some of the most common problems encountered by title examiners and also address some methods of overcoming those problems.

A. SUBDIVIDED PROPERTIES

It is a common practice to carve out smaller tracts from much larger ones. Real estate developers do this all the time. However, subdivided properties sometimes cause problems. For instance, the smaller properties may not be properly identified, leading to confusion about which property is which. It can be difficult to sift through all the properties to identify a particular parcel, especially in large developments.

When faced with this situation, always start with the most recent deed, if it is available. Many times the deed will contain language explaining how the original property was subdivided and how and when this particular tract was created. It is also helpful to locate the plat or survey of the subdivision. Besides presenting a visual depiction of the entire area, these drawings often contain additional information — such as bordering properties, existing easements, and water and sewer lines — that can help clear up many problems.

B. HOLES OR BREAKS IN THE CHAIN OF TITLE

In states that follow the grantor-grantee model, it is a common problem to have an apparent hole in the chain of title (in areas that follow the tract system, this is not a common problem). A title examiner will begin tracing back each of the owners until suddenly she cannot find a previous owner and there appears to be no deed granting property to a particular owner. What causes this apparent break in the chain of title? The most common reason is that the owner changed names while possessing the property, that is, the property was conveyed to the owner under one name and was then conveyed out from that owner under a different name. This happens more often than you might think. If a woman is single when she acquires property, then marries and takes her husband's last name, when she sells the property, her last name will be different.

What most title examiners do when they find an apparent missing transaction in the chain of title is to go to the marriage records. More often than not, they will discover that the missing transaction is a result of someone getting married. Less frequently, the missing transaction may be caused by someone incorrectly indexing the owner's name in the first place.

Case Excerpt

FID. NAT'L TITLE INS. CO. v. BUTLER
2017 Cal. App. Unpub. LEXIS 4380, 2017 WL 2774337

Plaintiff Fidelity National Title Insurance Company (Fidelity) sought a declaration that it had no duty under a title insurance policy to defend or indemnify defendants William R. Butler and his wife Peggy L. Butler in a quiet title action brought by the Butlers' neighbor because the Butlers had previously conveyed their interest in the disputed property to a third party thereby terminating any coverage that may have existed under the policy. The trial court issued the requested declaration after finding that the Butlers "failed to provide admissible evidence controverting a loss of coverage under the provisions of the title policy by their conveyance of their interest in their insured property, other than to claim, without authority, that retention of an easement was sufficient to keep the terms of the policy in effect." We shall affirm the judgment.

Factual and Procedural Background

In December 1980, the Butlers purchased real property commonly known as 462-030 Janesville Grade, Janesville, California. In connection with the transaction, the Butlers purchased a policy of title insurance from Western Title Insurance Company, which subsequently was acquired by Fidelity. The policy insures against loss by reason of "title to the estate or interest described in Schedule A being vested other than as stated herein." Schedule A states that "the estate or interest in the land described in Schedule C and which is covered by this policy is: A fee." The land described in Schedule C is "in Township 28 North, Range 13 East, Mount Diablo Meridian. Section 22: The W 1/2 of the NW 1/4." Section 2(b) of the conditions and stipulations attached to the policy provides in pertinent part: "CONTINUANCE OF INSURANCE AFTER CONVEYANCE OF TITLE The coverage of this policy shall continue in force as of Date of Policy, in favor of an insured so long as such insured retains an estate or interest in the land."

In January 2003, Lisa Souliere purchased real property located directly to the north of the Butlers' property. In August 2009, Souliere brought an action against the Butlers to quiet title to approximately one-eighth of an acre of property along the border between her property and the Butlers' property, and seeking damages for trespass. The operative second amended complaint alleges in pertinent part that the Butlers "claim some right, title, estate, lien, or interest in and to the Real Property and dispute the boundary line between Souliere's property and land owned to the south of Souliere's property by the Butlers."

In August 2009, the Butlers notified Fidelity of Souliere's lawsuit. More particularly, the Butlers advised Fidelity that they had "been served with a quiet title action filed by Lisa Souliere (their neighbor) in which she alleges that she owns property into Section 22, which is our property." After initially denying coverage based upon the terms of the policy, in May 2010, Fidelity offered to retain counsel to defend the Butlers under a reservation of rights.

In September 2010, Fidelity filed a declaratory relief action seeking a determination of its duties to defend and/or indemnify the Butlers for any liability arising from the Souliere lawsuit. Fidelity asserted several grounds for denial of coverage in its declaratory relief complaint, including that coverage for the disputed property was terminated in 2003 when the Butlers voluntarily conveyed their interest in that property to a third party. Fidelity apparently never retained coverage for the Butlers. The reasons for this are disputed and irrelevant to our resolution of this appeal.

The parties filed competing motions for summary judgment on Fidelity's declaratory relief action. In its motion for summary judgment, Fidelity argued, among other things, that it had no duty to defend or indemnify the Butlers in the Souliere lawsuit because "subsequent to the issuance of the subject policy of title insurance, the Defendants voluntarily divested themselves of the property that is the subject of this dispute. Under the policy terms, Defendants' act extinguished all Fidelity's duties to Defendants." Fidelity submitted affirmative evidence in support of its motion, including a request for judicial notice of the 2003 grant deed from the Butlers to Terry Smith and the declaration of its expert Gayle Picha. The Butlers objected to Fidelity's evidence on various grounds, including the declaration of Fidelity's expert Gayle Picha.

The Butlers disputed Fidelity's claim that they voluntarily divested themselves of any interest in the disputed property, claiming that they had temporarily conveyed the property to Smith for "financing purposes" and retained an easement in the disputed property following the conveyance to Smith. The Butlers' evidence consisted of the declaration of Terry Smith, a parcel map, and a letter from the Lassen County Planning Department to the Butlers regarding "Parcel Map Application #7-05-84." Fidelity objected to the Butlers' evidence on various grounds, including that the parcel map and letter had not been properly authenticated.

A hearing on both motions was scheduled for April 5, 2013, before Judge David A. Mason. Following the hearing, the trial court granted Fidelity's motion for summary judgment. In its written ruling, filed April 22, 2013, the trial court found that "Fidelity proffered sufficient admissible evidence to support each of its Undisputed Material Facts," "all of the Undisputed Material Facts alleged by Fidelity in support of Fidelity's Motion for Summary Judgment are true for purposes of the Motion," and the Butlers "failed to provide admissible evidence to dispute Fidelity's Undisputed Material Facts." More specifically, the trial court found that the Butlers "failed to provide admissible evidence controverting a loss of coverage under the provisions of the title policy by the Butlers' conveyance of their interest in their insured property, other than to claim, without authority, that retention of an easement was sufficient to keep the term of the policy in effect." The court further found that the Butlers' objections to Fidelity's evidence were not timely filed and served and declined to consider them. It also overruled in part and sustained in part Fidelity's objections to the Butlers' evidence, noting that the documents would be "received by the Court solely as evidence of their existence and not for the truth of their contents." With respect to the declaration of Fidelity's expert Gayle Picha, the trial court found that "her declaration was sufficient to establish — sufficient expertise for her to have made the claims that she made." The trial court did not rule on the Butlers' motion for summary judgment, concluding that it was moot in light of its ruling granting summary judgment in favor of Fidelity. The trial court ordered counsel for Fidelity to prepare an order.

After Judge Mason entered his written ruling granting summary judgment in Fidelity's favor, the Butlers moved to disqualify him. In response, Judge Mason recused himself, and the case was assigned to Judge C. Anders Holmer, who entered judgment in favor of Fidelity and against the Butlers on July 16, 2013.4 The Butlers timely appealed.

Discussion

I

Summary Judgment Was Properly Entered in Favor of Fidelity Because Coverage Under the Policy of Title Insurance Was Terminated by the Butlers' Conveyance of the Disputed Property to Smith

The Butlers contend that the trial court erred in granting summary judgment in Fidelity's favor because the Butlers never voluntarily divested themselves of an interest in the disputed property. As we shall explain, Fidelity produced evidence showing that the Butlers conveyed the disputed property to an uninsured third party in 2003 and in doing so did not retain an interest therein, and the Butlers failed to produce admissible evidence sufficient to establish a triable issue of material fact as to whether they retained an interest in the disputed property sufficient to continue coverage under the policy.

"The duty to defend in a title insurance case is governed by the same principles which govern the duty to defend under general liability policies." (*Lambert v. Commonwealth Land Title Ins. Co.* (1991) 53 Cal. 3d 1072, 1077, 282 Cal. Rptr. 445, 811 P.2d 737.) " 'A liability insurer owes a broad duty to defend its insured against claims that create a potential for indemnity.' " (*Montrose Chemical Corp. v. Superior Court* (1993) 6 Cal. 4th 287, 295, 24 Cal. Rptr. 2d 467, 861 P.2d 1153.) " 'The carrier must defend a suit which potentially seeks damages within the coverage of the policy.' Implicit in this rule is the principle that the duty to defend is broader than the duty to indemnify; an insurer may owe a duty to defend its insured in an action in which no damages ultimately are awarded." (*Ibid.*)

"In resolving the question of whether a duty to defend exists — tendered in the context of a . . . summary judgment motion in a declaratory relief action — the insurer has a higher burden than the insured. 'The insured need only show that the underlying claim may fall within policy coverage; the insurer must prove it cannot'; the insurer, in other words, must present undisputed facts that eliminate any possibility of coverage." (*American States Ins. Co. v. Progressive Casualty Ins. Co.* (2009) 180 Cal. App. 4th 18, 27, 102 Cal. Rptr. 3d 591, italics omitted, fn. omitted.)

Fidelity moved for summary judgment on the ground that any coverage related to the disputed property was terminated in 2003 when the Butlers voluntarily deeded a portion of their property, including the disputed property, to Terry Smith. In support of its motion, Fidelity produced the policy of title insurance, the recorded grant deed from the Butlers to Smith, and the declaration of its expert Gayle Picha. The policy provides that coverage shall continue "so long as an insured retains an estate or interest in the land." The grant deed, recorded on September 4, 2003, shows that the Butlers conveyed a portion of their property known as "Parcel A" to Smith "for valuable consideration, receipt of which is hereby acknowledged." In her declaration, Gayle Picha, who has over 35 years' experience in researching publicly recorded documents, searching titles to real property, and studying title issues involving California real estate, stated that she reviewed the chain of title as recorded in the Lassen County Recorder's Officer for the Butler and Souliere properties and read Souliere's complaint, filed August 18, 2009. According to Picha, the Lassen County Recorder's Office Official Records included the deed from the Butlers to Smith, which granted to Smith the portion of the Butlers' property described as "Parcel A." Picha opined that Parcel A included "all of the real property at the northern boundary of the Butler property nearest the land that Butler claims as his own within Section 22." Picha also indicated that the Lassen County Recorder's Official Records did not show that the Butlers retained any interest in the property deeded to Smith.

The evidence produced by Fidelity was sufficient to meet Fidelity's initial burden on presenting facts that eliminated any possibility of coverage. Thus, it was incumbent on the Butlers to demonstrate one or more triable issues of material fact as to that issue.

In opposing Fidelity's motion for summary judgment, the Butlers asserted that the conveyance to Smith did not terminate coverage under the policy because "said transfer was pursuant to a confidential agreement for financing purposes only." In support of their assertion, they cited to the declaration of Terry Smith. In his declaration, Smith confirmed that in August 2003, he entered into a confidential agreement with the Butlers "to assist them in refinancing their home." According to Smith, "it was necessary for refinancing of the Butler's [sic] home to list Smith's name on the title of the property, a requirement of the lender." He and the Butlers agreed that once the financing was in place, Smith would transfer "any and all of his interest" in the property back to the Butlers without any financial consideration. The financing was completed in September 2003, and in December 2003, Smith signed and notarized two grant deeds conveying the property to the Butlers. Copies of the confidential agreement and deeds were attached as exhibits to Smith's declaration. Consistent with Smith's declaration, the confidential agreement provided that "it is necessary for the refinancing that the subject property is in fee title ownership of Terry E. Smith." Smith never believed that he had an interest in the property. He never lived in the home or spent the night there.

Whether Smith believed he had an interest in the subject property or lived there is irrelevant, as is the purpose of the conveyance. The policy specifically states that coverage continues so long as the insured retains an estate or interest in the land. Thus, if the Butlers conveyed the property to a third party, i.e. someone such as Smith who is not named as an insured in the policy, without retaining any interest therein, coverage terminated as to the property conveyed.

Kwok v. Transnation Title Insurance Company (2009) 170 Cal. App. 4th 1562, 89 Cal. Rptr. 3d 141 (*Kwok*) is instructive. In April 2004, the Kwoks formed a limited liability company (LLC) and were its only members. (Id. at p. 1565.) The LLC purchased certain real property, and the defendant title insurance company issued a policy of title insurance for that property. (Ibid.) The LLC was the only named insured in Schedule A. (Ibid.) The policy defined "insured" as "the insured named in Schedule A, and, subject to any rights or defenses the Company would have had against the named insured, those who succeed to the interest of the named insured by operation of law. . . .'" (Ibid.) The policy provided that coverage would continue "so long as the insured retains an estate or interest in the land. . . .'" (Ibid.) In September 2005, the LLC transferred the property to the Kwoks as trustees of the Kwoks' revocable trust. (Ibid.) In December 2005, the LLC was dissolved. (*Id*. at pp. 1566-1567.)

Thereafter, the title insurance company denied coverage for an easement dispute between the Kwoks and their neighbors on the ground that the LLC's transfer of the property to the Kwoks as trustees was a voluntary act that terminated coverage under the policy. (*Kwok*, supra, 170 Cal. App. 4th at p. 1566.) The Kwoks sued the title insurance company for breach of contract and bad faith. (Ibid.) The title insurance company moved for summary judgment, arguing that it owed no duty to the Kwoks because the LLC voluntarily transferred the property to the Kwoks by grant deed prior to the LLC's dissolution, and therefore, the Kwoks did not become insureds by "operation of law'" under the terms of the policy. (Ibid.) The trial court granted summary judgment in favor of the title insurance company, and the Court of Appeal affirmed. (Id. at pp. 1567, 1573.) The Court of Appeal found that the transfer of the property to the Kwoks as trustees terminated coverage under the policy. (Id. at p. 1567.) The court rejected the Kwoks' claim that "the transfer of the property from the LLC directly to its members as trustees of a family trust effected only a change in the method of holding legal title, not a change in their proportional beneficial interest." (Id. at p. 1570.) The court explained, "The issue before us is not whether there was a change in the beneficial ownership of the property, but rather whether the Kwoks, as trustees of their family trust, succeeded as insureds under the terms of the policy. There is nothing in the policy definition of 'insureds' that identifies 'beneficial owners' as insureds. Under the terms of the policy, the Kwoks could only become insureds by operation of law. The transfer of property by an insured into a family trust is a voluntary act and not one that arises by operation of law." (Id. at p. 1571.)

Applying *Kwok*'s reasoning to the present case, it makes no difference whether the conveyance was for financing purposes or that Smith never believed that that he had an interest in the property. The salient point here, as in *Kwok*, is that the Butlers voluntarily transferred their interest in the subject property to Smith.

In opposing Fidelity's motion for summary judgment, the Butlers also asserted that their conveyance to Smith did not terminate coverage under the policy because they retained an easement in the property conveyed. Specifically, they asserted that the property "contains a forty foot easement for the access of Butler to adjacent parcels" which were not part transferred to Smith. They further asserted that "said easement still exists. The transfer was subject to this easement and was and is a retained interest in the Property by Butler." In support of their assertion, the Butlers relied on Smith's declaration, "Parcel Map No. 7-05-84," and a letter from the Lassen County Planning Department regarding "Parcel Map Application #7-05-84, Butler." Smith's declaration makes no mention of an easement, and the trial court overruled in part and sustained in part Fidelity's objections to the parcel map and the letter, ruling that such documents would be "received by the Court solely as evidence of their existence and not for the truth of their contents." The Butlers do not challenge the court's evidentiary ruling on appeal; thus, the parcel map and letter are not relevant, and we are precluded from considering them.

Assuming for argument's sake that the Butlers' appeal does include a challenge to the trial court's evidentiary ruling, we find the trial court acted within its discretion in refusing to consider the documents' contents. Neither document was properly authenticated. "Authentication of a writing is required before it may be received in evidence." (Evid. Code, § 1401, subd. (a).) "Authentication of a writing means (a) the introduction of evidence sufficient to sustain a finding that it is the writing that the proponent of the evidence claims it is or (b) the establishment of such facts by any other means provided by law." (Evid. Code, § 1400.) "Unless the opposing party admits the genuineness of the document, the proponent of the evidence must present declarations or other 'evidence sufficient to sustain a finding that it is the writing that the proponent of the evidence claims it is.'" (*Serri v. Santa Clara University* (2014) 226 Cal. App. 4th 830, 855, 172 Cal. Rptr. 3d 732.) Fidelity did not admit the genuineness of the documents, and the Butlers failed to offer any declarations or other evidence that would support a finding that the documents are what the Butlers claim them to be.

Even if the documents had been properly authenticated, the documents alone do not create a triable issue of material fact as to whether the Butlers retained an interest in the land. The Butlers failed to offer any expert testimony to explain the parcel map. Where the fact sought to be proved is not one within the general knowledge of laymen, expert testimony is required. (*Lara v. Nevitt* (2004) 123 Cal. App. 4th 454, 459, 19 Cal. Rptr. 3d 865.) We have reviewed the parcel map and find that the document does not speak for itself. As Fidelity points out, the map does not show the dominant or servient tenements benefitted and burdened by the easement. Thus, even if the parcel map were properly before us, which it is not, we are unable to determine whether it says what the Butlers say it says.

Finally, the letter from the Lassen County Planning Department to the Butlers, dated August 3, 1984, states that "the tentative parcel map submitted for Parcel Map Application #7-05-84 was approved subject to the following conditions: . . . Easement be created and shown on final map for potential future double access for a common approach." Again, even assuming for argument's sake that the letter was properly before us, which it is not, it is insufficient to create a triable issue of material fact as to whether the Butlers retained an interest in the disputed property after it was conveyed. This is true whether it is considered alone or in conjunction with the parcel map because additional information is necessary to explain the meaning and legal consequences of these documents.

On appeal, the Butlers argue that they "never 'voluntarily divested' themselves of an interest in their property" and assert that "this issue was resolved in May 2010 with Fidelity's Claims Counsel." In support of their assertion, they cite to a May 28, 2010, letter from Fidelity to the Butlers advising the Butlers that Fidelity "will accept the tender of defense on behalf of William and Peggy Butler in the Souliere litigation, subject to a reservation of rights as set forth below." The reservation of rights states that "to the extent that the Policy's coverage was not terminated by conveyances after the Date of the Policy, the cause of action would trigger coverage under the . . . Policy." The reservation of rights further provides that "if at some point in the future Fidelity concludes that it has no actual or potential obligation under the Policy to indemnify or provide legal representation to William and/or Peggy Butler in this matter, Fidelity expressly reserves the right to decide, after giving reasonable notice, to discontinue indemnification and/or discontinue providing William and/or Peggy Butler with a defense of the above-referenced litigation. The Company also reserves the right to seek a judicial declaration determining that it has no obligation to indemnify or provide a defense of the above-referenced litigation." (.) Even assuming for argument's sake that the contents of the letter are properly before us, Fidelity's acknowledgement that there existed a potential for coverage under the policy in May 2010 does not preclude a later determination that there is no actual or potential coverage under the policy, and the Butlers were so advised. In short, Fidelity's letter does not create a triable issue of material fact as to whether the Butlers' conveyance of the disputed property to Smith terminated coverage under the policy as to the portion conveyed.

For all the foregoing reasons, we conclude that summary judgment was properly entered in Fidelity's favor. In the absence of coverage, Fidelity had no duty to defend or indemnify the Butlers. Our decision is limited to the issue of whether Fidelity had a duty to defend and/or indemnify the Butlers in connection with the Souliere lawsuit. Whether Fidelity otherwise "violated insurance law" in its handling of the Butlers' claim is not before us.

Based on our independent review of the record, we conclude that the trial court properly granted summary judgment in Fidelity's favor. Accordingly, we need not reach any of the Butlers' procedural challenges.

Disposition

The judgment is affirmed. Fidelity shall recover its costs on appeal. (Cal. Rules of Court, rule 8.278(a)(1) & (2).)

Affirmed.

QUESTIONS ABOUT THE CASE

1   Under what grounds did the title insurance company claim that it no longer owed any duty to defend under its policy to the Butlers?
2   How did the Butlers respond to the allegation that they had conveyed the property to another party?
3   Were there any publicly recorded deeds or other instruments to show that the disputed property was in fact conveyed? If so, how did the Butlers respond?
4   Did Smith ever believe that he had title to the property? Were his beliefs germane to the issue before the court?
5   Did the fact that the Butlers retained an easement right to the property, even during the short time that Smith held title to the property, have an impact on whether the Butlers were covered under the policy?

COVID-19 CONCERN

In the age of the Internet and online records, it may be surprising to learn that not all records that deal with real estate are online. Many deed rooms and land offices provide free, online access to real estate records, but this access comes with some important limitations. For one thing, the records may only go back 10 or 20 years. That would seem more than sufficient, but for title examiners who often must peruse records 40 or 50 years old, online access does not provide what they need. Some of the other records that they need are not available online at all. Clerk's office records, which show details of lawsuits and whether someone received an award at trial or in a settlement that could affect title to real estate are not usually available online anywhere.

That means a trip to the courthouse. However, in the age of COVID, there are at least two prominent issues with a courthouse visit: access and exposure. During both 2020 and 2021 there were long stretches of time when courthouses were closed, and people doing title searches had no access. The second point is exposure: Even when courthouses are open, visitors and staff fear being in a small room surrounded by other people who may or may not be sick.

CHAPTER SUMMARY

Title insurance is an insurance policy with a very specialized function. It protects owners against claims made against the title to their property. Before a title insurance company will issue a policy, it requires an examination of the public records to make sure that there are no outstanding legal claims on the property. The mechanism to check the public records is a title examination. A title examiner is someone who is trained to review all public records in order to discover any potential claims against a parcel of real estate. The title examiner must review land records and civil and criminal actions to check for any outstanding legal claims on the property. The basic reason for a title examination is to protect the new owner from any claim that might affect her enjoyment of the property. Title examinations are required not only by title insurance companies but also by lenders who wish to safeguard their interest in the property.

A title examination is a multistep process. In states that follow the grantor-grantee index model, properties are listed by the names of the buyers and sellers. A title examiner in such a state is required to establish a chain of title, listing all the names of the owners of a particular tract going back for a specific period of time. In these states, attorneys are usually responsible for certifying the title as free and clear of all encumbrances. The attorney's opinion about the legal status of the property is grounds for a legal malpractice action if the attorney is incorrect. Not all states follow the attorney certification model. In some states, title examinations are performed by nonlawyers. Under either system, a title examiner must pay close attention to detail and make sure that all records are properly surveyed for any potential legal impact on the property.

SKILLS YOU NEED IN THE REAL WORLD

Double-Checking Your Own Title Work

One of the advantages to title searching is that there is a built-in mechanism to help you double-check your work. Because the grantor and grantee indexes are mirror images of one another, when you have a question about a particular conveyance, you can double-check the work by verifying the entry in the other indexes.

For example, suppose that the current owner of the property, John Doe, shows a deed book reference of volume 900, page 32, purchased from Joseph Wilson. The grantee index will show an entry from Joseph Wilson to John Doe. The grantor index, on the other hand, will show an entry under John Doe's name, receiving property from Joseph Wilson. Once a chain of title is established, the adverse conveyance worksheet is used to double-check the entries in the chain. At some point, a person listed as an owner in the chain will also be listed in the adverse conveyances. This helps you to cross-reference your work.

ETHICAL ISSUES FOR THE PARALEGAL

Tacking and Other Shortcuts

There is always a temptation to take shortcuts. This is especially true in title work. The reasoning that some title examiners use is, "If there is a problem with this property, it would have cropped up by now." So, they decide to shortcut the process and submit the title as free of any encumbrances so that they can shave some time off a title search and move on to the next one. This is an especially strong temptation when you consider that most title examiners are paid by the search, not by the hour. However, these shortcuts can have profound effects on other people. A missed lien, judgment, or assessment can mean that the new owner will be forced to pay thousands of dollars, or the title insurance company will have to pay thousands of dollars in defending the owner. In either event, the title examiner's reputation will be ruined. No matter how big a city you are in, the legal community is always small and word gets around quickly. Title examiners who skimp on the details and take chances on missing crucial information eventually get weeded out of the profession. Title insurance companies will refuse to work with them, attorneys will refuse to hire them, and what was a promising and potentially lucrative career has now been closed off forever, all for the sake of saving a little time on a single title search.

KEY TERMS AND CONCEPTS

Binder	Policy	Title abstract
Chain of title	Premium	Title examination
Grantor-grantee index	Tacking	Title insurance

END-OF-CHAPTER EXERCISES

Review Questions

See Appendix for answers.

1　What is title insurance?
2　How can title insurance assist in completing a real estate transaction?
3　What are some of the problems that title insurance protects against?
4　How does someone acquire title insurance?
5　How often must a person pay a title insurance premium?
6　What is the grantor-grantee index?
7　How can surveys and plats of property help in a title examination?
8　What are the basic steps involved in a title search?
9　What is a chain of title?
10　What information can a title examiner gather at the local tax office?
11　What are adverse or out conveyances?
12　Why is it important to determine if a previous mortgage has been canceled?
13　What are abstract forms?
14　What are the Uniform Commercial Code filings? Why are they important for title examinations?
15　How do probate, marriage, birth, and death records assist a title examiner?
16　What is the purpose of a preliminary title opinion?
17　Why is legal malpractice an issue in title searches in some states?
18　What is "tacking"? Why does it present ethical concerns?
19　Are attorneys required to certify titles in all states? Explain your answer.

DISCUSSION QUESTIONS

1   Different states follow different methods to certify that a title is free and marketable. Should there be a nationwide system that is used by all states that follows the same rules and procedures as there is with Truth-in-Lending and real estate settlements?

2   Can you access real estate records online in your county? If so, how far back can you go? Can you create a 30-year title search based solely on what you find online or would you have to visit the facility in order to get those records?

APPLYING WHAT YOU HAVE LEARNED

1   Should all states move to a system whereby an attorney certifies title to real property? What advantages and disadvantages would such a system have?

2   Using the forms provided in the figures throughout this chapter, prepare a title search on a piece of property. Create a chain of title going back for 40 years, then a list of adverse conveyances for each owner in the chain. Are there any Uniform Commercial Code listings for the current owner?

WEB SURFING

American Land Title Association
http://www.alta.org

Law.com Dictionary
http://www.law.com

Legal Explanations
http://www.legal-explanations.com

Tech Topic
TITLE INSURANCE CALCULATORS

**Old Republic National (http://www.oldrepublic
title.com/newnational/resources/locations.asp),
First American (http://facc.firstam.com), and
Fidelity National (http://ratecalculator.fnf.com) title**
**insurance companies each offer a title insurance
calculator, allowing you to compare rates between
the three companies.**

ANNOTATED DOCUMENT

Chain of Title

Current Owner(s): Cynthia Thompson Epps of 5402 Burkemont Road, Morganton, NC 28655

The chain of title begins by listing the current owner(s) (Cynthia Thompson Epps).

Grantor Name(s):	Colin D. Epps and wife Cindy Thompson Epps
Grantee Name(s):	Cynthia Thompson Epps
Date of Transaction:	October 14, 2022
Date Recorded:	November 5, 2022
Deed Book Reference:	Book 1412 pg 443-446
Brief description of property:	1.32 acres Southside of State RD 1957, Burkemont Mountain Rd.

Prior Transaction:

Grantor Name(s):	W.V. Home and wife Eula Denton Home, Wanda Home Elliot Nesbitt, Debbie Thompson McPeters, legally separated, and Cindy Thompson Epps and her husband Colin D. Epps
Grantee Name(s):	Colin D. Epps and wife Cindy Thompson Epps
Date of Transaction:	February 14, 2020
Date Recorded:	February 28, 2020
Deed Book Reference:	Book 942 pg 1599
Brief description of property:	1.32 acres Southside of State RD 1957, Burkemont Mountain Rd.

Prior Transaction:

Grantor Name(s):	W.V. Home and wife Eula Denton Home, Wanda Home Elliot Nesbitt, Debbie Thompson McPeters, legally separated, and Cindy Thompson Epps
Grantee Name(s):	Colin D. Epps and wife Cindy Thompson Epps
Date of Transaction:	December 17, 2009
Date Recorded:	December 30, 2009
Deed Book Reference:	Book 939 pg 2315
Brief description of the property:	1.32 acres Southside of State RD 1957, Burkemont Mountain Rd.

*Note: W.V. Home and wife Eula Denton Home gave their children Wanda and David Nesbitt, Debbie Thompson McPeters who is legally separated, and Cindy Thompson Epps and her husband a 1/3 undivided interest then the children signed their 1/3 undivided interest back to Cindy Thompson Epps and her husband Colin D. Epps.

The notes throughout clarify portions of the chain of title.

Prior Transaction:

Grantor Name(s):	W.V. Home
Grantee Name(s):	W.V. Home and wife Eula Denton Home
Date of Transaction:	November 2, 2001
Date Recorded:	February 16, 2002
Deed Book Reference:	Book 615 pg 536
Brief description of the property:	6.88 acres of S.R. 1957 on Burkemont Mountain Rd.

*Note: W.V. Home transferred his half interest to his wife Eula Denton Home so her name can be on the deed after they were married.

Prior Transaction:

Grantor Name(s):	Sherill H. Green and wife Quinn H. Green and Burlie L. Houk and his wife Grace G. Houk.
Grantees Name(s):	W.V. Home
Date of Transaction:	July 21, 1990
Date Recorded:	July 24, 1990
Deed Book Reference:	Book 589 pg 446
Brief description of property:	6.88 acres of S.R. 1957 on Burkemont Mountain Rd.

Prior Transaction:

Grantor Name(s):	Issiah Carswell and Wachovia Bank and Trust Company
Grantee Name(s):	Sherill H. Green and Burlie L. Houk
Date of Transaction:	August 1, 1989
Date Recorded:	August 14, 1989
Deed Book Reference:	Book 572 pg 808
Brief description of property:	Southwestern corner on Burkemont Rd.

Prior Transaction:

Grantor Name(s):	Iola P. Mace
Grantee Name(s):	Issiah Carswell
Date of Transaction:	August 9, 1970
Date Recorded:	August 10, 1970
Deed Book Reference:	Book 205 pg 628
Brief description of property:	Southwestern corner on Burkemont Rd.

*Note: Iola P. Mace died and Issiah Carswell and Wachovia bank transferred the property to the Greens and Houks.

Out Conveyance

Owner(s):	Colin D. Epps and wife Cindy Thompson Epps
	5402 Burkemont Road
	Morganton, NC 28655
	Taxes Paid on 7/30/2022 in the amount of $522.91
	Checked 3/15/23 at 9:00 am

The out conveyance is clearly noted.

Period checked: The period was checked from 1/1/2008 to 3/15/2023
Deed of Trust: Recorded 6/25/21 in Book 1255 pg 772-788

This deed has not yet been cancelled.
Right of Way Agreement: Recorded 8/18/2008 in Book 908 pg 2301
I checked the Clerk's office from 1/1/2008 to 3/15/23 and nothing was found except that
they had divorced.

PRACTICE QUESTIONS FOR TEST REVIEW

See Appendix for answers.

Essay Question

Explain title insurance.

True–False

1   **T   F**   Holes or breaks in the chain of title are a common problem faced by title
searchers.

2   **T   F**   Legal malpractice actions are rare in title examinations.

3   **T   F**   Attorneys conduct title examinations in many states.

Fill in the Blank

1   The term for updating a previous title search, without necessarily doing all of the
work of going back the required time: _____.

2   Some states require an attorney to certify the marketability of title. They do this
by issuing: _____.

3   In many states, this office is responsible for recording wills and handling issues
related to persons who died without a will: _____.

Multiple Choice

1   What is one of the biggest ethical dilemmas that often face title examiners?

   A   Payment for work that was not performed.
   B   Confidentiality.
   C   Taking short cuts on title work.
   D   All of the above.

2   What is one of the most common problems faced in a title search?

   A   Inability to identify the current owner of the parcel.
   B   Inability to determine that amount of taxes owed on a parcel.
   C   An apparent hole or break in the chain of title.
   D   All of the above.

3   In many states, title examinations are prepared by:

   A   Paralegals
   B   Attorneys
   C   Independent title examiners
   D   All of the above

The Closing

Chapter Objectives

- Describe the importance of a real estate settlement
- Explain the basic procedures involved in completing a real estate settlement
- List and describe the participants in the closing
- Define the important documents required at a closing
- Explain the ethical concerns that arise from the use of paralegals in real estate closings

Chapter Outline

I. Introduction

II. What is a Closing?

III. Preparing to Conduct a Closing
   A. Mortgages
   B. Attorney Representation
   C. Establishing the Date
   D. Gathering Documents and Information

IV. People Normally Present at the Closing
   A. Settlement Agent
   B. Buyer

C. Seller
D. Real Estate Agent

V. The Closing Procedure
   A. Preparing the Loan Package
   B. Verifying Hazard Insurance
   C. Exchanging Documents
   D. Disbursing the Funds

VI. Other Closing Issues
   A. "Escrow" Closings
   B. Dual Representation

VII. After the Closing

INTRODUCTION

A real estate closing is the point at which the parties to a real estate transaction come together, sign appropriate paperwork, and disburse funds. We examine the closing process in detail in this chapter, concentrating not only on the basic procedures but also on the critically important role played by paralegals in modern real estate closings.

Before we can begin describing the process of completing a real estate closing, it is important to address an issue about terminology. In some parts of the country, the final step to bring a real estate transaction to its completion is referred to as a "closing," while in other parts it is called a "settlement." The entire concept of the closing has undergone a radical change in recent years with the passage of the Dodd-Frank Act and the changes it has brought about to the Truth in Lending Act and the Real Estate Settlement Procedures Act, commonly shortened to "TRID."

We will address the commonplace actions surrounding a real estate closing and also focus on the changes brought about by new legislation that has changed the way that closings are carried out across the entire United States. However, before we can address those changes, we must first address the basic issues surrounding what a closing is and also learn some of the basic terminology involved.

WHAT IS A CLOSING?

Closing
Also known as a settlement, the final phase of a real estate transaction at which all deeds are signed and funds are distributed to complete the sale of real property.

A **closing** is the final step in a long process that began with a homeowner's decision to sell his house. The homeowner contacted a real estate agent, who entered into a listing agreement with the homeowner, placing the house for sale. At some point, a buyer made an offer on the house, and the stage was set for a closing. Between the time of the offer and acceptance, a great many things have happened. The buyer arranged for a mortgage with a lender. The house was inspected. The lender probably requested an appraisal. The buyer arranged for title insurance. The lender finalized its paperwork and prepared checks to disburse at the closing. A deed was prepared that will transfer the owner's interest in the property to the buyer. We have discussed all these elements in previous chapters. The closing is when all of the details finally come together.

REAL ESTATE BASICS AT A GLANCE

A closing brings together the buyer and the seller for the final stage in a real estate transaction.

Closings can be both complicated and time-consuming. Many different individuals are involved, and that is always a recipe for delay. Someone must take the responsibility of coordinating all the information to bring about the closing. In some states, attorneys are responsible for conducting closings, while in other states that duty falls to the lender or even a title insurance company representative. No matter who pulls the closing together, the actual process requires careful attention to detail. It is easy to make a mistake at a closing, and such a mistake can have enormous financial consequences. In states where attorneys conduct closings, it is very common for the attorney to rely on the services of a qualified paralegal to collect all the important documents and to coordinate the physical meeting of all concerned parties. Under TRID, the person designated to carry out the closing is referred to as the **settlement agent**, and we will use that terminology throughout this chapter.

Although TRID changes the name of the closing professional to settlement agent and no doubt that terminology will take hold, the same cannot be said of another change. Dodd-Frank makes a distinction between "consummation" and "closing." A **consummation** occurs when the buyer becomes contractually obligated to the lender to repay the loan. TRID uses different terms for these parties, and we will use those terms from now on. Instead of a "borrower," the legislation refers to these parties as "consumers."

Because a consummation and a closing are not the same thing, but occur at the same time, there is often confusion about these terms. As noted, consummation is a term that refers to the contractual obligation between the borrower and the lender, but the term "closing" refers to the entire process of finalizing a real estate transaction. "Closing" is a term so deeply embedded in the common parlance among title insurance companies, lawyers, paralegals, real estate agents, and lenders, to name just a few, that the idea that that term will change is probably unrealistic. The documents will all bear the name "consummation," but real estate professionals continue to use the age-old expression of "closing." For the purposes of clarity, we will use the terms "settlement agent" to refer to the person who handles the process of closing out a real estate sale, but use the term "closing" instead of consummation unless specifically referring to the legislation.

Settlement agent
Under TRID, the person designated to carry out all of the duties associated with closing a real estate transaction.

Consummation
Under TRID, the point where a consumer becomes contractually obligated to repay the mortgage to the lender.

PREPARING TO CONDUCT A CLOSING

Although different states follow different rules about who is authorized to conduct closings, there are similarities in the basic processes involved no matter where the closing is conducted. A settlement agent can be any of a number of different professionals, including title insurers, lenders, real estate attorneys, paralegals, and real estate agents.

A. MORTGAGES

The most obvious requirement of any transaction is payment for the property. Purchase contracts often contain express provisions requiring a loan commitment from the lender within 10 days of the contract date. Without this assurance, the transaction can never be completed. Once the loan commitment is given, it is up to the lender to make the funds available to complete the transaction at the closing.

B. ATTORNEY REPRESENTATION

Although many states do not require an attorney to conduct a closing, most buyers hire one anyway in order to safeguard their interests and handle any legal questions that come up during the negotiations and closing. In some states, there is a question about whether a nonlawyer can conduct a closing. States are split on this, with some allowing nonlawyers to conduct the entire closing and others claiming that handling a closing is essentially a legal process that requires the presence of an attorney. If a buyer hires an attorney, or if the closing occurs in a state where an attorney's involvement is mandatory, the attorney's fee is paid by the buyer from the proceeds at the sale. Most attorneys who handle closings are paid a flat fee or a percentage of the sales price.

REAL ESTATE BASICS AT A GLANCE

Attorneys are used in most, but not all, states to handle the details of a closing.

EXAMPLE 13-1

Sidebar

Another change that has spread throughout the culture of law firms is to move away from back-to-back, or "piggyback" closings. One way of describing a piggyback closing is when a seller closes on the sale of his home in the morning and buys a house in the afternoon. The buyer needs the proceeds of the morning sale to complete the afternoon closing. Before the days of Dodd-Frank, some banks would offer "bridge" loans or other incentives to help move these closings along. Those days are over. Because TRID requires a very strict interpretation of the three-day rule, the only way to conduct a piggyback closing is to ensure that all parties in both transactions, the morning and the afternoon closings, have been given the correct disclosures, the GFE, and the loan disclosures, and all at least three days prior to the date of the closing. It is not impossible, but with that many moving parts, it is easy for a mistake to be made.

THE ATTORNEY'S FEE

Ricardo has entered into a contract to purchase a home. He approaches a local law firm about representing him at the closing. The attorney explains that she will handle the closing, ensure that all documents are properly signed and recorded, and ensure that the deed and mortgage are properly recorded. Her fee is one-half of 1 percent of the sale price. The sale price is $92,000. How much is Ricardo's attorney fee?

  Answer: Multiply $92,000 by .5%. The answer is $460.

C. ESTABLISHING THE DATE

Because of the number of individuals who are involved in a typical real estate transaction, setting a closing date is not a simple matter. Many of these individuals must produce specific documents, and these documents must be completed prior to the closing date. Whoever is responsible for coordinating the closing must keep after all parties to make sure that checks, contracts, and other documents are ready in time.

1. THREE-DAY WINDOW

An additional factor must be considered when setting the date of the closing. Under TRID, the borrower (the "consumer") must be given all Truth-in-Lending disclosures, Good Faith Estimates, and loan disclosures at least three days prior to the date of the closing. This has put the nail in the coffin of the old custom of lenders providing these documents on the day of the closing, sometimes just hours ahead of the closing time. If any changes are made in the Good Faith Estimate, then a new three-day window is triggered.

The final date and time of the closing must take into account the needs of several different parties, including the client, the closing attorney (if any), the real estate agents, and the lender. If the funds are not available, for example, there is little point in scheduling a closing because the seller will certainly not execute a deed and sign over his rights without receiving payment.

Besides the practical issues of completing all the necessary paperwork, there is another important issue regarding closing dates: time is of the essence clauses.

2. TIME IS OF THE ESSENCE

We encountered time is of the essence clauses in Chapter 6. In that chapter, we saw that when a real estate contract contains such a clause, the closing must occur on the date set or the contract is void. Obviously, all parties wish to avoid that result, and this puts even greater pressure on the participants to complete all paperwork in time for the closing date.

TWO CLOSINGS

EXAMPLE 13-2

Renee is selling her home. She needs the funds from this sale in order to purchase a new home. She negotiated a closing date of the fifth day of the month for the sale of her old home and a closing date of the seventh day of the month for the purchase of her new home. She included a time is of the essence clause in the purchase contract for her old home. On the fifth, the attorney handling the closing calls to say that she has not received all the paperwork that she needs to conclude the closing. She says that the closing cannot be held until the sixth. What effect does this have on the contract?

Answer: It voids it. A time is of the essence clause specifically provides that the contract will be voided if the closing does not occur on a specific date. In this case, the attorney has indicated that the closing cannot be performed on that date, so the contract provision is triggered.

Sidebar

A party might insist on a time is of the essence clause when he is facing a set date in another closing and must have the funds from the first transaction before being able to complete the purchase of the new home.

D. GATHERING DOCUMENTS AND INFORMATION

The first and most important job in organizing a closing is gathering information. Many of the professionals responsible for coordinating the closing rely on forms to help them double-check all information needed to complete the closing. Not only will the settlement agent need everyone's full name and address, but also their telephone and cellphone numbers and email addresses as well. These days, it is often easier to reach someone through email or by cellphone than by other means. Many of the transactions that were formerly handled by couriers and faxes are now done by email. To successfully complete the closing, it is necessary for the settlement agent to gather information from a wide variety of sources (see Figure 13-1). The most common information needed to complete a closing includes:

1 Title search,
2 Legal description of the property,

3 Loan payoff amounts,

4 Tax information, and

5 Inspection reports.

REAL
ESTATE
BASICS AT
A GLANCE

Closings require close attention to detail, especially in regard to particular documents needed to complete the process.

FIGURE 13-1

Information Needed for Closing

- ▪ Title search
- ▪ Legal description of the property
- ▪ Loan payoff amounts
- ▪ Property survey
- ▪ Tax information
- ▪ Termite inspection and report
- ▪ House inspector's report
- ▪ Title insurance binder
- ▪ Information on any title problems
- ▪ Sewage certification or percolation test for unimproved property

1. TITLE SEARCH

The title search must be completed prior to closing. As we saw in the last chapter, a title search can be very involved and detailed. The purpose of the title search is to ensure that there are no legal claims that could affect the title to the property or prevent the finalization of the transaction.

When a title search has discovered potential title defects, such as liens, judgments, or any other issue that clouds title, it is up to the seller (and the seller's attorney) to clear up these title defects before the closing. One of the conditions that buyers, lenders, and title insurance companies insist on is that the title be free of defects.

As we saw in the previous chapter, some states use a system whereby the attorney certifies the status of the title. In those states, the attorney will issue two reports: the preliminary opinion and the final opinion. The preliminary opinion details any possible problems with the title and what the legal team will do to correct them. The final title opinion confirms that any legal problem has been cleared up and certifies that the title is free and clear of encumbrances.

The preliminary and final title opinions go not only to the client, but also to the title insurance company. It is these opinions that serve as the basis for the issuance of a title insurance policy, which the buyer is often required to obtain prior to the closing.

2. LEGAL DESCRIPTION OF THE PROPERTY

The legal description of the property is important for several reasons. First, it will be used in various documents, from the deed to the mortgage, to correctly identify the property. Researching and preparing the legal description often falls to the legal assistant or paralegal who works for the settlement agent. As we have seen in previous chapters, there are several different methods used to identify property, from tract indexes to metes and bounds descriptions. No matter what method is used, the settlement agent must make sure that the description is correct.

Understanding how property is described, either through metes and bounds or the tract system, can be a huge advantage to any legal professional, as well as consumers, investors, and homeowners.

REAL
ESTATE
BASICS AT
A GLANCE

---

3. LOAN PAYOFF AMOUNTS

Just before the actual closing, the settlement agent must obtain information about the exact amount owed on the seller's mortgage. The reason that the settlement agent must wait until the last possible moment is to ensure that this figure is accurate. Lenders charge daily interest rates on loans, and the settlement agent must confirm the amount owed up to the day of the closing so that the check written to pay off the mortgage is correct. This check will be disbursed at the closing.

To assist in this process, the seller should provide complete information about outstanding mortgages, including the lender's name, address, account numbers, and estimated payoff amounts. The settlement agent will pin down the actual payoff amounts, but it is always helpful to have a rough estimate from the seller to help double-check the information. It also helps to determine if there are one or two mortgages. Obviously, if there are two mortgages, both must be satisfied at the closing. When the seller's estimated payoff amount is wildly divergent from the actual amount, it can be a hint that there is more than one mortgage on the property.

One way of determining payoff amounts is by creating a standardized form that is sent to all lenders requesting this information. This letter may be followed up with a phone call shortly before the closing to determine the most up-to-the-minute payoff amount. Lenders will also often guarantee the loan payoff amount for a specific period of time. For instance, a lender might declare that the loan payoff amount is good for five business days only. If the closing occurs after that time, the settlement agent must call back and get new information.

4. TAX INFORMATION

One of the most important pieces of information that must be obtained prior to the closing is the tax bill for the property. Fortunately, a thorough title examination always discovers this information. If the taxes for the year have not yet been paid on the property, they must be paid at the closing. If they have already been paid, the seller will want reimbursement for the part of the year for which he did not live in the house. If the seller must be reimbursed, the settlement agent must prorate payments between the buyer and the seller. We discuss proration later in this chapter.

5. INSPECTION REPORTS

There are several different types of inspections that must occur prior to the actual closing. For instance, in Chapter 11 we examined the issue of the buyer's inspection of the premises by a certified housing inspector. However, the lender may also insist on a pest inspection.

A termite or pest inspection is a requirement imposed by most lenders. The reasons for the inspection are self-evident: The lender wants to make sure that there are no infestations that could ultimately affect the safety or stability of the structure. Lenders insist that a certified professional carry out this inspection. The inspector will examine the entire physical structure of the house, searching for any type of wood-boring insect. The inspector's final certification that the house is free of termites or other infestations is one of the documents required in order to conclude the closing.

Many real estate practitioners have predicted the end of quick closings, i.e., any closing where the date of the purchase and sale contract and the closing are 30 days or less. In fact, many closings now require at least 60 days in order to carry out the necessary steps required under Dodd-Frank.

Tech Topic
LOAN-CLOSING SOFTWARE

Modern computer software has made the job of loan closing considerably easier. Before the widespread use of the Department of Housing and Urban Development's HUD-1 Settlement Form, closings differed from state to state and even city to city. Closing paperwork was completed by hand and often involved time-consuming calculations, especially when it came to determining prorated payments for heating oil, taxes, and other expenses. Closing software has taken away much of the tedium involved in creating a settlement statement. Programs such as SoftPro and Display Soft can generate all the documents needed to complete the closing, including the new documents required by Dodd-Frank. The software also calculates the exact amount needed for disbursement checks, real estate commissions, and the settlement agent's fee. There are even precedents that argue that the failure to use closing software could be the basis of a legal malpractice claim against the closing attorney.

Because of the changes brought about by Dodd-Frank and TRID, the timeline for closing on a parcel of real estate has changed drastically. See Figure 13-2 for an overview of how long due diligence and preparation to close will probably take.

FIGURE 13-2

Probable Timeline for Due Diligence and Preparing for a Closing Under TRID

1st week:
    Receipt of offer to purchase and contract
    Client file created
    Tentative date of closing scheduled
2nd week: Inspections completed and reports submitted and filed. Any issues regarding repairs negotiated and finalized
    Loan commitment letter received and filed
    Appraisal request submitted
    Preliminary title examination
3rd week:
    Title examination completed and filed
    Appraisal received and filed
4th week:
    Broker's commission statement received and filed
    Insurance verified
    Payoff of existing loan verified and guaranteed through specific date
    First walk through of property
    Sellers' disclosures completed and filed
5th week:
    Creditor (Lender) issues Closing Disclosure
    Closing Disclosure given to client
6th week:
    Final walk through of property
    Closing or consummation scheduled and completed.

Various agencies and attorneys state that the best practice under TRID is to aim to have all information received and filed by the attorney who is handling the closing at least 20 days prior to the scheduled closing date. This is a radical departure from the way that closings were conducted in the past. In most situations, any last-minute changes to the Closing Disclosure will trigger at least a new three-day window before the closing can be completed, and some require a seven-day waiting period. As a result, lenders and settlement agents will not wish to make any alterations to the Closing Disclosure, meaning that the work that was formerly done at the last possible moment before the scheduled closing now must be completed at least three days prior to the closing.

The reason for creating TRID in the first place was to address some system-wide problems with real estate closings. Some of the problems were as mundane as last-minute changes to the HUD settlement statement, and some were as blatant as requiring last-minute "fees" and "charges" that could amount to hundreds, even thousands of dollars, all assessed when the parties have already begun to gather for the closing.

IV   PEOPLE NORMALLY PRESENT AT THE CLOSING

There are several people who are normally present at the closing. In states where non-lawyers are permitted to conduct the closing, there may not be an attorney present. However, other individuals will certainly be there. They include:

- The settlement agent,
- The buyer,
- The seller, and
- The real estate agent.

A. SETTLEMENT AGENT

Because TRID consistently refers to the person conducting the closing as a "settlement agent," we will follow that phrasing throughout this chapter in place of older terms such as "closing agent" or "closing attorney." Not only does this bring the information into compliance with new federal laws, it more closely reflects the day-to-day practice of closings across the United States. Although there are many states that use attorneys to act as settlement agents, there are also many that do not. In some parts of the country, closings are handled by escrow agents, title insurance companies, or others. Labeling them all as settlement agents helps clear up any issues and emphasizes that everyone who handles a closing is bound by the same set of rules, no matter what state he or she lives in.

1. ATTORNEY

In states that require attorneys to conduct closings, the attorney will obviously be present and will carry out all the actions that we have so far ascribed to the settlement agent. However, an attorney has one advantage over other types of settlement agents: He can answer legal questions that arise at the closing. In fact, it is this feature that many states still use as justification for permitting only attorneys to handle closings. Other settlement agents, such as lenders, title insurance agents, and real estate brokers, are not permitted to explain the legal significance of documents or to describe the impact that the closing will have on the legal rights of any of the parties. If any of these individuals did that, they would be guilty of practicing law without a license. An attorney obviously does not face that impediment. Attorneys who routinely handle closings have another distinct advantage over other settlement agents: paralegals.

2. PARALEGAL

The paralegal who works at a real estate firm carries out much, if not all, of the preparatory work to ensure that a closing goes off without a hitch. The paralegal may have personally handled the title search and will probably have completed all the documents necessary to conclude the closing. In addition to handling the paperwork, the paralegal is also the person who usually coordinates the actual meeting, making sure that all parties know when and where they are supposed to be. Usually, the paralegal is a notary public and can notarize legal documents. Finally, the paralegal will also be the person who takes the signed documents to the courthouse for filing.

Given all of the actions that paralegals routinely carry out in a real estate closing, some people have asked: What exactly does the attorney do to justify his fee? This question has particular relevance in states where the attorney may not be present at the closing. The paralegal may actually conduct the entire closing alone, with the attorney on the premises or available by telephone for a quick consultation.

B. BUYER

The buyer will be present at the closing because he must sign the paperwork necessary to complete the process. Even more important, he must be present to receive a signed and fully executed deed from the seller. As we have seen in previous chapters, a real estate transaction is only complete when a deed is delivered by the seller and accepted by the buyer.

C. SELLER

The seller will be present for the practical reason that she will be receiving a check for her profit from the sale. The seller is also present in order to deliver the deed to the buyer.

D. REAL ESTATE AGENT

There is no requirement for the real estate agent to be present at the closing if he or she is not conducting it. The settlement agent will write a check to the real estate agent and will forward this check to the agent. In fact, most real estate agents contact the settlement agent and request several different checks be written, each one reflecting the percentage of the commission that goes to the various individuals involved. As we saw in an earlier chapter, a real estate agent's final check will reflect commission-sharing with another agent and perhaps reductions for amounts paid to the real estate agent's company.

V   THE CLOSING PROCEDURE

All closings follow the same general procedures, but settlement agents know that no two closings are ever exactly the same. Real estate law offers an almost endless variation of issues and problems to be solved, and this is as true with closings as with any other aspect of the practice.

Immediately before the closing, the settlement agent is responsible for pulling all the documents together to ensure that the closing proceeds smoothly. During the closing, the parties will meet face-to-face and sign numerous documents. Keeping all these documents and disbursement checks organized can be daunting. The parties may also have questions about the legal impact of certain aspects of the closing. This is one reason why many states require attorneys to conduct the closing. In states where an attorney is not required, the parties are urged to have their questions answered by an attorney and the settlement agent is counseled not to give legal advice to any of the parties. Add to this the new requirements under Dodd-Frank, especially the mandate that the borrower receive Truth-in-Lending and other documents at least three days prior to the closing, and the settlement agent has a lot to keep track of.

In states where attorneys conduct the closings, real estate paralegals usually handle most of the details. The paralegal receives the loan packet from the lender and is responsible for making sure that all the lender's instructions are followed to the letter. It is also the paralegal who is often responsible for conducting the title examination and coordinating the attendance of the people necessary for a successful closing.

As the various documents are passed from party to party, there is often a need to have a signature notarized. Many settlement agents have notaries on staff to facilitate this aspect of the process. One of the most important aspects of the closing is the correct preparation of the loan package.

A. PREPARING THE LOAN PACKAGE

Loan package
A set of instructions from a lender about how financial documents should be prepared and distributed at the closing.

Several days prior to the closing, the lender should send the settlement agent a loan package that includes all the documents that must be completed during the closing. Many lenders have specific instructions and requirements for the way that their loan documents must be prepared and finalized. The **loan package** will include not only the documents that must be completed, but also an exhaustive set of instructions about how these documents should be completed and returned to the lender. Unfortunately, some lenders wait until the last minute — sometimes the actual day of the closing — before they send the loan package to the settlement agent. This puts a great deal of pressure on the team.

The loan package contains all the documents that the lender needs the buyer to complete at the closing. It also contains instructions for the law firm handling the closing.

B. VERIFYING HAZARD INSURANCE

The settlement agent must also verify that the new owner has obtained hazard insurance for the property. Hazard insurance, also known as homeowner's insurance, is required by the lender in order to safeguard the collateral for the loan. In addition to the loan package and hazard insurance, there are numerous other documents that will be exchanged during the closing.

C. EXCHANGING DOCUMENTS

In this section, we examine the most common documents that are exchanged at the closing. These documents must all be prepared prior to the closing and may require additional attention after the closing, such as filing at the local courthouse. The documents exchanged during the closing include:

- The general warranty deed,
- The mortgage,
- IRS forms,
- Lien waiver affidavits (if required),
- Closing Disclosure Form,
- a bill of sale for personal property,
- The compliance agreement,
- Credit insurance documents,
- The loan application,
- USA PATRIOT Act requirements,
- PMI disclosures,
- Trust disbursement records,
- TRID documentation,
- The termite inspection letter, and
- The survey.

1. GENERAL WARRANTY DEED

One of the responsibilities of the settlement agent is to make sure that the deed is drafted correctly. There are many issues involved in preparing the deed. For instance, the deed must contain appropriate language, use legal descriptions, and correctly identify parties, among other features that we discussed in depth in Chapter 8. This is where having an attorney prepare the deed is very useful. In states where attorneys conduct the closings, they also prepare the deeds.

2. MORTGAGE

As we have already seen, the mortgage (or deed of trust) is the financing document that sets out the arrangement between the buyer and the lender. The mortgage also gives the lender the right to foreclose on the property in the event that the buyer defaults. Another important aspect of the mortgage is the promissory note provision.

a. Promissory Note

The **promissory note** is the provision in a mortgage under which the borrower agrees to specific repayment terms, including the total amount of the loan, the monthly

Promissory note
A legal agreement whereby the borrower agrees to borrow a specific amount and also agrees to repay that amount.

interest payment, the annual percentage rate for the loan, the length of the loan, and other conditions. The promissory note provision is the binding agreement between the lender and the borrower whereby the borrower promises to repay the loan. Without this provision, a lender would have no way of enforcing a loan.

b. Subordination Agreements

We discussed subordination agreements in Chapter 9. In that chapter, we saw that a subordination agreement could be required in situations in which there is more than one mortgage on the property and there is an issue about priority. In situations involving owner financing, for instance, a lender might insist that the owner subordinate his mortgage to the lender's mortgage, especially when the lender is providing the bulk of the funds.

3. IRS FORMS

There are various Internal Revenue Service forms that may be required as part of the closing. One of the most important of these is Form 1099.

a. IRS Form 1099

This form has been required by the IRS since 1987; it details the total amount received by the seller during the closing. This document is important because it shows any profit that the seller has taken from the sale and will have important consequences for the seller's personal income tax return.

b. IRS Form 4506

In addition to Form 1099, other IRS forms may also be required. Another common one is Form 4506. This form allows the lender to request a copy of the borrower's income tax return from the IRS. This information is important in order to evaluate the borrower for a possible loan. Without this form, the IRS will not release a copy of an individual's income tax return.

c. W-9 Form

A W-9 verifies the borrower's Social Security number and is important not only as a means of tracking capital gains and other taxes, but also for reporting figures to other agencies. With modern concerns over identity theft and money laundering, the W-9 is a further safeguard that a person is who he claims to be.

4. LIEN WAIVER AFFIDAVITS

Title insurance companies routinely require lien waiver affidavits to show that there are no liens or other encumbrances against the property. This form is used as a safety net; by requiring the owner/seller to sign such an affidavit, the title insurance company can be assured that there are no outstanding or as yet unfiled liens that could affect title to the property at some later date. When sellers sign a lien waiver affidavit, they are swearing that they know of no judgments, encumbrances, liens, or other pending matters that could act as a bar to the transaction being completed. In states that use attorneys to conduct title examinations, lien waiver affidavits are often attached to the final title certificate.

5. DISCLOSURE FORM

As we saw in Chapter 9, new federal legislation has had significant impact on the practice of real estate for persons as diverse as real estate agents, lenders, borrowers, paralegals and attorneys, to name just a few. For the sake of simplicity, we will refer to the new legislation as "Dodd-Frank" instead of its more lengthy title, The Dodd-Frank Wall Street Reform and Consumer Protection Act, H.R. 4173 (2010). Among many things, Dodd-Frank reformed and changed many of the rules relating to real estate closings. It also created a new bureau, the Consumer Financial Protection Bureau (CFPB), which oversees the implantation and enforcement of Dodd-Frank rules and regulations.

6. BILL OF SALE FOR PERSONAL PROPERTY

In some situations, the seller and the buyer may have negotiated the purchase of items of personal property in addition to the real property. If, for instance, the seller has agreed to sell furniture, appliances, or other personal property, this sale must be set out in a separate bill of sale, independent of the other closing documents. Remember that the other documents are concerned with the transfer of title to real property. Any sale of personal property is separate and distinct from that transaction and must have its own supporting documentation.

7. COMPLIANCE AGREEMENT

A compliance agreement is a form signed by the borrower that permits the lender to request additional information or documents after the closing. The lender insists on this form in case there is some type of clerical error or missing paperwork from the closing. A compliance agreement is the borrower's agreement to provide any additional information requested by the lender after the closing has been completed.

8. CREDIT INSURANCE DOCUMENTS

It is very common for borrowers not only to negotiate the provisions of the real estate mortgage but also to request disability protection insurance. Disability insurance is a specific type of policy that will make a borrower's mortgage payments in the event that he is unable to meet that requirement because of illness or injury—basically ensuring that the borrower has good credit regardless of the circumstances. If disability insurance is part of the mortgage packet negotiated with the lender, the first premium is usually due at the closing and will be part of the disbursements that occur at that time.

9. LOAN APPLICATION

When the borrower first approached the lender about financing the purchase of real estate, he filled out an application and presented it to the lender. What lenders often do prior to the closing is to retype that application and put it in a final (and more easily read) form. During the closing, the borrower is often asked to sign this new loan application and to confirm that it contains all the same information that the borrower originally presented in the handwritten application.

Under Dodd-Frank, the loan application process itself is also modified. The Act requires six items in order to be considered a valid loan application, including:

1 Consumer's name,
2 Consumer's income,
3 Social Security number (for purposes of ordering a credit report),
4 Property address,
5 Estimate of the value of the property, and
6 Mortgage amount sought.

Lenders are permitted to ask for additional information, but these six items must be included in any loan application governed by Dodd-Frank, which essentially means any loan involving real estate.

10. USA PATRIOT ACT REQUIREMENTS

The USA PATRIOT Act was passed after the terrible events of September 11, 2001. Although terrorism would seem to be completely unrelated to a typical real estate transaction, the USA PATRIOT Act became a major factor in real estate closings by virtue of language contained in one clause of the act. The provision in question, Section 352, requires that certain financial institutions create anti–money laundering programs and certify that they have complied with the Act. More than bombs and hatred, terrorism thrives on money. It takes a great deal of money to keep a terrorist group functioning, and most of the money to support these efforts comes from laundered money from illicit activities as varied as producing counterfeit store coupons to making shady real estate deals. As a result, most settlement agents now include a provision in their closing documents to show that they have complied with the USA PATRIOT Act in determining the identities of the people involved and certifying, to the extent possible, that the transaction was not completed for money laundering purposes.

11. PMI DISCLOSURE

Private mortgage insurance (PMI)
An insurance policy that protects the lender and pays a specified amount in the event that the borrower defaults on the loan.

Private mortgage insurance (PMI) is insurance that protects the lender when the borrower has put down less than 20 percent of the loan purchase price. In the event that the borrower defaults on the mortgage, PMI will reimburse the lender for any money lost. It is referred to as "private" mortgage insurance to distinguish it from some public government programs under the FHA and VA that serve the same function.

The PMI disclosure brochure is a document that explains to the borrower what PMI is. The PMI disclosure form also informs the borrower how he can remove the

PMI premium from the loan and when the PMI is scheduled to terminate. While PMI is not designed to help the borrower, it can indirectly assist her. If a company is willing to issue a PMI policy in a particular transaction, it usually means that a borrower who might not have qualified for a mortgage under other circumstances will get one.

Private mortgage insurance protects the lender in the event of a borrower default. It is required whenever the borrower finances more than 80 percent of the purchase price.

REAL
ESTATE
BASICS AT
A GLANCE

---

12. TRUST DISBURSEMENT RECORDS

The trust disbursement record is a way for the settlement agent to keep track of all funds collected and disbursed before the closing. When the bank issues funds for the closing, they are normally deposited into the settlement agent's trust account, where they will remain until the day of the closing. At that time, the settlement agent will issue a series of checks from that trust account. Some of the funds will pay the real estate agent commissions, while others will pay a profit to the seller. The settlement agent must make a full accounting of the funds and show that none have been retained except for the settlement agent's fee. Closing software will generate these reports in a fraction of the time that it took before. See Figure 13-3 for an example of a record of trust disbursements.

FIGURE 13-3

Record of Trust Disbursements

Client: Juan Garcia
Re: Residence, purchase of
Closing date: April 6, 2021
Disbursement date: April 6, 2021
Amount received: $133,000, April 1, 2021

Disbursement Date	Payee	Amount
April 6, 2021	Bank of Placid	$508.50
April 6, 2021	Bank of Placid Escrow fee and taxes	$1,123.65
April 6, 2021	Placid County Registry	$61
April 6, 2021	Placid County tax collector (2021)	$624.22
April 6, 2021	First Citizens' Savings and Loan mortgage payoff, loan number 12345	$89,004
April 6, 2021	Attorney's fee	$824
April 6, 2021	Title insurance premium	$203.50
April 6, 2021	Cash out to seller	$8,457.20
April 6, 2021	Total disbursed amount	$100,806.07
April 6, 2021	Balance	$0

13. TRUTH-IN-LENDING DOCUMENTATION

TRID The Federal Truth in Lending Act (TILA) was originally created as a way to safeguard consumers from unscrupulous lenders. Like many other aspects of real estate financing, the old TILA rules have undergone a dramatic transformation as a result of the Dodd-Frank Act.

For one thing, the Act creates the Consumer Financial Protection Bureau. That Bureau has created a publication, "TILA-RESPA Integrated Disclosure Rule," which seeks to explain the changes brought about by Dodd-Frank in the area of financing in general and real estate mortgages and closings in particular. We will continue to refer to this stage as a "closing" even though the legislation changes the name to consummation. Closing disclosures begin on page 73 of that publication and a portion of the material is provided in Figure 13-4.

FIGURE 13-4

Page 73, "TILA-RESPA Integrated Disclosure Rule"

- **New three-day waiting period.** If the creditor provides a corrected disclosure, it may also be required to provide the consumer with an additional **three-business-day waiting period** prior to **consummation**. (§ 1026.19(f)(2)). (See section 12 below for a discussion of the redisclosure requirements for the **Closing Disclosure**)

10.2 The rule requires creditors to provide the Closing Disclosure three business days before consummation. Is "consummation" the same thing as closing or settlement? (§ 1026.2(a)(13))

No, **consummation** may commonly occur at the same time as closing or settlement, but it is a legally distinct event. **Consummation** occurs when the consumer becomes contractually obligated to the creditor on the loan, not, for example, when the consumer becomes contractually obligated to a seller on a real estate transaction.

The point in time when a consumer becomes contractually obligated to the creditor on the loan depends on applicable State law. (§ 1026.2(a)(13); Comment 2(a)(13)-1). Creditors and settlement agents should verify the applicable State laws to determine when **consummation** will occur, and make sure delivery of the **Closing Disclosure** occurs at least **three business days** before this event.

In addition to requiring different forms of disclosures to consumers/borrowers, Dodd-Frank also imposes strict limits on when, how and where consumer information can be stored and who has access to it in the creditor's office and the law office. The practical result of this is that many law offices will have to reconfigure both their information storage and the physical layout of their offices to prevent others from viewing sensitive information. The new rules require strict adherence to privacy concerns to the point of limiting which files can be open on a settlement agent's desk at any one time. Obviously, law firms will also have new issues about safeguarding the information provided on forms from potential hackers. After all, the information provided in a typical loan application is more than enough for someone to commit identity theft. Dodd-Frank addresses this in an extensive section about security that is too extensive to go into here.

The closing disclosure makes dramatic modifications to the old HUD-1 form. For one thing, it must contain the actual terms and costs of the transaction, not estimated or temporary numbers. Just as under the old legislation, all disclosures under the new Dodd-Frank bill must be in writing. The provisions governing closings went into effect on August 1, 2015.

The new disclosure forms require more information than has been traditionally made available to consumers. The idea is that more information helps consumers to compare various offers from lenders so that they can make the best choice for their specific needs. In Figure 13-5, we see the first page of the new disclosure form. What information appears on the first page? Among other items, the new documents require any general information about the loan or the lender and then specific information about:

- Loan terms,
- Projected payments, and
- Costs at closing (see Figure 13-5 for an example of the new form)

FIGURE 13-5

Page 75, "TILA-RESPA Integrated Disclosure Rule"

10.6 Page 1: General information, loan terms, projected payments, and costs at closing

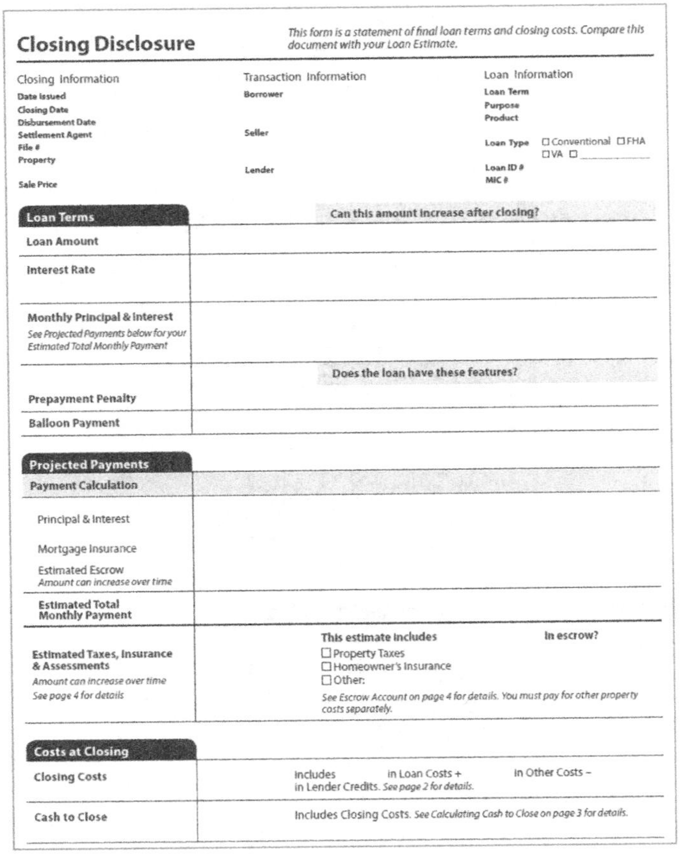

Closing Disclosure

This form is a statement of final loan terms and closing costs. Compare this document with your Loan Estimate.

Closing Information
Date Issued
Closing Date
Disbursement Date
Settlement Agent
File #
Property
Sale Price

Transaction Information
Borrower
Seller
Lender

Loan Information
Loan Term
Purpose
Product
Loan Type ☐ Conventional ☐ FHA ☐ VA ☐ ______
Loan ID #
MIC #

Loan Terms	Can this amount increase after closing?
Loan Amount	
Interest Rate	
Monthly Principal & Interest *See Projected Payments below for your Estimated Total Monthly Payment*	
	Does the loan have these features?
Prepayment Penalty	
Balloon Payment	

Projected Payments	
Payment Calculation	
Principal & Interest	
Mortgage Insurance	
Estimated Escrow *Amount can increase over time*	
Estimated Total Monthly Payment	
Estimated Taxes, Insurance & Assessments *Amount can increase over time* *See page 4 for details*	This estimate includes ☐ Property Taxes ☐ Homeowner's Insurance ☐ Other: — In escrow? *See Escrow Account on page 4 for details. You must pay for other property costs separately.*

Costs at Closing	
Closing Costs	Includes in Loan Costs + in Other Costs – in Lender Credits. *See page 2 for details.*
Cash to Close	Includes Closing Costs. *See Calculating Cash to Close on page 3 for details.*

Later pages in the disclosure form provide most of the information that was already required, but mandates that it be presented in a more user-friendly manner, such as breaking up the old HUD-1 form into much more understandable, bite-size pieces. Figure 13-6, for example, provides the following information specific the actual loan between the borrower and the lender, including:

- Assumption of pre-existing loans,
- Explanation of the demand feature,
- Prepayment penalty,
- Late payments,
- Explanation of negative amortization,
- The effect of partial payments, and
- Adjustable rate tables to explain payments and varying interest rates.

FIGURE 13-6
Page 80, "TILA-RESPA Integrated Disclosure Rule"

10.9 Page 4: Additional information about this loan

Page 4 of the Closing Disclosure form — "Additional Information About This Loan"

In the new disclosure form, lenders must provide:

- Summaries of transactions,
- Alternative for transactions, and
- Breaks down the old payoffs and payments can be substituted for summaries of transactions.

Further into the disclosure forms, lenders are required to provide extensive and precise information about all of the following:

- Total of payments (in a form that resembles the old TILA requirements),
- Finance charge,
- Amount financed,
- Contract details,
- Appraisal,
- Tax deductions,
- Contact information for all parties, and
- A "confirm receipt" provision.

Dodd-Frank provides that these disclosures must be provided to the consumer/borrower at least three business days prior to the closing. All of these forms can be provided in person, through the U.S. mail or through email. The settlement agent is required to provide this documentation to the consumer and the final provision in the disclosures reveals that the consumer has received the information and the date that it was provided.

TRID requires a lender to give specific information about percentage rates for a loan and the total amount that the borrower will repay should he make every payment for the life of the loan.

REAL
ESTATE
BASICS AT
A GLANCE

---

14. TERMITE INSPECTION LETTER

Lenders almost always require a termite inspection before they will finance the purchase of a residence. The termite inspector will issue a report, sometimes in the form of a letter that details exactly what the inspector found (see Figure 13-7 for an example). If any evidence of termite infestation was found, the termite inspector must issue a follow-up report showing that the infestation has been dealt with and no further evidence of termites can be found. Without this report, the lender will not go through with the closing. It is up to the seller to pay for the treatments to get rid of any infestations.

This report is prepared by a state-licensed inspector for the purposes of inspecting a residence for the presence of termites and other wood-boring insects. This inspection is not a warranty or a guarantee that no such insects exist on the premises. Instead, it is based on the inspector's access and due diligence in performing the inspection.

Section 1
Identifying Information

Seller's name: Sally Seller
Buyer's name: Brian Borrower
Property address: 1390 Placid Street, Anywhere, PL 00330
Structures inspected: residence at above location

Section 2
Exceptions and Exclusions

This inspection was limited because of the inaccessibility of certain portions of the residence. Inaccessible regions included: wall, floor, and ceiling.

Section 3
Presence of Termites or Other Wood-Boring Insects

The inspector found evidence of the following: Subterranean termites, Powder post beetles

Section 4
Treatment

The above-described property was treated in the following manner:
<u>Treatment for subterranean termites</u>
<u>Treatment for powder post beetles</u>

Section 5
Damage to Above-Described Property

There is visible damage from powder post beetles; this damage was discovered in the joists and steps leading from the basement.

Disclaimer: I have no interest in this property. My company has no interest in this property.

Signed: <u>Irving Inspector</u>
Placid Termite and Pest Company
Anywhere, PL 00330
1-912-555-1212

15. SURVEY

Surveys are physical measurements of the property and can reveal a host of problems, from inaccurate boundaries and unrecorded easements to encroachments. Most lenders require an accurate survey of the property before disbursing funds for the closing. Many lenders require a new survey every time that a property is resold (or even refinanced). Some lenders will allow the borrower to use a survey that is only a few years old. In other situations, the lender may accept a seller's affidavit in place of a new survey.

A seller's affidavit is a sworn statement that there have been no changes, improvements, or boundary line changes to the property since the date of the last survey. The problem with such affidavits is that the seller may have a good-faith but mistaken view of the facts. Many sellers are also reluctant to sign such affidavits, believing that such a statement might leave them open to civil liability later on.

D. DISBURSING THE FUNDS

The lender deposits the mortgage money into the settlement agent's trust account prior to the closing. The person conducting the closing then writes checks from that account, distributing the funds to the various parties. In this section, we detail some of the disbursements made at a typical real estate closing. In addition to the previous mortgage, the items that are paid at the closing include:

- The lender's fees,
- The attorney's fees,
- The recording fees,
- The seller's profit,
- The real estate agent's commission, and
- The real property taxes.

1. LENDER'S FEES

Among the fees that must be accounted for at the closing are the lender's fees. These include any fees associated with giving the loan, such as "points" (a fee based on a percentage of the total amount financed) and other fees assessed by the lender. In most mortgage situations, the lender requires a monthly payment that includes not only the monthly loan repayment, but also an additional amount that is set aside to pay the annual hazard insurance premiums and tax assessment. Dodd-Frank imposes limitations on the number and scope of the fees that can be charged in any loan processed after August 1, 2015. The lender will set aside these extra funds into what are commonly referred to as "escrow accounts" and then pay the insurance and taxes annually. However, not all lenders set up escrow accounts for their borrowers. Some lenders prefer to have the borrower pay his own insurance premiums and tax assessments as they come due.

Many lenders require the borrower to pay additional money each month for the annual hazard insurance premium and real property taxes.

2. ATTORNEY'S FEES

Other fees paid at the closing include the attorney's fee for handling the closing and carrying out the title search. This fee is usually a percentage of the total loan amount, such as one-half of 1 percent of the total purchase price. The attorney may also simply charge a flat rate for the service.

3. RECORDING FEES

The land or deed office charges a fee to record deeds and mortgages. These fees are added to the amount that the borrower must pay at the closing. Recording fees vary across the nation, from per-page fees of less than a dollar per page recorded to flat fees for recording specific types of documents.

4. SELLER'S PROFIT ON THE TRANSACTION

The seller's profit on the transaction will come in the form of a check drawn on the settlement agent's trust account. This profit is the amount that is left over after paying off the seller's mortgage, the real estate agent's commission, and any other charges assessed against the seller.

5. REAL ESTATE AGENT'S COMMISSION

One of the disbursements that must be made at the closing is the real estate agent's commission. We now know that instead of one check for the full commission amount, the commission is usually paid out in a series of smaller checks, all made out to the different individuals involved in the sale.

6. TAX PAYMENTS

If there are any outstanding real property taxes from prior years, those must be paid prior to the closing. Such payments would be the seller's responsibility. However, a different issue arises when the tax payment is for the current year's assessment. In that case, if the seller has paid the taxes for the entire year, he would be due a partial refund from the buyer. After all, without such a refund, the buyer would be taking advantage of the seller's prepayment. The same issue arises when the taxes have not yet been paid for the year. In that situation, the buyer's payment would reflect an entire year's residence when she only occupied it for part of the year. In both situations, taxes must be prorated.

7. PRORATION

Proration is the process of assessing payments based on the amount paid and the quantity of time that a party resides on the premises.

Proration
The distribution of payments based on a person's liability for the debt.

PRORATION

EXAMPLE 13-3

Placid County requires homeowners to pay their real estate taxes on the first business day of the year. This year, that day was January 3. When a homeowner pays these taxes, he is paying for the entire calendar year.

On January 3 of this year, Mary paid her real estate taxes of $459.12. However, she later put her house on the market and sold it on July 3. Because she paid the entire year's taxes in advance, she wants her tax payment prorated. How much will the new owners have to reimburse Mary for her taxes?

Answer: In order to prorate the taxes, we need some information. First of all, how many days passed from the day that Mary paid her taxes until the closing? If the year is not a leap year, there are 181 days between January 3 (not counting January 3) and July 3 (including the day of the closing). If we can determine a daily rate for the year, we can determine an exact amount for the proration.

$459.12 divided by 365 days in a year yields a daily tax rate of $1.26 (rounding off). Mary lived in the house for 181 days, so her portion of the taxes is: 181 days × $1.26 daily rate = $228.06.

Subtracting this amount from $459.12, Mary is due a refund from the buyers of $231.06. This is the amount that the buyers must transfer to Mary at the closing.

As you can see from this example, the calculations involved in proration can get complicated. To reach the answer in that example, we used the actual days method. However, there are other approaches. In the 30-day month method of proration, for example, the calculations assume that every month has exactly 30 days and the time period is calculated using those figures.

The settlement agent must work with the parties and lenders in order to determine which method of proration is preferred in a particular area. Closing software programs are also adaptable on this point. The user can select from any of a number of proration methods to calculate the final amounts.

Although we have used taxes as an example of a billed item that is prorated during a closing, the process applies to several other types of accounts. For instance, heating oil purchased in advance would be prorated, as would utility payments, city taxes, water, sewage, and trash services, among others.

8. CERTIFIED FUNDS FROM THE BUYER

One of the questions that buyers ask before a closing is how much money they should bring with them to the closing. Buyers are invariably required to bring certified funds to the closing, beyond what has been deposited into the trust account. These additional funds may be required for lender fees, inspections, or any of a number of services for which the buyer is responsible. Certified funds cannot be in the form of the buyer's personal checks. Instead, they must be in the form of a cashier's check, money order, or the like. The buyer may also simply pay the fees in cash, but that may be difficult as the amount in question could be several thousand dollars.

 **OTHER CLOSING ISSUES**

In addition to disbursements and documentation, there are other issues that commonly arise at closings. Among these issues are escrow closings and dual representation.

REAL WORLD PERSPECTIVES: *REAL ESTATE BROKER*

For me, the biggest change has been that the settlement statement used to be part of the overall package. Now, it's a separate document by buyer and seller. It's also known as the CD. There are terms and conditions that control the whole contract moving forward that would be on the other side of the settlement statement that I can't see. That might be that the seller is going to provide a concession for repairs or commission or provide a home warranty or provide any other concessions. The problem is, with the new settlement statement, I can't verify that any of those concessions are accurate. So, how do I do my job? I contact the closing agent and ask them directly, I just want to make sure that, for example the home warranty for six ninety-five fifty is on the seller side and that they are paying X contractor X amount of dollars for a specific repair. The closing agent can confirm that for me. Then, I'll also double-verify, in case someone drops the ball, and asked the other agent. I asked all of my questions in writing. Most of it is done by email.

— D. W., real estate broker

A. "ESCROW" CLOSINGS

Earlier in this chapter we used the word "escrow" to describe a system set up by lenders in which a borrower pays additional fees above the mortgage payment for the annual assessments for home insurance and taxes. However, "escrow" also refers to a type of closing.

Although face-to-face meetings are the preferred method used to close real estate transactions in many states, there is a provision that allows one or both parties to be absent on the actual day of the closing. In an escrow closing, a party signs an "escrow agreement" and completes all the necessary paperwork for the closing prior to the actual event. State law then applies a legal fiction to the agreement: that the signatures were actually completed at the closing, not before it. This legal fiction is a necessary feature of escrow closings and is referred to as the "doctrine of relation back."

1. RELATION BACK

The doctrine of relation back is used in escrow closings to satisfy specific legal requirements. As we have seen in previous chapters, a deed is not effective until it is signed by the seller, delivered by the seller to the buyer, and accepted by the buyer. When one of the parties is unable to attend the closing, this procedure cannot occur. The doctrine of relation back, however, states that when one of the parties signs an escrow agreement and completes paperwork prior to the actual closing, the signatures and actions will not have legal effect until the closing is completed, exactly as if the person were present to deliver or accept the deed in person.

The doctrine also helps settle some difficult questions. Suppose, for example, that the seller signs an escrow agreement and completes all paperwork but is killed before the closing can take place. In most ordinary situations, the seller's death would void the transaction; however, under the doctrine of relation back, the seller's actions are deemed to have occurred at the closing whether or not he was actually alive at that time.

Escrow closings were not created to satisfy this unusual situation, of course. The most common reason for an escrow closing is that one of the parties cannot be physically present at the closing and an escrow closing is the only way for the transaction to be completed. Escrow closings have become so popular in some states, though, that they are the most common type of closing even when the parties could be present at the closing.

When the sellers and buyers place signed documents into escrow, it is usually on the express condition that certain things must occur before the closing can be completed. For the seller, these conditions include presentation of the funds to conclude the transaction. For the buyer, these conditions include receiving a signed and delivered copy of the deed and any other preconditions that were negotiated in the offer to purchase and contract.

AN ESCROW CLOSING

EXAMPLE 13-4

On Tuesday, Daniel, the seller, attends an escrow closing and signs an escrow agreement, the deed, and other paperwork transferring title to Miranda, the buyer. On Wednesday, Daniel suffers a catastrophic stroke and is left in a permanent vegetative state. Miranda appears at the attorney's office on Thursday to sign the paperwork and receive title to the property. Can the transaction be completed?

Answer: Because this is an escrow closing, the fact that Daniel later suffered a stroke does not affect the transaction. The doctrine of relation back protects the transaction, and Miranda can receive title. Would the answer have been different if instead of suffering a stroke, Daniel had been declared mentally incompetent on Wednesday?

2. MODIFICATIONS TO ESCROW CLOSINGS UNDER DODD-FRANK

Dodd-Frank also makes changes to some of the existing procedures used in escrow closings. Under the new legislation, the creditor must tell the borrower the date that the account will be closed, and includes provisions detailing the exact amount that the borrower will pay in property costs, including taxes and insurance as well as an itemized statement about any fee imposed by the lender for servicing the escrow account. See Figure 13-8.

FIGURE 13-8

Escrow Closing Checklist

The creditor or servicer must disclose:
- The date on which the account will be closed,
- That an escrow account may also be called an impound or trust account,
- The reason why the escrow account will be closed,
- That without an escrow account, the consumer must pay all property costs, such as taxes and homeowner's insurance, directly, possibly in one or two large payments a year,
- A table, titled "Cost to you," that contains an itemization of the amount of any fee the creditor or servicer imposes on the consumer in connection with the closure of the consumer's escrow account, labeled "Escrow Closing Fee," and a statement that the fee is for closing the escrow account,

- Under the reference "In the future":

  The consequences if the consumer fails to pay property costs, including the actions that a State or local government may take if property taxes are not paid and the actions the creditor or servicer may take if the consumer does not pay some or all property costs;

- A telephone number that the consumer can use to request additional information about the cancellation of the escrow account;
- Whether the creditor or servicer offers the option of keeping the escrow account open and, as applicable, a telephone number the consumer can use to request that the account be kept open; and
- Whether there is a cut-off date by which the consumer can request that the account be kept open.

B. DUAL REPRESENTATION

In a typical real estate closing, the buyer and seller may request that one attorney represent them both. This can put an attorney in a potential ethical dilemma. After all, the buyer's and seller's interests are, by definition, adverse to one another. In certain situations, the attorney is allowed to represent both parties, but only after full disclosure and agreement from both sides. Dual representation, or dual agency, is also a problem for other professionals, such as real estate agents. In all states, full disclosure is the rule. The settlement agent must disclose to all parties whom the professional represents and who is paying that professional's fee.

VII   AFTER THE CLOSING

After the closing, the deeds and mortgages must be filed at the courthouse. The settlement agent or assisting paralegal will take the original deed and mortgage to the courthouse and make sure that they are properly recorded. The settlement agent often makes additional copies of these recorded documents to give to the buyer and the lender.

When filing the general warranty deed and mortgage, the sequence is important in order to guarantee priority. The deed must be filed first, showing the transfer of rights from the seller to the buyer. Immediately afterward, the mortgage must be filed. It is important that the mortgage be filed immediately to prevent any other creditors from obtaining a superior claim to the lender. The rule in most states is that whoever files first has the highest priority when it comes to foreclosures or judgments. Because the lender has loaned thousands, or even hundreds of thousands, of dollars on the sale, the lender will want to make sure that its mortgage has higher priority than any other claim. Filing it immediately after the general warranty deed is one way of making sure that happens.

See Figure 13-9 for a general checklist of items necessary for completion of a successful closing.

FIGURE 13-9

Closing Checklist

1. Sale contract
   a. Copy of tax record
   b. Are there any taxes outstanding?
2. Create client file
3. Names of parties
   a. Complete legal name of buyer:
   b. Realtor(s) names:
4. Lender
5. Seller's complete legal name:
   a. Seller's address:
6. Title insurance binder (policy number)
7. Mortgage
8. Termite letter
9. Survey
   a. Prepared by: _____
   b. Survey fee:
10. Lien waiver
11. W-9
12. General warranty deed
13. Restrictive covenants
14. Loan package (provided by lender)
15. Loan Disclosure Form
16. Checks
17. Will a courier be required?
18. Title insurance policy mailed to client and lender
19. Certified copies of the general warranty deed and mortgage provided to clients and lender
20. File closed out? Date:_____

One of the most important — and potentially dangerous — issues for law firms and other settlement agents is the protection of non-public information, or NPI. TRID defines NPI to include a wide range of information, not simply Social Security numbers. It also includes bank account information; the client's home address; financial information, including credit history; loan numbers; and any other information that could be used by identity thieves. The problem for settlement agents is that the old HUD Settlement Form and the new Closing Disclosure contain all of that information. As a result, law firms that specialize in real estate must take extra precautions with this data. A single breach under TRID could result in a $5,000 per day fine until the situation is fixed. If the data breach is considered reckless, the fine increases to $25,000 per day, and $1 million per day for knowingly violating the privacy rules.

TRID has an impact on other professionals involved in real estate. Real estate brokers, for instance, must now pay closer attention to the details provided in their multiple listing service (MLS) listings. It was common practice for real estate agents to use previous HUD settlement statements to glean information necessary to post on the MLS. Now, it would be considered a violation to pass these same documents on to real estate agents. Instead, the real estate agents find themselves having to rely more and more on information either in the public record or provided by the buyer or seller. Relying on one of the parties to the transaction for necessary information creates a whole new set of problems, as some people are not as forthcoming or as honest as they could be.

The American Land Title Association (ALTA) has developed a standardized settlement disclosure that works within the existing framework of TRID. It was specifically designed to avoid the release of NPI and so creates a work-around for real estate agents who need to provide as much information as possible in their listings, while also obeying the restrictions imposed by TRID.

Because law firms are required to safeguard their client information more than ever under TRID, some law firms have begun to adopt new guidelines to safeguard all of their information. Consider, for a moment, what information a hacker could learn by gaining access to a large law firm's database. The database contains a wealth of information about clients, including Social Security numbers, home addresses, cell phone numbers, email addresses, dates of birth, names of spouses and children, among many other items. Large firms that handle corporate mergers and acquisitions would have extremely sensitive information about upcoming corporate purchases, mergers, and even Securities and Exchange filings. How does a law firm protect itself from being hacked or even suffering from a drastic loss of data? There are several steps, from the mundane to the hi-tech. See Figure 13-10 for an overview of commonsense protections that all law firms should institute to protect client information.

FIGURE 13-10

Protecting Client Information

- No member of the legal team should open an email from an unknown sender and certainly not an attachment in that email.
- Employee phones should be password protected and safeguarded.
- Every firm, no matter how large or small, should have at least one person designated as the IT professional. This person would be responsible for maintaining the servers and the firewalls and ensuring that all programs are routinely updated for patches that have been discovered.
- The firm should have anti-virus programs running and constantly updated.
- The database should be routinely backed up, either to another computer or to a secure cloud server, and the backup should be encrypted.
- The firm could also use host intrusion software that logs every time the system is accessed and by whom.
- Passwords should be at least 12 characters long and should be changed routinely.
- There should never be a file anywhere in the system that lists the passwords, especially not a file named "passwords."
- Always change the default settings for routers and servers.
- Every computer used by the firm should have encryption software loaded on it.
- The physical server should be under an old-fashioned lock and key, not set up in the office space.
- Employees who are terminated should have all network privileges and access revoked immediately.
- Consider cyber insurance for your network.
- Wireless routers should be password protected.
- Thumb drives should be encrypted.

In 2009, the FBI issued a special advisory announcing that hackers have begun targeting law firms, often using a technique called "spear phishing" where the hacker sends an innocuously named email that may slip through the spam email filter and end up appearing in an employee's inbox, where it would be one click away from installing malware on the network's system. As an example, the FBI reported that a large law firm in New York was targeted by hackers allegedly from China.[1]

Case Excerpt

JOHNSON v. ALEXANDER
413 S.C. 196, 775 S.E.2d 697 (2015)

ON WRIT OF CERTIORARI TO THE COURT OF APPEALS

Justice HEARN: In this attorney malpractice case, Amber Johnson alleges her closing attorney, Stanley Alexander, breached his duty of care by failing to discover the house Johnson purchased had been sold at a tax sale the previous year. The trial court granted partial summary judgment in favor of Johnson as to Alexander's liability. On appeal, the court of appeals held Alexander could not be held liable as a matter of law simply because the attorney he hired to perform the title work may have been negligent. Instead, the court determined the relevant inquiry was "whether Alexander acted with reasonable care in relying on another attorney's title search"; accordingly, it reversed and remanded. *Johnson v. Alexander*, 408 S.C. 58, 64, 757 S.E.2d 553, 556 (Ct. App. 2014). We disagree and find the trial court properly granted summary judgment as to liability. We therefore remand to the trial court for a hearing on damages.

Factual/Procedural Background

Alexander acted as Johnson's closing attorney when she purchased a home in North Charleston on September 14, 2006. The title examination for the home had been performed by attorney Charles Feeley at the request of Johnson's previous attorney, Mario Inglese. Alexander purchased the title work from Inglese and relied on this title exam in concluding there were no back taxes owed on the property. Thereafter, Johnson learned the house had been sold at a tax sale and she did not have title to the property. In fact, the property had been sold October 3, 2005, almost a year prior to Johnson's purchase. Because of the title issue, the mortgage payments on the home ceased and the property eventually went to foreclosure.

Johnson brought this cause of action for malpractice, breach of fiduciary duty, and breach of contract against Alexander and Inglese. Specifically, Johnson alleged the attorneys owed her a duty to perform a complete title exam on the property to ensure she received good and clear title.

Johnson moved for partial summary judgment as to Alexander's liability. At the hearing, Johnson submitted the affidavit of Mary Scarborough, the Delinquent Tax Collector for Charleston County. She attested that she "had direct and personal knowledge that information regarding delinquent taxes for real properties located in

Charleston County, South Carolina, was readily and publicly available in July, August and September of 2006" in the Office of the Register Mesné Conveyance for Charleston County via a mainframe database. Furthermore, she stated that the Delinquent Tax data for Charleston County real properties has been publicly available on a mainframe database since 1997, when she helped design the system currently in use.

Alexander presented an affidavit from Feeley stating that although he could not remember the specific details of this title exam, he conducted all his examinations the same. Feeley further detailed his process at length, explaining his reliance on the Charleston County Online Tax Systems and his practice of searching back ten years of tax payments. He indicated his notes showed he found no back taxes due or owing. Feeley also attested that a prior tax sale would not have been disclosed in the chain of title for this property or made publicly available in the RMC office at the time of the title examination and closing in 2006 because the tax sale deed was not recorded until December 12, 2006.

The circuit court granted Johnson's motion as to Alexander's liability. The court relied heavily on Alexander's pleadings and admissions in his deposition that as a closing attorney he had a responsibility to ensure marketable title. Additionally, the court found Alexander had proximately caused Johnson's damages, but left the determination of the amount for a later hearing.

On appeal, the court of appeals reversed and remanded, holding the circuit court incorrectly focused "its inquiry on whether an attorney conducting a title search on this property should have discovered the delinquent taxes from 2003 and 2004 and the tax sale from 2005." *Johnson*, 408 S.C. at 62, 757 S.E.2d at 555. Instead, the court of appeals held the proper question was "whether Alexander acted reasonably under the existing circumstances in relying on the title search performed by Feeley." *Id.* at 63, 757 S.E.2d at 555. Finding there was a genuine issue of material fact as to whether Alexander acted reasonably, the court of appeals reversed the grant of summary judgment and remanded for trial. *Id.* at 64, 757 S.E.2d at 556. This Court granted certiorari to review the opinion of the court of appeals.

Issue Presented

Did the court of appeals err in reversing the circuit court's grant of summary judgment and remanding the case for trial?

Law/Analysis

Johnson argues the court of appeals erred in reversing the circuit court's grant of summary judgment because it misapprehended the proper standard of care. Specifically, Johnson argues the court of appeals erred in holding the requisite inquiry is whether an attorney reasonably relied on another attorney's work where that work is outsourced. Johnson contends that an attorney should be liable for negligence arising from tasks he chose to delegate unless he has expressly limited the scope of his representation. We agree.

In a claim for legal malpractice, the plaintiff must prove: (1) the existence of an attorney-client relationship; (2) a breach of duty by the attorney; (3) damage to the client; and (4) proximate cause of the client's damages by the breach. *Harris Teeter, Inc. v. Moore & Van Allen, PLLC*, 390 S.C. 275, 282, 701 S.E.2d 742, 745 (2010). An attorney is required to render services with the degree of skill, care, knowledge, and judgment usually possessed and exercised by members of the profession. *Holy Loch Distribs., Inc. v. Hitchcock*, 340 S.C. 20, 26, 531 S.E.2d 282, 285 (2000).

In determining the scope of Alexander's duty, we accept his consistent characterization of this responsibility—ensuring Johnson received good title. In her complaint, Johnson alleged "defendants had professional duties to ensure that Plaintiff was receiving good and clear title to the subject property free of any encumbrances, liens, or clouds on title before conducting the closing and if there was a problem after the closing, to correct said deficiencies and/or advise Plaintiff how to correct said deficiencies." In Alexander's answer he admitted those allegations. Parties are generally bound by their pleadings and are precluded from advancing arguments or submitting evidence contrary to those assertions. *Elrod v. All*, 243 S.C. 425, 436, 134 S.E.2d 410, 416 (1964) ("The general rule is that the parties to an action are judicially concluded and bound by such unless withdrawn, altered or stricken by amendment or otherwise. The allegations, statements or admissions contained in a pleading are conclusive as against the pleader. It follows that a party cannot subsequently take a position contradictory of, or inconsistent with, his pleadings and the facts which are admitted by the pleadings are to be taken as true against the pleader for the purpose of the action. Evidence contradicting such pleadings is inadmissible."). Additionally, during Alexander's deposition, he plainly conceded he owed a duty to Johnson to have clear title:

Q. Alright. And you were hired, or you were her attorney for this closing? Right?
A. Correct.
Q. And you had responsibility to make sure that she got good and marketable title? Correct?
A. Correct.
Q. And that's one of the responsibilities of a lawyer handling the closing, representing the purchaser? Right?
A. Correct.

Alexander cannot now assert his duty was anything other than what he has admitted—that he ensure good and clear title.

However, even absent Alexander's admissions, we find the court of appeals erroneously equated delegation of a task with delegation of liability. Certainly, Feeley's negligence is the issue here, but that does not displace Alexander's ultimate responsibility. While an attorney may delegate certain tasks to other attorneys or staff, it does not follow that the attorney's professional decision to do so can change his liability to his client absent that client's clear, counseled consent. See Rule 1.8(h), RPC, RULE 407, SCACR ("A lawyer shall not . . . make an agreement prospectively limiting the lawyer's liability to a client for malpractice unless the client is independently represented in making the agreement."). Thus, Alexander owed Johnson a duty and absent her agreement otherwise, he was liable for that responsibility regardless of how he chose to have it carried out.

We therefore agree with Johnson that an attorney is liable for negligence in tasks he delegates absent some express limitation of his representation. Stated another way, without an express limitation in representation, attorneys cannot delegate liability for tasks that are undertaken in carrying out the duty owed the client. A holding to the contrary would effectively allow an attorney to independently limit the scope of his representation through the manner in which he performs his duties instead of being bound by what the client understands his responsibilities to be.

Applying this standard to the facts, we find the grant of summary judgment was proper because there is no genuine issue of material fact as to liability. The circuit court relied on Scarborough's affidavit in concluding Johnson "proved to the Court what the public records reflected at the time of closing—taxes for the Property were delinquent for the tax years 2003 and 2004 and the Property had been sold on October 5, 2005 at a tax sale." Although Alexander submitted an affidavit by Feeley stating he would have discovered the information if it was public, we agree with the circuit court's ultimate conclusion that there was no issue of fact. Feeley admitted he did not remember the specifics of that transaction and provided no documentation supporting his assertion that he performed a ten year search and found no notice of the sale.

Furthermore, we find the circuit court properly held there was no genuine issue of material fact as to proximate cause. Because of Alexander's failure to discover the tax sale, Johnson did not receive marketable title—or any title—to the property she purchased. She was therefore unable to sell or rent the property. Alexander's arguments that the property foreclosure was due to Johnson's own negligence in failing to pay the mortgage will certainly be considered during the hearing on damages; however, that allegation does not alter the fact that Johnson's purchase of the property that had already been sold was a direct result of his failure to ensure she received good title.

Conclusion

Based on the foregoing, we reverse the opinion of the court of appeals and hold an attorney is liable for negligence in tasks he chooses to delegate absent an express limitation of his representation. Finding Alexander breached his duty and damages resulted, we reinstate the grant of partial summary judgment as to Alexander's liability and remand for a determination of damages.

TOAL, C.J., PLEICONES, KITTREDGE, JJ., and Acting Justice JAMES E. MOORE, concur.

QUESTIONS ABOUT THE CASE

1   What was the allegation of attorney malpractice in this case?
2   What was the finding of the trial court?
3   According to the court, what are the elements of legal malpractice?
4   Did Alexander ever dispute that he owed a duty to his clients to ensure that the title to the property was free and clear?
5   The court makes a distinction between delegation of a task and a delegation of duty. What does this mean?

COVID-19 CONCERN

As some of the excerpts from the real estate paralegal in this chapter show, it is becoming more common for the buyer and seller to not attend the closing at the same time — some even find this advisable. The COVID-19 pandemic has increased that trend. As some attorneys have gone to conducting closings in parking lots, shuffling from one car to another to get documents signed, it has become more than likely that a new infrastructure will need to be developed to streamline and "virtualize" closings. With e-notarization and Zoom conferences becoming the norm, going to the lawyer's office to conduct a closing may become the unusual procedure.

CHAPTER SUMMARY

A real estate closing is the final process in a real estate transaction that began when a homeowner decided to put his house up for sale. The closing is important for a number of reasons, not only because this is where the deed that transfers ownership to property is exchanged, but also because of the monetary disbursements that are made during the closing. Closings are handled in different ways around the country. In some states, for example, real estate attorneys and paralegals conduct closings. In other parts of the country, closings are conducted by title insurance companies, lenders, and others. No matter who conducts the closing, there are some basic features that all closings share. For example, mortgage documents will be signed at the closing. Truth-in-lending and other federal legislative initiatives must also be satisfied during the closing. Taxes must be paid. Real estate agents' commissions will be disbursed and several other important documents will also be exchanged during the course of the settlement process. It is important for any real estate professional to understand the legal significance of a real estate closing. In addition to legal concerns, there are also several ethical concerns that are often raised during the closing process. For instance, when a nonlawyer conducts a closing, this person is barred from giving legal advice about the impact of particular documents. In states that follow an attorney model for closings, ethical issues arise about the use of paralegals to conduct the closing. In some states, the practice is permissible, while in other states, it is not.

SKILLS YOU NEED IN THE REAL WORLD

Preparing Disclosure Forms

Preparing settlement forms can be one of the most challenging aspects of a closing, especially under the new Dodd-Frank rules. If you are the person who is responsible for tracking all the details and preparing the settlement statement, you should give consideration to acquiring one of the excellent software packages currently available. Not only will the software help you expedite a closing, but many title insurance companies and lenders have begun refusing to deal with settlement agents who do not use software. They have had too many bad experiences with settlement statements prepared by hand, and they may require you to certify which type of closing software you use before they will permit you to act as a settlement agent. The skill that you need here is the ability to weed through the many different programs now available to come up with the one that meets your clients' needs, offers you solid performance, and will keep you out of trouble. Talk with other legal professionals in your area. What program do they use? What are the program's advantages and disadvantages? (There are always disadvantages.) What kind of learning curve is involved in mastering the program? How user-friendly is it? What type of support does the company offer? Is the program subject to bugs or other actions that will cause it to freeze up? Does the company offer a license program that allows you to use the program on a network? These are all questions you should consider before acquiring any closing software package.

ETHICAL ISSUES FOR THE PARALEGAL

Delegating the Closing to the Paralegal

One of the most hotly contested issues in modern real estate practice concerns the use of paralegals to conduct real estate closings. As we have seen in this chapter, many states limit real estate closings to licensed attorneys. In those states, is it an ethical violation to allow the paralegal to conduct the entire real estate closing in the absence of the attorney? In some states, the answer is yes, while in other states, the answer is no. Unfortunately, there is no clear consensus. The safest practice is to locate ethics decisions from your state bar on this question to make sure that you stay on the right side of the ethical rules.

KEY TERMS AND CONCEPTS

Closing	Private mortgage	Proration
Consummation	insurance (PMI)	Settlement agent
Loan package	Promissory note	

END-OF-CHAPTER EXERCISES

Review Questions

See Appendix for answers.

1 List and explain the basic steps involved in conducting a closing.
2 Why is it difficult to schedule a closing?
3 Why is a contract clause that "time is of the essence" a particular challenge for settlement agents?
4 What are some of the important documents that are completed during a real estate closing?
5 What is a survey, and why is it important to the closing?
6 What are "loan payoff amounts," and why are they important?
7 Why is it important to know the tax payment status on a parcel of real estate prior to the closing?
8 What is the significance of the termite inspection report?
9 List some of the tax forms that may be required as part of the closing.
10 How has the USA PATRIOT Act affected real estate closings?
11 Explain records of trust disbursements. Describe private mortgage insurance (PMI).
12 What is a seller's affidavit, and how does it relate to surveys?
13 List the people who are typically present at the closing. What do these people normally do at the closing?
14 List and explain the documents that are usually required at the closing.
15 "Escrow" is used in two different contexts in this chapter. Explain both.
16 What are the ethical concerns surrounding dual representation at a closing?
17 What are some of the ethical concerns about allowing paralegals to conduct real estate closings?
18 Explain the impact that the Dodd-Frank Act has had on closings.
19 What are the some of the concerns in choosing a closing software package?

DISCUSSION QUESTIONS

1 Have the provisions of Dodd-Frank and the requirements of TRID gone too far? Some commentators have suggested that in attempting to protect consumers, regulations have made the business of closing on real estate too expensive and demanding for smaller firms. What do you think?

2 Based on what you have learned in this chapter, what is the most important quality of someone considering a career in real estate closings? Justify your answer.

APPLYING WHAT YOU HAVE LEARNED

Given the fact that so many states have different approaches to the use of lawyers and nonlawyers to conduct closings, is there an argument that you can make supporting the exclusive use of attorneys (and paralegals) at real estate closings?

WEB SURFING

Federal Deposit Insurance Corporation
www.fdic.gov

Federal Reserve
www.federalreserve.gov

Department of Housing and Urban Development
www.hud.gov

Consumer Financial Protection Bureau
http://www.consumerfinance.gov

Tech Topic
SETTLEMENT STATEMENTS UNDER DODD-FRANK

You can find a complete set of the new Dodd-Frank settlement procedures as a downloadable PDF file under the Consumer Financial Protection Bureau site.

ANNOTATED DOCUMENT

Settlement Statement

10.5 Page 1: General information, loan terms, projected payments, and costs at closing

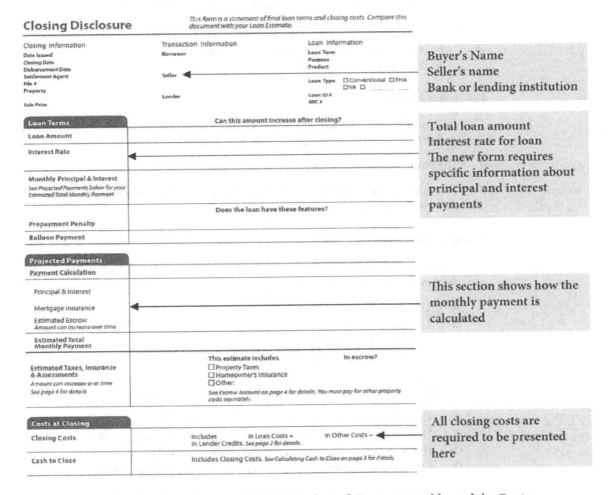

General information, the **Loan Terms** table, the **Projected Payments** table, and the **Costs at Closing** table are disclosed on the first page of the **Closing Disclosure**. (§ 1026.38(a), (b), (c), and (d))

PRACTICE QUESTIONS FOR TEST REVIEW

See Appendix for answers.

Essay Question

What is a closing?

True–False

1   **T   F**   Delegating duties to paralegals at closings raises few ethical concerns.

2   **T   F**   Real estate agents are normally present at closings.

3   **T   F**   Closing attorneys are not permitted to verify the borrower's Social Security Number.

Fill in the blank

1   In this style of pro-ration, the parties count the actual number of days involved and then calculate a daily rate based on that amount of time: _____.

2   The name for the real estate agent's payment: _____.

3   This is a fee that a lender charges that is based on a percentage of the total amount financed: _____.

Multiple Choice

1   When filing documents after a closing, the sequence is important. Which document is usually filed first?

   A   The mortgage.
   B   The deed.
   C   The financing statement.
   D   The attorney's affidavit.

2   Which of the following should appear on an Escrow Closing Checklist?

   A   The date on which the account will be closed.
   B   That an escrow account may also be called an impound or trust account.
   C   The reason why the escrow account will be closed.
   D   All of the above should appear on an Escrow Closing Checklist.

3   Under this doctrine, when one of the party's signs an escrow agreement and
completes paperwork prior to the actual closing, the signatures and actions will
not have legal effect until the closing is completed, exactly as if the person were
present.

    A   Doctrine of promissory estoppel.

    B   Doctrine of just cause.

    C   Doctrine of relation back.

    D   Doctrine of questionable practices.

ENDNOTE

[1] http://www.nbcnews.com/id/33991440/ns/technology_and_science-security/t/fbi-hackers-targeting-law-pr-firms/#.WoiJTUxFzIU (downloaded February 17, 2018).

Taxation Issues in Real Property

Chapter Objectives

- Explain the basis of a government's power to levy taxes
- Describe the types of properties that can be taxed
- Define the properties that are normally exempt from taxation
- Explain how tax regulations are enforced
- Describe the procedure involved in a tax auction

Chapter Outline

I. Introduction

II. Governmental Powers of Taxation
   A. What Can Be Taxed?
   B. Tax Exemptions

III. How Taxes are Assessed
   A. Determining the Property Values

B. Calculating the Tax Rate

IV. Paying Taxes
   A. Enforcing Tax Regulations
   B. Tax Liens

V. Assessments

INTRODUCTION

In this chapter we examine the important issue of real property taxation. Real estate remains an important source of tax revenue for state and local governments and may be one of the few sources of revenue for some governments. We explore not only a government's right to impose taxes, but also how tax rates are determined, the duty of tax assessors, and how tax regulations are enforced, including the use of tax auctions.

The topic of taxes has come up in several contexts throughout this book. In the chapter on title examinations, we mentioned that the status of real property taxes is one of the most important parts of a real estate title search. Taxes are important in many other contexts as well. However, before we can examine the complexities of government tax schemes, we must first address a more fundamental question: Where does the government get the power to assess taxes?

GOVERNMENTAL POWERS OF TAXATION

The power to levy a tax against citizens is set out in the U.S. Constitution, as well as in all state constitutions. State statutes authorize cities to impose taxes on real and personal property located within their geographic limits. Taxes can be assessed to pay for a wide variety of services and also to pay government salaries, service government debt, make up for government deficits, and meet law enforcement costs, among other uses.

A. WHAT CAN BE TAXED?

State constitutions authorize state and local governments to assess taxes against both real and personal property. This means that in addition to land, governments can tax a wide variety of other items. We restrict our discussion of taxes to the assessment of real property taxes, but keep in mind that there are many other types of taxes imposed against individuals. Essentially, the government has the power to tax anything that is not specifically exempt. See Figures 14-1 and 14-2 for examples of state laws regarding taxation.

FIGURE 14-1 Levy of Taxes (Nevada)	The boards of county commissioners shall have power and jurisdiction in their respective counties to levy, for the purposes prescribed by law, such amount of taxes on the assessed value of real and personal property in the county as may be authorized by law.[1]

FIGURE 14-2 Property Subject to Taxation (New York)	All real property within the state shall be subject to real property taxation, special ad valorem levies and special assessments unless exempt therefrom by law. Notwithstanding any provision of this chapter or of any other general, special or local law to the contrary, personal property, whether tangible or intangible, shall not be liable to ad valorem taxation.[2]

B. TAX EXEMPTIONS

State statutes provide **exemptions** for many types of properties. When a property is exempt, it means that the property owners are not required to pay real property taxes. There are many different types of exemptions, including:

Exemption
When an owner is not obligated to pay a specific tax.

- The homestead exemption,
- The charitable exemption,
- The nonprofit exemption, and
- The governmental exemption.

1. HOMESTEAD EXEMPTION

Many states allow permanent residents to qualify for a homestead exemption under the tax code. This means that a taxpayer can exempt up to a maximum percentage of the home's appraised value. Some states allow a homeowner to choose the larger of a maximum percentage and a total amount. To qualify for a homestead exemption, many states impose additional requirements, for example, that the taxpayer be at least 65 years of age and meet other income eligibility criteria.

2. CHARITABLE EXEMPTION

In all states, qualifying charitable and religious organizations receive tax-exempt status. The method to qualify as a charity or religious organization varies according to both state and federal law, but if an organization qualifies, it is not required to pay any real property taxes.

3. NONPROFIT EXEMPTION

Many states allow not only charitable and religious organizations but also nonprofit organizations to be exempt from the tax code. Under these rules, a qualifying nonprofit organization would be exempt from any real property tax assessments (see Figure 14-3).

FIGURE 14-3

Nonprofit Organizations (New York)

(a) Real property owned by a corporation or association organized or conducted exclusively for religious, charitable, hospital, educational, or moral or mental improvement of men, women or children purposes, or for two or more such purposes, and used exclusively for carrying out thereupon one or more of such purposes either by the owning corporation or association or by another such corporation or association as hereinafter provided shall be exempt from taxation as provided in this section.
(b) Real property such as specified in paragraph (a) of this subdivision shall not be exempt if any officer, member or employee of the owning corporation or association shall receive or may be lawfully entitled to receive any pecuniary profit from the operations thereof, except reasonable compensation for services in effecting one or more of such

FIGURE 14-3

(continued)

purposes, or as proper beneficiaries of its strictly charitable purposes; or if the organization thereof for any such avowed purposes be a guise or pretense for directly or indirectly making any other pecuniary profit for such corporation or association or for any of its members or employees; or if it be not in good faith organized or conducted exclusively for one or more of such purposes.[3]

4. GOVERNMENT EXEMPTION

In addition to exempting charity, religious, and nonprofit organizations, local governments also exempt government-owned property from taxation. In addition to government property, some tax codes also create specially protected areas, such as enterprise zones, that may receive favorable tax treatment.

Many local governments recognize that in order to improve living conditions and raise personal incomes (and to improve the tax base), it is important to attract businesses to economically depressed areas. One way of doing that is to create special zones wherein businesses receive favorable tax treatment. An enterprise zone is a common example. When a local government designates an enterprise zone, it sets off a specific geographic area and advertises the fact that businesses relocating to that area will have a lower tax bill. This usually results in a gradual buildup of the enterprise zone. Ultimately, offering a tax incentive proves to be a wise investment. By encouraging new businesses, the government is actually improving its tax base: More businesses mean more people and ultimately better tax revenues. See Figure 14-4 for an example of enterprise zone legislation.

FIGURE 14-4

Property Subject to Taxation (Ohio)

All real property in this state is subject to taxation, except only such as is expressly exempted therefrom.[4]

HOW TAXES ARE ASSESSED

Governments generally assess taxes based on an ad valorem tax scheme; that is, the government assesses a tax based on an item's value. Taxing by value is an ancient concept and relatively easy to impose. **Ad valorem taxes** can be applied to personal property, such as imported goods or automobiles. They can also be assessed against real property. The issue in any ad valorem tax scheme is the value of the property. In most cases, the government bases the tax on the fair market value of the property. The person responsible for determining fair market value of real property is the tax assessor.

Ad valorem taxes
Taxes assessed according to the value of the property.

REAL
ESTATE
BASICS AT
A GLANCE

Ad valorem taxes are based on the item's value.

A. DETERMINING THE PROPERTY VALUE

Before a property can be assessed for taxes, the local government must determine its value. The tax assessor's office is responsible for assigning a value to all eligible property in the jurisdiction. Tax assessment takes into account many different factors, including zoning, access, crop value, acreage, and any existing buildings and structures.

A tax assessment determines the value of all property in the jurisdiction as of a particular day. That day might be January 1 of the calendar year, or another date selected by the government. Assessors have strict rules that must be complied with in determining the value of property (see Figure 14-5). For instance, an assessor may be required to determine the fair market value of property based on a formula created by the state legislature.

An assessor, from the maps and descriptions furnished him by the county auditor and other sources of information, shall make a correct and pertinent description of each tract and lot of real property in his district. When he deems it necessary to obtain an accurate description of any separate tract or lot in his district, he may require the owner or occupier thereof to furnish such description, with any title papers he has in his possession. If such owner or occupier, upon demand, neglects or refuses to so furnish a satisfactory description of such parcel of real property, the assessor may employ a competent surveyor to make a description of the boundaries and location thereof, and a statement of the quantity of land therein. The expense of such survey shall be returned by such assessor to the county auditor, who shall add it to the tax assessed upon such real property, and it shall be collected by the county treasurer with such tax, and when collected, shall be paid, on demand, to the person to whom it is due.[5]

FIGURE 14-5

Duties of Assessor (Ohio)

Tax assessment takes into account several factors to calculate the value of a parcel of real estate.

REAL ESTATE BASICS AT A GLANCE

---

1. CHALLENGING AN ASSESSMENT

Taxpayers often complain about the taxes that they must pay. However, a taxpayer is allowed to challenge a tax assessment when she can show that the value reached was arbitrary or capricious. Only if the taxpayer can show that the assessor deviated from standard practices or carried out some other unauthorized activity will the taxpayer be successful in reducing the tax assessment on a particular property. Most taxpayers who challenge their assessments lose their suits.

Taxpayers can challenge a tax assessment, but only if they can show that the value reached was arbitrary.

REAL ESTATE BASICS AT A GLANCE

---

2. REASSESSMENT

Tax assessors could go through the lengthy process of assessing property every year in order to determine accurate values for that year's budget. However, the burden of reassessing every year might easily cost more money than it would generate in new taxes. Instead, many governments authorize their tax offices to reassess every few years, with some requiring no more than eight years between each reassessment.

B. CALCULATING THE TAX RATE

Millage rate
A tax rate that equates to a certain number of dollars per thousand dollars in value.

Assessment is only the first step in determining the tax bill for a particular parcel. The property value must be calculated against the local tax rate, sometimes known as the **millage rate**. When a local government creates its annual tax rates, it begins with the assessed value of all real property located within its geographic limits. Then it estimates the amount of money it will need to carry out all governmental activity for the year. Dividing one value into the other determines the tax rate. See Figure 14-6 for an example of legislation governing the setting of the tax rate.

EXAMPLE 14-1

Cost-a-lot County has assessed all of its qualifying real property and has determined that the total value is $250 million. The county has also calculated that in order to carry out all of its services and pay all of its employees, it will need $10 million. Using these numbers, the county divides $10 million by $250 million to determine its tax rate. In this case, that rate would be $.04, or $40 for every $1,000 in value. That would be a high, but not unheard of, tax rate. For a house valued at $100,000, the annual tax bill would be $4,000. Some states have passed legislation to prevent real estate tax bills from going beyond a specific millage rate. What would the tax amount be for a house worth $250,000 at a $20/$1,000 millage rate?

Answer: To calculate the tax amount for a $250,000 house at a $20/$1,000 millage rate, we would multiply $20 by 250, giving a tax amount of $5,000.

FIGURE 14-6

Duty of County Commissioners and School Board in Setting Rate of Taxation (Florida)

(1) The county commissioners shall determine the amount to be raised for all county purposes, except for county school purposes, and shall enter upon their minutes the rates to be levied for each fund respectively, together with the rates certified to be levied by the board of county commissioners for use of the county, special taxing district, board, agency, or other taxing unit within the county for which the board of county commissioners is required by law to levy taxes.[6]

REAL WORLD PERSPECTIVES: *REAL ESTATE BROKER*

These days, all the information about a property is available online, but that doesn't mean that it is accurate. The Tax Office is certainly accurate, at least as far as the tax value of the house. The Tax Office also gives a value of the property for tax purposes, but keep in mind, that's for taxes, not for sale. It's not fair market value, but it's often pretty close. Then, you have Zillow. You go there and get your Zestimate, which is either way too high or way too low. It can be largely inflated or underreported.

— D. W., real estate broker

PAYING TAXES

Each state handles paying taxes differently. Some states make taxes due in the fall, while others require them to be paid at the first of the year. Regardless of when the deadline is, the taxes must be paid by that time or the taxpayer faces sanctions, including interest charges, tax liens, and tax auctions. See Figure 14-7 for sample legislation regarding tax due dates.

All taxes shall be due and payable on November 1 of each year or as soon thereafter as the certified tax roll is received by the tax collector. Taxes shall become delinquent on April 1 following the year in which they are assessed or immediately after 60 days have expired from the mailing of the original tax notice, whichever is later. If the delinquency date for ad valorem taxes is later than April 1 of the year following the year in which taxes are assessed, all dates or time periods specified in this chapter relative to the collection of, or administrative procedures regarding, delinquent taxes shall be extended a like number of days.[7]

FIGURE 14-7

When Taxes Due; Delinquent (Florida)

A. ENFORCING TAX REGULATIONS

State statutes give governments the power to enforce their tax regulations through a wide assortment of remedies, including levies, garnishment, and attachments. Governments are also authorized to issue liens on property and to enforce those liens with tax auctions of the property.

B. TAX LIENS

A tax lien operates like any other lien: It prevents the sale of the property until the tax has been satisfied. But tax liens have important differences from other types of liens.

First, a tax lien remains on the property and is transferred when title is transferred. This means that a tax that was not paid by a previous owner can be assessed against a current owner. Tax liens also have the advantage of higher priority.

1. SETTING PRIORITIES IN TAX LIENS

Tax liens have special priority status under the law. Regardless of when a tax lien is filed, it automatically takes priority over other claims and must be paid in full before other judgments or liens. This gives the local taxing authority a powerful tool in collecting taxes. In addition to imposing a tax lien, the government can also foreclose on a tax lien.

2. FORECLOSING A TAX LIEN

When a tax lien has been outstanding for a specific period of time and remains unpaid, the local government is authorized to begin proceedings to foreclose the tax lien. The property will literally be auctioned off for back taxes (Figure 14-8). The auction is authorized like any other foreclosure auction, but these auctions have the added appeal that a successful bidder may acquire property for only a fraction of its true value. It is common for property valued at hundreds of thousands of dollars to be auctioned for back taxes in the amount of a few thousand dollars.

However, before anyone decides to bid at a tax auction, there are some complexities to consider. For instance, the successful bidder at a tax auction does not receive a general warranty deed to the property. The successful bidder doesn't even receive title in fee simple absolute. Instead, the bidder receives a deed that is referred to under a variety of names, such as "commissioner's deed" in some states and "sheriff's deed" in other states. The important point about these deeds is that they do not, by themselves, give the successful bidder absolute rights to the property. There is even a question about whether the deed authorizes the eviction of the current residents. Why, then, would anyone bid at a tax auction? The simple answer is that a tax auction deed could qualify as "colorable claim of title" for adverse possession purposes. Under that rule, a person can acquire title to property by open, notorious, hostile, and adverse possession of another's property under colorable claim of title. A tax auction deed could be exactly what a person needs in order to trigger the provisions of adverse possession. In some states, a tax auction deed can ripen into fee simple absolute after the passage of time and a court action by the successful bidder.

FIGURE 14-8	
Sale at Public Auction (Florida)	(1) The lands advertised for sale to the highest bidder as a result of an application filed under §197.502 shall be sold at public auction by the clerk of the circuit court, or his or her deputy, of the county where the lands are located on the date, at the time, and at the location as set forth in the published notice, which shall be during the regular hours the clerk's office is open. At the time and place, the clerk shall read the notice of sale and shall offer the lands described in the notice for sale to the highest bidder for cash at public outcry. The amount required to redeem the tax certificate, plus the amounts paid by the holder to the clerk of the circuit court in charges for costs of

sale, redemption of other tax certificates on the same lands, and all other costs to the applicant for tax deed, plus interest thereon at the rate of 1.5 percent per month for the period running from the month after the date of application for the deed through the month of sale and costs incurred for the service of notice provided for in §197.522(2), shall be considered the bid of the certificateholder for the property. However, if the land to be sold is assessed on the latest tax roll as homestead property, the bid of the certificateholder shall be increased to include an amount equal to one-half of the assessed value of the homestead property as required by §197.502. If there are no higher bids, the land shall be struck off and sold to the certificateholder, who shall forthwith pay to the clerk the documentary stamp tax and recording fees due, and a tax deed shall thereupon be issued and recorded by the clerk.[8]

Tech Topic
REAL ESTATE AND TAXATION

For the typical homeowner, property taxes are relatively straightforward. Each year, property taxes are calculated and assessed on the basis of current city, county, and state rates. Aside from the odd special assessment or incremental increase, residential property taxes remain fairly consistent from year to year.

Taxation on commercial property is vastly different, however. In an attempt to lure businesses to establish a presence, many states and localities offer tax incentives, particularly for employing advanced technology. For example, in Mississippi, a property tax exemption is available for telecommunications businesses when they purchase equipment for deploying broadband technology in the state. In Prince George's County, Maryland, any business primarily involved with the application of computer sciences can be eligible to receive a property tax credit.

Whether on the city, county, or state level, the value of technology is recognized and encouraged. The world of real estate is right in the thick of the technological revolution, a trend that will likely continue.

ASSESSMENTS

While taxes are applied to all qualifying real property within the county, an **assessment** is an individual charge placed against a particular parcel. The most common example of a special assessment arises when the local government installs a feature that benefits only a particular area. Constructing a playground, installing a sidewalk, and erecting streetlights are all examples of specific improvements that would justify an assessment. In such a case, all parcels that benefit from this improvement — and only those specific parcels that benefit — will often be assessed with a fee.

Assessment
The evaluation or estimation of the value of real property.

Case Excerpt

MILLER & RHOADS BUILDING, L.L.C. v. CITY OF RICHMOND
790 S.E.2d 484 (2016)

Opinion By Justice Cleo E. Powell

Miller & Rhoads Building, L.L.C. ("MRB") appeals the decision of the trial court ruling that the City of Richmond's (the "City") Tax Abatement for Rehabilitated Real Estate Program (the "Partial Exemption"), Richmond City Code §§ 98–149 to –159, does not apply to special district taxes.

I. Background

On March 17, 2006, MRB acquired the vacant Miller & Rhoads Building (the "building"). The building is located in a special service and assessment district of the City. Thus, in addition to being subject to the city-wide real estate tax, see Richmond City Code § 98–121, the building is also subject to an annual special district tax, see Richmond City Code § 98–842. Both taxes are calculated as a percentage of the property's "assessed evaluation." Richmond City Code §§ 98–121, –842.

MRB planned to rehabilitate the building and develop the property to include a hotel, residential condominiums, retail space and parking. MRB sought to recoup some of the costs of rehabilitation by seeking a partial exemption from real estate taxes for the property under the Partial Exemption. Although the City determined that MRB's planned rehabilitation of the building satisfied the basic requirements to qualify for the Partial Exemption, it only applied the Partial Exemption to the base real estate tax; the City refused to apply the partial exemption to the special district tax.

MRB paid the special district taxes under protest and brought an action to correct what it claimed were erroneous assessments. According to MRB, the City failed to properly calculate and apply the Partial Exemption. In its prayer for relief, MRB sought a refund of "any amounts of real property tax erroneously charged and paid that are attributable to the erroneous final value."

Prior to trial, the parties stipulated that "the only issue in disagreement is whether the Partial Exemption set forth in Richmond City Code §§ 98–149, 98–152 and 98–155 also applies to the City's computation of the special district tax as set forth in Richmond City Code §§ 98–816 and 98–842." After hearing argument on the matter, the trial court determined that the Partial Exemption did not apply to the special district tax. In a letter decision dated June 12, 2015, the trial court explained that, "according to the statutory origin for the imposition of the Special District Tax, its beginning method of calculation and its purposes, and use, the Special District Tax is not a real estate tax within the meaning and for the use of the Partial Exemption." On August 12, 2015, the trial court issued a final order that incorporated its letter opinion.

MRB appeals.

II. Analysis

On appeal, MRB argues that the trial court erred in ruling that the special district tax "is not a real estate tax within the meaning and for the use of" the Partial Exemption. In response, the City concedes that the special district tax is, in fact, a real estate tax, but claims that the special district tax is a different type of real estate tax that is not subject to the Partial Exemption. We agree with the City.

This Court has repeatedly admonished that, where, as here, a statute is clear and unambiguous, "the question . . . is not what the legislature intended to enact, but what is the meaning of that which it did enact. We must determine the legislative intent by what the statute says and not by what we think it should have said." *Carter v. Nelms*, 204 Va. 338, 346, 131 S.E.2d 401, 406–07 (1963). Thus, the paramount principle of statutory interpretation is "to interpret the statute as written." *City of Lynchburg v. Suttenfield*, 177 Va. 212, 221, 13 S.E.2d 323, 326 (1941).

In the present case, however, the trial court based its decision, not on the plain language of the Richmond City Code, but instead on "the statutory origin," the "beginning method of calculation," the "purposes" and the use of the special district tax. While consideration of these factors may be necessary in certain circumstances, such as when a literal reading of the statute would lead to absurd results, it has no place in the present case. Accordingly, the trial court erred in its analysis.

However, "appellate courts do 'not review lower courts' opinions, but their judgments." *Evans v. Commonwealth*, 290 Va. 277, 288 n.12, 776 S.E.2d 760, 766 n. 12 (2015). "In instances where a trial court's decision is correct, but its reasoning is incorrect, and the record supports the correct reason, we uphold the judgment pursuant to the right result for the wrong reason doctrine." *Haynes v. Haggert*, 291 Va. 301, 305, 784 S.E.2d 293, 294 (2016).

Under the right result for the wrong reason doctrine, "it is the settled rule that however erroneous . . . may be the reasons of the court for its judgment upon the face of the judgment itself, if the judgment be right, it will not be disturbed on account of the reasons." *Perry v. Commonwealth*, 280 Va. 572, 579, 701 S.E.2d 431, 435 (2010)

In the present case, both parties and the trial court focused primarily on the Partial Exemption and the special district tax, without giving proper consideration to the overarching statutory scheme. This Court has long recognized that "statutes are not to be considered as isolated fragments of law, but as a whole, or as parts of a great connected, homogeneous system, or a single and complete statutory arrangement." *Prillaman v. Commonwealth*, 199 Va. 401, 405, 100 S.E.2d 4, 7 (1957). Thus, in addition to those sections of the Richmond City Code that expressly enact the special district taxes and the Partial Exemption, it is also necessary to consider those sections that provide the overall framework for the levy and collection of special district taxes. In the present case, that framework is provided by Richmond City Code § 98–816.2.

Richmond City Code § 98–816 states:

> All assessments levied under Article XIV shall be added to the general real estate levy for the property and shall be subject to the following sections of Chapter 98 governing the levy and collection of real estate taxes and the penalties applicable thereto: sections 98–123, 98–124, 98–127 and 98–129.

It is of particular note that, in establishing the framework for levying and collecting special district taxes, the Richmond City Council cites only four specific sections of Article III of the Richmond City Code to which the special district taxes under Article XIV are "subject to." "In interpreting statutory language, we have consistently applied the time-honored principle *expressio unius est exclusio alterius*," because this maxim "recognizes the competence of the legislature to choose its words with care." *Virginia Department of*

Health v. NRV Real Estate, LLC, 278 Va. 181, 187–88, 677 S.E.2d 276, 279 (2009). Under this maxim, "when a legislative enactment limits the manner in which something may be done, the enactment also evinces the intent that it shall not be done another way." *Grigg v. Commonwealth*, 224 Va. 356, 364, 297 S.E.2d 799, 803 (1982). Stated another way, "the mention of specific items in a statute implies that all items omitted were not intended to be included." *NRV Real Estate*, 278 Va. at 188, 677 S.E.2d at 279.

While this maxim is not applicable in every situation, this Court has recognized that "no maxim of the law is of more general or uniform application, and it is never more applicable than in the construction and interpretation of statutes." *Whitehead v. Cape Henry Syndicate*, 105 Va. 463, 471, 54 S.E. 306, 308 (1906).

Applying this maxim to the present case demonstrates that, by enacting Richmond City Code § 98–816, the Richmond City Council intended for the special district taxes levied under Article XIV to only be "subject to" four specifically mentioned sections under Article III, Chapter 98 of the Richmond City Code. Similarly, by omitting the remaining sections of Article III, Chapter 98 of the Richmond City Code, the Richmond City Council has clearly indicated that it did not intend for special district taxes levied under Article XIV to be "subject to" those omitted sections. Conspicuously, the sections providing for the Partial Exemption are included in the omitted sections.

Accordingly, because the special district tax is not subject to the Partial Exemption, the trial court was correct, albeit for the wrong reason, in ruling that the special district tax "is not a real estate tax within the meaning and for the use of the Partial Exemption."

III. Conclusion

For the foregoing reasons, we affirm the decision of the trial court.

Affirmed.

QUESTIONS ABOUT THE CASE

1   The building at the center of this suit was assessed with two different taxes. What were they?
2   According to the plaintiff, what error did the city commit?
3   What is the main issue in this case?
4   What does the court say about interpreting statutes, such as the one at the center of this case?

COVID-19 CONCERN

In the era of the Internet, it may seem astounding that some processes still unfold just as they did hundreds of years ago. Tax auctions are one such event. Instead of opening up bids on the Internet, which only a few counties have attempted, most tax auctions today would appear very familiar to anyone who had participated in one at the beginning of the twentieth century. Someone calls the gathered people together, announces the property for auction and the tax amount owed, and then opens the auction up for bids. The bidder must be physically present — today, as always, the Internet is not used. There is no web conference, no Zoom link.

In the past two years, many counties simply cancelled or postponed their tax auctions, rather than consider upgrading the systems they use to conduct them. Some states have very strict statutes about how, when, and where an auction can take place, but surely it is time to avoid

bringing a large group of people together to loudly — and in close proximity — bid on property? A county gains no advantage by limiting tax auctions to local residents, and, in fact, some states deny counties the ability to limit bidding to local citizens only. The tax office simply wants its money. Why not create a simpler, safer, more productive method to bid? This is one of those areas where the conservative nature of real estate reveals itself.

The global pandemic is bringing about many changes. Perhaps it will even change how tax auctions are conducted.

CHAPTER SUMMARY

Governments are given the power to impose taxes by both federal and state constitutions. Most states base their real property taxes on an ad valorem system that taxes according to the value of the real estate. Tax assessors determine the value of all eligible properties in the jurisdiction, and then the government assesses a tax based on that rate multiplied by the millage rate. Some properties are exempt from taxation. These include religious organizations, nonprofit organizations, and government properties. Governments have the right to enforce their tax regulations by imposing tax liens on property and by eventually auctioning off property at tax auctions.

Assessments are similar to taxes except that they are placed against particular parcels that receive the benefit of nearby improvements.

SKILLS YOU NEED IN THE REAL WORLD

Researching Tax Issues

At some time or another all legal professionals who specialize in real property law will come into contact with tax issues. A client may wish to challenge an appraisal, or you may have to deal with the tax office on a particular issue. Keep in mind that tax issues in real estate are a world of their own. Case law on tax assessments and challenges involves terminology that may not be familiar from other real property issues. Taxes also involve issues on both federal and state levels. As a result, you must be able to research these issues on many different levels, from local tax ordinances to capital gains taxes on the federal level. Find a good reference on the issue of real estate taxes and hang on to it. You can annotate your copy as the tax rules change, and it will serve as a good backup whenever you are asked to research a particular complex tax issue.

ETHICAL ISSUES FOR THE PARALEGAL

Tax Dodges

Every few years, there are anti-tax movements. In recent decades, there have been groups that have claimed that the government does not have the power to assess taxes, or that specific provisions of the U.S. Constitution concerning income or property taxes were never properly enacted. As a legal professional, you may come into contact with individuals who have "foolproof" methods to avoid paying taxes. Always be cautious about any such scheme and remember the old saying that in life there are only two certainties: death and taxes. Anyone who claims to be able to avoid either one is probably selling something that is at best a fantasy and, at worst, a criminal enterprise.

KEY TERMS AND CONCEPTS

Ad valorem taxes	Exemption	Millage rate
Assessment		

END-OF-CHAPTER EXERCISES

Review Questions

See Appendix for answers.

1   What are ad valorem taxes?
2   How do governments enforce their tax rules and regulations?
3   Describe three types of property that are exempt from taxes.
4   What is a homestead exemption?
5   What are "enterprise zones"?
6   What is the difference between a property tax assessment and an appraisal?
7   What grounds can a taxpayer use to challenge a tax assessment?
8   What is the millage or tax rate?
9   What are some of the factors that tax assessors use to establish the value of property?
10   What is the difference between an assessment and a tax bill?
11   Why would a county only reassess its properties every few years?
12   What are the rules about lien priority when it comes to tax liens?
13   When are governments authorized to auction off property for back taxes?
14   What are some of the ethical concerns with "tax dodges"?
15   Why is it important to know how to research tax issues?
16   Why would someone challenge a tax bill?
17   What are the rules concerning when tax bills are due to be paid?
18   What is the procedure followed in a tax auction?
19   Explain the relationship between purchasing at a tax auction and adverse possession.

DISCUSSION QUESTION

Should there be a simpler way of collecting taxes? If you could make changes to the tax system, how would you structure it?

APPLYING WHAT YOU HAVE LEARNED

1   Every few years there are new proposals to revamp or completely change the tax codes. One such proposal is to eliminate real property taxes entirely and charge a flat tax of 10 percent on all purchases. Part of these taxes would go to the federal, state, and local governments. Can you fashion an argument for and against such a proposal?

2   Contact your local tax office and find out how they determine their tax rate. What is the tax rate? What types of properties are exempt in your area? What would the real property taxes be for a nonexempt property that is valued at $100,000? When would these taxes be due?

WEB SURFING

Real Property (Ad Valorem) Tax
http://public.findlaw.com/taxes/more-tax-topics/property-tax.html

Florida Millage Rates
www.pbcgov.org/papa/tax-roll.htm

Tech Topic
PROPERTY TAX COMPARISON AND CALCULATOR

The Tax Foundation offers a property tax comparison tool (http://interactive.taxfoundation.org/propertytax) that allows you to compare property tax rates in counties across the country.

Basic Mathematics offers a property tax calculator (http://www.basic-mathematics.com/property-tax-calculator.html) that allows you to calculate the property taxes for a given real estate parcel.

ANNOTATED DOCUMENT

County Tax Record

ENTIAL   123 MAPLE STREET   BARNES COUNTY, PLACID LRK 02972?   REVALUATION DATE OF: JANUARY 1, 2003   PAGE 1

ID   MAP# 044N -01-001-A -0 Card 1 Of 1   Neighborhood ID: 108.00   Zoning:RES   Class:R   Pin Number: 3639-12-97-0129.0000

ASSESSMENT INFORMATION:
Current Values:

Land Use Value	60,900	
Building	168,800	
Total	229,700	

Date   Type   Price   Source   Validity
1500   19850601 LAND + BLDG   117,000 BUYER   OO
PL   OO
28658-3643

Deed Book:1405
Deed Page:0333
Deed Date:19860101

Appraiser: JPT   229,700

Lister:JPT 20020125

PROPERTY FACTORS:
Topo: Util: St/Rd:
ROLLING ALL PUBLIC   PAVED

PERMIT RECORD: Purpose
Amount

LAND DATA AND COMPUTATION: 0   Land Use Code: 011   Township # 9

Type	Map Frtg Size	Rate	Influence Factors	Value
HOME SITE	X 1.000	21,000		16,590
FRONTAGE	X 2.000	21,000	VAL/LOC ADJ. -21	33,180
RESIDUAL	X 1.450	6,900	VAL/LOC ADJ. -21	11,110
			VAL/LOC ADJ. -11	
		SHAPE/SIZE		

Calc Acres: 4.450

Total Land Value   60,900
Use Value:

ADDITION DATA:

	LL	1st FL	2nd FL	3rd FL	Area	Value
A	LL					
B	OfP				396	11000
	1sMs				320	19100
C	EfP				80	3400
D	Cport				644	6400
E	1sMs	1sFr			300	29400
F	FrUt				60	700
G	Cnpy				144	1500

This presentation of information is considered a Restricted Appraisal Report used to appraise Fee Simple Interest of Real Property. The estimated Market Value is to be used for tax purposes only. This appraisal as required by General Statute 105-283 has been completed using Catabua County's 2003 Schedule of Values. Highest and Best Use for this property is RES. Market Value as defined by General Statute 105-283 has been determined by considering all three approaches to value: cost, market, and income. Additional information considered by the appraiser is in the work file of the appraiser. The COST VALUE approach has been used for this property.

DWELLING COMPUTATIONS

Base Price:	150,400
Attic:	11,850
Plumbing Adjustment:	7,840
Heat/Cent A/c Adj:	-5,290
Basement Adjustment:	-5,690
Exterior Trim:	
Finish Basement Living Area:	
Bsmt Recreation Area:	
Unfinished Area:	8,820
Well/Septic:	
Fireplaces:	71,500
Additions:	250,010
SUBTOTAL	
Grade Factor (X)	1.35
C & D Factor (X)	1.00
Replacement Cost New:	337,510
Percent Good:	0.50
Market Adjustment:	
RCNLD	168,800

LING DATA:
TWO STORY
2.00
PART FINISH
PART
4
9
3
Is: 1/40
1993
BRICK
1144
3-94

ng Area:
in Area:
openings:
acks: 2 / 2
CENTRAL A/C
HEAT PUMP
ELECTRIC
B+
Utility: AV
:   AVERAGE   48.31

OUTBUILDING DATA:

Size	Area	Grd Cond	MA	Mod Code	RCN	%d	%dd	Value
X								
X								
X								
X								
X								
X								

OBY MISC VALUE
15   Total Oby Value

PRACTICE QUESTIONS FOR TEST REVIEW

See Appendix for answers.

Essay

How are tax rates established?

True–False

1 T F Enterprise zones are unconstitutional.

2 T F Ad valorem taxes are assessed based on usage.

3 T F The U.S. and state constitutions authorize the collection of taxes.

Fill in the Blank

1 When a property falls into this category, property owners are not required to pay taxes: _____.

2 There are times when a local government wants to attract businesses to the area by creating tax incentives to attract businesses to specific areas. These areas are called: _____.

3 The term used by the tax office to determine a property's value: _____.

Multiple Choice

1 Tax based on an item's value.

    A Ad valorem taxes
    B subsequent taxes
    C Capital gains taxes
    D Personal taxes

2 In most cases, the government bases its tax on what type of valuation?

    A Resale value
    B Fair market value
    C Subjective value
    D None of the above

3 The person responsible for determining fair market value for tax purposes.

    A Clerk
    B Tax assessor
    C valuation officer
    D Judge

ENDNOTES

[1] Nev. Rev. Stat. § 244.150.
[2] N.Y. Real Prop. Tax Law (McKinney) § 300.
[3] N.Y. Real Prop. Tax Law (McKinney) § 420-a.
[4] Ohio Rev. Code Ann. § 5709.61(A).
[5] Ohio Rev. Code Ann. § 5713.02.
[6] Fla. Stat. Ann. (West's) § 200.011.
[7] Fla. Stat. Ann. (West's) § 197.333.
[8] Fla. Stat. Ann. (West's) § 197.542.

Appendix

Answers to Review Questions and Practice Questions for Test Review

CHAPTER 1. INTRODUCTION TO REAL PROPERTY

Review Questions and Answers

1 What is the definition of real property?

"Real property" refers to land and anything permanently attached to land.

2 What is the Statute of Frauds?

A statute that requires certain types of transactions, such as those involving the transfer of real property interest to be in writing before they will be enforceable.

3 What are some of the primary differences between real and personal property?

Real property consists of land and anything permanently attached to land; it is immobile and has a fixed point on the globe. Personal property is mobile and is not permanently attached to real estate.

4 What are some of the aspects of real property law that make it unique?

Land is fixed and immobile, unlike personal property which is, by its very nature, mobile and impermanent.

5 List and explain some of the physical characteristics of land.

Real property has several distinctive characteristics that separate it from personal property. For instance, land occupies a specific point on the globe.

Unlike personal property, land is fixed and immovable. It always remains where it is and cannot be relocated.

6   Describe the economic characteristics of real property.

Land generally appreciates in value over time and offers tax benefits to home-owners.

7   What makes real estate such an attractive investment?

Land usually appreciates in value and homeowners can often borrow against their equity.

8   Explain equity.

Equity is the difference between what a homeowner owes on his or her property and what the land is worth.

9   What is the real estate market?

The real estate market refers to the diverse buyers and sellers who acquire and dispose of property.

10   What is unimproved land?

Unimproved land refers to land that has no structures located on it.

11   List and explain the various classifications of real property.

Land can be classified as residential, commercial, industrial, rural, farmland, or government-owned land.

12   What are the elements that make a residence qualify as an apartment?

A residence qualifies as an apartment when it has five or more living units.

13   What is the difference between a condominium and a townhouse?

A condominium owner has rights to the interior of his or her unit, but not the exterior. A townhouse owner, on the other hand, has rights to both the interior and the exterior of the structure.

14   When does a mobile home or manufactured home qualify as real property?

Mobile homes or manufactured homes qualify as real property when they are permanently affixed to land.

15   What is the difference between residential and commercial property?

Residential property is designed for human habitation, while commercial property is designed for business transactions.

16   How much land does the government own?

Various federal and state governments own approximately one-third of all land located in the continental United States.

17   Why are ethical rules important for real estate practitioners?

Ethical rules are important to ensure fair and equitable procedures and to protect the rights of clients.

18   Explain how cloud computing impacts legal services.

Cloud-based computing allows lawyers and other legal professionals the ability to handle cases in a wide variety of settings by permitting them to access necessary information on a case on laptops and other devices.

PRACTICE QUESTIONS FOR TEST REVIEW

Essay Question

List and explain the various classifications of real property.

Real property can be classified as residential, commercial, industrial, rural, farmland or government-owned land. These classifications are important because they bring with them different terms, rights and means of conveying to others. Residential property is designed for living. Commercial categories were created as a way of designating various types of business establishments. The "industrial" classification is important not only because it designates either light or heavy manufacturing facilities but also because this classification can have an impact on zoning and other health regulations. Rural property consists of unimproved land, while farmland is designated for farms, ranches, and other real estate devoted to producing crops, timber, livestock, or some other product. Government-owned land consists of nearly one-third of the continental United States and encompasses military bases, government reserves, parks, federal and state government sites, among many others.

True–False

1   False
2   True
3   False

Fill in the Blank

1   Improved
2   Real property
3   Personal property

Multiple Choice

1 C

2 A

3 B

CHAPTER 2. ESTATES IN REAL PROPERTY

Review Questions and Answers

1 What is a real property estate?

An estate refers to the bundle of rights that the owner possesses.

2 What is the difference between a present estate and a future estate?

A present estate vests the owner with certain rights, while a future estate only provides ownership interests later or after specific conditions have occurred.

3 What are the rights that an owner in fee simple absolute enjoys?

An owner in fee simple enjoys the right to sell, giveaway, mortgage, and otherwise encumbered property for his or her own advantage.

4 What limitations are placed on the rights of a fee simple absolute owner?

An owner in fee simple absolute is not permitted to use his property in any way that he sees fit. The owner is limited by the rights of adjoining landowners as well as applicable laws.

5 What is a fee simple determinable estate and how does it compare to a fee simple absolute estate?

A fee simple determinable estate is one that provides a condition on the use of the property. This condition can be triggered at some future date and can transfer property ownership away from the owner. Fee simple absolute, on the other hand, places no such conditions on ownership.

6 What is a fee simple on a condition subsequent estate and how does it compare to a fee simple determinable and a fee simple absolute estate?

Fee simple on a condition subsequent estate is an arrangement where a person's ownership rights are condition on the use of the property for a specific reason. However, fee simple determinable estates will vest title automatically in a remainderman, while fee simple on a condition subsequent estates will only vest title after court action.

7   Why has the simple determinable estates fallen into disuse?

Fee simple determinable estates have fallen into disuse because there are better and more efficient methods for controlling the way that property is used.

8   Draft a deed provision that contains a fee simple determinable clause.

Student responses will vary, but should contain provisions applying conditions to the use of the premises, such as limitations in the way that property can be used.

9   What is a life estate?

A life estate is a temporary estate given to an individual for his or her life and then transferring the entire estate to another.

10   What limitations does a life tenant have in his or her ability to use the property subject to a life estate?

Life tenants are free to use the property in ways that approach those of fee simple absolute owners, except that they may not commit waste or transfer interests they do not possess.

11   Provide an example of a clause that would create a life estate.

To Mary, for her life, and then to my children.

12   What is a remainderman?

A remainderman is someone who has a future interest in property but no present interest.

13   What are *dower* and *curtesy*?

These are two traditional protections for spouses that allow them to take a portion of a deceased spouse's estate for their own use. They have been revoked in most states.

14   What is the historical basis for the creation of life estates?

Traditionally, life estates were created as a means to provide a home and security for a family member.

15   What is waste as that term applies to life estates?

Waste refers to the destruction of the property or the diminution in value by the actions of the life tenant.

16   What is a life estate *pur autre vie*?

This is a life estate measured by the life of another.

17   Compare and contrast tenancies in common with joint tenancies.

Tenancies in common give the tenants joined access and ownership to property but have no right of survivorship. Joint tenancies on the other hand, give tenants joint access to the property, but do have the right of survivorship.

18   What is the right of survivorship?

The right of survivorship is the right of the surviving tenant to take full title to the property, excluding the deceased tenant's heirs.

19   What is a tenancy by entirety?

A tenancy by entirety is a concurrent ownership estate reserved for married couples only.

20   What is a tenancy in partnership?

Tenancy in partnership is a legally recognized concurrent ownership reserved for business partners.

21   What is partition?

Partition is the physical separation of property by ownership percentage or the sale of property and the split of profits from the sale by ownership percentage.

PRACTICE QUESTIONS FOR TEST REVIEW

Essay Question

What are the rights and obligations that come with fee simple ownership?

An owner in fee simple enjoys the right to sell, give away, mortgage, and otherwise encumber property for his or her own advantage. Unlike other types of ownership, when someone owns real property, the rights conveyed are often depicted as a bundle. The owner can, and often does, transfer some of his or her rights to others for financial gain. The most common example is transferring the right to use and possess the property to a tenant in exchange for rent.

True–False

1   True
2   False
3   False

Fill in the Blank

1   Statutory share
2   Life estate *pur autre vie*
3   Partition

Multiple Choice

1 B
2 A
3 A

CHAPTER 3. PROPERTY DESCRIPTIONS AND DETERMINING PROPERTY BOUNDARIES

Review Questions and Answers

1 Why is it important to have an accurate property description for a real estate transaction?

An accurate property description is important in order to identify the real estate parcel that is the subject of the transaction and to alleviate any confusion that might arise in the real estate transaction.

2 Explain the difference between identifying real property and identifying personal property in a sale.

Identification of real property in the transaction is very different from identifying personal property. Real property must be described in such a way as to locate it on the surface of the earth, while personal property described with serial numbers or other identifying marks.

3 Describe the history of surveying real estate property boundaries.

Describing real estate property boundaries is thousands of years old. In ancient Egypt, surveyors were forced to describe real estate parcels to locate them again after the annual funds.

4 What are the two critical elements of any property description?

The two critical elements of any real property description include the distance and direction that the property boundary lines take. A valid property description must also describe the property in such a way as to making unique and identifiable.

5 Why is street address not sufficient to describe a parcel of real estate?

Street address is not sufficient to describe a parcel of real estate for the simple fact that there may be more than one street located in the area with identical name.

6 Explain the legal requirements for property descriptions in a deed.

Property descriptions must adequately describe the property and show how a parcel is unique when compared to all others.

7   What types of documents can a legal description referred to in creating a valid legal description?

Property descriptions can refer to other documents, including deeds, plats, surveys, and other publicly recorded documents.

8   What are patently ambiguous property descriptions?

A patently ambiguous property description is one that contains an obvious error or fails to adequately describe the property in such a way that parties can identify it.

9   What are latently ambiguous property descriptions?

A latently ambiguous property description is one in which the ambiguity is not obvious and only comes to light after a thorough review of the property description.

10   What is the parol evidence rule, and how does it apply to patently ambiguous and latently ambiguous property descriptions?

This is an evidentiary rule that prohibits oral testimony to modify a written property description.

11   What is a metes and bounds description?

This is a property description that gives distance and direction for all property boundary lines for a parcel of real estate.

12   How long is a "rod"? How long is a "chain"?

A rod is 16.5 feet. A chain is 66 feet.

13   What equipment do you need to draw a metes and bounds description?

To draw such a description, you need a circular land measure compass and a pencil.

14   What is a tract indexing system?

This is a property description method that relies on assigning a number to tracts of land located within a jurisdiction.

15   What is a plat?

A plat is a drawing based on a physical description of the property.

16   What is the Torrens registration system?

The Torrens registration system was originally created in Australia and later exported to other English-speaking countries. It is a method to register lands in a modified tract indexing system.

17 What are riparian rights?

These are the rights to water that come with ownership in a parcel of real estate.

18 Describe the natural forces that can affect property boundaries.

Natural forces, such as erosion, accretion, and other forces can gradually alter the boundaries of a parcel of real estate.

19 Compare and contrast accretion with erosion.

Accretion is the gradual deposit soil along a property boundary that expands overall size of the parcel. Erosion, on the other hand, is the gradual process of wearing away soil that slowly decreases the size of the parcel.

20 Explain the significance of this chapter's case excerpt.

Answers will vary. The court found that when someone attempts to foreclose on property, they must follow the correct procedures or it will be ruled a nullity.

PRACTICE QUESTIONS FOR TEST REVIEW

Essay Question

List and describe the natural forces that affect property boundaries.

Natural forces, such as erosion, accretion and other forces can gradually alter the boundaries of a parcel of real estate. When these processes occur as part of a natural continuation, then the property owners must accept the changes. However, when they occur as part of an unnatural process, such as damming a river or industrial processes or other man-made problems, the owners can bring suit against the wrongdoers to have the original boundaries restored or to be compensated for the loss.

True–False

1 False
2 True
3 False

Fill in the Blank

1 Patently ambiguous description
2 Parol evidence rule
3 Metes and bounds

Multiple Choice

1 D
2 C
3 B

CHAPTER 4. TRANSFERRING TITLE TO REAL ESTATE

Review Questions and Answers

1   What are some examples of voluntary transfer of real estate title?

Voluntary transfers include sale, gives, and transfer through probate.

2   Why is the question of the origin of title so important?

The question about the origin of title is important because of a rule in real property law that provides that a person can only receive the extent of title that the previous owner possessed. A new owner's rights do not improve after the sale; therefore, the original source of title helps determine the new owner's rights.

3   What are the minimum requirements of the legal sale?

The minimum requirements of a sale include an offer and an acceptance and legal capacity.

4   What basic elements must a will have before it is considered to be legally valid?

A will must be in writing, signed by the testator, witnessed, and show clearly that the testator had the intent to dispose of his or her property after death.

5   What are the differences between a will and a sale?

A will is a unilateral decision by an individual contemplating his or her own death and wishing to disburse property according to the person's wishes. A sale, on the other hand, is a bilateral agreement between two parties who engage in a transaction where one side gives up something of value in exchange for receiving something else of value. In a typical real estate transaction, the seller gives up title to his or her property in exchange for money, while the buyer gives up money in exchange for receiving title.

6   What is dedication as that term applies to real estate?

When land is dedicated, it means that the owner has given the land over to the government for a specific use.

7   How can a person acquire title to real estate through homesteading?

Some states allow persons to acquire title to real estate parcels by establishing homes on unclaimed land and maintaining possession for a fixed period. After that time, the state will award title to the possessors.

8   When and under what circumstances does foreclosure occur?

Foreclosure occurs when a borrower defaults on mortgage payments and the lender applies a clause in the mortgage that allows it to institute legal proceedings to have the property sold at auction.

9   Explain the basic steps involved in a foreclosure proceeding.

Once a borrower defaults, the lender sends the borrower notice of its intention to seek foreclosure, then posts a notice of the foreclosure in the legal classified section of the local newspaper. This notice advertises the sale of the home for the outstanding balance.

10   What is the right of redemption as that term applies to foreclosures?

The right of redemption is the borrower's right to pay the total amount of the outstanding indebtedness prior to the foreclosure auction and regain possession and title to his or her home.

11   What is eminent domain?

Eminent domain is the power of the government to seize real property for governmental purposes.

12   What is condemnation and how does it apply to eminent domain?

Condemnation is the action that governments use to exercise their power of eminent domain.

13   Explain partition.

Partition is the physical separation of a parcel based on the percentage of ownership that co-owners have in a parcel. It also refers to the act of selling the property and disbursing the profits along the percentage of ownership.

14   Describe escheat.

Escheat is the process of reverting property rights to the government when a person dies without a will and leaves no heirs who can receive the property. In that case, the local government will take title to the land.

15   How may a person lose title to property through the enforcement of a civil judgment?

A person can lose title to property when he or she loses a civil case and the court imposes a monetary judgment against the person's land to satisfy the amount of the monetary award.

16   What is adverse possession? List and explain the basic elements of adverse possession.

Adverse possession is the acquisition of title to property by a person with colorable claim of title who holds the property against the interests of the original owner, openly, notoriously, adversely, and for a specified period of time. After that period, the new owner can bring suit to have fee simple absolute title awarded to him or her.

17   What is color of title as that term applies to adverse possession?

Color of title is a phrase that describes the requirement that a person claiming through adverse possession have some legal claim to the property before the statutory provisions of adverse possession will be triggered.

18   What effect does a tax auction have on the original property owner's rights?

A tax auction can be used as the basis for a claim of adverse possession and may strip the original owner of title after a period of time.

19   Why is it important to be able to locate probate records?

Probate records are important for a wide range of real estate transactions and the ability to locate them will help legal professionals explain how property changed hands, and will also help explain provisions of a title examination.

20   Explain the information that can be found in a notice of foreclosure.

A notice of foreclosure will contain information identifying the borrower and lender, the amount of the loan, the terms, and the amount that the borrower owes, as well as the fact that the borrower defaulted and the type of foreclosure sale that the lender will conduct.

PRACTICE QUESTIONS FOR TEST REVIEW

Essay Question

What are the basic requirements of a will?

A will must be in writing, signed by the testator, witnessed, and show clearly that the testator had the intent to dispose of his or her property after death.

True–False

1   True
2   False
3   False

Fill in the Blank

1   Statute of Frauds
2   Publication
3   Dedication

Multiple Choice

1   B
2   D
3   A

CHAPTER 5. RIGHTS ASSOCIATED WITH REAL ESTATE

Review Questions and Answers

1 What is a fixture?

A fixture is an item of personal property that has become permanently attached to real property and has thus had its characterization changed to real property as well.

2 What are some of the tests that courts have used to determine when something qualifies as a fixture?

Courts have come up with several tests to determine when an item qualifies as a fixture, including: intent, manner of attachment, use and damage to remove it.

3 What is the difference between a fixture and a trade fixture?

A fixture is any personal property permanently attached to real property, while a trade fixture is an item of personal property that is necessary for a business, but is attached to real property. Trade fixtures may be removed by tenants.

4 What is an easement?

An easement is a person's right to use another person's property for a limited purpose, such as a driveway that provides access from a public road, across another person's property.

5 What are the two different types of easements?

The two different types of easements are appurtenant easements and easements in gross.

6 List and explain the way that easements can be created.

Easements can be created by dedication, agreement, implication, prescription, and eminent domain.

7 List and explain the way that easements can be terminated.

Easements can be terminated by merger, by circumstances that no longer require the easement, by agreement of the parties, and by abandonment.

8 What are assessments?

Assessments are bills for improvements installed by the local government that benefit a small class of homeowners or property owners.

9 How are licenses and easements different?

Licenses give a person the right to enter on the premises for a specific purpose, such as hunting, while easements give a person the right to use a portion of another person's property for access, without regard to the manner of use.

10   Explain "profits" from the land.

Profits refer to crops, timber, and any other substance grown, harvested, or mined on the land that can be sold.

11   Compare and contrast profits, licenses, and easements.

Profits refer to the right of a homeowner to harvest, mine, or gather items that have grown or developed on the property. Licenses give non-owners the right to enter onto another's property for a limited purpose. Easements give non-owners the right to use another's property for a specific purpose, such as access.

12   What is the difference between a materialmen's lien and a mechanic's lien?

A materialmen's lien is a lien filed by a person or company that has provided supplies to a homeowner; a mechanic's lien is a lien filed by someone who has provided a service to a homeowner.

13   What are air rights?

Air rights are the broad category of rights that owners have above the surface of their properties.

14   How would a real property owner's air rights in the Middle Ages compare to those same rights today?

In the Middle Ages, an owner's air rights were considered to extend into the sky; nowadays, an owner's rights are more limited, with the owner only having the right to use the surface above his or her property to a reasonable distance.

15   How did the development of air travel affect property owners' air rights?

Air travel had a direct impact on air rights by limiting the extent of an owner's individual rights. Because of air travel, owners were limited to reasonable distances above their properties and were prevented from filing trespass actions against planes that technically crossed over a person's property boundaries, but at such a high altitude that it caused no damage.

16   Why are water rights important?

In some areas, water is very scarce and access to it defines if property has any value. Right to draw water for home use is therefore critical and when property has no water rights of any kind, it is essentially worthless.

17   What rights does an owner of real property have to subterranean water?

Owners have the right to reasonable use to subterranean waters, to draw on them for personal use.

18   What are "percolating waters"?

Percolating waters are those waters that begin as surface waters and then percolate through the soil until they become subterranean waters.

19   Explain mineral rights.

Mineral rights are an owner's rights to mine minerals and other ingredients from the sub-surface in his or her property.

20   Explain the decision in this chapter's case excerpt.

Answers will vary. In this case, the court found that the easement in gross that was established continued to run with the land and would be enforceable against future owners.

PRACTICE QUESTIONS FOR TEST REVIEW

Essay Question

Describe how easements are created.

Easements can be created by dedication, agreement, implication, prescription, and eminent domain.

True–False

1   True
2   False
3   True

Fill in the Blank

1   Use test
2   Trade fixture
3   Easement

Multiple Choice

1   D
2   D
3   C

CHAPTER 6. REAL ESTATE CONTRACTS

Review Questions and Answers

1   What are the elements of a legally enforceable offer?

An offer must be specific about what is being offered and to whom it is being extended.

2   How does real property law define the "power of acceptance"?

The power of acceptance is created when a person receives a valid offer and can accept that offer and create a binding contract.

3   What is mutual assent?

Mutual assent consists of the agreement between the parties as to the terms and their obligations to one another created by the contract.

4   What is consideration and why is it a necessary component for contract?

Consideration is bargained for exchange between the parties to contract; it ensures that both parties have a legally binding interest in the transaction.

5   Explain how a contract may be unenforceable when it does not have a legal subject.

Contracts must be enforced through the court system. Courts will not enforce contracts that have illegal subjects. This would put the court in the untenable position of enforcing a criminal enterprise.

6   What is legal capacity to contract? Provide some examples of individuals who lack such capacity.

Capacity to contract is requirement that a party no one understand the legal consequences of entering into a binding contract. Individuals who lack capacity under the law include infants, people declared to be mentally incompetent, and those operating under the influence of alcohol or some other drug.

7   What is the Statute of Frauds and why is it important in real estate contracts?

The Statute of Frauds is a provision that requires that specific types of contracts must be in writing before they will be considered enforceable under the law. It applies to real estate law in several contexts, primarily because all transfer of ownership interests in real estate fall under the jurisdiction of the statute of frauds and because some leases fall under the jurisdiction of the statute as well.

8   How is contractual mistake defined in real property?

A "mistake" is an error that is made by both sides in the transaction.

9   What are the basic elements of an offer of purchase and contract?

An offer of purchase contract must contain the basic elements of who will be bound, what is being sold, the price, and the terms.

10 List and explain at least three important provisions of an offer to purchase and contract.

An offer to purchase and contract should contain provisions concerning the type of title that will be passed to the buyer, provisions concerning financing, closing date, and inspections.

11 Why does the law require that both the seller and the buyer sign the offer to purchase and contract?

Signature by both parties indicates their willingness to enter into the agreement.

12 What is an option?

An option is a contract between a potential buyer and a potential seller where the seller agrees, in exchange for money, to refuse to sell to other individuals without first offering the property to the potential buyer.

13 How is an offer to purchase and contract different from an option?

An offer to purchase and contract sets out the details of the buyer's offer to the seller, including provisions for sale price, financing, inspections, and closing date.

14 Explain the significance of a "time is of the essence" contract clause.

When a contract contains a provision that time is of the essence, it means that the real estate closing must occur on the date specified in the contract or transaction will be void.

15 What are some of the penalties that a seller can seek against the buyer for the buyer's wrongful refusal to perform under the offer to purchase and contract?

A seller is permitted to request that the court assessed damages against a noncomplying buyer. The seller can also request that the buyer be compelled to conclude the transaction as originally agreed, through the court's power to order specific performance.

16 What are some of the buyer's remedies against a seller who wrongfully refuses to perform under a contract of sale?

Buyers are also permitted to request specific performance. Buyers can also sue for damages.

17 What types of damages are a seller entitled to against a buyer who refuses to fulfill the obligations of an offer to purchase and contract?

The seller can retain the earnest money deposit and sue for any subsequent damages due to loss in price on a later sale.

18 Explain why it is so important to understand contract clauses.

Clauses are conditions developed between the parties that can have severe consequences if not followed. For instance, a "time is of the essence" contract can nullify a contract if the closing does not occur on a specific day.

19 Describe how you would begin to draft an offer of purchase and contract.

The best way to approach drafting an offer of purchase and contract would be to obtain a blank copy of your state's official form and then complete all the information requested. It would also be extremely wise to seek the advice of a real estate professional, especially an attorney.

20 What is specific performance?

Specific performance is a court's order compelling party to abide by the terms of contract the party initially agreed to.

PRACTICE QUESTIONS FOR TEST REVIEW

Essay Question

What are the basic elements of a legally binding contract?

A legally binding contract must have an offer, an acceptance, mutual assent, consideration, and capacity to enter into a contract. The contract must also have a legal object.

True–False

1 False
2 True
3 True

Fill in the Blank

1 Offer
2 Reasonable person standard
3 Terminates the original offer

Multiple Choice

1 C
2 C
3 C

CHAPTER 7. LANDLORD AND TENANT LAW

Review Questions and Answers

1   What rights does a landlord transfer to the tenant in a typical lease arrangement?

A landlord transfers the right to use and possess the leased premises to the tenant.

2   List the landlord's duties to the tenant.

The landlord must provide habitation that is clean, free of disease, infestation, has running hot and cold water, has a functioning H/V system, and meets all the basic conditions for habitation as set out in state law, including basic safety.

3   Explain the difference between a fixed rent lease and a percentage lease.

Net leases make the tenant responsible for not only pay rent, but also for paying all costs associated with the premises, including electric, water, sewage, and any other associated costs, while fixed rent leases a fixed rent lease assesses a flat fee that must be paid periodically and makes no provisions for the tenant's payment of utilities.

4   What is a ground lease?

A ground lease is arrangement between landlords and tenants where the tenant rents vacant land, often for farming or for constructing some building on the lot.

5   What is a mineral lease?

Mineral leases give the tenant the right to enter onto the property, test for the presence of various ores, sink mines, and carry out other actions to extract minerals and other materials from the soil.

6   What are the rules that govern pet and security deposits?

Pet and security deposits cannot be excessive and must be returned to a tenant upon the termination of the lease, once all damages above normal wear and tear have been calculated.

7   What is subletting?

Subletting occurs when a tenant leases the premises to another tenant.

8   Give an example of an action that would be permissible under a commercial lease but not a residential lease.

Under a commercial lease, a tenant would be allowed to remove a fixture, especially a trade fixture, while in a residential lease, fixtures become the property of the landlord.

9   How does the Statute of Frauds affect leases?

The Statute of Frauds applies to any lease that is for a period longer than 12 months.

10   What is the Uniform Residential Landlord and Tenant Act?

The Act provides a basic framework for the many issues that arise in landlord-tenant relationships, from creating the lease to the establishing the framework and procedures to evict a tenant.

11   Name at least three different statutes that are important in residential leasing and explain why they are important.

Landlords and tenants must be concerned with public policy concerns in residential leases, applicable state laws, the Residential Landlord and Tenant Act, and the Federal Residential Lead-Based Hazard Reduction Act of 1992.

12   What discriminatory practices are not prohibited under federal and state law?

Landlords are prohibited for barring tenants from their premises based on race, religion, or ethnic origin.

13   What is "ordinary wear and tear"?

"Wear and tear" is a phrase that covers all the normal dents and scrapes that come about through day-to-day living, including scratches, worn carpeting, and stains.

14   What is "self-help" eviction?

Self-help eviction is the process of allowing a landlord to physically eject non-paying tenants, thus running the risk of injury and potential danger to both the landlord and the tenant.

15   What are the characteristics of a tenancy for years?

A tenancy for years is any lease arrangement that will terminate on a specific date. Many of these tenancies run for set periods, such as one month or one year.

16   What are the characteristics of a tenancy from year to year?

A tenancy from year to year runs for a series of specific intervals. The most common example is a month-to-month lease.

17   How is a tenancy at will created?

The parties create a tenancy at will when they fail to specify the lease terms, regarding length, notice, renewal, or any other material terms usually found in a landlord-tenant relationship.

18   What is an estate at sufferance?

An estate at sufferance arises when a tenant remains beyond the lease term, with no new lease provision negotiated and the tenant fails to pay rent.

19   Create a table showing the different ways that the four tenancies discussed in this chapter can be terminated.

Student responses will vary, but should include provisions detailing whether termination is automatic or by action of the parties.

20   Summarize the chapter's case excerpt.

The court found that the CDC had exceeded its power by imposing a nation-wide moratorium on evictions.

PRACTICE QUESTIONS FOR TEST REVIEW

Essay Question

What rights does a landlord convey to the tenant in a typical landlord-tenant relationship?

A landlord conveys the right to use and possess real property to the tenant in a typical rental agreement. The landlord retains the other rights, such as the responsibility to pay taxes, make repairs, pay the mortgage and other items, but the right to use and possess are transferred to the tenant. Because the landlord has contractually transferred these rights to the tenant, then the landlord no longer has them.

True–False

1   False
2   True
3   True

Fill in the Blank

1   Tenants
2   Eviction
3   Sublet

Multiple Choice

1   C
2   D
3   A

CHAPTER 8. REAL ESTATE DEEDS

Review Questions and Answers

1   **List and explain at least five minimum requirements that any deed should have.**

Deeds must be in writing. They must identify the grantor and grantee. The grantor must sign the deed. Both parties must have legal capacity. The property conveyed must be adequately described.

2   **Who is required to sign a deed and why?**

The grantor is required to sign the deed to signify the transfer of his or her rights in the real property.

3   **Is the grantee required to sign the deed? Explain your answer.**

The grantee is not required to sign the deed. The reason is that the grantee does not convey any interest in the deed and therefore his or her signature is not required.

4   **What constitutes a valid legal description of the property conveyed in a deed?**

A valid legal description of property consists of a metes and bounds description, a tract index, or other approved description under state law.

5   **What is a habendum clause and what purpose does it serve?**

The habendum clause sets out the rights that the grantor transfers to the grantee.

6   **What is the difference between a habendum clause and a granting clause?**

A habendum clause transfers specific rights to a buyer, while a granting clause indicates the seller's intention to transfer the rights in the first place.

7   **Provide an example of "words of conveyance" that should be found in a deed.**

Words of conveyance include, "I hereby grant, sell, and convey" to the buyer.

8   **What is the significance of delivery and acceptance of a deed?**

Delivery by the grantor and acceptance by the grantee indicate the completion of the real estate transaction and also serve as the exact moment in time when title transfers from the grantor to the grantee.

9   **Compare and contrast attestation and acknowledgment.**

Attestation is another word for signature. Acknowledgment, on the other hand, is the grantors' proof that they are who they claim to be.

10   What is a seal?

Seals had an important role in previous decades; they supplemented the grantor's signature and enjoyed special protections under the law. For instance, they helped establish consideration for legal documents. They have become synonymous with signatures these days.

11   Is consideration required in a deed? Explain your answer.

Because deeds resemble contracts, many states have provisions in their deeds for a recital of the consideration between the grantor and the grantee.

12   What is the covenant of *seizin*?

The covenant of *seizin* is the grantor's assurance that he or she is in legal possession of the property and can transfer that right to the grantee.

13   What is the covenant against encumbrances?

The covenant against encumbrances is the grantor's promise that there are no outstanding encumbrances on the property that will affect the title.

14   What is the covenant of warranty forever?

The covenant of warranty forever is simply the grantor's guarantee that he or she will continue to support the grantee's claims at any point in the future, should it become necessary.

15   What is the difference between a special warranty deed and a general warranty deed?

A special warranty deed makes only one promise or warranty to the buyer while a general warranty deed provides a whole host of guarantees or promises to the buyer.

16   What are deeds of trust?

Deeds of trust are a form of mortgage used in some states in which a lender and a borrower authorize a third party, the trustee, to act on their behalf in the event of a loan default.

17   What function does a quitclaim deed serve?

A quitclaim deed surrenders any rights that the grantor may have in the property. It makes no guarantees or promises about the type or quality of the grantor's rights.

18   Under what circumstances would a quitclaim deed be used?

A quitclaim deed might be used in situations where there is a dispute arising from a probate matter and the parties wish to clear up any potential outstanding claims on the property.

19   Why would a buyer prefer a general warranty deed to a quitclaim deed?

A buyer would always prefer a general warranty deed over a quitclaim deed because a general warranty deed contains promises or conditions that the buyer can sue over if the buyer discovers that the seller has not been honest. However, in a quitclaim deed, the buyer accepts the property "as is" with no promises and no guarantees.

20   Describe the three statutory approaches to recording title.

First, there are "race" jurisdictions that hold that whoever records title at the courthouse first has possessory interests. Then, there are jurisdictions that follow a "race-notice" approach where the first person to record at the courthouse will still have possessory interest, unless he or she was under notice that someone else had or would acquire interest in the property. Finally, there are "notice" jurisdictions, where a person who gives notice of his or her possessory interest in property has a superior claim to the person who first records an interest at the courthouse.

PRACTICE QUESTIONS FOR TEST REVIEW

Essay Question

What are the minimum legal requirements of the deed conveying ownership interests from one person to another?

The minimum legal requirements for a valid deed include: identifiable parties, a valid, legal description, in writing, signed by the grantor, a grantor who has legal capacity to enter into a contract, and language contained in the deed that shows a clear intent on the grantor's part to convey ownership interests to the grantee.

True–False

1   True
2   True
3   False

Fill in the Blank

1   Capacity
2   Habendum clause
3   Deed

Multiple Choice

1   C
2   C
3   D

CHAPTER 9. MORTGAGES AND FINANCING THE PURCHASE OF REAL ESTATE

Review Questions and Answers

1 How is the secondary mortgage market different than the primary mortgage market?

The primary mortgage market is in the business of negotiating with borrowers, creating lending options, assessing borrowers for credit history, appraising the value of real estate, and presenting funds at the closing. Secondary mortgage participants do not work with individual borrowers, are not involved in the business of lending money to borrowers, and purchase mortgages already negotiated by primary lenders.

2 What is Fannie Mae?

Fannie Mae is an organization that was originally created following the Great Depression to purchase mortgages and ensure the availability of capital for banks and other lenders.

3 Explain the significance of the secondary mortgage market.

The secondary mortgage market is responsible for purchasing mortgages negotiated by primary lenders. The secondary mortgage market assures the continued availability of capital by paying primary lenders for the mortgages that they issue.

4 How has Dodd-Frank changed the way that mortgages are granted?

Dodd-Frank has brought about many changes in the way that closings are conducted, including simplifying the language that is used in closings, changing the terms involved and requiring additional information to be given to the consumer.

5 What is the difference between a mortgage and deed of trust?

Mortgages involve the lender and the borrower and set out the rights and obligations of both; deeds of trust, on the other hand, involve three parties: the lender, the borrower, and a trustee who acts to enforce the provisions of the deed of trust in the event of a default.

6 What is a granting clause in a mortgage?

A granting clause indicates the parties' intentions to transfer rights. The granting clause in a mortgage serves a similar purpose; it substantiates the borrower's intention of transferring the right to foreclose to the lender in exchange for the money provided for the purchase of the real estate.

7   What were the reasons for the creation of the Dodd-Frank Act?

Dodd-Frank was created in the wake of the Great Recession as a response to the rampant and unethical practices that permitted banks and other lenders to loan money to many consumers who were clearly unable to repay the loans.

8   What is a power of sale provision?

The power of sale provision authorizes the lender to begin foreclosure proceedings in the event of loan default.

9   What is an estoppel certificate?

An estoppel certificate is the borrower's certification of the amount that he or she has borrowed from the lender.

10   What are the rules of priority when it comes to mortgages?

The rules of priority for mortgages are very simple: The first to file at the courthouse generally receives the highest priority when it comes to paying out claims or distributing funds from a foreclosure sale.

11   What is a subordination agreement?

A subordination agreement is a lender's agreement to subordinate its higher priority mortgage to another lender, usually as part of an owner-financing arrangement.

12   What is the difference between a fixed-rate mortgage and an adjustable-rate mortgage?

A fixed-rate mortgage has terms that do not vary. The term of the mortgage, the amount borrowed and the annual interest rate are all fixed at the beginning of the mortgage and do not vary over time. However, an adjustable-rate mortgage has provisions that allow for changes in the interest rate or other terms for the entire length of the loan, or for the first few years before it converts into a fixed-rate mortgage.

13   How does Dodd-Frank affect Truth-in-Lending laws?

Dodd-Frank brought about enormous changes in Truth-in-Lending laws, requiring that all consumers be given specific information about the loans they were seeking and allowing them to back out of the loan before it was consummated (or closed). It also created a federal agency to help guard against consumer exploitation as well as imposing new requirements on banks to ensure that they met certain stress tests when it comes to paying back investors and meeting other financial obligations.

14   What is a wraparound mortgage?

A wraparound mortgage is a new mortgage that creates a double payment plan, one for the new mortgage and one for a pre-existing mortgage that was originally issued on very favorable terms.

15   What is mortgage underwriting?

Underwriting is the process of evaluating the potential risks in extending credit in a transaction. It relies on many factors, including the buyer's credit history, the value of the house, and the terms of the mortgage.

16   What qualifies as a default under a mortgage?

The most common type of default is the borrower's failure to pay regular, monthly payments on the mortgage. However, a default is any failure by the borrower to carry out agreed upon actions in the mortgage arrangement.

17   What are some of the common reasons for a borrower to default on a mortgage?

The most common reason for a borrower to default on a loan is because of lack of funds to pay the monthly mortgage payment. A borrower may also default due to failure to pay for insurance and/or taxes.

18   Explain the difference between judicial and power of sale foreclosure.

A judicial foreclosure is very similar to a lawsuit and requires many of the same steps that any lawsuit would require. However, a power of sale foreclosure allows the lender to sidestep many of the steps required in a civil suit and bring the foreclosure action faster than would be possible in a judicial foreclosure.

19   What is predatory lending?

Predatory lending consists of practices by unscrupulous lenders to take advantage of borrowers by assessing high fees and making no provisions concerning the borrower's ability to repay a loan.

PRACTICE QUESTIONS FOR TEST REVIEW

Essay Question

What are the basic elements of a mortgage?

The basic elements for any mortgage is that it must first be in writing. The lender and borrower must be clearly identified. The mortgage must contain specific language conveying the right to foreclose to the lender in exchange for the borrower receiving funds to purchase the real property. It should also contain a promissory note, a granting clause, a description of the debt, a power of sale provision, an acceleration clause, and a due on sale provision, among others.

True–False

1   False
2   True
3   False

Fill in the Blank

1 Secondary mortgage market
2 1968
3 Federal Reserve System

Multiple Choice

1 A
2 A
3 A

CHAPTER 10. PUBLIC AND PRIVATE RESTRICTIONS ON THE USE OF LAND

Review Questions and Answers

1   What is zoning?

Zoning consists of governmental rules and regulations limiting how owners of real estate can use their property.

2   What is aesthetic zoning?

Aesthetic zoning rules govern the appearance of structures in the covered areas.

3   How are zoning regulations enforced?

Zoning regulations are enforced through citations against offenders. These can include monetary sanctions or fines as well as orders that force offenders to abide by zoning rules.

4   What are the three broad categories of zoning regulations?

The three broad categories of zoning include residential, commercial, and industrial.

5   What is a non-conforming use?

The classification of "non-conforming use" is reserved for a structure that pre-dates the enactment of zoning regulation. When the structure is already in existence at the time the zoning ordinance is created, it can continue to exist even though its use violates the new rule.

6   What is a conditional use permit?

Conditional use permits allow a business entity to operate in an area that has been reserved for residential use. Conditional use permits allow the property to be used in a way that is not in strict compliance with the zoning classification, but that does provide an essential service.

7 What is a variance?

A variation is a zoning board's determination to allow a structure to operate in an area that has been zoned for other classifications. Zoning boards issue variances to allow for a degree of flexibility in zoning regulations, recognizing that it is extremely difficult to limit use entirely.

8 What are some examples of unconstitutional zoning regulations?

Zoning regulations that discriminate against residents based on religion, race, or ethnic origin are all examples of unconstitutional zoning regulations.

9 What is the "rational basis test" as it applies to zoning?

This is a rule that require all zoning rules and regulations to have a rational basis and that they directly apply to the purposes behind zoning, including health, safety, and welfare of citizens.

10 What is spot zoning?

Spot zoning is a practice used by zoning boards to single out a parcel for special treatment. An example of spot zoning would be the zoning board's action in selecting a residence and changing the zoning for that property but not the rest of the area.

11 How do building codes compare with zoning rules and regulations?

Building codes are local or state rules and regulations that have specific restrictions on the way that buildings can be constructed and how heating and air-conditioning systems and plumbing and electrical work can be installed and completed. Zoning, on the other hand, is directed at the way that owners use their property, not the way structures on the property are built.

12 What is an historic district?

An historic district is an area designated by the state for special treatment, usually because it contains buildings that have architectural or historical significance. Such areas often receive favorable tax treatment.

13 What is the Interstate Land Sales Full Disclosure Act?

The Interstate Land Sales Full Disclosure Act was passed in 1968 and requires land promoters to make specific disclosures about land on or near the Interstate Highway System.

14 What is the role of environmental issues in restricting a private landowners use of property?

Environmental acts, such as the Clean Water Act, provides strict guidelines for the use of wetlands and imposes limitations on how areas that qualify as wetlands can be used.

15   **Explain restrictive covenants.**

Restrictive covenants control issues such as minimum setbacks from road-ways, appearance, architecture, minimum lot sizes, and a host of other issues.

16   **What are some the methods used to create restrictive covenants?**

Restrictive covenants can be created by including them in a deed from the grantor to the grantee, by recording the restrictive covenants in the public records, and by recording a plat that contains the restrictive covenants.

17   **How can restrictive covenants be terminated?**

Restrictive covenants can be terminated when the restrictive covenants have a stated time period, when the restrictive covenants have been abandoned, when the neighborhood has incurred substantially changed conditions, and when the properties affected have merged.

18   **Provide examples of some of the typical provisions found in restrictive covenants.**

Restrictive covenants can establish minimum lot sizes, limit use of the prop-erty (such as for residential use only), limit the number of outbuildings on the parcel, restrict the types of animals that can live on the premises (such as forbidding farm animals), and require that all buildings conform to a general architectural theme.

19   **What does it mean when we say that restrictive covenants must "touch and concern" the land?**

This phrase means that the conditions remain on the parcel and are not specific to the owners. Once created, the restrictive covenants apply to all future owners.

20   **What are some examples of unconstitutional restrictive covenants?**

Any restrictive covenant that seeks to bar ownership to members of a specific religion, race, or ethnic origin will be considered unconstitutional and unen-forceable.

PRACTICE QUESTIONS FOR TEST REVIEW

Essay Question

Explain restrictive covenants.

Restrictive covenants can resemble zoning ordinances. Like zoning regulations, they control issues such as minimum setbacks from roadways, appearance, architec-ture, minimum lot sizes, and many other issues. However, while zoning regulations are implemented by the local government, restrictive covenants are created and enforced by private individuals on other private individuals.

True–False

1 True
2 True
3 True

Fill in the Blank

1 Residential
2 Conditional use permit
3 Private

Multiple Choice

1 B
2 D
3 C

CHAPTER 11. REAL ESTATE PROFESSIONS

Review Questions and Answers

1 What is an agent?

An agent is a person who represents the interests of another in a business transaction. Agents have specific duties that they owe to their principals.

2 Are agency relationships required to be in writing? Why or why not?

Generally, agency relationships are not required to be in writing unless they fall under the jurisdiction of the statute of frauds. However, many individuals put such agreements in writing to avoid confusion and potential litigation later.

3 List and explain the four duties that agent owes to a principal.

Agents owe the following duties to their principals: duty of care, duty of loyalty, duty of obedience, and duty to account.

4 What is a fiduciary?

A fiduciary is a person who holds a special position of trust and confidence to another.

5 What is "self-dealing"?

"Self-dealing" is using information provided by the principal to enrich the agent, usually at the expense of the principal. This would be a violation of the agent's duties.

6   **List and explain the three duties that agents owe to third parties.**

An agent owes the duties of care, obedience, and loyalty to the principal. Care refers to the duty to act in accordance with professional standards. Obedience means that the agent is supposed to follow the guidelines and orders of the principal. The agent must be loyal to the principal, which means that he or she must avoid self-dealing and conflicts of interest.

7   **What is fraud in the legal context?**

Fraud is the intentional misrepresentation of a material fact that is relied upon by the victim to make a critical decision.

8   **What duties does a principal owe to an agent?**

Principals have three general duties to agents: duty to compensate the agent, duty to cooperate, and the duty to refrain from injuring the agent's reputation.

9   **What is the difference between an agent and an independent contractor?**

An agent works for a principal. An independent contractor can be hired for a specific job, but the IC decides on his or her own course of conduct and how best to complete the job. Independent contractors can and often do work without direct supervision of the contractor.

10   **In a typical real estate transaction, who is the principal, who is the agent, and who is the third party?**

In a typical real estate transaction, the seller is the principal and the real estate broker (or agent) works as the agent for the seller, even though they may have never met. Other agents in the area also work for the seller in trying to produce a buyer who is ready, willing, and able to purchase the home. A third party is someone outside the principal-agent relationship. In this scenario, the buyer would be considered a third party.

11   **What is the difference between a real estate broker and a real estate agent?**

Although some states have eliminated the distinction, in states where it remains, a broker can carry out all actions associated with listing, advertising, showing, and receiving a commission for a real estate transaction. A real estate agent (or salesperson) has limited powers and cannot receive a commission without the involvement of a broker in the transaction.

12   **What is the Multiple Listing Service?**

The Multiple Listing Service is an arrangement among local brokers and agents that when a house is listed in the MLS, the listing broker is making an offer to others to split the commission 50-50.

13   What are some of the advantages of real estate as an investment?

There are specific tax advantages to owning real estate, such as the ability to write off the yearly interest payments for a mortgage from annual tax payments. In some instances, real property generally appreciates in value over time, although that is by no means certain.

14   What are some of the disadvantages of real estate as an investment?

Real estate is not a very liquid investment, meaning that it is difficult for an investor to get his or her money out of the investment in a short period of time. Although there are tax advantages, when the property is held as a residence, but for less than 24 months, there can be tax consequences. Finally, although there is a general tendency for real property to appreciate in value over time, that trend is certainly not guaranteed.

15   What are Real Estate Investment Trusts?

A REIT acts much like a mutual fund. Investors buy shares in the trust and the trust uses the accumulated money to buy real property in hopes of turning a profit on commercial ventures.

16   Explain the role of a real estate appraiser.

An appraiser reviews the property and comes up with an estimate of what the fair market value of the real property is. One method that an appraiser would use is to compare similar houses in the area and see how much they sold for recently.

17   What is a Comparative Market Analysis?

In a comparative market analysis, the appraiser reviews other recent sales of homes that are very similar to the house currently being evaluated. A CMA will take into account the sales of houses with the same number of bedrooms and bathrooms and other features and based on those sale prices, the appraiser will produce a CMA that lists what he or she believes is the fair market value of the property.

18   What are some of the duties carried out by real estate paralegals?

Real estate paralegals often conduct title searches before a property goes to closing. Paralegals often play a central role in the closing itself by bringing all the paperwork and disbursements together and making sure that each party receives not only the correct paperwork, but either submits certified funds or is paid with them.

19   Explain the role of a real estate inspector.

An inspector reviews the structure and other house systems to determine if any are not performing properly. A thorough inspection will look at the roof and basement structures, the air and heating systems, the electric systems, and the plumbing systems to determine if there any problems that could stop the final sale of the property.

20 Explain the commission system for paying real estate agents.

Typically, real estate agents charge a percentage of the overall sales price as their commission for the sale. In many parts of the country, for example, when a personal residence is sold, the listing agent is entitled to a total commission of 6 percent of the sale price of the home.

PRACTICE QUESTIONS FOR TEST REVIEW

Essay Question

Explain the law of agency.

An agency relationship is created when persons are unable or unwilling to conduct business on their behalf and instead retain another person to act for them. The person who hires an agent is referred to as the principal. The principal works out an arrangement with an agent, giving this agent the power to conduct certain transactions and the authority to see those transactions through to completion. The law of agency is very fluid and allows for a multitude of different relationships.

True–False

1 True
2 True
3 False

Fill in the Blank

1 Fiduciary
2 Care
3 Fraud

Multiple Choice

1 B
2 D
3 D

CHAPTER 12. TITLE INSURANCE AND TITLE EXAMINATION

Review Questions and Answers

1 What is title insurance?

A title insurance policy is designed to pay for any costs associated with claims raised against a title after the transaction has been completed.

2 How can title insurance assists in bringing about a real estate transaction?

Title insurance protects the interests of both the lender and the buyer and helps conclude the transaction by providing security for both.

3 What are some of the problems that title insurance protects against?

Title insurance protects against any claim made by someone claiming an ownership interest or other claim on the property's title.

4 How does someone acquire title insurance?

A person acquires title insurance by requesting a policy from a company and providing information about the state of the title.

5 How often must a person pay a title insurance premium?

The most common method to pay a title insurance premium is once: at the closing.

6 What is the grantor-grantee index?

This is a listing of all transactions where real estate interests were transferred from one individual to another.

7 How can surveys and plats of property help in a title examination?

Surveys and plats provide a visual record and reference for a title examiner and can help explain unusual features of written descriptions.

8 What are the basic steps involved in a title search?

The first step is to establish a chain of title, then the out or adverse conveyances. After that, the title examiner reviews tax and clerks' office records for any transaction that might affect the title. Finally, the title examiner ensures that there are no other encumbrances, such as liens, that might affect the transaction.

9 What is a chain of title?

A chain of title is a complete listing of every owner for the property going back a specific period of time.

10 What information can a title examiner gather at the local tax office?

The local Tax Office contains a wealth of information about real estate in the area, including owners' names, total acreage, PIN (Parcel Identification Number) or parcel ID numbers, tax maps, tax ID numbers, and deed references. In some states, this information is still stored on a paper "tax card," but in most it is available in a computer database that not only provides all the information set out above, but also basic floor plans, square footage, and even digital photos of the property in question.

11   What are adverse or out conveyances?

Adverse or out conveyances are any transaction that has transferred a potential ownership interest to someone other than an owner in the chain of title.

12   Why is it important to determine if a previous mortgage has been canceled?

An outstanding or uncanceled mortgage can create a lien or other encumbrance on the property that can effectively prevent it from being sold to anyone.

13   What are abstract forms?

Title abstract forms summarize the important features of a parcel, and encapsulate all the important information in such a way that it is readily available.

14   What are the Uniform Commercial Code filings? Why are they important for title examinations?

The Uniform Commercial Code listings are required whenever a borrower pledges personal property as collateral for a loan. There are times when a UCC filing is recorded on a fixture. The UCC filing may give a creditor the right to repossess or bring other actions to enforce payment.

15   How do probate, marriage, birth, and death records assist a title examiner?

Marriage, birth, and death records can provide vital information for a title examiner. Marriage records can show that a previous owner was married and can clear up an issue of whether the spouse should have signed the deed conveying it to the next owner in the chain. Birth and death records can establish family relationships and can clear up who has title to lands that have been transferred from family member to family member over the years.

16   What is the purpose of a preliminary title opinion?

The preliminary title certificate is issued prior to the closing and details any potential problems with the title and what actions the legal team will take to clear up these problems.

17   Why is legal malpractice an issue in title searches in some states?

When an attorney offers a final opinion on the nature of a real property title, the attorney is certifying that there are no legal impediments to the sale. If the attorney's opinion is wrong because the legal team has missed an important entry, or failed to notice an outstanding legal claim against the property, the borrower, lender, and title insurance company may all have causes of action against the attorney for legal malpractice.

18   What is "tacking" and why does it present ethical concerns?

Tacking is the process of checking a chain of title from the date of the last title search, not for the entire period mandated. It can raise ethical concerns when the client is not aware that the legal team is doing it and when the previous title examination was not thorough.

19 Are attorneys required to certify titles in all states? Explain your answer.

No, attorneys are not required to certify title in all states. In some states, closing professionals who are not lawyers can certify titles and in some states title insurance companies may do it.

PRACTICE QUESTIONS FOR TEST REVIEW

Essay Question

Explain title insurance.

Title insurance is an insurance policy. Instead of insuring an automobile for damages in a wreck or a life, it focuses on a very narrow issue: the marketability of the title to property. A title insurance policy is designed to pay for any costs associated with claims raised against a title after the transaction has been completed. It is title insurance that accounts for the need for a title examination.

True–False

1 True
2 False
3 True

Fill in the Blank

1 Tacking
2 A final title certificate
3 Probate Office

Multiple Choice

1 C
2 C
3 D

CHAPTER 13. THE CLOSING

Review Questions and Answers

1 List and explain the basic steps involved in conducting a closing.

The basic steps in a closing involve obtaining a loan package from the lender, completing the documentation necessary for the closing, contacting the various participants, and arranging for disbursement of funds during the closing.

2   Why is it difficult to schedule a closing?

A closing brings together several different individuals and also requires many different types of documentation. As a result, it is often difficult to coordinate both the persons and documentation for a particular date.

3   Why is a contract clause that "time is of the essence" a particular challenge for settlement agents?

This contract clause provides that the closing must occur on the date specified in the contract. If the closing does not occur on that date, the entire transaction is void.

4   What are some of the important documents that are completed during a real estate closing?

Important documents that are completed and closing include: title search, legal description of the property, loan payoff amounts, tax information, and termite inspection reports.

5   What is a survey and why is it important to the closing?

Surveys are physical measurements of the property and can reveal a host of problems, from inaccurate boundaries and unrecorded easements to encroachments. Most lenders require an accurate survey of the property before disbursing funds for the closing.

6   What are "loan payoff amounts" and why are they important?

The loan payoff amount is the amount of the borrower owes on the existing mortgage. It must be paid off as part of the closing.

7   Why is it important to know the tax payment status on a parcel of real estate prior to closing?

If there are any outstanding taxes, they must be paid before or as part of the closing.

8   What is the significance of the termite inspection report?

The termite inspection report is required for the closing and certifies that there is no pest infestation on the premises.

9   List some of the tax forms that may be required as part of the closing.

One of the most important of these is form 1099. This form has been required by the IRS since 1987; it details the total amount received by the seller during the closing. Other forms include: Form 4506, which allows the lender to request a copy of the borrower's income tax return from the IRS and Form W-9, which verifies the borrower's Social Security number.

10 How has the USA PATRIOT Act affected real estate closings?

The USA Patriot Act requires that financial institutions create an anti-money laundering program and certify that they have complied with the Act. They must certify compliance with every real estate closing.

11 Explain records of trust disbursements.

A record of trust disbursement tracks all money received by the closing professional and details how all this money was disbursed to the various participants. Private Mortgage Insurance (PMI) is insurance that protects the lender when the borrower has put down less than 20 percent of the loan purchase price. If the borrower defaults on the mortgage, PMI will reimburse the lender for money lost.

12 What is a seller's affidavit and how does it relate to surveys?

A seller's affidavit is a sworn statement that there have been no changes, improvements or boundary line changes to the property since the date of the last survey. It offers some legal protection to the buyer and also protects against any changes or other omissions in a survey.

13 List the people who are typically present at the closing. What do these people normally do at the closing?

An attorney or other closing professional is present to coordinate the closing and to ensure that all documents are prepared correctly. This person is also responsible for disbursing funds. The buyer is usually present and is often required to bring certified funds to complete the transaction. The seller is present to sign the deed and ensure that it is delivered to the buyer.

14 List and explain the documents that are usually required at the closing.

The various documents required at the closing include the title examination, title insurance policy, mortgage or deed of trust, and general warranty deed, among others.

15 "Escrow" is used in two different contexts in this chapter. Explain both.

Escrow refers to the extra payments that a borrower makes each month to defray the cost of taxes and hazard insurance. It also refers to the process of allowing buyers and sellers to complete the paperwork necessary for a closing prior to the actual date.

16 What are the ethical concerns surrounding dual representation at a closing?

There are always ethical pitfalls when an attorney represents both sides in the transaction. If the parties come into conflict, the attorney will be placed in a difficult position of having to decide which client to represent or withdrawing from representation of both.

17   What are some of the ethical concerns about allowing paralegals to conduct real estate closings?

There are numerous ethical concerns about using paralegals to conduct real estate closings, including the fact that the client has hired an attorney to conduct the closing, not to provide the paralegal who will act on the attorney's behalf. Other ethical concerns involve differences in the legal background and training of the paralegal and whether it is appropriate to use the paralegal to conduct the closing.

18   Explain the impact that the Dodd-Frank Act has had on closings.

Dodd-Frank made some dramatic changes to the traditional Good Faith Estimate and the initial Truth-in-Lending (TILA) disclosures. These have been modified into a single document, called the Loan Estimate. This document, along with the Closing Disclosure, must be provided to the consumer at least three business days before the closing is completed. The new rules apply to loan types not previously covered by TILA requirements, including construction loans, loans secured by vacant land, and trusts established for estate planning. No fees can be imposed on the borrower until the borrower has received the Loan Estimate and has indicated he or she wishes to proceed with the loan process. There are limits on fees for applications, appraisals, and underwriting.

19   What are the some of the concerns in choosing a closing software package?

Real estate closing software must be able to generate the appropriate documentation, checks, and other disbursements to complete the transaction in a way that guarantees accuracy.

PRACTICE QUESTIONS FOR TEST REVIEW

Essay Question

What is a closing?

A closing, or consummation, is the final step in a long process that began with a homeowner's decision to sell his house. The parties involved negotiated sale price and many other details, and the closing is where all of those details are put into place. At a closing, the borrowers sign documents that legally bind them to pay back the mortgage or lose the property through foreclosure. The closing is also where the final title documents are prepared and submitted to the parties for signature. The closing is when all of the details finally come together.

True–False

1 False
2 False
3 False

Fill in the Blank

1 Actual days method
2 Commission
3 Points

Multiple Choice

1 B
2 D
3 C

CHAPTER 14. TAXATION ISSUES IN REAL PROPERTY

Review Questions and Answers

1 **What are ad valorem taxes?**

These are taxes assessed according to the value of the property.

2 **How do governments enforce their tax rules and regulations?**

State statutes give governments the power to enforce their tax regulations through a wide assortment of remedies, including levies, garnishment, and attachments.

3 **Describe three types of property that are exempt from taxes.**

The most common exemptions include: homestead exemption, charitable exemption, and nonprofit exemption.

4 **What is a homestead exemption?**

A homestead exemption allows a homeowner to exempt some or all of the value of his or her home from assessment by the tax office and thus results in a lower tax bill.

5 **What are "enterprise zones"?**

Enterprise zones are areas that receive favorable tax treatment. The local government sets off a specific geographic area and advertises the fact businesses relocating to that area will have a lower tax bill. This usually results in a gradual build-up of the enterprise zone. Ultimately, offering a tax incentive proves to be a wise investment. By encouraging new businesses, the government is improving its tax base.

6   What is the difference between a property tax assessment and an appraisal?

A property tax assessment is the actual tax bill, while an appraisal is the value for the property determined by the tax office.

7   What grounds can a taxpayer use to challenge a tax assessment?

A taxpayer can challenge a tax assessment when he or she can show that the tax was assessed in an arbitrary or capricious way.

8   What is the millage or tax rate?

This is the tax rate that is calculated by the tax office based on the budgetary needs of the county and assessed against all qualifying properties.

9   What are some of the factors that tax assessors use to establish the value of property?

Tax assessors use some or all the following factors to reach assessment for a particular property: zoning, access, crop value, acreage, and the presence of buildings and structures on the property.

10   What is the difference between an assessment and a tax bill?

An assessment and a tax bill are essentially the same thing.

11   Why would a county only reassess its properties every few years?

Reassessment takes time and resources and doing it every year would eat up valuable time that could be spent collecting taxes.

12   What are the rules about lien priority when it comes to tax liens?

Tax liens always receive higher priority, no matter when they are actually filed. This rule ensures that tax liens are always paid first when the property is foreclosed.

13   When are governments authorized to auction off property for back taxes?

Whenever the taxpayer has failed to pay the taxes assessed and the taxpayer has received notice of a tax foreclosure sale.

14   What are some of the ethical concerns with "tax dodges"?

Tax dodges may involve the client in questionable practices that might easily result in criminal or civil actions by the IRS or other taxing body. Legal professionals must not encourage clients to break the law.

15 Why is it important to know how to research tax issues?

The ability to research tax issues is essential to safeguard a client's interests.

16 Why would someone challenge a tax bill?

A person would challenge a tax bill when he or she believes that the amount assessed is too high given the actual value of the property.

17 What are the rules concerning when tax bills are due to be paid?

In most situations, tax bills have priority over other debts and must be paid or the local government can bring a tax foreclosure action.

18 What is the procedure followed in a tax auction?

Property on which back taxes are owed can be auctioned off by the local government to individuals who can bid at the auction. They can bid more than the tax amount owed, and the successful bidder will receive a government deed, sometimes called a "tax commissioner's deed" that gives them certain rights to the property later.

19 Explain the relationship between purchasing at a tax auction and adverse possession.

The deed provided at a tax auction satisfies the element of "colorable claim of title" in order to establish one of the key elements of adverse possession.

PRACTICE QUESTIONS FOR TEST REVIEW

Essay Question

How are tax rates established?

Governments generally assess taxes based on an ad valorem tax scheme; that is, the government assesses a tax based on an item's value. Taxing by value is an ancient concept and relatively easy to impose. Ad valorem taxes can be applied to personal property, such as imported goods or automobiles. They can also be assessed against real property. Once the government calculates how much money it will need, it can review the eligible properties and assess a tax against them that will bring in sufficient revenue to meet the government's needs.

True–False

1 False
2 False
3 True

Fill in the Blank

1 Exemptions
2 Enterprise zones
3 Assessment

Multiple Choice

1 A
2 B
3 B

Abandonment   Giving up or surrendering all legal rights.

Accretion   The natural and gradual deposit of soil against a bank or other barrier.

Acknowledgment   Proof that the person who signed a document is who she claims to be.

Ad valorem taxes   Taxes assessed according to the value of the property.

Adverse possession   An action that can be brought by a person who possesses land owned by another, holds that land openly and against the claims of others, and continues in possession for a minimum period of time, such as seven years.

Aesthetic zoning   The requirement that all commercial and residential structures in a specified area have the same general appearance.

Agency   A business relationship between a principal (who is the source of the authority for the transaction) and the agent (who has the power to carry it out).

Amortization   The gradual paying down and elimination of a debt through an application of payments toward both principal and interest.

Apartment   A leased residence containing more than five living units sharing a single roof or foundation.

Appurtenant easement   An easement created for an adjoining or servient estate.

Assessment   The evaluation or estimation of the value of real property.

Attestation   Signing a document.

Avulsion   The sudden separation of land from its main body, usually by action of water.

Beneficiary   A person named in a will that the testator intends to receive an interest in property.

Binder   A preliminary agreement to issue an insurance policy.

Capacity   The ability to know and understand the consequences of entering a legally binding agreement.

Chain of title   A complete listing of all owners of a particular parcel of real estate for a specified time period.

Closing   Also known as a settlement, the final phase of a real estate transaction at which all deeds are signed and funds are distributed to complete the sale of real property.

Collateral   Any type of asset that is used to secure a loan.

Conditional use permit   An exception to a zoning classification granted by a zoning board, usually to benefit area residents.

Condominium   A form of real property in which the owner has full title to the interior, but not the exterior of the structure.

Consideration   The contractual requirement that both parties incur some form of legal detriment in exchange for receiving something of value; consideration ensures that both parties are bound to the contract.

Constructive eviction   A legal doctrine that holds that leased premises that are unfit for human habitation effectively prevent the tenant from continuing to live there.

Consummation   Under TRID, the point where a consumer becomes contractually obligated to repay the mortgage to the lender.

Contract   A legally recognized agreement that gives both parties the right to enforce the obligation through legal means.

Cooperative   A land holding arrangement often organized as a corporation where the owners have shares or ownership rights in the real estate, but do not hold title to the actual land itself.

Co-tenants   Two or more persons who have ownership interests in a single property.

Dedication   A grant of private land to the government.

Deed   The written instrument that conveys real property interests.

Deed of trust   A type of real estate financing in which a lender and a borrower authorize a third party, the trustee, to act on their behalf in the event of a loan default.

Default   Violation of a contractual duty.

Devise   Transfer property in a will.

Devisee   Another term for beneficiary.

Doctrine of laches   The legal principle that states that a person who fails to assert a legal right loses it.

Dower and curtesy   A provision of common law that provided a set portion of the marital property would automatically vest in a surviving spouse; *dower* referred to the portion allotted to a surviving wife, while *curtesy* referred to the portion allotted to a surviving husband.

Easement   The right of a person other than the landowner to use a portion of the owner's land, for example, a driveway or a right of way.

Equitable remedies   The power of a trial court to order a party to undertake specific actions, or to refrain from taking specific actions, such as injunctions and specific performance.

Equity   A person's value in property once he has subtracted the amount owed on the property from its current fair market value.

Erosion   The natural and gradual removal, usually by force of water, of soil from a bank or some other barrier.

Escheat   Transfer of title to local government when a person dies without heirs.

Estate   A right to use or enjoy real property.

Estoppel certificate   The borrower's acknowledgment of the total amount borrowed in the mortgage.

Eviction   The legal process of removing a tenant from the leased premises.

Exemption   When an owner is not obligated to pay a specific tax.

Farm and rural property   Property primarily designed for growing food, timber, or other products.

Fee simple absolute   The real property estate in which an owner has the right to give, sell, mortgage, and lease the property, among other rights.

Fiduciary   A person who holds a special position of trust and confidence to another.

Fixture   Personal property that has become permanently attached to real property.

Forced share   The statutory claim that a surviving spouse has in the marital estate.

Foreclosure   The right of a lender (mortgagor) to initiate an action to auction off property for outstanding indebtedness in a mortgage or deed of trust.

Fraud   An intentional deception that causes injury to another person.

Grantee   One who receives a real property interest.

Granting clause   A deed clause that demonstrates the grantor's willingness to engage in the transaction.

Grantor   One who conveys a real property interest.

Grantor-grantee index   A listing of all property by the names of individuals who buy and sell it.

Habendum clause   A deed clause that conveys specified rights to the grantee.

Holographic will   A will written entirely in the testator's handwriting.

HUD-1 Settlement Form   A real estate settlement and disbursement form that has been widely adopted by U.S. lenders.

Improvements   Buildings, fences, barns, and other structures that add value to raw land.

In gross easement   An easement that allows someone to enter onto the land; there are no servient estates with in gross easements.

In rem jurisdiction A court's power to render decisions based on the location of the land within the court's geographic boundaries.

Intestate The term for a person who dies without a will.

Intoxication A person who is suffering from the effects of alcohol or other drug to the point that he or she is unable to comprehend the legal obligations of entering into a legally binding agreement.

Joint tenancy A type of concurrent ownership in which two or more individuals own property together, with equal ownership rights and the right of survivorship.

Judicial foreclosure Foreclosure based on state statutes.

Laches The legal principle that states that a person who fails to assert a legal right loses it.

Landlord The owner of the premises. The landlord retains all the rights normally associated with ownership except use, possession, and enjoyment.

Latently ambiguous A description that appears to be invalid, but refers to a document through which the property can be adequately described.

Lease The contractual arrangement between a landlord and tenant.

Leasehold estate The body of rights conveyed to a tenant from the landlord.

Legality The requirement that a contract must have a legal subject or action as its subject.

License The right to the products of the land, but not the land itself. A licensee might have the right to enter the premises to harvest, but no right to any other use of the property.

Lien A monetary claim against property brought by a creditor that may ripen into judgment.

Life estate An estate granted to a specific person, allowing that person to use, possess, enjoy, and take profits from the real estate, but only as long as the person lives. On the possessor's death, title vests in a remainderman.

Life tenant The person who holds a life estate.

Liquidity The ease to which an investment can be converted into ready cash.

Listing agreement The contract between a seller and a real estate broker or agent where the broker agrees to make his or her best efforts to sell the house and the seller agrees to pay a commission when the sale is made.

Loan package A set of instructions from a lender about how financial documents should be prepared and distributed at the closing.

Material fact An important or central fact in the contract or business negotiations that, if fully revealed, would change the outcome of the transaction.

Materialman A creditor who has provided supplies for the benefit of real property.

Mechanic A creditor who has provided a service for the benefit of real property.

Merger The combination of two formerly separate tracts into a single unit.

Millage rate A tax rate that equates to one dollar per thousand dollars in value.

Mistake A misunderstanding or confusion about a material fact in a contract that is shared by both parties.

Mortgage A contractual agreement in which a borrower transfers specific real property rights to a lender in exchange for the lender's pledge of funds to purchase the real estate.

Mutual assent "Meeting of the minds"; the requirement that the parties to the contract have the same understanding about the contract.

Navigable water Water that can be used for navigation by boats.

Negligent misrepresentation Liability for a statement that proved to be untrue when the person making the statement had no reasonable belief in its accuracy.

Nonconforming use A structure that violates a zoning classification, but predated the enactment of the zoning rule.

Non-navigable water   A body of water so shallow or small that it is incapable of supporting navigation.

Nuisance   A cause of action that is authorized when the defendant's behavior results in a loss of enjoyment or value in the plaintiff's property.

Nuncupative will   An oral will, usually only permitted when the testator is in the last stages of life and is unable to draft a written will.

Option   A contract between a seller and buyer, whereby the seller agrees not to sell the property to another person for a stated period of time.

Ordinary wear and tear   The normal dents and scrapes that occur through daily use.

Parol evidence   Oral testimony offered to explain or interpret the provisions of a written document, such as the property description in a deed.

Partition   The right of co-tenants to divide up property according to their ownership interests.

Patently ambiguous   A description that is invalid on its face.

Personal jurisdiction   A court's power to render decisions based on an individual's personal connections and interactions within the court's geographic boundaries.

Policy   The contract of insurance between the insurance company and the insured.

Power of acceptance   The legally recognized capacity of a party to accept an offer and create a binding, enforceable contract.

Power of sale foreclosure   Foreclosure brought pursuant to a mortgage agreement.

Premium   The periodic payment to keep an insurance policy in effect.

Principal   The person for whom an agent works.

Private mortgage insurance   An insurance policy that protects the lender and pays a specified amount in the event that the borrower defaults on the loan.

***Profit à prendre* (French)**   The right of a person to enter onto the land owned by another and remove an item or items previously agreed upon.

Promissory note   A written document that binds the borrower to pay a specific amount at a specific time.

Proration   The distribution of payments based on a person's liability for the debt.

Publication   The announcement by a testator to witnesses that he or she has created a will and wishes to have it witnessed.

***Pur autre vie* (French)**   "For another's life"; a type of life estate.

Quiet enjoyment   The right of a tenant to use the leased premises unmolested.

Reliction   The sudden appearance of dry land from what was once covered by water.

Remainderman   A person with a future interest in property, but no present rights.

Restrictive covenant   A condition or restriction on the way that land may be used that is imposed by private individuals.

Right of survivorship   The right of a co-tenant to take fee simple title to property on the death of the other co-tenant.

Riparian rights   The right to use and draw water for the benefit of real property.

Run with the land   A right that transfers with the title to the property.

***Seizin* (French)**   Possession of real property.

Self-help eviction   The landlord acts without legal process to evict a tenant and instead relies on physical force; no longer permitted in most states, at least for residential leases.

Settlement agent   Under TRID, the person designated to carry out all of the duties associated with closing a real estate transaction.

Specific performance   A court's order compelling a party to abide by the terms of a contract to which that party was previously in agreement.

Spot zoning   A practice that is often ruled unconstitutional where a particular parcel is singled out for special treatment that does not further any of the stated goals of zoning regulations.

Statute of Frauds   Originally enacted in England and later adopted in all American states, it is a statute that requires certain types of contracts to be in writing before they can be enforced. Typical contracts covered by the Statute of Frauds include contracts to answer for the debt of another and transactions involving real estate.

Statutory share   Synonymous with *forced share*.

Sublet   One tenant rents the leased premises to another tenant.

Tacking   The process of updating a previous title search.

Tenancy by entirety   A joint tenancy available to married couples.

Tenancy in common   A type of concurrent ownership in which two or more people own property together without the right of survivorship.

Tenancy in partnership   A type of concurrent ownership among business partners, with the right of survivorship.

Tenant   The possessor of certain rights transferred away from the landlord; these rights include use, possession, and enjoyment.

Testate   A person who drafts a valid will before dying.

Title abstract   Forms that summarize important information about title to a particular piece of real estate.

Title examination   The process of reviewing public records to determine whether there are any outstanding claims that will affect the marketability of title to real property.

Title insurance   An insurance policy that protects against legal claims on title to real property.

Townhouse   A form of real property where the owner has title to both the interior and exterior of a structure that resembles an apartment instead of a traditional residence.

Trade fixture   A fixture that is necessary to the operation of a business.

Unimproved land   Raw land that contains no structures.

Variance   An exception to a zoning classification granted by a zoning board.

Warranty of habitability   A legal doctrine that imposes on landlords the implied duty to provide leased premises that are fit for human habitation.

Waste   An action by a life tenant that adversely affects the nature or quality of the remainderman's future interest in real property.

Zoning   The division of land in a local area into separate districts that are regulated by their use and development.

Index

A

Abandonment, easement 119
Abstracts, title 360
Acceleration clause, mortgages 252
Accretion 62
Acknowledgment 215
Ad valorem taxes 424
Adverse possession 95-98
    color of title 97
    doctrine of laches 96
    elements of 96-97
    open, continuous 96-97
    periods of time 97-98
    why doctrine exists 95-96
Agency
    accounting 310
    agent's duty to principal 309-310
    agent's duty to third parties 310-312
    care 310
    creating 308-309
    defined 308
    duty to principal 309-310
    fiduciary 309
    fraud 311
    honesty and fair dealing 311
    law of 308
    loyalty 310
    material fact 311
    negligent misrepresentation 312
    obedience 309
    principal 308
    principal's duty to agent 313-314
    reputation 314
    sales tactics 312
Agreement, easements 116
Air rights 122-125
Ambiguous property descriptions 53-55
Amortization 255
Apartments 9
Appraisal
    mortgages 261
    process of 325-326
    valuation 326
Appraisers 325-326
Appurtenant easements 114
Assessments 122, 429
Attestation, deeds 214

Attorney's fees
mortgages 247
    real estate 328
Auctions, tax 98
Avulsion 62

B

Beneficiary 86
Bill of sale, closing procedure 393
Binder, title insurance 345
Birth records, title search 359
Boards, planning 285
Breach of contract 154-155
    buyer's remedies 155
    seller's remedies 155
Buyer 155, 320-321, 380, 381, 382, 384, 386, 389, 391, 393, 400, 403, 404, 405, 406, 407, 408
Bridge loan 258
Building codes 284-285

C

Capacity to contract 144-145
Chain of title, title search 352
Charitable exemption, taxes 423
Civil judgment 95, 359-360
Clauses, contracts 153-151
Clean Water Act 284
Client file, creating 353
Closing procedure 381-387, 389-404
    agent 389, 395, 401, 402, 404
    agent's commission 389, 395, 401, 402, 404
    attorney 381, 382, 383, 384, 386, 387, 388-389, 390, 391, 393, 406
    attorney's fees 247, 253, 401, 402
    attorney representation 382
    bill of sale 393
    buyer 380, 381, 382, 384-386, 389, 391, 393, 400, 403, 404, 405, 406, 407, 408
    certified funds 404
    compliance agreement 393
    consummation 381
    credit insurance 393
    establishing the 382-383
    description of property 384-385

    disbursing the funds 401-404
    disclosure form 393
    dual representation 406
    escrow 388, 395, 401, 404-405, 406
    establishing date of 382-383
    exchanging documents 391-401
    fee
        escrow 395
        points 401
    gathering documents 383-387
    general warranty deed 391
    hazard insurance 390, 401
    HUD settlement form 383, 386, 387, 397, 407
    inspection reports 386-387
    introduction 380
    IRS forms 392
        1099 392
        4506 392
        W-9 392
    legal description of property 383, 384-385
    lender's fees 401
    lien waiver 391, 392-393, 407
    loan application 394
    loan-closing software 386
    loan package 390
    loan payoff amounts 385
    mortgage 381, 391
    paralegal 328, 361-363, 381, 384, 385, 388-389, 390, 393, 406-407
    preparing 381-387
    preparing loan package 390
    promissory note 391-392
    proration 403
    real estate agent 389, 395, 401, 402, 404
    real estate agent's commission 402
    recording fees 402
    seller 389
    seller's profit 402
    settlement agent 381, 388
    subordination agreements 392
    survey 401
    tax information 385-386
    tax payments 402-403
    termite inspection letter 399-400

Closing procedure (*continued*)
    three-day window 382-383
    time is of the essence 383
    title search 384
    trust disbursement records 395
    truth-in-lending documentation
        396-399
    USA Patriot Act 394
    verifying hazard insurance 390, 401
    what is? 380-381
Collateral, mortgages 251
Color of title 97
Commercial property 11-12
    malls 12
    retail/wholesale 12
    shopping centers 12
Compensatory damages, tenant 185
Compliance agreement, closing
    procedure 393
Concurrent ownership 35-39
joint tenancy 36-38
    right to partition 39
    right of survivorship 36
    tenancy by entirety 38-39
    tenancy in partnership 39
    tenants in common 36
Condemnation 94
Conditional use permit 280
Condominiums 10
Consideration 144
Constructive eviction 186-187
Consumer Reporting Agencies 260
Contract
    acceptance 141-143
    breach of 154-155
    capacity 144-145
    clauses 153-154
    closing provisions 152
    communicating offer 142
    conditions 151
    consideration 144
    counteroffers 143
    defined 141
    earnest money 151
    equitable remedies 154
    escrow 154
    formation issues 146-147
    insurance clause 154
    legality 144
    mailbox rule 142-143
    mistake 147
    mutual assent 143
    offer 139-141
    power of acceptance 141

property description 151
property disclosures 151
purchase of personal property 151
purchase price details 151
risk of loss 152
signature provisions 152
specific performance 154
time is of the essence 153
title 153
what is? 138
Contractors 329
    independent 314
Contracts
    fraud 147
    listing agreements 148
    offer of purchase and contract
        149-150
    real estate 149-152
Cooperatives 10
Credit insurance, closing procedure
    393-394
Creditors, terminating rights of 93

D

Death records, title search 359
Debt, description of 251-252
Dedication 88
Deed of trust 220, 249
Deed reservation, easement 116
Deeds
    acceptance by grantee 212-213
    acknowledgment 215
    adequate property description
        210-211
    ambiguous property descriptions
        53-55, 211
    attestation 214
    brief history of 204
    consideration 216
    conveyance 211-212
    date 217
    delivery by grantor 212-214
    delivery in escrow 214
    elements of 205-217
    exception and exclusions 216
    general warranty deed 217-218
    grantee 205
    granting clause 211
    grantor 205
    grantor's legal capacity 208
    habendum clause 211
    history of 205
    identify grantor and grantee 206-207
    introduction to 204

    legal capacity 208
    legal requirements for property
        descriptions 52
    must be signed by grantor 207-208
    must identify grantor and grantee
        206-207
    property description adequate
        210-211
    quitclaim 221
    seals 215
    signed by grantor 207-208
    special warranty 219
    trust 220
    types of 217-221
    witnesses 216-217
    words of conveyance 211-212
    writing 205-206
Default 90
Delivery
    deed 212-213
    escrow 214
Devise, wills 86
Districts, historic 285
Doctrine of laches 96
Dodd-Frank Act 243-248
    fees 247
    loan estimate 244-246
    potential problems 247-248
    sweeping changes 244
    three-day requirement 247
    violations 248
Dower and curtesy 33-34
Due on sale provision, mortgage 252

E

Earnest money 151
Easements 113-119
    abandonment 119
    agreement 116
    appurtenant 114
    creating 116-118
    deed reservation 116
    defined 113
    eminent domain 118
    implication 117
    in gross 115
    merger 119
    necessity 117
    prescription 117-118
    run with the land 116
    terminating 118-119
Economic characteristics of land 4-7
Eminent domain 92-94
    condemnation 94

easements 118
    inverse condemnation 94
Entirety, tenancy by 38-39
Environmental issues 286-287
Environmental Superfund 287
Equitable relief, tenant 185
Equitable remedies, breach of
    contract 154
Equity 5
Equity lines of credit 258
Erosion 62
Escheat 95
Escrow 388, 395, 401, 404-405, 406
    clause in contract 154
    closings 404-405
    delivery of deed in 214
Estate 29
    fee simple 28-32
    leasehold 168
    life 33-35
    real property 29-30
Estoppel certificate 252
Eviction 187-189
    constructive 186-187
    procedures 188
    retaliatory 189
    self-help 188
    wrongful 187
Exclusive listing 148
Exemption
    defined 423
    government 423
    homestead 423
    non-profit 423
    taxes 423-424

F

Fair Credit Reporting Act 260-261
Family, single residence 9
Fannie Mae 241
Farm property 13
Federal Reserve Board 242
Federal Truth in Lending Laws 244-248,
    396-399
    changes 247-248
Fee simple absolute 28
Fee simple conditional estates 30-32
Fee simple determinable 31
Fee simple estate 28-32
Fee simple on condition
    subsequent 31-32
Fee simple owners, rights of 30
Fiduciary 309
Final title certificate 361

Fixed-rent lease 171
Fixture, defined 110
Fixtures 110-113
    damage test 112-113
    intent test 111
    manner of attachment test 112
    trade 113, 184-185
    use test 112
Forced share 34
Foreclosing tax lien 428-429
Foreclosure 89-93, 262-263
    auction 91-92, 262-263
    default 90
    defined 89
    judicial 89, 262
    mortgages vs. deeds of trust 93
    notice to borrower 90-91
    power of sale 89-93, 262
    purchasing at sale 92-93
    rates of foreclosure 263
    right of redemption 92
    right to 90
    steps in 91
    terminating the rights of other
        creditors 93
Fraud 311
    contracts 147
    Statute of Frauds 145-146
Freddie Mac 242

G

General warranty deed 217-218
    against encumbrances 218
    further assurance 218
    quiet enjoyment 218
    seizin 218
    warranty forever 218
Gift 88
Ginnie Mae 241
Government survey system 59-61
Government-owned land 13
Grantee 205
Granting clause 219
    mortgages 251
Grantor 205
Grantor-grantee index 349
Ground lease 172

H

Habendum clause 211
Hazard insurance, closing procedure
    390-391
Historic districts 285
History of property boundaries 50-51

Holographic wills 85
Homes, mobile 11
Homesteading 88
HUD 242
HUD-1 settlement form 383, 386, 387,
    397, 407

I

Incompetent persons 81
Implication, easement 117
Improvements 9
Independent contractors 314-315
Indexing, tract 59-60
Industrial parks 12
Industrial property 12
Industry
    heavy 12-13
    light 12-13
Infants, sale of real property 81
Inspectors 329-330
Insurance, contract clause 154
Interest escalation clause, mortgages
    252-253
Interstate Land Sales Full Disclosure
    Act 286
Intestate 87
Intestate succession 87
Intoxicated persons, sale 81
Intoxication 81
Investing in real estate 321-323
    appreciation in value 322
    credit rating 322
    disadvantages to investing
        in 323
    down payment 323
    financing 323
    liquidity 323
    maintenance costs 323
    Real Estate Investment Trusts
        323-324
    source of funds 322
    tax advantages 322
    taxes 323
Investors, real estate 321-323
    "Do it yourselfers" 324
    Small investors 324
IRS form 1099 392
IRS form 4506 392

J

Joint tenancy 36-38
Judicial foreclosure 262
Judgment, civil 95, 359-360
Judgments, title search 359-360

Jurisdiction
    in rem 4
    personal 4

K
Kit homes 11

L
Land
    government-owned 13
    physical characteristics of 4
    unimproved 9
Landlord 168
Landlord's duties 178-181
Landlord-tenant relationships 169-170
    history of 169
    legal doctrines that affect 184
    modern changes 170
    remedies for breach of duty 184-187
    tenancy for years 189-190
    tenancy from year to year 190
    warranty of habitability 184
Landlord-tenant
    breach of duty, landlord 184-187
    damages awarded to tenant 185-186
    discriminatory practices 181
    duty of tenant 182-183
    duty to repair 179-180
    duty to third parties 181
    equitable relief 185
    historical background 169
    landlord's duties 179-181
    modern changes 170
    ordinary wear and tear 183
    pet deposits 184
    punitive damages 186
    quiet enjoyment 184
    right to enjoy 182
    right to re-enter 179
    safety deposits 183-184
    tenant duties 182-183
    warranty of habitability 184
Latently ambiguous property
    description 55
Lease 171-173
    commercial 176-177
    federal law 177
    fixed rent 171
    ground 172
    license 173
    mineral 172-173
    net 171
    oil and gas 173
    percentage 171

public policy concerns 177-178
    rent-to-own 172
    Statute of Frauds 145-146, 177-178
    timber 172
    Uniform Residential Landlord and
        Tenant Act 178
Lease provisions 173-177
    acceptance of premises 175
    eviction 187
    late payments 174
    modifying premises 175
    notice 175-176
    persons permitted on premises 174
    pet deposit 174
    renewal 174
    rent 173
    security deposit 174
    subletting 175
Leasehold estate 168
Legality, defined 144
Legal malpractice, title
    searches 361
Legal requirements of a mortgage/deed
    of trust 249-254
Lenders, internet 261
Licenses120
Liens 121-122
    defined 121
    materialman's 121
    mechanic's 121
    title search 357
Life estate 33-35
    court doctrines 35
    defined 33
    dower and curtesy 33
    forced share 33-34
    historical basis 33-34
    pur autre vie 35
    remaindermen 34
    tenant 33
    waste 34
Life tenant 33
Listing agreements 148
Listing
    exclusive 148
    multiple 148
    open 148
Loan application, closing
    procedure 394
Loan-closing software 386
Loan officers 324-325
    applications, online 325
    internet mortgage lenders 325
Loan package, closing procedure 390

M
Malls 12
Manager, property 329
Manufactured homes 11
Marriage records, title search 359
Material facts 311
Materialman's lien 121
Mechanic's lien 121
Mentally incompetent persons 81
Merger, easement 119
Metes and bound
    drafting 57-59
    property descriptions 55-59
    technology 59
Millage rate, taxes 426
Mineral lease 172-173
Mineral rights 124
Mistake, contracts 147
Mobiles homes 11
Money, earnest 151
Mortgage markets 237-248
    primary 237-239
    secondary 239-248
    secondary, federal agencies 240-242
Mortgages
    acceleration clause 252
    adjustable rate 255-256
    amortization 255
    appraisals 261
    attorney's fees 247, 253, 382, 401, 402
    balloon 243
    borrower's credit history 260
    bridge loans 258
    closing 391-392
    collateral 251
    deeds of trust versus 249
    defined 236
    description of debt 251-252
    discharging 261
    due on sale provision 252
    elements of 249-253
    equity lines of credit 258
    estoppel certificate 252
    Fair Credit Reporting Act 260
    fixed-rate 254-255
    granting clause 251
    identifying parties 250
    interest escalation clause 252-253
    internet lenders 261
    legal requirements of 249-254
    markets 237-248
    must be in writing 250
    points 261
    power of sale provision 252

prepayment clause 253
priority 253
promissory note 251, 391-392
property as collateral 251
purchase money 256-257
qualifying for 258-261
rate caps 256
recording statutes 253-254
second 257-258
specific clauses 251-253
taxes and insurance 252
types of 254-256
underwriting 260
wrap-around 257
writing requirement 250
Multiple Listing Service 319
Mutual assent 143

N
Navigable waters 63
Necessity, easement 117
Negligent misrepresentation 312
Net leases 171
Nonconforming use, zoning 281-282
Non-navigable waters 63
Nuisance actions 291-292
defined 291
private 292
public 291
Nuncupative will 85

O
Oil and gas lease 173
Offer 139-141
do not contain specific language 140
reasonable person standard 140
Offer of purchase and contract 149-150
Open listing 148
Options 152-153
Ordinary wear and tear 183

P
Paralegal 328, 361-363, 381, 385, 388, 389, 390, 406
Parks, industrial 12
Parol evidence 54
Partition 95
right to 39
Partnership, tenancy in 39
Patently ambiguous property description 54
Personal property 3
Pet deposit 184
Planning Boards 285

Plats 60
PMI (private mortgage insurance) 394-395
Points, mortgages 261
Policy, title insurance 345
Power of acceptance 141
Power of sale provision, mortgage 252
Prescription, easement 117-118
Preliminary certificate, title search 361
Premium, title insurance 346
Prepayment clause, mortgages 253
Private mortgage insurance (PMI) 394-395
Private nuisance actions 291
Probate records, title search 359
Profit à prendre 120-121
Promissory notes
closing procedure 391-392
mortgages 251, 291-392
Property
classifying by use 8-13
commercial 11-12
personal 3
real defined 1-2
Property boundaries
descriptions in deeds 51-55
history of 50-51
litigating 53
natural forces affecting 62-63
referring to other documents 52
Property description
ambiguous 53-55
elements of valid 5
latently ambiguous 55
legal requirements 54
parol evidence 54
patently ambiguous 54
referring to other documents 55
Property managers 329
Proration, closing procedure 403
Publication, will 85
Public nuisance actions 292
Punitive damages, tenant 186
Pur autre vie, life estate 35
Purchase money mortgage 256-257

Q
Qualifying for a mortgage 258-261
appraisal 261
borrower's credit history 260-261
Consumer Reporting Agencies 260
Fair Credit Reporting Act 260-261
points 261
underwriting 260

Quiet enjoyment 184, 218
Quitclaim deed 221

R
Real estate agent
becoming 317
classifications 316-317
duty of care 315-316
duty to disclose 316
locating buyers 320-321
regulations 318
Real estate agents
regulations 318
responsibility to disclose 316
rules governing 318
services provided 318-321
Real Estate Investment Trusts 323-324
Real estate market 7-8
Real Estate Settlement Procedures Act 248
Real estate title searchers 328
Real property defined 1-2
Recording statutes 221-222
mortgages 253-254
notice 221
race 222
race-notice 221-222
Recreational property 13
Redemption, foreclosure 92
Registration, Torrens 60-61
Reliction 63
Remaindermen, life estate 34
Rent 173
Rent-to-own lease 172
Residential property 9
Restrictive covenants 287-291
abandonment 290
changed conditions 290
creating 288
defined 287
enforcing 290
illegal 289
merger 291
stated time period 290
terminating 290-291
time period 290
"touch and concern" 288-289
typical covenants 289
unconstitutional 289
Retaliatory eviction 189
Rights
air 122-124
mineral 124
water 61-63, 124-125

Right of survivorship 36
Riparian rights 61

S

Sale of real estate 78-83
    capacity 81-82
    consideration 80
    infants 81
    mentally incompetent persons 81
    mutual assent 80, 143
    property description 82
Seals, deeds 215
Second mortgages 257-258
Seizin 218
Self-help eviction 188
Seller 155, 385, 389, 402
Shopping centers 16
Special warranty deed 219
Specific performance, breach of
    contract 154
Spot zoning 283
Statute of Frauds 2, 145-146
Statutes, recording 221-222
Subdivision rules and regulations 291
Sublet 175
Subordination agreements, closing
    procedure 392
Succession
    intestate 87
    testate 87
Sufferance, tenancy at 191
Superfund 287
Survey, closing procedure 401
Surveyors 326-328
Survivorship, right of 36

T

Tacking, title searches 361
Tax auctions 98
Tax liens 427-429
    foreclosing 428-429
    setting priorities 428
Taxes and insurance, mortgage 252
Taxes
    ad valorem 424
    assessments 122, 414-417
    calculating tax rate 426
    challenging assessment 425
    charitable exemption 423
    determining property value 425-436
    enforcing regulations 427
    exemptions 423-424
    government enterprise zones 424
    government's power to 422

homestead exemption 423
how assessed 424
millage rate 426
non-profit exemption 423
paying 427-428
priorities, tax liens 428
reassessment 426
setting priorities in tax liens 428
tax liens 427-429
Tax lien, 428-427
    foreclosing 428
Tenancy at sufferance 191
    creating 191
    terminating 191
Tenancy at will 191
    creating 191
    terminating 191
Tenancy by entirety 38-39
Tenancy for years 190
    creating 190
    terminating 190
Tenancy from year to year 190
    creating 190
    terminating 190
Tenancy in partnership 38-39
Tenancy, joint 36-38
Tenant 168
Tenants in common 36
Tenant remedies vs. landlord 185-187
    damages to tenant 185-186
Tenants' rights and duties 182-183
    damages 183
    duties 182-183
    ordinary wear and tear 183
    responsibility for damages
    right of enjoyment 182
    right to use 182
Termite inspection letter, closing
    procedure 399-400
Testate succession 87
Technology, role in real estate 329
Timber lease 172
Time is of the essence, closing 383
    contract clause 153
Title abstracts 360
Title examination 346-351
    current owners 349
    deed book and page number
        350-351
    defined 346
    description of property 350
    grantor-grantee index 349
    information needed 348-349
    names of current owners 349

surveys and plats 60, 351
tax ID number 350
time period 350
tract index 59-60, 349-350
what is? 347
Title insurance 344-346
    binder 345
    defined 344
    obtaining 345-346
    policy 345
    premium 346
    terminating 346
    what it does 344
Title search
    abstracts 360
    adverse conveyances 355-360
    birth records 359
    breaks in the chain of title 364
    chain of title 352
    common problems 363-364
    compiling information 360
    creating chain of title 352-355
    creating client file 353
    creating links in ownership 353-354
    death records 359
    final title certificate 361
    forms 360
    holes or breaks in chain 364
    judgments 359-360
    legal malpractice 361
    liens 121-122, 357
    links in chain of ownership 353-354
    marriage records 359
    out conveyances 355-360
    paralegal's role 361-363
    preliminary certificate 361
    probate records 359
    reviewing documents 356-357
    subdivided properties 363-364
    steps 351-363
    tacking 361
    tax office 353
    technological innovations 354-355
    title abstracts 360
    title documents 356-357
    UCC listings 358-359
Title searcher 328
Torrens registration 60-61
Townhouses 10
Tract index, title examination
    349-350
Tract indexing 59-60, 349-350
Trade fixtures 113, 184-185
Troubled Asset Relief Program 242

Trust disbursement records, closing
    procedures 395
Truth in Lending documentation,
    closing procedures 396-399
Truth in Lending Laws 244-248,
    396-399
    changes 247-248

U

UCC listings, title search 358-359
Underwriting, mortgages 260
Unimproved land 9
Urban planning 285-286
USA Patriot Act, closing procedure 394

V

Variance, zoning 280

W

W-9 392
Warranty of habitability 184
Waste 34
Water rights 61-63, 124-125
    court doctrines 61-62

limitations on 61
right to draw water 124
right to use 61-62
subterranean 124-125
Water
    accretion 62
    avulsion 62
    erosion 62
    property boundaries and 62-63
    reliction 63
    right to use 61-62
Waters
    navigable 63
    non-navigable 63
Will
    beneficiary 86
    capacity of testator 86-88
    devise 86
    devisee 86
    holographic 85
    minimum requirements 84-86
    nuncupative 85
    publication 85
    requirement to be in writing 84

sales versus 86-87
signed by testator 84-85
transfer of title by 84-86
witnesses 85-86
Wraparound mortgage 257
Wrongful eviction, action for 187

Z

Zoning 278-284
    aesthetic 279
    classifications 280-281
    commercial 281
    conditional use permit 280
    defined 278
    enforcing regulations 279-280
    exceptions 282
    industrial 281
    non-conforming use 281-282
    rational basis test 283
    residential 280
    "spot" 283
    unconstitutional ordinances
        283-284
    variance 280